# THE CLASSICAL TRADITION IN SOCIOLOGY

## THE AMERICAN TRADITION

# THE CLASSICAL TRADITION IN SOCIOLOGY

## THE AMERICAN TRADITION

### VOLUME IV

Edited by
JEFFREY ALEXANDER
RAYMOND BOUDON
MOHAMED CHERKAOUI

SAGE Publications
London • Thousand Oaks • New Delhi

Editorial arrangement © Jeffrey Alexander, Raymond Boudon, Mohamed Cherkaoui, 1997

First published 1997

All rights reserved. No part of this publication may be reproduced, stored in a retrieval system, transmitted or utilized in any form or by any means, electronic, mechanical, photocopying, recording or otherwise, without permission in writing from the Publishers.

Every effort has been made to trace all the copyright holders of the material reprinted herein, but if any have been inadvertently overlooked the publishers will be pleased to make the necessary arrangements at the first opportunity.

SAGE Publications Ltd
6 Bonhill Street
London EC2A 4PU

SAGE Publications Inc
2455 Teller Road
Thousand Oaks, California 91320

SAGE Publications India Pvt Ltd
32, M-Block Market
Greater Kailash
New Delhi 110 048

British Library Cataloguing in Publication Data

A catalogue record for this book is available from the British Library

ISBN 0-7619-5325-6 (set of four volumes)

Library of Congress Cataloging in Publication data has been applied for

Typeset in Berthold Baskerville by The Bardwell Press, Oxford, England
Printed in Great Britain at the Cambridge University Press, Cambridge, England

# CONTENTS

## VOLUME IV

### AMERICAN SOCIOLOGY IN THE TWENTIETH CENTURY: RECENT TRENDS IN SOCIOLOGICAL THEORY
(continued)

71. Neofunctionalism Today: Reconstructing a Theoretical Tradition  *Jeffrey C. Alexander and Paul Colomy* .... 1
72. The Post-Industrial Society  *Malcolm Waters* .... 33
73. The Iron Cage Revisited: Institutional Isomorphism and Collective Rationality in Organizational Fields  *Paul J. DiMaggio and Walter W. Powell* .... 50
74. Toward a Critique of Sociology  *Alvin W. Gouldner* .... 73
75. Individualism  *Robert N. Bellah, Richard Madsden, William M. Sullivan, Ann Swindler and Steven M. Tipton* .... 87
76. The New Forms of Control  *Herbert Marcuse* .... 108
77. Sociology's Historical Imagination  *Theda Skocpol* .... 120
78. The Rise and Future Demise of the World Capitalist System: Concepts for Comparative Analysis  *Immanuel Wallerstein* .... 138
79. The Peasants and Revolution  *Barrington Moore Jr.* .... 149
80. Sociology, Meet History  *Charles Tilly* .... 172
81. Introduction to *Frame Analysis*  *Erving Goffman* .... 221
83. Doing 'Being Ordinary'  *Harvey Sacks* .... 263
84. Treating Method and Form as Phenomena: An Appreciation of Garfinkel's Phenomenology of Social Action  *Lenore Langsdorf* .... 270
85. Drama as Life: The Significance of Goffman's Changing Use of the Theatrical Metaphor  *Phil Manning* .... 281
86. Rational Choice Theory in Sociology  *Robert J. Holton* .... 302
87. Feminism, Essentialism, and Historical Context  *Rosaria Champagne* .... 317
88. "I Can't Even Think Straight:" "Queer" Theory and the Missing Sexual Revolution in Sociology  *Arlene Stein and Ken Plummer* .... 330
89. Social Postmodernism: Beyond Identity Politics  *Linda Nicholson and Steven Seidman* .... 344

90. The Promise of a Cultural Sociology: Technological
    Discourse and the Sacred and Profane Information Machine
    *Jeffrey C. Alexander* 375

# AMERICAN SOCIOLOGY IN THE TWENTIETH CENTURY

## RECENT TRENDS IN SOCIOLOGICAL THEORY
(continued)

# 71

# Neofunctionalism Today: Reconstructing a Theoretical Tradition

*Jeffrey C. Alexander and Paul Colomy*

In 1979, Alexander acknowledged that "despite Parsons' enduring impression on the sociological tradition, it is too early to determine the ultimate fate of his theoretical legacy." There seemed a real possibility that "the Parsonian synthesis will break down completely." It was also possible, however, that in time a "more loosely-defined, less sectarian version of functionalist theory" might appear (Alexander 1979a, 355). In this essay we will try to demonstrate that it is the latter, not the former, of these possibilities that actually has come to pass.

When the initial volumes of *Theoretical Logic in Sociology* began to appear in 1982 (Alexander 1982a, 1982b, 1983a, 1983b), they were not greeted with unanimous approval. Incredulity, dismay, even indignation were prominently displayed. Marxist, humanist, constructivist, and positivist theorists, and even one older Parsonian, wrote negative reviews, warning the profession away from what they considered a retrograde development. The one thing about which these critics agreed was that the Parsonian foundation of *Theoretical Logic* represented a holdover from the past, rather than a new development in contemporary sociological thought.

These initial responses emerged from self-understandings of theoretical orientations that had been formed in a struggle against structural functional thought. Positivism, conflict theory, Marxism, exchange theory, symbolic interactionism, phenomenology – all had once been obstreperous challengers to the Parsonian edifice. By 1980, it might be said, with only some exaggeration, that they were triumphant, not challengers but the dominant theories in a new, if internally divided, establishment. Surely, if sociological progress was to have any meaning at all, the Parsonian approach could not be revived. The very *raisons d'etre* of these positions demanded that such an alternative not be raised.

In the January 1988 issue of *Contemporary Sociology*, Marco Orru describes the works he has under review as sharing an "enthusiastic reappraisal of

---

Source: George Ritzer (ed.), *Frontier of Socioglogical Theory*, (New York: Columbia University Press, 1990).

Parsonian sociology." He develops a perspective within which to view them by pointing precisely to the doubt their existence casts on linear conceptions of social scientific development.

> As social scientists, we wish for theories about the social world to build on each other in some linear fashion but more often than not we observe, instead, a cyclical pattern by which different schools of thought replace each other in commanding our attention over time. Leading figures in the various theoretical traditions follow this same pattern. (Orru 1988, 115)

Only after suggesting the validity of a more cyclical pattern can Orru conclude by suggesting that "the revival of Parsonian thought is one of the distinguishing features of 1980s sociology."

If Orru is right about the conspicuous importance of the Parsonian revival, and we think he is, there has been a sea change in sociology in the last half dozen years. In retrospect, at least, it seems clear that *Theoretical Logic* was not the final aftershock in response to the anti-Parsonian quake. As we will suggest later in this essay, it was not, in fact, an effort to revive earlier, orthodox Parsonian theory at all. It was, rather, a challenge to central tenets of the Parsonian orientation, an effort to revise it in a radical, post-Parsonian way. As such, it might better be seen as a preshock, a premonition of things to come. It has become evident in retrospect that *Theoretical Logic* was not anomalous. The previous year, indeed, Habermas had pointedly demanded the relegitimation of Parsonian theory in a not dissimilar way, as had Richard Munch in a powerful double set of articles in the *American Journal of Sociology*.[1]

When Alexander (1985a) subsequently introduced the term "neofunctionalism," it was in order to emphasize the double element of continuity and internal critique. This emphasis is revealed in his analogy to neo-Marxism. Current sociology a la Parsonian is to the earlier orthodoxy as neo-Marxism is to its orthodox earlier variant. Neo-Marxism has tried to overcome the mechanistic rigidities of Marx by incorporating the most important advances of twentieth-century social thought. The relation of neofunctionalism to the traditions that challenged early Parsonian theory, it was suggested, is much the same.

This public assertion of the continuing vitality of the Parsonian tradition drew, once again, a decidedly mixed response. In *Footnotes*, an elder statesman (Page 1985) wrote an open letter to warn his colleagues about the dangers of revivifying functionalism. A younger theorist, Charles Camic (1986), in his review of *Neofunctionalism*, reassured his readers that the revivalists had learned nothing from the criticisms of Parsons and that in their theorizing one could find nothing new. Another contemporary, George Ritzer (1985), reinforced this skepticism, while offering that he was willing to wait and see.

Today, while fundamental doubts about the validity and desirability of neofunctionalism have not disappeared, the disciplinary community is gradually coming to terms with the fact that something new has appeared on the sociological scene. Orru's observation attests to this recognition. So does Giddens and Turner's (1987, 3) reference to the recent "considerable revival" of Parsonian thought in their introduction to *Social Theory Today*. Contemporary textbooks in sociological theory (e.g., Ritzer 1988; Collins 1988a) are being revised to reflect this shift in the theoretical map.[2]

In the course of the twentieth century, critics and sympathizers of neo Marxism have often asked, "What is Marxist about it?" In so doing, they have indicated the extent of the critical departure from the original form. In Jonathan Turner and Alexandra Maryanski's (1988) "What is Functionalist about Neofunctionalism?" the same doubt is raised about recent neofunctionalist work. There is no doubting that in certain respects Turner and Maryanski have grounds for complaint. Neofunctionalism differs from orthodox Parsonian thought in decisive and often radical ways. Even while it disputes the discipline's evaluation of earlier functionalism, it does not itself accept some of the central tendencies of that earlier thought. Even while it sustains fundamental links with Parsons' earlier work, therefore, it does not conceive of itself as an attempt to resuscitate an older orthodoxy. Whether its originality is undermined by its continuing roots in Parsonian thought is, of course, a matter of debate. The claim can be made, however, that neofunctionalism is the only new theoretical movement to have emerged in Western sociology in the 1980s.[3]

One of our ambitions in this paper is to indicate the substance of this new theoretical movement in sociology – its general discursive structure, its interpretations of the classics, the scope of its research programs, and its relation to other theoretical discourse and research programs in the field. This will involve a critical look at the wide variety of work that is currently underway. We would like to begin, however, by exploring some of the reasons why this unexpected revival has come about. In this regard, to point to the intrinsic interest of current neofunctionalist works is besides the point. Their very appearance has been a response to underlying developments in sociology. Neofunctionalism, we will argue, is only one indication of a deep groundshift in the entire sociological field. To understand its relevance on the contemporary scene one must understand the new and different theoretical situation that is emerging today.

## The Emerging Third Phase of Postwar Sociology

Since World War II, Western sociology has passed through two periods, and it is entering a third. In the first phase, which lasted into the 1960s, structural-functionalism, in its Parsonian and Mertonian form, could be said to be the dominant force. Whatever its ideological weaknesses, its anti-empirical stance, its naive confidence in equilibrium – and we will talk about all these below – that functionalism was committed to the syntheses of what Parsons called the "warring schools" of sociological thought seems impossible to deny. This orientation toward theoretical integration and synthesis was one casualty of the rebellion against functionalism that began in the 1960s and continued triumphantly into the early 1980s.

Two major battle lines were drawn. On the one side, microsociology set contingent action against social structure in the name of creativity and individual freedom. On the other side, conflict sociology argued that social change could be explained only by emphasizing material rather than ideal forces. These propositions denied the central tenets of Parsons' work. Thus, as Goffman, Homans, and Garfinkel gained increasing authority, interest in socialization and personality structure correspondingly declined. As Rex, Lockwood, and Dahrendorf became central figures, with Collins, Giddens, Wright, and Skocpol following in their stead, macrosociological interest in culture and symbolic legitimacy dramatically declined.

Yet even as these brilliant challengers became the new establishment, even as the "multiparadigmatic" character of sociology passed from daring prophecy (e.g., Friedrichs 1970) to conventional wisdom (e.g., Ritzer 1975), the vital and creative phase of these theoretical movements was coming to an end. Stimulated by the premature theoretical closure of the micro and macro traditions, a new phase is beginning. It is marked by an effort to relink theorizing about action and order, conflict and stability, structure and culture. Such efforts have been made from within each of the newly dominant theoretical traditions, from both sides of the great micro/macro divide. They are also the most clearly distinguishing characteristics of the new directions in general theory. The old lines of confrontation are being discredited. There is a movement back to synthesis once again. We believe that it is this development that marks the third phase of postwar sociology.

In symbolic interaction, a whole spate of work has challenged the emphasis on individualistic contingency that, under Blumer's leadership, marked this tradition's earlier development. Goffman's writing (1974) on frame analysis and Becker's (1982) on the social organization of art can be seen as marked departures from earlier, much more negotiation-oriented work. Stryker (1980) has called for a reintegration of interactionism with systems theory, Lewis and Smith (1980) have argued that Mead was a collectivist, and Fine (1984, 1988) has moved forcefully into the area of cultural and organizational studies.

In the exchange tradition, leading theorists (e.g., Coleman 1986a, 1986b, 1987; Wippler and Lindenberg 1987) increasingly reject the notion that the individual/structure relation can be seen as a causal relation between discrete empirical events. Because there is empirical simultaneity, the linkage between micro and macro must be seen as an analytical one sustained by larger systemic processes. This analytical linkage is achieved by the application of what are called "transformation rules," such as voting procedures, to individual actions. In the work of theorists like Goode, Blau, and Coleman, structural explanations – about the rules of constitutions (e.g., Coleman 1987), the dynamics of organizations and intergroup relations (Blau 1977), and the system of prestige allocation (Goode 1978) – have begun to replace utility arguments.

Within ethnomethodology, one can point to similar developments in the work of Cicourel, who has recently pushed for a linkage with macrosociological work (Knorr-Cetina and Cicourel 1981). Recent work by Molotch (Molotch and Boden 1985) and Schegloff (1987) demonstrates how discursive practices are structured by organizational context and the distribution of power, even while their analytical autonomy is maintained. Heritage and Greatbatch's (1986) research on political conventions makes a similar effort to establish micro-macro links.

When one examines the structural or conflict position, one finds similar efforts to overcome the splits of the second phase. Moore (1978) has turned from objective to subjective injustice, Skocpol and Finegold (1982) have raised the possibility that religion may be an independent cause of social policy and political change. Sewell (1980, 1985), once a devoted Tilly student, and Darnton (1982), once a leading *Annaliste*, are now developing cultural approaches to social change and history. Calhoun (1982) and Prager (1986) have published polemically antistructural works of historical sociology. Meyer and Scott (1983) link organizations to cultural structures rather than technical ones. This cultural turn in macrosociology is responsible, we believe, for the emergence of a new disciplinary specialty, cultural sociology, which has just become the newest American Sociological Association section. It is instructive that theorists who associate themselves with this specialty argue that culture cannot be understood in terms of what we have called the dichotomies of the second phase. Wuthnow (1988) argues that culture need not be understood individualistically or even subjectively, Swidler (1986) for culture's opening to contingency, Archer (1988) for its sensitivity to change, Eisenstadt (1986) for its link to material force and institutional life.

Within general theory there is an equally strong movement away from the one-sided polemics of earlier theoretical work. Where Giddens' earlier work (1971) was part of conflict and neo-Marxist theorizing, in the last decade he (1984) has sought to interweave contingency, material structure, and normative rules. Collins' (1975) earlier work was paradigmatic of conflict sociology; in recent years, by contrast, he has embraced microsociology (1981), the later Durkheimian emphasis on rituals (1987, 1988b), and even the framing concept of multidimensionality (1988a). Habermas, too, began his career with a typical Frankfurt school emphasis on the destructively capitalist features of modern life; more recently, he (1984) has theorized about the normative and micro processes that underline and often oppose the macrostructure of capitalist societies, making these cultural forces "equal but separate" subsystems.[4]

We earlier pointed to premature theoretical closure as the intellectual reason for the denouement of phase two. One-sided theories are effective polemical means; they are decidedly less successful when they must function as sources of theoretical cohesion, if not disciplinary integration, in their own right. Social and institutional factors, however, are also involved. One certain factor is the changing political climate in the United States and Europe.

Revolutionary social movements have faded away; because of developments like Solidarity and revelations about the Chinese Cultural Revolution, in the eyes of many critical intellectuals Marxism itself has been morally delegitimated.

The ideological thrust that fueled post-Parsonian discourse in its micro and macro form and that justified Marxist structuralism on the Continent is largely spent. There is a new realism, even pessimism, about the possibilities for social change, which has manifest itself in two very different ways. On the one hand, there is the resignation, even fatalism of so much postmodern thought, with its nostalgic return to localism (Lyotard 1984) and its abandonment of the possibility of a more rational social life (Foucault 1984). On the other hand, there is the search for less apocalyptic ways of institutionalizing rationality, approaches which concentrate on the difficulties of preserving political democracy rather than on the unlikely, and perhaps undesirable, possibility of some socialist transformation (Lefort 1986; Alexander 1988a).

## Parsons' New Relevance in the Contemporary Phase

Is it any wonder that neofunctionalism has flourished in this changing social and disciplinary environment? Parsons' original work contained within it a wide and contradictory range of theoretical ideas. There are central areas in his corpus, however, that complement this third phase. Developing in a period of reaction against the limits of the second phase, neofunctionalists have interpreted the "natural concerns" of Parsons' thought in just this way. They have argued that it provides critical theoretical resources for addressing the concerns of this new period in postwar sociological work.

More than anything else, perhaps, neofunctionalism has presented itself as a prototypically synthetic form of theorizing. After all, it was Parsons' original and flawed effort at theoretical integration – and what were seen as its attendant weaknesses – that provoked micro and macro theorists to launch the one-sided theories that themselves have recently come under increasing doubt. It is not surprising, therefore, that as contemporary theorists have returned to the project of synthesis, they have often returned to some core element in Parsons' earlier thought. It is striking that this return is manifest in the work of theorists who have never had any previous association with Parsonian thought. The motive is theoretical logic, not personal desire.

No more clear example of this theoretical pressure can be found than Habermas' *Legitimation Crisis* (1975). Departing from the safe harbor of critical theory, Habermas wanted to incorporate into his model of economic contradictions factors like personality strain, the universalist potential of value commitments, and the latently anticapitalist pressures that emanate from the formal equality of political and legal institutions. What he ends up employing, de facto if not de jure, is Parsons' AGIL model and also his division between culture, personality, and social system. Similar examples can be found in a wide range of recent theoretical work. When Schluchter (1979, 1981) wants to present a newly integrated view of Weber's civilizational work, he makes use of the evolutionary and developmental language of Parsons' differentiation theory. When Collins (1988b) pushes to expand his "conflict-Durkheimian" theory of social rituals into the realm of democratic politics, he is forced to acknowledge the importance of Parsons' multidimensional theory of political support. In Holton's (1986) effort to transcend both market and Marxist approaches to political economy, he turns with relief to the rich conceptual legacy of Parsons and Smelser's model of the economy–society relation. To reaffirm the delicate but distinctive pluralism of Western social systems, Turner (1986a, 1986b, 1987) extends the concepts of inclusion, citizenship, and value generalization from Parsons' theory of social change. In our own efforts (Alexander and Giesen 1987; Alexander 1987a; Colomy and Rhoades 1988) to construct a model of the micro–macro link – efforts that challenge orthodox functionalism in fundamental ways – we have found that Parsons' analytic model provides the only viable foundation for a new synthesis.

This new relevance of Parsonian thought can also be seen in the renewed theorizing about culture and society. It is not accidental, in this regard, that it has been the former students and coworkers of Parsons who have assumed a central role in the revival of macrocultural studies. Geertz (1973) initiated this "cultural revolution" with his essays in the 1960s, which stood firmly upon Parsons' insistence on the analytical autonomy of the cultural realm. Bellah's (1970, 1973) argument for the relationship between symbolic realism and democratic social integration can also be traced back to key themes in Parsons' normative work. When Eisenstadt criticizes contemporary structuralist approaches to historical and contemporary sociology for their "ontological" rather than analytical approach to culture and society relations (1986), he is drawing from Parsons' theory of the institutionalization of values. Archer's (1985, 1988) ambitious metatheory of culture begins from the Parsonian distinction between culture, action, and social system. Robertson's (1987) work on global culture issues in critical respects (Robertson 1982; cf. Robertson 1988) from Parsons' concepts of value generalization and societal community. In Alexander's (1982b, 211–296; 1984; 1988b) own effort to construct a model of cultural structures and processes, he, too, begins with the analytic differentiation of symbolic patterns from the exigencies of social and personality systems.

We have indicated here the convergence between the interests that mark the current, third phase of sociological thought and some of the earlier concerns of Parsonian work. We have demonstrated this coincidence in terms of the desire for theoretical synthesis and the new attempt to theorize culture. The third element of this third phase – the clearly changing ideological environment of sociology – will be taken up below, in the context of a more systematic discussion of neofunctionalist work. Up until this point, we have noted the convergence between developments in neofunctionalism and more general movements in the theoretical field, but we have not looked at specific arguments or tried to construct the details of a new disciplinary map.

Before taking up these tasks, we need a framework within which to consider issues of disciplinary conflict and change.

## Social Science as Discourse and Research Program[5]

To understand correctly the issues involved in the emergence and decline of theoretical orientations, we must see that social science is neither the fact-bound nor middle-level enterprise that empiricists describe. Social science is organized by traditions, and traditions, whatever their aspirations for rationality, are founded by charismatic figures. At the beginnings of a discipline, powerful intellectual figures are regarded as classical founders (Alexander 1987b); at later points, they are accorded quasi-classical status and treated as founders of powerful schools. Social reality, then, is never confronted in and of itself. Because perception is mediated by the discursive commitments of traditions, social scientific formulations are channeled within relatively standardized, paradigmatic forms. The matrix social scientists inhabit need not be drawn from a single tradition or be wholly of a piece, but inhabit it they must, aware of it or not.

While traditionalism implies habitual behavior, it need not imply stasis or lack of change. In social science, this openness to change is intensified by the universalism of institutionalized standards that mandate impersonal rationality and push against the particularism of a traditional first response. Social science traditions define themselves by staking out theoretical cores that are highly resistant to change. The substantial areas surrounding these nuclei, however, are subject to continuous variation. In ideal-typical terms, changes in the peripheral areas of traditions can be conceived as proceeding along two lines, "elaboration" and "revision." While both lines of development present themselves as loyally carrying out traditional commitments, they differ in the creativeness with which they pursue this task. Because elaborative sociological work proceeds from the assumption that the original tradition is internally consistent and relatively complete, it aims primarily at refinement and expansion of scope. In revisionist work, by contrast, there is a greater sense of the vulnerabilities of the established tradition; in the guise of loyal specification, an often implicit effort is made to address these strains and offer formulations that can resolve them (see, e.g., Alexander 1979a; Colomy 1986).

Elaboration and revision are lines of specification that recur periodically in a tradition's history, not only in the period of routinization that immediately follows the charismatic founding but in the wake of the powerful reformulations that must emerge if a tradition is to remain intact.[6] It is this latter possibility that points to a third ideal-typical form of theoretical change. Insofar as cores themselves undergo substantial shifts – without abandoning their association with the overarching tradition – there occurs the theoretical activity we will call "reconstruction." Reconstruction differs from elaboration and revision in that differences with the founder of the tradition are clearly acknowledged and openings to other traditions are explicitly made. Reconstruction can revive a theoretical tradition, even while it creates the opportunity for the kind of development out of which new traditions are born.[7] Finally, of course, traditions can be destroyed. This does not happen because core and peripheral commitments are falsified, but because they have become delegitimated in the eyes of the scientific community. Even in this situation, however, traditions do not so much disappear as become latent; the possibility always remains that they may be picked up once again.[8]

According to this model, then, social science does not grow simply because of the compulsion to understand empirical reality; nor can its growth be measured merely in relation to the expansion of empirical knowledge or conceptual scope. The primary motor of social scientific growth is conflict and competition between traditions. The primary reference points for measuring scientific growth are established by the relations between traditions and by signposts internal to a given tradition itself. Instead of speaking about theoretical or empirical progress per se, one must speak of relative explanatory and theoretical success vis-à-vis one's own tradition or competing ones.[9]

Elaboration, revision, and reconstruction are concepts that describe the closeness of fit between subsequent theoretical work and original tradition. They do not describe the degree of real advance. Elaboration, for example, may be thin or thick, to redeploy Geertz's ethnographic standards. Traditions may be enriched and elevated by these processes of theoretical change; they may also be impoverished and simplified, robbed of their sophistication and denuded of some of their most powerful intellectual sustenance.[10] If social science change can be progressive, therefore, it can be reactionary as well. It is rare, moreover, for these modes of theoretical development to proceed in either an entirely progressive or reactionary way.

A disciplinary community's switch from one theoretical position to another is determined neither by the theoretical effectiveness and sophistication of the respective positions nor by their objective empirical scope. It is usually motivated, rather, by broad shifts in what might be called the disciplinary community's "scientific sensibility."[11] Shifts in disciplinary sensibility put different questions on the floor. They place a premium on the development of different modes of discourse. Indeed, it is often only after new discursive commitments are made to an approach that increased theoretical sophistication and empirical scope emerge. It is in this sense that one can speak less of social scientific "development" than of social scientific "movements." Disciplines should not be understood as being organized primarily by specialties defined by their empirical objects of investigation, into Mertonian middle-range subfields like deviance, stratification, or political sociology. The deep structure of a discipline consists of the networks and literatures that are produced by the contact between empirical objects, ongoing traditions, and new disciplinary movements.

By this route we can return to the topic of neofunctionalism. In the phase of routinization that followed the emergence of Parsons' founding work, functionalism was presented as a consistent and increasingly completed theory, and elaboration and revision were the order of the day. In the second phase of postwar sociology, shifts in the disciplinary sensibility delegitimated these efforts and functionalism as a vital tradition came near to extinction. In the emerging third phase, scientific sensibility has shifted once again. In an altered theoretical and historical climate, new questions are being asked. These questions represent opportunities for dramatic disciplinary shift. In response, the functionalist tradition has entered a phase of reconstruction. Neo-functionalism is the result.

To fully elaborate the changes that have occurred within the functionalist tradition would be a complex and detailed task, for one would have to examine developments at every level of the scientific continuum. The discussion can be simplified by examining the process in terms of two basic genres, generalized discourse and research programs. By generalized discourse, we refer to discussions that argue about presuppositions, about ontology and epistemology, about the ideological and metaphysical implications of sociological argument, and about its broad historical grounding. Within the context of research programs, by contrast, such generalized issues are assumed to be relatively unproblematic. What becomes problematic, what propels this mode of scientific activity, is the need to provide interpretations or explanations of specific empirical structures and processes.

The discourse/research program distinction must not be confused with the distinctions introduced above. It is not isomorphic, for example, with core and peripheral concerns. The specific commitments that are pursued by research programs may be considered vital to the core of a tradition. Generalized discourse, for its part, is often directed to peripheral elements. Thus, in twentieth-century Marxism, in contrast to that of the nineteenth century, presuppositions about materialism and idealism have been considered part of the core; shifts toward idealism are not conceived of as threatening the "Marxist" character of theorizing. As for our model of scientific development, the processes we have identified as elaboration, revision, and reconstruction can occur through both discourse and research programs alike. In practice, it is usually discourse about more general issues that announces and introduces a reconstructive phase, for it is generalized issues that provide a framework within which more specific explanatory concerns can be conceived.[12] Indeed, in our consideration of neofunctionalism, we will focus primarily on the new kind of generalized discourse that has challenged the core. Following that discussion, we will present a brief overview of the research programs that have followed in its wake.

### The Generalized Discourse of Neofunctionalism

Generalized discourse occurs in both interpretive and expository modes. Via interpretation, theorists treat the work of the founder and other major figures in the tradition as difficult and problematic texts. Interpretive challenges are also mounted against the primary and secondary texts of other classical traditions and against the secondary literature that has developed within the home tradition as well. In the expository mode, by contrast, discourse is conducted on its own terms, general principles are set out and comparative frameworks established. While these modes of generalized discourse can be carried out by different theorists or at different points in the same discussion by a single person, they are connected to one another in an intimate way. No matter how apparently scholastic an interpretive discussion, the broader context of disciplinary struggle ensures that texts will never be considered simply for their own sake. Arguments about the meaning and validity of various texts represent one alternative, and sometimes the most effective one (Alexander 1987b) for engaging in substantive theoretical debate.

Generalized discourse makes arguments within the framework of, and in reference to, presuppositions, models, metamethodological commitments, and *Weltanschauung*, or world views. While it is possible to argue that Parsons took definite positions on each of these elements, we would argue, as neofunctionalists, that on each of these levels Parsons' orientation was ambiguous (Alexander 1983b). In terms of the problem of action, Parsons committed himself to a synthesis of material and idealist presuppositions; yet he consistently deviated from this professed aim in an idealist way. In terms of order, he aimed at linking individual actions and social structures, but from within his collectivist position he never theorized contingent effort. In terms of Parsons' theoretical model, functional and systems terminology are employed to describe a society of interrelated yet relatively independent parts. None of these are conceptualized as dominant, and equilibrium is considered an analytic reference point for evaluating social systems, not an empirical description of them. When Parsons' converted this model into a cybernetic system, however, he tilted toward one set of social system parts, the normative, raising it to a vertical position over another set, the material. He had great difficulty, moreover, in maintaining the analytic status of his model, often conflating the conceptualized ideal of equilibrium with the condition of an empirical society. Finally, there are extremely significant ambiguities in Parsons' ideology or *Weltanschauung*. Over the course of his long career, his ideological outlook shifted from critical to quiescent liberalism. What was a hopeful pessimism in the 1930s and 1940s became full-throated optimism in the 1950s and 1960s as a dedicated social scientist who aimed at constructing general covering laws, Parsons denied the connection of facts and values. Yet his growing confidence in modern, and particularly American, society made his work significantly less sensitive to the darker sides of modernity, to a wide range of depressing but undeniable facts about contemporary life.

What is perhaps most distinctive about the initial phases in the elaboration and revision of a sociological tradition is that they typically do not occur in a discursive mode. If we examine the three or four decades of Parsons' students' works, most of it, whether elaborative or revisionist, takes place within the school's research program. One need only think here of Bellah's *Tokugawa Religion* and *Beyond Belief*, Smelser's *Social Change in the Industrial Revolution* and *Theory of Collective Behavior*, and Eisenstadt's *The Political Systems of Empires*. In each of these works there is a powerful challenge to an element in the tradition's ambiguous core (Alexander 1979a, 1983b), but it is expressed in the mode of an implicit revision of explanatory apparatus, not in the framework of general discourse. [13]

When generalized discourse does emerge in this initial period, it is almost entirely affirmative, its aim being to explain the intricacies of a difficult text to students or outsiders. Good illustrations of such occasional discursive references are the Devereaux (1961) and Williams (1961) contributions to the Max Black volume on Parsons, various sections in Harry Johnson's (1960) once popular introductory textbook, and the initial chapters to the seminal books by Parsons' students we have listed above. Only in the waning days of functionalism's initial period, when Parsons came under increasing attack, did consistent exercises in generalized discourse appear. Victor Lidz's (1970, 1972) rejoinders to Albert Syzmanski's (1970a, 1970b, 1972) attacks on the value-laden character of Parsonian theory are a case in point. For the first time, Lidz raised the metamethodological underpinnings of Parsons' work in an explicit way. His rejoinders were brilliant elaborations and generalized defenses of Parsons' value-neutral stance, strictly from within the confines of the technical theory. The editors' introductions to the various sections of the two-volume Free Press festschrift for Parsons can be read in much the same way, as the last attempts by the last generation of "real Parsonians" to develop a general discourse that could affirm, elaborate, and revise the founder's work (Loubser et al. 1976).

Neofunctionalism can be distinguished from functionalism by its effort to reconstruct the core of the Parsonian tradition. Elaborative and revisionist efforts remain; indeed, the emergence of reconstructive efforts have relegitimated these more moderate, internalist lines of development. It is reconstruction, however, that has established the framework for a "neo" functionalism in the contemporary phase. Among those loosely associated with this movement, there is virtually no effort to return to the research program or discourse of the earlier period. A surprisingly large portion of earlier peripheral criticism has been accepted, just as the core itself is being reshaped in a responsive way. From this perspective, neofunctionalism is post-Parsonian. Its aim is to go beyond both the first and second phase of postwar sociology and to construct a new synthesis on the basis of the contributions of each.

It should not be surprising, then, that in contrast to the earlier phase of functionalist theorizing, generalized discourse has been central in the development of neofunctionalist work. Primarily, this has been in the service of reconstructive arguments about the core, but it has appeared also in the more affirmative practices of revisionism and even elaboration. Alexander's (1983b) work has explicitly attacked the idealist tendencies in Parsons' approach to action and argued that this reduction was responsible for many defects in Parsons' work, such as its tendency to see change in teleological terms and its relative slighting of economic rewards and political coercion. In a series of articles and working papers, Gould also sought to reemphasize material factors, in order similarly to reconstruct a more truly multidimensional tradition. His explicit challenge to Parsons remained reserved for his more specific and explanatory work (Gould 1987); in this more generalized domain, he chose revisionism (Gould, 1976), arguing that Parsons had issued an "urgent warning" against neglecting the material domain (Gould 1981).

In the initial period of neofunctionalism, the order issue seemed less salient. Here too, however, explicitly reconstructive discourse has strongly emerged. Recently, Alexander (1988c) has sharply criticized Parsons for his failure to bring contingency back into his theorizing of collective order. In response to this "black box" of individual action, Alexander has suggested formulations that are modeled on theories of individual exchange, interpretation, and pragmatic experience. In complementary efforts, Colomy (1982, 1985, 1990a, 1990b) has argued against the lack of attention to open-ended group processes in the functionalist understanding of change; in a series of theoretical and historical papers, he has developed systematic theories integrating work on collective behavior with structural approaches to social differentiation. Motivated by a similar interest to bring the individual back into functionalist work, Sciulli (1986, 1988) has argued that the early and the later Parsons himself understood voluntarism in a manner that emphasized its protean and individualistic qualities. Strongly criticizing Parsons' emphasis on socialization in his middle period work, Sciulli has argued for a convergence between Blumer's understanding of public negotiation and a neofunctionalist theory of public political life. Finally, though Munch's (1981, 1982) early articles on Parsons' neo-Kantian core were couched in the language of affirmative revision rather than reconstruction,[14] they, too, can be seen as a powerful attempt to bring effort and individual will back into the center of functionalist work.

There has also been an efflorescence of general and often polemical discussions about the model level of functional theory. Alexander (1983b) made a series of criticisms about the reification of functionalist and systems reasoning in Parsons' work. He also criticized the conflation between the AGIL divisions in the model and the empirical differentiation of contemporary society. Because these problematic applications of the model made it difficult to avoid the identification of functionalism with stasis and conflation, Alexander called for a return to the more concrete, group-oriented, early-middle phase of Parsons' work, in which the institutional content of a particular social system was clearly differentiated from its abstract mechanisms.

While in Germany it is actually the functionalized Weberianism of Schluchter and the Parsonian Marxism of Habermas that comes closest to this ideal, the German neofunctionalists have also altered Parsons' model in a revealing way.[15] Luhmann (1982), too, has criticized Parsons for reducing the dynamism of systems analysis by reifying it as a fourfold table; with his insistence on the tension between the internal and external environments of systems, he has developed a more supple and dynamic model.[16] Munch (1987a, 1988) has also changed the model forcefully, renaming the four subsystems in a manner that emphasizes contingency and the ideological and cultural imperative of rational communication.

Powerful and complementary challenges to Parsons' systems model have come from Gould and Colomy. In an ambitious challenge to Parsons, Gould (1985) has argued that functional models, drawn from systems or organicist theories, are necessary but limited. Developmental models must also be employed: abstract sketches of phases through which particular historical societies must pass if specified levels of development are to be achieved. Finally, in an argument that parallels Alexander's criticism of conflation, Gould insists that neither of these models should be confused with the actual structure of historical societies. This is provided by a "structural" model of particular institutional and group relations in a given period. For his part, Colomy (1985) has directed his efforts at altering Parsons' differentiation theory in a neofunctionalist way. He has argued that differentiation should be treated as a sharply delimited model; it is a "master trend" rather than an actual empirical description, much less an explanation for change. Within this altered framework, Colomy has offered a series of specific models of the structure and process of social change.

In the realm of ideology, the most radical break with orthodox funtionalism has simply been to make the ideological dimension of this tradition explicit. While arguing for the generally progressive and humanistic thrust of Parsons' work, Alexander has agreed with many of Parsons' critics about some of its conservative features. He himself has sought to politicize functionalism and tie it to the normative issues of the day. In his eulogy for Parsons in *The New Republic*, Alexander (1979b) described Parsons as providing "a sociology for liberals," stressing the normative and critical potential of Parsons' concepts of inclusion, differentiation, and value-generalization. Since that time he has tried to push neofunctionalism in a left-leaning but not radical direction. In an independent contribution to this effort, Colomy (1990c) has discussed this neofunctionalist orientation under the rubric of "critical modernism." Mayhew's (1982, 1984, 1990) work on the centrality of the public in democratic polities elaborates a similar normative-cum-empirical claim, as does Robertson's (1988) developing theory of globalization, which argues simultaneously for a new worldwide cosmopolitanism and for an increased tolerance for national variance, which, he suggests, Parsons' own modernization theory overlooked.

Sciulli and Gould have staked out more radical ideological claims. Operating in the space provided by his voluntaristic interpretation of Parsons' macrosociology, Sciulli (1989a) has developed empirical criteria for evaluating democratization in his theory of "societal constitutionalism." Arguing that modern industrial societies are threatened by political and economic oligarchies, on the one hand, and by a pacified citizenry on the other, he finds a countervailing force in Parsons' understanding of the increasing importance of collegial, self-governing communities. Gould (1987, 1985) embraces an even more restrictive and critical conception of capitalist political economy, and he has reconstructed a model of contemporary societies whose strains can be alleviated only through the transformation of property relations.

The most ambitious effort to transform disciplinary understandings of the functionalist *Weltanschauung* can be found in Holton and Turner's (1986) work. Describing Parsons as the only major theorist rooted in a society that did not experience the damaging transition from feudalism to capitalism, they argue that he has been the only theorist to conceptualize the positive possibilities of a progressive and stable modernity. Compared to Marx, Weber, and Durkheim, Parsons escapes from nostalgia because he sees the moral and pluralistic possibilities of *Gesellschaft*.

> An alternative option is to consider the possibility that *Gesellschaft* permits authentic expressions of values, rather than the "false," or "fetished" forms of consciousness as diagnosed by exponents of the Frankfurt school. In addition, value-pluralism under *Gesellschaft* need be considered neither as a series of narcissistic worlds, in retreat from the public domain, nor as an irreducible battle of Nietzschian wills. Rather it can be conceived as generating a normative basis for the orderly resolution of pluralism and diversity. (Holton and Turner 1986, 215–216)

In the second phase discourse of postwar work, Parsons was a conservative because he was not a radical. Arguing against the picture of Parsons as "an apologist for that kind of crass economic individualism that is often taken to underlie the capitalist economy," Holton and Turner portray Parsons' optimism, to the contrary, as reflecting "a profoundly moral and political identification with liberal democratic values" (216–217). In their view, it is Parsons, not his second phase critics, who now must be seen as occupying the higher moral ground.

> Parsons emerges from most confrontations with his critics as both morally engaged and politically committed, not as an apologist for capitalism, but as an anti-elitist and anti-Utopian social theorist. This standpoint moves us beyond the ambivalence of the classical sociologists toward modernity . . . . In all these respects Parsons' social theory announces the end of the classical phase of sociological thought. (218)

Earlier in this paper we spoke of the significance of the new ideological and political environment in generating the contemporary, third phase of sociological work. For neofunctionalism, the effect of this altered environment has been most powerfully crystallized by Holton and Turner; indeed, they present an argument that simply could not have been made at any earlier point. While offered as an affirmative elaboration and revision of the original rather than its reconstruction, their argument can take this position only because it is neofunctionalism, not orthodoxy, that now provides the framework for discourse in the Parsonian mode.[17] The powerfully reconstructive effects of their Parsons' portrait helps to renew the kind of critical modernism that is necessary to reform and sustain a liberal and democratic society.

The interpretive mode of generalized discourse is intimately tied to the expository mode we have just discussed. We have earlier pointed to the affirmative quality of the orthodox Parsonians' elaborations and revisions of their founder's texts. More interesting, perhaps, was this group's approach to classical texts outside the home tradition. Parsons (1937) had set the tone in *The Structure of Social Action*, when he stressed convergence within the work of his "group of recent European writers." That Parsons had himself constructed this convergence through powerful interpretation was never acknowledged, nor was the crucial fact that what they converged with was Parsons' emergent social theory rather than their own. Parsons often "revisited" Durkheim, Weber, and Freud, as his theory continually evolved. He needed to incorporate new elements from their work, but he could do so only by presenting these elements as if they converge with the new elements in his own. Between those theorists admitted to the classical canon of sociology there could be no fundamental strains, nor could there be any unresolvable strains between these theories and Parsons' own. This affirmative approach to interpretation – its expression as elaboration and revision – reached its apogee in Parsons and his collaborators' *Theories of Societies* (1961). In its depiction of the convergence of the entire history of social thought with action theory, this work was either extraordinarily naive or disingenuous.

Still, interpretive discourse did not flourish in the orthodox phase of functionalism any more than did discourse in the expository mode. When Parsonians engaged in interpretation, moreover, they modeled their discussions on Parsons' convergence model. Bellah's (1959) penetrating early article on Durkheim as a differentiation theorist is a case in point. Smelser's (1973) edition of Marx, Eisenstadt's (1971) of Weber, and the Lidz brothers' (1976) treatment of Piaget are similarly powerful examples.

Interpretation in the contemporary phase has, by contrast, been much more central and aggressively reconstructive. We have indicated above how Parsons' own work has been the object of several neofunctionalist critiques. In discussing classical works outside the home tradition, neofunctionalists have adopted a decidedly un-Parsonian line. They have stressed divergence rather than convergence, for they have need of theoretical resources beyond the home tradition itself.

We will take up the neofunctionalist dialogue with the classics of macrosociology first. Where Parsons not only neglected but in effect tried to repress Marx, Alexander (1982b) makes Marx paradigmatic of the material and instrumental theorizing that he criticizes Parsons for trying to ignore. He (1983a) sets Weber against Parsons in much the same way, arguing that Parsons underplayed the objectification that for Weber was the necessary underside of individuation. In a similar vein, Alexander (1988b) has stressed the symbolic and culturalistic elements in Durkheim, playing them off against the culturally reductionist tendencies in the orthodox functionalist concentration on "value." Gould (1987) has treated Marx, Hegel, Keynes, and Piaget in much the same way, stressing their distance from Parsons in the first instance, and the need to incorporate their "antifunctionalism" in the second. His theory of revolution and radical collective behavior has emerged from this reconstructed mix. For Sciulli (1985), the absence that interpretation must overcome is Habermas. While stressing in a revisionist mode the areas of convergence between Parsons and Habermas, he has also interpreted Habermas in a manner that exposes the self-limitations of Parsons' orthodox work. He has interpreted the legal theorist Lon Fuller in the same reconstructive way. Both Habermas and Fuller (Sciulli, 1989, 1990) provide critical resources for Sciulli's neofunctionalist theory of societal constitutionalism.

There has also emerged within neofunctionalist interpretation a significant dialogue with the central texts of the microsociological tradition. Because Parsons did not recognize the problem of contingent action, it is not surprising that his relation to these traditions never went beyond ceremonial remarks on their convergence with his own. For neofunctionalism, by contrast, it has become important to understand the divergence between microsociology and the orthodox tradition, in order to develop theoretical resources for opening neofunctionalism up to contingency in the ways we have discussed above.

Alexander (1985b, 1987c, 195–280) has emphasized, for example, a collective thrust in Mead, Peirce, and Goffman, and also in the phenomenological theory of Husserl, Schutz, and the early Garfinkel, arguing that such theoretical resources have been largely ignored by these traditions' contemporary interpreters. While Munch (1986, 1987b) and Sciulli (1988), by contrast, do not refer to this thrust in their interpretations of interactionist theory, all three theorists agree that neofunctionalism must draw upon these traditions in order to incorporate considerations of contingency and voluntarism. These theoretical appropriations are openly presented as remedies to the acknowledged shortcomings of orthodoxy, and defended as a means by which the more original, creative, and synthesizing project of neofunctionalists can be advanced.

Within the new environments of the third postwar phase, and in response to the opportunities and provocations provided by the new generalized discourse, there has been an outpouring of neofunctionalist research that, if this term is taken in its broad rather than restricted sense, can be called a research program. Earlier functionalist research was guided by a reaffirmative strategy, envisioning a single, all-embracing conceptual scheme that tied areas of specialized research into a tightly wrought package. What neofunctionalist empirical work points to, by contrast, is a package loosely organized around a general logic and possessing a number of rather autonomous "proliferations" and "variations" at different levels and in different empirical domains (Wagner 1984; Wagner and Berger 1985).

## A Note on Research Programs in Neofunctionalism

In the preceding sections we have described the emergence of neofunctionalism, treating it as a central feature of the third phase of postwar sociology and identifying the intellectual and socio-political grounds for its resurgence. Neofunctionalism's discursive elements – its presuppositions, ontology, epistemology, and ideological implications – have been outlined. But neofunctionalism is more than generalized discourse. It also seeks to explain particular facets of the social world.

The most developed neofunctionalist research programs have emerged in the areas of social change, cultural sociology, political sociology, mass communications, feminist studies, the professions, and economic sociology. While a detailed examination of these programs cannot be presented here, an overview highlighting the most prominent contours of this work is in order.[18]

Much of neofunctionalist research has charted a decidedly revisionist course. Studies of structural differentiation, for instance, revise orthodox functionalism's approach to change in four ways: 1) they supplement descriptions of the "master trend" toward increasingly specialized institutions by developing models of patterned departures from that trend (e.g., Alexander 1981; Lechner 1984, 1985, 1990; Tiryakian 1985, 1990; Champagne 1990; Colomy 1982, 1985, 1990a, 1990b; Hondrich 1990; Surace 1982; Smelser 1985, 1990; Colomy and Tausig 1988); 2) they move beyond purely systemic and evolutionary explanations of differentiation toward accounts that stress contingency, concrete groups, conflict, and social movements and collective behavior (e.g., Eisenstadt 1980; Colomy 1985, 1990a, 1990b; Colomy and Rhoades 1988; Colomy and Tausig 1988; Rhoades 1990; Mayhew 1990; Alexander 1980; Smelser 1985); 3) they recognize that the orthodox emphasis on adaptive upgrading, inclusion, and value generalization represents but one configuration among a much broader array of the possible outcomes of social differentiation (e.g., Luhmann 1982, 1990a, 1990b; Alexander 1978, 1983b, 1984; Eder 1990; Rhoades 1990; Munch 1981, 1982, 1983, 1987a, 1988, 1990a, 1990b; Sciulli 1985, 1990b; Mayhew 1984, 1990); 4) they replace a complacent liberal optimism concerning the process and consequences of differentiation with a critical modernism that is more attuned to the dark sides that are ineluctably related to it (e.g., Sciulli 1990a, 1990b; Mayhew 1984, 1990; Munch 1987a, 1988; Colomy 1990c).[19]

Conventional functionalist research into the culture–society relation has also been critiqued and revised. The orthodox approach posited a cultural system neatly institutionalized in the social system through values that the personality internalized via socialization. Archer (1985, 1988) argues that this model is guilty of "downward conflation," for it holds that an integrated cultural system engulfs the social and personality systems. Alexander (1984) suggests that this conventional approach to institutionalization, which he calls the cultural specification model, represents only one form culture–society relations can assume. He proposes two additional modes. In cultural refraction, conflicting social groups and functions produce antagonistic subcultures that continue to draw upon a value system that is integrated at the cultural level. In cultural columnization, by contrast, there are fundamental antagonisms in both the social and cultural systems, interest groupings have no significant common beliefs, and genuinely antagonistic political cultural groupings emerge.[20]

In their effort to develop a broadly neofunctionalist feminist sociology, Miriam Johnson and her colleagues (Johnson 1975, 1977, 1981, 1982, 1988a, 1988b; Johnson et al. 1975, 1981; Gill et al. 1987; Stockard and Johnson 1979) reappropriate and revise elements of the Parsonian legacy others have left behind. They reconceptualize the traditional distinction between instrumentality and expressiveness, the structural differentiation model of the family, socialization, and Parsons' particular application of his culture, society and personality model to account for the origins and reproduction of gender inequality. When considered in isolation, each of their reconceptualizations can be accurately characterized as revisionist. Taken together, however, it is readily apparent that this research program is animated by a reconstructionist thrust. It aims not at describing how the family "produces" human personalities capable of assuming adult roles in a complex, differentiated society – the orthodox Parsonian issue – but at explaining the radically different question of how a cultural and social system subordinates and distorts a particular class of personalities.

Johnson and her colleagues not only revise and reconstruct Parsons, they also wed their reconfiguration of orthodox functionalism to other intellectual traditions, especially psychoanalysis and feminist scholarship. Jeffrey Prager (1986) has extended and revised the functionalist treatment of political sociology in an analogous way. He draws on Parsons' discussion of a differentiated societal community to devise a neofunctionalist conception of the public sphere. He ties that structural concept to the more concrete and processual symbolic interactionist approach that emphasizes the content, dynamics and effects of actual public discourse. With the aid of this powerful theoretical link between functionalism and interactionism, Prager's investigation of Ireland's movement toward democracy demonstrates not only how democratic institutions operate, but also how they are created in the first place.

In addition to its reconstructionist and revisionist thrust, neofunctionalist research also contains an elaborationist current. For instance, Robertson's (1985, 1986, 1987, 1990; Robertson and Chirico 1985; Robertson and Lechner 1985) analyses of the relationship between globalization and cultural change carries the Parsonian theme of value generalization to the level of the world system. At the same time, because he is sensitive to the wide diversity of cultural responses engendered by globalization, Robertson revises Parsons by eschewing the notion that these changes amount merely to a global version of cultural specification and normative integration.

More recently, such elaborative research has occurred less against the backdrop of earlier orthodox functionalism, but in relation to the rapidly developing body of neofunctionalist theory itself. Rothenbuhler (1986a, 1986b, 1987, 1988a, 1988b, 1988c, 1988d, n.d.; Peters and Rothenbuhler 1988) draws on general statements of the neofunctionalist position as well as on neofunctionalist treatments of culture to fashion an impressive research program in mass communications. Drawing upon highly abstract neofunctionalist discussions of the micro–macro link, Colomy and Rhoades (1988) develop a series of ideal-typical models and causal hypotheses to explain educational change in the late nineteenth century United States. In a similar way, Lehman (1988) uses Alexander's analysis of presuppositions about action and order to generate a new and more complex empirical research program on political power and the state. Rambo's (1988) work in economic sociology elaborates neofunctionalist treatments of culture, while Edles (1988) draws on the same neofunctionalist literature to analyze Spain's civil religion and its recent transition to democracy.

In sum, while a central part of neofunctionalism has been carried out at the level of general theory, there is a complementary, and rapidly growing, body of more empirically oriented work. This work supplements the reconstructionist thrust of neofunctionalist metatheory with several significant revisions of orthodox functionalism and has even begun to elaborate neofunctionalist general theory itself.

## Conclusion

Our task in this paper has been to demonstrate that neofunctionalism is delivering on its promissory notes. Today, neofunctionalism is much more than a promise; it has become a field of intense theoretical discourse and growing empirical investigation. We have conducted this demonstration within the framework of a nascent model of social scientific knowledge. Because sociological knowledge is generated by traditions, the most compelling criteria for evaluating scientific progress is comparative, in terms of different phases in the life of a particular tradition and in terms of the relations between competing traditions. By making such comparisons we can measure social scientific progress, although, to be sure, this is progress in a postpositivist sense.

In this paper, we assessed neofunctionalism's advances primarily by comparing them to the older orthodoxy. Toward that end several terms – reconstruction, expropriation, revision, and elaboration – have been employed. Our thesis has been that, at both discursive and more empirical levels, neofunctionalism has produced significant advances relative to earlier renditions of the tradition. We have tried to show that the reconstructions, revisions, and elaborations that compose neofunctionalism have been directed precisely at those areas of the orthodox tradition that critics, both internal and external, earlier identified as theoretically or empirically suspect. If neofunctionalism represents theoretical progress – and we think it does – this reflects its ability to produce satisfactory reconstructions and revisions in response to critiques that once threatened to destroy the functionalist tradition altogether.

Of course, theoretical progress cannot be judged on internal grounds alone. Comparisons must also be made with competing traditions. Certainly the "critics of functionalism" will respond with new kinds of ripostes. Some will try to ignore the vast changes that neofunctionalism has wrought. Others will recognize that fundamental shifts have occurred and will reformulate the nature of their critiques. We eagerly await these reformulations. The conventional debates have become stale and dry. We are in the midst of a sea change in sociological theory. Old alignments are dissolving; new configurations are being born. "Neofunctionalism" cannot be stuffed back into the old box.

## Notes

1. Now that the second volume of Habermas' *Theory of Communicative Action* has been translated into English (Habermas 1987), the seriousness of his encounter with Parsons will clearly be seen. We would argue, in fact, that the framework Habermas employs in both volumes of this work can be seen as a neo-Marxist revision of Parsonian concepts.

2. But not revised enough, from our point of view. Ritzer, for example, simply places "neofunctionalism" as the concluding section to "functionalism," following it with sections on conflict theory and so forth. We will argue below that the vitality of neofunctionalism casts doubt on this conventional division of theory texts. Neofunctionalism has taken as its project to open itself up to social conflict and contingent interaction. Insofar as it does so, then certainly "conflict theory" and "ethnomethodology" cannot be presented as responses to contemporary functionalist work. These reified divisions were never theoretically accurate ones (Alexander 1982a), but they did represent at least the historical self-consciousness of the profession in what we will below call the second phase of postwar sociology. At this point, we believe, they do not even do that. Sociology is embarked upon a third phase of postwar development which is in the process of making these textbook divisions obsolete.

3. After making this claim, we want immediately to stress that neofunctionalism, while a genuine intellectual movement, is not an integrated theory. There is much disagreement between those who we would classify under this rubric, and some, in fact, do not welcome the general designation as such. We will talk more openly about this unformed and emergent character below.

4. We have limited our discussion only to developments within what American sociologist consider to be the matrix of their discipline. Outside of it, of course, there are also extremely important illustrations of this third phase. In France, for example, we would point to the poststructuralist movement, where cultural structures – discursive formations (Foucault 1984), cultural capital (Bourdieu), and political narratives (Lyotard 1984) – have replaced material ones.

5. We are drawing here from a work on sociological theory in preparation for the Prentice-Hall *Foundations of Sociology* series.

6. After Marx, there are the elaborations and revisions of writers like Engels, Kautsky, Otto Bauer, Labriola, and others. These specifications were interrupted, however, by the more radical reconstructionist efforts of the World War I generation, theorists like Lenin, Gramsci, Lukacs, Korsch, and others. Subsequent specification of Marxism often occurred within these reformulated Marxian traditions of Lenin-Marx, Gramsci-Marx, Lukacs-Marx, etc., whether or not the reconstruction was explicitly recognized. Later in the history of the Marxian tradition, thinkers like Sartre, Althusser, E. P. Thompson, and those associated with the Frankfurt School introduced a new round of more radical reformulation.

7. Thus, theorists who created new traditions were at an earlier point usually important reconstructors of the traditions out of which their new theories were formed. Marx is a case in point. In the early 1840s he was a "Young Hegelian," which was a radical, quasi-religious movement of Hegel's last students to reopen the master's theory to critical strands of the Enlightenment and even to socialist thought. When Marx encountered political economy, he felt compelled to leave the Hegelian fold and created historical materialism. Interesting parallels can be drawn for Parsons. For the first ten years of his scholarly life, through the very publication of *The Structure of Social Action*, he seemed devoted to reconstructing the classical sociological traditions. He became more ambitious only at a later point in his career. One should be careful not to see the ideal-typical sequences – elaboration–revision–reconstruction–tradition creation – as a scale of theoretical contribution. Most of the greatest minds in social science, for example, never make the transition from reconstruction to tradition creation, and many who have made the transition were much the worse for it. The works of Von Wiese are long forgotten, but the writings of Gramsci, Lukacs, Mannheim, and Mauss continue to be intently pursued.

8. Vico's work represents just such an example from classical traditions, Spencer's from the sociological.

9. For an excellent discussion from a very similar point, see the detailed critiques Bryan Turner makes of the efforts at theoretical cumulation that comprise the collection of ASA miniconference papers Jonathan Turner (1989) has collected in *Theory Building in Sociology*. Bryan Turner (1989, 132) concludes: "In sociology, we appear to have more dispersal and fragmentation of approaches than cumulation and organized growth, and these theoretical fragmentations are products of institutional fragmentation and competition between intellectuals for audience and patronage. . . . Analytical rupture rather than theory cumulation is the decisive aspect of sociology's history in the twentieth century."

10. Think here of vulgar Marxism, which actually encompasses most of what has been accepted as legitimate Marxist work, or of the reductionistic and mechanistic applications of Durkheim and Weber, which have been offered by some of their most devoted followers. It need hardly be said that Parsonian functionalism had its own large share of simplifiers.

11. For a discussion that highlights the concept of "sensibility" in the investigation of the shifting commitments of a major contemporary theorist *see* Alexander (1986).

12. This is by no means always true, however. Bernstein's empirical challenge to the reigning Marxist proposition about the falling rate of profit – an issue of research program rather than generalized discourse – struck at the core of the tradition and initiated the reconstruction that came to be called the "social democratic" tendency in Marxism. This tendency was accompanied, however, by a great deal of generalized discourse.

13. Bellah's essays for "symbolic realism" would have to be read as an exception in this regard, they were discursive, generalized arguments. Yet they remained revisionist. Rather than critically confronting Parsons' cultural theory, Bellah argued symbolic realism was one clear implication of it.

14. In this regard, Munch's articles of this period, and some of his later work as well, resemble Alexander's (1978) own earlier discursive defense of Parsons. Though clearly engaging in revision, Alexander did not choose to confront Parsons' theory in a reconstructive way. In the late 1970s, the second phase of postwar theorizing was still a vigorous rising tide, and those sympathetic to Parsons' tradition confronted his critics in the polemical spirit of the time. It may have been Parsons' death in 1979 as well as the changing theoretical and political climate that allowed a less defensive and more reconstructive posture to be assumed.

15. It might be useful, in fact, to introduce the concept "expropriation" to refer to the incorporation by one tradition of key elements of an opposing tradition in order to elaborate, revise, and reconstruct the home tradition itself. Thus, while Schluchter and Habermas express a sharp antipathy to functionalism, in this third phase of theorizing they have expropriated Parsons' theory in creative and quite thorough-going ways. Expropriation is one sign of the expansionary phase of a tradition.

16. The problem for Luhmann is quite different: he has not developed a theory of institutions, groups, and concrete interaction. The differences between Luhmann's and Munch's work, on the one hand, and the American and English neofunctionalists', on the other, is a topic which must soon be taken up. The differences stem less from differences in national traditions, perhaps, than from the contrasts in the disciplinary environments within which each emerged. In Germany, neither conflict nor micro sociology ever became as strongly institutionalized.

17. "Since the death of Talcott Parsons in Munich in 1979, it has become clear that a significant re-appraisal of Parsons' sociology and his impact on modern sociology is well underway.... This volume ... may appropriately be regarded as part of this new wave of re-evaluation" (Holton and Turner 1986, 1). The movement beyond affirmative revision is demonstrated by the fact that in his review of Holton and Turner's book in the *American Journal of Sociology*, Lechner (1988) – himself an active theorist in the reconstructionist movement – offers the criticism that it is "too positive" about Parsons!

18. For a detailed discussion of these research programs, *see* Alexander and Colomy (forthcoming).

19. For a much more detailed analysis of recent developments in differentiation theory, *see* Colomy (1986, 1990c). For discussions that situate the emergence and development of differentiation theory in a broader historical and theoretical context *see* Giesen (1988, 1990) and Alexander (1988d).

20. Our discussion here has focused only on the primordial issue of culture–society boundary relations. Once the possible attenuation of this boundary relation has been acknowledged, however, a more internalist and less socially circumscribed understanding of the cultural system can begin to be developed. In his efforts to incorporate semiotic and hermeneutic models, and to elaborate the "late Durkheimian" approach to cultural studies, Alexander's research has recently moved in this direction (1988b). *See also* Edles (1988) and Rambo and Chan (1988).

## References

Alexander, Jeffrey C. 1978. "Formal and Substantive Voluntarism in the Work of Talcott Parsons: A Theoretical and Ideological Reinterpretation." *American Sociological Review* 43: 177–198.

Alexander, Jeffrey C. 1979a. "Paradigm Revision and 'Parsonianism.'" *Canadian Journal of Sociology* 4: 343–357.

Alexander, Jeffrey C. 1979b. "Sociology for Liberals." *The New Republic* (June 2) 1: 10–12.

Alexander, Jeffrey C. 1980. "Core Solidarity, Ethnic Outgroups, and Social Differentiation: A Multi-Dimensional Model of Inclusion in Modern Societies." In Jacques Dofny and Akinsola Akiwowo, eds., *National and Ethnic Movements*. Beverly Hills: Sage.

Alexander, Jeffrey C. 1981. "The Mass Media in Systemic, Historical and Comparative Perspective." In Elihu Katz and Thomas Szeckso, eds., *Mass Media and Social Change*. Beverly Hills: Sage.

Alexander, Jeffrey C. 1982a. *Theoretical Logic in Sociology. Volume 1: Positivism, Presuppositions, and Current Controversies*. Berkeley: University of California Press.

Alexander, Jeffrey C. 1982b. *Theoretical Logic in Sociology. Volume 2: The Antinomies of Classical Thought: Marx and Durkheim*. Berkeley: University of California Press.

Alexander, Jeffrey C. 1983a. *Theoretical Logic in Sociology. Volume 3: The Classical Attempt at Theoretical Synthesis: Max Weber*. Berkeley: University of California Press.

Alexander, Jeffrey C. 1983b. *Theoretical Logic in Sociology. Volume 4: The Modern Reconstruction of Classical Thought: Talcott Parsons*. Berkeley: University of California Press.

Alexander, Jeffrey C. 1984. "Three Models of Culture and Society Relations: Toward an Analysis of Watergate." *Sociological Theory* 2: 290–314.

Alexander, Jeffrey C. 1985a. "Introduction." In J. Alexander, ed., *Neofunctionalism*. Beverly Hills: Sage.

Alexander, Jeffrey C. 1985b. "The Individualist Dilemma in Phenomenology and Interactionism: Toward a Synthesis with the Classical Tradition." In S. N. Eisenstadt and H. I. Helle, eds., *Perspectives on Sociological Theory*. Vol. 1. Beverly Hills: Sage.

Alexander, Jeffrey C. 1986. "Science, Sense, and Sensibility." *Theory and Society* 15: 443–463.

Alexander, Jeffrey C. 1987a. "Action and Its Environments." In Jeffrey C. Alexander, Bernhard Giesen, Richard Munch, and Neil J. Smelser, eds., *The Micro–Macro Link*. Berkeley: University of California Press.

Alexander, Jeffrey C. 1987b. "On the Centrality of the Classics." In Anthony Giddens and Jonathan Turner, eds. *Social Theory Today*. London: Polity Press.

Alexander, Jeffrey C. 1987c. *Twenty Lectures*. New York: Columbia University Press.

Alexander, Jeffrey C. 1988a. "Between Progress and Apocalypse: Social Theory and the Dream of Reason in the Twentieth Century." Paper presented at the conference, "Social Progress and Sociological Theory: Movements, Forces, and Ideas at the End of the Twentieth Century." Krakow, Poland.

Alexander, Jeffrey C. 1988b. "Culture and Political Crisis: Watergate and Durkheimian Sociology." In Jeffrey C. Alexander, ed., *Durkheimian Sociology: Cultural Studies*. New York: Columbia University Press.

Alexander, Jeffrey C. 1988c. *Action and Its Environments.* New York: Columbia University Press.
Alexander, Jeffrey C. 1988d. "Durkheim's Problem and Differentiation Theory Today." In Jeffrey C. Alexander, *Action and Its Environments.* New York: Columbia University Press.
Alexander, Jeffrey C., and Paul Colomy. 1985. "Toward Neofunctionalism: Eisenstadt's Change Theory and Symbolic Interactionism." *Sociological Theory* 2: 11–23.
Alexander, Jeffrey C., and Bernhard Giesen. 1987. "From Reduction to Linkage: The Long View of the Micro–Macro Debate." In Jeffrey C. Alexander, Bernhard Giesen, Richard Munch, and Neil J. Smelser, eds., *The Micro–Macro Link.* Berkeley: University of California Press.
Archer, Margaret S. 1985. "The Myth of Cultural Integration." *British Journal of Sociology* 36: 333–353.
Archer, Margaret S. 1988. *Culture and Agency: The Place of Culture in Social Theory.* Cambridge: Cambridge University Press.
Becker, Howard. 1982. *Art Worlds.* Berkeley: University of California Press.
Bellah, Robert N. 1957. *Tokugawa Religion: The Values of Pre-Industrial Japan.* Glencoe, Ill.: Free Press.
Bellah, Robert N. 1959. "Durkheim and History." *American Sociological Review* 24: 447–461.
Bellah, Robert N. 1970. *Beyond Belief.* New York: Harper and Row.
Bellah, Robert N. 1973. "Introduction." In Robert N. Bellah, ed., *Emile Durkheim: On Morality and Society.* Chicago: University of Chicago Press.
Blau, Peter M. 1977. *Inequality and Heterogeneity: A Primitive Theory of Social Structure.* New York: Free Press.
Calhoun, Craig. 1982. *The Question of Class Struggle: Social Foundations of Popular Radicalism during the Industrial Revolution.* Chicago: University of Chicago Press.
Camic, Charles. 1986. "The Return of the Functionalists." *Contemporary Sociology* 15: 692–695.
Champagne, Duane. 1990. "Culture, Differentiation, and Environment: Social Change in Tlingit Society." In Jeffrey C. Alexander and Paul Colomy, eds., *Differentiation Theory and Social Change: Historical and Comparative Perspectives.* New York: Columbia University Press.
Coleman, James S. 1986a. "Social Theory, Social Research, and a Theory of Action." *American Journal of Sociology* 91: 1309–1335.
Coleman, James S. 1986b. *Individual Interests and Collective Action: Selected Essays.* New York: Cambridge University Press.
Coleman, James S. 1987. "Microfoundations and Macrosocial Behavior." In Jeffrey C. Alexander, Bernhard Giesen, Richard Munch, and Neil J. Smelser, eds., *The Micro–Macro Link.* Berkeley: University of California Press.
Collins, Randall. 1975. *Conflict Sociology: Toward an Explanatory Science.* New York: Academic Press.
Collins, Randall. 1981. "On the Micro-Foundations of Macro-Sociology." *American Journal of Sociology* 86: 984–1014.
Collins, Randall. 1987. "Interaction Ritual Chains, Power and Property: The Micro–Macro Connection as an Empirically Based Theoretical Problem." In Jeffrey C. Alexander, Bernhard Giesen, Richard Munch, and Neil J. Smelser, eds., *The Micro–Macro Link.* Berkeley: University of California Press.

Collins, Randall. 1988a. *Theoretical Sociology*. San Diego: Harcourt Brace Jovanovich.
Collins, Randall. 1988b. "The Durkheimian Tradition in Conflict Sociology." In Jeffrey C. Alexander, ed., *Durkheimian Sociology: Cultural Studies*. New York: Cambridge University Press.
Colomy, Paul. 1985. "Uneven Structural Differentiation: Toward a Comparative Approach." In Jeffrey C. Alexander, ed., *Neofunctionalism*. Beverly Hills: Sage.
Colomy, Paul. 1986. "Recent Developments in the Functionalist Approach to Change." *Sociological Focus* 19: 139–158.
Colomy, Paul. 1990a. "Uneven Differentiation and Incomplete Institutionalization: Political Change and Continuity in the Early American Nation." In Jeffrey C. Alexander and Paul Colomy, eds., *Differentiation Theory and Social Change: Comparative and Historical Perspectives*. New York: Columbia University Press.
Colomy, Paul. 1990b. "Strategic Groups and Political Differentiation in the Antebellum United States." In Jeffrey C. Alexander and Paul Colomy, eds., *Differentiation Theory and Social Change: Comparative and Historical Perspectives*. New York: Columbia University Press.
Colomy, Paul. 1990c. "Revisions and Progress in Differentiation Theory." In Jeffrey C. Alexander and Paul Colomy, eds., *Differentiation Theory and Social Change: Comparative and Historical Perspectives*. New York: Columbia University Press.
Colomy, Paul and Gary Rhoades. 1988. "Specifying the Micro–Macro Link: An Application of General Theory to the Study of Structural Differentiation." Paper presented at the Annual Meetings of the American Sociological Association, Atlanta,
Colomy, Paul and Mark Tausig. 1988. "The Differentiation of Applied Sociology: Prospects and Problems." Manuscript.
Coser, Lewis A. 1956. *The Functions of Social Conflict*. New York: Free Press.
Darnton, Robert. 1982. *The Literary Underground of the Old Regime*. Cambridge, Mass.: Harvard University Press.
Devereux, Edward C., Jr. 1961. "Parsons' Sociological Theory." In Max Black, ed. *The Social Theories of Talcott Parsons*. Carbondale and Edwardsville: Southern Illinois University Press.
Eder, Klaus. 1990. "Contradictions and Social Evolution." In Hans Haferkamp and Neil J. Smelser, eds., *Social Change and Modernity*. Berkeley: University of California Press.
Edles, Laura D. 1988. "Political Culture and the Transition to Democracy in Spain." Ph.D. dissertation, University of California, Los Angeles.
Eisenstadt, S. N. 1963. *The Political Systems of Empires*. New York: Free Press.
Eisenstadt, S. N. 1971. "Introduction." In S. N. Eisenstadt, ed., *Weber on Charisma and Institution Building*. Chicago: University of Chicago Press.
Eisenstadt, S. N. 1980. "Cultural Orientations, Institutional Entrepreneurs, and Social Change: Comparative Analyses of Traditional Civilizations." *American Journal of Sociology* 85: 840–869.
Eisenstadt, S. N. 1986. "Culture and Social Structure Revisited." *International Sociology* 1: 297–320.
Fine, Gary Alan. 1984. "Negotiated Orders and Organizational Cultures." *Annual Review of Sociology* 10: 39–262.
Fine, Gary Alan. 1988. "Symbolic Interactionism in the Post-Blumerian Age." Paper presented at the Maryland Theory Conference.
Foucault, Michel. 1984. *The Foucault Reader*. Edited by Paul Rabinow. New York: Pantheon.

Friedrichs, Robert. 1970. *A Sociology of Sociology*. New York: Free Press.
Geertz, Clifford. 1973. *The Interpretation of Cultures*. New York: Basic Books.
Giddens, Anthony. 1971. *Capitalism and Modern Social Theory*. Cambridge: Cambridge University Press.
Giddens, Anthony. 1984. *The Constitution of Society*. Berkeley: University of California Press.
Giddens, Anthony, and Jonathan Turner, eds. 1987. *Social Theory Today*. London: Polity Press.
Giesen, Bernhard. 1987. "Media and Markets." In M. Schmid and F. M. Wuketits, eds., *Evolutionary Theory in Social Science*. West Germany: Reidel.
Giesen, Bernhard. 1988. "The Autonomy of Social Change." *International Review of Sociology*, forthcoming.
Giesen, Bernhard. 1990. "The Change in 'Change': An Evolution Theoretical View on the History of the Concept." In Hans Haferkamp and Neil J. Smelser, eds. *Social Change and Modernity*. Berkeley: University of California Press.
Gill, Sandra, Jean Stockard, Miriam Johnson, and Suzanne Williams. 1987. "Measuring Gender Differences: The Expressive Dimension and Critique of Androgyny Scales." *Sex Roles* 17: 375-400.
Goffman, Erving. 1974. *Frame Analysis*. New York: Harper and Row.
Goode, William. 1978. *The Celebration of Heroes: Prestige as a Social Control System*. Berkeley: University of California Press.
Gould, Mark. 1981. "Parsons versus Marx: An Earnest Warning." *Sociological Inquiry* 51: 197-218.
Gould, Mark. 1985. "Prolegomena to Any Future Theory of Societal Crisis." In Jeffrey C. Alexander, ed., *Neofunctionalism*. Beverly Hills: Sage.
Gould, Mark. 1987. *Revolution in the Development of Capitalism*. Berkeley: University of California Press.
Habermas, Jürgen. 1975. *Legitimation Crisis*. Translated by Thomas McCarthy. Boston: Beacon Press.
Habermas, Jürgen. 1984. *The Theory of Communicative Action, Volume 1: Reason and Rationalization of Society*. Translated by Thomas McCarthy. Boston: Beacon Press.
Habermas, Jürgen. 1987. *The Theory of Communicative Action, Volume 2: Lifeworld and System: A Critique of Functionalist Reason*. Translated by Thomas McCarthy. Boston: Beacon Press.
Heritage, John, and David Greatbatch. 1986. "Generating Applause: A Study of Rhetoric and Response at Party Political Conferences." *American Journal of Sociology* 92: 110-157.
Holton, Robert J. 1986. "Talcott Parsons and the Theory of Economy and Society." In Robert J. Holton and Bryan S. Turner, *Talcott Parsons: On Economy and Society*. London: Routledge and Kegan Paul.
Holton, Robert J., and Bryan S. Turner. 1986. *Talcott Parsons: On Economy and Society*. London: Routledge and Kegan Paul.
Hondrich, Karl Otto. 1990. "World Society versus Niche Societies: Paradoxes of Undirectional Evolution." In Hans Haferkamp and Neil J. Smelser, eds., *Social Change and Modernity*. Berkeley: University of California Press.
Johnson, Harry M. 1960. *Sociology: A Systematic Introduction*. New York: Harcourt, Brace.
Johnson, Miriam M. 1963. "Sex Role Learning in the Nuclear Family." *Child Development* 34: 319-333.
Johnson, Miriam M. 1975. "Fathers, Mothers, and Sex Typing." *Sociological Inquiry* 45: 15-26.

Johnson, Miriam M. 1977. "Androgyny and the Maternal Principle." *School Review* 86: 50–69.
Johnson, Miriam M. 1981. "Heterosexuality, Male Dominance, and the Father Image." *Sociological Inquiry* 51: 129–139.
Johnson, Miriam M. 1982. "Fathers and Femininity in Daughters: A Review of the Research." *Sociology and Social Research* 67: 1–17.
Johnson, Miriam M. 1988a. *Strong Mothers, Weak Wives: The Search for Gender Equality.* Berkeley: University of California Press.
Johnson, Miriam M. 1988b. "Feminism and the Theories of Talcott Parsons." Paper presented at the American Sociological Association meetings, Atlanta, Ga.
Johnson, Minam M., Jean Stockard, Joan Acker, and Claudeen Naffziger. 1975. "Expressiveness Reevaluated." *School Review* 83: 617–644.
Johnson, Miriam M., Jean Stockard, Mary K. Rothbart, and Lisa Friedman. 1981. "Sexual Preference, Feminism, and Women's Perceptions of Their Parents." *Sex Roles* 7: 1–18.
Knorr-Cetina, K., and Aaron V. Cicourel, eds. 1981. *Advances in Social Theory and Methodology: Toward an Integration of Micro- and Macro- Sociologies.* Boston: Routledge and Kegan Paul.
Lechner, Frank. 1984. "Ethnicity and Revitalization in the Modern World System." *Sociological Focus* 17: 243–256.
Lechner, Frank. 1985. "Modernity and Its Discontents." In Jeffrey C. Alexander, ed., *Neofunctionalism.* Beverly Hills: Sage.
Lechner, Frank. 1990. "Fundamentalism as Path Away from Differentiation." In Jeffrey C. Alexander and Paul Colomy, eds., *Differentiation Theory and Social Change: Comparative and Historical Perspectives.* New York: Columbia University Press.
Lefort, Claude. 1986. *The Political Forms of Modern Society: Bureaucracy, Democracy, Totalitananism.* Edited and with an introduction by John B. Thompson. Cambridge, Mass.: MIT Press.
Lehman, Edward W. 1988. "The Theory of the State versus the State of Theory." *American Sociological Review* 53: 807–823.
Lewis, David J., and Robert L. Smith. 1980. *American Sociology and Pragmatism: Mead, Chicago Sociology, and Symbolic Interaction.* Chicago: University of Chicago Press.
Lidz, Charles W., and Victor M. Lidz. 1976. "Piaget's Psychology of Intelligence and the Theory of Action." In J. Loubser et al., eds., *Explorations in General Theory in Social Science.* New York: Free Press.
Lidz, Victor. 1970. "Values in Sociology: A Critique of Szymanski." *Sociological Inquiry* 40: 13–20.
Lidz, Victor. 1972. "On the Construction of Objective Theory: Rejoinder to Syzmanski." *Sociological Inquiry* 42: 51–64.
Loubser, J. J., R. C. Baum, A. Effrat, and V. M. Lidz, eds. 1976. *Explorations in General Theory in Social Science.* Vols. 1 and 2. New York: Free Press.
Luhmann, Niklas. 1982. *The Differentiation of Society.* Translated by Stephen Holmes and Charles Larmore. New York: Columbia University Press.
Luhmann, Niklas. 1990a. "The Paradox of System Differentiation and the Evolution of Society." In Jeffrey C. Alexander and Paul Colomy, eds., *Differentiation Theory and Social Change: Comparative and Historical Perspectives.* New York: Columbia University Press.
Luhmann, Niklas. 1990b. "The Direction of Evolution." In Hans Haferkamp and Neil J. Smelser, eds., *Social Change and Modernity,* Berkeley: University of California Press.

Lyotard, Jean Francois. 1984. *The Postmodern Condition: A Report on Knowledge.* Translated by Geoff Bennington and Brian Massumi. Minneapolis: University of Minnesota Press.
Mayhew, Leon, ed. 1982. *Talcott Parsons: On Institutions and Social Evolution.* Chicago: University of Chicago Press.
Mayhew, Leon. 1984. "In Defense of Modernity: Talcott Parsons and The Utilitarian Tradition." *American Journal of Sociology* 89: 1273–1305.
Mayhew, Leon. 1990. "The Differentiation of the Solidary Public." In Jeffrey C. Alexander and Paul Colomy, eds., *Differentiation Theory and Social Change: Comparative and Historical Perspectives.* New York: Columbia University Press.
Meyer, John W., and W. Richard Scott. 1983. *Organizational Environments: Ritual and Rationality.* Beverly Hills: Sage.
Molotch, Harvey L., and Deirdre Boden. 1985. "Talking Social Structure: Discourse, Domination and the Watergate Hearings." *American Sociological Review* 50: 273–288.
Moore, Barrington, Jr. 1978. *Injustice: The Social Bases of Obedience and Revolt.* New York: Pantheon.
Munch, Richard. 1981. "Talcott Parsons and the Theory of Action I: The Structure of Kantian Lore." *American Journal of Sociology* 86: 709–739.
Munch, Richard. 1982. "Talcott Parsons and the Theory of Action II: The Continuity of Development." *American Journal of Sociology* 87: 771–826.
Munch, Richard. 1983. "Modern Science and Technology: Differentiation or Interpenetration?" *International Journal of Comparative Sociology* 24: 157–175.
Munch, Richard. 1986. "The American Creed in Sociological Theory." *Sociology Theory* 4: 41–60.
Munch, Richard. 1987a. *Theory of Action.* London: Routledge and Kegan Paul.
Munch, Richard. 1987b. "The Interpenetration of Microinteraction and Macrostructures in a Complex and Contingent Institutional Order." In Jeffrey C. Alexander, Bernhard Giesen, Richard Munch, and Neil J. Smelser, eds., *The Micro-Macro Link.* Berkeley: University of California Press.
Munch, Richard. 1988. *Understanding Modernity.* London: Routledge and Keagan Paul.
Munch, Richard. 1990a. "Social Change and Modernity in America: The System of Equality and Inequality." In Hans Haferkamp and Neil J. Smelser, eds., *Social Change and Modernity.* Berkeley: University of California Press.
Munch, Richard. 1990b. "Differentiation and Rationalization of Society: Recent German Debates." In Jeffrey C. Alexander and Paul Colomy, eds., *Differentiation Theory and Social Change: Comparative and Historical Perspectives.* New York: Columbia University Press.
Orru, Marco. 1988. "Review of *Talcott Parsons: On Economy and Society* (by Robert J. Holton and Bryan S. Turner) and *The Integration of Economic and Sociological Theory* (The Marshall Lectures, University of Cambridge, 1953)." *Contemporary Sociology* 17: 115–117.
Page, Charles H. 1985. "On Neofunctionalism." *Footnotes* 13: 10.
Parsons, Talcott. 1937. *The Structure of Social Action.* New York: Free Press.
Parsons, Talcott, Edward Shils, Kaspar D. Naegele, and Jesse R. Pitts, eds. 1961. *Theories of Society.* New York: Free Press.
Peters, John D., and Eric W. Rothenbuhler. 1988. "The Reality of Construction." In H. Simons, ed., *Perspectives on the Rhetoric of the Human Sciences.* London: Sage.
Prager, Jeffrey. 1986. *Building Democracy in Ireland: Political Order and Cultural Integration in a Newly Independent Nation.* Cambridge: Cambridge University Press.

Rambo, Eric. 1988. "Economic Culture." Ph.D. dissertation, University of California, Los Angeles.
Rhoades, Gary. 1990. "Differentiation in Four Higher Educational Systems." In Jeffrey C. Alexander and Paul Colomy, eds., *Differentiation Theory and Social Change: Comparative and Historical Perspectives.* New York: Columbia University Press.
Ritzer, George. 1975. *Sociology: A Multiple Paradigm Science.* Boston: Allyn and Bacon.
Ritzer, George. 1985. "The Rise of Micro-Sociological Theory." *Sociological Theory* 3: 88–98.
Ritzer, George. 1988. *Sociological Theory.* 2d ed. New York: Knopf.
Robertson, Roland. 1982. "Parsons on the Evolutionary Significance of American Religion." *Sociological Analysis* 43: 307–326.
Robertson, Roland. 1985. "The Sacred and the World-System." In Phillip Hammond, ed., *The Sacred in a Post-Secular Age.* Berkeley: University of California Press.
Robertson, Roland. 1986. "Sociological Theory and Images of World Order: A Working Paper." Paper presented at the American Sociological Association and German Sociological Association Conference on Development and Change, Berkeley, California.
Robertson, Roland. 1987. "Globalization Theory and Civilizational Analysis." *Comparative Civilizations Review* 17: 20–30.
Robertson, Roland. 1988. "The Sociological Significance of Culture: Some General Considerations." *Theory Culture and Society* 5: 3–23.
Robertson, Roland. 1990. "Globality, Global Culture and Images of World Order." In Hans Haferkamp and Neil Smelser, eds., *Social Change and Modernity.* Berkeley: University of California Press.
Robertson, Roland, and Jo Ann Chirico. 1985. "Humanity, Globalization and Worldwide Religious Resurgence." *Sociological Analysis* 46: 219–242.
Robertson, Roland, and Frank Lechner. 1985. "Modernization, Globalization and the Problem of Culture in World-Systems Theory." *Theory, Culture and Society* 2: 103–118.
Rothenbuhler, Eric W. 1986a. "A Cross-National Analysis of Communication in Social Conflict." Paper presented to the Annual Convention of the American Association for Public Opinion Research, St. Petersburg Beach, Florida.
Rothenbuhler, Eric W. 1986b. "Media Events and Social Solidarity: An Updated Report on the Living Room Celebration of the Olympic Games." Paper presented to the Annual Convention of the International Communication Association, Chicago.
Rothenbuhler, Eric W. 1987. "Neofunctionalism for Mass Communication." In M. Gurevitch and M. R. Levy, eds., *Mass Communication Review Yearbook.* Volume 6. Newbury Park, Cal.: Sage.
Rothenbuhler, Eric W. 1988a. "Live Broadcasting, Media Events, Telecommunication, and Social Form." In David R. Maines and Carl Couch, eds., *Information, Communication, and Social Structure.* Springfield, IL.: Charles C. Thomas.
Rothenbuhler, Eric W. 1988b. "The Liminal Flight: Mass Strikes as Ritual and Interpretation." In Jeffrey C. Alexander, ed., *Durkheimian Sociology.* New York: Columbia University Press.
Rothenbuhler, Eric W. 1988c. "The Living Room Celebration of the Olympic Games." Manuscript.
Rothenbuhler, Eric W. 1988d. "Values and Symbols in Public Orientations to the Olympic Media Event." Manuscript.
Rothenbuhler, Eric W. n.d. "Collective Action and Communication." Paper, Department of Communication Studies, University of Iowa.

Schegloff, Emanuel A. 1987. "Between Macro and Micro: Context and Other Connections." In Jeffrey C. Alexander, Bernard Giesen, Richard Munch, and Neil J. Smelser, eds., *The Micro-Macro Link*. Berkeley: University of California Press.

Schluchter, Wolfgang. 1979. "The Paradox of Rationalization." In Guenther Roth and Wolfgang Schluchter, *Max Weber's Vision of History*. Berkeley: University of California Press.

Schluchter, Wolfgang. 1981. *The Rise of Western Rationalism: Max Weber's Developmental History*. Translated by Guenther Roth. Berkeley: University of California Press.

Sciulli, David. 1984. "Talcott Parsons' Analytic Critique of Marxism's Concept of Alienation." *American Journal of Sociology* 90: 514-540.

Sciulli, David. 1985. "The Practical Groundwork of Critical Theory: Bringing Parsons to Habermas (and Vice Versa)." In J. Alexander, ed., *Neofunctionalism*. Beverly Hills: Sage.

Sciulli, David. 1986. "Voluntaristic Action." *American Sociological Review* 51: 743-767.

Sciulli, David. 1988. "Reconsidering Interactionism's Corrective Against the Excesses of Functionalism." *Symbolic Interaction* 11: 69-84.

Sciulli, David. 1989. "Theory of Societal Constitutionalism: Foundations of a Non-Marxist Critical Theory." Manuscript.

Sciulli, David. 1990. "Differentiation and Collegial Formations: Implications of Societal Constitutionalism." In Jeffrey C. Alexander and Paul Colomy, eds., *Differentiation Theory and Social Change: Comparative and Historical Perspectives*. New York: Columbia University Press.

Sewell, William, Jr. 1980. *Work and Revolution in France: The Language of Labor From the Old Regime to 1848*. Cambridge: Cambridge University Press.

Sewell, William, Jr. 1985. *Structure and Mobility: The Men and Women of Marseille, 1820-1870*. Cambridge: Cambridge University Press.

Skocpol, Theda, and Kenneth Finegold. 1982. "State Capacity and Economic Intervention in the Early New Deal." *Political Science Quarterly* 97: 255-278.

Smelser, Neil J. 1959. *Social Change in the Industrial Revolution*. Chicago: University of Chicago Press.

Smelser, Neil J. 1962. *Theory of Collective Behavior*. New York: Free Press.

Smelser, Neil J., ed. 1973. *Karl Marx: On Society and Societal Change*. Chicago: University of Chicago Press.

Smelser, Neil J. 1985. "Evaluating the Model of Structural Differentiation in Relation to Educational Change in the Nineteenth Century." In Jeffrey C. Alexander, ed., *Neofunctionalism*. Beverly Hills: Sage.

Smelser, Neil J. 1990. "The Contest Between Family and Schooling in Nineteenth Century Britain." In Jeffrey C. Alexander and Paul Colomy, eds., *Differentiation Theory and Social Change: Comparative and Historical Perspectives*. New York: Columbia University Press.

Stockard, Jean, and Miriam M. Johnson. 1979. "The Social Origins of Male Dominance." *Sex Roles* 5: 199-218.

Stryker, Sheldon. 1980. *Symbolic Interactionism: A Social Structural Version*. Menlo Park, Cal.: Benjamin Cummings.

Surace, Samuel. 1982. "Incomplete Differentiation." Manuscript.

Swidler, Ann. 1986. "Culture in Action." *American Sociological Review* 51: 273-286.

Syzmanski, Albert. 1970a. "Toward a Radical Sociology." *Sociological Inquiry* 40: 3-13.

Syzmanski, Albert. 1970b. "The Value of Sociology: An Answer to Lidz." *Sociological Inquiry* 40: 21-25.

Syzmanski, Albert. 1972. "Dialectical Functionalism: A Further Answer to Lidz." *Sociological Inquiry* 42: 145–153.

Tiryakian, Edward A. 1985. "On the Significance of Dedifferentiation." In S. N. Eisenstadt and H. J. Helle, eds., *Macro-Sociological Theory: Perspectives on Sociological Theory*. Volume 1, Beverly Hills: Sage.

Tiryakian, Edward A. 1990. "Reenchantment and Dedifferentiation as Counter Processes of Modernity." In Hans Haferkamp and Neil J. Smelser, eds., *Social Change and Modernity*. Berkeley: University of California Press.

Turner, Bryan S. 1986a. *Citizenship and Capitalism*. London: Allen and Unwin.

Turner, Bryan S. 1986b. "Personhood and Citizenship." *Theory, Culture, and Society* 3: 1–16.

Turner, Bryan S. 1987. "Marx, Weber, and the Coherence of Capitalism." In Norbert Wiley, ed., *The Marx–Weber Debate*. Beverly Hills: Sage.

Turner, Bryan S. 1989. "Commentary: Some Reflections on Cumulative Theorizing in Sociology." In Turner, ed., *Theory Building in Sociology*.

Turner, Jonathan H., ed. 1989. *Theory Building in Sociology*. Beverly Hills: Sage.

Turner, Jonathan H., and Alexandra Maryanski. 1988. "Is 'Neofunctionalism' Really Functional?" *Sociological Theory* 6: 110–121.

Wagner, David G. 1984. *The Growth of Sociological Theories*. Beverly Hills: Sage.

Wagner, David G., and Joseph Berger. 1985. "Do Sociological Theories Grow?" *American Journal of Sociology* 90: 697–728.

Williams, Robin M., Jr. 1961. "The Sociological Theory of Talcott Parsons." In Max Black, ed., *The Social Theories of Talcott Parsons*. Carbondale and Edwardsville: Southern Illinois University Press.

Wippler, Reinhard, and Siegwart Lindenberg. 1987. "Collective Phenomena and Rational Choice." In Jeffrey C. Alexander, Bernhard Giesen, Richard Munch, and Neil J. Smelser, eds., *The Micro–Macro Link*. Berkeley: University of California Press.

Wuthnow, Robert. 1988. *Meaning and Moral Order: Explorations in Cultural Analysis*. Berkeley: University of California Press.

# 72

# The Post-Industrial Society

## Malcolm Waters

This chapter introduces the first of Daniel Bell's 'big ideas', the notion that ideology has been exhausted as a principle for the organization of political life. In this chapter we address perhaps the biggest of his ideas, the one that has become the most influential both inside sociology and in wider intellectual circles, the idea that society is becoming 'post-industrial'. The term 'post-industrial society' has become common conceptual currency because of Bell's construction of it, even where that construction is not acknowledged, much as the concept of 'charisma' is invoked without making reference to Weber. This alone is a tribute to the effectiveness of the conceptualization.

The term 'post-industrial society' is used to describe a series of contemporary macro-social changes. Bell had sensed that such changes were occurring as early as 1950. One of the historical shifts that was contributing to the decomposition of Marxist ideology was the reconstruction of the techno-economic structure. Bell gropes for a term to describe it:

> In the dimly-emerging social structure, new power sources are being created and new power sources are being formed. Whatever the character of that new social structure may be – whether state capitalism, managerial society, or corporative capitalism – by 1950 American socialism as a political and social fact had become simply a notation in the archives of history. [MS: 193]

By the late 1950s he had the terminology within his grasp. In 1959 he gave lectures using the term 'post-Industrial society' at the Salzburg Seminar in Austria and in 1962 he wrote a long paper on the topic under the title 'The Post-Industrial Society: A Speculative View of the United States and Beyond'. This must be one of the most influential unpublished papers ever written because it circulated widely in academic and public policy circles. It was pirated both in *Current* and in *Dun's Review* and it moved the journal *Science* (12/6/64) to comment:

---

Source: Malcolm Waters, *Daniel Bell*, (London: Routledge, 1995).

> One of the prophets most honoured by quotation and imitation is Daniel Bell, Columbia University sociologist and a former labor editor of *Fortune* who drew a convincing and intimidating picture of what is coming, barring war, in a paper called "The Post-industrial Society". [in Bell 1971a: 167n]

Bell decided not to publish at the time, however, 'because I felt that the idea was unfinished' (1971: 167n). However, the temptations of public exposure could not be resisted for long and several papers incorporating the original idea appeared in the mid- to late 1960s. One such that must be close to original appeared in a volume on scientific progress (1967a) and a set of more developed 'notes' on the concept appeared in *The Public Interest* at about the same time (1967b; 1967c). The 'notes' had a widespread, international impact. The various essays that Bell wrote on the topic were collected and published as *The Coming of Post-Industrial Society: a Venture in Social Forecasting* (COPIS) in 1973.

Bell is hesitant about taking credit for the invention of the term. He developed it originally, self-consciously to debate Dahrendorf's claims about changes in the class structure of contemporary industrial society (1959). However, it had been used by Riesman in an essay called 'Leisure and Work in Post-industrial Society' published in 1958. Bell admits: 'I had, quite likely, read Riesman's essay at the time and the phrase undoubtedly came from him, though I have developed it in various writings in a vastly different way' (1971a: 167n). Certainly, Bell does not intend the term to mean a post-work society as Riesman did. In any event, the issue of terminological originality is redundant because it was first used by a now obscure British socialist theorist, Arthur Penty, as early as 1917 [COPIS: 37n].[1]

Curiously, Bell received little credit among his immediate contemporaries for his development of the idea. Kuhns' *The Post-industrial Prophets* (1971) does not include or even reference Bell. Kleinberg gives large coverage to Bell's end-of-ideology thesis and even makes reference to the 'notes', but for him the concept of 'post-industrial society' is evanescent, having 'become widely ad[o]pted as a basic term of reference for discussions of the new society' (1973: 1). Touraine's book entitled *The Post-industrial Society* (1971), originally published in French in 1969, makes no reference to Bell.[2]

Bell outlines four intellectual influences on the formulation (1971a: 165–7):

- his own analysis of the break-up of family capitalism in which he proposes that societies are no longer ruled by business managers but by a technical-intellectual elite (EI: 39–16) – 'the perennial interest of a sociologist in scanning the historical skies for a "new class" was the starting point of the argument' (1971a: 165–6);
- studies of the changing composition of the labour force done at *Fortune* that drew on Clark's classification of employment into three

sectors (primary, secondary and tertiary) (1957) and a subsequent study by Foote and Hatt (1953) that extended the idea into quaternary and quinary sectors;
- a reading of Schumpeter (1942) that turned his mind to technological forecasting; and
- a paper by a historian of science, Gerald Holton (1962), that emphasized that the path of innovation in science was best reflected in the codifications of theory.

The post-industrial-society concept put these ideas, a new ruling elite, the movement of the labour force into service sectors, technology as the driving force of change and theory as the most important type of knowledge, into an entirely novel and challenging sociological account of changing social structure.

Before proceeding to an outline of the theory it needs to be located generally within the three-realms paradigm introduced in Chapter 2. Bell insists throughout his analysis, and against the understandings of many of his critics, that it is only the techno-economic realm of society, the realm that he often calls the 'social structure', that can become post-industrial. Social structure can become post-industrial regardless of political regime or cultural configuration. Indeed, he goes further in distinguishing two dimensions *within* social structure, the socio-economic (patterns of economic ownership) and the socio-technical, and it is only in the second of these that the transition to post-industrialism can occur (COPIS: ix–xii). The issue of whether a society is post-industrial is therefore not only independent of whether it is Christian or Islamic, democratic or totalitarian, but also of whether it is capitalist or socialist. Indeed, if these dimensions are truly autonomous, one might presumably encounter a feudal post-industrial society or even a tribal post-industrial society (although Bell does not admit to either of these possibilities). The line Bell takes is not only an attack on the holistic and deterministic theories to which he is opposed, but also serves to defend him against critics who accuse him of constructing a convergence thesis.

## The Conceptual Prism

The 'post-industrial society', then, is a theory of social change. It argues that contemporary societies are or will be going through a shift so that the post-industrial society that emerges will be as different from industrial society as industrial society is from pre-industrial society. We can perhaps begin by considering the distinctions that Bell makes between these three (COPIS: 116–19, 126–9). It must be remembered that Bell intends this distinction only to be analytic, which, in his terms, means that while societies may appear different when viewed through this particular 'prism' or typology they may be similar when viewed through another. Also, Bell does not argue that one type displaces the preceding one but that rather: 'Like palimpsests, the new developments overlie the previous layers, erasing some features and thickening the texture of society as a whole.' (COPIS: xvi)

A *pre-industrial society* can be characterized as 'a game against nature' that centres on attempts to extract resources from the natural environment. Primary-sector occupations and industries (hunting, foraging, farming, fishing, mining, forestry) dominate its economy. Economic activity is carried out according to custom and tradition and faces severe limitations from the supply of land and resources. The level of economic activity varies according to the seasons and to global fluctuations in demand. The possession of land determines the pattern of stratification. The unit of social life is the extended household which, above the level of manual labour, often includes a relatively large number of domestic servants.

An *industrial society* is a 'a game against fabricated nature' that centres on human-machine relationships and applies energy to the transformation of the natural into a technical environment. Economic activity focuses on the manufacturing and processing of tangible goods. The central occupations are the secondary sector ones of semi-skilled factory worker and engineer.[3] The chief economic problem is the mobilization of sufficient capital to establish manufacturing enterprises. By contrast, the main social problem is located in the stratification system. That system depends on the differential ownership of capital and is likely to give rise to industrial or class conflict about the distribution of returns to capital and labour. So another key problem is the coordination of differentiated activities and interests around machine technology.

By contrast, a *post-industrial society* is 'a "game between persons" in which an "intellectual technology," based on information, rises alongside of machine technology' (COPIS: 116).[4] The post-industrial society involves industries from three sectors: the tertiary industries of transportation and utilities; the quaternary industries of trade, finance and capital exchange; and the quinary industries of health, education, research, public administration and leisure. Among these, the last is definitive because the key occupations are the professional and technical ones, with scientists at the core. Given that the generation of information is the key problem and that science is the most important source of information, the organization of the institutions of science, the universities and research institutes is the central problem in the post-industrial society. The strength of nations is given in their scientific capacity and: 'For this reason the nature and kinds of state support for science, the politicization of science, the sociological problems of the organization of work by science teams, all become central policy issues in a post-industrial society' (COPIS: 117–18).

Bell elaborates his ideal-typical construct of the post-industrial society in terms of five dimensions, a methodology that presumably emulates Weber's dimensions of the ideal type of bureaucratic administrative staff. They are as follows (COPIS: 14–33):

- *Creation of a service economy.* Here Bell conceptualizes social change in terms of what Miles and Gershuny (1986) call 'a march through the sectors'. As discussed in Chapter 2, the techno-economic structure of a society changes according to an economizing principle in which more efficient and productive techniques and production systems replace less efficient and productive ones. Drawing on Clark (1957), Bell argues that change therefore involves unilinear progression between the sectors (primary through quinary) and a corresponding shift in the labour force. Accordingly: 'the first and simplest characteristic of a post-industrial society is that the majority of the labor force is no longer engaged in agriculture or manufacturing but in services, which are defined, residually, as trade, finance, transport, health, recreation, research, education, and government' (COPIS: 15). On this criterion the USA had the first service economy by the mid-1950s but it has now been joined by much of the Western world, Japan and some of the Asian dragons. Bell cautions about the particular use that he gives to the word 'services' (against misreadings by such critics as Kumar 1978: 242ff). He intends it to apply not to personal and manual services but only those found in health, education, research and public administration.
- *The pre-eminence of the professional and technical class.* Here Bell tells us that the predominant, although not necessarily the majority of, occupations in the society will be professional and technical occupations requiring a tertiary level of education. The core will be scientists and engineers and together they will become a knowledge class that displaces the propertied bourgeoisie.[5]
- *The primacy of theoretical knowledge.* This is the defining 'axial principle' of the post-industrial society, the organization of the society around knowledge that becomes the basis for social control, the direction of innovation and the political management of new social relationships. Bell stresses that in a post-industrial society this knowledge is theoretical, rather than traditional or practical, in character. It involves the codification of knowledge into abstract symbolic systems that can be applied in a wide variety of situations. The scientist displaces the inventor; the econometrician displaces the political economist.
- *The planning of technology.* The advance of theoretical knowledge allows technological forecasting, that is, the planning of change, including forward assessments of its risks, costs and advantages.[6] The control and regulation of the future introduction of technologies becomes feasible.
- *The rise of a new intellectual technology.* Against usual understandings of technology as physical, as to do with tools or machines, Bell introduces the idea of an intellectual technology, a system of abstract

symbols that can model those 'games between people' and allow one to make decisions without intuition: 'An intellectual technology is the substitution of algorithms (problem-solving rules) for intuitive judgements' (COPIS: 29). The computer is a physical technology that is necessary to this development because only by the use of a computer can the multiple complexities involved be calculated. However the critical intellectual technology is the software and the statistical or logical formulae that are entered into the computer.

In a foreword written for a new edition of COPIS published in 1978 Bell alters this list of dimensions. The planning dimension is eliminated and seven new dimensions are added. These are (COPIS: xvi–xix):

- *A change in the character of work.* Work focuses not on the manipulation of objects but on an engagement in relationships with other people.
- *The role of women.* The expansion of the services sector provides a basis for the economic independence of women that had not previously been available.[7]
- *Science as the imago.* Scientific institutions and their relationship with other institutions are the central, emergent and 'perfect' feature of the post-industrial society.
- *Situses as political units.* A situs is defined as a vertical order of a society, as opposed to the horizontal orders of classes or strata. Bell specifies four functional situses (scientific, technological, administrative and cultural) and five institutional situses (business, government, university/research, social welfare and military). Major conflicts will occur between situses rather than between classes and, indeed, class formation may well be prevented.
- *Meritocracy.* Position is allocated on the basis of education and skill rather than wealth or cultural advantage.
- *The end of scarcity?* Scarcity of goods will disappear in favour of scarcities of information and time. A key problem may be the allocation of leisure time.
- *The economics of information.* Because information is essentially a collective rather than a private good, it will be necessary to follow a co-operative, rather than an individualistic strategy in the generation and use of information (perhaps the creation of a 'public household' – see Chapter 4).

The dimensions are now multiplying like rabbits and Bell seeks to bring us back to the core of his proposal by specifying that there are two 'large' dimensions by which one decides whether a social structure has yet entered a post-industrial phase. These are, the centrality of theoretical knowledge (including by implication, the employment of science as a means to technological change) and the expansion of the quinary service sector. We can now move on to examine the consequences of these two shifts in some detail.

## A Service Society

Bell disentangles the move towards a service economy into several components (COPIS: 127–9). First, industrial society itself presupposes an expansion of certain 'manual' service industries, transportation, communication, public utilities and wholesale and retail distribution. Second, white-collar employment grows in the 'co-ordinating' sectors of the economy, banking and finance. Third, as goods production begins to exceed immediate needs and as individual incomes rise, personal and leisure services (grooming, dining, leisure travel, entertainment, sport, etc.) expand. Fourth, the conception of rights to health and education expands. Last, the increasing complexity of society and the increasing politicization of rights and entitlements leads to an expansion of public-sector services.

In so far as the USA is the emerging post-industrial society, Bell (COPIS: 129–33) can now move on to examine the march through the sectors in that society. The overall picture confirms the existence of such a trend: in 1900 30 per cent of American workers were employed in service-sector industries (tertiary, quaternary, quinary); in 1940 50 per cent were so employed; and by 1980 the proportion had reached 70 per cent. Until 1920 this development was the consequence of declining agricultural employment and service employment grew only in the tertiary sector. Thereafter, the share of secondary sector employment itself began to shrink, even though its absolute numbers increased. After 1947 the most important area of service employment growth was government, so that by 1980 it accounted for about 16 per cent of the labour force although a major component of this was the expansion in the area of education. Bell is also acutely aware that sectoral distribution does not necessarily inform us about the distribution of manual vs. non-manual labour. Many employees in the service sector are manual workers and about one-third of the manufacturing employees are non-manual. He forecasts that not only will the secondary-sector share of employment decline but that the proportion of manual workers in manufacturing will also decline as automation takes hold.

This leads Bell (COPIS: 134–7) into an analysis of the occupational distribution of the American labour force. The proportion of the labour force in white-collar (excluding personal service) occupations rose from 17 per cent in 1900 to 50 per cent in 1980. He admits that much of this change has been due to the absorption of women into routine white-collar employment. However, even if one looks solely at male employment the transformation has been remarkable; the share in white-collar occupations increased from 15 to 42 per cent between 1900 and 1970. By comparison, blue-collar (manual-industrial) occupations peaked at about 40 per cent in 1940 before declining to 32 per cent in 1980; and agricultural employment slid from 37 per cent in 1900 to 2 per cent in 1980. A key element in Bell's argument is that the fastest-growing occupational group of all is the professional and technical group. It was less than a million in 1890 and now numbers over 12 million, or 16 per cent of the labour force. Four million of these are teachers and health workers but 2.3 million are in science and engineering.

This development poses severe difficulties for the trade union movement which Bell clearly regards as a phenomenon of industrial society (COPIS: 137–42). American union membership advanced rapidly between 1935 and 1947 but since then the level of union density has declined from 30 to 27 per cent in 1980.[8] This slight shift masks some considerable internal redistributions of membership. The causes of the reduction lie in declining blue-collar employment (where unionization continues to stand at about 60 per cent) and in rising female employment. The only real area of union growth is in the area of government employment, but private-sector, white-collar employment is a difficult arena of recruitment. Financial service employees remain largely unorganized.

Bell can now examine some of the issues that arise from the emergence of a service labour force and that differentiate it from an industrial labour force. He discusses five such issues, focusing on their implications for social division and conflict:

- *Education and status* (COPIS: 143–5) The post-industrial labour force is highly educated and, in so far as it is decreasingly fed by migration, culturally homogeneous. This allows Bell to ask whether this might provide the basis for the emergence of a new proletarian consciousness of a type envisioned by Marx, but he remains agnostic on the issue. Indeed, he is agnostic on the exact form of labour organization that new professional employees will set up.
- *Blacks* (COPIS: 145) Bell recalls that in his first specification of the post-industrial-society concept in 1962 he had suggested that class would disappear in favour of a system of social inequality based primarily on race. In 1973 he sees little reason to change his mind, although the stress of post-industrial occupations on performance criteria has provided a slightly increased measure of equality.
- *Women* (COPIS: 146) The service economy is highly feminized. About half the workers in the services sector are women, compared with 20 per cent of employees in the goods-producing sectors. Women employees present a particular recruitment problem for organized labour that historically has excluded them.
- *The non-profit sector* (COPIS: 146–7) The non-profit sector of the service economy is growing much faster than the private sector. Indeed, it is the major area for the net growth of new jobs, so that by 1980 about 20 per cent of the labour force was in non-profit-sector jobs. In so far as many of these workers are middle class they will have

both an increased appetite for cultural products and a more liberal set of social and political attitudes.
- *The 'new' working class* (COPIS: 148–54) The educated and professionalized sections of the working class are unlikely to become a militant and radicalized vanguard for the rest of the (disappearing) proletariat. Rather, they are likely to be drawn into the system of professional situses which is a more likely possibility for socio-economic conflict.

Bell sums up the character of the emerging service economy in the following passage:

> [W]hat is central to the new relationship is encounter or communication, and the response of ego to alter, and back – from the irritation of a customer at an airline-ticket office to the sympathetic or harassed response of teacher and student. But the fact that individuals now talk to other individuals rather than interact with a machine, is the fundamental fact about work in the post-industrial society. [COPIS: 163]

For Bell, this means profound implications for the central conflicts and divisions in society. He recognizes the possibility that particular events, such as foreign competition, may occasionally heighten labour militancy but, in a return to an earlier theme, he thinks it unlikely that this will constitute ideologically organized class warfare. Politics is likely to focus on what he calls communal issues – health, education, the environment and crime – on which labour may often be divided or, indeed, allied with capital.

## A Knowledge Society

We can now turn to the second 'large dimension' of the post-industrial society, the centrality of theoretical knowledge and the institutions of science. In an unusual step Bell gives a formal definition of knowledge, 'a set of organized statements of facts or ideas, presenting a reasoned judgement or an experimental result, which is transmitted to others through some communication medium in some systematic form' (COPIS: 175; italics deleted). However, because he proposes to measure the growth of knowledge, he needs an operational rather than a formal definition, which he also offers: 'Knowledge is that which is objectively known, an intellectual property, attached to a name or group of names and certified by copyright or some other form of social recognition (e.g. publication)' (COPIS: 176). He insists that such knowledge is social, as opposed to individual, in terms of both its production and cost and in terms of its evaluation by the market.

Bell more or less accepts a formulation from Price that the rate of growth of scientific papers and of books has always been exponential rather than lineal, with a doubling time of about fifteen years. However, growth in any field of science always hits limits[9] and outputs of knowledge actually increase as the consequence of the differentiation or 'branching' of science, 'the creation of new and numerous subdivisions or specialties within fields' (COPIS: 186). This happens continuously: in 1948 the *National Register of Scientific and Technical Personnel* listed 54 scientific specializations; by 1968 there were 900.

Technology has grown equally rapidly. Bell surveys several estimates of the rate of technological change, measured largely by general increases in productivity (average output per worker). Productivity typically increases by roughly 2 per cent per year, give or take 0.5 per cent. Before the Second World War it was usually below 2 per cent, and after that war it was usually above 2 per cent (COPIS: 189–95). However, Bell claims that in the post-industrial society something radically new is occurring in the area of technology, 'the changed relationship between science and technology, and the incorporation of science through the institutionalization of research into the ongoing structure of the economy . . . as a normal part of business organization' (COPIS: 196). Research is becoming organized systematically rather than operating on a piecemeal basis and industries are becoming more science-based. Productivity is therefore likely to escalate.

Taking these developments together Bell argues that the post-industrial society is a knowledge society. In a knowledge society science and technology become intimately related because technology is driven by theoretical as opposed to practical knowledge; and the shares of employment of GDP in the knowledge field become relatively large (COPIS: 212). Bell seeks to show that the USA is moving into just such a configuration. For example, the proportion of GDP devoted to education doubled from 3.5 to 7.5 per cent between 1949 and 1969 (COPIS: 216–20).[11] More impressively, the proportion of GNP devoted to research and development multiplied fifteen times between 1948 and 1965 to reach 3 per cent. Most of this funding came from government, so that a large proportion was committed to defence and atomic energy research. However, almost all of the rest went into physical and medical sciences. Spending in these areas is growing much faster than in defence and atomic energy research (COPIS: 250–62).

The development of a knowledge society incorporates 'a democratization of higher education on a scale that the world has never seen before'. The proportion of 18–21-year-olds enrolled in education doubled between 1946 and 1964 to 44 per cent. The average doubling time for the American university population is 20 years (since 1879), but since the Second World War the rate of increase accelerated rapidly by virtue of enrolments in graduate degrees. So by 1970 the doubling time had come down to ten years. Importantly, while only about a quarter of first degrees are in science, more than half the doctorates are in natural science and mathematics (COPIS: 216–20).

From a sociological point of view, Bell makes a more important claim that those who work in the knowledge sectors come to constitute a 'knowledge class'. The members are some of those he has already discussed in his analysis of the service economy teachers, engineers, technicians and scientists. The last is the most 'crucial group'. Whereas the work-force increased by 50 per cent between 1930 and 1975, and the number of engineers increased by 370 per cent, the number of scientists increased by 930 per cent (475,000). In 1970 the 'scientific population' was about four million or 4.7 per cent of the workforce (COPIS: 216–17).

Bell works through a conceptual filtering process to identify the scientific elite, the equivalent of the capitalist bourgeoisie, by progressively eliminating teachers, those without doctorates and those not engaged in research. The resulting select group of perhaps 120,000 scientific and technical personnel is very different from the population as a whole in so far as less than a quarter are employed in (industrial) business and more than a half in universities. Here he shows that he really does mean that this elite is a knowledge *class*:

> If one believes . . . that the expansion of science and scientifically based technology is creating the framework for a new social order that will erode capitalism, as the activities of the merchants and the bourgeois outside the landed economy undermined feudalism, then the significant fact is that most of the activities of science are outside the business system and the organization of science policy is not, in the first instance, responsive to business demand. The necessary foundation for any new class is to have an independent institutional base outside the old dominant order. For the scientist this base has been the university. [COPIS: 232]

While Bell is in no doubt that scientists constitute a new class he remains uncertain about whether they can maintain sufficient independence ever to undermine capitalism.

It follows though that the university is a critical institution. Certainly, current rates of expansion might give Bell cause to believe that an institutional base for the knowledge class will continue to be available. More importantly, he is able to isolate a smallish group of largish universities, perhaps 100 or 150 of the 2,500 in the USA, that teach most of the undergraduates and do nearly all the graduate teaching and research. Indeed, twenty-one such universities carried out 54 per cent of the research. It is critical to the pre-eminence of the knowledge class that this core should maintain the relatively high level of autonomy that derives from private sources of funding, and Bell sees a threat to such autonomy in the declining share of enrolment received by the major private universities (Harvard, Stanford, etc.).

## A Communal Society

Bell's claims about the rise of a knowledge class appear problematic to many sociologists. The argument that social inequality might be based on the intangibles of theory and information rather than on the solidities of material property or even occupation runs counter to a century of sociological tradition.

In a nutshell, Bell's stratification claim is twofold: first, that the basis of stratification in the post-industrial society will shift from property to knowledge, and thus from class to status, so that the knowledge 'class' becomes the most powerful status-group in society; and second, that there will be intersecting dimensions of inequality such that no particular cleavage can be regarded as fundamental.[11] Society will come to approximate a community not merely because inequalities cross-cut but because the form of decision-making changes as social structures enter the post-industrial phase. Industrial society is organized as a market in which the intersection of multiple individual choices determines outcomes, but the post-industrial society requires social decisions, that is, consensus on planning future developments. However, as the discussion of Bell's concept of the public household in the preceding chapters indicates, consensus is extraordinarily difficult to achieve in the context of an escalation of claims and entitlements. A conflict between populist claims and professional expertise is a real possibility. So the post-industrial society need not be communal in the sense that it realizes a utopian harmony:

> If the struggle between capitalist and worker, in the locus of the factory, was the hallmark of industrial society, the clash between the professional and the populace, in the organization and in the community is the hallmark of conflict in the post-industrial society. [COPIS: 129]

Rather, it is a community only in so far as many of its decisions need to be made by collectivized groups.

We can now examine these claims in more detail. At the gross level of the ideal type, the sources of power and who wields it are quite clear. In an industrial society the key issue is control of capital plant and machinery and it is the business class that controls these, exercising political power through indirect influence on governmental decisions and reproducing itself through direct inheritance, patronage and educational inheritance. In a post-industrial society the key resource is knowledge and this is under the control of scientists and researchers influencing political processes by being engaged and incorporated in governmental decisions and reproducing itself largely through education (COPIS: 359). However, because contemporary social structure is not completely post-industrial it combines a mixture of power and mobility mechanisms including wealth and property, political position and credentialized skill. Nevertheless, two features of this complex confirm a shift in the power structure: the common interest of the scientific elite in promoting professional or ethical rather than material outcomes; and the reconstitution of individual and private property into organizational property. (COPIS: 360–2)

These developments do not imply that politics will become less important but rather the reverse. The reasons are that: society must be organized on a national rather than a regional or local basis if planning and co-ordination are to prove effective; and multiplying claims for entitlements are made through politics. Decisions about planning and entitlements cannot be made simply on the basis of technical rationality but imply political value-judgements (COPIS: 364). Politics therefore becomes the 'cockpit' of the post-industrial society, the visible hand that co-ordinates where the market no longer can be effective. Its activities have been enlarged and problematized by five developments[12] (COPIS: 468–71):

- the openness of government has increased and avenues for access have multiplied;
- telecommunications have increased the frequency of interaction between the members of society;
- families are more mobile and more technologized so their members engage in more frequent exchanges with others;
- there is an increased need for planning; and
- advancing levels of consumption make imperative an increased regulation of competition between individuals and groups for resources.

It follows from this that:

> In terms of status (esteem and recognition, and possibly income) the knowledge class may be the highest class in the new society, but there is no intrinsic reason [that it should] become a new economic interest class, or a new political class which would bid for power. [COPIS: 374–5]

Bell's overall scheme for the 'societal structure' of the post-industrial society therefore includes three dimensions that are somewhat reminiscent of Weber's class-status-party triplet. These are status, situs and control, although in Bell they are all dimensions of 'the classes'. Status is the 'horizontal' dimension that sets up the knowledge strata. There are four such strata: the professional class, technicians and semi-professionals, clerical and sales workers, and craftsmen and semi-skilled workers. In a mix-and-match of stratification terminology, the professional 'class' is subdivided into four 'estates': scientific, that develops basic knowledge and is autonomous; technical, that applies knowledge to practical problems; administrative that manages organizations; and cultural, that is involved with the expressive symbolization of forms and meanings. Conflict is possible between these estates on the basis of ethical differences: e.g. between a professional ethos and an ethos of self-interest; or between a rational ethos and an expressive ethos (COPIS: 375–6).

Bell uses the term 'situs' to indicate the 'vertical' structures of society that are 'the actual locuses of occupational activities and interests'. There are five: economic enterprises; government; universities and research institutes; social service organizations; and the military. A peculiar feature of the post-industrial society is that statuses are not concentrated within situses but are scattered across them. In an industrial society, capital and labour are defined by the economic situs alone, but scientists in a post-industrial society can be found in any situs.

As the preceding discussion indicates, a new feature of post-industrial society is the importance of government. Whereas, in previous configurations, distributional disputes were fought out between capital and labour in the economic enterprise they are now being fought out within the 'control system' between an expanded number of interest groups that are frequently situs-based. The control system is broadly divided between a 'directorate' of senior government officials and 'the polities' including parties, non-governmental elites, interest and lobby groups, and mobilized claimants (COPIS: 375–7).

## Conclusion

One of the reasons that Weber's work has had a particularly seminal effect is that, although he often engages in a tedious semanticism, his work is also often loose and incomplete as well as being extraordinarily suggestive and insightful. Neo-Weberians can spend many happy hours, indeed whole careers, of scholarship chasing down alternative possible conceptualizations and typological arrangements. Bell offers those who study him similar opportunities and nowhere is this more true than in the case of the post-industrial society. To be frank, the concept is slippery, not through any attempt at dissimulation but rather because the essayistic style that Bell adopts encourages expressiveness at the possible expense of analytic precision.

Analytic imprecision is not difficult to find. The very term 'post-industrial society' is imprecise because Bell frequently insists that he is not arguing about all three realms of society but only about the techno-economic or social structure. The polity and the culture are supposed to turn through their own cycles in blissful isolation. Even so, Bell cannot resist telling us that the form of the polity will be communal in the post-industrial society. Equally we cannot be entirely clear about his methodology. Perhaps the clearest statement of intent is on the first page of the 1978 Foreword, where he says that it is a speculative construct that identifies emergent features against which future reality can be measured. But there is an awful lot of straightforward narrative and description in the book that has little to do with ideal types or prisms and a lot to do with the peculiarities of American social development. Another inconsistency surrounds the discussion of axial principles and structures. In the three-realms argument (published in full after COPIS), the axial principle of the TES is economizing and its axial structure is bureaucracy. However, bureaucracy loses top billing in COPIS to the collegial structures of the university and the axial principle is variously specified as 'intellectual technology' (COPIS: ix), 'the centrality of theoretical knowledge' (COPIS: 115) or both (COPIS: 212). We can easily find other inconsistencies, about whether the post-industrial society has actually arrived or is merely a typological construct, and, if it has arrived, when it began, or about the usage of such terms as 'class', 'status' and 'polity', but this would be fruitless because the importance of the book lies in its capacity to sensitize us to a significant social shift rather than in laying out an analytical grid.

This sort of quibbling is common in relation to Bell and in relation to this book in particular and frequently tempts somewhat uncharitable responses (see e.g. Archer 1990; Kumar 1978; Miller 1975; Pahl 1975). If we are to criticize we might more profitably concentrate on whatever theoretical weakness there is in the argument. These seem to be twofold. First, as Nichols (1975: 350) has it, Bell by assertion shuts tight all the doors on any claim that he is theorizing an end to capitalism and class, especially in so far as he claims that technology is on a different dimension from property ownership. However, throughout the book, and particularly in the sections on stratification, it is clear that, in Bell's view, neither society as a whole nor the TES alone will be structured by capital accumulation in the future. This formulation surely must be designed to deny the reality of business power in a claim that is perhaps a little too anti-Marxist. Second, and to return to a criticism raised in the preceding chapter, Bell forecasts the development of an enlarged communal state as if it can only happen in some future society. In fact, liberal corporatist states have long existed elsewhere than in the USA that have frequently successfully managed to balance claims within a reasoned political philosophy. The underdevelopment of the state has been both the poverty and the strength of American society, but it should not be taken to be a general feature of all advanced societies.

Notwithstanding these qualifications, the force of much of the argument cannot be denied. As Bell himself says, almost with surprise, the phrase 'post-industrial society' has passed quickly into the sociological literature (COPIS: ix).[13] The argument must be regarded as strongest in its stress on the emergence of the quinary service sector and the development of information as a resource, and perhaps weakest in its claims for a scientocracy and the centrality of universities. Certainly, few scientists would see themselves as members of a dominant or even rising social group, and universities twist and turn in the winds of governmental and private-sector funding flows. These strengths and weaknesses are perhaps reflected in the ways in which sociologists conventionally use the term. Every sociologist knows that 'post-industrialization' means the displacement of manufacturing occupations by service occupations, and indeed the description of such jobs as 'post-industrial occupations' is common parlance.

## Notes

1. Bell refers to *Old Worlds for New: A Study of the Post-Industrial State*. Here, Penty conceptualizes the post-industrial state as a primitive communist or anarchist utopia of small artisanal workshops (COPIS: 37n). Penty had earlier published a volume of

essays with Ananda K. Coomaraswamy entitled *Essays in Post-Industrialism: A Symposium of Prophecy on the Future Society* (1914) and he also published a subsequent monograph called simply *Post-Industrialism* (1922) (Rose 1991: 21-4).

2. Touraine (1977) later protests that he can get no credit for the conceptualization against Bell. However, this is not surprising because he only uses the term as the title for his book. It does not appear at all in the text where he prefers the term, 'the programmed society'. Touraine's choice of title therefore leaves an impression of opportunism.

3. Elsewhere (COPIS: 13), he lists engineers with scientists and technocrats among 'the hierophants of the new [post-industrial] society'.

4. This is the closest thing Bell provides to a formal definition of 'post-industrial society' that I can find. Leibowitz (1985: 176) estimates that there are nine definitions in COPIS but this may be both an over- and an underestimate. Bell does not formally define the concept at all but the descriptions of the post-industrial society are multiple. Pahl (1975: 347) counts over fifty different uses of the term.

5. Here Bell slips into a substantive description of the growth of these groups in the USA rather than giving ideal-typical details. He is quite clear that dominance does not translate into rule (interview 9/11/94) so it is unclear what he means by 'pre-eminence'.

6. Bell's view can be contrasted with that of Beck (1990) who argues that risk in contemporary society is inherently incalculable and uncontrollable.

7. The few lines in this foreword represent one of the rare occasions on which Bell mentions women at all. For another see COPIS: 146.

8. The unionization rate declined very rapidly in the USA during the 1980s, after Bell wrote COPIS. By the end of the decade it had reached 15 per cent (Crook, Pakulski and Waters 1992: 134n).

9. Bell gives an extensive discussion of the way in which the expansion of outputs within a closed system follows a sigmoid or S curve (COPIS: 179-85). The limits are reached at the top of the curve. Branching involves the multiplication and overlapping of S curves.

10. The use of proportions can be misleading. For example, a Third-World society with a small GDP and a commitment to educating its population might well spend a high proportion in that area but this would scarcely qualify it as a 'knowledge society'.

11. Bell defines class thus: 'Class, in the final sense, denotes not a specific group of persons but a system that has institutionalized the ground rules for acquiring, holding, and transferring differential power and its attendant privileges' [COPIS: 361].

12. Bell introduces these issues to indicate that the area of coordination is one of the new scarcities of post-industrial society, along with information, and time (COPIS: 466-74).

13. Appropriately he also regrets being the beneficiary of any fashion for an interest in social change, any association with what he calls 'future schlock' (COPIS: xi).

# References

(COPIS) *The Coming of Post-Industrial Society: A Venture in Social Forecasting*, pbk edn with new foreword. New York: Basic (Harper Torchbook), 1976 [1st edn, New York: Basic 1975; 1st British edn, London: Heinemann, 1974].

(MS) *Marxian Socialism in the United States,* Princeton: Princeton University Press, 1967 [originally published in D. Egbert and S. Persons (eds) *Socialism and American Life* (Princeton Studies in American Civilization, Number 4), Princeton: Princeton University Press, 1952].

Archer, M. (1990) 'Theory, Culture and Post-industrial Society' in M. Featherstone (ed.) *Global Culture*, London: Sage: 207–36.
Bell, D. (1967b) 'Notes on the Post-Industrial Society (I)' *The Public Interest* (6 Winter): 24–35.
Bell, D. (1967c) 'Notes on the Post-Industrial Society (II)' *The Public Interest* (7 Spring): 102–18.
Bell, D. (1971a) 'The Post-Industrial Society: The Evolution of an Idea' *Survey* 16(1): 102–68.
Clark, C. (1957) *The Conditions of Economic Progress*, London: Macmillan.
Crook, S., J. Pakulski and M. Waters (1992) *Postmodernization*, London: Sage.
Holton, G. (1962) 'Scientific Research and Scholarship: Notes Towards the Design of Proper Scales' *Daedalus* 91(2): 362–99.
Kuhns, W. (1971) *The Post-industrial Prophets*, New York: Harper.
Kumar, K. (1978) *Prophecy and Progress. The Sociology of Industrial and Post-industrial Society*, Harmondsworth: Penguin.
Leibowitz, N. (1985) *Daniel Bell and the Agony of Modern Liberalism*, Westport: Greenwood.
Miles, I., and J. Gershuny (1986) 'The Social Economics of Information Technology' in M. Ferguson (ed.) *New Communication Technologies and the Public Interest*, London: Sage.
Miller, S. (1975) 'Notes on Neo-Capitalism' *Theory and Society* 2(1): 1–35.
Nichols, T. (1975) 'Review of COPIS' *Sociology* 9: 349–52.
Offe, C. (1984) *Contradictions of the Welfare State*, London: Hutchinson.
Pahl, R. (1975) 'Review of COPIS' *Sociology* 9: 347–9.
Rose, M. (1991) *The Post-modern and the Post-industrial*, Cambridge: Cambridge University Press.
Schumpeter, J. (1942) *Capitalism, Socialism and Democracy*, New York: Harper.
Touraine, A. (1977) 'Crisis or Transformation?' in N. Birnbaum (ed.) *Beyond the Crisis*, New York: Oxford University Press: 17–49.

# 73

# The Iron Cage Revisited: Institutional Isomorphism and Collective Rationality in Organizational Fields

*Paul J. DiMaggio and Walter W. Powell*

In *The Protestant Ethic and the Spirit of Capitalism,* Max Weber warned that the rationalist spirit ushered in by asceticism had achieved a momentum of its own and that, under capitalism, the rationalist order had become an iron cage in which humanity was, save for the possibility of prophetic revival, imprisoned "perhaps until the last ton of fossilized coal is burnt" (Weber, 1952:181–82). In his essay on bureaucracy, Weber returned to this theme, contending that bureaucracy, the rational spirit's organizational manifestation, was so efficient and powerful a means of controlling men and women that, once established, the momentum of bureaucratization was irreversible (Weber, 1968).

The imagery of the iron cage has haunted students of society as the tempo of bureaucratization has quickened. But while bureaucracy has spread continuously in the eighty years since Weber wrote, we suggest that the engine of organizational rationalization has shifted. For Weber, bureaucratization resulted from three related causes: competition among capitalist firms in the marketplace; competition among states, increasing rulers' need to control their staff and citizenry; and bourgeois demands for equal protection under the law. Of these three, the most important was the competitive marketplace. "Today," Weber (1968:974) wrote:

> it is primarily the capitalist market economy which demands that the official business of administration be discharged precisely, unambiguously, continuously, and with as much speed as possible. Normally, the very large, modern capitalist enterprises are themselves unequalled models of strict bureaucratic organization.

We argue that the causes of bureaucratization and rationalization have changed. The bureaucratization of the corporation and the state have been achieved.

---

Source: *American Sociological Review,* 1983, vol. 48, no. 2, pp. 147–160.

Organizations are still becoming more homogeneous, and bureaucracy remains the common organizational form. Today, however, structural change in organizations seems less and less driven by competition or by the need for efficiency. Instead, we will contend, bureaucratization and other forms of organizational change occur as the result of processes that make organizations more similar without necessarily making them more efficient. Bureaucratization and other forms of homogenization emerge, we argue, out of the structuration (Giddens, 1979) of organizational fields. This process, in turn, is effected largely by the state and the professions, which have become the great rationalizers of the second half of the twentieth century. For reasons that we will explain, highly structured organizational fields provide a context in which individual efforts to deal rationally with uncertainty and constraint often lead, in the aggregate, to homogeneity in structure, culture, and output.

## Organizational Theory and Organizational Diversity

Much of modern organizational theory posits a diverse and differentiated world of organizations and seeks to explain variation among organizations in structure and behavior (e.g., Woodward, 1965; Child and Kieser, 1981). Hannan and Freeman begin a major theoretical paper (1977) with the question, "Why are there so many kinds of organizations?" Even our investigatory technologies (for example, those based on least-squares techniques) are geared towards explaining variation rather than its absence.

We ask, instead, why there is such startling homogeneity of organizational forms and practices; and we seek to explain homogeneity, not variation. In the initial stages of their life cycle, organizational fields display considerable diversity in approach and form. Once a field becomes well established, however, there is an inexorable push towards homogenization.

Coser, Kadushin, and Powell (1982) describe the evolution of American college textbook publishing from a period of initial diversity to the current hegemony of only two models, the large bureaucratic generalist and the small specialist. Rothman (1980) describes the winnowing of several competing models of legal education into two dominant approaches. Starr (1980) provides evidence of mimicry in the development of the hospital field; Tyack (1974) and Katz (1975) show a similar process in public schools; Barnouw (1966–68) describes the development of dominant forms in the radio industry; and DiMaggio (1981) depicts the emergence of dominant organizational models for the provision of high culture in the late nineteenth century.

What we see in each of these cases is the emergence and structuration of an organizational field as a result of the activities of a diverse set of organizations; and, second, the homogenization of these organizations, and of new entrants as well, once the field is established.

By organizational field, we mean those organizations that, in the aggregate, constitute a recognized area of institutional life: key suppliers, resource and product consumers, regulatory agencies, and other organizations that produce similar services or products. The virtue of this unit of analysis is that it directs our attention not simply to competing firms, as does the population approach of Hannan and Freeman (1977), or to networks of organizations that actually interact, as does the interorganizational network approach of Laumann et al. (1978), but to the totality of relevant actors. In doing this, the field idea comprehends the importance of both *connectedness* (see Laumann et al., 1978) and *structural equivalence* (White et al., 1976).[1]

The structure of an organizational field cannot be determined a priori but must be defined on the basis of empirical investigation. Fields only exist to the extent that they are institutionally defined. The process of institutional definition, or "structuration," consists of four parts: an increase in the extent of interaction among organizations in the field; the emergence of sharply defined interorganizational structures of domination and patterns of coalition; an increase in the information load with which organizations in a field must contend; and the development of a mutual awareness among participants in a set of organizations that they are involved in a common enterprise (DiMaggio, 1982).

Once disparate organizations in the same line of business are structured into an actual field (as we shall argue, by competition, the state, or the professions), powerful forces emerge that lead them to become more similar to one another. Organizations may change their goals or develop new practices, and new organizations enter the field. But, in the long run, organizational actors making rational decisions construct around themselves an environment that constrains their ability to change further in later years. Early adopters of organizational innovations are commonly driven by a desire to improve performance. But new practices can become, in Selznick's words (1957:17), "infused with value beyond the technical requirements of the task at hand." As an innovation spreads, a threshold is reached beyond which adoption provides legitimacy rather than improves performance (Meyer and Rowan, 1977). Strategies that are rational for individual organizations may not be rational if adopted by large numbers. Yet the very fact that they are normatively sanctioned increases the likelihood of their adoption. Thus organizations may try to change constantly; but, after a certain point in the structuration of an organizational field, the aggregate effect of individual change is to lessen the extent of diversity within the field.[2] Organizations in a structured field, to paraphrase Schelling (1978:14), respond to an environment that consists of other organizations responding to their environment, which consists of organizations responding to an environment of organizations' responses.

Zucker and Tolbert's (1981) work on the adoption of civil-service reform in the United States illustrates this process. Early adoption of civil-service reforms was related to internal governmental needs, and strongly predicted by such city characteristics as the size of immigrant population, political reform movements, socio-economic composition, and city size. Later adoption, however, is not predicted by city characteristics, but is related to institutional definitions of the legitimate structural form for municipal administration.³ Marshall Meyer's (1981) study of the bureaucratization of urban fiscal agencies has yielded similar findings: strong relationships between city characteristics and organizational attributes at the turn of the century, null relationships in recent years. Carroll and Delacroix's (1982) findings on the birth and death rates of newspapers support the view that selection acts with great force only in the early years of an industry's existence.⁴ Freeman (1982:14) suggests that older, larger organizations reach a point where they can dominate their environments rather than adjust to them.

The concept that best captures the process of homogenization is *isomorphism*. In Hawley's (1968) description, isomorphism is a constraining process that forces one unit in a population to resemble other units that face the same set of environmental conditions. At the population level, such an approach suggests that organizational characteristics are modified in the direction of increasing compatibility with environmental characteristics; the number of organizations in a population is a function of environmental carrying capacity; and the diversity of organizational forms is isomorphic to environmental diversity. Hannan and Freeman (1977) have significantly extended Hawley's ideas. They argue that isomorphism can result because nonoptimal forms are selected out of a population of organizations or because organizational decision makers learn appropriate responses and adjust their behavior accordingly. Hannan and Freeman's focus is almost solely on the first process: selection.⁵

Following Meyer (1979) and Fennell (1980), we maintain that there are two types of isomorphism: competitive and institutional. Hannan and Freeman's classic paper (1977), and much of their recent work, deals with competitive isomorphism, assuming a system rationality that emphasizes market competition, niche change, and fitness measures. Such a view, we suggest, is most relevant for those fields in which free and open competition exists. It explains parts of the process of bureaucratization that Weber observed, and may apply to early adoption of innovation, but it does not present a fully adequate picture of the modern world of organizations. For this purpose it must be supplemented by an institutional view of isomorphism of the sort introduced by Kanter (1972:152–54) in her discussion of the forces pressing communes toward accommodation with the outside world. As Aldrich (1979:265) has argued, "the major factors that organizations must take into account are other organizations." Organizations compete not just for resources and customers, but for political power and institutional legitimacy, for social as well as economic fitness.⁶ The concept of institutional isomorphism is a useful tool for understanding the politics and ceremony that pervade much modern organizational life.

### Three Mechanisms of Institutional Isomorphic Change

We identify three mechanisms through which institutional isomorphic change occurs, each with its own antecedents: 1) *coercive* isomorphism that stems from political influence and the problem of legitimacy; 2) *mimetic* isomorphism resulting from standard responses to uncertainty; and 3) *normative* isomorphism, associated with professionalization. This typology is an analytic one: the types are not always empirically distinct. For example, external actors may induce an organization to conform to its peers by requiring it to perform a particular task and specifying the profession responsible for its performance. Or mimetic change may reflect environmentally constructed uncertainties.[7] Yet, while the three types intermingle in empirical setting, they tend to derive from different conditions and may lead to different outcomes.

*Coercive isomorphism.* Coercive isomorphism results from both formal and informal pressures exerted on organizations by other organizations upon which they are dependent and by cultural expectations in the society within which organizations function. Such pressures may be felt as force, as persuasion, or as invitations to join in collusion. In some circumstances, organizational change is a direct response to government mandate: manufacturers adopt new pollution control technologies to conform to environmental regulations; nonprofits maintain accounts, and hire accountants, in order to meet tax law requirements; and organizations employ affirmative-action officers to fend off allegations of discrimination. Schools mainstream special students and hire special education teachers, cultivate PTAs and administrators who get along with them, and promulgate curricula that conform with state standards (Meyer et al., 1981). The fact that these changes may be largely ceremonial does not mean that they are inconsequential. As Ritti and Goldner (1979) have argued, staff become involved in advocacy for their functions that can alter power relations within organizations over the long run.

The existence of a common legal environment affects many aspects of an organisation's behavior and structure. Weber pointed out the profound impact of a complex, rationalized system of contract law that requires the necessary organizational controls to honor legal commitments. Other legal and technical requirements of the state – the vicissitudes of the budget cycle, the ubiquity of certain fiscal years, annual reports, and financial reporting requirements that ensure eligibility for the receipt of federal contracts or funds – also shape organizations in similar ways. Pfeffer and Salancik (1978:188–224) have discussed how organizations faced with unmanageable interdependence seek to use the greater power of the larger social system and its government to eliminate difficulties or provide for needs. They observe that politically constructed environments have two characteristic features: political decisionmakers often do not experience directly the consequences of their actions; and political decisions are applied across the board to entire classes of organizations, thus making such decisions less adaptive and less flexible.

Meyer and Rowan (1977) have argued persuasively that as rationalized states and other large rational organizations expand their dominance over more arenas of social life, organizational structures increasingly come to reflect rules institutionalized and legitimated by and within the state (also see Meyer and Hannan, 1979). As a result, organizations are increasingly homogeneous within given domains and increasingly organized around rituals of conformity to wider institutions. At the same time, organizations are decreasingly structurally determined by the constraints posed by technical activities, and decreasingly held together by output controls. Under such circumstances, organizations employ ritualized controls of credentials and group solidarity.

Direct imposition of standard operating procedures and legitimated rules and structures also occurs outside the governmental arena. Michael Sedlak (1981) has documented the ways that United Charities in the 1930s altered and homogenized the structures, methods, and philosophies of the social service agencies that depended upon them for support. As conglomerate corporations increase in size and scope, standard performance criteria are not necessarily imposed on subsidiaries, but it is common for subsidiaries to be subject to standardized reporting mechanisms (Coser et al., 1982). Subsidiaries must adopt accounting practices, performance evaluations, and budgetary plans that are compatible with the policies of the parent corporation. A variety of service infrastructures, often provided by monopolistic firms – for example, telecommunications and transportation – exert common pressures over the organizations that use them. Thus, the expansion of the central state, the centralization of capital, and the coordination of philanthropy all support the homogenization of organizational models through direct authority relationships.

We have so far referred only to the direct and explicit imposition of organizational models on dependent organizations. Coercive isomorphism, however, may be more subtle and less explicit than these examples suggest. Milofsky (1981) has described the ways in which neighborhood organizations in urban communities, many of which are committed to participatory democracy, are driven to developing organizational hierarchies in order to gain support from more hierarchically organized donor organizations. Similarly, Swidler (1979) describes the tensions created in the free schools she studied by the need to have a "principal" to negotiate with the district superintendent and to represent the school to outside agencies. In general, the need to lodge responsibility and managerial authority at least ceremonially in a formally defined role in order to interact with hierarchical organizations is a constant obstacle to the maintenance of egalitarian or collectivist organizational forms (Kanter, 1972; Rothschild-Whitt, 1979).

*Mimetic processes.* Not all institutional isomorphism, however, derives from coercive authority. Uncertainty is also a powerful force that encourages imitation. When organizational technologies are poorly understood (March and Olsen, 1976), when goals are ambiguous, or when the environment creates symbolic uncertainty, organizations may model themselves on other organizations. The advantages of mimetic behavior in the economy of human action are considerable; when an organization faces a problem with ambiguous causes or unclear solutions, problemistic search may yield a viable solution with little expense (Cyert and March, 1963).

Modeling, as we use the term, is a response to uncertainty. The modeled organization may be unaware of the modeling or may have no desire to be copied; it merely serves as a convenient source of practices that the borrowing organization may use. Models may be diffused unintentionally, indirectly through employee transfer or turnover, or explicitly by organizations such as consulting firms or industry trade associations. Even innovation can be accounted for by organizational modeling. As Alchian (1950) has observed:

> While there certainly are those who consciously innovate, there are those who, in their imperfect attempts to imitate others, unconsciously innovate by unwittingly acquiring some unexpected or unsought unique attributes which under the prevailing circumstances prove partly responsible for the success. Others, in turn, will attempt to copy the uniqueness, and the innovation-imitation process continues.

One of the most dramatic instances of modeling was the effort of Japan's modernizers in the late nineteenth century to model new governmental initiatives on apparently successful western prototypes. Thus, the imperial government sent its officers to study the courts, Army, and police in France, the Navy and postal system in Great Britain, and banking and art education in the United States (see Westney, forthcoming). American corporations are now returning the compliment by implementing (their perceptions of) Japanese models to cope with thorny productivity and personnel problems in their own firms. The rapid proliferation of quality circles and quality-of-work-life issues in American firms is, at least in part, an attempt to model Japanese and European successes. These developments also have a ritual aspect; companies adopt these "innovations" to enhance their legitimacy, to demonstrate they are at least trying to improve working conditions. More generally, the wider the population of personnel employed by, or customers served by, an organization, the stronger the pressure felt by the organization to provide the programs and services offered by other organizations. Thus, either a skilled labor force or a broad customer base may encourage mimetic isomorphism.

Much homogeneity in organizational structures stems from the fact that despite considerable search for diversity there is relatively little variation to be selected from. New organizations are modeled upon old ones throughout the economy, and managers actively seek models upon which to build (Kimberly, 1980). Thus, in the arts one can find textbooks on how to organize a community arts council or how to start a symphony women's guild. Large organizations choose from a relatively small set of major consulting firms, which, like Johnny Appleseeds, spread a few organizational models throughout the land. Such models are powerful because structural changes are observable, whereas changes in policy and strategy are less easily noticed. With the advice of a major consulting firm, a large metropolitan public television station switched from a functional design to a multidivisional structure. The stations' executives were skeptical that the new structure was more efficient; in fact, some services were now duplicated across divisions. But they were convinced that the new design would carry a powerful message to the for-profit firms with whom the station regularly dealt. These firms, whether in the role of corporate underwriters or as potential partners in joint ventures, would view the reorganization as a sign that "the sleepy nonprofit station was becoming more business-minded" (Powell, forthcoming). The history of management reform in American government agencies, which are noted for their goal ambiguity, is almost a textbook case of isomorphic modeling, from the PPPB of the McNamara era to the zero-based budgeting of the Carter administration.

Organizations tend to model themselves after similar organizations in their field that they perceive to be more legitimate or successful. The ubiquity of certain kinds of structural arrangements can more likely be credited to the universality of mimetic processes than to any concrete evidence that the adopted models enhance efficiency. John Meyer (1981) contends that it is easy to predict the organization of a newly emerging nation's administration without knowing anything about the nation itself, since "peripheral nations are far more isomorphic – in administrative form and economic pattern – than any theory of the world system of economic division of labor would lead one to expect."

*Normative pressures.* A third source of isomorphic organizational change is normative and stems primarily from professionalization. Following Larson (1977) and Collins (1979), we interpret professionalization as the collective struggle of members of an occupation to define the conditions and methods of their work, to control the "production of producers" (Larson, 1977:49–52), and to establish a cognitive base and legitimation for their occupational autonomy. As Larson points out, the professional project is rarely achieved with complete success. Professionals must compromise with nonprofessional clients, bosses, or regulators. The major recent growth in the professions has been among organizational professionals, particularly managers and specialized staff of large organizations. The increased professionalization of workers whose futures are inextricably bound up with the fortunes of the organizations that employ them has rendered obsolescent (if not obsolete) the dichotomy between organizational commitment and professional allegiance that characterized traditional professionals in earlier organizations (Hall, 1968). Professions are subject to the same coercive and mimetic pressures as are organizations. Moreover, while various kinds of professionals within an organization may differ from one another, they exhibit much similarity to their professional counterparts in other organizations. In addition, in many cases, professional power is as much assigned by the state as it is created by the activities of the professions.

Two aspects of professionalization are important sources of isomorphism. One is the resting of formal education and of legitimation in a cognitive base produced by university specialists; the second is the growth and elaboration of professional networks that span organizations and across which new models diffuse rapidly. Universities and professional training institutions are important centers for the development of organizational norms among professional managers and their staff. Professional and trace associations are another vehicle for the definition and promulgation of normative rules about organizational and professional behavior. Such mechanisms create a pool of almost interchangeable individuals who occupy similar positions across a range of organizations and possess a similarity of orientation and disposition that may override variations in tradition and control that might otherwise shape organizational behavior (Perrow, 1974).

One important mechanism for encouraging normative isomorphism is the filtering of personnel. Within many organizational fields filtering occurs through the hiring of individuals from firms within the same industry; through the recruitment of fast-track staff from a narrow range of training institutions; through common promotion practices, such as always hiring top executives from financial or legal departments; and from skill-level requirements for particular jobs. Many professional career tracks are so closely guarded, both at the entry level and throughout the career progression, that individuals who make it to the top are virtually indistinguishable. March and March (1977) found that individuals who attained the position of school superintendent in Wisconsin were so alike in background and orientation as to make further career advancement random and unpredictable. Hirsch and Whisler (1982) find a similar absence of variation among *Fortune* 500 board members. In addition, individuals in an organizational field undergo anticipatory socialization to common expectations about their personal behavior, appropriate style of dress, organizational vocabularies (Cicourel, 1970, Williamson, 1975) and standard methods of speaking, joking, or addressing others (Ouchi, 1980). Particularly in industries with a service or financial orientation (Collins, 1979, argues that the importance of credentials is strongest in these areas), the filtering of personnel approaches what Kanter (1977) refers to as the "homosexual reproduction of management." To the extent managers and key staff are drawn from the same universities and filtered on a common set of attributes, they will tend to view problems in a similar fashion, see the same policies, procedures and structures as normatively sanctioned and legitimated, and approach decisions in much the same way.

Entrants to professional career tracks who somehow escape the filtering process – for example, Jewish naval officers, woman stockbrokers, or Black insurance executives – are likely to be subjected to pervasive on-the-job socialization. To the extent that organizations in a field differ and primary socialization occurs on the job, socialization could reinforce, not erode, differences among organizations. But when organizations in a field are similar and occupational socialization is carried out in trade association workshops, in-service educational programs, consultant arrangements, employer-professional school networks, and in the pages of trade magazines, socialization acts as an isomorphic force.

The professionalization of management tends to proceed in tandem with the structuration of organizational fields. The exchange of information among professionals helps contribute to a commonly recognized hierarchy of status, of center and periphery, that becomes a matrix for information flows and personnel movement across organizations. This status ordering occurs through both formal and informal means. The designation of a few large firms in an industry as key bargaining agents in union-management negotiations may make these central firms pivotal in other respects as well. Government recognition of key firms or organizations through the grant or contract process may give these organizations legitimacy and visibility and lead competing firms to copy aspects of their structure or operating procedures in hope of obtaining similar rewards. Professional and trade associations provide other arenas in which center organizations are recognized and their personnel given positions of substantive or ceremonial influence. Managers in highly visible organizations may in turn have their stature reinforced by representation on the boards of other organizations, participation in industry-wide or inter-industry councils, and consultation by agencies of government (Useem, 1979). In the nonprofit sector, where legal barriers to collusion do not exist, structuration may proceed even more rapidly. Thus executive producers or artistic directors of leading theatres head trade or professional association committees, sit on government and foundation grant-award panels, or consult as government- or foundation-financed management advisors to smaller theatres, or sit on smaller organizations' boards, even as their stature is reinforced and enlarged by the grants their theatres receive from government, corporate, and foundation funding sources (DiMaggio, 1982).

Such central organizations serve as both active and passive models, their policies and structures will be copied throughout their fields. Their centrality is reinforced as upwardly mobile managers and staff seek to secure positions in these central organizations in order to further their own careers. Aspiring managers may undergo anticipatory socialization into the norms and mores of the organizations they hope to join. Career paths may also involve movement from entry positions in the center organizations to middle-management positions in peripheral organizations. Personnel flows within an organizational field are further encouraged by structural homogenization, for example the existence of common career titles and paths (such as assistant, associate, and full professor) with meanings that are commonly understood.

It is important to note that each of the institutional isomorphic processes can be expected to proceed in the absence of evidence that they increase internal organizational efficiency. To the extent that organizational effectiveness is enhanced, the reason will often be that organizations are rewarded for being similar to other organizations in their fields. This similarity can make it easier for organizations to transact with other organizations, to attract career-minded staff, to be acknowledged as legitimate and reputable, and to fit into administrative categories that define eligibility for public and private grants and contracts. None of this, however, insures that conformist organizations do what they do more efficiently than do their more deviant peers.

Pressures for competitive efficiency are also mitigated in many fields because the number of organizations is limited and there are strong fiscal and legal barriers to entry and exit. Lee (1971:51) maintains this is why hospital administrators are less concerned with the efficient use of resources and more concerned with status competition and parity in prestige. Fennell (1980) notes that hospitals are a poor market system because patients lack the needed knowledge of potential exchange partners and prices. She argues that physicians and hospital administrators are the actual consumers. Competition among hospitals is based on "attracting physicians, who, in turn, bring their patients to the hospital." Fennell (p. 505) concludes that:

> Hospitals operate according to a norm of social legitimation that frequently conflicts with market considerations of efficiency and system rationality. Apparently, hospitals can increase their range of services not because there is an actual need for a particular service or facility within the patient population, but because they will be defined as fit only if they can offer everything other hospitals in the area offer.

These results suggest a more general pattern. Organizational fields that include a large professionally trained labor force will be driven primarily by status competition. Organizational prestige and resources are key elements in attracting professionals. This process encourages homogenization as organizations seek to ensure that they can provide the same benefits and services as their competitors.

## Predictors of Isomorphic Change

It follows from our discussion of the mechanism by which isomorphic change occurs that we should be able to predict empirically which organizational fields will be most homogeneous in structure, process, and behavior. While an empirical test of such predictions is beyond the scope of this paper, the ultimate value of our perspective will lie in its predictive utility. The hypotheses discussed below are not meant to exhaust the universe of predictors, but merely to suggest several hypotheses that may be pursued using data on the characteristics of organizations in a field, either cross-sectionally or, preferably, over time. The hypotheses are implicitly governed by *ceteris paribus* assumptions, particularly with regard to size, technology, and centralization of external resources.

A. *Organizational-level predictors.* There is variability in the extent to and rate at which organizations in a field change to become more like their peers. Some organizations respond to external pressures quickly; others change only after a long period of resistance. The first two hypotheses derive from our discussion of coercive isomorphism and constraint.

Hypothesis A-1: *The greater the dependence of an organization on another organization, the more similar it will become to that organization in structure, climate, and behavioral focus.* Following Thompson (1957) and Pfeffer and Salancik (1978), this proposition recognizes the greater ability of organizations to resist the demands of organizations on whom they are not dependent. A position of dependence leads to isomorphic change. Coercive pressures are built into exchange relationships. As Williamson (1979) has shown, exchanges are characterized by transaction-specific investments in both knowledge and equipment. Once an organization chooses a specific supplier or distributor for particular parts or services, the supplier or distributor develops expertise in the performance of the task as well as idiosyncratic knowledge about the exchange relationship. The organization comes to rely on the supplier or distributor and such transaction-specific investments give the supplier or distributor considerable advantages in any subsequent competition with other suppliers or distributors.

Hypothesis A-2: *The greater the centralization of organization A's resource supply, the greater the extent to which organization A will change isomorphically to resemble the organizations on which it depends for resources.* As Thompson (1967) notes, organizations that depend on the same sources for funding, personnel, and legitimacy will be more subject to the whims of resource suppliers than will organizations that can play one source of support off against another. In cases where alternative sources are either not readily available or require effort to locate, the stronger party to the transaction can coerce the weaker party to adopt its practices in order to accommodate the stronger party's needs (see Powell, 1983).

The third and fourth hypotheses derive from our discussion of mimetic isomorphism, modeling, and uncertainty.

Hypothesis A-3: *The more uncertain the relationship between means and ends the greater the extent to which an organization will model itself after organizations it perceives to be successful.* The mimetic thought process involved in the search for models is characteristic of change in organizations in which key technologies are only poorly understood (March and Cohen, 1974). Here our prediction diverges somewhat from Meyer and Rowan (1977) who argue, as we do, that organizations which lack well-defined technologies will import institutionalized rules and practices. Meyer and Rowan posit a loose coupling between legitimated external practices and internal organizational behavior. From an ecologist's point of view, loosely coupled organizations are more likely to vary internally. In contrast, we expect substantive internal changes in tandem with more ceremonial practices, thus greater homogeneity and less variation and change. Internal consistency of this sort is an important means of interorganizational coordination. It also increases organizational stability.

Hypothesis A-4: *The more ambiguous the goals of an organization, the greater the extent to which the organization will model itself after organizations that it perceives to be successful.* There are two reasons for this. First, organizations with ambiguous or disputed goals are likely to be highly dependent upon appearances for legitimacy. Such organizations may find it to their advantage to meet the expectations of important constituencies about how they should be designed and run. In contrast to our view, ecologists would argue that organizations that copy other organizations usually have no competitive advantage. We contend that, in most situations, reliance on established, legitimated procedures enhances organizational legitimacy and survival characteristics. A second reason for modeling behavior is found in situations where conflict over organizational goals is repressed in the interest of harmony; thus participants find it easier to mimic other organizations than to make decisions on the basis of systematic analyses of goals since such analyses would prove painful or disruptive.

The fifth and sixth hypotheses are based on our discussion of normative processes found in professional organizations.

Hypothesis A-5: *The greater the reliance on academic credentials in choosing managerial and staff personnel, the greater the extent to which an organization will become like other organizations in its field.* Applicants with academic credentials have already undergone a socialization process in university programs, and are thus more likely than others to have internalized reigning norms and dominant organizational models.

Hypothesis A-6: *The greater the participation of organizational managers in trade and professional associations, the more likely the organization will be, or will become, like other organizations in its field.* This hypothesis is parallel to the institutional view that the more elaborate the relational networks among organizations and their members, the greater the collective organization of the environment (Meyer and Rowan, 1977).

B. *Field-level predictors.* The following six hypotheses describe the expected effects of several characteristics of organizational fields on the extent of isomorphism in a particular field. Since the effect of institutional isomorphism is homogenization, the best indicator of isomorphic change is a decrease in variation and diversity, which could be measured by lower standard deviations of the values of selected indicators in a set of organizations. The key indicators would vary with the nature of the field and the interests of the investigator. In all cases, however, field-level measures are expected to affect organizations in a field regardless of each organization's scores on related organizational-level measures.

Hypothesis B-1: *The greater the extent to which an organizational field is dependent upon a single (or several similar) source of support for vital resources, the higher the level of isomorphism.* The centralization of resources within a field both directly causes homogenization by placing organizations under similar pressures from resource suppliers, and interacts with uncertainty and goal ambiguity to increase their impact. This hypothesis is congruent with the ecologists' argument that the number of organizational forms is determined by the distribution of resources in the environment and the terms on which resources are available.

Hypothesis B-2: *The greater the extent to which the organizations in a field transact with agencies of the state, the greater the extent of isomorphism in the field as a whole.* This follows not just from the previous hypothesis, but from two elements of state/private-sector transactions: their rule-boundedness and formal rationality, and the emphasis of government actors on institutional rules. Moreover the federal government routinely designates industry standards for an entire field which require adoption by all competing firms. John Meyer (1979) argues convincingly that the aspects of an organization which are affected by state transactions differ to the extent that state participation is unitary or fragmented among several public agencies.

The third and fourth hypotheses follow from our discussion of isomorphic change resulting from uncertainty and modeling.

Hypothesis B-3: *The fewer the number of visible alternative organizational models in a field, the faster the rate of isomorphism in that field.* The predictions of this hypothesis are less specific than those of others and require further refinement; but our argument is that for any relevant dimension of organizational strategies or structures in an organizational field there will be a threshold level, or a tipping point, beyond which adoption of the dominant form will proceed with increasing speed (Granovetter, 1978; Boorman and Leavitt, 1979).

Hypothesis B-4: *The greater the extent to which technologies are uncertain or goals are ambiguous within a field, the greater the rate of isomorphic change.* Somewhat counterintuitively, abrupt increases in uncertainty and ambiguity should, after brief periods of ideologically motivated experimentation, lead to rapid isomorphic change. As in the case of A-4, ambiguity and uncertainty may be a function of environmental definition, and, in any case, interact both with centralization of resources (A-1, A-2, B-1, B-2) and with professionalization and structuration (A-5, A-6, B-5, B-6). Moreover, in fields characterized by a high degree of uncertainty, new entrants, which could serve as sources of innovation and variation, will seek to overcome the liability of newness by imitating established practices within the field.

The two final hypotheses in this section follow from our discussion of professional filtering, socialization, and structuration.

Hypothesis B-5: *The greater the extent of professionalization in a field, the greater the amount of institutional isomorphic change.* Professionalization may be measured by the universality of credential requirements, the robustness of graduate training programs, or the vitality of professional and trade associations.

Hypothesis B-6: *The greater the extent of structuration of a field, the greater the degree of isomorphics.* Fields that have stable and broadly acknowledged centers, peripheries, and status orders will be more homogeneous both because the diffusion structure for new models and norms is more routine and because the level of interaction among organizations in the field is higher. While structuration may not lend itself to easy measurement, it might be tapped crudely with the use of such familiar measures as concentration ratios, reputational interview studies, or data on network characteristics.

This rather schematic exposition of a dozen hypotheses relating the extent of isomorphism to selected attributes of organizations and of organizational fields does not constitute a complete agenda for empirical assessment of our perspective. We have not discussed the expected nonlinearities and ceiling cf fects in the relationships that we have posited. Nor have we addressed the issue of the indicators that one must use to measure homogeneity. Organizations in a field may be highly diverse on some dimensions, yet extremely homogeneous on others. While we suspect, in general, that the rate at which the standard deviations of structural or behavioral indicators approach zero will vary with the nature of an organizational field's technology and environment, we will not develop these ideas here. The point of this section is to suggest that the theoretical discussion is susceptible to empirical test, and to lay out a few testable propositions that may guide future analyses.

## Implications for Social Theory

A comparison of macrosocial theories of functionalist or Marxist orientation with theoretical and empirical work in the study of organizations yields a paradoxical conclusion. Societies (or elites), so it seems, are smart, while organizations are dumb. Societies comprise institutions that mesh together comfortably in the interests of efficiency (Clark, 1962), the dominant value system (Parsons, 1951), or, in the Marxist version, capitalists (Domhoff, 1967; Althusser, 1969). Organizations, by contrast, are either anarchies (Cohen et al., 1972), federations of loosely coupled parts (Weick, 1976), or autonomy-seeking agents (Gouldner, 1954) laboring under such formidable constraints as bounded rationality (March and Simon, 1958), uncertain or contested goals (Sills, 1957), and unclear technologies (March and Cohen, 1974).

Despite the findings of organizational research, the image of society as consisting of tightly and rationally coupled institutions persists throughout much of modern social theory. Rational administration pushes out nonbureaucratic forms, schools assume the structure of the workplace, hospital and university administrations come to resemble the management of for-profit firms, and the modernization of the world economy proceeds unabated. Weberians point to the continuing homogenization of organizational structures as the formal rationality of bureaucracy extends to the limits of contemporary organizational life. Functionalists describe the rational adaptation of the structure of firms, schools, and states to the values and needs of modern society (Chandler, 1977; Parsons, 1977). Marxists attribute changes in such organizations as welfare agencies (Pivan and Cloward, 1971) and schools (Bowles and Gintis, 1976) to the logic of the accumulation process.

We find it difficult to square the extant literature on organizations with these macrosocial views. How can it be that the confused and contentious bumblers that populate the pages of organizational case studies and theories combine to construct the elaborate and well-proportioned social edifice that macrotheorists describe?

The conventional answer to this paradox has been that some version of natural selection occurs in which selection mechanisms operate to weed out those organizational forms that are less fit. Such arguments, as we have contended, are difficult to mesh with organizational realities. Less efficient organizational forms do persist. In some contexts efficiency or productivity cannot even be measured. In government agencies or in faltering corporations selection may occur on political rather than economic grounds. In other contexts, for example the Metropolitan Opera or the Bohemian Grove, supporters are far more concerned with noneconomic values like aesthetic quality or social status than with efficiency per se. Even in the for-profit sector, where competitive arguments would promise to bear the greatest fruit, Nelson and Winter's work (Winter, 1964, 1975; Nelson and Winter, 1982) demonstrates that the invisible hand operates with, at best, a light touch.

A second approach to the paradox that we have identified comes from Marxists and theorists who assert that key elites guide and control the social system through their command of crucial positions in major organizations (e.g., the financial institutions that dominate monopoly capitalism). In this view, while organizational actors ordinarily proceed undisturbed through mazes of standard operating procedures, at key turning points capitalist elites get their way by intervening in decisions that set the course of an institution for years to come (Katz, 1975).

While evidence suggests that this is, in fact, sometimes the case – Barnouw's account of the early days of broadcasting or Weinstein's (1968) work on the Progressives are good examples – other historians have been less successful in their search for class-conscious elites. In such cases as the development of the New Deal programs (Hawley, 1966) or the expansion of the Vietnamese conflict (Halperin, 1974), the capitalist class appears to have been muddled and disunited.

Moreover, without constant monitoring, individuals pursuing parochial organizational or subunit interests can quickly undo the work that even the most prescient elites have accomplished. Perrow (1976:21) has noted that despite superior resources and sanctioning power, organizational elites are often unable to maximize their preferences because "the complexity of modern organizations makes control difficult." Moreover, organizations have increasingly become the vehicle for numerous "gratifications, necessities, and preferences so that many groups within and without the organization seek to use it for ends that restrict the return to masters."

We reject neither the natural-selection nor the elite-control arguments out of hand. Elites do exercise considerable influence over modern life and aberrant or inefficient organizations sometimes do expire. But we contend that neither of these processes is sufficient to explain the extent to which organizations have become structurally more similar. We argue that a theory of institutional isomorphism may help explain the observations that organizations are becoming more homogeneous, and that elites often get their way, while at the same time enabling us to understand the irrationality, the frustration of power, and the lack of innovation that are so commonplace in organizational life. What is more, our approach is more consonant with the ethnographic and theoretical literature on how organizations work than are either functionalist or elite theories of organizational change.

A focus on institutional isomorphism can also add a much needed perspective on the political struggle for organizational power and survival that is missing from much of population ecology. The institutionalization approach associated with John Meyer and his students posits the importance of myths and ceremony but does not ask how these models arise and whose interests they initially serve. Explicit attention to the genesis of legitimated models and to the definition and elaboration of organizational fields should answer this question. Examination of the diffusion of similar organizational strategies and structures should be a productive means for assessing the influence of elite interests. A consideration of isomorphic processes also leads us to a bifocal view of power and its application in modern politics. To the extent that organizational change is unplanned and goes on largely behind the backs of groups that wish to influence it, our attention should be directed to two forms of power. The first, as March and Simon (1958) and Simon (1957) pointed out years ago, is the power to set premises, to define the norms and standards which shape and channel behavior. The second is the point of critical intervention (Domhoff, 1979) at which elites can define appropriate models of organizational structure and policy which then go unquestioned for years to come (see Katz, 1975). Such a view is consonant with some of the best recent work on power (see Lukes, 1974); research on the structuration of organizational fields and on isomorphic processes may help give it more empirical flesh.

Finally, a more developed theory of organizational isomorphism may have important implications for social policy in those fields in which the state works through private organizations. To the extent that pluralism is a guiding value in public policy deliberations, we need to discover new forms of intersectoral coordination that will encourage diversification rather than hastening homogenization. An understanding of the manner in which fields become more homogeneous would prevent policy makers and analysts from confusing the disappearance of an organizational form with its substantive failure. Current efforts to encourage diversity tend to be conducted in an organizational vacuum. Policy makers concerned with pluralism should consider the impact of their programs on the structure of organizational fields as a whole, and not simply on the programs of individual organizations.

We believe there is much to be gained by attending to similarity as well as to variation among organizations and, in particular, to change in the degree of homogeneity or variation over time. Our approach seeks to study incremental change as well as selection. We take seriously the observations of organizational theorists about the role of change, ambiguity, and constraint and point to the implications of these organizational characteristics for the social structure as a whole. The foci and motive forces of bureaucratization (and, more broadly, homogenization in general) have, as we argued, changed since Weber's time. But the importance of understanding the trends to which he called attention has never been more immediate.

## Notes

A preliminary version of this paper was presented by Powell at the American Sociological Association meetings in Toronto, August 1981. We have benefited considerably from careful readings of earlier drafts by Dan Chambliss, Randall Collins, Lewis Coser, Rebecca Friedkin, Connie Gersick, Albert Hunter, Rosabeth Moss Kanter, Charles E. Lindblom, John Meyer, David Morgan, Susan Olzak, Charles Perrow, Richard A. Peterson, Arthur Stinchcombe, Blair Wheaton, and two anonymous *ASR* reviewers. The authors' names are listed in alphabetical order for convenience. This was a fully collaborative effort.

1. By *connectedness* we mean the existence of transactions tying organizations to one another: such transactions might include formal contractual relationships, participation of personnel in common enterprises such as professional associations, labor unions, or boards of directors, or informal organizational-level ties like personnel flows. A set of organizations that are strongly connected to one another and only weakly connected to other organizations constitutes a *clique*. By *structural equivalence* we refer to similarity of position in a network structure: for example, two organizations are structurally equivalent if they have ties of the same kind to the same set of other organizations, even if they themselves are not connected: here the key structure is the *role* or *block*.

2. By organizational change, we refer to change in formal structure, organizational culture, and goals, program, or mission. Organizational change varies in its responsiveness to technical conditions. In this paper we are most interested in processes that affect organizations in a given field: in most cases these organizations employ similar technical bases; thus we do not attempt to partial out the relative importance of technically functional versus other forms of organizational change. While we shall cite many examples of organizational change as we go along, our purpose here is to identify a widespread class of organizational processes relevant to a broad range of substantive problems, rather than to identify deterministically the causes of specific organizational arrangements.

3. Knoke (1982), in a careful event-history analysis of the spread of municipal reform, refutes the conventional explanations of culture clash or hierarchal diffusion and finds but modest support for modernization theory. His major finding is that regional differences in municipal reform adoption arise not from social compositional differences, "but from some type of imitation or contagion effects as represented by the level of neighboring regional cities previously adopting reform government" (p. 1337).

4. A wide range of factors – interorganizational commitments, elite sponsorship, and government support in form of open-ended contracts, subsidy, tariff barriers and import quotas, or favorable tax laws – reduce selection pressures even in competitive organizational fields. An expanding or a stable, protected market can also mitigate the forces of selection.

5. In contrast to Hannan and Freeman, we emphasize adaptation, but we are not suggesting that managers' actions are necessarily strategic in a long-range sense. Indeed, two of the three forms of isomorphism described below – mimetic and normative – involve managerial behaviors at the level of taken-for-granted assumptions rather than consciously strategic choices. In general, we question the utility of arguments about the motivations of actors that suggest a polarity between the rational and the nonrational. Goal-oriented behavior may be reflexive or prerational in the sense that it reflects deeply embedded predispositions, scripts, schema, or classifications; and behavior oriented to a goal may be reinforced without contributing to the accomplishment of that goal. While isomorphic change may often be mediated by the desires of managers to increase the effectiveness of their organizations, we are more concerned with the menu of possible options that managers consider than with their motives for choosing particular alternatives. In other words, we freely concede that actors' understandings of their own behaviors are interpretable in rational terms. The theory of isomorphism addresses not the psychological states of actors but the structural determinants of the range of choices that actors perceive as rational or prudent.

6. Carroll and Delacroix (1982) clearly recognize this and include political and institutional legitimacy as a major resource. Aldrich (1979) has argued that the population perspective must attend to historical trends and changes in legal and political institutions.

7. This point was suggested by John Meyer.

## References

Alchian, Armen, 1950, "Uncertainty, evolution, and economic theory." Journal of Political Economy 58:211–21.

Aldrich, Howard, 1979, Organizations and Environments. Englewood Cliffs, NJ: Prentice-Hall.

Althusser, Louis, 1969, For Marx. London: Allan Lane.

Barnouw, Erik, 1966–68, A History of Broadcasting in the United States, 3 volumes. New York: Oxford University Press.

Boorman, Scott A. and Paul R. Levitt, 1979, "The cascade principle for general disequilibrium dynamics." Cambridge/New Haven: Harvard-Yale Preprints in Mathematical Sociology. Number 15.

Bowles, Samuel and Herbert Gintis, 1976, Schooling in Capitalist America. New York: Basic Books.

Carroll, Glenn R. and Jacques Delacroix, 1982, "Organizational mortality in the newspaper industries of Argentina and Ireland: an ecological approach," Administrative Science Quarterly 27:169–98.

Chandler, Alfred D., 1977, The Visible Hand: The Managerial Revolution in American Business. Cambridge: Harvard University Press.

Child, John and Alfred Kieser, 1981, "Development of organizations over time." Pp. 28–64 in Paul C. Nystrom and William H. Starbuck (eds.), Handbook of Organizational Design. New York: Oxford University Press.

Cicourel, Aaron, 1970, "The acquisition of social structure: toward a developmental sociology of language." Pp. 136–68 in Jack D. Douglas (ed.), Understanding Everyday Life. Chicago: Aldine.

Clark, Burton R., 1962, Educating the Expert Society. San Francisco: Chandler.

Cohen, Michael D., James G. March and Johan P. Olsen, 1972, "A garbage can model of organizational choice." Administrative Science Quarterly 17:1–25.

Collins, Randall, 1979, The Credential Society. New York: Academic Press.

Coser, Lewis, Charles Kadushin and Walter W. Powell, 1982, Books: The Culture and Commerce of Book Publishing. New York: Basic Books.

Cyert, Richard M. and James G. March, 1963, A Behavioral Theory of the Firm. Englewood Cliffs, NJ: Prentice-Hall.

DiMaggio, Paul, 1981, "Cultural entrepreneurship in nineteenth-century Boston. Part 1: The creation of an organizational base for high culture in America." Media, Culture and Society 4:33–50.

DiMaggio, Paul, 1982, "The structure of organizational fields: an analytical approach and policy implications." Paper prepared for SUNY-Albany Conference on Organizational Theory and Public Policy. April 1 and 2.

Domhoff, J. William, 1967, Who Rules America? Englewood Cliffs, NJ: Prentice-Hall.

Domhoff, J. William, 1979, The Powers That Be: Processes of Ruling Class Domination in America. New York: Random House.

Fennell, Mary L., 1980, "The effects of environmental characteristics on the structure of hospital clusters." Administrative Science Quarterly 25:484–510.

Freeman, John H., 1982 "Organizational life cycles and natural selection processes." Pp. 1–32 in Barry Staw and Larry Cummings (eds.), Research in Organizational Behavior. Vol. 4, Greenwich, CT: JAI Press.

Giddens, Anthony, 1979, Central Problems in Social Theory: Action, Structure, and Contradiction in Social Analysis, Berkeley: University of California Press.

Gouldner, Alvin W., 1954, Patterns of Industrial Bureaucracy. Glencoe, IL: Free Press.

Granovetter, Mark, 1978, "Threshold models of collective behavior." American Journal of Sociology 83:1420–43.

Hall, Richard, 1968, "Professionalization and bureaucratization." American Sociological Review 33:92–104.

Halperin, Mortin H., 1974, Bureaucratic Politics and Foreign Policy. Washington, D.C.: The Brookings Institution.

Hannan, Michael T. and John H. Freeman, 1977, "The population ecology of organizations." American Journal of Sociology 82:929–64.

Hawley, Amos, 1968, "Human ecology." Pp. 328–37 in David L. Sills (ed.), International Encyclopedia of the Social Sciences. New York: Macmillan.

Hawley, Ellis W., 1966, The New Deal and the Problem of Monopoly: A Study in Economic Ambivalence. Princeton: Princeton University Press.

Hirsch, Paul and Thomas Whisler, 1982, "The view from the boardroom." Paper presented at Academy of Management Meetings, New York, NY.

Kanter, Rosabeth Moss, 1972, Commitment and Community. Cambridge, MA: Harvard University Press.

Kanter, Rosabeth Moss, 1977, Men and Women of the Corporation. New York: Basic Books.

Katz, Michael B., 1975, Class, Bureaucracy, and Schools: The Illusion of Educational Change in America. New York: Praeger.

Kimberly, John, 1980, "Initiation, innovation and institutionalization in the creation process." Pp. 18–43 in John Kimberly and Robert B. Miles (eds.), The Organizational Life Cycle. San Francisco: Jossey-Bass.

Knoke, David, 1982, "The spread of municipal reform: temporal, spatial, and social dynamics." American Journal of Sociology 87:1314–39.

Larson, Magali Sarfatti, 1977, The Rise of Professionalism: A Sociological Analysis. Berkeley: University of California Press.

Laumann, Edward O., Joseph Galaskiewicz and Peter Marsden, 1978, "Community structure as interorganizational linkage." Annual Review of Sociology 4:455–84.

Lee, M. L., 1971, "A conspicuous production theory of hospital behavior." Southern Economic Journal 38:48–58.

Lukes, Steven, 1974, Power: A Radical View. London: Macmillan.

March, James G. and Michael Cohen, 1974, Leadership and Ambiguity: The American College President. New York: McGraw-Hill.

March, James C. and James G. March, 1977, "Almost random careers: the Wisconsin school superintendency, 1940–72." Administrative Science Quarterly 22:378–409.

March, James G. and Johan P. Olsen, 1976, Ambiguity and Choice in Organizations. Bergen, Norway: Universitetsforlaget.

March, James G. and Herbert A. Simon, 1958, Organizations. New York: Wiley.

Meyer, John W., 1979, "The impact of the centralization of educational funding and control on state and local organizational governance." Stanford, CA: Institute for Research on Educational Finance and Governance, Stanford University, Program Report No. 79-B20.

Meyer, John W., 1981, Remarks at ASA session on "The Present Crisis and the Decline in World Hegemony." Toronto, Canada.

Meyer, John W. and Michael Hannan, 1979, National Development and the World System: Educational, Economic, and Political Change. Chicago: University of Chicago Press.

Meyer, John W. and Brian Rowan, 1977, "Institutionalized organizations: formal structure as myth and ceremony." American Journal of Sociology 83:340–63.

Meyer, John W., W. Richard Scott and Terence C. Deal, 1981, "Institutional and technical sources of organizational structure explaining the structure of educational organizations." In Herman Stein (ed.), Organizations and the Human Services: Cross-Disciplinary Reflections. Philadelphia, PA: Temple University Press.

Meyer, Marshall, 1981, "Persistence and change in bureaucratic structures." Paper presented at the annual meeting of the American Sociological Association, Toronto, Canada.

Milofsky, Carl, 1981, "Structure and process in community self-help organizations." New Haven: Yale Program on Non-Profit Organizations, Working Paper No. 17.

Nelson, Richard R. and Sidney Winter, 1982, An Evolutionary Theory of Economic Change. Cambridge: Harvard University Press.

Ouchi, William G., 1980, "Markets, bureaucracies, and clans." Administrative Science Quarterly 25:129–41.

Parsons, Talcott, 1951, The Social System. Glencoe, IL: Free Press.

Parsons, Talcott, 1977, The Evolution of Societies. Englewood Cliffs, NJ: Prentice-Hall.

Perrow, Charles, 1974, "Is business really changing?" Organizational Dynamics Summer:31–44.

Perrow, Charles, 1974, "Control in organizations." Paper presented at American Sociological Association annual meetings, New York, NY.

Pfeffer, Jeffrey and Gerald Salancik, 1978, The External Control of Organizations: A Resource Dependence Perspective. New York: Harper & Row.

Piven, Frances Fox and Richard A. Cloward, 1971, Regulating the Poor: The Functions of Public Welfare. New York: Pantheon.

Powell, Walter W., 1983, "The Political Economy of Public Television." New Haven: Program on Non-Profit Organizations.

Powell, Walter W., 1983, "New solutions to perennial problems of bookselling: whither the local bookstore?" Daedalus: Winter.

Ritti, R. R. and Fred H. Goldner, 1979, "Professional pluralism in an industrial organization." Management Science 16:233–46.

Rothman, Mitchell, 1980, "The evolution of forms of legal education." Unpublished manuscript. Department of Sociology, Yale University, New Haven, CT.

Rothschild-Whitt, Joyce, 1979, "The collectivist organization: an alternative to rational bureaucratic models." American Sociological Review 44:509–27.

Schelling, Thomas, 1978, Micromotives and Macrobehavior. New York: W. W. Norton.

Sedlak, Michael W., 1981, "Youth policy and young women, 1950–1972: the impact of private-sector programs for pregnant and wayward girls on public policy." Paper presented at National Institute for Education Youth Policy Research Conference, Washington, D.C.

Selznick, Philip, 1957, Leadership in Administration. New York: Harper & Row.

Sills, David L., 1957, The Volunteers. Means and Ends in a National Organization. Glencoe, IL: Free Press.

Sumon, Herbert A., 1957, Administrative Behavior. New York: Free Press.

Starr, Paul, 1980, "Medical care and the boundaries of capitalist organization." Unpublished manuscript. Program on Non-Profit Organizations, Yale University, New Haven, CT.

Swidler, Ann, 1979, Organization Without Authority: Dilemmas of Social Control of Free Schools. Cambridge: Harvard University Press.

Thompson, James, 1967, Organizations in Action. New York: McGraw-Hill.

Tyack, David, 1974, The One Best System: A History of American Urban Education. Cambridge, MA: Harvard University Press.

Useem, Michael, 1979, "The social organization of the American business elite and participation of corporation directors in the governance of American institutions." American Sociological Review 44:553–72.

Weber, Max, 1952, The Protestant Ethic and the Spirit of Capitalism. New York: Scribner.

Weber, Max, 1968, Economy and Society: An Outline of Interpretive Sociology. Three volumes. New York: Bedminster.

Weick, Karl, 1976, "Educational organizations as loosely coupled systems." Administrative Science Quarterly 21:1–19.

Weinstein, James, 1968, The Corporate Ideal in the Liberal State, 1900–1918. Boston, MA: Beacon Press.

Westney, D. Eleanor, forthcoming. Organizational Development and Social Change in Meiji, Japan.

White, Harrison C., Scott A. Boorman and Ronald L. Breiger, 1976, "Social structure from multiple networks. I. Blockmodels of roles and positions." American Journal of Sociology 81:730–80.

Williamson, Oliver E., 1975, Markets and Hierarchies, Analysis and Antitrust Implications: A Study of the Economics of Internal Organization. New York: Free Press.

Williamson, Oliver E., 1979, "Transaction-cost economics: the governance of contractual relations." Journal of Law and Economics 22:233–61.

Winter, Sidney G., 1964, "Economic 'natural selection' and the theory of the firm." Yale Economic Essays 4:224–72.

Winter, Sidney G., 1975, "Optimization and evolution in the theory of the firm." Pp. 73–118 in Richard H. Day and Theodore Graves (eds.), Adaptive Economic Models. New York: Academic Press.

Woodward, John, 1965, Industrial Organization, Theory and Practice, London: Oxford University Press.

Zucker, Lynne G. and Pamela S. Tolbert, 1981, "Institutional sources of change in the formal structure of organizations: the diffusion of civil service reform, 1880–1935." Paper presented at American Sociological Association annual meeting, Toronto, Canada.

# 74

# Toward a Critique of Sociology

*Alvin W. Gouldner*

The criticism and transformation of society can be divorced only at our peril from the criticism and transformation of theories about society. Yet the gap between theory and practice, so common in the history of American radical movements, is in some quarters growing wider. Some of the most militant of American radicals, in the New Left or in the movement for Black liberation, have at least temporarily avoided any serious concern with social theory.

This neglect of theory doubtless has various origins. In some part it is due to the fact that these social movements are still new and their political activism consumes their necessarily limited energies and resources; the new radicalisms will, in short, need time to produce their new theories. Although the neglect of theory is scarcely peculiar to Americans, it is in part also due to the fact that American radicals are often more American than they know and may prefer the tangible outcomes of pragmatic politics to the intangible outputs of theory. Again, part of their neglect of theoretical problems is probably due to the close links that some young radicals have with the "hippie" contingent of their generation, whose more expressive and aesthetic styles of rejecting American culture dispose them to avoid what they take to be the sterile "hassles" of intellectual confrontation. There is also a vocal minority who, as has been said, feel personally excluded when they hear an appeal to reason.

There are, however, other important sources of theoretical apathy among young American radicals today, and these, among other things, distinguish them from the radicals of the 1930's. One of these may well be the emergence of sociology, between the 1940's and the 1960's, as part of popular culture. Sociology then came of age, institutionally if not intellectually. It became a viable part of the academic scene: hundreds of thousands of American college students took courses in sociology; literally thousands of sociology books were written. At the same time, the newly emerging paperback book industry made these available as mass literature. They were sold in drugstores, railway stations, air terminals, hotels, and grocery stores, while, at the same time,

---

Source: Alvin W. Gouldner, *The Coming Crisis of Western Sociology*, (London: Heinemann, 1971).

increasing middle-class affluence made it easier for students to purchase them, even when not required as textbooks.

This mass availability of sociology (and the other social sciences) as part of everyday culture has had a paradoxical effect on the attitudes that some young people developed toward social theory and social problems. On the one side, the bookstore mingling of social science with other expressions of popular literature identified social science, by association, as part and parcel of the larger culture that the radicals rejected. Some young radicals thus came to distrust social theory because they experienced it as part of the prevailing culture. On the other side, however, sheer familiarity with the social sciences led some to accept it uncritically. For some young people the paperback sociology of the bookstore began to take the place of the earlier literature of radical criticism and protest.

Assimilating the social sciences as part of everyday culture, reading books about the nature of prejudice or poverty, the facts of life in America often seemed quite clear to them. Efforts to discuss theory might then seem to be an unnecessary obfuscation, a substitution of talking about problems for doing something about them. Viewing these researches against the background of their own values, they often experienced a simple moral revulsion rather than an intellectual stimulation. Theorizing, some came to believe, was a form of escapism, if not of moral cowardice.

Yet the neglect of self-conscious theory by radicals is both dangerous and ironic, for such a posture implies that – although they lay claim to being radical – they have in effect surrendered to one of the most vulgar currents of American culture: to its small-town, Babbitt-like anti-intellectualism and know-nothingism. Moreover, if radicals wish to change their world, they must surely expect to do so only against the resistance of some and with the help of others. Yet those whom they oppose, as well as those with whom they may wish to ally themselves, will in fact often be guided by certain theories. Without self-conscious theory, radicals will be unable to understand, let alone change, either their enemies or their friends. Radicals who believe that they can separate the task of developing theory from that of changing society are not in fact acting without a theory, but *with* one that is tacit and therefore unexaminable and uncorrectable. If they do not learn to use their theory self-consciously, they will be used by it. Unable either to control or to understand their theories, radicals will thus in effect submit to one form of the very alienation that they commonly reject.

The profound transformation of society that many radicals seek cannot be accomplished by political means alone; it cannot be confined to a purely political embodiment. For the old society is not held together merely by force and violence, or expedience and prudence. The old society maintains itself also through theories and ideologies that establish its hegemony over the minds of men, who therefore do not merely bite their tongues but submit to it willingly. It will be impossible either to emancipate men from the old society or to build a humane new one, without beginning, here and now, the construction of a total counter-culture, including new social theories; and it is impossible to do this without a critique of the social theories dominant today.

The ambivalence toward theory among some sectors of the New Left, the simultaneous sense of its irrelevance and of its necessity, was clearly expressed by Daniel Cohn-Bendit, one of the leading activists in the French student rebellion that began at Nanterre in the spring of 1968: the anarchists, he remarked, "have influenced me more by certain activities than by their theories . . . theoreticians are laughable." At the same time, however, Cohn-Bendit also observed "the existence of a gap between theory and practice . . . we are trying to effectively develop a theory."[1]

That theory has had an effect upon the emerging New Left, whatever the attitude toward it, is evidenced, among other things, by the role of the "Frankfurt school of critical sociology" – including Jurgen Habermas, Theodor Adorno, and Max Horkheimer – which has been said to be "as important as any single event"[2] in the political revitalization of the *Sozialisticher Deutscher Studentbund* from 1961–1965. Also, there is the international responsiveness of the new radicals to the work of another member of that school, Herbert Marcuse, whose practical importance was backhandedly acknowledged by recent Soviet critiques of his theory. Yet even here, within the critical school of sociology, the continuing tension between theory and practice was evidenced by the polemical exchange between Habermas and the young militants during the fall of 1968, after their demonstrations at Frankfurt.

Lacking the time or the impulse to reformulate old theories or to develop their own new theories, the radicals' need of a theory is today sometimes satisfied by a hastily gulped, vulgar Marxism. Yet even this seems better than another alternative often taken today, namely, merely to label one's own views as "Marxist." This self-characterization may express solidarity with a powerful intellectual tradition but, lacking any true assimilation of it, provides no real help. Indeed, this "magic naming" may do harm, since it can distract critical attention from the rather different theory that the individual may, in point of fact, actually be using. Thus, on one occasion I heard a young radical deliver an extended critique of modern sociology, particularly of Talcott Parsons' version of Functionalism, from what he claimed to be a Marxist standpoint, when he was actually viewing it only from the standpoint of another, somewhat different version of Functional theory.

At its best, such uses of Marxism by American radicals, even when they are more than merely invocatory, are fundamentally regressive and primitivistic. This is particularly true in the United States, where, apart from a very few economists and a slightly larger number of capable historians, Marxism itself has developed hardly at all; where its intellectual caliber remains fixated on the stunted level of the 1930's, when it was blighted by Stalinism; and where it has hardly begun to assimilate even the older contributions of a Georg Lukacs or an Antonio Gramsci, let alone those of the brilliant German, Italian, and French contemporaries. American Marxists have been among the less original and creative contingents of world Marxism; they have usually only applied, but practically never deepened, Marxist theory. Unless one is willing to believe that the academic social sciences have contributed nothing of value to an understanding of modern society during the last thirty years, the flight back to an unreconstructed Marxism is an act, at best, of desperation, and at worst, of irresponsibility or bad faith. Many young radicals today, however, have no impulse to retreat to a rote Marxism. Indeed, many are deeply critical of what they take to be its ingrained disposition toward a totalitarian *Realpolitik;* for some, this becomes still one further reason to suspect and avoid theory.

### New Sentiments, Old Theories

My reading of the contemporary radical condition is that we are now living in a fluid transitional era when a younger generation has emerged with a sharply different structure of sentiments, with collective feelings that are not resonated by the very different kinds of sentiments that have been historically deposited in older theories, and this makes some among the younger generation either coldly indifferent or hotly antagonistic to the older theories. There is, in short, a gap between the newly emerging structure of sentiments among young radicals and the older "languages" or theories, a gap that has not yet been bridged by the development of a new theoretical language in which young radicals might more fully express themselves and their own conception of reality.

From this standpoint, the crux of the issue is the lack of "fit" between new sentiments and old theories. It is precisely because of this that certain young radicals do not simply feel the old theories are "wrong" and should be criticized in detail; their more characteristic response to the older theories is a feeling of their sheer *irrelevance*. Their inclination is not to disprove or argue with the old theories, but to ridicule or avoid them.

At this juncture, academic social theorists might reply that in this respect the New Left is simply being wrong-headed, for what have theories and personal sentiments to do with one another? One should not assume, the academic sociologist might say, that theories need to be consonant with men's sentiments before they are accepted or rejected. However, my own contrary assumption – to be elaborated later – is that the fit between theories and sentiments has a good deal to do with the career of a theory. Much of the theoretical apathy of some young radicals, their ritual Marxism, their efforts to restore the young Marx of alienation, or their clutching at new theories such as ethnomethodology, all are, I believe, various expressions of the existence of an unfilled theoretical need that derives from the gap between their own new structure of sentiments or their own sense of what is real, on the one hand, and, on the other hand, the older theories now available in the academic and social surround.

As some young American radicals now experience it, their important need at this moment in history is to activate and to assert their emerging radical sentiments, and to consolidate and to preserve their new radical identity. It may be that in the beginning this can be done by a militant politics of activistic demonstration. R. D. Laing, whose views have often articulated the feelings of young radicals, has expressed this well in his *Politics of Experience*, where he remarks: "No one can begin to think, feel or act now except from the starting point of his own alienation . . . we do not need theory so much as the experience that is the source of the theory."[3]

The feeling that one's sentiments are valid, that one has a right to have and to hold them, is rooted partially in the sense of reality that derives from personal experience and in the solidarity with others who share these experiences and sentiments. The felt validity of sentiments is thus fundamentally a matter of consensual validation, not of analytic power, or refined conceptualization, or even of "evidence." The young radical thus draws lines in terms of generational solidarities and cleavages, of emotional rather than ideological affinities: "trust no one over thirty." Whether or not it "should be," social theory is always rooted in the theorist's experiences. Whether or not it should be, the sensed validity of a theory depends therefore upon the sharing of experience and of the sentiments to which such experience gives rise, among those who offer and those who listen to the theory.

Apart from the sheer cultural obsolescence of traditional social theories because of their rooting in older personal realities, and apart from the inability of old theories to resonate new sentiments, theory is sometimes suspect today because it is something received from the past. Theory is commonly transmitted by older men to younger men who are in some way dependent upon them. The theoretical apathy of a young radical is thus sometimes an expression of his vigorous striving toward individuality and autonomy, and of his need to become and live as a man, and, if possible, as a better man than his elders have been. Somewhere in the young radical's thoughts is the suspicion that not only are received, traditional theories wrong or irrelevant, but that they are also *unmanly;* he sees them as the timidity-generating creations of timid men.

Still not "professionalized," the young radical does not view a theory as pure, isolated, and alone, but sees through the theory to the theorist. He sees theory as a communication by a whole man. His judgment about a theory and theorizing will be influenced by his feeling about the whole man who produces it. And he often sees this man as someone who has "copped out," retreated from life's struggles, compromised his own highest ideals, accommodated himself to injustice and suffering, and made a comfortable career out of studying the misery of others. The young radical observes that, for all his sympathetic writing about the "culture of poverty," the social scientist, nevertheless, does not share his book royalties even with the poor whom he has studied and who have made them possible. The young radical observes that, for all his sympathetic commentary about the suffering of Blacks, hardly any sociologist of repute can be recruited to teach in Black colleges in the south. The young radical's grievance is often, then, that the sociologist and social theorist is not a whole man, and that his life does not give consistent expression to his own values. In short, he is prone to see the sociologist as he sees other elders, as something of an exploiter and hypocrite. He observes that there are no martyrs among sociologists.

Interpreting social theory in terms of what he sees in the theorist, and viewing it as a falsification of what he himself has seen in the social world, the young radical often defines *all* of Academic Sociology and social theory as an undifferentiated obfuscation of life, as an ideology discolored by a pervasive conservative bias in the service of the status quo.

### Sociology and the New Left: A Paradox

Yet there is a deepgoing paradox here, and the young radical himself has already begun to confront it. Some, for example, have noticed that in the past decade or so an Academic Sociology akin to that in the United States has also emerged in the Soviet Union, alongside of traditional Marxism–Leninism. This development has been intellectually troublesome to those radicals who, out of a rote Marxism, have concluded that American Academic Sociology is an instrument of American corporate capitalism. For clearly the conservative character of American sociology cannot be attributed to its subservience to corporate capitalism if an essentially similar sociology has emerged where, as in the Soviet Union, there is no corporate capitalism.

But this is only one of the paradoxes generated by a blanket critique that views all of sociology as the conservative instrument of a repressive society. For example, many of the most visible leaders of student rebellions throughout the world, from Nanterre to Columbia Universities, have been students of sociology. France's Cohn-Bendit is just one of the most obvious cases in point. Leslie Fiedler has more generally observed that "at the root of any [student] demonstration there is a character who is . . . a student of sociology . . . [and] a Jew . . . [and] an outsider," or who possesses at least two of these characteristics.[4] Without endorsing the validity of all of Mr. Fiedler's designations, I do believe that there is considerable merit in his observation of the prominent role of young sociologists in current student rebellions. Yet, if this is so, how can sociology be an unmitigated expression of political conservatism?

Another version of this paradox was evidenced at the Boston meetings of the American Sociological Association in August 1968. There were, in a way, actually two concurrent meetings at Boston: the official one, routinely managed by the American Sociological Association; and, alongside of it, a series of unscheduled "shadow" meetings, organized by the young men and women of the "radical caucus," the Sociology Liberation Movement, with a noticeable leavening of Columbia University militants. These two tracks paralleled one another without touching until the climactic plenary session of the ASA meetings, when more than a thousand gathered to hear the Secretary of Health, Education, and Welfare. Scheduled to have been a dull, honorific occasion, it became what may in a modest way be an historic event when ASA President Philip M. Hauser, having heard that the radical caucus planned to demonstrate at the secretary's talk, invited the caucus to express its dissenting views from the platform.

The key dissenting talk was made by a young sociologist, Martin Nicolaus, then from Canada's Simon Fraser University and one of the contributing editors of the New Left journal, *Viet Report*. In icy, measured tones, Mr. Nicolaus declared:

> The Secretary of HEW is a military officer in the domestic front of the war against the people . . . the Department of which the man is head is more accurately described as the agency which watches over the inequitable distribution of preventable diseases, over the funding of domestic propaganda and indoctrination, over the preservation of a cheap and docile labor force. . . . This assembly [of sociologists] here tonight . . . is a conclave of high and low priests, scribes, intellectual valets, and their innocent victims, engaged in the mutual affirmation of a falsehood . . . the profession is an outgrowth of nineteenth-century European traditionalism and conservatism, wedded to twentieth-century American corporation liberalism . . . the professional eyes of the sociologist are on the down people, and the professional palm of the sociologist is stretched toward the up people . . . he is an Uncle Tom not only for this government and ruling class but for any.

These harsh words were applauded vigorously by the caucus and its sympathizers, hissed by a few of the older ex-radicals, and met by a larger group with shocked, stony forbearance. Now, even those who concur, as I do, in many of Mr. Nicolaus' acerbic judgments, must also acknowledge that their sheer utterance implies a dilemma. It is not so much that he was allowed to speak by officials of the ASA that expresses this dilemma, but, rather, that he wanted to speak. It was not so much that he was allowed to say what he saw, but that he saw as much as he did, that expresses the dilemma. For Nicolaus' very utterances, as well as the vigor and activity of the radical caucus at this same convention, themselves demonstrate that not all sociologists are "intellectual valets" and that not all are "Uncle Toms" of the ruling class.

There is a problem here: How can one account for the very radicalism of those sociologists who accuse sociology of being conservative? Much of what I say in subsequent chapters will, indeed, stress the conservative character of certain dominant trends in American sociology. At the same time, however, the fact that it is often sociologists themselves who criticize sociology for being conservative implies that sociology may produce radicals as well as conservatives.

My point then is that sociology may produce, not merely recruit, radicals, that it may generate, not merely tolerate, radicalization.

It is undoubtedly correct that sociology often attracts young men and women of reformist inclination and prior radical outlook, and that some of their subsequent criticism of sociology may indeed derive from their frustrated expectations. Yet I doubt that this is the whole story. For there are other questions that need to be considered: If sociology often attracts radicals, what is there about sociology itself that attracts them? Can we believe that the young reformer's initial attraction to sociology was simply a case of mistaken identity?

Moreover, it is certain that many, but not all, of the radicals attracted become conservative. Not all the young socialists of the 1930's who became sociologists also became pillars of the status quo, and neither will all those of the New Left of today. While it cannot be central to the volume that follows and will not be examined here in any detail, I believe that there are aspects of the character of and outlook intrinsic to Academic Sociology itself that sustain rather than tame the radical impulse. I believe that, in the normal course of working as a sociologist, there are things that happen that may radicalize a man and have a liberating rather than repressive effect upon him. In brief, and in the language of a non-Academic Sociology, I believe that sociology has its own "internal contradictions," which, despite its powerful link to the status quo and its deepgoing conservative bent, have the unwitting but inherent consequence of fostering anti-Establishment and radicalizing tendencies, particularly among young people.

The relationship between sociology and the New Left is a complex one. Certainly I do not intend to imply that it was the emergence of sociology and its penetration into popular culture that energized the New Left. Nonetheless, the sheer visibility of sociologists in the student revolts at various universities, the importance of the German school of critical sociology for the New Left in Germany and elsewhere, as well as the early role of C. Wright Mills in articulating the emerging sentiments of the new American radicalism, all suggest that sociology has not simply served as a foil for the New Left. They suggest the possibility that some styles and aspects of sociology have also, wittingly and unwittingly, contributed productively to it. This in turn implies that sociology is by no means totally repressive or uniformly conservative in character, but possesses also a liberating or radicalizing potential, susceptible to further growth.

Sociology has a dialectical character and contains both repressive and liberative dimensions. The extrication and further development of its liberative potential will depend, in important part, on the penetration of an historically informed critique of sociology as a theory and as a social institution.

Sociology today is akin to early nineteenth-century Hegelianism, especially in the ambivalence of its political implications. Despite Hegelianism's predominantly conservative and authoritarian cast, it contained powerful radical implications that Marx was able to extricate and to incorporate into a transcending system of thought. The extrication of the liberative potential of modern Academic Sociology from its encompassing conservative structure is a major task of contemporary cultural criticism. It is a task that parallels the similar effort of some of the new radicals today, to extricate Marxism itself from its own conservative and repressive components, and in particular from the bureaucratic and totalitarian proclivities to which it is vulnerable. In neither case, however, will this be possible apart from the sharpest and most probing of criticism. In neither case will it be possible simply to assume that the only important question is the empirical validity or factuality of the intellectual systems involved, and that the viable parts of each theoretical system can be sifted out by "research" alone. The question here is not simply which parts of an intellectual system are empirically true or false, but also which are liberative and which repressive in their consequences. In short, the problem is: What are the social and political consequences of the intellectual system under examination? Do they liberate or repress men? Do they bind men into the social world that now exists, or do they enable men to transcend it?

Any and every statement about the social world, as well as the methodologies by which it is reached, has consequences that may be viewed quite apart from its intellectual validity. When it is said that a social science should be appraised solely in terms of its own autonomous standards, this is a value choice that cannot be justified by "purely scientific" considerations alone; it depends upon anterior, nonscientific assumptions about what a social science is for. That the ideological implications and social consequences of an intellectual system do not determine its validity, for theory does indeed have a measure of autonomy, is not in the least denied here. Certainly the *cognitive* validity of an intellectual system cannot and should not be judged by its ideological implications or its social consequences. But it does not follow from this that an intellectual system should be (or, for that matter, ever is) judged only in terms of its cognitive validity, its truth or falsity. In short, it is never simply a question of whether an intellectual system, or a statement that it implies, is true or false. Those who affirm that it is are simply choosing to ignore or to devalue other meanings and consequences of theories, and are in effect refusing to take responsibility for them even though they do exist.

There is no reason why one should be required to evaluate the formula for a new poison gas solely in terms of its mathematical elegance or of other purely technical criteria. And there is little point in pretending that such a formula is a purely neutral bit of information, useful for the furtherance of any and all social values: the thing is meant to kill and, precisely because it is technically adequate, it does so. To limit judgment solely to "autonomous" technical criteria is in effect not only to allow but to require men to be moral cretins in their technical roles. It is to make psychopathic behavior culturally required in the conduct of scientific roles. Insofar as our culture conventionally construes technical, scientific, and professional roles as those that obligate men to ignore all but the technical implications of their work, the very social structure itself is inherently pathogenic. The social function of such a segmented role structure is akin to that of the reflexive obedience induced by military training. The function of such a technical role structure, as of military discipline, is to sever the normal moral sensibilities and responsibilities of civilians and soldiers, and to enable them to be used as deployables, willing to pursue practically any objective. In the last analysis, such arrangements produce an unthinking readiness to kill or to hurt others – or to produce things that do so – on order.

The extrication of the liberative potential of Academic Sociology, no less than that of historical Marxism, is not to be accomplished by research alone. It will also require action and criticism, efforts to change the social world and efforts to change social science, both of which are profoundly interconnected, if for no other reason than that social science is a *part* of the social world as well as a *conception* of it.

In a later study I hope to be able to contribute to a sociologically informed critique of Marxism. In this volume, however, I shall seek to contribute to a critique of modern sociology in some of its dominant institutional and intellectual characteristics, as a part of a larger critique of modern society and culture. The critique of contemporary society cannot be deepened except insofar as the intellectual instruments of this critique, including sociology and the other social sciences, are themselves critically sharpened. Correspondingly, a critique of sociology will be superficial unless the discipline is seen as the flawed product of a flawed society and unless we begin to specify the details of this interconnection. What is required therefore is an analysis on different levels, in which sociology is seen in its relation to larger historical trends, to the macro-institutional level, and especially to the state; it also means seeing sociology in the setting of its most immediate locale, the university; it means seeing it as a way in which men work as teachers and researchers, and operate within an intellectual community with a received occupational culture, where they pursue careers, livelihoods, material ambitions, as well as intellectual aspirations.

Finally, and centrally, a critique of sociology also requires detailed and specific analysis of the dominant theoretical and intellectual products that sociology has created. It is these intellectual products that distinguish sociology from other activities, that justify its existence, and that produce its distinctive impact on the larger surrounding society. There can be no serious critique of sociology without a fine-grained, close analysis of its theories and its theorists.

The intellectual scope and output of modern sociology, let alone the sheer size of its operating establishments and the number of its personnel, are vast and complex; there can be no question, therefore, of exhaustive coverage of all its varying expressions and tendencies, here in this volume. Rather than a superficial effort at pseudo-systematic and exhaustive coverage, what I have therefore essayed is a close critique of a few important standpoints and issues: in particular, of what is by far the dominant system of American social theory, namely, that created by Talcott Parsons. Laborious though this effort will doubtless seem at times, let me repeat that I view it only as a very partial contribution to a critique of American sociology.

I am convinced that the extrication of the liberative potential of sociology today cannot be effected by sweeping generalizations that ignore detail; it must proceed by confronting the theories, point by point, and the theorists, man by man. This process, of working through the details of these theories and our own reactions to them, is necessary if we are to transcend them, liberate ourselves from their penetrating conservative influence, and incorporate their viable dimensions in new standpoints. Without this painful process, a radical criticism of society or sociology runs the continual risk of falling into a sterile polemicism that yields no enduring guidance and will be dangerously lacking in self-awareness.

Just as the sharpest critics of Marxism have usually been Marxists, the keenest critics of sociology today have usually been sociologists and students of sociology. They have commonly been men who regard themselves as sociologists and who have critically evaluated sociology from a sociological perspective. Their prototype, of course, is C. Wright Mills. Thus even the most polemical of their criticisms have an ambiguous implication. At one and the same time, they testify both to the profound flaws and to the continuing value, to the painful predicaments and to the perduring potentialities, of the sociological perspective.

Often enough the men whose rejection of such criticism is most vehement are those who live *off* sociology, while the most vehement critics are those who live *for* it. Often, but not always. For it is well to notice that there are critics and critics. They too may be divided among those who live for and those who live off sociology. Criticism is sometimes a way in which men can draw a quick notice to themselves without making solid contributions of their own. In short, men sometimes play the critic because they expect that the door to repute can be opened with a key of brass. The serious critics, however, are those marked by an ability to resist conventional success or by an ability to transcend failure as conventionally defined. C. Wright Mills never became a full professor; his "failure" may remind us that the serious players are always those who have an ability to pay costs.

## Criticism and the Historical Perspective

We might suggest that those who live off sociology in the most opportunistic ways, in brief, the careerists who accept sociology very largely as it is, are not, strangely enough, the most ambitious. In a way, their very careerism tokens a low level of ambition, or at least a type of ambition relatively easily satisfied within the framework of a routine career. The most unswerving critics of an intellectual establishment, those who cannot be satisfied by and within it, are usually those who do not treasure the coin of its realm, but value other, rather different kinds of fulfillments. Often these are attainable only by men with a vivid historical sense, who view themselves as historical actors and as part of a longer social and intellectual tradition. In effect, the gratifications they seek cannot be given them by their contemporaries, and the responsibilities they feel are not to contemporaries alone. They are therefore less vulnerable to the temptations and seductions of the present. From the standpoint of their more conventional contemporaries, such men are often seen as flawed. Yet they are frequently flawed in a productive manner; for being less subject to the influence of the dominant surround, they are often critically sensitive to the limitations of established intellectual paradigms and can work in a manner that is creatively at variance with them.

One of the most important functions of the "classics" in sociology is to root the sociologist in history and to enable him to live among and to take the role of truly great men. The classics implant standards of great, though often unfulfillable, achievement; they make it difficult for a man to be impressed or intimidated by those around him. An historical approach to theory puts one in the company of greatness, and it inevitably raises the standard by which one measures accomplishment. History thus insulates us from the vulgarities, no less than the gratifications, of the present.

Yet to be in love with history is dangerous, for in delivering us from the present, it may also place us in bondage to the past. It may induce an insensitivity to the new problems or needs of the present as well as to the novelty and genuine creativity of new responses to these new needs. It may produce an interminable, pedantic exegesis of the past and encourage a petulant refusal to acknowledge contemporary achievement as valuably new. The historically sensitive critic who lives too much in the shadow of the great may suffer a failure of nerve that paralyzes his creative originality; he may therefore devalue the achievements of his peers and contemporaries. In short, his criticism of contemporaries may be animated not only by *their* failure to measure up to the standards of greatness but also by his *own*. The life of criticism is therefore a precarious one not only because those criticized take a dim view of the critic, but also because it produces inner vulnerabilities that easily sour the critic. Yet the continuing development of the social sciences and its liberative potential cannot be accomplished without risking the sharpest criticism.

During an earlier period, prior to the present full-scale effort to professionalize sociology, career-seeking young men often manifested their mettle by assaulting the ideas of their seniors and, what some thought to be safer, those of classical sociologists now safely deceased. With the growth of professionalization, however, young sociologists were increasingly encouraged to seek out what was "right" in the work of others, not what was wrong. In effect they were enjoined to adopt a constructive attitude, a positive rather than a critical or negative attitude. Rather than a call for criticism, the watchwords of professionalized sociology became: continuity, codification, convergence, and cumulation. Talcott Parsons' *Structure of Social Action* was the paradigm of such a posture, and its ideology of "continuity" was taken up and amplified by his students.

This ideology is essentially an extension of the perspective that nineteenth-century sociological Positivism developed in the course of its opposition to what it regarded as the "negative" criticism of the French Revolution and the *philosophes*. The modern ideology of continuity is an extension of this earlier Positivist view of *society* into a view of *sociology* itself, into the methodology of scholarly practice, and into the training of the young scholar. The search for convergences with and in the past, for which it calls, seeks to reveal a tacit consensus of great minds and, by showing this, to lend credence to the conclusions that they are held to have converged upon unwittingly. Convergence thus becomes a rhetoric, a way of persuading men to accept certain views. The implication is that if these great men, tacitly or explicitly, agreed on a given view, it must have a *prima facie* cogency. Convergence, then, is one way in which views come, in practice, to be "tested," even though this is at variance with the canons of scientific method formally espoused by these same men.

The ideology of convergence implies that if great theorists can be shown to have come to a consensus unbeknownst to themselves, then it is these tacit *agreements* that are theoretically productive, rather than the polemics to which the men themselves often gave focal attention. Underneath the manifest disagreements of theory, the cunning of history – it is implied – has contrived to produce a truly valuable residue of intellectual consensus. This is an Americanized version of Hegelianism, in which historical development presumably occurs not through polemic, struggle, and conflict, but through consensus.

The theorist proceeding in this manner has found an ingenious way of linking his own position to the past, while at the same time manifesting his own superiority to it. Seemingly subordinating his own claims to personal priority, in apparent conformity to a higher, selfless principle, the theorist puts himself forward modestly, as a discoverer of consensus rather than as an originator of ideas. Yet in the very act of "discovering" theoretical convergences and continuities in the work of earlier men, and in particular by holding that these were unwitting, the modern theorist tacitly presents himself as now revealing things hitherto hidden from the founding fathers, and as saying them more precisely and clearly. For all his decorous regard for the past, the contemporary exponent of continuity thus manages to communicate his own originality and creativity.

The call to intellectual convergence and cumulation began to crystallize in the United States under certain distinctive social conditions. It began to emerge with – and it congenially resonated – sentiments appropriate to the "united front" solidarity of the political and military struggle against Nazism. It was in effect the academic counterpart of wartime domestic unity and of international unity between the Western powers and the Soviet Union. In short, the American call to convergence and continuity in social theory had its social foundation in collective sentiments that favored all kinds of social unity, and which had developed in response to the military and political exigencies of World War II. Correspondingly, however, with the breakdown of national unity after the war as well as with the later growth of widespread racial conflict and student rebellion, the ideology of convergence and continuity no longer resonated collective sentiment. A more critical standpoint could re-emerge.

The ideology of convergence and continuity, however, did not only reflect general national and international conditions, but was also congenial to the drive to professionalize sociology that was mounted about the same time. For such an ideology is less congenial to men who see themselves as intellectuals than to those who aspire to be professionals and technicians. The call to continuity and convergence is a methodological slogan more congenial to the guild-like sentiments of professionals, who commonly affirm their solidarity and who deplore the indecorous public display of their internal disputes. If this slogan of "continuity-convergence" serves to strengthen the mutual solidarity of professionals, it most often does so, however, at the cost of a blanketing mood of consensus that smothers intellectual criticism and innovation. If it opens some bridges to the past, it does so at the cost of barricading bridges to the future. There is no possible way of transcending the present and the past from which it derives, without a thoroughgoing criticism of it. And there is no way of moving beyond contemporary sociology without a criticism of its theory and its practice, its establishments and its ideas.

## Notes

1. "Interview with Daniel Cohn-Bendit," *Our Generation*, VI, Nos. 1–2 (May, June, July 1968), 98–99.

2. John and Barbara Ehrenreich, "The European Student Movements," *Monthly Review*, XX (September 1968), 17.

3. R. D. Laing, *The Politics of Experience* (New York: Ballantine Books, 1968), pp. 12, 17.

4. *Village Voice*, September 19, 1968, p. 59.

# 75

# Individualism

*Robert N. Bellah, Richard Madsden, William M. Sullivan, Ann Swindler and Steven M. Tipton*

### The Ambiguities of Individualism

Individualism lies at the very core of American culture. Every one of the four traditions we have singled out is in a profound sense individualistic. There is a biblical individualism and a civic individualism as well as a utilitarian and an expressive individualism. Whatever the differences among the traditions and the consequent differences in their understandings of individualism, there are some things they all share, things that are basic to American identity. We believe in the dignity, indeed the sacredness, of the individual. Anything that would violate our right to think for ourselves, judge for ourselves, make our own decisions, live our lives as we see fit, is not only morally wrong, it is sacrilegious. Our highest and noblest aspirations, not only for ourselves, but for those we care about, for our society and for the world, are closely linked to our individualism. Yet, as we have been suggesting repeatedly in this book, some of our deepest problems both as individuals and as a society are also closely linked to our individualism. We do not argue that Americans should abandon individualism – that would mean for us to abandon our deepest identity. But individualism has come to mean so many things and to contain such contradictions and paradoxes that even to defend it requires that we analyze it critically, that we consider especially those tendencies that would destroy it from within.

Modern individualism emerged out of the struggle against monarchical and aristocratic authority that seemed arbitrary and oppressive to citizens prepared to assert the right to govern themselves. In that struggle, classical political philosophy and biblical religion were important cultural resources. Classical republicanism evoked an image of the active citizen contributing to the public good and Reformation Christianity, in both Puritan and sectarian forms, inspired a notion of government based on the voluntary participation of

---

Source: Robert N. Bellah *et al.*, *Habits of the Heart: Individualism and Commitment in American Life*, (Berkeley: University of California Press, 1996).

individuals. Yet both these traditions placed individual autonomy in a context of moral and religious obligation that in some contexts justified obedience as well as freedom.

In seventeenth-century England, a radical philosophical defense of individual rights emerged that owed little to either classical or biblical sources. Rather, it consciously started with the biological individual in a "state of nature" and derived a social order from the actions of such individuals, first in relation to nature and then in relation to one another. John Locke is the key figure and one enormously influential in America. The essence of the Lockean position is an almost ontological individualism. The individual is prior to society, which comes into existence only through the voluntary contract of individuals trying to maximize their own self-interest. It is from this position that we have derived the tradition of utilitarian individualism. But because one can only know what is useful to one by consulting one's desires and sentiments, this is also ultimately the source of the expressive individualist tradition as well.

Modern individualism has long coexisted with classical republicanism and biblical religion. The conflict in their basic assumptions was initially muted because they all, in the forms commonest in America, stressed the dignity and autonomy of the individual. But as modern individualism became more dominant in the United States and classical republicanism and biblical religion less effective, some of the difficulties in modern individualism began to become apparent. The therapeutic ethos to which we have devoted so much attention is suggestive of these because it is the way in which contemporary Americans live out the tenets of modern individualism. For psychology, as Robert Coles has written, the self is "the only or main form of reality."[1]

The question is whether an individualism in which the self has become the main form of reality can really be sustained. What is at issue is not simply whether self-contained individuals might withdraw from the public sphere to pursue purely private ends, but whether such individuals are capable of sustaining either a public or a private life. If this is the danger, perhaps only the civic and biblical forms of individualism – forms that see the individual in relation to a larger whole, a community and a tradition – are capable of sustaining genuine individuality and nurturing both public and private life.

There are both ideological and sociological reasons for the growing strength of modern individualism at the expense of the civic and biblical traditions. Modern individualism has pursued individual rights and individual autonomy in ever new realms. In so doing, it has come into confrontation with those aspects of biblical and republican thought that accepted, even enshrined, unequal rights and obligations – between husbands and wives, masters and servants, leaders and followers, rich and poor. As the absolute commitment to individual dignity has condemned those inequalities, it has also seemed to invalidate the biblical and republican traditions. And in undermining these traditions, as Tocqueville warned, individualism also weakens the very meanings that give content and substance to the ideal of individual dignity.

We thus face a profound impasse. Modern individualism seems to be producing a way of life that is neither individually nor socially viable, yet a return to traditional forms would be to return to intolerable discrimination and oppression. The question, then, is whether the older civic and biblical traditions have the capacity to reformulate themselves while simultaneously remaining faithful to their own deepest insights.

Many Americans would prefer not to see the impasse as starkly as we have put it. Philosophical defenders of modern individualism have frequently presumed a social and cultural context for the individual that their theories cannot justify, or they have added ad hoc arguments that mitigate the harshness of their theoretical model. Therapists see a need for the social ties that they cannot really comprehend – they cry out for the very community that their moral logic undercuts. Parents advocate "values" for their children even when they do not know what those "values" are. What this suggests is that there is a profound ambivalence about individualism in America among its most articulate defenders. This ambivalence shows up particularly clearly at the level of myth in our literature and our popular culture. There we find the fear that society may overwhelm the individual and destroy any chance of autonomy unless he stands against it, but also recognition that it is only in relation to society that the individual can fulfill himself and that if the break with society is too radical, life has no meaning at all.

## Mythic Individualism

A deep and continuing theme in American literature is the hero who must leave society, alone or with one or a few others, in order to realize the moral good in the wilderness, at sea, or on the margins of settled society. Sometimes the withdrawal involves a contribution to society, as in James Fenimore Cooper's *The Deerslayer*. Sometimes the new marginal community realizes ethical ends impossible in the larger society, as in the interracial harmony between Huckleberry Finn and Jim. Sometimes the flight from society is simply mad and ends in general disaster, as in *Moby Dick*. When it is not in and through society but in flight from it that the good is to be realized, as in the case of Melville's Ahab, the line between ethical heroism and madness vanishes, and the destructive potentiality of a completely asocial individualism is revealed.

America is also the inventor of that most mythic individual hero, the cowboy, who again and again saves a society he can never completely fit into. The cowboy has a special talent – he can shoot straighter and faster than other men – and a special sense of justice. But these characteristics make him so unique that he can never fully belong to society. His destiny is to defend society without ever really joining it. He rides off alone into the sunset like Shane, or like the Lone Ranger moves on accompanied only by his Indian companion. But the cowboy's importance is not that he is isolated or antisocial. Rather, his significance lies in his unique, individual virtue and special skill and it is because of those qualities that society needs and welcomes him. Shane, after all, starts as a real outsider, but ends up with the gratitude of the community and the love of a woman and a boy. And while the Lone Ranger never settles down and marries the local schoolteacher, he always leaves with the affection and gratitude of the people he has helped. It is as if the myth says you can be a truly good person, worthy of admiration and love, only if you resist fully joining the group. But sometimes the tension leads to an irreparable break. Will Kane, the hero of *High Noon,* abandoned by the cowardly townspeople, saves them from an unrestrained killer, but then throws his sheriff's badge in the dust and goes off into the desert with his bride. One is left wondering where they will go, for there is no longer any link with any town.

The connection of moral courage and lonely individualism is even tighter for that other, more modern American hero, the hard-boiled detective. From Sam Spade to Serpico, the detective is a loner. He is often unsuccessful in conventional terms, working out of a shabby office where the phone never rings. Wily, tough, smart, he is nonetheless unappreciated. But his marginality is also his strength. When a bit of business finally comes their way, Philip Marlowe, Lew Archer, and Travis McGee are tenacious. They pursue justice and help the unprotected even when it threatens to unravel the fabric of society itself. Indeed, what is remarkable about the American detective story is less its hero than its image of crime. When the detective begins his quest, it appears to be an isolated incident. But as it develops, the case turns out to be linked to the powerful and privileged of the community. Society, particularly "high society," is corrupt to the core. It is this boring into the center of society to find it rotten that constitutes the fundamental drama of the American detective story. It is not a personal but a social mystery that the detective must unravel.[2]

To seek justice in a corrupt society, the American detective must be tough, and above all, he must be a loner. He lives outside the normal bourgeois pattern of career and family. As his investigations begin to lead him beyond the initial crime to the glamorous and powerful center of the society, its leaders make attempts to buy off the detective, to corrupt him with money, power, or sex. This counterpoint to the gradual unravelling of the crime is the battle the detective wages for his own integrity, in the end rejecting the money of the powerful and spurning (sometimes jailing or killing) the beautiful woman who has tried to seduce him. The hard-boiled detective, who may long for love and success, for a place in society, is finally driven to stand alone, resisting the blandishments of society, to pursue a lonely crusade for justice. Sometimes, as in the film *Chinatown,* corruption is so powerful and so total that the honest detective no longer has a place to stand and the message is one of unrelieved cynicism.

Both the cowboy and the hard-boiled detective tell us something important about American individualism. The cowboy, like the detective, can be valuable to society only because he is a completely autonomous individual who stands outside it. To serve society, one must be able to stand alone, not needing others, not depending on their judgment, and not submitting to their wishes.

Yet this individualism is not selfishness. Indeed, it is a kind of heroic selflessness. One accepts the necessity of remaining alone in order to serve the values of the group. And this obligation to aloneness is an important key to the American moral imagination. Yet it is part of the profound ambiguity of the mythology of American individualism that its moral heroism is always just a step away from despair. For an Ahab, and occasionally for a cowboy or a detective, there is no return to society, no moral redemption. The hero's lonely quest for moral excellence ends in absolute nihilism.[3]

If we may turn from the mythical heroes of fiction to a mythic, but historically real, hero, Abraham Lincoln, we may begin to see what is necessary if the nihilistic alternative is to be avoided. In many respects, Lincoln conforms perfectly to the archetype of the lonely, individualistic hero. He was a self-made man, never comfortable with the eastern upper classes. His dual moral commitment to the preservation of the Union and the belief that "all men are created equal" roused the hostility of abolitionists and Southern sympathizers alike. In the war years, he was more and more isolated, misunderstood by Congress and cabinet, and unhappy at home. In the face of almost universal mistrust, he nonetheless completed his self-appointed task of bringing the nation through its most devastating war, preaching reconciliation as he did so, only to be brought down by an assassin's bullet. What saved Lincoln from nihilism was the larger whole for which he felt it was important to live and worthwhile to die. No one understood better the meaning of the Republic and of the freedom and equality that it only very imperfectly embodies. But it was not only civic republicanism that gave his life value. Reinhold Niebuhr has said that Lincoln's biblical understanding of the Civil War was deeper than that of any contemporary theologian. The great symbols of death and rebirth that Lincoln invoked to give meaning to the sacrifice of those who died at Gettysburg, in a war he knew to be senseless and evil, came to redeem his own senseless death at the hand of an assassin. It is through his identification with a community and a tradition that Lincoln became the deeply and typically American individual that he was.[4]

## The Social Sources of Ambivalence

Individualism is deeply rooted in America's social history. Here the bondservant became free, the tenant became a small landowner, and what Benjamin Franklin called the self-respecting "middling" condition of men became the norm. Yet the incipient "independent citizen" of colonial times found himself in a cohesive community, the "peaceable kingdoms" that were colonial towns, where ties to family and church and respect for the "natural leaders" of the community were still strong.[5] Individualism was so embedded in the civic and religious structures of colonial life that it had not yet found a name, even though John Locke's ideas about individual autonomy were well known. It took the geographical and economic expansion of the new nation, especially in the years after 1800, to produce the restless quest for material betterment that led Tocqueville to use the word "individualism" to describe what he saw.[6] The new social and economic conditions did not create the ideology of modern individualism, most of whose elements are considerably older than the nineteenth century, but those conditions did make it possible for what we have called utilitarian and, later, expressive individualism to develop their own inherent tendencies in relative independence from civic and religious forms of life, important though those still were.

Tocqueville was quick to point out one of the central ambiguities in the new individualism – that it was strangely compatible with conformism. He described the American insistence that one always rely on one's own judgment, rather than on received authority, in forming one's opinions and that one stand by one's own opinions. We have already heard many examples of this attitude in the conversations recorded in earlier chapters – in the assertion, for example, that compromise with others is desirable, but not if you sacrifice your own "values." But, as Tocqueville observed, when one can no longer rely on tradition or authority, one inevitably looks to others for confirmation of one's judgments. Refusal to accept established opinion and anxious conformity to the opinions of one's peers turn out to be two sides of the same coin.[7]

There has been a long-standing anxiety that the American individualist, who flees from home and family leaving the values of community and tradition behind, is secretly a conformist. Mark Twain depicted the stultifying conformity of the mid-nineteenth-century town of his youth in recounting the adventures of boys who tried to break free of it and never quite succeeded. As late as the 1920s, Sinclair Lewis identified a classic American type in his portrait of *Babbitt,* the small town businessman too afraid of censure from neighbors and family to develop his political convictions or pursue his own happiness in love. The advice Babbit gives his son not to make the mistake he has made is typical: "Don't be scared of the family. No, nor all of Zenith. Nor of yourself, the way I've been."

In the past hundred years, individualism and its ambiguities have been closely linked to middle-class status. The "middle class" that began to emerge in the later part of the nineteenth century differed from the old "middling condition." In the true sense of the term, the middle class is defined not merely by the desire for material betterment but by a conscious, calculating effort to move up the ladder of success. David Schneider and Raymond Smith usefully define the middle class as a "broad but not undifferentiated category which includes those who have certain attitudes, aspirations, and expectations toward status mobility, and who shape their actions accordingly." Status mobility has increasingly depended on advanced education and competence in managerial and professional occupations that require specialized knowledge. For middle-class Americans, a calculating attitude toward educational and occupational choice has been essential and has often spilled over into determining criteria for the choice of spouse, friends, and voluntary associations. From the point of view of lower-class Americans, these preoccupations do not necessarily seem natural. As one of Schneider and Smith's informants put it, "To be a square dude is hard work, man."[8]

For those oriented primarily to upward mobility, to "success," major features of American society appear to be "the normal outcome of the operation of individual achievement." In this conception, individuals, unfettered by family or other group affiliation, are given the chance to make the best of themselves, and, though equality of opportunity is essential, inequality of result is natural. But the ambiguities of individualism for the middle-class person arise precisely from lack of certainty about what the "best" we are supposed to make of ourselves is. Schneider and Smith note that "there are no fixed standards of behavior which serve to mark status. The only clearly defined cultural standards against which status can be measured are the gross standards of income, consumption, and conformity to rational procedures for attaining ends." Middle-class individuals are thus motivated to enter a highly autonomous and demanding quest for achievement and then left with no standard against which achievement is to be measured except the income and consumption levels of their neighbors, exhibiting anew the clash between autonomy and conformity that seems to be the fate of American individualism.[9]

But perhaps Schneider and Smith's third cultural standard, "rational procedures for attaining ends," offers a way of asserting individual autonomy without the anxious glance at the neighbor. In the case of middle-class professionals whose occupation involves the application of technical rationality to the solution of new problems, the correct solution of a problem or, even more, an innovative solution to a problem, provides evidence of "success" that has intrinsic validity. And where such competence operates in the service of the public good – as, for example, in medical practice at its best – it expresses an individualism that has social value without being conformist.[10]

But to the extent that technical competence is enclosed in the life pattern that we have designated "career," concern for rational problem solving (not to speak of social contribution) becomes subordinated to standards of success measured only by income and consumption. When this happens, as it often does to doctors, lawyers, and other professionals, it raises doubts about the intrinsic value of the work itself. These doubts become all the more insistent when, as is often the case, the professional must operate in the context of a large public or private bureaucracy where much ingenuity must be spent, not on solving external problems, but on manipulating the bureaucratic rules and roles, both in order to get anything done and in order to move ahead in one's career. Anxieties about whether an "organization man" can be a genuine individual long predate William H. Whyte's famous book *The Organization Man*.[11] The cowboy and the detective began to appear as popular heroes when business corporations emerged as the focal institutions of American life. The fantasy of a lonely, but morally impeccable, hero corresponds to doubts about the integrity of the self in the context of modern bureaucratic organization.

The irony of present-day middle-class American individualism derives from the fact that while a high degree of personal initiative, competence, and rationality are still demanded from individuals, the autonomy of the successful individual and even the meaning of "success" are increasingly in doubt. It is as though the stress on the rationality of means and on the importance of individual wants, the primary emphases of utilitarian and expressive individualism, have come loose from an understanding of the ends and purposes of life, in the past largely derived from the biblical and republican traditions. One response to this situation is to make occupational achievement, for so long the dominating focus of middle-class individualism, no longer an end in itself, but merely an instrument for the attainment of a private lifestyle lived, perhaps, in a lifestyle enclave. Yet this solution is subject to doubt. The same inner contradictions that undermined occupational success as a life goal also threaten to deprive private life of meaning when there is no longer any purpose to involvement with others except individual satisfaction.

The ambiguity and ambivalence of American individualism derive from both cultural and social contradictions. We insist, perhaps more than ever before, on finding our true selves independent of any cultural or social influence, being responsible to that self alone, and making its fulfillment the very meaning of our lives. Yet we spend much of our time navigating through immense bureaucratic structures – multiversities, corporations, government agencies – manipulating and being manipulated by others. In describing this situation, Alasdair MacIntyre has spoken of "bureaucratic individualism," the form of life exemplified by the manager and the therapist.[12] In bureaucratic individualism, the ambiguities and contradictions of individualism are frighteningly revealed, as freedom to make private decisions is bought at the cost of turning over most public decisions to bureaucratic managers and experts. A bureaucratic individualism in which the consent of the governed, the first demand of modern enlightened individualism, has been abandoned in all but form, illustrates the tendency of individualism to destroy its own conditions.

But in our interviews, though we saw tendencies toward bureaucratic individualism, we cannot say that it has yet become dominant. Rather we found all the classic polarities of American individualism still operating: the deep desire for autonomy and self-reliance combined with an equally deep conviction that life has no meaning unless shared with others in the context of community; a commitment to the equal right to dignity of every individual combined with an effort to justify inequality of reward, which, when extreme, may deprive people of dignity; an insistence that life requires practical effectiveness and "realism" combined with the feeling that compromise is ethically fatal. The inner tensions of American individualism add up to a classic case of ambivalence. We strongly assert the value of our self-reliance and autonomy. We deeply feel the emptiness of a life without sustaining social commitments. Yet we are hesitant to articulate our sense that we need one another as much as we need to stand alone, for fear that if we did we would lose our independence altogether. The tensions of our lives would be even greater if we did not, in fact, engage in practices that constantly limit the effects of an isolating individualism, even though we cannot articulate those practices nearly as well as we can the quest for autonomy.

## The Limits of Individualism

We have pointed out the peculiar resonance between middle-class life and individualism in America. We have also stressed the special nature of the middle class, the fact that it is not simply a "layer" in a "system of stratification" but rather a group that seeks to embody in its own continuous progress and advancement the very meaning of the American project. To a large extent, it has succeeded in this aspiration. It so dominates our culture that, as Schneider and Smith put it, "middle-class values can be said to encompass both lower- and upper-class values." This is true for the lower class in that not only are middle-class values understood and respected but "lower-class people explain their inferior position in terms of circumstances that have prevented them from behaving in a middle-class fashion." The upper class sometimes takes comfort in its special sense of family and tradition, but it does not try to substitute its values for the dominant ones. On the contrary, its members praise middle-class rationality and achievement as the values on which our society is based, even when they do not choose to follow them.[13]

The nature of middle-class individualism becomes even clearer when we contrast it to lower-class and upper-class culture. Schneider and Smith describe the contrast very suggestively when they say that the middle class sees "individual and social behavior as predominantly determined by the application of technical rules to any situation that arises," whereas the lower class (and, interestingly enough, the upper class) have a more "dramaturgical view of social action." By "dramaturgical" they mean action that takes on meaning because of a particular history of relationships. Abstract rules are less important than the examples set by individuals. Schneider and Smith argue, for example, that it is in the lower class that ethnicity, as a specific pattern of cultural life, survives in America, and that as individuals enter the middle class, ethnicity loses distinctive social content even when it is symbolically emphasized.[14] The point is not that lower- and upper-class Americans are not individualistic, but rather that their individualism is embedded in specific patterns of relationship and solidarity that mitigate the tendency toward an empty self and empty relationships in middle-class life. The contrast is expressed by middle-class Americans themselves when they entertain envious fantasies about more "meaningful community" among lower-class racial and ethnic groups or among (usually European) aristocracies.

Important though the distinctions we have been drawing are, we should not overemphasize the degree to which rationality and technical rules govern middle-class life. Children do not grow up through abstract injunctions. They identify with their parents, they learn through role modeling, and they are influenced by the historic specificity of their family, church, and local community. It is the middle-class orientation toward technical education, bureaucratic occupational hierarchies, and the market economy that encourages the greater emphasis on universal rules and technical rationality. The upper and lower classes can maintain greater cultural specificity (though in the United States that specificity is only relative) because they are less oriented to these rationalizing institutions.

Since middle-class people, too, are embedded in families, churches, and local communities, they also experience conflict between the more rational and the more dramaturgic spheres of life. The tensions that divide middle-class Americans from other Americans also exist within the middle class itself. Much is said about the cultural diversity and pluralism of American life. But perhaps what divides us most is not that diversity, but the conflict between the monoculture of technical and bureaucratic rationality and the specificity of our concrete commitments.[15]

## Communities of Memory

In chapter 3 we discussed at length the process by which a primary emphasis on self-reliance has led to the notion of pure, undetermined choice, free of tradition, obligation, or commitment, as the essence of the self. We pointed out that the radical individualist's sincere desire to "reconnect" with others was inhibited by the emptiness of such an "unencumbered" self. It is now time to consider what a self that is not empty would be like – one that is constituted rather than unencumbered, one that has, let us admit it, encumbrances, but whose encumbrances make connection to others easier and more natural. Just as the empty self makes sense in a particular institutional context – that of the upward mobility of the middle-class individual who must leave home and church in order to succeed in an impersonal world of rationality and competition – so a constituted self makes sense in terms of another institutional context, what we would call, in the full sense of the word, community.

Communities, in the sense in which we are using the term, have a history – in an important sense they are constituted by their past – and for this reason we can speak of a real community as a "community of memory," one that does not forget its past. In order not to forget that past, a community is involved in retelling its story, its constitutive narrative, and in so doing, it offers examples of the men and women who have embodied and exemplified the meaning of the community. These stories of collective history and exemplary individuals are an important part of the tradition that is so central to a community of memory.[16]

The stories that make up a tradition contain conceptions of character, of what a good person is like, and of the virtues that define such character. But the stories are not all exemplary, not all about successes and achievements. A genuine community of memory will also tell painful stories of shared suffering that sometimes creates deeper identities than success, as we saw when Ruth Levy recognized her own identity with a community of shared love and suffering in the number on her baby-sitter's arm. And if the community is completely honest, it will remember stories not only of suffering received but of suffering inflicted – dangerous memories, for they call the community to alter ancient evils. The communities of memory that tie us to the past also turn us toward the future as communities of hope. They carry a context of meaning that can allow us to connect our aspirations for ourselves and those closest to us with the aspirations of a larger whole and see our own efforts as being, in part, contributions to a common good.[17]

Examples of such genuine communities are not hard to find in the United States. There are ethnic and racial communities, each with its own story and its own heroes and heroines. There are religious communities that recall and reenact their stories in the weekly and annual cycles of their ritual year, remembering the scriptural stories that tell them who they are and the saints and martyrs who define their identity. There is the national community, defined by its history and by the character of its representative leaders from John Winthrop to Martin Luther King, Jr. Americans identify with their national community partly because there is little else that we all share in common but also partly because America's history exemplifies aspirations widely shared throughout the world: the ideal of a free society, respecting all its citizens, however diverse, and allowing them all to fulfill themselves. Yet some Americans also remember the history of suffering inflicted and the gap between promise and realization, which has always been very great. At some times, neighborhoods, localities, and regions have been communities in America, but that has been hard to sustain in our restless and mobile society. Families can be communities remembering their past, telling the children the stories of parents' and grandparents' lives, and sustaining hope for the future – though without the context of a larger community that sense of family is hard to maintain. Where history and hope are forgotten and community means only the gathering of the similar, community degenerates into lifestyle enclave. The temptation toward that transformation is endemic in America though the transition is seldom complete.

People growing up in communities of memory not only hear the stories that tell how the community came to be, what its hopes and fears are, and how its ideals are exemplified in outstanding men and women; they also participate in the practices – ritual, aesthetic, ethical – that define the community as a way of life. We call these "practices of commitment" for they define the patterns of loyalty and obligation that keep the community alive. And if the language of the self-reliant individual is the first language of American moral life, the languages of tradition and commitment in communities of memory are "second languages" that most Americans know as well, and which they use when the language of the radically separate self does not seem adequate.

The empty self, as we said in chapter 3, is an analytic concept, a limit toward which we tend, but not a concrete reality. A completely empty self could not exist except in the theory of radical individualism. It is theoretically imaginable but performatively impossible. The constituted self is also an analytic concept, a limit that is never quite reached. It is true that we are all children of specific parents, born in a particular locality, inheritors of those group histories, and citizens of this nation. All of these things tell us who we are in important ways. But we live in a society that encourages us to cut free from the past, to define our own selves, to choose the groups with which we wish to identify. No tradition and no community in the United States is above criticism, and the test of the criticism is usually the degree to which the community or tradition helps the individual to find fulfillment. So we live somewhere between the empty and the constituted self.

The tension can be invigorating, helping to keep both individual and community vital and self-critical. But the tension is also anxious and sometimes leads to the potentially explosive conflicts between technical rationality and concrete commitments we mentioned earlier. Liberal intellectuals, in their own minds devoted to individual freedom, sometimes caricature regional or religious groups whose traditions and communities they find ignorant and potentially authoritarian. And since liberal intellectuals have considerable influence on public policy, both through the courts and through legislation, they have on occasion forced their own enlightened views on their fellow citizens. On the other hand, some conservative groups, dismayed by rapid social change and by the social consequences of radical individualism, simplify and objectify their traditions with fundamentalist inflexibility and then condemn those of their fellow citizens who hold differing views, sometimes joining political action committees in the attempt to legislate their convictions. We have used the terms *liberal* and *conservative* here because they are frequently used in this context, but they do not serve well. The conflict is cultural more than political, though it can have serious political consequences. Another way of speaking of these antagonists is to call them "modernists" and "antimodernists," but this, too, is of only limited utility. Rather than relying on simplistic labels, we should recognize that some of our deepest cultural conflicts arise from differing understandings of our common individualism.

For a long time, our society was held together, even in periods of rapid change, by a largely liberal Protestant cultural center that sought to reconcile the claims of community and individuality. Rejecting both chaotic openness and authoritarian closure, representatives of this cultural center defended tradition – some version of the civic republican and biblical traditions – but not traditionalism. They sought to reappropriate the past in the light of the present, mindful of the distortions that mar the past of every tradition. That task has become increasingly difficult, but it has by no means been abandoned. In the rest of this chapter, we will consider a few examples of those who have attempted to articulate a socially responsible individualism within the context of communities of memory and the second languages and practices of commitment they carry. We will see that this is no easy task in a society in which the first language of modern individualism, fusing utilitarian and expressive components, and the practices of separation that go with it, are so dominant that alternatives are hard to understand. Yet as the ambivalence that we have repeatedly noticed in this chapter indicates, even those most exclusively caught in the first language seem to be yearning for something more.

### Community, Commitment, and Individuality

Les Newman, very much a middle-class American, has found a home in the church, one that allows him to take a critical view of the environing society. He says that "American society is becoming very self-oriented, or very individual-oriented: what's in it for me, how much do I get out of it, am I getting everything I'm entitled to in my life? It is tearing down a lot that is right about the country. People don't look at the repercussions of their individual actions outside of themselves."

For this evangelical Baptist, reared in the South, just graduated from a well-known business school, and now working as an executive in the California suburbs, such sweeping criticism becomes more specific in characterizing his fellow-alumni. Most of them "felt they didn't need God, didn't need religion. There was a strong impression in business school, the self-made individual, being able to do it all yourself if you just work hard enough and think hard enough, and not having to rely on other people." It is precisely because such self-made individuals don't appreciate their need for God that they don't appreciate their need for other people, Les Newman observes. He experiences both needs in the active life of his church congregation. Its members aren't "the standard go-to-church Sunday-morning people" who practice "a ritual as opposed to a lifestyle." For them religion is more than just saying "Here's a set of morals to live by and here's this great example of 2,000 years ago." The heart of their shared life and teaching "is that Jesus Christ is a person. He's alive today, to relate to today. He works in your life today, and you can talk to Him through the week in prayer." Church for this believer, therefore, "isn't just a place, it's a family" that has given him the closest friends he has. Despite leaving home, moving to California, and entering the competitive world of business, he has found a new family-like anchor for his life, a new bond to other people through the shared celebration of a "personal relationship with Jesus Christ."

In this traditional Christian view, what connects one self to another is the objectively given reality of their creation as God's children and God's own continuing presence in the world in Jesus Christ. This reality is one each person freely accepts, thus establishing the bonds of the Christian congregation while affirming individual identity. Reflecting on this process of self-integration, the Baptist businessman testifies, "I got my personal Christian relationship with Jesus and that has sort of been the ongoing thing that has tied together a whole bunch of different things. That relationship with Christ has changed me somewhat as an individual when it comes to my outlook on the world. He is the person who has steadied my emotion. Before, I was kind of unstable, and I've had some pretty good lows, and now I find that doesn't happen. It has strengthened my commitment in my marriage, and it's had a great deal of impact on the way I relate to other people at work. My life is such a combination of disjointed events. My childhood was just a whole series of moves." Relating oneself to Christ, even in the disjointed course of social uprooting and cultural conflict, yields an experience of the self's integrity.

His church community has helped Les Newman find a language and a set of practices that have strengthened his marriage, aided him in dealing with his work situation, and given him a more coherent sense of self, as well as providing him with some critical distance from the environing society. Ted Oster has no such community and seems much more at ease in the first language of modern individualism, a language he uses to explain most of what goes on around him. Yet when pressed to explain why he remains in a long marriage, his several attempts to do so in cost/benefit terms finally break down. His happiness with his wife comes from "proceeding through all these stages of life together. . . . It makes life meaningful and gives me the opportunity to share with somebody, have an anchor, if you will, and understand where I am. That for me is a real relationship." Here Ted Oster seems to be groping for words that could express his marriage as a community of memory and hope, a place where he is not empty, but which essentially defines who he is. It is as though he had to invent a second language out of the failing fragments of his usual first language.

Although we did not see it in the case of Ted Oster, and only tentatively in the case of Les Newman, communities of memory, though often embedded in family experiences, are an important way in which individuals are led into public life. Angelo Donatello, a successful small businessman who has become a civic leader in a suburb of Boston, tells how a reluctant concern for the ethnic heritage rooted in his family finally led him into public life: "One of the important things that got me into politics was that I was a confused individual. I came from a real old-fashioned Italian family in East Boston. We spoke both languages at home, but I was more Americanized than my brothers or sisters, so to speak. We were forgetting our heritage – that meant becoming more free, more liberal, being able to express myself differently. Thirteen or fourteen years ago, there was a group of people in town who talked about forming a chapter of the Sons of Italy. I would not have been one of the first ones to propose such a thing. My wife was Irish – I was one of the first ones in my family to marry out. But I went to these meetings. Before I had gotten into this I had forgotten my heritage." What catalyzed Angelo's involvement was the unexpected appearance of prejudice when the group tried to buy a piece of land for the Sons of Italy hall. In fighting the opposition, which seemed to focus on the belief that Italians are drunken and rowdy, Angelo became involved with the town government. Remembering his heritage involved accepting his origins, including painful memories of prejudice and discrimination that his earlier efforts at "Americanization" had attempted to deny.

The experience of ethnic prejudice helped Angelo see that there is more to life than leaving behind the past, becoming successful on his own, and expressing himself freely. But as he became more involved with the community he had tried to forget – more active, that is, in the Sons of Italy – he also became more involved with his town. Elected a selectman, he saw it his duty to represent not only Italian-Americans but also the welfare of the town as a whole. Abandoning one kind of individualism, he was led toward a civic individualism that entailed care for the affairs of his community in both the narrower and wider senses. While leaving behind "Americanization," he became American.

Marra James provides an interesting contrast to Angelo Donatello. Born in a small town in West Virginia, she has lived for some years in a Southern California suburb, where she has become active in a variety of causes focussing around environmental issues such as saving wild land from development. Marra was raised in the Catholic church and was active in her parish when she first came to California. She does not go to church anymore as she has gone beyond what she calls "structural religion." Yet she has carried a sensitivity to ritual over into her new concerns. She dates her involvement in the environmental movement from the celebration of the first Earth Day at a local college, and she was, when interviewed some ten years later, actively planning the local tenth anniversary celebration.

Marra has a strong and explicit understanding of the importance of community: "Many people feel empty and don't know why they feel empty. The reason is we are all social animals and we must live and interact and work together in community to become fulfilled." But she sees serious impediments to the realization of community in America: "Most people have been sold a bill of goods by our system. I call it the Three C's: cash, convenience, consumerism. It's getting worse. The reason you don't feel a part of it is that nobody is a part of it. Loneliness is a national feeling." But Marra has not reacted to this realization with despair. She is intensely active and returns to the fray whether she wins or loses. In her years as city council member and chair of a county planning commission, she has suffered plenty of defeats. "I sometimes describe myself as a rubber ball," she says. "I've been pushed down sometimes to where I've almost been pressed flat, but I've always been able to bounce back." For Marra, politics is a worthwhile educational endeavor, win or lose, perhaps especially when you lose.

Marra James is remarkable in the scope with which she defines her community: "I feel very much a part of the whole – of history. I live in a spectrum that includes the whole world. I'm a part of all of it. For what I do impacts the whole. So if I'm going to be wasteful, misuse resources – that will impact the whole world." Marra identifies herself as a moderate Republican, but her politics go beyond any such label. For her, the "whole world" is a community of memory and hope and entails practices of commitment that she assiduously carries out. Undoubtedly, there has been involvement in many communities along the way, each one important in constituting her as the person she is – her family, the church, the network of her fellow environmental activists. In trying to give substance to what is as yet an aspiration by defining her community as the whole world, she runs the risk of becoming detached from any concrete community of memory.

Finally, let us consider the example of Cecilia Dougherty, in whose life a series of communities of memory have played a part in leading to her present political commitment in ways even clearer than in the case of Marra James. Cecilia lives in a part of Santa Monica whose landscape is shaped by shade trees, schools, and churches. She, like Wayne Bauer, is an active member of the Campaign for Economic Democracy. At present she works for a local attorney involved in progressive causes, and in addition serves as an elected official of city government. Despite these rather daunting commitments, Cecilia is the single mother of four teenagers, her husband having died several years ago, an event that was for her at once traumatic and transformative.

Cecilia Dougherty began her political activism in her forties following the great break caused in the continuity of her life by her husband's death. She started out by working on the congressional campaign of a local candidate, in part because his opponent supported many things she opposed, but also to try out her capacities to engage in political life on her own. Cecilia had begun to think about taking more public initiative while her husband was living.

The critical event was meeting a colleague of her husband, a woman of their age, who told Cecilia that having heard good things about her from her husband, she was eager to learn more about her. Cecilia says that she began, "I have four children . . ." but the woman persisted, saying. "Wait just a minute. I didn't ask about your children, I asked about you. Where are you coming from? " At this Cecilia was stunned. " I mean, my role was a housewife and I didn't quite grasp what she was really talking about." But the woman told her: "I'm not talking about your identity as Greg's wife. I'm concerned with your identity as a human being, as a person, and as an individual, and as a woman." She invited Cecilia to join a consciousness-raising group, "a turning point in my life, a real change for me."

Once into the consciousness-raising group, Cecilia Dougherty experienced herself as waking up as if from a sleep, reaching back to hopes and aspirations she had had as a girl, before becoming a wife and mother. Cecilia rediscovered that she had wanted to become a teacher, and at first thought about going to college to fulfill that dream. She was already working as a clerk for a labor union, however, and she decided to tailor her educational aspirations around that. "I decided that I would work with what I had already." Whatever earlier "gut feelings" Cecilia may have discovered in consciousness raising, her decision to build on the past, on what she "had already," is characteristic of the way she has acted on her new sense of freedom and efficacy.

In fact, for all their importance as catalysts, contact with feminist consciousness raising and discovering her identity "as a person and as an individual" have not been the determining factors in Cecilia Dougherty's activist commitments. Rather, as she describes it, the new sense of efficacy that she learned from consciousness raising in a real sense returned her to earlier commitments and an identification with the cause of the dignity of working people that was deeply rooted in her family's experience. Her sense of purpose in political involvement is not based simply on radical individualism but grounded in the continuity of generations: "I want to see the have-nots have power that reflects their numbers, and I want to protect the future of my children and my grandchildren. I feel a historical family responsibility for continuing to be working for progressive causes."

When Cecilia was asked to explain her commitment to activism, she responded, characteristically, with the story of how her ideals of self developed through the experience of her family. That is, she employed a "second language" that organizes life by reference to certain ideals of character – virtues such as courage and honor – and commitments to institutions that are seen as embodiments of those values. For example, Cecilia's feminism is in part emulation of her mother in a different context. Her mother was an Italian immigrant who married at eighteen and did not go to college, but became the first woman in her county to be elected chair of the state Democratic Central Committee. "So," commented Cecilia, "she made me realize a commitment at a very early age. By eight years old, I was working in party headquarters, licking stamps and answering the phone."

But the paradigmatic event that gave Cecilia a deep sense of identity with the labor movement and its goals of a more just and inclusive society involved her father. When Cecilia was fourteen, her father, an Irish Catholic immigrant working for an energy corporation, went on strike. This was shortly after World War II. Cecilia vividly recalls the weeks of the strike, especially the union solidarity that got the family through it. "We went every night to the town where the union hall was," she recounted, "for dinner in the soup kitchen kind of thing, and my mother would help cook." However, the decisive event occurred six weeks into the strike, when her father was arrested on charges of throwing rocks at strikebreakers.

The shock was that Cecilia's father "who'd been such a good citizen; so honest, and so conscientious, the American-way type person" should be not only arrested, but attacked in court as a communist and rabble-rouser. The revelation of the low tactics of the corporation's lawyers had a strong impact on her, resulting in a sense of moral outrage that continues to frame her political concerns. She was also deeply impressed by her father's courage and sense of honor under attack by the "company attorneys, with their suits and everything." Most of all, she was impressed by the strength of the solidarity in the labor movement. "I realized then the value of the union and how we were utterly dependent on the union for our very sustenance."

Thus when Cecilia Dougherty returned to politics in the Democratic party, and when she decided to become heavily involved in local activism, she could, and did, draw upon a considerable heritage. She describes her transition from working wife and mother to her present, much more public involvements not so much as a choice – in the sense that one might choose to take up painting versus taking up bowling – but as a response to part of her identity, as fulfilling a responsibility to which her life, her heritage, and her beliefs have called her.

Asked what she sees her activism achieving, Cecilia responded by saying that she hopes to "bring people away from concern only about their own lives, to a sense of much, much broader, greater responsibility. It sounds very grandiose! Probably the most I'm going to be able to do is sustain and build better community in Santa Monica, you know, and that's certainly a life's work." The image of community contained in Cecilia's account of the strike is quite different from the association of like-minded individuals advocated by others we talked to.

The fundamental contrasts between Cecilia Dougherty's self-understanding and the first language of modern individualism can be narrowed to three. First, Cecilia articulates her sense of self by reference to a narrative illustrative of long-term commitments rather than desires and feelings. While she sees certain breaks with her past as crucial "turning points" in her life, she interprets the resulting freedom as an opportunity for new commitments, often "working from what I had already." Thus, unlike the radical individualistic notion of a life course based on leaving home in order to become a free self, Cecilia's self-image is rooted in a concept of the virtues that make an admirable life, especially those exemplified in the lives of her mother and father. This is the second contrast: that her sense of self is rooted in virtues that define a worthwhile life and have been passed on and modeled by others who have shared that tradition, not in a contentless freedom attained by leaving concrete commitments behind.

The third distinguishing feature of Cecilia's "second language" is her notion that community means a solidarity based on a responsibility to care for others because that is essential to living a good life. She describes her solidarity with working people and "the have-nots" as an expression of a concern for human dignity, the violation of which sparked her first anger at the abuse of power. This sense of a community of solidarity recalls the classical civic contrast between the private person who thinks first of himself alone and the citizen who knows himself to be a participant in a form of life through which his own identity is fulfilled. The civic vision is quite different from the image of a gathering of like-minded individuals whose union depends entirely on their spontaneous interest. Indeed thinking about this contrast tends to confirm Tocqueville's claim that public order and trust cannot spring from individual spontaneity alone, but require the kind of cultivation that only active civic life can provide.

The lived source of the civic language in Cecilia Dougherty's life is not hard to identify: it was her and her parents' lifelong commitments to the labor movement. It was probably reinforced by a similar emphasis on solidarity in the Catholicism she shared with parents and husband. It is this that she has been able to expand into a general concern for "economic democracy."[18]

It is characteristic of Cecilia Dougherty and the others we have just considered that they define themselves through their commitments to a variety of communities rather than through the pursuit of radical autonomy. Yet Cecilia, like the others, exhibits a high degree of self-determination and efficacy. She exemplifies a form of individualism that is fulfilled in community rather than against it. Conformism, the nemesis of American individualism, does not seem to be a problem for Cecilia and the others. Their involvement in practices of commitment makes them able to resist pressures to conform. On occasion, they show great resilience in so doing, as when Marra James bounces back after being "pressed flat." Our examples suggest that Tocqueville was probably right in believing that it was isolation, not social involvement, that led to conformism and the larger danger of authoritarian manipulation.

There are authoritarian groups in the United States, sometimes devoted to destructive ends. What makes them different from genuine communities is the shallowness and distortion of their memory and the narrowness of what they hope for. A radically isolating individualism is not a defense against such coercive groups. On the contrary, the loneliness that results from isolation may precipitate the "hunger for authority" on which such groups feed.

## Private and Public

Sometimes Americans make a rather sharp dichotomy between private and public life. Viewing one's primary task as "finding oneself" in autonomous self-reliance, separating oneself not only from one's parents but also from those larger communities and traditions that constitute one's past, leads to the notion that it is in oneself, perhaps in relation to a few intimate others, that fulfillment is to be found. Individualism of this sort often implies a negative view of public life. The impersonal forces of the economic and political worlds are what the individual needs protection against. In this perspective, even occupation, which has been so central to the identity of Americans in the past, becomes instrumental – not a good in itself, but only a means to the attainment of a rich and satisfying private life. But on the basis of what we have seen in our observation of middle-class American life, it would seem that this quest for purely private fulfillment is illusory: it often ends in emptiness instead. On the other hand, we found many people, some of whom we introduced earlier in this chapter, for whom private fulfillment and public involvement are not antithetical. These people evince an individualism that is not empty but is full of content drawn from an active identification with communities and traditions. Perhaps the notion that private life and public life are at odds is incorrect. Perhaps they are so deeply involved with each other that the impoverishment of one entails the impoverishment of the other. Parker Palmer is probably right when he says that "in a healthy society the private and the public are not mutually exclusive, not in competition with each other. They are, instead, two halves of a whole, two poles of a paradox. They work together dialectically, helping to create and nurture one another."[19]

Certainly this dialectical relationship is clear where public life degenerates into violence and fear. One cannot live a rich private life in a state of siege, mistrusting all strangers and turning one's home into an armed camp. A minimum of public decency and civility is a precondition for a fulfilling private life. On the other hand, public involvement is often difficult and demanding. To engage successfully in the public world, one needs personal strength and the support of family and friends. A rewarding private life is one of the preconditions for a healthy public life.

For all their doubts about the public sphere, Americans are more engaged in voluntary associations and civic organizations than the citizens of most other industrial nations. In spite of all the difficulties, many Americans feel they must "get involved." In public life as in private, we can discern the habits of the heart that sustain individualism and commitment, as well as what makes them problematic.

## Notes

1. Robert Coles, "Civility and Psychology," *Daedalus* (Summer 1980), p. 137.

2. On individualism in nineteenth-century American literature see D. H. Lawrence, *Studies in Classic American Literature* (1923; Garden City, N.Y.: Doubleday, Anchor Books, 1951). On the image of the cowboy see Will Wright, *Sixguns and Society: A Structural Study of the Western* (Berkeley and Los Angeles: University of California Press, 1975). On cowboys and detectives see John G. Cawelti, *Adventure, Mystery, and Romance: Formula Stories as Art and Popular Culture* (Chicago: University of Chicago Press, 1976).

3. On the hero's avoidance of women and society see Leslie Fiedler, *Love and Death in the American Novel* (New York: Stein and Day, 1966), and Ann Swidler, "Love and Adulthood in American Culture," in *Themes of Work and Love in Adulthood*, ed. Neil J. Smelser and Erik H. Erikson (Cambridge, Mass.: Harvard University Press, 1980), pp. 120–47.

4. The best book on Lincoln's meaning for American public life is Harry V. Jaffa, *Crisis of the House Divided: An Interpretation of the Lincoln-Douglas Debates* (Garden City, N.Y.: Doubleday, 1959). Reinhold Niebuhr's remarks appear in his essay "The Religion of Abraham Lincoln," in *Lincoln and the Gettysburg Address*, ed. Allan Nevins (Urbana, Ill.: University of Illinois Press, 1964), p. 72.

5. See, particularly, Michael Zuckerman, *Peaceable Kingdoms: New England Towns in the Eighteenth Century* (New York: Random House, 1970). The phrase "peaceable kingdom" is, of course, eschatological in its reference. It is what the New Englanders aspired to be, not what they claimed they were.

6. On the introduction of the term individualism by Tocqueville and the American response see Yehoshua Arieli, *Individualism and Nationalism in American Ideology*

(Cambridge, Mass.: Harvard University Press, 1964), pp. 183–210, 246–76. On the emergence of the term in the European context see Koenraad W. Swart, "Individualism in the Mid-Nineteenth Century," *Journal of the History of Ideas* 23 (1962): 77–90.

7. Alexis de Tocqueville, *Democracy in America,* trans. George Lawrence, ed. J. P. Mayer (New York: Doubleday, Anchor Books, 1969), vol. 2, part 1, chapters 1 and 2.

8. David M. Schneider and Raymond T. Smith, *Class Differences and Sex Roles in American Kinship and Family Structure* (Englewood Cliffs, N.J.: Prentice-Hall, 1973), pp. 19, 20.

9. Ibid., p. 24.

10. Ibid., p. 46.

11. William H. Whyte, *The Organization Man* (New York: Simon and Schuster, 1956).

12. Alasdair MacIntyre, *After Virtue* (South Bend, Ind.: University of Notre Dame Press, 1981), p. 33.

13. Schneider and Smith, *Class Differences*, p. 27.

14. Ibid., pp. 107, 39. "The direct experience of our field research was that, while consciousness of ethnic identity persists at all levels of society, it is of rapidly decreasing significance as a factor affecting the behavior of those who are middle class. In fact, one aspect of becoming middle class is the abandonment of most of the behavioral characteristics of ethnicity, a process considerably aided by orientation toward individual achievement, the rational control of events and things, and looking to the future rather than to the past" (pp 35–36).

15. Richard M. Merelman in *Making Something of Ourselves: On Culture and Politics in the United States* (Berkeley and Los Angeles: University of California Press, 1984) defines this conflict as between loose-boundedness and tight-boundedness. He sees it as the major conflict in American life today.

16. See MacIntyre, *After Virtue,* chapter 15.

17. On the memory of suffering and the importance of keeping such memories alive see Johann Baptist Metz, *Faith in History and Society: Toward a Practical Fundamental Theology* (New York: Seabury, 1980). Freud, in "Mourning and Melancholia," (1917) *Collected Papers* (London: Hogarth Press, 1956), 4: 152–70, points out that if the memory of suffering is suppressed it continues to dominate a person in unhealthy ways. This suggests a dialectic of forgetting and remembering: only by remembering can we be free to act without being dominated by unconscious memory.

18. Cecilia Dougherty might be surprised to know that the early twentieth-century Catholic social thinker Monsignor John A. Ryan, author of *Distributive Justice* (New York, 1927), was already using the term "economic democracy."

19. Parker J. Palmer, *The Company of Strangers: Christians and the Renewal of America's Public Life* (New York: Crossroad, 1981), p. 31.

# 76

# The New Forms of Control

*Herbert Marcuse*

A comfortable, smooth, reasonable, democratic unfreedom prevails in advanced industrial civilisation, a token of technical progress. Indeed, what could be more rational than the suppression of individuality in the mechanization of socially necessary but painful performances; the concentration of individual enterprises in more effective, more productive corporations; the regulation of free competition among unequally equipped economic subjects; the curtailment of prerogatives and national sovereignties which impede the international organization of resources. That this technological order also involves a political and intellectual coordination may be a regrettable and yet promising development.

The rights and liberties which were such vital factors in the origins and earlier stages of industrial society yield to a higher stage of this society: they are losing their traditional rationale and content. Freedom of thought, speech, and conscience were – just as free enterprise, which they served to promote and protect – essentially *critical* ideas, designed to replace an obsolescent material and intellectual culture by a more productive and rational one. Once institutionalized, these rights and liberties shared the fate of the society of which they had become an integral part. The achievement cancels the premises.

To the degree to which freedom from want, the concrete substance of all freedom, is becoming a real possibility, the liberties which pertain to a state of lower productivity are losing their former content. Independence of thought, autonomy, and the right to political opposition are being deprived of their basic critical function in a society which seems increasingly capable of satisfying the needs of the individuals through the way in which it is organized. Such a society may justly demand acceptance of its principles and institutions, and reduce the opposition to the discussion and promotion of alternative policies within the status quo. In this respect, it seems to make little difference whether the increasing satisfaction of needs is accomplished by an authoritarian or a non-authoritarian system. Under the conditions of a rising standard of living,

---

Source: Herbert Marcuse, *One Dimensional Man*, (London: Routledge and Kegan Paul, 1964).

non-conformity with the system itself appears to be socially useless, and the more so when it entails tangible economic and political disadvantages and threatens the smooth operation of the whole. Indeed, at least in so far as the necessities of life are involved, there seems to be no reason why the production and distribution of goods and services should proceed through the competitive concurrence of individual liberties.

Freedom of enterprise was from the beginning not altogether a blessing. As the liberty to work or to starve, it spelled toil, insecurity, and fear for the vast majority of the population. If the individual were no longer compelled to prove himself on the market, as a free economic subject, the disappearance of this kind of freedom would be one of the greatest achievements of civilization. The technological processes of mechanization and standardization might release individual energy into a yet uncharted realm of freedom beyond necessity. The very structure of human existence would be altered; the individual would be liberated from the work world's imposing upon him alien needs and alien possibilities. The individual would be free to exert autonomy over a life that would be his own. If the productive apparatus could be organized and directed toward the satisfaction of the vital needs, its control might well be centralized; such control would not prevent individual autonomy, but render it possible.

This is a goal within the capabilities of advanced industrial civilization, the "end" of technological rationality. In actual fact, however, the contrary trend operates: the apparatus imposes its economic and political requirements for defence and expansion on labour time and free time, on the material and intellectual culture. By virtue of the way it has organized its technological base, contemporary industrial society tends to be totalitarian. For "totalitarian" is not only a terroristic political coordination of society, but also a non-terroristic economic–technical coordination which operates through the manipulation of needs by vested interests. It thus precludes the emergence of an effective opposition against the whole. Not only a specific form of government or party rule makes for totalitarianism, but also a specific system of production and distribution which may well be compatible with a "pluralism" of parties, newspapers, "countervailing powers," etc.[1]

Today political power asserts itself through its power over the machine process and over the technical organization of the apparatus. The government of advanced and advancing industrial societies can maintain and secure itself only when it succeeds in mobilizing, organizing, and exploiting the technical, scientific, and mechanical productivity available to industrial civilization. And this productivity mobilizes society as a whole, above and beyond any particular individual or group interests. The brute fact that the machine's physical (only physical?) power surpasses that of the individual, and of any particular group of individuals, makes the machine the most effective political instrument in any society whose basic organization is that of the machine process. But the political trend may be reversed; essentially the power of the machine is only the stored-up and projected power of man. To the extent to which the work world is conceived of as a machine and mechanized accordingly, it becomes the *potential* basis of a new freedom for man.

Contemporary industrial civilization demonstrates that it has reached the stage at which "the free society" can no longer be adequately defined in the traditional terms of economic, political, and intellectual liberties, not because these liberties have become insignificant, but because they are too significant to be confined within the traditional forms. New modes of realization are needed, corresponding to the new capabilities of society.

Such new modes can be indicated only in negative terms because they would amount to the negation of the prevailing modes. Thus economic freedom would mean freedom *from* the economy – from being controlled by economic forces and relationships; freedom *from* the daily struggle for existence, from earning a living. Political freedom would mean liberation of the individuals *from* politics over which they have no effective control. Similarly, intellectual freedom would mean the restoration of individual thought now absorbed by mass communication and indoctrination, abolition of "public opinion" together with its makers. The unrealistic sound of these propositions is indicative, not of their utopian character, but of the strength of the forces which prevent their realization. The most effective and enduring form of warfare against liberation is the implanting of material and intellectual needs that perpetuate obsolete forms of the struggle for existence.

The intensity, the satisfaction and even the character of human needs, beyond the biological level, have always been preconditioned. Whether or not the possibility of doing or leaving, enjoying or destroying, possessing or rejecting something is seized as a *need* depends on whether or not it can be seen as desirable and necessary for the prevailing societal institutions and interests. In this sense, human needs are historical needs and, to the extent to which the society demands the repressive development of the individual, his needs themselves and their claim for satisfaction are subject to overriding critical standards.

We may distinguish both true and false needs. "False" are those which are superimposed upon the individual by particular social interests in his repression: the needs which perpetuate toil, aggressiveness, misery, and injustice. Their satisfaction might be most gratifying to the individual, but this happiness is not a condition which has to be maintained and protected if it serves to arrest the development of the ability (his own and others) to recognize the disease of the whole and grasp the chances of curing the disease. The result then is euphoria in unhappiness. Most of the prevailing needs to relax, to have fun, to behave and consume in accordance with the advertisements, to love and hate what others love and hate, belong to this category of false needs.

Such needs have a societal content and function which are determined by external powers over which the individual has no control; the development and satisfaction of these needs is heteronomous. No matter how much such needs may have become the individual's own, reproduced and fortified by the conditions of his existence; no matter how much he identifies himself with them and finds himself in their satisfaction, they continue to be what they were from the beginning – products of a society whose dominant interest demands repression.

The prevalence of repressive needs is an accomplished fact, accepted in ignorance and defeat, but a fact that must be undone in the interest of the happy individual as well as all those whose misery is the price of his satisfaction. The only needs that have an unqualified claim for satisfaction are the vital ones – nourishment, clothing, lodging at the attainable level of culture. The satisfaction of these needs is the prerequisite for the realization of *all* needs, of the unsublimated as well as the sublimated ones.

For any consciousness and conscience, for any experience which does not accept the prevailing societal interest as the supreme law of thought and behaviour, the established universe of needs and satisfactions is a fact to be questioned – questioned in terms of truth and falsehood. These terms are historical throughout, and their objectivity is historical. The judgement of needs and their satisfaction, under the given conditions, involves standards of priority – standards which refer to the optimal development of the individual, of all individuals, under the optimal utilization of the material and intellectual resources available to man. The resources are calculable. "Truth" and "falsehood" of needs designate objective conditions to the extent to which the universal satisfaction of vital needs and, beyond it, the progressive alleviation of toil and poverty, are universally valid standards. But as historical standards, they do not only vary according to area and stage of development, they also can be defined only in (greater or lesser) *contradiction* to the prevailing ones. What tribunal can possibly claim the authority of decision?

In the last analysis, the question of what are true and false needs must be answered by the individuals themselves, but only in the last analysis; that is, if and when they are free to give their own answer. As long as they are kept incapable of being autonomous, as long as they are indoctrinated and manipulated (down to their very instincts), their answer to this question cannot be taken as their own. By the same token, however, no tribunal can justly arrogate to itself the right to decide which needs should be developed and satisfied. Any such tribunal is reprehensible, although our revulsion does not do away with the question: how can the people who have been the object of effective and productive domination by themselves create the conditions of freedom?[2]

The more rational, productive, technical, and total the repressive administration of society becomes, the more unimaginable the means and ways by which the administered individuals might break their servitude and seize their own liberation. To be sure, to impose Reason upon an entire society is a paradoxical and scandalous idea – although one might dispute the righteousness of a society which ridicules this idea while making its own population into objects of total administration. All liberation depends on the consciousness of servitude, and the emergence of this consciousness is always hampered by the predominance of needs and satisfactions which, to a great extent, have become the individual's own. The process always replaces one system of preconditioning by another; the optimal goal is the replacement of false needs by true ones, the abandonment of repressive satisfaction.

The distinguishing feature of advanced industrial society is its effective suffocation of those needs which demand liberation – liberation also from that which is tolerable and rewarding and comfortable – while it sustains and absolves the destructive power and repressive function of the affluent society. Here, the social controls exact the overwhelming need for the production and consumption of waste; the need for stupefying work where it is no longer a real necessity; the need for modes of relaxation which soothe and prolong this stupefication; the need for maintaining such deceptive liberties as free competition at administered prices, a free press which censors itself, free choice between brands and gadgets.

Under the rule of a repressive whole, liberty can be made into a powerful instrument of domination. The range of choice open to the individual is not the decisive factor in determining the degree of human freedom, but *what* can be chosen and what *is* chosen by the individual. The criterion for free choice can never be an absolute one, but neither is it entirely relative. Free election of masters does not abolish the masters or the slaves. Free choice among a wide variety of goods and services does not signify freedom if these goods and services sustain social controls over a life of toil and fear – that is, if they sustain alienation. And the spontaneous reproduction of superimposed needs by the individual does not establish autonomy; it only testifies to the efficacy of the controls.

Our insistence on the depth and efficacy of these controls is open to the objection that we overrate greatly the indoctrinating power of the "media", and that by themselves the people would feel and satisfy the needs which are now imposed upon them. The objection misses the point. The preconditioning does not start with the mass production of radio and television and with the centralization of their control. The people enter this stage as preconditioned receptacles of longstanding; the decisive difference is in the flattening out of the contrast (or conflict) between the given and the possible, between the satisfied and the unsatisfied needs. Here, the so-called equalization of class distinctions reveals its ideological function. If the worker and his boss enjoy the same television programme and visit the same resort places, if the typist is as attractively made up as the daughter of her employer, if the Negro owns a Cadillac, if they all read the same newspaper, then this assimilation indicates not the disappearance of classes but the extent to which the needs and satisfactions that serve the preservation of the Establishment are shared by the underlying population.

Indeed, in the most highly developed areas of contemporary society, the transplantation of social into individual needs is so effective that the difference between them seems to be purely theoretical. Can one really distinguish between the mass media as instruments of information and entertainment, and as agents of manipulation and indoctrination? Between the automobile as nuisance and as convenience? Between the horrors and the comforts of functional architecture? Between the work for national defence and the work for corporate gain? Between the private pleasure and the commercial and political utility involved in increasing the birth rate?

We are again confronted with one of the most vexing aspects of advanced industrial civilization: the rational character of its irrationality. Its productivity and efficiency, its capacity to increase and spread comforts, to turn waste into need, and destruction into construction, the extent to which this civilization transforms the object world into an extension of man's mind and body makes the very notion of alienation questionable. The people recognize themselves in their commodities; they find their soul in their automobile, hi-fi set, split-level home, kitchen equipment. The very mechanism which ties the individual to his society has changed, and social control is anchored in the new needs which it has produced.

The prevailing forms of social control are technological in a new sense. To be sure, the technical structure and efficacy of the productive and destructive apparatus has been a major instrumentality for subjecting the population to the established social division of labour throughout the modern period. Moreover, such integration has always been accompanied by more obvious forms of compulsion: loss of livelihood, the administration of justice, the police, the armed forces. It still is. But in the contemporary period, the technological controls appear to be the very embodiment of Reason for the benefit of all social groups and interests – to such an extent that all contradiction seems irrational and all counteraction impossible.

No wonder then that, in the most advanced areas of this civilization, the social controls have been introjected to the point where even individual protest is affected at its roots. The intellectual and emotional refusal "to go along" appears neurotic and impotent. This is the socio-psychological aspect of the political event that marks the contemporary period: the passing of the historical forces which, at the preceding stage of industrial society, seemed to represent the possibility of new forms of existence.

But the term "introjection" perhaps no longer describes the way in which the individual by himself reproduces and perpetuates the external controls exercised by his society. Introjection suggests a variety of relatively spontaneous processes by which a Self (Ego) transposes the "outer" into the "inner". Thus introjection implies the existence of an inner dimension distinguished from and even antagonistic to the external exigencies – an individual consciousness and an individual unconscious *apart from* public opinion and behaviour.[3] The idea of "inner freedom" here has its reality: it designates the private space in which man may become and remain "himself".

Today this private space has been invaded and whittled down by technological reality. Mass production and mass distribution claim the *entire* individual, and industrial psychology has long since ceased to be confined to the factory. The manifold processes of introjection seem to be ossified in almost mechanical reactions. The result is, not adjustment but *mimesis*: an immediate identification of the individual with *his* society and, through it, with the society as a whole.

This immediate, automatic identification (which may have been characteristic of primitive forms of association) reappears in high industrial civilization; its new "immediacy", however, is the product of a sophisticated, scientific management and organization. In this process, the "inner" dimension of the mind in which opposition to the status quo can take root is whittled down. The loss of this dimension, in which the power of negative thinking the – critical power of Reason – is at home, is the ideological counterpart to the very material process in which advanced industrial society silences and reconciles the opposition. The impact of progress turns Reason into submission to the facts of life, and to the dynamic capability of producing more and bigger facts of the same sort of life. The efficiency of the system blunts the individuals' recognition that it contains no facts which do not communicate the repressive power of the whole. If the individuals find themselves in the things which shape their life, they do so, not by giving, but by accepting the law of things – not the law of physics but the law of their society.

I have just suggested that the concept of alienation seems to become questionable when the individuals identify themselves with the existence which is imposed upon them and have in it their own development and satisfaction. This identification is not illusion but reality. However, the reality constitutes a more progressive stage of alienation. The latter has become entirely objective; the subject which is alienated is swallowed up by its alienated existence. There is only one dimension, and it is everywhere and in all forms. The achievements of progress defy ideological indictment as well as justification; before their tribunal, the "false consciousness" of their rationality becomes the true consciousness

This absorption of ideology into reality does not, however, signify the "end of ideology". On the contrary, in a specific sense advanced industrial culture is *more* ideological than its predecessor, inasmuch as today the ideology is in the process of production itself.[4] In a provocative form, this proposition reveals the political aspects of the prevailing technological rationality. The productive apparatus and the goods and services which it produces "sell" or impose the social system as a whole. The means of mass transportation and communication, the commodities of lodging, food, and clothing, the irresistible output of the entertainment and information industry carry with them prescribed attitudes and habits, certain intellectual and emotional reactions which bind the consumers more or less pleasantly to the producers and, through the latter, to the whole. The products indoctrinate and manipulate; they promote a false consciousness which is immune against its falsehood. And as these beneficial products become available to more individuals in more social classes, the indoctrination they carry ceases to be publicity; it becomes a way of life. It is a good way of life – much better than before – and as a good way of life, it militates against qualitative change. Thus emerges a pattern of *one-dimensional thought and behaviour* in which ideas, aspirations, and objectives that, by their content, transcend the established universe of discourse and action are either repelled or reduced to terms of this universe. They are redefined by the rationality of the given system and of its quantitative extension.

The trend may be related to a development in scientific method: operationalism in the physical, behaviourism in the social sciences. The common feature is a total empiricism in the treatment of concepts; their meaning is restricted to the representation of particular operations and behaviour. The operational point of view is well illustrated by P. W. Bridgman's analysis of the concept of length:[5]

> We evidently know what we mean by length if we can tell what the length of any and every object is, and for the physicist nothing more is required. To find the length of an object, we have to perform certain physical operations. The concept of length is therefore fixed when the operations by which length is measured are fixed: that is, the concept of length involves as much and nothing more than the set of operations by which length is determined. In general, we mean by any concept nothing more than a set of operations; *the concept is synonymous with the corresponding set of operations.*

Bridgman has seen the wide implications of this mode of thought for the society at large:[6]

> To adopt the operational point of view involves much more than a mere restriction of the sense in which we understand "concept", but means a far-reaching change in all our habits of thought, in that we shall no longer permit ourselves to use as tools in our thinking concepts of which we cannot give an adequate account in terms of operations.

Bridgman's prediction has come true. The new mode of thought is today the predominant tendency in philosophy, psychology, sociology, and other fields. Many of the most seriously troublesome concepts are being "eliminated" by showing that no adequate account of them in terms of operations or behaviour can be given. The radical empiricist onslaught (I shall subsequently, in chapters VII and VIII, examine its claim to be empiricist) thus provides the methodological justification for the debunking of the mind by the intellectuals – a positivism which in its denial of the transcending elements of Reason, forms the academic counterpart of the socially required behaviour.

Outside the academic establishment, the "far-reaching change in all our habits of thought" is more serious. It serves to coordinate ideas and goals with those exacted by the prevailing system, to enclose them in the system, and to repel those which are irreconcilable with the system. The reign of such a one-dimensional reality does not mean that materialism rules, and that the spiritual, metaphysical, and bohemian occupations are petering out. On the contrary, there is a great deal of "Worship together this week", "Why not try God", Zen, existentialism, and beat ways of life, etc. But such modes of protest and transcendence are no longer contradictory to the status quo and no longer negative. They are rather the ceremonial part of practical behaviourism, its harmless negation, and are quickly digested by the status quo as part of its healthy diet.

One-dimensional thought is systematically promoted by the makers of politics and their purveyors of mass information. Their universe of discourse is populated by self-validating hypotheses which, incessantly and monopolistically repeated, become hypnotic definitions or dictations. For example, "free" are the institutions which operate (and are operated on) in the countries of the Free World; other transcending modes of freedom are by definition either anarchism, communism, or propaganda. "Socialistic" are all encroachments on private enterprises not undertaken by private enterprise itself (or by government contracts), such as universal and comprehensive health insurance or the protection of nature from all too sweeping commercialization, or the establishment of public services which may hurt private profit. This totalitarian logic of accomplished facts has its Eastern counterpart. There, freedom is the way of life instituted by a communist regime, and all other transcending modes of freedom are either capitalistic, or revisionist, or leftist sectarianism. In both camps, non-operational ideas are non-behavioural and subversive. The movement of thought is stopped at barriers which appear as the limits of Reason itself.

Such limitation of thought is certainly not new. Ascending modern rationalism, in its speculative as well as empirical form, shows a striking contrast between extreme critical radicalism in scientific and philosophic method on the one hand, and an uncritical quietism in the attitude toward established and functioning social institutions. Thus Descartes' *ego cogitans* was to leave the "great public bodies" untouched, and Hobbes held that "the present ought always to be preferred, maintained, and accounted best." Kant agreed with Locke in justifying revolution *if and when* it has succeeded in organizing the whole and in preventing subversion.

However, these accommodating concepts of Reason were always contradicted by the evident misery and injustice of the "great public bodies" and the effective, more or less conscious rebellion against them. Societal conditions existed which provoked and permitted real dissociation from the established state of affairs; a private as well as political dimension was present in which dissociation could develop into effective opposition, testing its strength and the validity of its objectives.

With the gradual closing of this dimension by the society, the self-limitation of thought assumes a larger significance. The interrelation between scientific–philosophical and societal processes, between theoretical and practical Reason, asserts itself "behind the back" of the scientists and philosophers. The society bars a whole type of oppositional operations and behaviour; consequently, the concepts pertaining to them are rendered illusory or meaningless. Historical transcendence appears as metaphysical transcendence, not acceptable to science and scientific thought. The operational and behavioural point of view, practiced as a "habit of thought" at large, becomes the view of the established universe of discourse and action, needs and aspirations. The "cunning of Reason" works, as it so often did, in the interest of the powers that be. The insistence on operational and behavioural concepts turns against the efforts to free thought and behaviour *from* the given reality and *for* the suppressed alternatives. Theoretical and practical Reason, academic and social behaviourism meet on common ground: that of an advanced society which makes scientific and technical progress into an instrument of domination.

"Progress" is not a neutral term; it moves toward specific ends, and these ends are defined by the possibilities of ameliorating the human condition. Advanced industrial society is approaching the stage where continued progress would demand the radical subversion of the prevailing direction and organization of progress. This stage would be reached when material production (including the necessary services) becomes automated to the extent that all vital needs can be satisfied while necessary labour time is reduced to marginal time. From this point on, technical progress would transcend the realm of necessity, where it served as the instrument of domination and exploitation which thereby limited its rationality; technology would become subject to the free play of faculties in the struggle for the pacification of nature and of society.

Such a state is envisioned in Marx's notion of the "abolition of labour". The term "pacification of existence" seems better suited to designate the historical alternative of a world which – through an international conflict which transforms and suspends the contradictions within the established societies – advances on the brink of a global war. "Pacification of existence" means the development of man's struggle with man and with nature, under conditions where the competing needs, desires, and aspirations are no longer organized by vested interests in domination and scarcity – an organization which perpetuates the destructive forms of this struggle.

Today's fight against this historical alternative finds a firm mass basis in the underlying population, and finds its ideology in the rigid orientation of thought and behaviour to the given universe of facts. Validated by the accomplishments of science and technology, justified by its growing productivity, the status quo defies all transcendence. Faced with the possibility of pacification on the grounds of its technical and intellectual achievements, the mature industrial society closes itself against this alternative. Operationalism, in theory and practice, becomes the theory and practice of *containment*. Underneath its obvious dynamics, this society is a thoroughly static system of life: self-propelling in its oppressive productivity and in its beneficial coordination. Containment of technical progress goes hand in hand with its growth in the established direction. In spite of the political fetters imposed by the status quo, the more technology appears capable of creating the conditions for pacification, the more are the minds and bodies of man organized against this alternative.

The most advanced areas of industrial society exhibit throughout these two features: a trend toward consummation of technological rationality, and intensive efforts to contain this trend within the established institutions. Here is the internal contradiction of this civilization: the irrational element in its rationality. It is the token of its achievements. The industrial society which makes technology and science its own is organized for the ever-more-effective domination of man and nature, for the ever-more-effective utilization of its resources. It becomes irrational when the success of these efforts opens new dimensions of human realization. Organization for peace is different from organization for war; the institutions which served the struggle for existence cannot serve the pacification of existence. Life as an end is qualitatively different from life as a means.

Such a qualitatively new mode of existence can never be envisaged as the mere by-product of economic and political changes, as the more or less spontaneous effect of the new institutions which constitute the necessary prerequisite. Qualitative change also involves a change in the *technical* basis an which this society rests – one which sustains the economic and political institutions through which the "second nature" of man as an aggressive object of administration is stabilized. The techniques of industrialization are political techniques: as such, they prejudge the possibilities of Reason and Freedom.

To be sure, labour must precede the reduction of labour, and industrialization must precede the development of human needs and satisfactions. But as all freedom depends on the conquest of alien necessity, the realization of freedom depends on the *techniques* of this conquest. The highest productivity of labour can be used for the perpetuation of labour, and the most efficient industrialization can serve the restriction and manipulation of needs.

When this point is reached, domination – in the guise of affluence and liberty – extends to all spheres of private and public existence, integrates all authentic opposition, absorbs all alternatives. Technological rationality reveals its political character as it becomes the great vehicle of better domination, creating a truly totalitarian universe in which society and nature, mind and body are kept in a state of permanent mobilization for the defence of this universe.

## Notes

1. H. Marcuse, *One Dimensional Man*, (London: Routledge and Kegan Paul, 1964), p. 53.
2. H. Marcuse, *One Dimensional Man*, loc. cit., p. 47.
3. The change in the function of the family here plays a decisive role: its "socializing" functions are increasingly taken over by outside groups and media. See my *Eros and Civilization* (Boston: Beacon Press, 1955), p. 96 ff.
4. Theodor W. Adorno, *Prismen, Kulturkritik und Gesellschaft*, (Frankfurt: Suhrkamp, 1955), p. 24 f.
5. P. W. Bridgman, *The Logic of Modern Physics* (New York: Macmillan, 1928), p. 5. The operational doctrine has since been refined and qualified. Bridgman himself has extended the concept of "operation" to include the "paper-and-pencil" operations of the theorist (in Philipp J. Frank, *The Validation of Scientific Theories* [Boston: Beacon Press, 1954], Chap. II). The main impetus remains the same: it is "desirable" that the paper-and-pencil operations "be capable of eventual contact, although perhaps indirectly, with instrumental operations."
6. P. W. Bridgman, *The Logic of Modern Physics*, loc. cit., p. 31.

# Sociology's Historical Imagination

## Theda Skocpol

> Every social science – or better, every well considered social study – requires an historical scope of conception and a full use of historical material.
>
> C. Wright Mills[1]

In a basic sense, sociology has always been a historically grounded and oriented enterprise. As wise commentators have pointed out again and again, all of the modern social sciences, and especially sociology, were originally efforts to come to grips with the roots and unprecedented effects of capitalist commercialization and industrialization in Europe. What accounted for the special dynamism of Europe compared to other civilizations, of some parts of Europe compared to others? How were social inequalities, political conflicts, moral values, and human lives affected by the unprecedented changes in economic life? Would industrializing capitalist societies break asunder or generate new forms of solidarity and satisfaction for their members? How would changes proceed in the rest of the world under the impact of European expansion? The major works of those who would come to be seen as the founders of modern sociology, especially the works of Karl Marx, Alexis de Tocqueville, Emile Durkheim, and Max Weber, all grappled with such questions.[2] To varying degrees, all offered concepts and explanations meant to be used in truly historical analyses of social structures and social change.

Truly historical sociological studies have some or all of the following characteristics. Most basically, they ask questions about social structures or processes understood to be concretely situated in time and space. Second, they address processes over time, and take temporal sequences seriously in accounting for outcomes. Third, most historical analyses attend to the interplay of meaningful actions and structural contexts, in order to make sense of the unfolding of unintended as well as intended outcomes in individual lives and social transformations. Finally, historical sociological studies highlight the *particular* and *varying* features of specific kinds of social structures and patterns of change.

---

Source: Theda Skocpol (ed.), *Vision and Method in Historical Sociology*, (Cambridge: Cambridge University Press, 1984).

Along with temporal processes and contexts, social and cultural differences are intrinsically of interest to historically oriented sociologists. For them, the world's past is not seen as a unified developmental story or as a set of standardized sequences. Instead, it is understood that groups or organizations have chosen, or stumbled into, varying paths in the past. Earlier "choices," in turn, both limit and open up alternative possibilities for further change, leading toward no predetermined end.

To be sure, some of sociology's founders focused more closely than others on explaining particular sequences of historical events. And some founders, or their followers, turned more readily than others to the fashioning of transhistorical generalizations and teleological schemas. Thus, strictly speaking, Tocqueville and Weber – and Marx in his essays on current events – were more "historical" in the senses I have listed than Durkheim, or Marx in his more philosophical writings. Yet each of the founders was so committed to making sense of the key changes and contrasts of his own epoch that he was a historically oriented social analyst according to at least some of the basic criteria just mentioned.[3] None of the founders ever got entirely carried away by a philosophy of universal evolution, by formal conceptualization, or by theoretical abstraction for its own sake. Each devoted himself again and again to situating and explaining modern European social structures and processes of change.

## The Partial Eclipse of Historical Sociology

Despite its roots in the works of the founders, by the time sociology became fully institutionalized as an academic discipline in the United States after World War II, its historical orientation and sensibilities were partially eclipsed. Important scholars such as Robert Bellah, Reinhard Bendix, and Seymour Martin Lipset continued to do historical work in the direct tradition of the founders,[4] but the most prestigious theoretical and empirical paradigms broke with the tradition. The anti-historicism of "grand theory" and "abstracted empiricism" was lamented by C. Wright Mills in *The Sociological Imagination*, his passionate dissent from establishment trends in American sociology of the 1950s.[5] Although Mills pointed out that qualitative investigations of social problems could exhibit equal disregard for temporal and structural contexts, empiricist antihistoricism was chiefly exemplified in Mills's account by quantitative studies of specific social patterns, in which U.S. realities of the moment were naively treated out of context as proxies for all of human social life. At the opposite, though complementary, extreme of the sociological practice of his day, the antihistoricism of grand theory was for Mills supremely epitomized in Talcott Parsons's *The Social System*, published in 1951.[6] That prestigious work set forth a grid of abstract categories through which all aspects of social life, regardless of times and places, could be classified and supposedly explained in the same, universal theoretical terms.

*The Social System* elaborated a theoretical edifice overwhelmingly devoted to accounting for societal equilibria, with only passing nods to phenomena of social change. Yet Parsons himself was too great a theorist, and structural functionalism too ambitious as a world view and a scholarly approach, not to take on more directly issues of societal transformation. Evolutionist theories of "development" or "modernization" proliferated in the later 1950s and in the 1960s, all of them treating "societal differentiation" as the master key to classifying and ordering all types of societies and accounting for transformations from traditional to modern social orders.[7] Given the hegemony of the United States in the international order it shaped after World War II, and given the Cold War rivalry between the United States and the Soviet Union, it was perhaps not surprising that these theories of societal change as modernization mapped standardized lines of change along which all normally developing nations would sooner or later move. In due course, they would supposedly come to resemble what the United States was happily conceptualized to be in the 1950s and early 1960s: economically expanding and innovative, highly educated and achievement-oriented, politically pluralistic, and pragmatically nonideological.

Meanwhile, in the Soviet Union, Stalinist readings of Marxist grand theory had already established a twisted mirror image of this evolutionist scheme. In the Soviet version of modernization, economic progress inevitably drove all nations through fixed stages.[8] Each stage was a mode of production with its own characteristic technological level and associated patterns of class domination and class conflict. Nations would move through successive stages toward a classless "socialist" order and would ultimately arrive at a conflict-free "Communist" utopia.

This is not the place to discuss in detail how and why. Yet between the 1950s and the 1980s, the implicit world views embodied in both static and developmentalist versions of structural functionalism were rendered less meaningful by the reverberations of political conflicts inside the United States and across the globe. Economic-determinist and linear evolutionist readings of Marxism also lost any appeal they once held for most Western intellectuals. Meanwhile, however, different versions of Marxist ideas, stressing class consciousness, historical process, and the roles of varying cultural and political structures, became attractive to younger scholars looking for ways to criticize social scientific orthodoxies. Not only did the historically oriented Western Marxist theorist Antonio Gramsci gain enormously in visibility and popularity, Marx's own writings were also selectively reexamined to plumb their resources for handling issues of consciousness and political struggle.[9]

During this same period, the ideas of Alexis de Tocqueville and (especially) Max Weber have also sparked renewed interest for students of social change and comparative social structures. Simply put, people have turned to the particular works or readings of classical sociologists that could best help them reintroduce concerns for sociocultural variety, temporal process, concrete events, and the dialectic of meaningful actions and structural determinants into macrosociological explanations and research. For these purposes, the methodological ideas and historical works of Max Weber are especially relevant, so it is hardly surprising that the small coterie of sociologists who, in 1982 and 1983, launched a new section of the American Sociological Association dedicated to fostering Comparative and Historical Sociology devoted their early efforts to reconsiderations of themes from Weber's scholarly corpus.

## Are Revivals of the Classics the Essence?

If reconsiderations of Weber were the essence of the increasing interest in historically oriented theorizing and research in contemporary sociology, this interest could be treated simply as an intellectual revival. The renewed interest in Weber's historical writings could be seen as accompanied by, and furthering, a de-Parsonizing of our understanding of Weber's ideas, essentially the kind of project to which Anthony Giddens and Randall Collins have devoted significant efforts.[10] We could speak of an era of Weberian historical interpretation taking over the baton of macrosociological explanation from Durkheim and Parsons, on the one hand, and snatching it from the waiting arms of various neo-Marxists, on the other. And that would be that.

There are able commentators who advocate this way of understanding what the spreading interest in historical work in sociology is all about.[11] Others would respond to this identification of historical sociology with Weber's legacy by constructing Durkheimian or Marxian historical sociologies as alternatives or supplements.[12] In my view historical sociology is better understood as a continuing, ever-renewed tradition of research devoted to understanding the nature and effects of large-scale structures and fundamental processes of change. Compelling desires to answer historically grounded questions, not classical theoretical paradigms, are the driving force. To be sure, there have always been, and always will be, sociologists who do not ask or seek to answer historically grounded, macroscopic questions. Although none can afford to ignore structural and historical contexts, all sociologists need not investigate directly matters such as the origins and development of capitalism and nation-states; the spread of ideologies and religions; the causes and consequences of revolutions; and the relationship of ongoing economic and geopolitical transformations to the fates of communities, groups, and types of organizations. Moreover, there certainly have been moments when many scholars interested in macroscopic questions attempted antihistorical modes of addressing them. The brief credibility of Parsonian structural functionalism as an all-encompassing theory of society was one such moment.

But the realities of modern social life are so fundamentally rooted in ongoing conflicts and changes in communities, regions, nations, and the world as a whole, that sociologists have never stopped – and will never want to stop – fashioning fresh theories and interpretations that highlight the variety of social structures, the epochal constraints and alternative possibilities for change, the intersections of structural contexts and group experiences, and the unfolding of events and actions over time. Indeed, historically oriented analyses in sociology are bound to be especially attractive in periods such as our own, when for the world as a whole – for the leaders and victors in earlier phases of economic development and geopolitical conflict, as well as for the peripheral and newly industrializing nations – there are such obvious uncertainties about the continuation of existing trends and relationships into the future. Broadly conceived historical analyses promise possibilities for understanding how past patterns and alternative trajectories might be relevant, or irrelevant, for present choices. Thus excellent historical sociology can actually speak more meaningfully to real-life concerns than narrowly focused empiricist studies that pride themselves on their "policy relevance."[13]

## Research Agendas in Historical Sociology

The classical questions and answers of Weber, Marx, Tocqueville, Durkheim, and others naturally live on in the ongoing enterprise of historical sociology. This happens partly because the founders' answers to the important questions they asked about their own and earlier times were not always correct or complete. Even more it happens because the ideas of the founders rightly continue to serve as fruitful benchmarks for much sociological theorizing. Yet it is a sign of the continuing vitality of historical sociology in the twentieth century, right down to the present, that new questions and ideas, beyond the letter if not the spirit of the founders, are always being addressed by sociologists with comparable vision and will to understand social structures and transformations from the vantage points of their own times and places.

The nine scholars whose working lives and major projects constitute the focus of the chapters in this book all operate on terrain shared with the founders. Most of the major works of the scholars discussed here, from Marc Bloch's *Feudal Society* and *French Rural History* to Barrington Moore's *Social Origins of Dictatorship and Democracy*, and from Karl Polanyi's *The Great Transformation* to Immanuel Wallerstein's *The Modern World-System*, continue to explore the antecedents, nature, and consequences of the original capitalist and democratic revolutions of Europe.[14] The specific problems addressed, however, are often distinct from those of the founders, and fresh answers are certainly offered.

English industrialization, the French Revolution, and German bureaucratization were, one might say, the events and processes that preoccupied the founders. Their basic shared concern was to conceptualize the distinctiveness and dynamics of capitalist industrialism and democracy in contrast to other orders of social life. Among the scholars surveyed here, Reinhard Bendix, Perry Anderson, E. P. Thompson, and Charles Tilly draw both their questions and their answers almost entirely from this classical agenda. Bendix and Anderson build on Weber's arguments about bureaucratization and transformations of political regimes. Thompson reworks the quintessential Marxian ideas about industrialization and the formation of the working class in England. Tilly probes the tensions between the explanations offered by Durkheim and Marx for the changing forms of group conflict that accompanied European revolutions, statemaking, and capitalistic development. Even so, each of these contemporary historical sociologists offers new blends of, or counterpoints to, the classical arguments. And each deploys his own distinctive methods for mediating between theories and historical facts.

Beyond these four, the twentieth-century scholars break new ground in their questions as well as arguments and ways of arriving at them. Karl Polanyi's *The Great Transformation* deals not only with the establishment of capitalist market society in England but also with the national and international crises of the market order from the early to middle twentieth century. Marc Bloch's historical agenda focuses mainly on European and French feudal patterns as worthy of explanation in their own right. In three very different ways, S. N. Eisenstadt, Immanuel Wallerstein, and Barrington Moore, Jr., seek to encompass and explain in the same conceptual terms broad swatches of non-Western along with Western history. Eisenstadt's most important book, *The Political Systems of Empires*, analyzes the emergence and long-term fates of historical bureaucratic empires throughout world history. Wallerstein explores the origins, structure, history, and projected future demise of the capitalist world economy. Moore probes the patterns and moral significance of the alternative paths that agrarian states have traversed into the modern world. These grand subject matters have pushed Eisenstadt, Wallerstein, and Moore well beyond Marx's and (even) Weber's strategies of using the non-West mainly to validate by contrast arguments about the special dynamism of the West.

The chapters to come take very seriously the particular problems explored by the nine scholars, for their arguments and methods certainly cannot be understood apart from the questions they address and their individual reasons for caring to ask those questions. So the authors probe their subjects in different ways, not only because authors write from their own individual points of view, but more fundamentally because each major historical sociologist is (or was) concerned with a distinctive set of problems, forming his own special lifelong research agenda. Still, some important common themes emerge, telling us about the special qualities shared by these scholars and the similar theoretical and methodological challenges all of them have faced in their research and writing.

### Vantage Points for Thinking Big

In the twentieth century, the Western social sciences have been centered in universities and professional associations. Both research and teaching have been, as they say, institutionalized in an array of specialized disciplines, and often in very narrowly or technically focused compartments within those academic disciplines. Even so, major unspecialized works by every single one of the nine men examined here have been celebrated in the institutional worlds of academic social science. Professional associations have awarded their highest prizes to books by Bendix, Eisenstadt, Anderson, Wallerstein, and Moore, and both graduate and undergraduate reading lists have, again and again, given pride of place to Bloch's *Feudal Society*, Polanyi's *The Great Transformation*, Eisenstadt's *The Political Systems of Empires*, Bendix's *Work and Authority in Industry*, Anderson's *Lineages of the Absolutist State*, Thompson's *The Making of the English Working Class*, Tilly's *The Vendée* and many theoretical or quantitative articles, Wallerstein's *The Modern World-System*, and Moore's *Social Origins of Dictatorship and Democracy*. What is more, many of these scholars have sought and attained great institutional influence within academia: Bloch helped to found the internationally prestigious French *Annales* school and attained the most coveted prize in French academic life, a professorial chair in Paris. Eisenstadt holds Germanic sway at the Hebrew University, has been visiting professor at the Western world's most prestigious universities, and participates in every important international conference conceivably related to his breathtakingly broad interests. Bendix, a professor at the University of California, Berkeley, is honored by established sociologists, political scientists, and historians alike, and gained sufficient professional visibility to be elected president of the American Sociological Association. Tilly has attracted large amounts of research funding over the years, built a major research center at the University of Michigan, and serves as a professional gatekeeper in three or four disciplines. Wallerstein enjoys broad international prestige comparable to Eisenstadt's, and has managed to embody his world-system perspective in a research center and journal at the State University of New York at Binghamton, in yearly conferences at revolving university locations around the United States, and in a section of the American Sociological Association that controls several sessions for every year's annual meeting.

Despite these evidences of mainstream academic and professional attainments, every one of our nine scholars has been in some sense marginal or opposed to orthodox academic ways of doing things. Their marginality or opposition has been intimately related, as both cause and effect, to their ability to ask bigger questions than most social scientists ever dream of posing. In turn, asking big questions has led them toward the various blends of general theorizing, totalizing or comparative historical analysis, and sensitivity to contextual details and temporal processes that make their scholarly achievements so compelling.

The connection between genuinely oppositional marginality to mainstream academia and asking big questions and devising unorthodox ways to pursue the answers is most obvious – and certainly most clearly highlighted in the subsequent chapters – for those scholars who have also been politically engaged leftists. Karl Polanyi was and Perry Anderson, E. P. Thompson, and Immanuel Wallerstein all are committed socialists of one variety or another, although, significantly, none of these four has been permanently associated with any established Communist or Socialist party. Polanyi, according to Block and Somers, wrote *The Great Transformation*, "the book that brought together all of the themes of a lifetime" for this humanist socialist, as a "conscious political intervention . . . to influence the shape of the post-World War II world."[15] And Polanyi completed this masterwork *before* he moved into a more specialized academic niche in economic anthropology.

Anderson has not pursued a regular academic career in any sense. As Fulbrook and I stress, he has formulated his "totalizing" questions and answers in historical sociology in close conjunction with his effort to reorient revolutionary socialist intellectual life in Britain through the *New Left Review*. Similarly, as Kay Timberger elaborates, E. P. Thompson did not become a historian through graduate work at a university. He has conceived all of his major scholarly projects not in the course of a regular professorial career but through involvements in adult worker education and the Communist Historians' Group of 1946–56, followed by participation in the British New Left after his break with the Communist Party, and culminating, now, in his plunge back into the crusade for nuclear disarmament. In general, this trajectory has left Thompson free to pursue intensely felt, politically relevant subjects with polemic gusto and insouciance, defying narrow academic conventions. *The Making of the English Working Class* reflects this freedom in both its grand design and its detailed arguments.

Unlike Polanyi, Anderson, and Thompson, Immanuel Wallerstein *has* pursued an academic career; thus his situation is perhaps the most revealing tale of marginality among the leftists. Wallerstein's intention in conceptualizing and studying the modern world system of capitalism has been, Ragin and Chirot maintain, fundamentally political. They tell the fascinating story of Wallerstein's step-by-step movement away from modernization theory and empiricism, toward the more holistic and historical approach embodied in the world-system perspective. For his Ph.D. and his first books, Wallerstein studied the early hopes and later travails of decolonized African nations; thereafter he experienced some of the most intense battles of the American student rebellion of the 1960s. Simultaneously, he moved from the role of loyal Columbia graduate student into the uncomfortable position of a young associate professor who (from the point of view of the Columbia establishment) sympathized too much with student New Leftists. Thus, at the very intellectual juncture when he arrived at his vision of the world system, launched his own major historical projects, and "set himself the task of becoming the academic spokesman and promoter of the vision of world history that lay behind the Third World's revolutionary ideologies," Wallerstein's collegial life at Columbia became "increasingly unpleasant" and he relinquished his tenure there. Since 1975, the perhaps inevitable relationship between Wallerstein's politically leftist big thinking and his marginality to the most orthodox centers of academic and professional life has been aptly expressed by his semiperipheral empire building through the Braudel Center at Binghamton and through the Political Economy of the World System Section of the American Sociological Association.

In some ways, the issue of how distance is gained from academic orthodoxies becomes even more interesting when we turn from those scholars who have explicitly combined scholarship and leftist politics to those whose extraacademic involvements, while often important (think of Bloch's work in the Resistance), have come in forms more acceptable to their respective national academic establishments. Participating in government service or military activities during legitimate national emergencies, or engaging in intellectual journalism and the giving of speeches on issues of current interest to educated publics are, after all, entirely respectable forms of academic political involvement. No doubt they are conducive to a certain breadth of scholarly vision, but they hardly give us a sufficient view of the special critical vantage points attained by Bloch, Eisenstadt, Bendix, Tilly, and Moore. Varying factors, it seems to me, came into play for each of these scholars.

The careers of Marc Bloch and Charles Tilly reveal the special concomitants of unusual thinking for two scholars who eventually became very successful shapers of collective research agendas at the centers of established academia. Bloch finally "arrived" at a professorship in Paris, where he had originally received his graduate education. But his highly unorthodox ideas about methods of historiography, and his unusually cosmopolitan and transnational sense of the scope appropriate to the study of medieval Europe, germinated while this man from a Jewish family with roots in Alsace was a professor at the University of Strasbourg, an Alsatian university considered quite peripheral in the French system, as it had been earlier in the German system. Bloch, moreover, drew (selectively and cautiously, as Chirot shows) on sociological ideas to broaden his agenda of historical questions and explanations.

Decades later in the United States, as Lynn Hunt skillfully argues, Charles Tilly would fashion an unusually broad and temporally deep agenda for his historical sociology by simultaneously using archival methods to do French history and quantitative statistical techniques to test sociological hypotheses and develop an innovative theory of collective political violence. Moreover, while Tilly's eventual research base was at a major American university and in a leading sociology department, his blend of French history and quantitative sociology relegated him to a minor department for his first job, after he did graduate work at Harvard during the era of Talcott Parsons's dominance, not under Parsons but under George Homans and Barrington Moore. (Later on, Harvard brought Tilly back as a nontenured professor, but then, to its later chagrin, failed to retain him with tenure.) Tilly has been the closest to a straightforward academic among all of the scholars assessed in this book. Yet his attempt from the very beginning of his intellectual career to combine issues and methods central to more than one discipline has kept him at the disciplinary margins of both sociology and history, even as it simultaneously allowed him to put himself and his students at some of the most innovative cutting edges in the American social sciences of the last two decades.

Hamilton and Rueschemeyer tell us practically nothing about the biographies and careers of Eisenstadt and Bendix, preferring to concentrate on the critical intellectual stances these men developed toward structural functionalism, the paradigm that dominated American macrosociology for their intellectual generation. Both Eisenstadt and Bendix have certainly become established professors, yet they drew upon Weber's concepts and comparative historical studies to criticize Talcott Parsons. In seeking the roots of their critical stances, I do not think we should ignore the fact that both came from European Jewish backgrounds. Like the other Central European, Polanyi, Eisenstadt and Bendix were émigrés from what was, before World War II, the most civilized arena of high culture in the West. Both also received very cosmopolitan and wide-ranging European-style higher educations. Eisenstadt and Bendix therefore carried their own understandings of European ideas and history into international sociological debates. Moreover, Eisenstadt's major permanent university position has been in Israel, that remarkable home of intellectuals who are at once extraordinarily cosmopolitan and attuned to Western orthodoxies and inescapably aware that not all of world history happens in big, core nations.

Barrington Moore, finally, was never an international emigrant, but he became, in a sense, another sort of émigré. Drawing on the kind of self-confidence bred by a privileged background, by a secure association with elite universities, and by an education in the classics, including Greek and Latin, Moore became an internal émigré away from the distractions of career building in American academia, deliberately giving up the professional influence he might have had if he had been willing to chair departments, build his own research center, promote the careers of his students, and shape the agendas of journals and professional associations. Although he taught at Harvard and was based in that university's Russian Research Center until his recent retirement, Moore quit the Social Relations Department many years ago and thereafter became only nominally affiliated with the Government Department. Moore's one sustained commitment to collegial pedagogy at Harvard was in the Social Studies Program, an elite interdisciplinary honors program dedicated (like the course in which many of the program's founders taught, "Soc. Sci. 2" in the College at the University of Chicago) to teaching the classics of modern social theory: Marx, Weber, Durkheim, and Freud. Beyond this, Moore has always insisted on a fiercely private life.

Moore's scholarly agenda, as Dennis Smith shows, has been as remarkable for its sustained pursuit of consistent intellectual and moral concerns as for its breadth. Moore's books are written in profound solitude – for example, on a yacht in the waters off Maine – with criticism only from Elizabeth Moore and a very few friends or associates. Thinking of himself as an intellectual artisan in an era of bureaucratized research, Moore has worked singly or in small groups only with carefully selected graduate and undergraduate students. He has conveyed to them, not a theory or a method, but his own exacting standards of scholarly craftsmanship and his sense that the unflinching pursuit of answers to large, humanly significant questions is all that really matters in the life of the mind.

## Historical Critiques of Functionalism, Economism, and Evolutionism

Thinking big and approaching social analysis historically need not go together, of course. During the decades when our nine scholars have been at work, the grand paradigms of Parsonian structural functionalism, liberal economics, and economic-determinist Marxism, along with their applications to problems of development through modernization theories and Marxist evolutionism, have dominated much of academic discourse about societal structures and socioeconomic change. Again and again in the chapters to come, we see how all of the major scholars discussed here have shaped their arguments partly or overwhelmingly in critical response to the abstract generalizations offered by proponents of one or more of these perspectives. For many of these scholars, the very shape of their historical studies seems to have been significantly determined by dialogues with existing grand theories. For others, concern with historical problems as such has been primary, and their critical dialogues with the general theories have been correspondingly more nuanced.

The chapters on Eisenstadt, Bendix, Anderson, and Thompson provide a fascinating set of insights into the parallel ways in which these scholars have attempted to introduce historical variety and particularity into grand theories. Eisenstadt and Bendix orient themselves to structural functionalism, while Anderson and Thompson are engaged in critiques of Marxist economism and evolutionism. What I find especially interesting is not the similarities within these pairs but the parallels between Eisenstadt and Anderson on the one hand and Bendix and Thompson on the other.

Eisenstadt and Anderson are friendly critics of structural functionalism and Marxism, respectively. Each is determined to use the basic theoretical perspective to explain large-scale structures and long-term developments, and each is equally committed to using the variety of the world-historical record to criticize overly general readings of the theory. Not incidentally, Eisenstadt chooses to conceptualize and explain "historical bureaucratic empires," which fit poorly into a simple modernization framework opposing traditional to modern societies. Similarly, Anderson tackles "the absolutist state," which has been a source of controversy for Marxists unable to decide whether it was feudal or capitalist.

Both scholars proceed to conceptualize the particular historical periods and political regimes that interest them as what Gary Hamilton aptly calls "configurations in history." These are systemic constructs, defined for Eisenstadt in terms of "levels of differentiation" and "modes of societal integration," and defined for Anderson as "modes of production" and patterns of "class dominance and class struggle." Having done this conceptual work, it becomes possible to account for *aspects* of world history in terms of the structures and dynamics posited by functionalism or Marxist theory. Eisenstadt accounts for a major type of sociopolitical regime, the bureaucratic empire. Anderson accounts for the central, dynamic trajectory of Western European history in contrast to other histories. Neither Eisenstadt nor Anderson, however, claims that all of world history can be encompassed in a single scheme of societal stages or a single master logic of change.

In large part because both are unusually sensitive to subjective meanings and cultural variety in history, Reinhard Bendix and E. P. Thompson are more skeptical than Eisenstadt and Anderson of the utility of structural functionalist and Marxist theories for explaining historical patterns. I would argue, nevertheless, that Bendix and Thompson remain just as closely oriented to the respective grand theories. They proceed by bouncing particular historical cases off theoretical concepts rather than by finding clever new ways to make basic structural functionalist and Marxist concepts and propositions work to explain societal types and long-term change.

Bendix's work has become, as Dietrich Rueschemeyer shows, increasingly concerned simply with descriptively contrasting historical cases to one another. According to Bendix, structural functionalist and modernization theories overgeneralize patterns of structure and change by applying concepts (often abstract versions of Weber's concepts) that are ethnocentric and that inevitably fail to capture the full particularity of any country's history, even within the West. Bendix therefore advocates turning theoretical ideas into ideal types – optimally, into polar pairs of "contrast conceptions," such as "contractual authority" versus personal "fealty." Such concepts can then be used as benchmarks to help in the accurate characterization of historical instances. In this way, Bendix avoids overgeneralization – and indeed downplays explanation as such – in favor of the use of theoretical ideas purely as sensitizing devices for case-by-case historical discussions.

In remarkably analogous ways, E. P. Thompson uses theoretical ideas as benchmarks in his study, *The Making of the English Working Class*. Economic-determinist notions of class, or narrowly economic arguments about how working people were supposedly affected by industrialization, are introduced by Thompson to dramatize their failure to capture the cultural, political, and subjective dimensions of the events through which the English working class both was made and made itself. Thompson does not try to displace old general theories with a more rigorous new one, for he views even his own favored theoretical concepts as "elastic" devices for illuminating the particulars of each historical instance. "They do not impose a rule, but they hasten and facilitate the interrogation of the evidence, even though it is often found that each case departs, in this or that particular, from the rule."[16] Likewise, Kay Trimberger's discussion of Thompson's "dialectical" arguments reminds one of Bendix's preference for using contrast conceptions to sensitize himself to combinations of opposite tendencies in particular instances.

Thus Eisenstadt and Anderson, on the one hand, and Bendix and Thompson, on the other, have reacted in alternative ways to the challenges of bringing existing grand theories and historical variety to bear upon one another. Notice, however, that all four of these scholars have remained closely engaged in their respective dialogues with the grand theories. They have been so closely engaged in these dialogues, in fact, that the arguments they have developed about historical problems have either been specifications and reworkings of structural functionalist and Marxist ideas or else assertions that the complexity, particularity, and subjective meaningfulness of historical instances cannot be adequately encompassed by the grand theories in question. None of these scholars, I would maintain, has used the confrontation of existing theories and history to generate a new set of explanatory generalizations.

Immanuel Wallerstein and Charles Tilly have been just as closely engaged in critical dialogues with existing grand theories as the four scholars just discussed. Yet these historical sociologists indubitably *have* used the confrontation of theory and history to generate new theoretical arguments.

Wallerstein has used historical critiques of modernization theories and Marxist evolutionism almost single-mindedly for the purpose of devising a new grand paradigm to displace the discredited old ones. This is the picture that comes through in Ragin and Chirot's thoughtful discussion of Wallerstein's historical sociology of the capitalist world system. Determined to displace generalizing theories that conceptualize social change as a series of stages through which all nations pass, and yet not willing to surrender to purely idiographic history or journalism, Wallerstein posited the capitalist world system as a single totality. This totality is to be understood simultaneously through theorizing about its structure and dynamics and through tracing the history of the system as a whole from its emergence in early modern times through the present. According to Wallerstein, the varied histories of regions, nations, classes, and peoples also need to be fully explored in all of their concreteness and variety, but not by using the methods of cross-national causal analysis associated in his mind with modernization theory. Instead, investigations and comparisons of these histories serve, as Ragin and Chirot put it, "to illustrate general features of the world system" as a whole. For Wallerstein, the antinomies between theoretical generalization and historical analysis are overcome once and for all through the world-system perspective.

The primary thread of Charles Tilly's historical sociology over the last two decades can be understood as an argument with Durkheim and with his modern intellectual successors, the structural functionalists and "relative deprivation" theorists. The argument is over the connections between such long-term processes as commercialization, industrialization, urbanization, and the rise of national states and the changing forms and objectives of collective action, including violent actions. Like Wallerstein, in other words, Tilly has been disputing the standard sociological wisdom of his time. But he has certainly gone about this task in a different way. Instead of positing a new grand theoretical paradigm and doing historical reinterpretations in terms of its conceptual dictates, Tilly has, as Lynn Hunt recounts, assembled quantitative data bases for long stretches of historical time, especially French historical time. He has then bombarded the data bases with alternative causal hypotheses, some of them purportedly deduced from Durkheimian and modernization premises, others developed from the "political mobilization" model for explaining collective action devised by Tilly himself (partly on the basis of Marxist premises).

Especially in the last few years, Tilly has also carried on more of a grand theoretical battle – a battle of labels and concepts, at least – with modernization theories. He has begun to insist that there is no such thing as social change in general, whether for nations or for world systems. Rather, there are epochal processes, such as the processes of statemaking and capitalist accumulation that have remade the modern world in the last several hundred years. The historical sociologist's task is to analyze the relationships between these epochal processes and to probe their consequences for forms of group action.[17] Thus far, however, Tilly himself has only attempted this for one national history. He has not actually generalized about macroscopic structures or trends through comparative-historical analyses, in ways comparable to his use of intranational comparison of groups, regions, and time periods to arrive at generalizations about the causes of collective action.

If we look back over the six scholars we have just surveyed, it is striking how thoroughly the historical work of all of them has been permeated by their arguments with structural functionalists and modernization theorists, or with economic-determinist and evolutionist Marxists. In varying ways, all of these historical sociologists have been theory driven. This is perhaps clearest for Eisenstadt, Anderson, and Wallerstein. But I think it also holds for the others, even though the modes they respectively chose for arguing with existing grand theories spurred Tilly to do quantitative data analysis and drove Bendix and Thompson to renounce the very goal of explanatory generalization in favor of meaningful characterizations and interpretations of particular histories. Anderson, Bendix, Eisenstadt, Thompson, Tilly, and Wallerstein alike have all pursued their historical studies in close, albeit critical, relationship to the dominant macrotheoretical paradigms of contemporary sociology.

## Developing Explanations for Historical Patterns

Critical dialogues with ahistorical grand theories are also important in the work of Karl Polanyi, Marc Bloch, and Barrington Moore, Jr. Yet each of these three scholars primarily practices historical social analysis in what I would call a *problem-oriented* way. The primary aim is not to rework or reveal the inapplicability of an existing theoretical perspective, nor is it to generate an alternative paradigm to displace such a perspective. Rather, the primary aim is to make sense of historical patterns, using in the process whatever theoretical resources seem useful and valid.

Much of Karl Polanyi's scholarship, Block and Somers explain, was devoted to criticizing the overgeneralizations of liberal economics or the economic determinism of certain Marxists and to developing, instead, concepts that would allow analysis of historically varying economic institutions in the entire societal contexts in which they functioned. In *The Great Transformation*, however, the work that Block and Somers call Polanyi's most important contribution to historical sociology, the object of explanation was a specific world-historical process, the emergence and eventual crisis of nineteenth-century capitalist "market society," centered in Britain. Not unlike Wallerstein, although on a different scale, Polanyi was faced with the challenge of explaining a single case, a single totality of structure and process. Block and Somers tell us that Polanyi used a "metaphor of organic misdevelopment" to help him conceptualize the emergence and development-into-crisis of market society. Yet, they point out, Polanyi constantly moved back and forth from the metaphor to concrete causal arguments referring to particular sequences of historical events in Britain and on the international scene. For he knew (in Block and Somers's words) that "metaphor can only operate as an heuristic; it cannot be used to carry the argument," as Wallerstein's world-system model all too often seems to do. This contrast between Wallerstein and Polanyi is easily understandable, however, when we realize that Wallerstein's goal is the development of an overarching paradigm to displace modernization theory, while Polanyi's goal in *The Great Transformation* was to make unified sense of a concrete set of institutions and events.

Marc Bloch and Barrington Moore, the first and last scholars discussed in the chapters of this volume, seem to me quite similar to Polanyi, and especially similar to one another, in the spirit and methods of their historical work. Both are theoretically well informed and eclectic: Chirot points out that Bloch knew and drew on the sociological ideas of the Durkheim school, as well as Marxian ideas about classes. Smith tells us of Moore's willingness to borrow ideas from structural functionalism and from evolutionism, as well as (more obviously) from Marx and Weber. Like all of the other scholars, moreover, Bloch and Moore are critical of overly abstract and single-factor-determinist theories. Yet neither spends very much effort arguing with, or trying to displace, such theories. Instead, both are more committed to making sense of important historical realities; for the most part, they simply ignore totally unhelpful theories, no matter how fashionable. To help devise good questions to put to history, as well as good answers to explore with various kinds of evidence, both Bloch and Moore accept the aid of whatever theoretical propositions they can borrow from others or devise themselves in the ongoing course of their historical investigations. Both use comparative historical analysis as one of their primary techniques for examining hypotheses and exploring patterns of historical causation.

Bloch's commitment, Chirot writes, "was to tell us what had happened and to explain why." As a historian, his interest lay in understanding medieval European society as a significant totality, finding the temporal and spatial boundaries within which relatively enduring and regular patterns of economic, social, political and cultural life had prevailed. In Bloch's view, the task of theories was "only to help the historian look for better evidence about the past," including evidence from sources not usually tapped by historians. Comparisons among regional or national patterns could be just as useful for rejecting bogus general explanations and getting an accurate sense of causal sequences particular to given cases, as for generating valid causal generalizations that might apply to more than one instance.

As a sociologist rather than a historian by discipline, Barrington Moore is naturally more interested than Bloch in using historical evidence to develop general arguments. He seeks generalizations, for example, about alternative "routes" for agrarian states to the modern world and about human reactions to unjust social situations. But even when he poses a rather abstract issue for investigation, such as the second one just mentioned, Moore always moves quickly into concrete historical instances. Like Bloch, he teases his sense of particular and general causal connections out of explorations of case histories and out of comparisons of relevant aspects of similar and different cases. In *Social Origins of Dictatorship and Democracy*, Dennis Smith points out, "Moore's discussion of each national case is punctuated with detailed and subtle cross-references to other societies. These references are brought in not as a mere adornment but as essential material for an argument being constructed before the reader's eyes." When Moore runs up against a particularly difficult case from the point of view of his own emerging general argument, he spends extra time on it – for example, with India in *Social Origins* – rather than downplaying or ignoring it, as other analysts might do.

Both Bloch and Moore are more interested in the use or development of explanatory generalizations than are Bendix or Thompson, yet the possible theoretical gains from their kind of approach may seem much more modest and restricted than those attained by, say, Wallerstein or Eisenstadt. This appearance could be misleading. Daniel Chirot argues that Marc Bloch was able to suggest "an important general rule of social change" through his comparative study of what may seem a very arcane historical problem: intra-European variations of beliefs about "the royal touch," the capacity attributed to kings to heal diseases. Although Bloch's argument "has not lent itself to flashy theory construction," it is, Chirot argues, the most "scrupulous study of a case of the routinization of charisma." Chirot emphasizes that the generalizable results of this study can "allow those who study other periods and times to ask interesting questions and suggest tentative answers." This, surely, is what any good macrosociological theory should do. It may be all that it can ever reasonably aspire to do.

In the final reckoning, problem-oriented historical sociologists like Marc Bloch and Barrington Moore may tell us even more about social structures and social change than do historical sociologists who rework, or argue with, overarching theoretical paradigms.

## Notes

1. C. Wright Mills, *The Sociological Imagination* (New York: Oxford University Press, 1959), p. 145.

2. See the discussions in Anthony Giddens, *Capitalism and Modern Social Theory* (Cambridge, U.K., and New York: Cambridge University Press, 1971); Philip Abrams, *Historical Sociology* (Ithaca, N.Y.: Cornell University Press, 1982), chaps. 1–4; Robert Nisbet, *The Sociological Tradition* (New York: Basic Books, 1966); Gianfranco Poggi, *Images of Society: Essays on the Sociological Theories of Tocqueville, Marx, and Durkheim* (Stanford, Calif.: Stanford University Press, 1972); and Neil J. Smelser and R. Stephen Warner, *Sociological Theory: Historical and Formal* (Morristown, N.J.: General Learning Press, 1976), pt. 1.

3. Durkheim is the founder most often considered ahistorical, but see Robert Bellah, "Durkheim and History," *American Sociological Review* 24(4) (1959) 447–61. For discussions of the other founders as historically oriented analysts, see especially Melvin Richter, "Comparative Political Analysis in Montesquieu and De Tocqueville," *Comparative Politics* 1 (1969): 129–60; Neil Smelser, "Alexis De Tocqueville as Comparative Analyst," in *Comparative Methods in Sociology*, ed. Ivan Vallier (Berkeley: University of California Press, 1971), pp. 19–48; R. Stephen Warner, "The Methodology of Marx's Comparative Analysis of Modes of Production," in *Comparative Methods*, ed. I. Vallier, pp. 49–74; Leonard Krieger, "The Uses of Marx for History," *Political Science Quarterly* 75 (1960): 355–78; E. J. Hobsbawm, "Karl Marx's Contribution to Historiography," in *Ideology in Social Science: Readings in Critical Social Theory*, ed. Robin Blackburn (New York: Vintage Books, 1973), pp. 265–83; Reinhard Bendix, *Max Weber: An Intellectual Portrait* (Garden City, N.Y.: Doubleday Anchor, 1960); Gunther Roth, "Max Weber's Comparative Approach and Historical Typology," in *Comparative Methods*, ed. I. Vallier, pp. 75–96; and David Zaret, "From Weber to Parsons and Schutz: The Eclipse of History in Modern Social Theory," *American Journal of Sociology* 85(5) (1980): 1180–1201.

4. See Robert N. Bellah, *Tokugawa Religion: The Values of Pre-Industrial Japan* (Boston: Beacon Press, 1970; orig. 1957); Reinhard Bendix, *Work and Authority in Industry* (Berkeley: University of California Press, 1974; orig. 1956); and Seymour Martin Lipset, *Agrarian Socialism* (Berkeley: University of California Press, 1950).

5. Mills, *Sociological Imagination*, chaps. 2 and 3.

6. Talcott Parsons, *The Social System* (Glencoe, Ill. Free Press, 1951).

7. For major examples, see Neil J. Smelser, "Mechanisms of Change and Adjustment to Change," in *Industrialization and Society*, ed. Bert F. Hoselitz and Wilbert E. Moore (The Hague, Mouton, 1963), pp. 32–54; Marion J. Levy, Jr., *Modernization and the Structure of Societies* (Princeton, N.J.: Princeton University Press, 1966); Talcott Parsons, "Evolutionary Universals," *American Sociological Review* 29 (1964): 339–57; Talcott Parsons, *Societies: Evolutionary and Comparative Perspectives* (Englewood Cliffs, N.J.: Prentice-Hall, 1966); Karl W. Deutsch, "Social Mobilization and Political Development," *American Political Science Review* 55 (1961): 493–514; Gabriel A. Almond, "A Developmental Approach to Political Systems," *World Politics* 16 (1965): 183–214; and Gabriel A. Almond

and G. Bingham Powell, Jr., *Comparative Politics: A Developmental Approach* (Boston: Little, Brown, 1966).

8. An orthodox statement of Soviet "modernization" theory appears in Joseph Stalin, *Dialectical and Historical Materialism* (New York: International Publishers, 1940); reprinted in *The Essential Stalin: Major Theoretical Writings 1905-52*, ed. Bruce Franklin (Garden City, N.Y.: Doubleday Anchor, 1972). For an early precursor, see Nikolai Bukharin, *Historical Materialism* (Ann Arbor: University of Michigan Press, 1969; orig. 1921).

9. Perry Anderson's *Considerations on Western Marxism* (London: New Left Books, 1976) discusses the development of Western Marxist theories in the twentieth century. For one of the most popular of all Western Marxist texts, see Antonio Gramsci, *Selections from the Prison Notebooks*, trans. Quentin Hoare and Geoffrey N. Smith (New York: International Publishers, 1971). On the revival of Marxist ideas among young sociologists, see Michael Burawoy, "Introduction: The Resurgence of Marxism in American Sociology," in *Marxist Inquiries: Studies of Labor, Class, and States*, supp. to vol. 88 of *American Journal of Sociology*, ed. Michael Burawoy and Theda Skocpol (Chicago: University of Chicago Press, 1982), pp. 1-30.

10. See Giddens, *Capitalism and Modern Social Theory*; Randall Collins, "Weber's Last Theory of Capitalism: A Systematization," *American Sociological Review* 45(6) (1980): 925-42; and Randall Collins, *Conflict Sociology: Toward an Explanatory Science* (New York: Academic Press, 1975).

11. See especially Charles Ragin and David Zaret, "Theory and Method in Comparative Research: Two Strategies," *Social Forces* 61(3) (1983): 731-54.

12. In effect, Robert Bellah and those working with him are currently pursuing a kind of Durkheimian historical sociology, and Jeffrey Alexander's *Theoretical Logic in Sociology*, 4 vols. (Berkeley: University of California Press, 1982-84) may be laying the basis for another version of this kind of enterprise. Marxian historical sociologies have been cogently advocated by, among others, Eric J. Hobsbawm, "From Social History to the History of Society," *Historical Studies Today, Daedalus* 100 (1971): 20-45; and Gareth Stedman Jones, "From Historical Sociology to Theoretical History," *British Journal of Sociology* 27(3) (1976): 295-304. Some people might consider Charles Tilly and his collaborators to be practitioners of a certain kind of Marxian historical sociology.

13. For example, Charles Sabel's historical sociology of industrial relations from the nineteenth century to the present offers a vivid sense of alternative policy possibilities in the present for the advanced capitalist democracies including the United States. See Charles Sabel, *Work and Politics: The Division of Labor in Industry* (Cambridge, U.K., and New York: Cambridge University Press, 1982) and Michael Piore and Charles Sabel, *The Second Industrial Divide* (New York: Basic Books, forthcoming).

14. Full citations for the books I mention are given in the notes and bibliographies of the chapters dealing with each respective author, Theda Skocpol (ed.), *Vision and Method in Historical Sociology*, (Cambridge: Cambridge University Press, 1984)

15. For this quotation from the chapter on Polanyi by Block and Somers I see no need to give a formal citation.

16. E. P. Thompson, "The Poverty of Theory," in *The Poverty of Theory and Other Essays* (London: Merlin Press, 1978), p. 237.

17. See especially Charles Tilly, *Big Structures, Large Processes, Huge Comparisons* (New York: Russell Sage Foundation, forthcoming).

# 78

# The Rise and Future Demise of the World Capitalist System: Concepts for Comparative Analysis

*Immanuel Wallerstein*

The structural differences of core and periphery are not comprehensible unless we realize that there is a third structural position: that of the semi-periphery. This is not the result merely of establishing arbitrary cutting-points on a continuum of characteristics. Our logic is not merely inductive, sensing the presence of a third category from a comparison of indicator curves. It is also deductive. The semi-periphery is needed to make a capitalist world-economy run smoothly. Both kinds of world-system, the world-empire with a redistributive economy and the world-economy with a capitalist market economy, involve markedly unequal distribution of rewards. Thus, logically, there is immediately posed the question of how it is possible politically for such a system to persist. Why do not the majority who are exploited simply overwhelm the minority who draw disproportionate benefits? The most rapid glance at the historic record shows that these world-systems have been faced rather rarely by fundamental system-wide insurrection. While internal discontent has been eternal, it has usually taken quite long before the accumulation of the erosion of power has led to the decline of a world-system, and as often as not, an external force has been a major factor in this decline.

There have been three major mechanisms that have enabled world-systems to retain relative political stability (not in terms of the particular groups who will play the leading roles in the system, but in terms of systemic survival itself). One obviously is the concentration of military strength in the hands of the dominant forces. The modalities of this obviously vary with the technology, and there are to be sure political prerequisites for such a concentration, but nonetheless sheer force is no doubt a central consideration.

A second mechanism is the pervasiveness of an ideological commitment to the system as a whole. I do not mean what has often been termed the 'legitimation' of a system, because that term has been used to imply that the lower strata of a system feel some affinity with or loyalty towards the rulers, and I doubt that this has ever been a significant factor in the survival of world-systems. I mean rather the degree to which the staff or cadres of the system (and I leave this term deliberately vague) feel that their own well-being is wrapped up in the survival of the system as such and the competence of its leaders. It is this staff which not only propagates the myths; it is they who believe them.

But neither force nor the ideological commitment of the staff would suffice were it not for the division of the majority into a larger lower stratum and a smaller middle stratum. Both the revolutionary call for polarization as a strategy of change and the liberal encomium to consensus as the basis of the liberal polity reflect this proposition. The import is far wider than its use in the analysis of contemporary political problems suggests. It is the normal condition of either kind of world-system to have a three-layered structure. When and if this ceases to be the case, the world-system disintegrates.

In a world-empire, the middle stratum is in fact accorded the role of maintaining the marginally-desirable long-distance luxury trade, while the upper stratum concentrates its resources on controlling the military machinery which can collect the tribute, the crucial mode of redistributing surplus. By providing, however, for an access to a limited portion of the surplus to urbanized elements who alone, in pre-modern societies, could contribute political cohesiveness to isolated clusters of primary producers, the upper stratum effectively buys off the potential leadership of coordinated revolt. And by denying access to political rights for this commercial-urban middle stratum, it makes them constantly vulnerable to confiscatory measures whenever their economic profits become sufficiently swollen so that they might begin to create for themselves military strength.

In a world-economy, such 'cultural' stratification is not so simple, because the absence of a single political system means the concentration of economic roles vertically rather than horizontally throughout the system. The solution then is to have three *kinds* of states, with pressures for cultural homogenization within each of them – thus, besides the upper-stratum of core-states and the lower stratum of peripheral states, there is a middle stratum of semi-peripheral ones.

The semi-periphery is then assigned as it were a specific economic role, but the reason is less economic than political. That is to say, one might make a good case that the world-economy as an economy would function every bit as well without a semi-periphery. But it would be far less *politically* stable, for it would mean a polarized world-system. The existence of the third category means precisely that the upper stratum is not faced with the *unified* opposition of all the others because the *middle* stratum is both exploited and exploiter. It follows that the specific economic role is not all that important, and has thus changed through the various historical stages of the modern world-system. We shall discuss these changes shortly.

Where then does class analysis fit in all of this? And what in such a formulation are nations, nationalities, peoples, ethnic groups? First of all, without arguing the point now, I would contend that all these latter terms denote variants of a single phenomenon which I will term 'ethno-nations'.

Both classes and ethnic groups, or status-groups, or ethno-nations are phenomena of world-economies and much of the enormous confusion that has surrounded the concrete analysis of their functioning can be attributed quite simply to the fact that they have been analyzed as though they existed within the nation-states of this world-economy, instead of within the world-economy as a whole. This has been a Procrustean bed indeed.

The range of economic activities being far wider in the core than in the periphery, the range of syndical interest groups is far wider there. Thus, it has been widely observed that there does not exist in many parts of the world today a proletariat of the kind which exists in, say, Europe or North America. But this is a confusing way to state the observation. Industrial activity being disproportionately concentrated in certain parts of the world-economy, industrial wage-workers are to be found principally in certain geographic regions. Their interests as a syndical group are determined by their collective relationship to the world-economy. Their ability to influence the political functioning of this world economy is shaped by the fact that they command larger percentages of the population in one sovereign entity than another. The form their organizations take has, in large part, been governed too by these political boundaries. The same might be said about industrial capitalists. Class analysis is perfectly capable of accounting for the political position of, let us say, French skilled workers if we look at their structural position and interests in the world-economy. Similarly with ethno-nations. The meaning of ethnic consciousness in a core area is considerably different from that of ethnic consciousness in a peripheral area precisely because of the different class position such ethnic groups have in the world-economy.

Political struggles of ethno-nations or segments of classes within national boundaries of course are the daily bread and butter of local politics. But their significance or consequences can only be fruitfully analyzed if one spells out the implications of their organizational activity or political demands for the functioning of the world-economy. This also incidentally makes possible more rational assessments of these politics in terms of some set of evaluative criteria such as 'left' and 'right'.

The functioning then of a capitalist world-economy requires that groups pursue their economic interests within a single world market while seeking to distort this market for their benefit by organizing to exert influence on states, some of which are far more powerful than others but none of which controls the world-market in its entirety. Of course, we shall find on closer inspection that there are periods where one state is relatively quite powerful and other periods where power is more diffuse and contested, permitting weaker states broader ranges of action. We can talk then of the relative tightness or looseness of the world-system as an important variable and seek to analyze why this dimension tends to be cyclical in nature, as it seems to have been for several hundred years.

We are now in a position to look at the historical evolution of this capitalist world-economy itself and analyze the degree to which it is fruitful to talk of distinct stages in its evolution as a system. The emergence of the European world-economy in the 'long' sixteenth century (1450–1640) was made possible by an historical conjuncture: on those long-term trends which were the culmination of what has been sometimes described as the 'crisis of feudalism' was superimposed a more immediate cyclical crisis plus climatic changes, all of which created a dilemma that could only be resolved by a geographic expansion of the division of labor. Furthermore, the balance of inter-system forces was such as to make this realizable. Thus a geographic expansion did take place in conjunction with a demographic expansion and an upward price rise.

The remarkable thing was not that a European world-economy was thereby created, but that it survived the Hapsburg attempt to transform it into a world-empire, an attempt seriously pursued by Charles V. The Spanish attempt to absorb the whole failed because the rapid economic-demographic-technological burst forward of the preceding century made the whole enterprise too expensive for the imperial base to sustain, especially given many structural insufficiencies in Castilian economic development. Spain could afford neither the bureaucracy nor the army that was necessary to the enterprise, and in the event went bankrupt, as did the French monarchs making a similar albeit even less plausible attempt.

Once the Hapsburg dream of world-empire was over – and in 1557 it was over forever – the capitalist world-economy was an established system that became almost impossible to unbalance. It quickly reached an equilibrium point in its relations with other world-systems: the Ottoman and Russian world-empires, the Indian Ocean proto-world-economy. Each of the states or potential states within the European world-economy was quickly in the race to bureaucratize, to raise a standing army, to homogenize its culture, to diversify its economic activities. By 1640, those in northwest Europe had succeeded in establishing themselves as the core states; Spain and the northern Italian city-states declined into being semi-peripheral; northeastern Europe and Iberian America had become the periphery. At this point, those in semi-peripheral status had reached it by virtue of decline from a former more pre-eminent status.

It was the system-wide recession of 1650–1730 that consolidated the European world-economy and opened stage two of the modern world-economy. For the recession forced retrenchment, and the decline in relative surplus allowed room for only one core state to survive. The mode of struggle was mercantilism, which was a device of partial insulation and withdrawal from the world market of *large* areas themselves hierarchically constructed – that is, empires within the world-economy (which is quite different from world-empires). In this struggle England first ousted the Netherlands from its commercial primacy and then resisted successfully France's attempt to catch up. As England began to speed up the process of industrialization after 1760, there was one last attempt of those capitalist forces located in France to break the imminent British hegemony. This attempt was expressed first in the French Revolution's replacement of the cadres of the regime and then in Napoleon's continental blockade. But it failed.

Stage three of the capitalist world-economy begins then, a stage of industrial rather than of agricultural capitalism. Henceforth, industrial production is no longer a minor aspect of the world market but comprises an ever larger percentage of world gross production – and even more important, of world gross surplus. This involves a whole series of consequences for the world-system.

First of all, it led to the further geographic expansion of the European world-economy to include now the whole of the globe. This was in part the result of its technological feasibility both in terms of improved military firepower and improved shipping facilities which made regular trade sufficiently inexpensive to be viable. But, in addition, industrial production *required* access to raw materials of a nature and in a quantity such that the needs could not be supplied within the former boundaries. At first, however, the search for new markets was not a primary consideration in the geographic expansion since the new markets were more readily available within the old boundaries, as we shall see.

The geographic expansion of the European world-economy meant the elimination of other world-systems as well as the absorption of the remaining mini-systems. The most important world-system up to then outside of the European world-economy, Russia, entered in semi-peripheral status, the consequence of the strength of its state-machinery (including its army) and the degree of industrialization already achieved in the eighteenth century. The independences in the Latin American countries did nothing to change their peripheral status. They merely eliminated the last vestiges of Spain's semi-peripheral role and ended pockets of non-involvement in the world-economy in the interior of Latin America. Asia and Africa were absorbed into the periphery in the nineteenth century, although Japan, because of the combination of the strength of its state-machinery, the poverty of its resource base (which led to a certain disinterest on the part of world capitalist forces), and its geographic remoteness from the core areas, was able quickly to graduate into semi-peripheral status.

The absorption of Africa as part of the periphery meant the end of slavery world-wide for two reasons. First of all, the manpower that was used as slaves was now needed for cash crop production in Africa itself, whereas in the eighteenth century Europeans had sought to *discourage* just such cash crop production. In the second place, once Africa was part of the periphery and not the external arena, slavery was no longer economic. To understand this, we must appreciate the economics of slavery. Slaves receiving the lowest conceivable reward for their labor are the least productive form of labor and have the shortest life span, both because of undernourishment and maltreatment and because of lowered psychic resistance to death. Furthermore, if recruited from areas surrounding their workplace the escape rate is too high. Hence, there must be a high transport cost for a product of low productivity. This makes economic sense only if the purchase price is virtually nil. In capitalist market trade, purchase always has a real cost. It is only in long-distance trade, the exchange of preciosities, that the purchase price can be in the social system of the purchaser virtually nil. Such was the slave trade. Slaves were bought at low immediate cost (the production cost of the items actually exchanged) and none of the usual invisible costs. That is to say, the fact that removing a man from West Africa lowered the productive potential of the region was of *zero* cost to the European world-economy since these areas were not part of the division of labor. Of course, had the slave trade totally denuded Africa of all possibilities of furnishing further slaves, then a real cost to Europe would have commenced. But that point was never historically reached. Once, however, Africa was part of the periphery, then the real cost of a slave in terms of the production of surplus in the world-economy went up to such a point that it became far more economical to use wage-labor, even on sugar or cotton plantations, which is precisely what transpired in the nineteenth-century Caribbean and other slave-labor regions.

The creation of vast new areas as the periphery of the expanded world-economy made possible a shift in the role of some other areas. Specifically, both the United States and Germany (as it came into being) combined formerly peripheral and semi-peripheral regions. The manufacturing sector in each was able to gain political ascendancy, as the peripheral subregions became less economically crucial to the world-economy. Mercantilism now became the major tool of semi-peripheral countries seeking to become core countries, thus still performing a function analogous to that of the mercantilist drives of the late seventeenth and eighteenth centuries in England and France. To be sure, the struggle of semi-peripheral countries to 'industrialize' varied in the degree to which it succeeded in the period before the First World War: all the way in the United States, only partially in Germany, not at all in Russia.

The internal structure of core states also changed fundamentally under industrial capitalism. For a core area, industrialism involved divesting itself of substantially all agricultural activities (except that in the twentieth century further mechanization was to create a new form of working the land that was so highly mechanized as to warrant the appellation industrial). Thus whereas, in the period 1700–40, England not only was Europe's leading industrial exporter but was also Europe's leading agricultural exporter – this was at a high point in the economy-wide recession – by 1900, less than 10 per cent of England's population were engaged in agricultural pursuits.

At first under industrial capitalism, the core exchanged manufactured products against the periphery's agricultural products – hence, Britain from 1815 to 1873 as the 'workshop of the world'. Even to those semi-peripheral countries that had some manufacture (France, Germany, Belgium, the US), Britain in this period supplied about half their needs in manufactured goods. As, however, the mercantilist practices of this latter group both cut Britain off from outlets and even created competition for Britain in sales to peripheral areas, a competition which led to the late nineteenth century 'scramble for Africa', the world division of labor was reallocated to ensure a new special role for the core: less the provision of the manufactures, more the provision of the machines to make the manufactures as well as the provision of infrastructure (especially, in this period, railroads).

The rise of manufacturing created for the first time under capitalism a large-scale urban proletariat. And in consequence for the first time there arose what Michels has called the 'anti-capitalist mass spirit',[1] which was translated into concrete organizational forms (trade-unions, socialist parties). This development intruded a new factor as threatening to the stability of the states and of the capitalist forces now so securely in control of them as the earlier centrifugal thrusts of regional anti-capitalist landed elements had been in the seventeenth century.

At the same time that the bourgeoisies of the core countries were faced by this threat to the internal stability of their state structures, they were simultaneously faced with the economic crisis of the latter third of the nineteenth century resulting from the more rapid increase of agricultural production (and indeed of light manufactures) than the expansion of a potential market for these goods. Some of the surplus would have to be redistributed to someone to allow these goods to be bought and the economic machinery to return to smooth operation. By expanding the purchasing power of the industrial proletariat of the core countries, the world-economy was unburdened simultaneously of two problems: the bottleneck of demand, and the unsettling 'class conflict' of the core states – hence, the social liberalism of welfare-state ideology that arose just at that point in time.

The First World War was, as men of the time observed, the end of an era; and the Russian Revolution of October 1917 the beginning of a new one – our stage four. This stage was to be sure a stage of revolutionary turmoil but it also was, in a seeming paradox, the stage of the *consolidation* of the industrial capitalist world-economy. The Russian Revolution was essentially that of a semi-peripheral country whose internal balance of forces had been such that as of the late nineteenth century it began on a decline towards a peripheral status. This was the result of the marked penetration of foreign capital into the industrial sector which was on its way to eliminating all indigenous capitalist forces, the resistance to the mechanization of the agricultural sector, the decline of relative military power (as evidenced by the defeat by the Japanese in 1905). The Revolution brought to power a group of state-managers who reversed each one of these trends by using the classic technique of mercantilist semi-withdrawal from the world-economy. In the process of doing this, the now USSR mobilized considerable popular support, especially in the urban sector.

At the end of the Second World War, Russia was reinstated as a very strong member of the semi-periphery and could begin to seek full core status.

Meanwhile, the decline of Britain which dates from 1873 was confirmed and its hegemonic role was assumed by the United States. While the US thus rose, Germany fell further behind as a result of its military defeat. Various German attempts in the 1920s to find new industrial outlets in the Middle East and South America were unsuccessful in the face of the US thrust combined with Britain's continuing relative strength. Germany's thrust of desperation to recoup lost ground took the noxious and unsuccessful form of Nazism.

It was the Second World War that enabled the United States for a brief period (1945–65) to attain the same level of primacy as Britain had in the first part of the nineteenth century. United States growth in this period was spectacular and created a great need for expanded market outlets. The Cold War closure denied not only the USSR but Eastern Europe to US exports. And the Chinese Revolution meant that this region, which had been destined for much exploitative activity, was also cut off. Three alternative areas were available and each was pursued with assiduity. First, Western Europe had to be rapidly 'reconstructed', and it was the Marshall Plan which thus allowed this area to play a primary role in the expansion of world productivity. Secondly, Latin America became the reserve of US investment from which now Britain and Germany were completely cut off. Thirdly, Southern Asia, the Middle East and Africa had to be decolonized. On the one hand, this was necessary in order to reduce the share of the surplus taken by the Western European intermediaries, as Canning covertly supported the Latin American revolutionaries against Spain in the 1820s. But also, these countries had to be decolonized in order to mobilize productive potential in a way that had never been achieved in the colonial era. Colonial rule after all had been an *inferior* mode of relationship of core and periphery, one occasioned by the strenuous late-nineteenth century conflict among industrial states but one no longer desirable from the point of view of the new hegemonic power.

But a world capitalist economy does not permit true imperium. Charles V could not succeed in his dream of world-empire. The Pax Britannica stimulated its own demise. So too did the Pax Americana. In each case, the cost of *political* imperium was too high economically, and in a capitalist system, over the middle run when profits decline, new *political* formulae are sought. In this case the costs mounted along several fronts. The efforts of the USSR to further its own industrialization, protect a privileged market area (Eastern Europe), and force entry into other market areas led to an immense spiralling of military expenditure, which on the Soviet side promised long-run returns whereas for the US it was merely a question of running very fast to stand still. The economic resurgence of Western Europe, made necessary both to provide markets for US sales and investments and to counter the USSR military thrust, meant over time that the Western European state structures collectively became as strong as that of the US, which led in the late 1960s to the 'dollar and gold crisis' and the retreat of Nixon from the free-trade stance which is the definitive mark of the self-confident leader in a capitalist market system. When the cumulated Third World pressures, most notably Vietnam, were added on, a restructuring of the world division of labor was inevitable, involving probably in the 1970s a quadripartite division of the larger part of the world surplus by the US, the European Common Market, Japan, and the USSR.

Such a decline in US state hegemony has actually *increased* the freedom of action of capitalist enterprises, the larger of which have now taken the form of multinational corporations which are able to maneuver against state bureaucracies whenever the national politicians become too responsive to internal worker pressures. Whether some effective links can be established between multinational corporations, presently limited to operating in certain areas, and the USSR remains to be seen, but it is by no means impossible.

This brings us to the seemingly esoteric debate between Liu Shao-Chi and Mao Tse-Tung as to whether China was, as Liu argued, a socialist state, or whether, as Mao argued, socialism was a *process* involving continued and continual class struggle. No doubt to those to whom the terminology is foreign the discussion seems abstrusely theological. The issue, however, is real. If the Russian Revolution emerged as a reaction to the threatened further decline of Russia's structural position in the world-economy, and if fifty years later one can talk of the USSR as entering the status of a core power in a *capitalist* world-economy, what then is the meaning of the various so-called socialist revolutions that have occurred in a third of the world's surface? First let us notice that it has been neither Thailand nor Liberia nor Paraguay that has had a 'socialist revolution' but Russia, China and Cuba. That is to say, these revolutions have occurred in countries that, in terms of their internal economic structures in the pre-revolutionary period, had a certain minimum strength in terms of skilled personnel, some manufacturing, and other factors which made it plausible that, within the framework of a capitalist world-economy, such a country could alter its role in the world division of labor within a reasonable period (say 30–50 years) by the use of the technique of mercantilist semi-withdrawal. (This may not be all that plausible for Cuba, but we shall see.) Of course, other countries in the geographic regions and military orbit of these revolutionary forces had changes of regime without in any way having these characteristics (for example, Mongolia or Albania). It is also to be noted that many of the countries where similar forces are strong or where considerable counterforce is required to keep them from emerging also share this status of minimum strength. I think of Chile or Brazil or Egypt – or indeed Italy.

Are we not seeing the emergence of a political structure for *semi-peripheral* nations adapted to stage four of the capitalist world-system? The fact that all enterprises are nationalized in these countries does not make the participation of these enterprises in the world-economy one that does not conform to the mode of operation of a capitalist market-system: seeking increased efficiency of production in order to realize a maximum price on sales, thus achieving a more favorable allocation of the surplus of the world-economy. If tomorrow US Steel became a worker's collective in which all employees without exception received an identical share of the profits and all stockholders were expropriated without compensation, would US Steel thereby cease to be a capitalist enterprise operating in a capitalist world economy?

What then have been the consequences for the world-system of the emergence of many states in which there is no private ownership of the basic means of production? To some extent, this has meant an internal reallocation of consumption. It has certainly undermined the ideological justifications in world capitalism, both by showing the political vulnerability of capitalist entrepreneurs and by demonstrating that private ownership is irrelevant to the rapid expansion of industrial productivity. But to the extent that it has raised the ability of the new semi-peripheral areas to enjoy a larger share of the world surplus, it has once again depolarized the world, recreating the triad of strata that has been a fundamental element in the survival of the world-system.

Finally, in the peripheral areas of the world-economy, both the continued economic expansion of the core (even though the core is seeing some reallocation of surplus internal to it) and the new strength of the semi-periphery have led to a further weakening of the political and hence economic position of the peripheral areas. The pundits note that 'the gap is getting wider', but thus far no one has succeeded in doing much about it, and it is not clear that there are very many in whose interests it would be to do so. Far from a strengthening of state authority, in many parts of the world we are witnessing the same kind of deterioration Poland knew in the sixteenth century, a deterioration of which the frequency of military coups is only one of many signposts. And all of this leads us to conclude that stage four has been the stage of the *consolidation* of the capitalist world-economy.

Consolidation, however, does not mean the absence of contradictions and does not mean the likelihood of long-term survival. We thus come to projections about the future, which has always been man's great game, his true *hybris*, the most convincing argument for the dogma of original sin. Having read Dante, I will therefore be brief.

There are two fundamental contradictions, it seems to me, involved in the workings of the capitalist world-system. In the first place, there is the contradiction to which the nineteenth-century Marxian corpus pointed, which I would phrase as follows: whereas in the short-run the maximization of profit requires maximizing the withdrawal of surplus from immediate consumption of the majority, in the long-run the continued production of surplus requires a mass demand which can only be created by redistributing the surplus withdrawn. Since these two considerations move in opposite directions ( a 'contradiction'), the system has constant crises which in the long-run both weaken it and make the game for those with privilege less worth playing.

The second fundamental contradiction, to which Mao's concept of socialism as process points, is the following: whenever the tenants of privilege seek to co-opt an oppositional movement by including them in a minor share of the privilege, they may no doubt eliminate opponents in the short-run; but they also up the ante for the next oppositional movement created in the next crisis of the world-economy. Thus the cost of 'co-option' rises ever higher and the advantages of co-option seem ever less worthwhile.

There are today no socialist systems in the world-economy any more than there are feudal systems because there is only *one* world-system. It is a world-economy and it is by definition capitalist in form. Socialism involves the creation of a new kind of *world-system*, neither a redistributive world-empire nor a capitalist world-economy but a socialist world-government. I don't see this projection as being in the least utopian but I also don't feel its institution is imminent. It will be the outcome of a long struggle in forms that may be familiar and perhaps in very new forms, that will take place in all the areas of the world-economy (Mao's continual 'class struggle'). Governments may be in the hands of persons, groups or movements sympathetic to this transformation but *states* as such are neither progressive nor reactionary. It is movements and forces that deserve such evaluative judgements.

## Note

1. Robert Michels, 'The Origins of the Anti-Capitalist Mass Spirit', in *Man in Contemporary Society* (Columbia University Press, New York, 1955), vol. 1, pp. 740–65.

# 79

# The Peasants and Revolution

## Barrington Moore Jr.

The process of modernization begins with peasant revolutions that fail. It culminates during the twentieth century with peasant revolutions that succeed. No longer is it possible to take seriously the view that the peasant is an "object of history," a form of social life over which historical changes pass but which contributes nothing to the impetus of these changes. For those who savor historical irony it is indeed curious that the peasant in the modern era has been as much an agent of revolution as the machine, that he has come into his own as an effective historical actor along with the conquests of the machine. Nevertheless the revolutionary contribution has been very uneven: decisive in China and Russia, quite important in France, very minor in Japan, insignificant in India to date, trivial in Germany and England after initial explosions had been defeated. In this concluding chapter our task will be to relate these facts to each other systematically in the hope of discovering what kinds of social structures and historical situations produce peasant revolutions and which ones inhibit or prevent them.

The undertaking is not an easy one. The traditional general explanations run into important exceptions within the range of materials examined here. No theory emphasizing a single factor appears to be satisfactory. Since negative findings have their uses, I will begin with a brief summary of theories it has been necessary to discard.

The first one that a modern investigator might choose is a simple economic interpretation in terms of deterioration in the peasants' situation under the impact of commerce and industry.

Where such deterioration has occurred on a marked scale, it seems plausible to expect revolutionary outbreaks. Once again the case of India provides a useful check, especially when set alongside that of China. There is no indication that the deterioration in the economic position of the Indian peasantry has been worse than that of the Chinese during the nineteenth and twentieth centuries. Admittedly the evidence is far from perfect in both cases. Local and ineffective peasant upheavals there were in India. Still it is highly unlikely that

---

Source: Barrington Moore, Jr., *Social Origins of Dictatorship and Democracy* (London: Peregrine Books, 1969).

whatever difference there may be is adequate to account for the contrast in the political behaviour of Chinese and Indian peasants during the past century and a half. Since these differences also extend backward in time for centuries, it becomes obvious that no simple economic explanation will do.

One might object that this form of the economic explanation is too simple. Could it be that not merely a decline in the peasants' material situation but a massive threat to their entire mode of life, to the very foundations of peasant existence – property, family, and religion – brings about a revolutionary situation? Once more the evidence is clearly negative. It was not the English peasants turned adrift by enclosures who rose in massive revolt but the French ones who were merely threatened by them. Russian peasant society in 1917 was mainly intact. Again, as I shall have occasion to point out in more detail later in this chapter, it was not the peasants of eastern Germany rolled under by the manorial reaction and the reintroduction of serfdom who turned to bloody revolt in the sixteenth century but those of the south and west, who by and large retained and even extended their old way of life. Indeed the very opposite hypothesis comes closer to the truth, as we shall see in due course.

From the romantic and conservative tradition of the nineteenth century comes another familiar thesis that where the noble aristocrat lives in the countryside among his peasants there is less likelihood of acute peasant outbreaks than where he becomes a lover of luxury, living in the capital. Contrasts between the fate of the French and English aristocracy during the eighteenth and nineteenth centuries seem to be the origin of this notion. However, the Russian landlord of the nineteenth century often lived a large part of his life on his estate, a fact that did not deter peasants from burning manors and finally driving the *dvorianstvo* from the historical stage. Even for France itself, the thesis is doubtful. Modern research has shown that by no means all the nobility were hangers-on at the court; many lived morally exemplary lives in the countryside.

The notion that a large rural proletariat of landless labor is a potential source of insurrection and revolution may be somewhat closer to the truth. The huge size and appalling misery of India's rural proletariat might seem to refute the thesis. Many of these are, on the other hand, tied to the prevailing system through possession of a tiny plot of land and by the caste system. Where such bonds have been snapped or never existed at all, as in plantation economies operated with very cheap hired labor of a different race or by slaves, the possibilities of insurrection are much greater. Though slave owners in the American South seem to have had exaggerated fears, there has been reason enough elsewhere to fear insurrection: in ancient Rome, Haiti and other parts of the Caribbean during the eighteenth and nineteenth centuries, parts of Spain in modern times, and quite recently on the sugar plantations of Cuba. But, even if the hypothesis should turn out on more careful inquiry to be correct, it would not account for the historically significant cases. No rural proletariat of this type was important in the Russian Revolutions of 1905 or 1917.[1] Though the Chinese case is less well documented, and bands of wandering peasants driven from their land by a variety of causes have been important there, the revolutionary upsurges of 1927 and 1949 were certainly not those of a rural proletariat working huge landed estates. Nor was this the case in the revolutionary outbreaks of the nineteenth century. As a general explanation, this conception simply will not do.

Driven back from material explanations one might turn naturally to hypotheses about the role of religion. At first glance this seems a promising tack. Hinduism might go a long way toward explaining the passivity of the Indian peasantry. More generally an organic cosmology that conferred legitimacy on the role of the ruling classes, couched in some theory of the harmony of the universe that stressed resignation and the acceptance of individual fate, might conceivably serve as a strong bar to insurrection and rebellion if the peasants accepted its norms. Here at once a difficulty appears. Such religions are the product of urban and priestly classes. The extent of their acceptance among peasants is problematic. In general the existence of an undercurrent of belief distinct from that of the educated strata, often in direct opposition to it, characterizes peasant societies. Passed along by word of mouth from generation to generation, only fragments of this underground tradition are likely to find their way into the historical record, and then very likely in a distorted form.

Even in religion-soaked India there are numerous indications of widespread hostility to the Brahman. Possibly Indian and other peasants believe in the effectiveness of magic and ritual as such, while at the same time they resent the human agent who performs the rituals and the price that he exacts for their performance. Movements to do away with the priest, to attain direct access to the deity and the source of magic, have simmered underground in both Europe and Asia for long periods, to burst forth from time to time in heretical and rebellious movements. In this connection, too, we would want to know what circumstances make peasants receptive to these movements at some times and not at others. Nor are they a universal accompaniment of the more important peasant upheavals. There is little indication of any religious component in the peasant disturbances that preceded and accompanied the French Revolution. In the Russian Revolution it is highly unlikely that revolutionary notions from the towns, either religious or secular, were of any importance. G.T. Robinson in his study of Russian peasant life before 1917 points out that the religious and other intellectual currents impinging on the peasants from the outside were wholly on the side of conservatism and strongly discounts the role of revolutionary ideas from the towns.[2] Conceivably further research may reveal the role of underground traditions indigenous to the peasantry and couched in religious terms. Nevertheless, to be meaningful, such an explanation in the case of Russia, or of any society, requires information about the way in which ideas were related to concrete social circumstances. Religion by itself clearly provides no key.

The shortcoming of all these hypotheses is that they focus too much attention on the peasantry. A moment's reflection on the course of any specific preindustrial rebellion reveals that one cannot understand it without reference to the actions of the upper classes that in large measure provoked it. Another noticeable feature of rebellions in agrarian societies is their tendency to take on the character of the society against which they rebel. In modern times this tendency is obscured because successful rebellion has been the prelude to thorough and violent overhaul of the entire society. In earlier peasant rebellions, it is much more obvious. The insurgents battle for the restoration of the "old law," as in the *Bauernkrieg*, for the "real Tsar" or the "good Tsar" in Russian peasant upheavals. In traditional China the outcome has often been the replacement of a decaying dynasty by a new and vigorous one, that is, a restoration of essentially the same social structure. Before looking at the peasantry, it is necessary to look at the whole society.

With these considerations in mind we may raise the question whether certain types of agrarian and premodern societies are more subject to peasant insurrection and rebellion than others and what structural features may help to explain the differences. The contrast between India and China is sufficient to show that the differences exist and have prolonged political consequences. Likewise the existence of even one substantiated attempt at peasant revolt in India, that of Hyderabad in 1948, even leaving aside other smaller upheavals, strongly suggests that no social structure can be totally immune to revolutionary tendencies set up in the course of modernization. On the other hand, some societies are obviously much more vulnerable than others. For the moment we may set aside all problems that arise during the course of modernization and concentrate specifically on structural differences in premodern societies.[3]

The contrast between India and China suggests an hypothesis perhaps more tenable than those just discussed. Indian society, as many scholars have remarked, resembles some huge yet very simple invertebrate organism. A central coordinating authority, a monarch, or to continue the biological analogy, a brain, was not necessary to its continued operation. Through much of Indian history down to modern times, there was no central authority imposing its will on the whole subcontinent. Indian society reminds one of the starfish whom fishermen used to shred angrily into bits, after which each fragment would grow into a new starfish. But the analogy is inexact. Indian society was even simpler and yet more differentiated. Climate, agricultural practices, taxation systems, religious beliefs, and many other social and culture features differed markedly from one part of the country to another. Caste, on the other hand, was common to them all and provided the framework around which all of life was everywhere organized. It made possible these differences and a society where a territorial segment could be cut off from the rest without damage, or at least without fatal damage, to itself or the rest of the society. Far more important, from the standpoint of our immediate problem, is the reverse of this feature. Any attempt at innovation, any local variation, simply became the basis of another caste. This has not been merely a matter of new religious beliefs. Since the distinction between sacred and profane is very dubious for Indian society, and since religiously tinged caste codes cover practically the whole range of human activities, any innovation or attempted innovation in premodern times was likely to become the basis for another caste. Thus opposition to society and preying on society became a part of society in the form of bandit castes or castes in the form of religious sects. In China, too, hereditary bandits were known.[4] In the Chinese context, their significance was quite different, aside from the fact that the absence of caste made recruitment easier. In China the landlord needed a strong central authority as part of the arrangement for extracting the surplus from the peasants. Until quite recent times, caste made this arrangement unnecessary in India. Chinese society for this reason required something resembling a brain, a more than rudimentary coordinating authority at the center. Bandits were a threat in China and could grow into peasant insurrections.

The general hypothesis that emerges from this brief recapitulation, hedged with that familiar ritual phrase *ceteris paribus* used by scholars to avoid thorny issues, might be put in the following way: A highly segmented society that depends on diffuse sanctions for its coherence and for extracting the surplus from the underlying peasantry is nearly immune to peasant rebellion because opposition is likely to take the form of creating another segment. On the other hand, an agrarian bureaucracy, or a society that depends on a central authority for extracting the surplus, is a type most vulnerable to such outbreaks. Feudal systems, where real power is diffused into several centers under the nominal authority of a weak monarch, belong somewhere in between. This hypothesis at least fits the main facts in this study. Peasant rebellion was a severe problem in traditional China and tsarist Russia; was somewhat less severe but frequently beneath the surface in medieval Europe; was quite noticeable in Japan from the fifteenth century onwards; and finds almost no mention in histories of India.[5]

Turning to the process of modernization itself, we notice once again that the success or failure of the upper class in taking up commercial agriculture has a tremendous influence on the political outcome. Where the landed upper class has turned to production for the market in a way that enables commercial influences to permeate rural life, peasant revolutions have been weak affairs. There are several very different ways in which this antirevolutionary transition has been able to take place. In early Meiji Japan, a landed upper class that was being rapidly renewed preserved much of the traditional peasant society as the mechanism for extracting a surplus. In other key cases, peasant society was destroyed, either by breaking the connection with the land as in England or by intensifying the connection as in the reintroduction of serfdom in Prussia. Conversely the evidence indicates that a revolutionary movement is much more likely to develop and become a serious threat where the landed aristocracy fails to develop a really powerful commercial impulse within its own ranks. Then it may leave beneath it a peasant society damaged but intact, with which it has few connecting links. Meanwhile it is likely to try to maintain its style of life in a changing world by extracting a larger surplus out of the peasantry. By and large this was the case in eighteenth-century France and in Russia and China during the nineteenth and twentieth centuries.[6]

The great German peasant war, the *Bauernkrieg* of 1524–1525, illustrates these relationships in a striking fashion, especially if one compares the areas in which it broke out violently with those parts of Germany where it was not more than a minor episode. Since it was the most important peasant revolution of early modern times in Europe, it will be well to discuss it briefly here. Once again its meaning becomes clearest through contrast with changes in English society. An influential sector of the landed upper classes in England wanted, not men, but land for sheep raising. The German Junkers, on the other hand, wanted men, more specifically men attached to the land, in order to grow the grain which they exported. Much of the subsequent history of the two countries goes back to this homely difference.

In Prussia the coming of grain exports brought about a sharp reversal of earlier trends that had been similar to those in Western Europe, where parliamentary democracy eventually triumphed. By the middle of the fourteenth century, Prussia still resembled Western Europe, even if it had reached this stage by a different route. Then it was a land of prosperous and relatively free peasants. As in the rest of what later became northeastern Germany, the necessity to grant favorable conditions to immigrating German colonists had, along with the development of a strong central authority in the form of the Teutonic Order and a vigorous town life, been the main cause of this freedom. German peasants had the right to sell and bequeath their lands, as well as to market their produce in the nearby towns. Their dues to the overlord in both money and labor were small, the authority of the lord in village affairs was strictly limited, mainly to "higher justice," i.e., the more serious crimes. For the rest, villagers managed their own affairs.[7]

The villages throughout the colonized area were settled by the *locator*, often employed by the noble landholders, who procured the settlers, led them from their place of origin, allocated to them their holdings, measured the village fields, and in return became the hereditary mayor with larger holdings than the rest.[8] In a sense, therefore, the villages of northeastern Germany were artificial communities that received their rights in the form of charters (*Handfesten*) from above. Their situation on this score differed from that of southern German-speaking villages, which won their rights in the course of a prolonged struggle with the overlord. This difference may be partly responsible for the lack of resistance to later subjugation in the northeast, though other factors were probably more significant. Another difference from the south was the ethnically mixed character of the population, as Germans settled in Slavic territories. However, German villages were usually settled on unoccupied land, and the Slavic peasants soon gained the same favorable legal status as the Germans.[9]

Toward the end of the fourteenth century, certain changes began that later led to the enserfment of the peasants. The towns declined; the central authority weakened. But most important of all, there appeared the beginnings of an export market for grain. Together these forces altered the political balance in the countryside. Other parts of Germany and Europe were also hit by a debasement of the currency as part of a weakening of royal authority and by an agrarian crisis that led the nobility to press hard on the peasants, events that helped to produce the Peasants' War.[10] But only in the northeast did an important export trade in grain put in an appearance.

The consequences for the peasants were disastrous. The lords ceased to be interested in money dues from the peasants and turned instead to cultivating and increasing the demesne. For this the labor of the peasants was necessary. Labor services were extended; the peasants tied to the soil. Their rights to sell and bequeath their property were all but abolished, and they were no longer allowed to marry off the estate. Most of these changes took place during the sixteenth century, an era of booming grain prices. It is worth noticing that in this situation the scarcity of labor did not aid the peasants but led to severe discipline in order to prevent flight and that a numerous though rather poor nobility was able to establish a labor-repressive system without the assistance of a powerful central government. In fact the formal end of the Teutonic Order in 1525 was one of the more important political events that led to the results just mentioned.[11]

During the period of colonization, peasant villages had often been physically separate from the noble's estate and had been largely independent organisms. In the second half of the fifteenth century, this situation ceased,[12] as the lords penetrated the villages, economically by taking over peasant property, especially the larger holdings of the mayor, and politically by establishing a monopoly of justice.[13] Without this capture of the village community and the destruction of its autonomy, it is difficult to understand how a mass of scattered nobles could have imposed their will.

By the end of the seventeenth century, most of the nobles had become petty despots in the area of their estates, checked by no formal authority from above or below. The "capitalist" revolution of the sixteenth- and seventeenth-century Junker was almost entirely a social and political one. There is no indication in the literature of any important technical changes in agriculture that accompanied the Junker's rise to supremacy. The three-field system was still almost universal up until about the time of the Seven Years' War, and, by the eighteenth century, agricultural practices, especially on the big Junker estates, were far behind those in Germany's western provinces.[14]

The peasants did offer limited resistance. The only revolt of importance broke out in the vicinity of Königsberg in 1525, shortly after the abolition of the Teutonic Order. It is not surprising that the impetus came partly from the town itself and from those who had most to lose – the more prosperous free peasants. Its rapid suppression was due to weak support from the towns, where, in contrast to the *Bauernkrieg* area, guild life was relatively feeble.[15]

The situation that led to the *Bauernkrieg* of 1524–1525 was in its most important aspects almost the opposite of that in northeastern Germany and calls to mind some of the features that more than two centuries later produced the French Revolution. Since the *Bauernkrieg* and the numerous upheavals that led up to it were spread over a wide area, from what is now western Austria, through nearly all of Switzerland, parts of southwestern Germany, and a large area of the upper Rhine Valley, there was naturally considerable variation in local conditions, a variation that has added to the difficulty in determining its causes and kept alive a vigorous controversy over them up to the present time.[16]

Nevertheless there is widespread agreement among a variety of scholars along the following lines. The territorial princes in this part of Germany were getting stronger, not weaker as in the northeast, and taking some of the early steps toward controlling their own nobility and setting up a modern uniform administration. This form of absolutism was, however, a petty, fragmented variety, as the Emperor had dissipated German energies in a vain struggle with the papacy. Town life flourished in this part of Germany; the late Middle Ages were the golden age of the German *Bürger*.

Thus the peasants could at times draw on the urban plebs for support. But to generalize about what social strata the peasants allied themselves with and which ones they opposed is very risky. At different times and places they were in opposition to nearly every conceivable group and in alliance with some other: in the Rhineland with the nobles against the monastic holdings,[17] against the nobility at others, with the nobility at still others, yet again in opposition to the bourgeoisie and the territorial prince.[18] All that one can say with confidence is that the conflict began chiefly with the moderate demands of well-to-do peasants and became more radical as it developed, turning later into the apocalyptic visions of Thomas Münzer. Partly this progressive radicalization was due to the refusal of early moderate demands,[19] partly to the tendency of peasants to turn to new religious notions emanating from the Reformation in justification of their economic, political, and social grievances.[20] The connection with the towns probably contributed to this radicalization, of which there were some foreshadowings at an early date.[21] It may also have derived from the complaints of lower strata among the peasantry, who were dividing into rich and poor much as in France of the late eighteenth century, though I have not found any explicit statement of this connection.

The nobility of the time were facing a double squeeze: from the efforts of the territorial princes to establish their authority and from the more general effects of the spread of a commercial economy. They needed money and tried in a variety of ways to get it, reviving where they could ancient rights, or – as it seemed to the peasants – trying to create new obligations. Indeed the first stirrings of peasant discontent took the form of efforts to retain or return to "das alte Recht."[22] What the nobles did *not* do, except here and there on a small scale, was to undertake farming for the market. Here lies the crucial difference between the area of the *Bauernkrieg* and Junker Germany.

As for the peasants themselves, the economic and social position of a large sector had been improving for some time. As one scholar observed more than twenty years ago, the evidence of prosperity among the peasants and *Bürger* in this part of Germany at the end of the Middle Ages has become so abundant that it is no longer possible to believe that general economic deterioration caused the revolt.[23] This fact is of course quite consistent with the view that hard pressed nobles tried to put the screw on the peasants in whatever way they could.[24] For centuries a see-saw struggle had been taking place between the peasant community and the overload over their respective rights, a struggle that did not exclude shared interests on many issues. Periodically the outcome crystallized in a written record known as a *Weistum*, the codification of customary law (*Rechtsgewohnheiten*) which was written down from answers to questioning under oath of the experienced older men of the community. The surviving records show a big increase in the number of *Weistümer* after 1300 with the largest number falling between 1500 and 1600, after which they fall off rapidly.[25] What these documents and other similar evidence reveal is a tightly knit village community, albeit one with increasing property differentials, existing in a slowly changing situation of antagonistic cooperation with the overlord.[26] Labor dues and the cultivation of the demesne appear to have been declining in importance and money dues increasing, the reverse of the situation in the northeast. A good many peasants had come close to attaining *de facto* property rights, having shaken off most of the stigmata of feudal tenure, though there were many pockets where the latter remained.[27]

In the early stages of the revolt, peasant demands often repeated themes taken from older *Weistümer*.[28] This fact is one more strong indication that the revolt began with the "legitimate" grievances of respected and substantial members of the village community.[29]

The *Bauernkrieg* was a failure and bloodily suppressed. Both its radical and conservative manifestations were driven underground. Partly because of the aristocratic victory, which as we have seen took place in the northeast for different reasons and against little resistance, the prospects for the emergence of liberal democracy in Germany were cut off for centuries. Not until the nineteenth century did Germany again take halting and, as it turned out, still unsuccessful steps in this direction.

The respective victories of the English squire and the German Junker constitute almost exactly opposite forms in which a landed upper class might make a successful transition to commercial agriculture. They also constitute exactly opposite ways of destroying the basis of political action by the peasantry. Even if defeated, this action was vigorous in the *Bauernkrieg* areas where the upper classes did not make an economic onslaught on peasant society but apparently tried to increase the amount of money it took from the peasants.

This excursion into a concrete case is sufficient, I hope, to indicate the main ways in which the response of the landed upper classes to the challenge of commercial agriculture creates situations that are favorable or unfavorable to revolts by the peasantry. The main areas where peasant revolutions have in modern times had the greatest importance, China and Russia, were alike in the fact that the landed upper classes by and large did not make a successful transition to the world of commerce and industry and did not destroy the prevailing social organization among the peasants.

Now we may leave the actions of the aristocracy aside to undertake a more analytic discussion of factors at work among the peasantry itself. Just what does modernization mean for the peasantry beyond the simple and brutal fact that sooner or later they are its victims? On general grounds, it seems obvious that the different types of social organization found in various peasant societies, together with the timing and character of the modernization process itself, can be expected to have considerable influence on whether or not the response will be a revolutionary or a passive one. But just what is the connection among these variables? Let us see first what general changes take place in this complex process.

In agriculture economic modernization means the extension of market relationships over a much wider area than before, and the replacement of subsistence farming more and more by production for the market.[30] Secondly, in politics successful modernization involves the establishment of peace and order over a wide area, the creation of a strong central government. There is no universal connection between the two processes: Rome and China both established powerful and far-flung governments for their time without generating any significant impetus toward a modern society. It is the combination of the two, nevertheless, that has yielded modernization in various parts of the world since the fifteenth century. The spread of the state's authority and the intrusion of the market, which may occur at quite different times, affect the bonds of the peasant to the overlord, the division of labor within the village, its system of authority, class groupings within the peasantry, tenure and property rights. At some point the influence of these external forces may produce changes in the technology and level of productivity in agriculture. To my limited knowledge, there is no instance of a major technical revolution in agriculture arising among the peasantry, though moderately important ones are reported for Japan, as we have seen, toward the end of the Tokugawa era. Technological changes so far have been far more important in the West; in the rice economies of Asia, added productivity has come mainly through intensified human labor.

In this complex of related changes three aspects are especially important politically: the character of the link between the peasant community and the overlord, property and class divisions within the peasantry, and the degree of solidarity or cohesiveness displayed by the peasant community. Because these three aspects are so closely related to each other, it is impossible to avoid some overlap and repetition in an effort to trace out characteristic patterns of modernization in each of them.

To return to the starting point of the process, one finds that there are certain very broad similarities among peasant communities or villages and their relationships to the outside world in many agrarian civilizations. It will be helpful to begin by sketching the general ground plan of these communities in very general terms, realizing that there are numerous politically significant departures from this plan. Indeed it is easier to perceive the meaning of these departures if we first grasp the general model. I shall limit the discussion to villages, conceived as compact settlements surrounded by cultivated fields. Though the system of scattered individual settlements also occurs quite widely, it was not the predominant form anywhere except perhaps in parts of the United States in colonial and frontier times. In itself this is one of the grounds for refusing the designation peasant to American farmers.

Either directly or indirectly the immediate overlord played a vital part in the life of the village. In feudal societies he was the seigneur; in bureaucratic China he was the landlord dependent on the Imperial bureaucracy; in parts of India the *zamindar*, a figure roughly halfway between the bureaucratic official and the feudal seigneur. The general task of the secular overlord was to provide security against the external enemies. Often, but not universally, he rendered justice and settled disputes among the inhabitants of the village. Alongside the secular overlord, there has often been the priest. His task has been to help give legitimacy to the prevailing social order and to provide a way of both explaining and coping with those misfortunes and disasters for which the individual peasant's traditional economic and social techniques were inadequate. In return for the performance of these functions, the overlord with the priest extracted an economic surplus from the peasants in the form of labor, agricultural products, or even money, though this was generally less important in precommercial times. How these obligations were distributed among the peasants varied considerably. The peasants' right to cultivate the soil and keep a portion of the products for their own use generally depended on fulfilling the above obligations.

There is considerable evidence to support the thesis that, where the links arising out of this relationship between overlord and peasant community are strong, the tendency toward peasant rebellion (and later revolution) is feeble. In both China and Russia, the links were tenuous and peasant upheavals endemic to these states, even though the structure of the peasant communities themselves were about as different as could be imagined. In Japan, where peasant revolution was kept under control, the linkage was very effective. There are some puzzles and contradictions in the evidence. In India, strictly political power did not reach into the village except in certain areas in pre-British times. But there was a strong linkage to authority through the priesthood.

Two conditions are probably essential for the link to be an effective agent of social stability. One is that there should not be severe competition for land or other resources between the peasants and the overlord. This is not simply a matter of how much land is available. Social institutions are just as important as the amount of land in determining whether or not peasants become land hungry. Thus, a second and closely related condition, I would suggest, is the following: political stability requires the inclusion of the overlord and/or the priest as members of the village community who perform services necessary for the agricultural cycle and the social cohesion of the village for which they receive roughly commensurate privileges and material rewards. This point requires more extensive discussion since it raises general issues that are a matter of lively dispute.

The difficulty arises from the notion of rewards and privileges commensurate with the services rendered by the upper class. In a feudal society just how many hens and eggs at stated times in the year, how many days of work on the lord's fields, would be a "fair" repayment for the lord's protection and justice? Is the matter not wholly arbitrary, one that can only be decided by a test of strength? More generally, is not the concept of "exploitation" a purely subjective one, no more than a political epithet, that cannot receive any objective pinning down or measurement? Very likely a majority of social scientists today would answer these questions with an affirmative. If one takes this position, the proposition just suggested becomes a trivial tautology. It means that peasants do not revolt as long as they accept the privileges of the aristocracy and their own obligations to them as legitimate. *Why* the peasants accept them remains as much of a problem as ever. Within the framework of this position, force and deception can be the only possible answers to this question because one set of rewards is just as arbitrary as any other. It seems to me that at this point the whole subjective interpretation of exploitation breaks down and becomes flagrantly self-contradictory. How can nine-tenths of the peasants' crop be no more and no less arbitrary an exaction than a third?

The opposite point of view, that exploitation is in principle an objective notion, I submit, makes better sense generally and at least provides the possibility of an explanation. The point at issue is whether or not one can make an objective assessment of the contributions of qualitatively different activities, such as fighting and tilling the soil, to the continued existence of a specific society. (Economists used to tell us that this was possible, at least through a competitive market, but would, I take it, be reluctant to go that far now.) It seems to me that this is possible for a detached observer and that he does so by asking the traditional questions 1) Is this activity necessary to the society? What would happen if it stopped or changed? 2) What resources are necessary in order to enable people to carry out this activity effectively? Though the answers to such questions must always have a substantial margin of uncertainty, they also have a common objective core.

Within limits broad enough for society to work, the objective character of exploitation seems so dreadfully obvious as to lead to the suspicion that the denial of objectivity is what requires explanation. It is not hard to tell when a peasant community gets real protection from its overlord and when the overlord is either unable to keep enemies out or is in league with them. An overlord who does not keep the peace, who takes away most of the peasants' food, seizes his women – as happened over wide areas of China in the nineteenth and twentieth centuries – is clearly exploitative. In between this situation and objective justice are all sorts of gradations where the ratio between services rendered and the surplus taken from the peasants is open to dispute. Such disputes may intrigue philosophers. They are not likely to rip society apart. The thesis put forward here merely holds that the contributions of those who fight, rule, and pray must be obvious to the peasant, and the peasants' return payments must not be grossly out of proportion to the services received. Folk conceptions of justice, to put the argument in still another way, do have a rational and realistic basis; and arrangements that depart from this basis are likely to need deception and force the more they do depart.

Certain forms of modernization are especially likely to upset any form of equilibrium that may establish itself in the relationship between the peasant community and the landed upper classes and to put new strains on the mechanisms linking them together. Where the royal authority has increased and intensified the burden on the peasantry in order to meet the costs of an expanding military establishment and administrative bureaucracy, as well as an expensive policy of courtly magnificence, the growth of royal absolutism may contribute heavily to peasant explosions.[31] The Bourbon kings and the Russian tsars each in their very different ways used this combination of devices to tame their respective nobilities at the cost of substantial suffering among the peasants. The reaction was intermittent eruptions, much more severe in Russia than in France. The Tudors and Stuarts in England faced an entirely different situation, and lost a royal head, partly because they attempted to protect the peasants against the "antisocial" behavior of a commercializing nobility. In Japan the Tokugawa *Shogun* resolutely turned their backs on the outside world and therefore did not have to create as expensive a military and administrative establishment as did absolute monarchs in Europe. Peasant disturbances did not become important until the latter part of the era.

Generally the creation of centralized monarchy has meant that the peasants' immediate overlord lost his protective functions to the state. In both France and Russia this change took place in such a way as to leave still in large measure intact the rights of the lord to a series of obligations from the peasants. These lordly rights were backed up by the new power of the state because the royal authority could not afford to alienate the nobility altogether. In turn, gradual infiltration into the countryside of goods made in the towns that the lord needed or thought he needed, together with the requirements of conspicuous consumption at court, increased the lord's need to squeeze more out of the peasantry. The failure of commercial farming to take hold on any very wide scale made the situation worse, since it meant that there was scarcely any alternative to squeezing the peasant. As we have seen, what trends there were toward commercial agriculture were labor-repressive. In France, Russia, and other parts of eastern Europe, the small lord became the most reactionary figure, perhaps because all alternatives were closed to him, such as the court, a good marriage, or an attempt at commercial farming. There is no need to labor the connection between these trends and peasant discontent, which have been pointed out by numerous historians.

Where the peasants have revolted, there are indications that new and capitalist methods of pumping the economic surplus out of the peasantry had been added while the traditional ones lingered on or were even intensified. This was true in eighteenth-century France, where the peasant movement that helped to bring down the *ancien régime* had strong anticapitalist as well as strong antifeudal features. In Russia the tsar's action in dismounting serfdom from above failed to satisfy the peasants. The redemption payments were too high and the grants of land too small, as the subsequent accumulation of arrears soon showed. In the absence of any thoroughgoing modernization of the countryside, the redemption payments merely became new ways of taking a surplus from the peasant while keeping him from getting the land that was "rightfully" his. Again, in China the peasant showed by his behavior that he resented the combination of the old tax-collecting official and commercial landlord embodied in the Kuomintang regime.

These facts do not imply that the total burden on the peasantry *necessarily* increased under these circumstances. Indeed it is an historical commonplace that improvement in the economic situation of the peasantry may be a prelude to revolt.[32] The fact seems moderately well established for the English countryside prior to the upheaval of 1381, for the *Bauernkrieg* in sixteenth-century Germany, and for the French peasantry prior to 1789. In other cases, the most important ones, Russia and China, the burden on the peasants very likely increased.

In any event, one of the greatest dangers for an *ancien régime* during the earlier phases of transition to the world of commerce and industry is to lose the support of the upper crust of the peasantry. One common explanation is a psychological one, to the effect that limited improvement in the economic position of this stratum leads to greater and greater demands and eventually to a revolutionary outbreak. This notion of a "revolution of rising expectations" may have some explanatory power. It will not do as a general explanation. For both Russia and China, even in the twentieth century, it strains the evidence beyond recognition. There are several different ways in which the richer peasants may turn upon the old order, depending on specific historical circumstances and the impact of these on different forms of peasant society.

The timing of changes in the life of the peasantry, including the number of people simultaneously affected, are crucial factors in their own right. I suspect that they are more important than the material changes in food, shelter, clothing, except for very sudden and big ones. Economic deterioration by slow degrees can become accepted by its victims as part of the normal situation. Especially where no alternative is clearly visible, more and more privation can gradually find acceptance in the peasants' standards of what is right and proper. What infuriates peasants (and not just peasants) is a new and sudden imposition or demand that strikes many people at once and that is a break with accepted rules and customs. Even the traditionally docile Indian peasants struck *en masse* and raised the specter of agrarian revolt over much of Bengal in the

1860s when English overlords tried to force them to grow indigo at starvation prices for the suddenly booming textile market.[33] Revolutionary measures against the priests in the Vendée had a very similar effect. To multiply instances is hardly necessary. The significant point is that under these conditions individual grievances in a flash become apparent as collective ones. If the impact is of the right kind (sudden, widespread, yet not so severe as to make collective resistance seem hopeless from the start), it can ignite the solidarity of rebellion or revolution in any kind of a peasant society. No type, as far as I can perceive, is immune. Nevertheless there are variations in the explosive potential that can be connected with types of peasant society.

In the course of this study we have noticed a substantial range of differences in the degree of cooperation and the associated division of labor in peasant communities. At one extreme one might place the peasants of the Vendée with their isolated farmsteads, rather atypical for peasants in civilized societies. At the other extreme might be the highly integrated Japanese village, an integration that has persisted through modern times. On general grounds, it seems obvious that the degree of solidarity displayed by peasants, since it is an expression of the entire network of social relationships within which the individual lives out his life, would have an important bearing on political tendencies. Nevertheless, because this factor is intertwined with so many others, the assessment of its importance presents difficulties. As I read the evidence, the absence of solidarity (or more precisely a state of weak solidarity, since some cooperation always exists) puts severe difficulties in the way of *any* political action. Hence its consequence is conservative, though the type of sudden shock just discussed can override this conservative tendency and arouse the peasants to violent action. Where solidarity is on the other hand strong, it is possible to distinguish between conservative forms and those favoring rebellion or revolution.

In a rebellious and revolutionary form of solidarity, institutional arrangements are such as to spread grievances through the peasant community and turn it into a solidarity group hostile to the overlord There are strong indications that this was happening in the late nineteenth and early twentieth centuries in Russian villages. One of the main consequences of the periodic redivision of property in the *mir*, or peasant commune, seems to have been to generalize land hunger, to align the richer peasants with the poorer ones. Certainly this was the conclusion of Stolypin, who reversed earlier official support for the *mir* and tried to establish a Russian version of sturdy yeomanry to prop up the tottering throne of the Romanoffs.[34] It is also worth recalling that the Chinese Communists, before they took power, had to create this kind of solidarity out of refractory social materials.

The opposite kind of solidarity, the conservative one, derives its cohesion by tying those with actual and potential grievances into the prevailing social structure. This takes place, as Japanese and Indian materials show, through a division of labor that has behind it strong sanctions while at the same time it provides a recognized if humble niche for those with little property. Quite possibly the key to the difference between radical and conservative forms of solidarity rests on this point. Radical solidarity, as in the Russian system, may represent an attempt to find an equitable distribution of a scarce resource, namely land; conservative solidarity was based on the division of labor. In general it seems easier to get people to cooperate on a common task than to cooperate peaceably in the use of scarce resources.[35]

To put the same point in a slightly different fashion, property arrangements vary a great deal in the way they tie the peasants to the prevailing society and hence in their political effects. In order to be a full member of the Chinese village and come under the conservative influences of the network of kinship and religious obligations, it was necessary to have a certain rough minimum of property. The process of modernization apparently increased very considerably the number of those peasants below this minimum, something that may well have happened in premodern times as well, and hence the radical potential. Japanese and Indian villages, on the other hand, provided a legitimate if lowly status for those with little or no property both in premodern and later times.

The type of weak solidarity that inhibits political action of any variety is mainly a modern phenomenon. After the establishment of a capitalist legal framework and after commerce and industry have made a substantial impact, peasant society may reach a new form of conservative stability. This happened in much of France, parts of western Germany, and elsewhere in western Europe during the first half of the nineteenth century. Marx caught the essence of the situation when he compared French villages made up of small peasant holdings to sacks of potatoes.[36] The key feature is the absence of a network of cooperative relationships. This makes the modern peasant village the opposite of a medieval one. A recent study of a village of this type in southern Italy shows how the competition among the family units that make up the village inhibits any form of effective political action. The origin of "amoral familism" – a caricature of capitalism – is rooted in the specific history of this village, an extreme development that contrasts with more cooperative relationships in other parts of Italy.[37] More important and more general factors may be the disappearance of common rights and of the performance in common of certain tasks during the agricultural cycle; the overwhelming importance of the small plot worked by family labor; and the competitive relationships introduced by capitalism. At a more advanced stage of industrial development, this type of atomised small peasant village may, as we have seen in parts of Germany, become the seedbed of reactionary anticapitalist sentiment in the countryside.

To sum up, the most important causes of peasant revolutions have been the absence of a commercial revolution in agriculture led by the landed upper classes and the concomitant survival of peasant social institutions into the modern era when they are subject to new stresses and strains. Where the peasant community survives, as in Japan, it must remain closely linked to the dominant class in the countryside if revolution is to be avoided. Hence an important contributing cause of peasant revolution has been the weakness of the institutional links binding peasant society to the upper classes, together with the exploitative character of this relationship. Part of the general syndrome has been the regime's loss of the support of an upper class of wealthy peasants because these have begun to go over to more capitalist modes of cultivation and to establish their independence against an aristocracy seeking to maintain its position through the intensification of traditional obligations, as in eighteenth-century France. Where these conditions have been absent or reversed, peasant revolts have failed to break out or have been easily suppressed.

The great agrarian bureaucracies of royal absolutism, including China, have been especially liable to the combination of factors favoring peasant revolution. Their very strength enables them to inhibit the growth of an independent commercial and manufacturing class. At most, they are likely to encourage one that is fragmented and tied to royal apronstrings for the sake of magnificence and war as in seventeenth-century France. By taming the bourgeoisie, the crown reduces the impetus toward further modernization in the form of a bourgeois revolutionary breakthrough. This effect was very noticeable even in France. Russia and China, in escaping bourgeois revolution, became more vulnerable to peasant evolutions. Furthermore, an agrarian bureaucracy, through its heavy demands for taxes, risks driving the peasants into alliance with local élites in the towns, a particularly dangerous situation as it separates royal officialdom from the mass of the population.[38] Finally, to the extent that it takes over the protective and judicial functions of the locally residing overlord, royal absolutism weakens the crucial link that binds the peasants to the upper classes. Or if it takes over these functions only partly and haphazardly it is likely to find itself in competition with local élites in extracting resources from the peasants. In such circumstances there is a temptation for the local notables to side with the peasants.

Variations in the types of solidary arrangements among the peasants, to continue with general factors, are important mainly insofar as they constitute focal points for the creation of a distinct peasant society in opposition to the dominant class and as the basis for popular conceptions of justice and injustice that clash with those of the rulers. Conservative or radical consequences depend on the specific forms of the institutions promoting peasant cohesion. Solidarity among the peasants could help the dominant classes or be a weapon against them, sometimes changing from one to the other. In some premodern societies one may also find, as seems to have been the case in China, a division of labor that creates much less cohesion. Hence, the revolutionary potential under the impact of modernization varies greatly from one agrarian society to another. On the other hand, the more extreme forms of atomization that severely inhibit any effective political action and that have powerful conservative results seem to occur at a somewhat later stage of capitalism. Such a culture of selfish poverty may be only a transitional stage in backwaters not yet reached by advanced industrialism.

The preceding factors may explain how a revolutionary potential arises among the peasantry. Whether or not this potential becomes politically effective depends on the possibility of a fusion between peasant grievances and those of other strata. By themselves the peasants have never been able to accomplish a revolution. On this point the Marxists are absolutely correct, wide of the mark though they are on other crucial aspects. The peasants have to have leaders from other classes. But leadership alone is not enough. Medieval and late medieval peasant revolts were led by aristocrats or townsmen and still were crushed. This point should serve as a salutary reminder to those modern determinists, by no means all Marxists, who feel that once the peasants have become stirred up, big changes are necessarily on the way. Actually peasant revolts have been repressed far more often than they have succeeded. For them to succeed requires a somewhat unusual combination of circumstances that has occurred only in modern times. Success itself has been of a strictly negative sort. The peasants have provided the dynamite to bring down the old building. To the subsequent work of reconstruction they have brought nothing; instead they have been – even in France – its first victims. The upper classes have to display a substantial degree of blindness, mainly the product of specific historical circumstances and to which there have always been some important individual exceptions, before a revolutionary breakthrough becomes feasible.

Naturally the peasant movement will not find its allies among the élite, though it may draw upon a section of it, especially a handful of discontented intellectuals in modern times, for its leaders. The intellectuals as such can do little politically unless they attach themselves to a massive form of discontent. The discontented intellectual with his soul searchings has attracted attention wholly out of proportion to his political importance, partly because these searchings leave behind them written records and also because those who write history are themselves intellectuals. It is a particularly misleading trick to deny that a revolution stems from peasant grievances because its leaders happen to be professional men or intellectuals.

The allies that peasant discontent can find depends upon the stage of economic development that a country has reached and more specific historical circumstances; these factors also determine the point at which the allies turn on the peasant movement to draw its teeth or suppress it. German peasants in the *Bauernkrieg* got some help from the towns as well as from dissident landed aristocrats but accomplished nothing; the collective power that the landed élite could bring to bear was still overwhelming. In France the peasant movement fused with bourgeois demands, mainly because the preceding feudal reaction had antagonized the well-to-do peasants. The connection seems to me to have been precarious and might have gone the other way, since many bourgeois had property in the countryside and were disturbed by peasant disorders. Another major revolutionary ally was the urban crowd in Paris, though the term ally should not be taken to mean that their policies were coordinated or that either stratum, for that matter, had a really coherent policy. The *sans-culottes* were mainly smaller artisans and journeymen, who have generally played a much more important revolutionary role than Marxist theory might lead us to believe.

In Russia of 1917 the commercial and industrial classes were not a suitable ally for the angry peasants. The Russian bourgeoisie was much smaller and weaker in the country as a whole than had been the case in France, despite a higher level of technology where trade and industry did exist. Though there had been flirtations with Western constitutional notions, the Russian bourgeoisie was tied by many strings to the tsarist government, which had encouraged, largely for military reasons, a certain amount of hothouse capitalist development. Perhaps most important of all, no significant segment of the Russian peasantry was interested in securing property rights against the remnants of feudalism, as had been the case in France. The demands of the Russian peasant were brutally simple: to get rid of the landlord, divide up the land, and of course stop the war. The Constitutional Democrats, the main party with a bourgeois flavor, had earlier considered giving in to peasant demands. But the peasants' frontal attack on property was too much for its stomach when the issue had to be faced squarely. On the other hand, there was nothing in the notion of dividing up the land to disturb the industrial workers, at least not for the moment. Stopping the war appealed to the peasants who were the main victims of the slaughter and had little interest in defending a government that refused concessions. Among the peasants, the Bolsheviks had no real following. But as the only party without ties to the existing order they could afford to give in temporarily to their demands for the sake of seizing power. This they did on taking over the government and again after the chaos of the Civil War. Subsequently of course the Bolsheviks found it necessary to turn on those who had brought them to power and to drive the peasants into collectives in order to make them the main basis and victims of the socialist version of primary capitalist accumulation.

In China we see still another combination of circumstances, about which less is known, partly because the events are still too recent to have been the subject of extensive historical investigation. It is difficult to point to any clearcut stratum as an ally of the peasants, on whose backs the Communists finally rode to victory, even though, or perhaps partly because, disaffection with the Kuomintang had spread through all classes. As a contemporary scholar has convincingly demonstrated, the Communists made little headway as long as they clung to Marxist notions about the importance of the proletariat as the vanguard of the revolutionary and antiimperialist struggle.[39] In time they did get massive peasant support. Still, without urban leaders, it is unlikely that the peasants could have organized the Red Army and carried on the partisan warfare that distinguished this revolution from its predecessors and has set a model for subsequent attempts. The effect on their opponents has been curious; some of the Western enthusiasm for learning the "lessons" of guerilla warfare recalls nineteenth-century Japanese notions about democracy: the belief that it is a simple technique one can borrow that will bring in its train all the other advantages that the opponent enjoys.

In both Russia and China, the chances of halting the process of decay at some point short of peasant revolution were very slim, mainly due to the lack of any strong basis for either liberal or reactionary capitalism in the trading and manufacturing classes. Whether the same will be true of India is a question to which only the future will give a firm answer. To jump to conclusions about India on the basis of China is foolish, since their agrarian social structures are in major respects exactly opposite to one another. If the agrarian program of the present Indian government fails to solve India's food problem, and there is substantial evidence for a pessimistic evaluation, a political upheaval of some sort will become highly likely. But it will not necessarily take the form of a communist-led peasant revolution. A turn to the right or fragmentation along regional lines, or some combination of these two, seems much more probable in the light of India's social structure. The situation in India leads one to ask whether the great wave of peasant revolutions, so far one of the most distinctive features of the twentieth century, may not have already spent its force. Any attempt to consider the question seriously would require detailed study of Latin America and Africa, a huge task that must be left to others. Nevertheless one consideration is worth pointing out. By and large, during the process of modernization the circumstances of peasant life have seldom made peasants the allies of democratic capitalism, an historical formation that in any case is now past its zenith. If the revolutionary wave continues to sweep through the backward world in the years to come, that is scarcely the form it is likely to take.

## Notes

1. Robinson, *Rural Russia*, 206, is explicit on this point.
2. *Rural Russia*, 144.
3. As the expressions "immune" and "vulnerable" show, English usage imposes a conservative bias on the analysis of revolutions: the implicit assumption is that a "healthy" society is immune to revolution. Hence it becomes necessary to make explicit the author's rejection of this assumption. The analysis of why revolutions do and do not occur carries no *logical* implication of approval or disapproval, even if no investigator is free of such preferences. Without trying to develop the argument here, I suspect that a strong case can be made for the thesis that sick societies are ones in which revolutions are impossible.
4. Hsiao, *Rural China*, 462.
5. Japanese revolts show some of the signs characteristic of the early phase of modernization in Europe, a fact compatible with Japan's more centralized feudalism, which resembled European efforts under absolute monarchies to preserve privilege and the *status quo*. See Sansom, *History of Japan*, II, 208–210.

6. India may seem an exception to this generalization about the survival of peasant society as a cause of modern revolution. It is partly explicable in terms of the impediments to rebellion and revolution inherent in India's premodern social structure, partly the way modernization has proceeded up to now. Most important of all, modernization has but barely begun in the Indian countryside. Such are the main grounds for holding that it is not really an exception. Perhaps it will become one. Historical generalizations are not immutable laws like those of physics: the course of history reflects mainly an effort to escape the bounds imposed by previous conditions expressed in such generalizations.

7. Carsten, *Origins of Prussia*, pt 1, esp 29–31, 41, 62, 64, 73–74, for details of the peasants' situation. Stein, *Agrarverfassung*, I, 431, 434, adds in a concise fashion some legal materials.

8. Carsten, *Origins of Prussia*, 30–31.

9. Carsten, *Origins of Prussia*, 32, 34–5, 37–39.

10. Carsten, *Origins of Prussia*, 115.

11. Carsten, *Origins of Prussia*, chap XI, esp 149–150, 154, 163–164.

12. Aubin, *Geschichte des gutsherrlich-bäuerlichen Verhältnisses*, 155–156.

13. Stein, *Agrarverfassung*, I, 437–439.

14. Stein, *Agrarverfassung*, I, 463–464.

15. Carsten, "Bauernkrieg," 407. The weak resistance in Germany to the establishment of serfdom presents a sharp contrast with the peasant unrest and revolts that accompanied and followed its establishment during the same time period in Russia. The main reason for the difference is probably a fact to which attention has been drawn before: serfdom in Russia arose in response to a political situation. As part of the process by which absolutism established itself, Russian serfdom provided a method of working the lands granted to support the tsar's officials. Also serfdom in Russia seems to have damaged the peasant village far less than in Prussia. Though it lost much of its autonomy, the Russian village commune (*mir*, or more accurately *sel'skoe obshchestvo*) remained very much a going concern. For an excellent treatment of the changes during the sixteenth and seventeenth centuries in Russia, see Blum, *Lord and Peasant*, chaps 8–14; on peasant unrest, 258, 267–268; on the *mir*, 510–512.

16. See the three maps at the end of Franz, *Bauernkrieg*.

17. Waas, *Grosse Wendung*, 13–15, 19.

18. Franz, *Bauernkrieg*, 84, 32, 26.

19. The thesis of Waas, in *Grosse Wendung*.

20. Nabholz, "Ursachen des Bauernkriegs," 144–167 brings out this connection very clearly for the Zürich area. Note especially 162–163, 165, 167.

21. E.g., in the piper of Niklashausen. See Franz, *Bauernkrieg*, 45–52.

22. Franz, *Bauernkrieg*, 1–40.

23. Waas, *Grosse Wendung*, 40–42.

24. Evidence on this score is presented by a Soviet scholar Smirin, *Ocherki istorii politicheskoi bor'by v Germanii*, chap 11. Smirin does everything he can to prove the existence of a "seigneurial reaction" and at times strains the evidence to the point of being silly: as when he cites (p. 60) labor dues of three days a year as an indication of their importance. But he is probably correct in his assertion (p. 85) that the peasants were upset by the uncertainty and variation in their obligations.

25. Wiessner, *Sachinhalt und Wirtschaftliche Bedeutung der Weistümer*, 26–29.

26. Wiessner, "Geschichte des Dorfes," 43–44, 60, 63, 70–71. Though the account is limited to Austria, it is highly likely that the same type of differences was appearing elsewhere.

27. For the Zürich area, Nabholz, "Ursachen des Bauernkriegs," 158–159; for Austria, Wiessner, "Geschichte des Dorfes," 49, 50, 67; for Germany, Waas, *Grosse Wendung,* 37–38.

28. Waas, *Grosse Wending,* 34–35.

29. Cf Franz, *Bauernkrieg,* 1–40.

30. Markets were by no means absent in premodern peasant villages. And even the modern suburban businessman may take pride in a few tomatoes grown in his backyard. It would not be necessary to mention these points were it not for anticonceptual scholarship that delights in the effort to trample down historical distinctions by pointing to such trivialities. Obviously what matters is the qualitative role played by the market in the countryside: its effect on social relationships.

31. For a detailed account of the relationship in seventeenth-century France, see Porchnev, *Soulèvements populaires.*

32. Such improvement would seem to contradict the thesis that objective exploitation is a cause of revolt. This is not necessarily so. The relationship between the overlord and the peasant community can become more exploitative without the peasants becoming any poorer, indeed even if their material situation improves. This would happen wherever the lord's exactions increased and his contribution to the welfare of security of the village declined. A decline in the lord's contribution, along with general economic improvement and efforts by the lord to increase his "take," could be expected to generate tremendous resentment. To test this conception of objective exploitation carefully against several cases would be a very difficult but rewarding undertaking. I have not done this; the notion came to me in the course of a prolonged effort to make sense of the data, and I present it as a working hypothesis that finds some support in the evidence.

33. An instructive account from a radical standpoint in Natarajan, *Peasant Uprisings,* chap IV.

34. Robinson, *Rural Russia,* 153, points out that among the twenty *guberniias* where landlords suffered heaviest losses during the peasant upheavals of 1905, sixteen showed a predominance of repartitional tenure over hereditary holdings by individual peasant households. On the government's fear of solidarity among the peasants, see ibid, 264.

35. For a humble illustration compare what happens when a large family has to arrange a complicated picnic on a beach, where one child gathers firewood, another builds the fire, etc, with what happens during the morning rush for the bathroom.

36. See "Eighteenth Brumaire," 415.

37. See Banfield, *Moral Basis of a Backward Society,* chap 8, esp 147, 150–154.

38. This is especially clear in the disturbances preceding and accompanying the *Fronde.* See Porchnev, *Soulèvements populaires,* 118–131, 392–466. The author has demonstrated beyond any possible doubt that the *Fronde* was much more than a piece of aristocratic mischief. For reasons that need no repetition here as they are part of the entire argument I have tried to present, I reject his effort and that of other Marxist writers to identify royal absolutism with feudalism.

39. See Schwartz, *Chinese Communism.*

# References

Aubin, Gustav, *Zur Geschichte des gutsherrlich-bäuerlichen Verhältnisses in Ostpreussen von der Gründung des Ordensstaates bis zur Steinschen Reform,* Leipzig, 1911.

Banfield, Edward C., *The Moral Basis of a Backward Society.* Glencoe, 1958.

Blum, Jerome, *Lord and Peasant in Russia: From the Ninth to the Nineteenth Century.* Princeton, 1961.

Carsten, F.L., "Der Bauernkrieg in Ostpreussen 1525," *International Review for Social History*, III (1938), 398–409.

Carsten, F.L., *The Origins of Prussia.* London, 1954, reprinted 1958.

Franz, Günther, *Der deutsche Bauernkrieg.* Darmstadt, 1956.

Hsiao, Kung-chuan, *Rural China: Imperial Control in the Nineteenth Century.* Seattle, 1960.

Nabholz, Hans, "Zur Frage nach den Ursachen des Bauernkriegs 1525," reprinted in *Ausgewählte Aufsätze zur Wirtschaftsgeschichte* (Zürich, 1954). First published in 1928.

Natarajan, L., *Peasant Uprisings in India 1850–1900.* Bombay, 1953.

Porchnev, Boris, *Les Soulèvements populaires en France de 1623 à 1648.* Paris, 1963.

Robinson, Geroid T., *Rural Russia Under the Old Regime: A History of the Landlord Peasant World and a Prologue to the Peasant Revolution of 1917.* New York, 1932.

Sansom, Sir George, *A History of Japan.* 3 vols. Vol. I: *To 1334* (Stanford, 1958). Vol. II: *1334–1615* (Stanford, 1961). Vol. III: *1615–1867* (Stanford, 1963).

Schwartz, Benjamin I., *Chinese Communism and the Rise of Mao.* Cambridge, Massachusetts, 1951.

Smirin, M.M., *Ocherki istorii politicheskoi bor'by v Germanii pered reformatsiei.* 2nd ed., Moscow, 1952.

Stein, Robert, *Die Umwandlung der Agrarverfassung Ostpreussens durch die Reform des neunzehnten Jahrhunderts.* Vol. I, Jena, 1918.

Waas, Adolf, *Die Grosse Wendung im deutschen Bauernkrieg.* München, 1939.

Wiessner, Hermann, *Beiträge zur Geschichte des Dorfes und der Dorfgemeinde in Österreich,* Klagenfurt, 1946.

Wiessner, *Sachinhalt und Wirtschaftliche Bedeutung der Weistümer im Deutschen Kulturgebiet.* Baden, 1934.

# 80

# Sociology, Meet History

## *Charles Tilly*

### Mercurial Views of the Seventeenth Century

*Durant l'Esté de ceste annee le Roy estant à Paris fut adverty par un nommé le capitaine Belin, qu'en Limosin, Perigord, Quercy, & en quelques provinces des environs, plusieurs Gentils-hommes faisoient des assemblées pour relever les fondemens de rebellion, que le feu Mareschal de Biron & ceux qui estoient de sa conspiration y avoient jettez; & ce fut le pretexte ordinaire des rebelles, scavoir, pour descharger le peuple, & pour faire que la Justice fust mieux administrée a l'advenir par ceux qui l'exercaient: & toutes fois leur dessein n'estoit q pour pescher en eau trouble, & sous l'apparence du bien public s'engraisser des ruines du pauvre peuple.*

During the summer of this year the King, who was in Paris, was warned by a certain captain Belin that in Limousin, Perigord, Quercy, and other nearby provinces a number of Gentlemen were meeting to restore the bases of the rebellion that the late Marshal Biron and his co-conspirators had laid down. They had the rebels' usual pretext: to lighten the people's burden, and to make sure that those who were charged with the administration of justice would do better in the future. Nonetheless their real hope was to fish in troubled water and, in the guise of the public good, to fatten themselves up at the expense of the poor people [*Mercure françois* 1605: 11–12].

The year is 1605; the king, Henry IV of France; the source, the *Mercure françois*, an ancestor of the daily newspaper. For a twentieth-century reader, it is a curious, exhilarating experience to savor the *Mercure:* to have the noble rebellions, the assassination of Henry IV, the Thirty Years' War coming in as current news.

If the twentieth-century reader is a sociologist, this curious experience offers a challenge to reflection on the character of the reader's discipline and on

---

Source: Charles Tilly, *As Sociology Meets History: Studies in Social Discontinuity*, (New York: Academic Press, 1981).

sociology's relationship to history. The *Mercure's* reporter, after all, is proposing an age-old interpretation of rebellion. The interpretation runs like this:

1. Self-serving, manipulative troublemakers drawn from discontented segments of the dominant classes enlist gullible rebels from the common people.
2. The common people pay all the cost and get none of the benefit – if any – of rebellion.

Elites and authorities often hold that theory today.

In its context, the *Mercure's* interpretation is not absurd. A major form of rebellion in sixteenth- and seventeenth-century France was, indeed, an alliance between a small group of discontented, self-seeking nobles and a large group of aggrieved commoners. The weight of taxes and the maladministration of justice were, indeed, widespread grievances and frequent justifications for rebellion. The organizers of rebellion, indeed, often decamped with the gains and escaped before royal vengeance struck them down. So far as it goes, in fact, the *Mercure's* analysis only contains one substantial error: It underestimates the extent to which the "common people" acted knowingly on their interests; it treats ordinary rebels as a shapeless, manipulable mass. That error, many twentieth-century analysts of twentieth-century rebellion have made as well.

The *Mercure* offers many more occasions for sociological reflection. In 1608, for example, we have the story of the Guilleris, three noble brothers from Brittany. During the recent Wars of Religion, the brothers "had followed the League party under the Duke of Mercoeur, and had performed under his leadership as valiant, brave soldiers." On demobilization, they had formed a robber band. "The promenade of all these robbers crossed many parts of France," reported the *Mercure*, "all the way to Normandy, the Lyon region, and Guyenne. On the highways leading to the fairs and markets of Poitou they posted notices on trees, reading PEACE TO GENTLEMEN, DEATH TO PROVOSTS AND ARCHERS, AND THE PURSE FROM MERCHANTS. ("Provosts and archers" were essentially the royal and municipal police of the time.) The governor of the Niort military district called together a force of provosts, besieged the Guilleris' castle, and finally took 80 prisoners. The youngest Guilleri brother was executed (*Mercure françois* 1608: 289–290).

Shades of Robin Hood! Although we have no evidence that the Guilleri bandits gave to the poor, they certainly assumed the right to take from the rich. In the context of the time, their quick change from valiant soldiers to dangerous criminals was rather more a shift in attitude, name, and coalition than an alteration in their day-to-day behavior. As the people of the ravaged French countryside testified repeatedly, it was often hard to tell the difference between troops and bandits. The transformation from cavalryman to highwayman, the formation of a roving band, the posting of declarations, the siege, and the execution all portray for us a world in which a model of armed conquest was readily available. By no means did the national state have the monopoly on armed conquest.

Not that the state was powerless. The king, his retainers, his clients, and his bureaucracy formed a greater, stronger cluster than any other in France. He who touched the royal person or prerogative paid the price. When Ravaillac assassinated Henry IV in 1610, the king's counselors rolled out the terrible, clanking apparatus of royal justice. In a public execution before the Paris city hall, the hangman assaulted Ravaillac's body with molten lead and red-hot iron. Then it was time for drawing and quartering. "After the horses had pulled for a good hour," reported the *Mercure*,

> Ravaillac finally gave up the ghost without having been dismembered. The executioner having broken him and cut him into quarters, people of all sorts went at the four parts with swords, knives and staves; they snatched the parts from the executioner so eagerly that after having beaten, cut and torn them, the people dragged the pieces here and there through the streets on all sides, in such a frenzy that nothing could stop them [1610: 457].

As was customary on such occasions, the day ended with the burning of the bloody remains in bonfires throughout Paris.

The lurid killing of Ravaillac and the many other public executions recounted in the *Mercure* add two more elements to our understanding of seventeenth-century France. First, we appreciate the importance of exemplary justice and punishment, as opposed to an effort to apprehend all violators of the law. Seventeenth-century authorities did not seek to punish all offenders, by any means. They did not, in general, use jailing as a punishment, although they sometimes incarcerated people as a form of extortion or preventive detention. They lacked the means to send many criminals to the galleys or the gallows. Judges and other officials sought, instead, to deter potential delinquents by the quick and visible chastisement of a few. The mounting of bloody examples dramatized the power of the authorities without overtaxing their limited judicial capacities.

Second, we recognize the participation of ordinary people – as spectators and, to some degree, as critics and participants – in the process of retribution. On other occasions, that popular participation in justice provided a warrant, or at least a model, for the people's taking the law into its own hands. Tax rebellions and attacks on profiteering officials took the forms of assemblies, deliberations, declarations, condemnations, and, sometimes, executions. Exemplary justice and popular participation faded away in later years, as the government's repressive power grew and the separation between accusers and accused increased.

Later in that same year the *Mercure* reported yet another execution at Paris's Place de Grève, in front of the city hall. This time the victims were three gentlemen of Poitou: du Jarrage, Chef-bobbin and Champ-martin. The courts had convicted them of

> preparing a Manifesto which tried to stir the people of Poitou into rebellion, and to induce the people to join [the three gentlemen] in taking up arms, in order (they said) to change the state into an Oligarchy – France, they imagined, not being well governed. Unworthy to die by the sword like nobles, they received the wages of their disgrace: the hangman's rope [1610: 512].

Thus we learn that the law decapitated nobles and hanged commoners. We glimpse the standard routine in which rebels, like highwaymen, posted declarations of intent before striking at their enemies. And we begin to sense the prevalence of rebellion in the early seventeenth century.

These news flashes from 1605, 1608, and 1610 present more than one challenge to the sociologist. The first challenge is to say how the nearly 400 years of experience and thought that have intervened since then have improved our understanding of rebellion and of other sorts of conflict. (The answer, I regret to say, is precious little, and that little comes mainly through (*a*) conceptual refinements; and (*b*) clarification of the connections between major conflicts and the routine pursuit of everyday interests.)

The second challenge is to lay out categories within which the general changes occurring in the France of 1605 will make sense: modernization, class struggle, agrarian bureaucracy, something else. (Although any reply we make to that challenge today is bound to be controversial and incomplete, I favor stressing the development of capitalism and the growth of national states as the contexts of seventeenth-century struggles.)

The third challenge is to examine what difference, if any, it makes whether we approach the events of seventeenth-century France as sociologists or as historians – and whether some sort of synthesis is feasible. (My answer is that in practice sociologists and historians approach the analysis of such events rather differently, but in principle there are good reasons for seeking, not one grand Synthesis, but several different syntheses of sociological and historical practice, all having in common a historical grounding of social theory.) For reasons that will become clearer as we proceed, we might call the three challenges the problems of *collective action,* of *structural change,* and of *historical practice*. These three problems have brought the varied chapters in this book into being.

## Historical Practice

For the moment, let us concentrate on the problem of historical practice. Although I will yield occasionally to the joy of needling fellow historians, my sermons are aimed at sociologists. More than anything else, I want to dispel the illusion that historical practice amounts to failed sociology. Although few sociologists lay out their belief in quite those insulting terms, a belief in the intellectual feebleness of historical practice lies implicit in sociologists' readiness to capture cases from the historical record without considering the existing historiography, and without grounding their own analyses in systematic knowledge of the contexts from which the cases come. S. M. Lipset offers us a characteristic summary:

> From an ideal-typical point of view, the task of the sociologist is to formulate general hypotheses, hopefully set within a larger theoretical framework, and to test them. His interest in the way in which a nation such as the United States formulated a national identity is to specify propositions about the general processes involved in the creation of national identities in new nations. Similarly, his concern with changes in the patterns of American religious participation is to formulate and test hypotheses about the function of religion for other institutions and the social system as a whole. The sociologist of religion seeks to locate the conditions under which chiliastic religion occurs, what kinds of people are attracted to it, what happens to the sects and their adherents under various conditions, and so on. These are clearly not problems of the historian. History must be concerned with the analysis of the particular set of events or processes. Where the sociologist looks for concepts which subsume a variety of particular descriptive categories, the historian must remain close to the actual happenings and avoid statements which, though linking behavior at one time or place to that elsewhere, lead to a distortion in the description of what occurred in the set of circumstances being analyzed. [from *Sociology and History: Methods* by Seymour Martin Lipset and Richard Hofstadter (eds.) © 1968 by Basic Books, Inc., Publishers, New York: 22–23. Reprinted by permission.]

The division of labor, then, resembles the division between the mycologist and the mushroom collector, between the critic and the translator, between the political analyst and the city hall reporter, between brains and brawn. History does the transcription, sociology the analysis.

Historians have sometimes collaborated in this mystification. As Gareth Stedman Jones, an outstanding historian of nineteenth-century Great Britain, complains:

> Attitudes toward sociological theory among sociologically inclined historians have often verged on the credulous, and although more critical sociologists might have rejected as naively positivist any distinction between history and sociology which sees the one as "idiographic" and the other as "nomothetic", many of these historians have behaved in practice as if they considered such a division of labour to be legitimate Defensive about their own subject and repelled by an inadequately

understood marxism which appeared to be the only other contender, they have looked uncritically to sociology as a theoretical storehouse from which they could simply select concepts most serviceable for their individual needs [1976: 300].

On the technical side as well, sociologists and historians have often behaved as though historians had nothing to teach and everything to learn. The wholesale application of sociological statistics to historical analyses, the forcing of historical data into computer formats designed for survey results, the adoption in historical work of occupational coding schemes derived from contemporary censuses all embody the idea of raw historical material, ready for processing.

History is not failed sociology, and historical materials are not raw evidence awaiting sociological analysis. Let me divide my arguments on those scores, for the sake of emphasis, into matters of *fact* and matters of *principle*. As a matter of fact, historians conduct their inquiries according to rules that differ significantly from those sociologists follow in their own work, and which may well puzzle or surprise the unsuspecting sociologist who wanders into their territory. Some sections of this chapter will present a sort of primer of historical practice for the sake of puzzled sociologists. As a matter of fact, the materials of history differ, on the average, from those of sociology. Within the limits set by all residues of past behavior, furthermore, historians' current conventions and procedures reduce radically the evidence that is currently susceptible to historical treatment. Again, parts of this chapter will review the character of historical material, for the benefit of sociologists who confront that material.

As a matter of principle, all analyses of social processes are not equally historical. An analysis is historical to the extent that the place and time of the action enter into its explanations: Spengler's fanciful account of Western ills as consequences of the playing out of a particular civilization has more historical bite, in this sense, than Kuznets's more accurate account of the correlates of economic growth in a wide variety of countries. The distinction, then, does not depend on the accuracy of the observation. It has little or nothing to do with the conventional division between "generalizing" and "particularizing" disciplines: Hardly any statement about social processes, for example, could be more general than Sorokin's attempt to sweep all of human history into ideational, idealistic, and sensate phases of specific societies. Yet Sorokin's scheme, in its curious way, builds in place and time; it has historical grounding. Nor does the hoary contrast between the "cultural" sciences and the "natural" sciences – the *Geisteswissenschaften* and the *Naturwissenschaften* – capture what I have in mind. Indeed, "natural" sciences such as geology, palaeontology, and evolutionary biology sometimes proceed quite historically. The integration of time and place into the very argument marks off historical analysis. Later on, I will argue that sociological analyses of large-scale change suffer, by and large, from being insufficiently historical. Sociological theory needs more historical grounding. Failed sociology? No, in important ways sociological practice comes down to failed history.

## Stinchcombe's Challenge

Traveling a different trajectory, Arthur Stinchcombe has arrived at a similar conclusion. When it comes to "epochal theories of social change," Stinchcombe argues, sociologists have commonly blundered by attempting to force large models onto history, instead of interacting intelligently with the historical evidence. Stinchcombe's *Theoretical Models in Social History* pursues the theme that "one does not apply theory to history; rather one uses history to develop theory [1978: 1]." General ideas are illusory:

> The argument here is that such ideas are flaccid, that they are sufficient neither to guide historical research nor to give the resulting monograph the ring of having told us about the human condition. These ideas are good for introductions and conclusions, for 1-hour distinguished lectureships, for explaining briefly what our profession is all about, and for other functions in which easily comprehensible and inexact ideas are useful They are not what good theory applied to historical information looks like, and consequently their being psychologically anterior has no epistemological significance. It is the fact that "theories of social change" consist of such flaccid general notions that makes them so much less interesting than studies of social changes [Stinchcombe 1978:116–117].

Later, I will give some reasons for being a bit more enthusiastic about general theories than Stinchcombe declares himself to be Nevertheless, I cannot help cheering his admonition to ground theories of social change in genuine historical analyses.

Effective studies of social change, according to Stinchcombe, identify deep causal analogies among sets of facts, then build the sets of facts thus established into cumulative causal analyses of the particular processes of change under study. Facts are deeply analogous if they have similar causes and similar effects. Here is a possible example: We might build a deep analogy among different forms of time discipline and work discipline imposed on workers by pointing out that they all result from the same cause – the effort of owners to increase their discretionary control over the factors of production. We would then point to their similar effects: They all tend to sharpen the division between work and nonwork.

Stinchcombe goes farther; he argues that proper causal analogies identify "similarity in what people want and what they think they need to do to get it [1978: 120]." Thus in our analysis of time discipline and work discipline, we might claim that in case after case owners and workers are locked in the same strategic conflict – each side seeking to extend its control over the factors of production but adopting a distinctly different strategy for doing so. By such a deep analogy we anchor a fact in a particular historical situation: These owners and workers in this place and time are locked in a characteristic struggle over time discipline and work discipline. The core of an effective historical analysis, however, is not the establishment of single facts. It is, in Stinchcombe's view, the construction of a sequence of facts (each established as a fact by means of proper causal analogy) into a cumulative causal process in which each fact creates the conditions for the next. Thus we might find a new market opening up, entrepreneurs increasing the work they farm out to local weavers in order to meet the expanded demand, entrepreneurs making profits and accumulating capital, some entrepreneurs trying to increase their volume and their profits by standardizing the product and the conditions of production, those same entrepreneurs inventing or adopting such means of time discipline and work discipline as grouping previously dispersed workers into the same shop, workers resisting by means of sabotage, mutual pressure and strike activity, and so on indefinitely. The mark of a good Stinchcombian analysis is not that the whole sequence repeats itself in many different situations. It is that the causal status of each step in the sequence is established by a deep analogy with other similar situations elsewhere, and that the effects of one step are the causes of the next.

Most narrative history, thinks Stinchcombe, is seductively misleading. It gives the appearance, but not the substance, of such causal sequences. Most narrative history is superficial because the deep analogies are missing; the author substitutes an easy, unverified reading of the intentions of the chief actors or (worse still) a presentation of the sequence of events as the working out of a dominant Force or Plan. Sociologists who stumble into history, Stinchcombe suggests, commonly go wrong because the conventions of narrative history mislead them into thinking they can substitute their own (presumably superior) Forces, Plans, or readings of intentions for the historians' pitiful versions. The sociologists' pretentions convert a harmless, if ineffectual, literary device into a pernicious mishandling of the historical record.

Stinchcombe attaches his provocative arguments to detailed, ingenious exegeses of the work of four historical analysts: Leon Trotsky, Alexis de Tocqueville, Neil Smelser, and Reinhard Bendix. None of the four qualifies as an archive-mongering professional historian – Smelser and Bendix even less so than Trotsky or Tocqueville. For Stinchcombe's main argument, however, it matters little whether the analysts' raw materials are texts or other historians' glosses on texts. In fact, one hears in Stinchcombe's arguments strong echoes of Tocqueville's reflections on the same subject:

> For my part, I hate those absolute systems which make all historical events depend on great primary causes, and link the events into an

unbreakable chain, thereby eliminating people from the history of humanity. I find them narrow in their false grandeur, and false beneath their appearance of mathematical truth. Unlike the writers who invent sublime theories to nourish their vanity and ease their labor, I find that many important historical events can only be explained by accidental circumstances, and that many others remain inexplicable. I find, finally, that chance – or, rather, that network of secondary causes which we call chance for lack of ability to untangle them – matters a great deal in everything we see on the world's stage. But I believe strongly that chance does nothing which is not prepared in advance. Previous events, the nature of institutions, states of mind, moral conditions are the materials with which chance devises impromptus that astonish and frighten us [Tocqueville 1978 (1850) © Editions Gallimard 1964:112-113].

Thus Stinchcombe comes out a bit more optimistic – or, at least, a bit more ambitious – than Tocqueville; with proper deep analogies, Stinchcombe argues, we can untangle chance. This is, indeed, his account of what good social historians do. When they are good, Trotsky, Tocqueville, Smelser, Bendix, and other strong historical analysts work effectively with deep analogies. When they try to apply very general models to large historical sequences, conversely, their results are as vacuous and misleading as anyone else's. *Theoretical Methods in Social History* ends with these words:

The moral of this book is that great theorists descend to the level of such detailed analogies in the course of their work. Further, they become greater theorists down there among the details, for it is the details that theories in history have to grasp if they are to be any good [Stinchcombe 1978: 124].

Now, *there* is a conclusion calculated to offend almost everyone – historians, historiographers, theorists, history-seeking sociologists. Even if it is wrong, any statement that strikes at so many cherished interests with the same blow deserves serious attention.

It is not wrong. There is much truth in Stinchcombe's cantankerous argument. Much supposed application of general theories to history does consist of assigning resounding names – rationalization, modernization, secularization, hegemony, imperialism – to known facts. The search for deep analogies is, indeed, a key to effective historical explanation. Narrative history does commonly give an illusory appearance of causal solidity – an appearance that shatters as we reach out to grasp the connections. Stinchcombe's main points are correct.

Yet those points are only correct within stringent limits. Let us distinguish between two processes: the one by which historians arrive at conclusions, and the one by which they make those conclusions intelligible and convincing to other people. The two processes intertwine, but they are never identical, and they sometimes differ greatly from each other. Stinchcombe's analysis of historical practice deals almost exclusively with the second process – how historians make their conclusions intelligible and convincing to others. The central issues, furthermore, are epistemological; the point is not to say how most run-of-the-mill historians do their work from day to day but to identify the conditions under which we could reasonably accept historical accounts – and instructions for producing historical accounts – as valid.

When it comes to arriving at conclusions, as opposed to validating them, historians can and do rely on broad theories. They do so in two ways: (*a*) the agenda for any particular subfield of history has a theoretical edge; the student of demographic history, for instance, can hardly escape the influence of the ever-present theory of demographic transition; and (*b*) haphazardly or rigorously, the search for evidence relevant to the subfield's questions entails a theoretical choice. The American historian who examines the treatment of slaves by undertaking a detailed study of slaveholders' diaries, while neglecting the records of slave auctions, makes an implicit choice favoring a theory in which slaveholders' attitudes are significant determinants of slave experience. Historians may arrive at deep analogies, but they begin with theories, crude or refined.

Even in the area of validation, real historians rarely conform to Stinchcombe's prescriptions. Their practice is narrower in some regards and broader in others. It is narrower in that historians ordinarily require validation that goes beyond logical conviction. The two most pressing requirements are that the analysis be relevant to the existing historical agenda and that it be based on irrefutable texts. It is broader in that historians commonly grant validity to forms of argument that Stinchcombe forcefully rejects – psychologically compelling narrative and effective naming of an era, a group, or an intellectual current. That such practices are widespread does not, of course, make them sound. Still, their prevalence makes it clear that (for all the delightful exegesis of Trotsky, Tocqueville, Smelser, and Bendix) Stinchcombe's main business is not description but prescription.

Within Stinchcombe's chosen limits, however, I have only one substantial objection to his argument. The general theories that Stinchcombe dismisses as irrelevant to historical explanation commonly contain instructions for the identification of deep causal analogies. Theories are tool kits, varying in their range and effectiveness but proposing solutions to recurrent explanatory problems. Some of those instructions are worthless, some are misleading, and some are good. But it is normally better to have a bad tool than none at all.

Why? Because explanatory problems recur in history as they do elsewhere. When a problem recurs, why make the same mistakes over again? Even a bad theory generates standard ways of solving recurrent problems, reminders of difficulties on the way to the solutions, and a record of past results. Toward the end of the nineteenth century, Emile Durkheim elaborated a theory of social differentiation and its consequences. The theory includes, among other things, a sort of race between differentiation and shared beliefs: If a society's shared beliefs accumulate faster than it differentiates, change is orderly; if differentiation proceeds faster than shared belief, disorder (suicide, industrial strife, protest, sometimes even revolution) results. Durkheim's theory is bad. As Chapter 4, "Useless Durkheim," in this volume indicates, it not only generates invalid historical analogies (for example, between individual crime and collective protest) but also misstates the causal similarities among situations (for example, different streams of rural-to-urban migration) that are, in fact, analogous.

Yet even this bad theory has advantages as a tool of historical analysis. First, it crystallizes a line of argument that is pervasive in Western folk sociology, and therefore quite likely to turn up when historians confront suicide, industrial strife, protest, and other presumed varieties of disorder. It saves time, effort, and confusion to identify the main lines of the argument at the outset, rather than to have it enter the account piecemeal. Second, it contains instructions for analogizing and marshaling evidence in support of the analogy: The user must at a minimum make a showing that the people detached from existing systems of shared belief have a particular propensity to disorder. Finally, its repeated explicit use produces a record of successes and failures (in the case of Durkheim's theory, I believe, mostly failures) in arriving at satisfactory causal analogies. The record should eventually teach the users of that particular tool kit something about the scope and value of the solutions it contains.

And there are good theories. Leon Trotsky (to take one of Stinchcombe's favorite theorists) proposed a theory of dual power – loosely stated, that an essential precondition of revolution is the emergence of an alternative concentration of power, a countergovernment, to which the bulk of the population can switch its allegiance if the existing government demonstrates its incapacity or intolerability. That is, I think, quite a good theory. It contains a set of instructions for analyzing a prerevolutionary situation: Look for the dual power, check the conditions for acquiescence of the population to the existing government, watch for defections, and so on. In short, press this particular analogy.

Trotsky's theory of dual power is an especially appropriate example. It is not just a good theory but also a historically grounded theory. Trotsky grounds his analysis on an explicit comparison of the English Revolution of the seventeenth century, the French Revolution of the eighteenth, and the Russian Revolution of 1917. That sets limits to the theory's domain; as Trotsky formulates it, the theory is not likely to operate well outside the world of fairly strong, centralized, and autonomous national states. The restriction is the price we pay for a theory that works effectively *within* those limits.

According to this account of the place of theory, and according to Stinchcombe's treatment of deep analogies, the potential place of the social sciences in historical work is large. Whatever else they do, the social sciences serve as a giant warehouse of causal theories and of concepts involving causal analogies; the problem is to pick one's way through the junk to the solid merchandise. Stinchcombe rightly scores the "flaccidity" of our general theories of social change. He wrongly obscures the significance of good theory to effective historical analysis. Sociologists and historians alike, however, should be searching for theories that have adequate historical grounding.

## History's Place

Before seeking that historical grounding, let us explore the terrain of history. The word *history* refers to a phenomenon, to a body of material, and to a set of activities. As a *phenomenon*, history is the cumulative effect of past events on events of the present – any present you care to name. To the extent that *when* something happens matters, history is important. Analysts of industrialization, for example, divide roughly into (*a*) people who think that essentially the same process of capital accumulation, technological innovation, labor force recruitment, and market growth repeats itself in country after country; and (*b*) those who think that the process changes fundamentally as a function of which other countries have industrialized and established their shares of the world market before a new section of the world starts industrializing. Only members of the first group can, in good conscience, adopt a common procedure – using a comparison among a number of different countries, ranging from agrarian to industrial, at the same point in time in order to identify the standard correlates of industrialization. Members of the second group should abhor that sort of cross-sectional comparison; they attach greater importance to the phenomenon of history than the first group does.

As a *body of material*, history consists of the durable residues of past behavior. The vignettes from the *Mercure françois* with which we began are misleading in this regard. They perpetuate an easy misunderstanding, one that often wanders into manuals of historiography, that "historical records" consist mainly of narratives of various kinds. Chronicles, confessions, autobiographies, eyewitness reports, and other sorts of narratives are actually a tiny portion of historical material. Most historical material consists of fragmentary by-products of social routines: the remains of stone walls, trash heaps, tools, beaten paths, graffiti, and so on. As it happens, historians have concentrated on the written materials remaining from the past. But the written materials, too, are mainly fragmentary by-products of social routines: birth records, judicial proceedings, financial accounts, administrative correspondence, military rosters, and bills of lading are far more numerous than are narratives of any sort.

All documents are not equally valuable in reconstructing the past. If we are trying to understand the pattern of rebellion in seventeenth-century France, one memorandum from Richelieu will be worth a thousand biblical glosses (or, for that matter, pornographic poems) from the monks of Saint-Germain-des-Prés. Still, coming to terms with the historical record means, among other things, appreciating how much of the seventeenth century writing went into pious essays and pornography.

What of history as a *set of activities?* The central activity is reconstructing the past. That activity, too, easily lends itself to misunderstanding, to the supposition that the main historical problem is to establish the facts of what happened in the past. Establishing what happened is a hopeless program. It is hopeless for two reasons, which become obvious after a little reflection. First, the supply of information about the past is almost inexhaustible. It far exceeds the capacity of any historian to collect, absorb, synthesize, and relate it. Historians have no choice but to select a small portion of the available documentation.

Second, what matters, among the innumerable things that happened in the past, is a function of the questions and assumptions the historian brings to the analysis. To the historian who concentrates on the histories of regimes, and who believes that in any particular regime the attitudes and decisions of a few statesmen make all the difference, records of births, deaths, and marriages are trivial. Records of births, deaths, and marriages are crucial, on the other hand, to the historian who is trying to explain why industrialization occurred when and where it did, and who believes that fluctuations in the labor supply strongly affect the feasibility of industrialization. Historians therefore select radically among available sources and facts.

Other specialists – geologists, archaeologists, classicists, paleobotanists, for example – also draw selectively on the past. Yet they are not, in general, historians. The distinguishing features of the historical profession are these:

1. Its members specialize in reconstructing past human behavior.
2. They use written residues of the past: texts.
3. They emphasize the grouping and glossing of texts as the means of reconstructing past events.
4. They consider where and, especially, when an event occurred to be an integral part of its meaning, explanation, and impact.

Historians are people who do these four things. Professional historians are simply the people who certify one another as competent to do the four things.

As in other fields, the Ph.D. degree serves as the chief certificate of competence in history. The history Ph.D. is a peculiar experience in one regard: Although the reconstruction of past behavior, the location and transcription of relevant texts, and the analysis of those texts are the historian's distinguishing skills, the average historian-in-the-making has almost no serious practice in these skills until the last phase of his or her training. Very few historians, for example, ever enter an archive before they begin work on their doctoral dissertations. Before that time, they are busy learning other people's syntheses: basic sequences, critical events, rival interpretations, major books. Within a limited number of time–space blocks (Classical Greece, Latin America since

1816, etc.) they are learning what they might later have to teach to undergraduates. They are also, it is true, learning to write expository prose and to criticize other people's arguments. But their teachers only give them serious exposure to the basic historical skills after they, the students, have mastered their share of the discipline's ideas and beliefs. Within any particular speciality, that is, the professionals recognize one another by means of their orientation to a common literature.

In the United States, professional history is a large field, and predominantly a teaching field. At its peak in 1970, the American Historical Association had about 20,000 members. The demographic and economic contraction of the following years brought the number a little below 16,000 by 1977. That was still a great many professionals. History was smaller than the giants among research fields: chemistry, engineering, biology, and psychology. Yet it approached the size of physics and stood in the same range as such fields as mathematics and Anglo-American literature. In 1977, some 17,000 people who had received Ph.D.'s in history from 1934 through 1976 were known to be living in the United States. During the early 1970s, the profession was grinding out about 1000 new Ph.D.'s each year. In 1976–1977, the figure was still 961, with 36% in American history, 27% in European history, and the remaining 37% in a great variety of other fields.

The great bulk of historians who make their livings as historians do so as teachers. In 1976–1977, of all history Ph.D.'s known to be employed, 96% worked for educational institutions. Of all working Ph.D.'s, 79% were in teaching, 6% in research, 6% in management and administration, another 6% in writing and editing, and the final 3% in other sorts of jobs (all figures are from *AHA Newsletter*, December 1978, or National Research Council 1978). Of these thousands of practitioners, most spent most of their time teaching American or European history to young people who had no intention of specializing in history. Many devoted some of their nonteaching time to research and writing. A few hundred of them actually published books and articles reporting their historical work. Those writers were the profession's nucleus. They provided the chief connections among previous work, current research, what students were learning, and what the general public was reading about history. They set the tone of historical practice.

## The Historical Zoo

I hope my description does not make the historical profession seem smoothly organized, neatly hierarchical, or deeply coherent. In reality, the practice of history resembles a zoo more than a herbarium, and a herbarium more than a cyclotron. In a cyclotron a huge, costly, unified apparatus whirs into motion to produce a single focused result; history does not behave like that. In a herbarium, a classificatory order prevails; each dried plant has its own niche. Historians divide their subject matter and their styles of thought into diplomatic, economic, intellectual, and other sorts of history, but the divisions are shifting, inexact . . . and often ignored in practice.

A zoo? Yes, watching historians at work does have something in common with strolling from the polar bears to the emus to the armadillos. Each species of historian is confined to an artificially reduced habitat, fenced off from its natural predators and prey. In the historical zoo, however, the inmates often leap the barriers to run through the spectators, to invade other cages, and even occasionally to change themselves from one sort of beast into another. Intellectual history becomes cultural history, social history edges over into economic. Nevertheless, at any given point in time the boundaries are real and significant: Practitioners on one side of a line or the other have their own journals, their own associations, their own jargons, their own professional agendas. That they should be further subdivided by time and place (Modern American Intellectual History being one recognized speciality, Medieval European Economic History another) only accentuates the fragmentation of historical practice.

What happens in the zoo? Do not trust studies of historiography to tell you. Historiographers rely almost exclusively on the skills of biographers, intellectual historians, and philosophers: They analyze history not as a concrete social activity but as the development and application of general ideas. For every discussion of how Lewis Namier actually did his work, we have a dozen discussions of the possibility, in principle, of contributing to historical knowledge by means of the sort of collective biography that Namier created. Jerzy Topolski's massive *Methodology of History*, for example, begins with the complaint that

> earlier statements by historians on their own research techniques reveal the nature and degree of their methodological awareness. A few decades ago when Marc Bloch was writing his *The Historian's Craft* and the science of scientific method was not so far advanced as now, historians took little interest in explicit problems of methods. Since then, much has been said about the science of history without the participation of historians. Today the practitioners of historiography have to be more aware of methodological considerations [1976:3].

To remedy earlier oversights, Topolski devotes 600 pages or so to "Patterns of Historical Research," "Objective Methodology of History," "Pragmatic Methodology of History," and "Apragmatic Methodology of History." He energetically reduces the problem of historical knowledge to a special case of the problem of knowledge in general. But he writes nary a page on an actual historian's workaday approach to his or her research.

If we are to believe the historiographers who do portray flesh-and-blood historians, on the other hand, then historians spend most of their time forming, joining, or combating Schools of Thought, focus their analytic efforts on puzzles posed by history, and do most of their own analyses by thinking themselves into the circumstances of historical actors in order to reconstruct the states of mind that led them to act as they did. We might reflect on this characterization of E. P. Thompson's work:

> Attempts to partition society for purposes of analysis often build upon Marx's insight that a group's economic function generates a distinctive class culture and social system as well as particular economic interests. In *The Making of the English Working Class* (1963), E. P. Thompson brilliantly used the Marxist notion of class to analyze the class consciousness or culture of British workers in the eighteenth and nineteenth centuries. Thompson contended that class is not an abstract concept that can be lifted out of context and treated as a static category. If class consciousness is "largely determined by the productive relations into which we are born," he wrote, it still develops over time and is conditioned by particular experiences. Class consciousness cannot be deduced from general principles, but must be studied historically. Thompson insisted that although the rise of class consciousness follows similar patterns in different times and places, it never occurs "in just the same way" [Lichtman and French 1978: 110–111].

Thompson did, indeed, use the Marxist notion of class brilliantly. He did, in fact, emphasize the conditioning of class consciousness by particular experiences. Yet the summary suggests that Thompson chose (for unstated reasons) to study British working-class culture, then chose to set up his study as an analysis of class consciousness, then developed a theory of class consciousness in order to deal with the available evidence. The intellectual context is missing. Especially lacking are two sorts of controversy – about whether England somehow escaped from a revolutionary situation in the first half of the nineteenth century, about the conditions under which workers develop militant class consciousness. Those controversies entail further questions – about the distinctness of the English experience, about the character of social class, about the extent to which English workers formed a single class with its own autonomous, self-sustaining culture. The questions, furthermore, form part of a contemporary political debate, as well as belonging to the historians' agenda. The Thompson of *The Making of the English Working Class* took a strong stand for class as a process and relationship rather than as a category, for the relative autonomy of working-class culture and consciousness, for the development of a domestic revolutionary tradition within the English working class. A reader of Thompson who ignores this context is likely to be puzzled by his repeated, vigorous, indignant, sometimes dazzling critiques of nineteenth-century observers (such as Francis Place and Andrew Ure) as well as of twentieth-century historians (for instance, John Clayham, R.F.W. Wearmouth, George Rudé, and Neil Smelser). Thompson must knock down a lot of bystanders in order to make his own way to the reviewing stand.

E. P. Thompson is not only a talented historian but also an adroit polemicist. With a flick of his pen he can summon an image of an entire worker's movement, or dispatch an opponent to oblivion. Most historians fall short of his accomplishments in either regard. Yet they try. Historiographers tend to ignore, or conceal, how much historical writing consists of documented commentary on previous historical writing. Instead, they give us a historian who dreams up questions and then goes to the sources to find the answers to those questions.

### Historical Practice as Social Structure

Real historians behave rather differently. In order to be clear and concrete, let me concentrate for a while on American historical practice. In the United States, by and large, a practicing historian embeds himself or herself in a segment of the profession: modern Latin American economic history, Tokugawa urban history, or something of the sort. The basic differentiation is three-dimensional:

1. Place (Africa Asia, Brazil, etc.)
2. Time (Medieval, Renaissance, Early Modern, Modern, Contemporary, to take a common way of dividing European history)
3. Subject matter (political, intellectual, diplomatic, social, etc.)

Courses and graduate programs in American universities are divided in roughly the same ways. As a result, most historians work mainly in one time–place–subject subdivision of the profession but are comfortably familiar with one or two more. Someone who works competently in four or five of the hundreds of pigeonholes defined by these dimensions is considered broad indeed.

As a social structure, each historical subdivision has two main elements: an interpersonal network and a shared agenda. The network's nodes consist of major teachers and their former students. The shared agenda has several components: a set of pressing questions, an array of recognized means for answering those questions, and a body of evidence agreed upon as relevant to the questions. Some, but not all, networks formalize their existence by giving themselves a name, an association, a journal, or other professional impedimenta.

American specialists in the history of the family, to take one case, long plied their trade as no more than a particularly well-connected clump in the network of social historians. At the end of the 1960s family historians – encouraged by the success of their European counterparts – began to differentiate themselves more decisively from other social historians. This historical network (like others tainted with social science) connected people who were interested in the same phenomena across a wide variety of times and places; historians of modern Africa talked to historians of ancient Rome. During the early 1970s, American historians of the family created conferences, an association, and a journal of their own. By that time, a well-demarcated subdivision of the profession had come into existence; a college department could say it wanted to hire a historian of the family, and a well-oiled mechanism of communication and validation would whir into action.

Historians with an entrepreneurial flair ordinarily play important parts in this sort of institution building. By these means (as well as by editing, reviewing, refereeing, and other time-honored means of scholarly promotion and control) they help set the intellectual agenda. In history, specialists who are well connected outside their own country – particularly those who are connected with scholars in parts of the world whose history they are studying – carry significant extra weight; even if they have few ideas of their own, they commonly serve as conduits and interpreters of work being done elsewhere. Because of this structure, historians who are already well placed find it fairly easy to reproduce themselves by connecting their own graduate students (and, sometimes, a few other carefully selected clients) to the structure.

The intellectual agenda itself consists of questions, means for answering questions, and a body of evidence. As in many other disciplines, the historians in a given speciality implicitly orient the bulk of their work to a handful of crucial questions. In American political history, for example, whether the War of Independence constituted a full-fledged popular revolution, whether the Civil War was the inevitable denouement of a long struggle between two antithetical ways of life, and why no durable socialist movement arose in the United States stand high on the agenda; they compel much more attention than such questions as whether nineteenth-century changes in suffrage altered the national structure of power. A young historian who wants to make an impact on other historians will pose a fresh answer to part of one of the crucial old questions, will help refute one of the established answers, or will assemble a new body of evidence supporting an answer that is already in competition.

Orientation to a compelling set of questions, however, creates an interesting ambivalence. On one side, the historical profession lies in wait, posing compelling questions, demanding new answers, and insisting on a demonstration of familiarity with previous work in the field as well as with the available evidence. On the other side, a larger public calls for interpretations that are lively, lucid, and self-contained. What is more, professionals reserve a particular admiration for the historian who reaches that larger public without compromising technical standards. In that, they resemble many of their colleagues in the humanities but differ from most of their colleagues in the natural and social sciences. Natural and social scientists tend to doubt the seriousness of anything that reads easily and sells well. Humanists tend to think of the supreme accomplishment as a work that is at once accessible and profound. Humanists and historians are bookish; although they prize the well-turned essay, they cherish the well-read book.

Major book awards reinforce the prestige of accessible history. Biographies and broad new interpretations of American experience dominate the lists.

Recent Pulitzer Prizes, for example, have gone to biographies or autobiographies of Dean Acheson, Franklin Roosevelt, Thomas Jefferson, Lamy of Santa Fe, and Leo Baeck, plus a half-dozen general essays on American history. The American Historical Association's Bancroft Prize runs a bit differently:

1973 *Fire in the Lake: The Vietnamese and Americans in Vietnam*
*The United States and the Origins of the Cold War*
*Booker T. Washington*
1974 *Frederick Jackson Turner*
*The Other Bostonians*
*The Devil and John Foster Dulles*
1975 *Time on the Cross*
*Roll Jordan, Roll*
*Deterrence in American Foreign Policy: Theory and Practice*
1976 *The Problem of Slavery in the Age of Revolution*
*Edith Wharton*
1977 *Class and Community: The Industrial Revolution in Lynn*
*Slave Population and Economics in Jamaica*
1978 *The Visible Hand: The Managerial Revolution in American Business*
*The Transformation of American Law, 1790–1860*
1979 *Allies of a Kind: The United States, Britain, and the War against Japan, 1941–45*
*Rockdale: The Growth of an American Village in the Early Industrial Revolution*

Biographies still stand out among the prizewinners, but general reinterpretations of American life appear to attract the Bancroft judges less than they do the Pulitzer Prize committees. Fresh answers to old questions on the historical agenda win praise from the insiders. As the inclusion of Robert Fogel and Stanley Engerman's *Time on the Cross* (with its econometric analyses of the profitability of American slavery) indicates, the fresh answers may even be controversial and may even build on the social sciences. Yet on the whole technical *tours de force* take second place to graceful expositions of subjects that interest the literate public. Thus the historical scholar who craves esteem from peers must find a way to surmount the dilemma: solidity versus accessibility.

The newly trained historian faces the dilemma in its extreme form. The doctoral dissertation in which he or she has just invested 4 or 5 years ordinarily addresses a precise subquestion of one of the Big Questions, reviews previous answers to that subquestion meticulously, catalogs and arrays the available sources, and cautiously lays out the evidence for a new reply to the subquestion – in short, situates itself exactly with respect to an existing literature. But now, the dissertation completed, the young historian's career depends on publishing a book. A few fresh Ph.D.'s have the good fortune of access to monograph series that publish books greatly resembling dissertations. Or they have a topic and a dissertation committee that permit them to make light work of the connections with the field. Most of them, however, must think about turning a manuscript heavy with scholarly apparatus into something quite different: a book whose buyers generally care little about the state of the literature but are looking for a rounded, convincing, comprehensible treatment of the subject at hand. As editors and thesis advisors learn to their pain, the transformation commonly requires the dismantling not only of the dissertation but also of the former graduate student's training in documentation and cross-reference. To become working historians, the newcomers must unlearn their graduate educations.

But not completely. The skillful manipulation of acceptable sources remains an essential part of the craft. The problem for the professional is how to convey the insider's signs of authenticity without impeding the outsider's access. The book must contain enough "primary" sources – texts produced as a direct effect or observation of the historical circumstances under analysis – to demonstrate the author's familiarity with the era and its materials. Yet the writer must weave the sources into a coherent argument. The argument, in turn, must differ in some significant way from those proposed by earlier authors. The entire procedure requires a lawyerly handling of the evidence.

### Handling the Evidence

What is that evidence? At the borderland of anthropology and history, potsherds, wall paintings, and paving stones serve as the historical record of distant civilizations. Some historians of art and culture work with buildings, sculptures, and pictures. Students of the recent past have tape recordings and films at their disposal. Philippe Ariès and Lawrence Stone have made funerary sculpture speak to us about the family life of earlier centuries. Yet the great bulk of the evidence that historians learn to use – and do use, in fact – consists of texts. Historians are the specialists par excellence in reconstructing social life from its written residues.

Within any particular historical speciality, however, practitioners tend to recognize only a limited range of texts as useful to their enterprise. In most subdivisions of history, ostensibly direct testimonies by major actors – autobiographies, depositions, private letters, and so on – have long held pride of place. In the history of the family, such testimonies complement marriage contracts, birth registers, household property inventories, and other records of routine transactions. A military historian, on the other hand, is unlikely to pay much attention to routine domestic transactions. At least a military historian is unlikely to pay much attention until someone else shows that birth registers and the like yield fresh answers to the questions the discipline is already posing.

A significant part of historical innovation consists, indeed, of showing that new sources will answer old questions better, or differently. During the 1960s, Stephan Thernstrom almost single-handedly reoriented American urban history by demonstrating that with appropriate statistical processing readily available city directories and similar enumerations of the local population would yield estimates of the rates and directions of occupational mobility among different segments of the population. He created skeletal individual biographies by following the same person from one record to the next, summary collective biographies by collating the experiences of all members of a given cohort, class, or ethnic category. Thernstrom modeled many of his procedures on those of sociologists who had been studying twentieth-century mobility patterns and found ways to make them work in a nineteenth-century context with nineteenth-century evidence. He cannily chose to study the very Newburyport, Massachusetts – "Yankee City" in pseudonym – whose twentieth-century class structure Lloyd Warner and associates had examined in such detail, and whose nineteenth-century class structure Warner had sketched from the local people's memory and myth.

Thernstrom's findings countered the notion of a slowing of mobility from a fluid nineteenth century to a rigid twentieth century. They also suggested different *patterns* of mobility for different ethnic groups. His analysis therefore bore on two classic questions of American urban history: whether the nineteenth-century city was a sort of opportunity machine that gradually slowed down, whether the ethnic and racial diversity of the American working class hampered the development of common living conditions, class consciousness, and collective action. Other historians immediately took up Thernstrom's challenge and his model of analysis; not only city directories but also manuscript censuses and a variety of other records suddenly became relevant to pressing questions of the field.

Today's historiography grows from yesterday's history; just as previous historians have set the current questions, they have identified the proper means for answering them. The means vary from one historical subdivision to another. Because so many major questions in American political history turn on the mentalities and calculations of the chief actors – the Founding Fathers, Abraham Lincoln, or, more rarely, The People – the favored means consist either of documenting those mentalities or of rearranging the existing evidence in a new interpretation of mentalities and calculations that appears to be more consistent, economical, and/or plausible than the available interpretations. The conventional means of documenting mentalities proceed through the exposition of correspondence, of public writings, of utterances, or perhaps of the materials of folk culture: songs, slogans, tales, pictures, and the like. Some historians have lavished attention on voting records and have built up large quantitative analyses of the correlates of one voting preference or another. Three of America's most energetic organizers of quantitative electoral studies speak of "the electoral statement as a means of penetrating the outer structure of political life and charting the subterranean arena of conflicting values, interests, and desires that exist in most societies [Silbey, Bogue, and Flanigan 1978: 4]." The persistent secret hope of voting analysts is, I think, not to absorb political history into political science. It is to establish a new, reliable means of documenting popular mentalities.

Reinterpretation, however, scores more points with fellow historians than does documentation. Historians share with artists and literati a deep admiration for the ability to state and defend an "original thesis." An able young scholar must, in consequence, take the greatest care to differentiate his or her arguments from those of his or her mentor; there is nothing worse in history than to be thought imitative – better dull than dependent! That drive to identify a topic and an approach, then to make them your own, accounts for a feature of historians' behavior that frequently puzzles outsiders. If two people discover that they are working on the same topic, instead of competing to solve the problem faster and/or differently (as people in many other fields would do), they tend to divide up the territory: one drops the topic, both redefine, or they work out a division of labor A "responsible" thesis director will not let a student continue working on a topic if it is discovered that someone else is further along on the same topic.

Historians commonly rationalize this behavior by saying that it takes a long time to become familiar with a topic and that competition for the same unique body of evidence is likely to hamper the work of both investigators; it is therefore doubly inefficient to have two people working on the same problem. But such arguments apply *a fortiori* in fields where research is more expensive and in which no such rule applies. In fact, the rule resembles the rule of serial monogamy: Adultery is unacceptable, but divorce and remarriage are desirable solutions to marital discord. Once Historian A has written his or her book, it is fair play – even high adventure – for Historian B to go back to the sources and tear up A's argument. The stress on originality and the emphasis on reinterpretation dovetail.

### Reinterpretations and Theories

This complex social structure helps explain how historians can so easily shrug off work by nonhistorians that, from the outside, looks highly relevant to their concerns. It helps account for the mystique of primary sources and archives. It clarifies why the recurrent call for something like a "general history of civilizations" (e.g., Marrou 1961: 1475) attracts polite applause but no action. Even the "total history" advocated by a Fernand Braudel turns out in practice to be time–place history that broadens the range of sources and processes under examination. Historians recognize fellow specialists by their familiarity with a set of conventional categories and facts concerning a particular ensemble of places and periods, their competence in locating and using a set of sources (usually writings of various sorts) agreed upon as relevant to the events that took place in those periods and places, and their orientation to the current body of doctrine and controversy about those periods and places. The worker who deals familiarly with those categories, facts, sources, doctrines, and controversies, who builds an argument and a body of evidence that reinterpret some or all of the categories, facts, sources, doctrines, and controversies, gains recognition as a genuine historian. The reinterpretation starts from the knowledge that previous practitioners have left behind.

And why not? Any coherent field proceeds by elaboration and criticism of previous work. Even poems and symphonies often define themselves in relation to previous poems and symphonies. I stress the connection between current and previous work in history only because historians have worked out their own distinctive version of that connection: cutting the past into time–place blocks, posing a limited set of questions about each block, paying exceptional attention to the questions the literate public is asking about that period and place, giving priority to politics, being concerned about the didactic, moral, and political implications of the historical experience under analysis, insisting on the virtues of familiarity with a basic set of texts concerning that experience, and valuing the individual mastery, understanding, and interpretation of the available texts. Given this organization of inquiry, we should not be surprised to find historians proceeding in something like the fashion of literary critics: moving, *textes à l'appui*, from reinterpretation to reinterpretation. Not for most historians is the economist's derivation and estimation of a model from neoclassical economic theory, or the sociologist's effort to bring data to bear on two conflicting hypotheses. No, a historical reinterpretation should produce a new understanding of the place, time, phenomenon, and underlying question under study.

Nevertheless, the means of reinterpretation vary from field to field within history. Demographic history, for example, has a technical edge: One shows that the methods by which earlier historians arrived at crucial conclusions were faulty and that other methods produce substantially different conclusions. Thus Thomas McKeown begins his challenging reinterpretation of the causes of modern Western population growth with a modest demurrer:

> Demographers and historians interested in the pre-registration period have attempted to provide a substitute for national records by exploiting the information available in parish registers and bills of mortality. Can we, from such sources, expect to get a reliable national estimate of fertility, mortality and cause of death? I do not think so [McKeown 1976: 7].

This hesitant seed explodes into a giant shade tree, cutting the sun from all its competitors. McKeown systematically sets up the accounting problem, steadily counters alternative accounts of population growth (he is especially deft at cutting down arguments that stress the early contributions of medical improvements to life expectancy), and gradually builds up a case in which better nutrition plays a central part.

Reorientations in political history, on the other hand, rarely spring from methodological innovations. An impressive case in point is quantitative political history. Although dozens of historians have undertaken the measurement and modeling of elections, of legislative behavior, and of political elites, and although the advocates of quantitative analysis have been among the most vociferous critics of narrative and biographical approaches to political history, the field continues serenely to reward studies of Thomas Jefferson and of the American political temper.

The variation in question posing from one subfield in history to another gives the lie to two easy interpretations of the role of theory in historical analysis. (I am not speaking of the role that theory could or should play but of theory's actual place in the routine activities of working historians.) The first easy interpretation is that history is essentially atheoretical – a miscellany of facts and opinions. The second is its contrary – that theory plays about the same part in history as in any other analysis of human affairs, except that historians' general theories are usually commonsense, or poorly explicated, or both.

Neither is correct. The practitioners in each subfield of history create their own agenda and establish a limited number of theories as relevant to the answering of questions on the agenda. Both the agenda and the available theories change in spurts, as new reinterpretations come along. The reinterpretations, in their turn, respond to the internal agenda, to new ideas in adjacent fields, and to events in the world at large. Ultimately, the most consistent points of reference for all these agendas and theories are the political histories of large time–space blocks: Why did European states and their extensions come to dominate Asia and the rest of the world after the eighteenth century? Why did "traditional" China give rise to a far-reaching socialist revolution? Such master questions give rise to the subquestions on which most historical work actually focuses: Why, for example, Great Britain became the dominant colonial power in the eighteenth and nineteenth centuries, or whether the Chinese revolution of 1911 somehow anticipated, or even caused, the struggles that eventually produced a Communist regime. Theories of capitalism, of liberalism, of industrialism, of class struggle ultimately guide historians' inquiries into the multiple subquestions. Elsewhere in history, the master questions and relevant theories are different, but just as well defined.

Many of the relevant theories are themselves historically grounded. "Historically grounded" means embedded in time: focused on some historically specific setting or process, such as the growth of a capitalist world-economy after 1500, or at least postulating some important alteration in a process depending on where it occurs in a time sequence. (Alexander Gerschenkron's discussions of the "advantages of backwardness" in industrialization – the chief advantage being that a latecomer can profit by the successes and failures of early industrializers – provide an example of the second sort of historically grounded theory.) The historical grounding of historians' theories is neither self-evident nor universal; general psychological theories, timeless models of organizational structure, and historical conceptions of political processes show up regularly in historical analysis. Nevertheless, the historical grounding of the historians' master questions also predisposes historians toward historically grounded theories proposing answers to the questions.

### "Social Science History"

Yet, something called "social science history" has arisen. There is even a journal by the name *Social Science History*, in addition to journals of economic history, demographic history, social history, and the like. How is that possible? The topics of articles in the first volume of *Social Science History* give an idea:

"The Institutional Context of Crossfiling"
"Urbanization, Industrialization and Crime in Imperial Germany"
"The Evolution of Public Perceptions of Adenauer as a Historic Leader"
"The Congressional Game: A Prospectus"
"Sampling for a Study of the Population and Land Use of Detroit in 1880–1885"
"The Social Functions of Voluntary Associations in a Nineteenth-Century American Town"
"Town and Country in Nineteenth-Century Germany: A Review of Urban–Rural Differentials in Demographic Behavior"
"Black Yellow Fever Immunities, Innate and Acquired, as Revealed in the American South"
"The Growth of English Agricultural Productivity in the Seventeenth Century"
"The Changing Context of British Politics in the 1880s: The Reform Acts and the Formation of the Liberal Unionist Party"

This incomplete list shows the variety of topics that crowd in under the name of social science history: elections, public opinion, legislators, urban structure, fertility, disease, and so on. The list does not show the unusual features of the style and contents: full of tables and graphs; frequently summarizing results or hypotheses as equations; selfconscious about techniques of analysis; speaking frequently of models, hypotheses, and problems of measurement; obsessed by comparisons over time and over space. These are the stigmata of social science history. And social science history is flourishing.

Social science history is flourishing for two main reasons: (*a*) a number of social scientists have become interested in working seriously with historical materials, and some of the leaders in American social science history are actually based in departments of political science, sociology, and economics; and (*b*) a few special fields of history have invested heavily in social science approaches to their problems and their evidence. A small proportion of a large discipline, augmented by outsiders, is enough people to create and sustain the institutional apparatus of a subdiscipline. Of the 15,000–20,000 professional historians in the United States, perhaps 1000 consider themselves to be practitioners of social science history.

The subdiscipline of social science history is unusual. It is one of the few specialties in history not defined by a time, a place, and an aspect of social life. Although they come disproportionately from the fields that are otherwise known as social, economic, and political history, the topics that comprise social science history do not form a logically coherent block. Historians have not previously considered most of them to belong together. Nor are they simply the topics that come, in principle, closest to the preoccupations of the adjacent social sciences. The spread of social science practice has not even followed a principle of adjacency *within* history; separate geysers of social science history have erupted through plains of conventional historical practice.

The subdiscipline has other peculiar features. The common literature to which its members are oriented is rather thin and mainly methodological. Since no single, coherent social science exists, the historians involved attend to different literatures within the social sciences, depending on the special historical topics that concern them. Almost all the historians in the discipline have dual or triple allegiances, for in addition to being devoted to social science history as such, they work in specific time–place fields and often seek to make contributions to the social science disciplines – economics, anthropology, demography, and so on – with which they are most closely associated.

People trained outside of history commonly play important roles in social science history. Technical innovations frequently come from outside the subdiscipline; new ways of storing evidence, new statistical techniques, and new models often migrate in from nonhistorical work in the adjacent social sciences. The common ground of social science history, in the last analysis, is not substantive; instead of being committed to common problems, however defined, its members share an attitude, a relationship to the historical profession as a whole, and a small amount of technical lore.

If this shaky common ground were the whole of social science history, one could readily understand the suspicion that greets it elsewhere in history and easily predict its rapid disappearance. What gives social science history its strength, however, is that it is composed of a number of smaller clusters, each of which does share problems, materials, and procedures. As a practical approximation of these clusters, we might take the topics officially represented on the program committee of the 1979 meeting of the Social Science History Association: theory; methods and teaching of social science history; labor history; social structure and mobility; family history; ethnicity; urban history; history of education; economic history; demography; electoral, party and legislative history; bureaucracy; elites; international relations; diplomatic history; violence; public disorder; criminal justice; legal history. (Among the dozen members of the committee, incidentally, six were based in departments of history, four in departments of political science, one in a department of economics, and one in a department of sociology.) The clusters are of two overlapping kinds: historical specialties that have long existed but that have developed close working relationships with one or another of the social sciences; specialties that essentially came into being as a result of the interaction of history and one of the social sciences.

In the first category the most prominent case is economic history. During the 1960s, economic historians began adopting economic models and econometric methods as standard elements of their intellectual armamentarium; it is now hard to enter the field at all without having considerable training in economics. In the category of new specialties, the most dramatic case is demographic history. (Many of its practitioners call the field historical demography; the changed emphasis itself tells us something about the field's character; see Gaunt 1973). Although the specialty's intellectual origins go back to the political arithmeticians of the eighteenth century, demographic history has only existed as a substantial, distinctive body of knowledge since the 1960s.

Somewhere between the cases of economic history and demographic history fall the other major enterprises of social science history: quantitative urban history, the study of social mobility, and so on. Each of these specialties has its own relationship to some portion of the social sciences, and each shares some pool of problems, materials, and procedures. Each has the makings of a distinct subdiscipline.

## How Do History and Social Science Coalesce?

Why these areas and not others? From a logical point of view, they are no more obvious candidates for social science work than other subjects that have remained inhospitable to social science – military history, the history of science, the history of popular culture, agricultural history, and biography are cases in point. In all of these fields, there exists a body of related systematic work somewhere in the social sciences, and some scholars have made the effort to apply the approaches of social science to the historical problem. Yet, unlike economic history or the history of the family, these fields have not moved noticeably toward the social sciences.

It is possible, in principle, that the explanation lies in the relative power of the ideas and procedures available inside and outside of history. Fields whose guiding ideas are relatively weak, one might think, tend to succumb to social-scientific enchantment. I think, however, that it has more to do with the compatibility between the existing structure of the historical field and the styles of analysis that prevail in the adjacent areas of social science. The crucial question is this: Will existing social scientific approaches to a given problem yield fresh and/or superior answers to the questions that historians *are already asking?* If the answer is yes, and if someone with sufficient credentials as a historian to attract other historians' attention demonstrates the way to fresh and/or superior conclusions, others will follow quickly. Graduate students begin proposing investigations to confirm, duplicate, elaborate, or refute the new conclusions. Since revised doctoral dissertations make up the bulk of the monographs published in history, the new approach has a considerable impact on the books historians are reading 5 or 10 years later. The easier and the more general the procedures involved, the more quickly graduate students and junior scholars follow.

The study of American slavery illustrates the point well. The efficiency and profitability of slavery in America's cotton regions before the Civil War are crucial problems because they bear directly on several fundamental questions: whether Southern planters had a strong economic interest in slavery; whether the Peculiar Institution was likely to collapse of its own weight; whether the greater efficiency of Northern agriculture and of free labor were further threats to the economic viability of the South; whether the Civil War was a logical outcome of the confrontation between incompatible sectional interests. These questions stirred American politicians and historians from the time of the Civil War onward. In the late 1950s, however, Alfred Conrad and John Meyer began to redefine the profitability of slavery as a question of formal economics and began to derive estimates of that profitability from evidence on costs, prices, and production in the South. Their estimates portrayed slave-powered agriculture as a relatively efficient and profitable system. That work shifted the terms of the debate and started the stream of econometric research on slavery that eventually included the efforts of Robert Fogel, Stanley Engerman, Gavin Wright, Richard Sutch, and a number of other expert economists. Although noneconomists such as Eugene Genovese and Herbert Gutman continued to play important parts in the assessment of the character and consequences of American slavery, the proposal of an economic answer to an old historical question opened the way to an invasion of that part of history by economists.

The invasion resembled the great migrations of the Mongols or the Normans. Although their arrival deeply transformed the social structure at their destination, eventually the newcomers and the older settlers assimilated to each other. The economists began by acting as if they were simply going to incorporate American economic history into neoclassical economics and leave nothing worthwhile for the historians to do. Eventually, however, the economists began to respond to the peculiarities of the American nineteenth century, even to interest themselves in the historical problems posed by that time and place. At the same time, historians began to learn the strengths and weaknesses of econometric analysis, even on occasion to learn how to do it. As Eugene Genovese once wrote,

> The finest products of the new school have transformed themselves from economists who work on data from the past into economic historians in the full sense – into historians who are primarily concerned with economic processes within larger social processes and who therefore struggle to define the extent to which economic processes are autonomous and the ways in which they are contingent. The better

traditional historians, analogously, did not deny a degree of autonomy to the economic sector and did not reject the new methods; they tried to take full account of the new work while reevaluating the relationship between economic behavior and social behavior as a whole [1975: 533].

By 1978 – 20 years after Conrad and Meyer – Gavin Wright was prefacing an important econometric study of the Cotton South with the declaration that the fruits of econometric economic history "have frequently been valuable and stimulating, but I now believe that it is a mistake for economic history to define itself merely as economics applied to old data. Instead, economic history offers a distinctive intellectual approach to the study of economics, a view of the economic world in which historical time plays a fundamental role [1978: xiii]."

American economic history is in no sense reverting to the status quo ante. Any historian who now wants to be heard on the viability of slavery or any number of other topics in nineteenth-century history has to be familiar with the econometric work on the subject and may well have to undertake his or her own econometric analysis. The basic training in the field now includes a substantial amount of economics; indeed, many of the new people in the field are getting their training in departments of economics. But four further changes have taken the field past the point at which it seemed that economic history might simply vanish into economics:

1. The economists began to act as if the time and place – the historical setting – significantly constrained the operation of economic processes that had previously appeared to be timeless and universal.
2. The economists began to respond to the questions historians in general were asking about the time and place.
3. The historians became sufficiently familiar with the procedures, products, and pitfalls of econometric work that they could assimilate and criticize its results.
4. Historians and economists alike began to identify problems that were crucial but not easily handled by the available economics.

In the process, as Genovese says, a distinct specialty of economic history – neither strictly economics nor strictly history – began to form.

The changing historiography of slavery provides a paradigm for the diffusion of social-scientific approaches into historical inquiry. Similar, less complete transformations have occurred in the historical study of family structure, cities, social class, and a number of other topics. That highly selective coalescence of portions of history with segments of the social sciences accounts for the curious structure of social science history as a whole. Instead of being the edge of the social sciences as a whole with history as a whole, it is a collection of many different edges.

Still, the social science historians have the common ground of prisoners of war – the common ground that results from originating in one broad tradition and being confronted with another. On the one side, there is the historical tradition, with its rooting of analysis in a time and a place by means of a defined set of products, mostly texts, of that time and place. On the other side, there is the social-scientific tradition, with its distinguishing features: explicit conceptualization and modeling of the phenomena under study, a strong emphasis on measurement, the deliberate use of comparison – often quantitative comparison – to establish the strength and direction of important relationships. The attempt to reconcile these two traditions gives social science history a certain methodological unity.

The subdiscipline also bears a paradoxical strain of populism; paradoxical because other historians often resist the numbers and abstractions of the social sciences on the ground that they are inhumane. Yet in field after field the appeal of social-scientific approaches has been that they facilitate the bringing of ordinary people back into the historical record, permit the historian to rescue them from abstraction and to gain a sense of the day-to-day conditions of their lives. Ordinary people leave few diaries, letters, and novels, but their experiences leave documentary evidence nonetheless. The documentary evidence shows up in birth certificates, marriage contracts, notarized transactions, conscription registers, tax rolls, rent books, censuses, catechetical records, and other routine sources. One of the greatest contributions of the social sciences to historical practice has been to suggest means of combining the fugitive mentions of individuals in such sources into biographies – individual biographies, and collective ones as well.

The most obvious example of that populist use of collective biography is one we have already discussed: the systematic study of political militants and revolutionary crowds. In the 1950s, Albert Soboul, Kåre Tønnesson, Richard Cobb, George Rudé, and other students of revolutionary France followed the lead of Georges Lefebvre in attempting exhaustive enumerations and descriptions of different important groups of activists. Their quantitative work was simple and not very extensive, but it demonstrated the existence of abundant evidence concerning ordinary participants in the revolution. Although entirely nonquantitative, the rich essays of E. P. Thompson and E. J. Hobsbawm on the lives of workers likewise displayed the promise of history "from the bottom up." It did not take social scientists long to see that the resulting redefinition of the historical agenda gave them an opportunity to apply their own skills to the available evidence. A segment of social science history devoted to the study of crowds, militants, and ordinary workers grew up.

The growth of demographic history was in some ways contrary to that of crowd studies, yet it produced a similar result. Whereas the urge to study crowds originated within history, the historical study of vital processes grew very largely from the concerns of demographers. French demographer Louis Henry, in particular, sought to pinpoint the conditions under which deliberate fertility limitation became part of a way of life. The search for the origins of unreversed declines in fertility has long been one of demography's dominant preoccupations. Henry's pivotal insight was to realize that the same sorts of materials that antiquarians used for the construction of genealogies would, with great care, yield fine measures of fertility, mortality, and nuptiality. He and his collaborators developed a form of collective biography – "family reconstitution" – using the registers of births, deaths, and marriages the Roman Catholic church had established for its parishioners. The method yielded important results, including indications of much greater variability in preindustrial fertility than had previously been thought to be the case. Other research groups (notably the group working with economic historian E. A. Wrigley and intellectual historian Peter Laslett at Cambridge University) took up similar inquiries. The early agenda was largely demographic; it was, in essence, an effort to modify and refine the theory of demographic transition.

The crossover into history occurred when Wrigley, Pierre Goubert, and other economic historians began to interpret fluctuating vital rates as indicators of welfare and to examine the covariation of demographic fluctuations with swings in the economy. Goubert, for example, traced the devastating effect of periodic food shortages on the death rate in parishes of the Beauvais region, as well as the remarkable recuperation of fertility once the crisis was past. That line of analysis articulated neatly with the already-established interpretation of French economic history as a series of well-defined cycles. In France and elsewhere, the inquiry broadened from there. Some investigators refined the study of demographic processes, others worked at bringing other routinely produced documents into the analysis of everyday experience, still others concentrated on the connections between demographic processes and their economic context. By this time, formal demography, economic modeling, and statistical analysis were becoming commonplaces in this particular branch of historical research. A new variety of social science history was emerging.

## Is Quantification the Essence?

In field after field, the leading edge of the change was some form of quantification. Because of that uniformity, many nonquantitative historians mistook the prow for the whole ship: They thought that quantification was the essence of the new movement, that its proper name was "quantitative history," that its practitioners claimed everything could and should be counted. The advocates themselves compounded the misunderstanding. They delighted in showing how much historical reasoning that appears in nonnumerical prose is nonetheless crudely quantitative: More or less, growing or contracting, crisis or continuity recur throughout historical writing. Each of them has an implicitly quantitative content (cf. Fogel 1975). Such arguments invite deliberate quantification.

The point is important, for it provides the demonstration that the quantifiers are not simply amusing (or abusing) themselves but are pursuing significant questions that are already on the historical agenda. Yet the argument is misleading, for two reasons:

1. Available quantitative models and statistical techniques are inadequate to deal with many of the more-or-less statements, which do, indeed, abound in historical argument.
2. Quantification is only the most visible piece of a much larger analytical apparatus – an apparatus of deliberate conceptualization, explicit modeling, painstaking measurement, and self-conscious comparison.

The defense of quantification therefore both oversells and understates the likely impact of social-scientific approaches on historical practice.

Critics of social science history have gradually come around to the realization that quantification is not the essence. As quantitative economic history and historical studies of social mobility first lumbered into the light, defenders of history as art stared at the new beasts with distaste... and what they saw first was numbers. Jacques Barzun wrote an elegant variant of a standard judgment: "Technical diagnosis or statistical analysis does not amplify understanding or finally explain persons and events, because it abstracts from their particularity in order to put in their place common denominators, mechanisms, averages, or trends [Barzun 1974:148]." Quantitative history, he thought, violated true principles of historical knowledge.

Later, however, a more explicitly political critique of social science history began to take shape. That critique deflected attention from numbers as such toward the presumptions concerning history which the use of numbers was supposed to reveal: various shades of positivism, an unwarranted confidence in the models and methods of social science, a populism which treated all features of everyday life as equally worthy of investigation, an avoidance of exploitation and class struggle. Even antiquantitative anthropological approaches to history came in for scathing denunciation. As Fox-Genovese and Genovese summed it up:

> As admirable as much of the recent social history has been and as valuable as much of the description of the life of the lower classes may eventually prove, the subject as a whole is steadily sinking into a neo-antiquarian swamp presided over by liberal ideologues, the burden of whose political argument – notwithstanding the usual pretense of not having a political argument – rests on an evasion of class confrontation [1976: 214].

Fox-Genovese went on to complain that former leftists and pseudoleftists were trying to maintain their credentials by clinging to the study of popular culture while abandoning the political struggle a true left perspective entails. Similarly, Tony Judt declared that history is not only about politics, it is politics, and that one "consequence of the divorce of political from social history is the insulting denial to people in the past of their political and ideological identity [1979: 68]." In short, by not organizing their inquiries around class struggle, social historians betray the class struggle.

The critique contains some grains of truth. It is true that social history which relies heavily on the social sciences tends to shake the dominance of political history by attributing importance to population changes, to economic transformations, to such esoteric matters as alterations in nutrition. It is also true that populist examinations of political life itself often turn up people who suffered exploitation, yet did not articulate their suffering in terms of class. But the critique is doubly incorrect. First, social-scientific historians have proved themselves fully capable of following the leads of Rudé, Hobsbawm, Thompson, and other students of class struggle into systematic reconstructions of everyday political and social life; they have not abandoned the study of class or of struggle. Second, social-scientific historians have rendered a great service to political history by making class action simultaneously problematic and accessible to closer scrutiny: identifying circumstances in which ordinary people had an apparent class interest in action and yet acted on bases other than class, or did not act at all; beginning to inventory and connect the concrete means – not only strikes and rebellions but also festivals, mocking ceremonies, and other forms of protest – by which exploited people stated their demands and complaints. That is no mean accomplishment.

Not all the criticism of social science history has come from proponents of class struggle. Partly because of the inevitable discrepancy between early claims and late realities, erstwhile leaders of the movement toward social science have taken to writing disclaimers. The disclaimers commonly say, in effect, "I never promised you a rose garden." Lawrence Stone – an early and influential advocate of quantification in English history – has observed that

> disillusionment with economic or demographic monocausal determinism and with quantification has led historians to start asking a quite new set of questions, many of which were previously blocked from view by the preoccupation with a specific methodology, structural, collective and statistical. More and more of the "new historians" are now trying to discover what was going on inside people's heads in the past, and what it was like to live in the past, questions which inevitably lead back to the use of narrative [1979:13].

In an earlier statement of the same theme, Stone took a more prophetic tone. He portrayed most of the social sciences as treacherous allies on their way to internal collapse. He deplored the heedless adoption of quantification, especially as the core of large-scale research projects and specialized graduate programs.

He castigated the excesses of psychohistory. And he criticized the tendency to apply simple, one-way, causal explanations to the complexities of history.

"The basic objection to these threats to the historical profession," preached Stone, "is that they all tend to reduce the study of man, and the explanation of change, to a simplistic, mechanistic determinism based on some preconceived theoretical notion of universal applicability, regardless of time and space, and allegedly verified by scientific laws and scientific methods [1977: 38]." "It may be," he continued,

> that the time has come for the historian to reassert the importance of the concrete, the particular and the circumstantial, as well as the general theoretical model and the procedural insight; to be more wary of quantification for the sake of quantification; to be suspicious of vast cooperative projects of staggering cost; to stress the critical importance of a strict scrutiny of the reliability of sources; to be passionately determined to combine both quantitative and qualitative data and methods as the only reliable way even to approach truth about so odd and unpredictable and irrational a creature as man; and to display a becoming modesty about the validity of our discoveries in this most difficult of disciplines [1977: 39].

Veterans of revival meetings will immediately recognize this passage as a deployment of the "Sinner, Beware!" technique. The preacher fixes his gaze over the congregation's head, points a prophetic finger, and forecasts doom for unrepentant sinners. He names no names, and the sins in question appear as ominous labels – lust, greed, gluttony – rather than as concrete actions. Most of the congregation receive the double thrill of self-satisfaction and righteous indignation, a few thin-skinned souls feel guilty, and the emptiness of the condemnation passes unnoticed. No reader, after all, is likely to cheer "quantification for the sake of quantification," much less "projects of staggering cost." The social scientists and historians who are the objects of these complaints are likely to reply, hurt and puzzled, "Who, me?" Few readers will dare deny the importance of the concrete, the value of strict scrutiny of the sources, the attractiveness of modesty, and so on. Yet Stone's sermon is a disservice to historians. It is a disservice because it misrepresents how the interaction between history and the social sciences has usually worked itself out and misstates the choices now before the profession. The critical choice, indeed, is one I have barely mentioned: whether to help the social scientists make proper use of historical materials and historical analysis.

## Sociology Reaches for History

The choice is more critical today because several social science disciplines that had long operated far from history – notably, anthropology, sociology, and political science – have reached out to reestablish their historical connections. Let us focus on sociology. The discipline of sociology grew out of history – especially, I think, out of the nineteenth century effort to grasp and control the origins, character, and consequences of industrial capitalism. In this broad sense, such otherwise contrasting thinkers as Marx, Tönnies, and Durkheim joined in the same enterprise. The early, self-conscious practitioners of sociology, however, specialized in large schemes designed to place all historical experience into coherent master sequences. August Comte's Theological, Metaphysical and Positive stages of thought and Herbert Spencer's grand march of human societies along the road of differentiation from "militant" to "industrial" were simply two of the most prominent among many such schemes. Since Comte coined the term *sociology* and Spencer gave it wide currency, however, the two schemes helped define the infant discipline. Quickly the historical content drained out of sociology in favor of an effort to create a timeless natural science of society. Although Weber and some of his successors were zealous historical practitioners, on the whole, twentieth-century sociologists committed themselves to the study of the present; they showed less and less inclination to consider history important, either as a set of influences on contemporary social processes or as a field of inquiry worthy of sociological attention.

Yet in the 1960s and, especially, in the 1970s, sociologists did begin to reach for history. Historical analyses of industrialization, of rebellion, of family structure began to appear in the journals that sociologists read. Departments of sociology began hiring specialists in something called "historical and comparative analysis." Sociological authors began to write as if *when* something happened seriously affected *how* it happened. Some few sociologists actually began to learn the basic historical skills: archival exploration, textual analysis, and the like. History began to matter.

What happened? Among many strands, I see two as strongest. First, the social-scientific work that had been proceeding in history doubled back on the social sciences. The successes of historical demography provided a model for contemporary students of marriage and the family, as well as for other demographers. Historical studies of crime, of voting, of urban structure, of social mobility were sufficiently fruitful and/or provocative with respect to prevailing sociological doctrines that sociologists started to think of them as more than mere *tours de force*. Second (and more important), disillusion with models of modernization and development turned students of large-scale social change toward history.

The disillusion with developmental theories followed a decade or two of enthusiasm after World War II. During the palmy days of developmentalism, Western economists hoped to export the secrets of economic growth to the "underdeveloped" world, and sociologists imagined other forms of development – political, social, educational, urban, and so on – to accompany the economic growth. The reaction against developmental theories had several different origins. Development of any sort proved difficult to engineer. Capital accumulation, family planning, land reform, and other desiderata of development turned out to meet more powerful resistance, and to have more extensive political ramifications, than optimistic Western theories promised. The theories themselves fell on hard times. On the whole, they were inadequate to the task of explaining what was actually happening in the Third World. Their political premises – especially the implication that Western-style party politics was an inevitable, desirable concomitant of other forms of development – excited the anger of Third World intellectuals and powerholders alike. Among other things, the standard conceptions of political development clashed with the explanation of the disadvantages of poor countries as consequences of Western imperialism; that was, after all, an attractive alternative in the many former colonies that were acquiring statehood and undertaking planned national development. In the course of the widespread opposition to American warmaking in Southeast Asia during the 1960s, many social scientists in the West (including the United States) became aware of, and sympathetic to, the antiimperial and neo-Marxist alternatives to development theories. They even began to contribute to the building of those alternative theories themselves. Developmentalism fell into disrepute.

But why and how were the alternatives to developmentalism *historical?* Largely because, in one way or another, they portrayed the current situation of poor countries as the outcome of a long, slow, historically specific process of conquest, exploitation, and control. Thus André Gunder Frank and other students of Latin America spoke of "underdevelopment," not as the primeval condition from which the still-poor areas of the world had to be rescued, but as a product of the dependency of their economies on those of the world's dominant powers. "The expansion of the capitalist system over the past centuries," wrote Gunder Frank,

> effectively and entirely penetrated even the apparently most isolated sectors of the underdeveloped world. Therefore, the economic, political, social, and cultural institutions and relations we now observe there are the products of the historical development of the capitalist system no less than are the seemingly more modern or capitalist features of the national metropoles of these underdeveloped countries. Analogously to the relations between development and underdevelopment on the international level, the contemporary underdeveloped institutions of the so-called backward or feudal domestic areas of an underdeveloped country are no less the product of the single historical process of capitalist development than are the so-called capitalist institutions of the supposedly more progressive areas [1972: 4–5].

Such an argument denied the idea of a developmental process that repeated itself over and over in different parts of the world, denied the division of the world into "traditional" and "modern" sectors, with the modern transforming the traditional into itself, and denied the validity of any analysis that took a single self-contained society as its unit of analysis. All these denials moved analysts of the contemporary world closer to an explanation of the present as the outcome of a historically specific struggle for power and profit. That Marx and Lenin provided the theoretical linchpins of the whole alternative system of thought further promoted the concern with history.

A prestigious example of the move toward history appears in the work of Immanuel Wallerstein. Wallerstein, an Africanist, published sympathetic studies of decolonization: *Africa: The Politics of Independence, The Road to Independence: Ghana and the Ivory Coast*, and others. As of 1966, he was arguing that

> the imposition of colonial administration created new social structures which took on with time increasing importance in the lives of all those living in them. The rulers of the colonial system, as those of all social systems, engaged in various practices for their own survival and fulfillment which simultaneously resulted in creating movements which in the long run undermined the system. In the case of the colonial situation, what emerged as a consequence of the social change wrought by the administration was a nationalist movement which eventually led a revolution and obtained independence [1966: 7].

In his arguments of the time, history's role was limited. In any particular colony, the past practices of the colonizers accounted for the current political situation. Later, Wallerstein came to see the entire sequence of colonization, exploitation, and decolonization as part of a single historical process: the incorporation of peripheral areas into the expanding capitalist world-system.

Wallerstein tells us that he first explored Western history in a search for parallels with the African experience, in hopes of identifying a standard process of modernization. But the difficulties of drawing boundaries around the societies in question, of identifying the stages in their development, and of making meaningful comparisons of seventeenth-century with twentieth-century states eventually appeared to be more than technical problems to overcome; they grew into fundamental objections to the enterprise. "It was at this point," writes Wallerstein, "that I abandoned the idea altogether of taking either the sovereign state or that vaguer concept, the national society, as the unit of analysis. I decided that neither one was a social system and that one could only speak of social change in social systems. The only social system in this scheme was the world-system [1974: 7]." By this path he arrived at a deeply historical conception of the problem – what happened before made all the difference to what happened next. That new conception drew the onetime Africanist back to a general study of the origins of the capitalist world system in the European sixteenth century.

As Christian Palloix said of Gunder Frank:

That emphasis on the capitalist world economy instead of the national economy – the central concept of bourgeois political economy until now – is not new to Marxist thought, since the phrase "capitalist world economy" is due to Rosa Luxemburg, and the concept is ever-present by implication in the work of Bukharin. Rosa Luxemburg was the first to call clearly for the displacement of Marxist analysis from the national to the world level in order to understand contemporary capitalism [1971: I, 8].

Eastern European historians such as Marion Malowist have long used a similar set of ideas to explain the connections between the commercial capitalism of north-western Europe and the agrarian economies of the East during the fifteenth and sixteenth centuries. Wallerstein takes an extreme Luxemburgian position. He also commits himself firmly to one side of a long-raging debate within Marxist analysis, stressing the relations of exchange, rather than the relations of production, as the distinctive features of alternative modes of production. He therefore rejects the traditional Marxist centerpiece in the tableau of capitalism: the confrontation of a capitalist who owns and controls the means of production with a proletarian who receives wages for the yielding of labor power. "To oversimplify," says Wallerstein in a summary of his argument, "capitalism is a system in which the surplus value of the proletarian is appropriated by the bourgeois [1979: 293]." The bourgeois and the proletarian are often half a world apart, and the complex of relations between them is a complex of unequal exchange. A system of production for exchange, rather than production for use, forges those long, long chains of exploitation. Some significant, controversial conclusions follow: that distant subsistence farmers participate fully in the capitalist world-economy; that so long as a capitalist core sets the terms of international exchange, semiperipheral socialist countries remain integral elements of a capitalist system; and that capitalism did not spread through the world little by little, as one firm, farm, or plantation after another took up wage labor and capitalist control, but took charge in a great, worldwide structural transformation. Thus the history of capitalism occupies a large share of the total history of the last five centuries.

A reader who persists to the end of this book will find that in tracing the development of European capitalism I have seized the other horn of the Marxist dilemma, emphasizing the immediate relations of production as the defining features of capitalism. That choice produces a narrower, later catalog of capitalist development. Wallerstein's broad definition, it seems to me, sacrifices the sort of insight concerning the logic of capitalist social relations that Marx unfolded in his analyses of agrarian change in England – especially the insight into the way in which the capitalist's pursuit of profit helped transform workers into proletarians. For those who, like me, want to examine how the development of capitalism affected the collective action of ordinary people, that insight is essential, its loss critical.

Despite these reservations, let me acknowledge Wallerstein's powerful contribution to sociological practice. For one thing, Wallerstein managed to draw sociologists' attention to a fruitful line of thought they had previously ignored. "Since the publication of Immanuel Wallerstein's *The Modern World System*," Albert Bergesen observes, "there has been an explosion of interest and research on this topic [1980: xiii]." The "explosion" has promoted serious historical work within sociology. Although a number of sociologists have taken world-system ideas as the frame for large, quantitative, cross-sectional comparisons of many contemporary national states (a practice that makes me fear a repetition of mistakes made long since by modernization theorists), time and history have moved onto the practical research agenda as never before.

Not all the sociologists following Wallerstein's lead, furthermore, take his conclusions for granted. In *Labor, Class, and the International System*, for example, Alejandro Portes and John Walton display considerable impatience with Wallersteinian neglect of the concrete connections between world-system processes and the actual workings of such phenomena as international migration. Yet without Wallerstein's forceful posing of the problem, books such as theirs would have been much less likely to appear – and find an audience – within sociology. The dialectic has begun.

Within history as well, Wallerstein's work has made a difference. From the historical perspective, Wallerstein's special contribution is to propose a synthesis – a synthesis between a well-known line of thought about the capitalist world-economy and Fernand Braudel's broad treatment of the entire Mediterranean world during the formative years of European capitalism as a single, interdependent system. Braudel has returned the favor. His sprawling, three-volume *Civilisation matérielle, économie, et capitalisme* explores the history of the entire world during the ascent of capitalism; to the extent that it has a unifying framework, the framework consists of a succession of world-economies, culminating in the capitalist world-economy. He adopts, furthermore, Wallerstein's emphasis on large-scale exchange as the essence of capitalism and likewise places within the capitalist system many people and situations other historians locate outside the system's perimeter. In response to Witold Kula's claim that the landlords who "refeudalized" eastern Europe did not, and could not, calculate as capitalists, Braudel declares:

> To be sure, that is not the argument I wish to challenge. It seems to me, however, that the second serfdom was the counterpoint of a merchant capitalism which took advantage of the situation in the East, and even, to some extent, based its operation there. The great landlord was not a capitalist, but he was a tool and a collaborator at the service of the capitalism of Amsterdam and other places. *He was part of the system* [1979: II, 235].

If Braudel has long insisted on the interconnectedness of the world, his latest treatments of the connections have taken on a decidedly Wallersteinian air.

Indeed, Braudel's grand synthesis and Wallerstein's magnum opus appear increasingly to be complementary efforts, with the one making unexpected connections in great profusion and the other supplying the long-lacking systematic narrative of the world-economy's historical development. In his swing from single-country studies of political modernization to worldwide studies of capitalism's development, Wallerstein epitomizes the substitution of historical analysis for the developmentalism of the 1950s and 1960s.

Wallerstein's world-system analysis keeps to the enormous scale of the developmental schemes it is meant to replace. He aspires to stuff the whole of human history since 1500 into a single sack. Except when writing textbooks or end-of-career reflections, professional historians almost never work at that scale. Most other sociologists who have taken up historical analyses in recent years have also chosen a smaller scope than Wallerstein. Comparative history has been an important choice; S. N. Eisenstadt's *The Political Systems of Empires* has served as one sort of model, Barrington Moore's *Social Origins of Dictatorship and Democracy* as another. Those are formidable models for emulation, but talented newcomers have met the challenge; Theda Skocpol's searching comparison of the French, Russian, and Chinese revolutions, in *States and Social Revolutions*, is a case in point. Other sociologists have turned down the scale yet another notch or two: Michael Hechter on internal colonialism in Great Britain, Daniel Chirot on the politics of Rumania, Michael Schwartz on a single important farmer's movement in the American South, and so on down to the level of a single community. Some of America's best sociological talent is going into historical studies

The movement has caught on and is likely to be around for some time. Elsewhere in sociology, historical approaches to crime, collective action, power structures, occupational differentiation, and a host of other topics are becoming commonplace. The sociologists in question are not turning into historians. As a rule, they are not learning to do archival research; nor are they taking their questions from the prevailing historical agenda, or suppressing their inclinations to explicit modeling, careful measurement, and deliberate comparison. They are, on the other hand, edging toward the adoption of genuinely historical arguments – arguments in which where and, especially, when something happens seriously affects its character and outcome. The result, I predict, will not be a general rapprochement of sociology and history but a counterpart to the earlier development of separate social-scientific specialties within history: a highly selective shift of particular topics to historical analyses and historical materials.

Selective or not, the shift is important. It is enlarging the place of historically grounded theories, and challenging the place of theories that disregard time, in sociology: the development of capitalism instead of modernization, the growth of an international state-system instead of political development. It is expanding the opportunities to formulate and test models of long-term change on reliable evidence concerning substantial blocks of time instead of on the sham comparison of presumably "backward" and "advanced" areas of the same point in time. And it is increasing the number of sociologists who, instead of treating the works of historians as if they were raw but solid evidence simply awaiting a sociological gloss, detect what is problematic in existing historical interpretations and know how to go about correcting them. Even if social science history, within history, is reaching a plateau, historical work within sociology is continuing to grow.

## Historical Analyses of Structural Change and Collective Action

Two areas of sociological analysis that stand to gain significantly from the swing toward history are studies of large-scale structural change and of collective action. The search for timeless general models of industrialization, rationalization, or political development will yield to twin efforts to identify the master change processes in particular historical eras and to connect specific transformations occurring in those eras to the master processes of change. The attempt to formulate general laws of revolution, of social movements, or of worker organization will give way to a quest for regularities in the collective action of particular historical eras.

For our own era, the two master processes are no doubt the expansion of capitalism and the growth of national states and systems of states. The expansion of capitalism combined the accumulation of capital with proletarianization of producers; increasingly, workers with little or no capital sold their labor power to people who controlled substantial capital and who decided how the capital and labor would be combined for their profit. From a small European base, the capitalists extended their decision-making power to the entire world. Wallerstein's *The Modern World-System* sums up one major interpretation of how that process worked, but there are others – notably, the idea that capitalism was a sort of invention that worked so well that one country after another adopted it. The historical problem is, then, to determine why and how capital accumulation-cum-proletarianization occurred, why and how the system of productive relations expanded, and what were the consequences of that expansion. Time is of the essence, historical analysis indispensable to the enterprise. Yet there remains room for the classic problems that have concerned students of "modernization": why, how, and with what effects production moved into large, capital-intensive organizations; what caused the industrial city to come into being; what happened to the peasantry; and so on. All these follow easily from the historical analysis of capitalism's development.

As counterpoint to that analysis, we have the growth of national states and systems of states. An organization is a *state*, let us say, in so far as (*a*) it controls the principal organized means of coercion in some territory; (*b*) that territory is large and contiguous; (*c*) the organization is differentiated from other organizations operating in the same territory; (*d*) it is autonomous; (*e*) it is centralized; and (*f*) its divisions are formally coordinated with one another.

In that sense of the word, states were rare phenomena anywhere in the world before a few hundred years ago. Yet by the twentieth century states had become the dominant organizations almost everywhere in the world. What is more, states struggled with one another, borrowed one another's organizational innovations, formed hierarchies and interdependent clusters, and worked collectively at creating new states, containing old states, and realigning the weaker states to meet the interests of the stronger. In short, not only states but also systems of states came to dominate the world.

Again, the historical analysis begins with the Europe of the Renaissance, fragmented into hundreds of nominally autonomous political units, none of which resembled a twentieth-century national state. For convenience, without insisting stubbornly on the distinction, we can distinguish between the internal and the external history of statemaking — how particular organizations grew up that asserted dominance over their "own" populations and how those organizations established their power with respect to competing organizations outside. Warmaking then becomes crucial on both sides of the divide: internally, as the activity that drove the statemakers to tax, conscript, commandeer, and disarm a subject population, and thus build up their coercive power; externally, as the primary means by which statemakers established their exclusive rights within their own areas, expanded those areas, and reshaped the form, personnel, and policies of other states. How states acquired control over education, welfare, marriage, natural resources, and economic activity poses the next round of questions. We move easily to the examination of the central problems of contemporary political sociology: to what extent and how the economically dominant classes control the political apparatus as well; under what conditions a national population is active, organized, and informed with respect to national politics; how riots, rebellions, and revolutions occur; and so forth. But we take up the problems with a difference. We take up the analysis of power, of participation, of rebellion as historical problems, ultimately attaching them to the expansion of capitalism and the growth of systems of national states.

Capitalism and statemaking provide the context for a historically grounded analysis of collective action — of the ways in which people act together in pursuit of shared interests. Grounding the analysis historically, again, means fleeing universal categories. Instead of the eternal behavior of crowds, we study the particular forms of action that people use to advance claims or register grievances. Instead of laws of social movements, we study the emergence of the social movement as a political phenomenon. Instead of power in general, we study the modalities of power within a certain mode of production.

Capitalism and statemaking provide another sort of grounding as well, for their rhythms and directions dominated the changes in collective action's three fundamental components: the *interests* around which people were prepared to organize and act; their *capacity* to act on those interests; and the *opportunity* to defend or advance those interests collectively. Concretely, we find ourselves examining how and why strikes became standard vehicles for labor–management struggles, the ways in which the expanding intervention of states in everyday life (by taxing, drafting, regulating, or seizing control of crops) excited resistance from peasants and artisans, the conditions under which patron–client networks lost their political effectiveness, and similar problems. These problems are, to my mind, sufficiently broad and important to compensate sociologists for the fall from timeless universalism that pursuit of these problems entails.

## What's Going on Here?

With minor exceptions, the later chapters of this book report ideas and provisional conclusions from the historically grounded study of statemaking, the development of capitalism, and popular collective action in Europe over the last four centuries. Chapters 2 ("Computing History") and 3 ("Homans, Humans, and History") deviate most from that program – the first because it reflects in general about the impact of computers on historical practice before arriving at the specific uses of computers in my group's studies of collective action, and the chapter on Homans because it sketches a style of historical analysis that contrasts with my own. "Useless Durkheim" (Chapter 4), on the other hand, not only presents materials for the study of popular collective action but also examines the weaknesses of standard sociological notions concerning the central problems in the research program.

Chapters 5 and 6 ("War and Peasant Rebellion in Seventeenth-Century France" and "How [And, to Some Extent, Why] to Study British Contention") combine ideas, materials, methods, and provisional results from two inquiries within that research program. Those two inquiries tend to take the processes of statemaking and capitalism for granted and to aim their questions at collective action. Then attention shifts to the historical processes by which capitalism developed and states grew. "Proletarianization: Theory and Research" and "States, Taxes, and Proletarians" (Chapters 7 and 8) follow a somewhat more critical, synthetic, and speculative mode of analysis, in an effort to set priorities for the next round of historically grounded theory and research. And the book's conclusion ("Looking Forward . . . Into a Rearview Mirror") traces continuities among these varied sociological expeditions into historical terrain.

May I mention something else I have found on that terrain? It is, to quote George Homans, "the joy sheer, single facts can give of their own sweet selves." The historically grounded inquiry into statemaking, popular collective action, and the development of capitalism in Europe offers the additional compensation of bringing the sociologist into the rich historical residues of everyday social life. The sorts of residues, for example, that we encountered at the start of the discussion, in the *Mercure françois*.

Let us return to the *Mercure*, to see where a program of historical analysis leads us. Now we can reverse the angle of our approach. Earlier we looked at a text and asked what it could tell us about the era. Now we are in a position to ask how the evidence in the text bears on the analysis of capitalism, statemaking, and collective action. Properly read, the *Mercure* fairly bursts with relevant evidence.

In 1615, Louis XIII (son and successor of the assassinated Henry IV) was 14 years old; his mother, Marie de Medici, was regent. Louis and Marie faced three linked challenges from within his turbulent kingdom. The great sovereign courts, especially the Parliament of Paris, were trying to consolidate their own autonomy by such means as guaranteeing the heredity of offices and to extend their power to review and veto royal actions. The king's close kin and rival princes, including the prince of Condé, alternated between grudging acquiescence and armed rebellion. Protestant consistories in Guienne were organizing to resist by force the very Catholic marriages of the king to a Spanish princess and of his sister to the Spanish crown prince. The resistance of the courts deprived the king of their sanction for new taxes with which to pay the troops required to put down the rebellions. The king and the queen mother turned to cruel old expedients, such as expelling all practicing Jews and confiscating their property. Meanwhile, the rebellious princes faced a parallel problem: how to squeeze the wherewithal for expensive armies from a reluctant population without driving the population itself into rebellion against them. On 22 October 1615 the army of the princes

> went to lodge themselves at the little city of Espougny, two leagues from Auxerre. The inhabitants wanted to hold them off, but the city was forced and pillaged. People have written that rape and violence, more than barbarous, took place, in the church as well as elsewhere. Complaints and murmurs reached all the way to the Prince and to the Duke of Mayenne. They had two soldiers, accused of rape and violence, hanged [*Mercure françois* 1615: 260].

When they had to (which was often), the princes let the troops wrest their food, lodging, arms, and sexual satisfaction from the local population; when the exactions threatened to turn the locals into rebels, the military commanders checked their troops by means of exemplary punishment. When they could, the princes established a more regular system of taxation, parallel to that of the king. As the *Mercure*'s writer commented,

> It is very hard on the poor peasants to be trampled by the military, and to pay a double *taille* [the basic property tax] as well; they were obliged to do so by the revenue officers set up by the Princes in the provinces of Picardy, Ile de France, Champagne, Auxerrois, Berry, Touraine and Anjou below the Loire. The officers sent their garrisons to seize the richest peasants, and held them prisoner until they had paid not their own share of the *taille*, but that of the entire village, which they were then supposed to collect from the others [1615: 305–306].

That technique, the princes had learned directly from the crown's own tax officers.

Now, it would take a great many more texts to reconstruct the changes going on in the France of 1615. In context, however, these two are enough to identify an unexpected convergence between the interests of capitalists and the interests of statemakers. Capitalists specialized in setting prices on goods, land, and labor, in exchanging them, and in bringing them into larger and larger markets; that is how they accumulated capital. Capitalists had a powerful interest in destroying the capacity of local people to produce for themselves, to barter goods and services, to keep land off the market. Statemakers needed resources that were embedded in local communities – especially the food, supplies, and manpower required to keep large armies going. To the extent that goods, land and labor were being exchanged via a monetized market, and thus had visible prices, it was easier for the statemakers to seize resources: They taxed the exchanges themselves, they used market-derived values to judge the capacity of people to pay, they grabbed the money people accumulated from selling their goods, and they used the tax revenues to buy food, supplies, and manpower on the market instead of commandeering them directly from unwilling households. The process had its converse: The enforcement of taxation in money forced people to sell goods, services, or land, and thus to expand the market.

Capitalists played facilitating roles at all levels of the process: as local merchants interested in making a profit on the sale of cattle, as purchasers of tax-collecting offices on which it was possible to make a profit, as creditors who advanced large sums to the crown in return for the rights to shares of future tax revenues, enforceable by means of the royal military power. In other regards the capitalists, too, fought the state's advance. At these crucial points, however, the interests of capitalists and statemakers coincided and led to an effective coalition – a coalition that, for the most part, excluded the statemakers' rivals and victimized the subject population.

The coalition worked. "Financiers" (as they were called at the time) and royal officials succeeded in greatly expanding royal revenues, and thus made possible the building of large, stable, and reliable armies that were largely independent of the great magnates – the king's rivals. Under that sort of effort, the French national budget nearly doubled, rising from about 27 million to about 50 million lives, between 1614 and 1622. The process of building a regular army occupied a full century, and the financing of the army staggered from expedient to expedient up to the Revolution of 1789. Yet the expedients worked, most of the time, and the state swelled in size and power.

The statemakers and financiers faced formidable opposition. Ordinary people resisted the rising taxes, especially when the taxes cut into the necessities of local life and when they visibly profited the local bourgeoisie. Nobles, great and small, fought the growth of a rival civil power and a threat to their own power to tax and exploit the local population. On the principle that the enemy of my enemy is my friend, the rather different interests aligning both nobles and poor commoners against the crown sometimes produced a powerful alliance. The alliance could mean a regional rebellion far fiercer than the typical noble conspiracy or the commonplace popular resistance to the tax collector. As the *Mercure*'s commentator said back in 1605, the rebels' usual "pretext" was, indeed, "to lighten the people's burden, and to make sure that those who were charged with the administration of justice would do better in the future." If he was also right that "their real hope was to fish in troubled water and, in the guise of the public good, to fatten themselves up at the expense of the poor people," then we can see why the "pretext" had wide popular appeal. Popular rebellions, many of them tied to the conspiracies of great nobles, racked the French seventeenth century. The greatest cluster of them all – the series of popular, noble, and judicial struggles with the crown that we call the Fronde – almost destroyed the monarchy. With this background, it is easier to understand several puzzling features of France in the seventeenth century: (*a*) the extent to which popular collective action consisted of resistance to someone else's attempt to take something away – the recurrent rebellions against taxation being the most dramatic cases; (*b*) the coexistence of incessant rebellion with successful statemaking; (*c*) the persistent, and ultimately successful, efforts of the crown to neutralize a fractious nobility via cooptation, concession, and repression; and (*d*) the curious coalitions that sometimes sprang up among Protestant zealots, Catholic nobles, and nominally Catholic citizens of the towns. All of these make sense in the light of a vigorously expanding state, seconded by a growing bourgeoisie whose interests coincided temporarily with those of the state.

Consider the province of Quercy in 1623. Bypassing the previous arrangement by which the provincial estates granted tax revenues to the crown, the king had established the Election to collect taxes directly. The officers of the Election had bought their offices and gained their incomes from the taxes they brought in for the crown. Word spread, says the *Mercure*, that the region's powerful people would support a popular rising to abolish the Election. When the new officers came to take office,

> a certain Douat, a Quercy native . . . about fifty-five or so (who fooled with horoscopes, was a great physiognomist, and fortune-teller, and had always said he would die in action), having gone from parish to parish secretly agitating the populace, put himself into the field at the head of five thousand men, both peasants and other good-for-nothings who had been discharged from the armies since the peace. The specious pretext of this great rising was the establishment of the new Elections, by which they said the province would he overburdened with *tailles*, and with the salaries, benefits, fees for signing the rolls, and other revenues that had been assigned to the Election officers. Furthermore, that the richest people of the province, who had previously paid the heaviest *taille*, up to

three or four hundred livres, having bought the offices for their exemption from the *taille*, they would push the *taille* onto the little people, including the *pro rata* surtaxes which are now due on past and present assessments [*Mercure françois* 1623: 473–474].

The rebels attacked the houses of the new officers; their force grew to 16,000 men. But the military governor of Quercy attacked them near Cahors, broke them up, and captured their leaders.

The next day, the 8th of June, the Marshal had Douat and Barau [a second chief] taken to Figeac for trial. The Provost sentenced Douat to have his head cut off, his body quartered, and his head impaled on a post at Figeac, and also that his four quarters would be taken to four of the principal cities of Quercy and suspended there. This was done the same day [*Mercure françois* 1623: 477].

Barau was hanged in his hometown 10 days later. Thus the Quercy rebellion ended like many others, with a few of its leaders punished spectacularly and the fiscal power of the crown (not to mention the privileges of the bourgeois who had bought the royal offices) confirmed by military force.

Except through the presence of the profiteering bourgeoisie, the experience of Quercy in the 1620s does not trace the trajectory of expanding capitalism very clearly. It does, on the other hand, show the interplay of statemaking and popular collective action. Statemaking impinged deeply and directly on the interests of ordinary people. When they could, ordinary people resisted the threat to their interests. But time and military might were on the side of the statemakers; the people tried repeatedly, and lost repeatedly. Before long, their favored allies, the provincial nobility, had been checked as well. From that point on, such popular rebellions as occurred posed a diminishing threat to the state. In fact, as France rolled into the eighteenth century popular collective action against the state declined somewhat, and action against profiteering landlords and merchants became more prominent. Whereas in the seventeenth century the tax rebellion and the attack on occupying troops or grasping officials had been the more visible forms of popular resistance, the eighteenth century brought food riots, occupations of disputed land, and struggles against the landlord's exactions to the fore. Once we see that the food riots acted against merchants and officials who backed merchants and that the landlords who stirred up the greatest dissension were those who bought most eagerly into the expanding cash-crop market, the shift away from statemaking to capitalism as the focus of popular collective action becomes manifest. The changes in collective action responded sensitively to the trends of structural change.

Do not take this sketch of seventeenth-century France as a model for the historically grounded sociological analysis I am advocating. It lacks the painstaking confrontation of the sources with alternative interpretations in which historians excel. It lacks the explicit modeling, precise conceptualization, careful measurement, and deliberate comparison that are the emblems of good social-scientific work. It lacks the essential specification of the forms and changes of statemaking, capitalism, and collective action from one era to the next. Later chapters in this book – "War and Peasant Rebellion in Seventeenth-Century France," "How . . . to Study British Contention," and others – set out fragments of the approach that I have in mind. This preliminary sketch simply evokes the problem – to situate social processes in time and place. The work requires a permanent encounter of sociology and history.

## Bibliography

Barzun, Jacques, 1974, *Clio and the Doctors: Psycho-History, Quanto-History, and History*. Chicago: University of Chicago Press.

Bergesen, Albert (ed.), 1980, *Studies of the Modern World-System*. New York: Academic Press.

Braudel, Fernand, 1979, *Civilisation matérielle, économie, et capitalisme, XV$^e$–XVIII$^e$ siècle*. 3 vols. Paris: Colin.

Fogel, Robert William, 1975, "The limits of quantitative methods in history." *American Historical Review* 80: 329–350.

Fox-Genovese, Elizabeth, and Eugene Genovese, 1976, "The political crisis of social history." *Journal of Social History* 10: 205–221.

Gaunt, David, 1973, Historisk demografi eller demografisk historia? En Oversikt och ett debattinlagg om ett tvarventenskapligt dilemma." *Historisk Tidskrift* 1973: 382–405.

Genovese, Eugene D., 1975, "Concluding remarks." In Stanley L. Engerman and Eugene D. Genovese (eds.), *Race and Slavery in the Western Hemisphere. Quantitative Studies*. Princeton, N.J.: Princeton University Press.

Gunder Frank, André, 1972, "The development of underdevelopment." In James D. Cockcroft *et al.* (eds.), *Dependence and underdevelopment: Latin America's political economy*. Garden City, N.Y.: Doubleday.

Judt, Tony, 1979, "A clown in regal purple: Social history and the historians." *History Workshop* 7: 66–94.

Lichtman, Alan J., and Valerie French, 1978, *Historians and the Living Past*. Arlington Heights, Ill.: AHM Publishing Corp.

Lipset, Seymour Martin, 1968, History and sociology: Some methodological considerations. In Seymour M. Lipset and Richard Hofstadter (eds.), *Sociology and History: Methods*. New York: Basic Books.

McKeown, Thomas, 1976, *The Modern Rise of Population*. New York: Academic Press.

Palloix, Christian, 1971, *L'économie mondiale capitaliste*. 2 vols. "Economie et Socialisme," 16, 17. Paris: François Maspero.

Portes, Alejandro, and John Walton, 1981, *Labor, Class, and the International System*. New York: Academic Press.

Silbey, Joel H., Allan G. Bogue, and William H. Flanigan (eds.), 1978, *The History of American Electoral Behavior*. Princeton, N.J.: Princeton University Press.

Stedman Jones, Gareth, 1976, 'From historical sociology to theoretical history." *British Journal of Sociology* 27:295–305.

Stinchcombe, Arthur L., 1978, *Theoretical Methods in Social History*. New York: Academic Press.
Stone, Lawrence, 1977, "History and the social sciences in the twentieth century." In Charles F. Delzell (ed.), *The Future of History*. Nashville: Vanderbilt University Press.
Tocqueville, Alexis de, 1978, *Souvenirs*. Paris: Gallimard. [1850]
Topolski, Jerzy, 1976, *Methodology of History*. Warsaw: Polish Scientific Publishers; Dordrecht: D. Reidel.
Wallerstein, Immanuel, 1966, "Introduction" to Immanuel Wallerstein (ed.), *Social Change: The Colonial Situation*. New York: Wiley.
Wallerstein, Immanuel, 1974, *The Modern World-System: Capitalist Agriculture and the Origins of the European World-Economy in the Sixteenth Century*. New York: Academic Press.
Wallerstein, Immanuel, 1979, *The Capitalist World-Economy*. Cambridge: Cambridge University Press.
Wright, Gavin, 1978, *The Political Economy of the Cotton South: Households, Markets, and Wealth in the Nineteenth Century*. New York: W. W. Norton.

# 81

# Introduction to *Frame Analysis*

## *Erving Goffman*

There is a venerable tradition in philosophy that argues that what the reader assumes to be real is but a shadow, and that by attending to what the writer says about perception, thought, the brain, language, culture, a new methodology, or novel social forces, the veil can be lifted. That sort of line, of course, gives as much a role to the writer and his writings as is possible to imagine and for that reason is pathetic. (What can better push a book than the claim that it will change what the reader thinks is going on?) A current example of this tradition can be found in some of the doctrines of social psychology and the W. I. Thomas dictum: "If men define situations as real, they are real in their consequences." This statement is true as it reads but false as it is taken. Defining situations as real certainly has consequences, but these may contribute very marginally to the events in progress; in some cases only a slight embarrassment flits across the scene in mild concern for those who tried to define the situation wrongly. All the world is not a stage – certainly the theater isn't entirely. (Whether you organize a theater or an aircraft factory, you need to find places for cars to park and coats to be checked, and these had better be real places, which, incidentally, had better carry real insurance against theft.) Presumably, a "definition of the situation" is almost always to be found, but those who are in the situation ordinarily do not *create* this definition, even though their society often can be said to do so; ordinarily, all they do is to assess correctly what the situation ought to be for them and then act accordingly. True, we personally negotiate aspects of all the arrangements under which we live, but often once these are negotiated, we continue on mechanically as though the matter had always been settled. So, too, there are occasions when we must wait until things are almost over before discovering what has been occurring and occasions of our own activity when we can considerably put off deciding what to claim we have been doing. But surely these are not the only principles of organization. Social life is dubious enough and ludicrous enough without having to wish it further into unreality.

---

Source: Erving Goffman, *Frame Analysis*, (Harmondsworth: Penguin Press, 1975).

Within the terms, then, of the bad name that the analysis of social reality has, this book presents another analysis of social reality. I try to follow a tradition established by William James in his famous chapter "The Perception of Reality,"[1] first published as an article in *Mind* in 1869. Instead of asking what reality is, he gave matters a subversive phenomenological twist, italicizing the following question: *Under what circumstances do we think things are real?* The important thing about reality, he implied, is our sense of its realness in contrast to our feeling that some things lack this quality. One can then ask under what conditions such a feeling is generated, and this question speaks to a small, manageable problem having to do with the camera and not what it is the camera takes pictures of.

In his answer, James stressed the factors of selective attention, intimate involvement, and noncontradiction by what is otherwise known. More important, he made a stab at differentiating the several different "worlds" that our attention and interest can make real for us, the possible subuniverses, the "orders of existence" (to use Aron Gurwitsch's phrase), in each of which an object of a given kind can have its proper being: the world of the senses, the world of scientific objects, the world of abstract philosophical truths, the worlds of myth and supernatural beliefs, the madman's world, etc. Each of these subworlds, according to James, has "its own special and separate style of existence,"[2] and "each world, *whilst it is attended to*, is real after its own fashion; only the reality lapses with the attention."[3] Then, after taking this radical stand, James copped out; he allowed that the world of the senses has a special status, being the one we judge to be the realest reality, the one that retains our liveliest belief, the one before which the other worlds must give way.[4] James in all this agreed with Husserl's teacher, Brentano, and implied, as phenomenology came to do, the need to distinguish between the content of a current perception and the reality status we give to what is thus enclosed or bracketed within perception.[5]

James' crucial device, of course, was a rather scandalous play on the word "world" (or "reality"). What he meant was not *the* world but a particular person's current world – and, in fact, as will be argued, not even that. There was no good reason to use such billowy words. James opened a door; it let in wind as well as light.

In 1945 Alfred Schutz took up James' theme again in a paper called "On Multiple Realities."[6] His argument followed James' surprisingly closely, but more attention was given to the possibility of uncovering the conditions that must be fulfilled if we are to generate one realm of "reality," one "finite province of meaning," as opposed to another. Schutz added the notion, interesting but not entirely convincing, that we experience a special kind of "shock" when suddenly thrust from one "world," say, that of dreams, to another, such as that of the theater:

> There are as many innumerable kinds of different shock experiences as there are different finite provinces of meaning upon which I may bestow

> the accent of reality. Some instances are: the shock of falling asleep as the leap into the world of dreams; the inner transformation we endure if the curtain in the theater rises as the transition into the world of the stageplay; the radical change in our attitude if, before a painting, we permit our visual field to be limited by what is within the frame as the passage into the pictorial world; our quandary, relaxing into laughter, if, in listening to a joke, we are for a short time ready to accept the fictitious world of the jest as a reality in relation to which the world of our daily life takes on the character of foolishness; the child's turning toward his toy as the transition into the play-world; and so on. But also the religious experiences in all their varieties – for instance, Kierkegaard's experience of the "instant" as the leap into the religious sphere – are examples of such a shock, as well as the decision of the scientist to replace all passionate participation in the affairs of "this world" by a disinterested contemplative attitude.[7]

And although, like James, he assumed that one realm – the "working world" – had a preferential status, he was apparently more reserved than James about its objective character:

> We speak of provinces of *meaning* and not of subuniverses because it is the meaning of our experience and not the ontological structure of the objects which constitute reality,[8]

attributing its priority to ourselves, not the world:

> For we will find that the world of everyday life, the common-sense world, has a paramount position among the various provinces of reality, since only within it does communication with our fellow-men become possible. But the common-sense world is from the outset a sociocultural world, and the many questions connected with the intersubjectivity of the symbolic relations originate within it, are determined by it, and find their solution within it,[9]

and to the fact that our bodies always participate in the everyday world whatever our interest at the time, this participation implying a capacity to affect and be affected by the everyday world.[10] So instead of saying of a subuniverse that it is generated in accordance with certain structural principles, one says it has a certain "cognitive style."

Schutz's paper (and Schutz in general) was brought to the attention of ethnographic sociologists by Harold Garfinkel, who further extended the argument about multiple realities by going on (at least in his early comments) to look for rules which, when followed, allow us to generate a "world" of a given kind. Presumably a machine designed according to the proper specifications could grind out the reality of our choice. The conceptual attraction here is obvious. A game such as chess generates a habitable universe for those who can follow it, a plane of being, a cast of characters with a seemingly unlimited number of different situations and acts through which to realize their natures and destinies. Yet much of this is reducible to a small set of interdependent rules and practices. If the meaningfulness of everyday activity is similarly dependent on a closed, finite set of rules, then explication of them would give one a powerful means of analyzing social life. For example, one could then see (following Garfinkel) that the significance of certain deviant acts is that they undermine the intelligibility of everything else we had thought was going on around us, including all next acts, thus generating diffuse disorder. To uncover the informing, constitutive rules of everyday behavior would be to perform the sociologist's alchemy – the transmutation of any patch of ordinary social activity into an illuminating publication. It might be added that although James and Schutz are convincing in arguing that something like the "world" of dreams is differently organized from the world of everyday experience, they are quite unconvincing in providing any kind of account as to how many different "worlds" there are and whether everyday, wide-awake life can actually be seen as but one rule-produced plane of being, if so seen at all. Nor has there been much success in describing constitutive rules of everyday activity.[11] One is faced with the embarrassing methodological fact that the announcement of constitutive rules seems an open-ended game that any number can play forever. Players usually come up with five or ten rules (as I will), but there are no grounds for thinking that a thousand additional assumptions might not be listed by others. Moreover, these students neglect to make clear that what they are often concerned with is not an individual's sense of what is real, but rather what it is he can get caught up in, engrossed in, carried away by; and this can be something he can claim is really going on and yet claim is not real. One is left, then, with the structural similarity between everyday life – neglecting for a moment the possibility that no satisfactory catalog might be possible of what to include therein – and the various "worlds" of make-believe but no way of knowing how this relationship should modify our view of everyday life.

Interest in the James-Schutz line of thought has become active recently among persons whose initial stimulus came from sources not much connected historically with the phenomenological tradition: The work of those who created what has come to be called "the theater of the absurd," most fully exhibited in the analytical dramas of Luigi Pirandello. The very useful paper by Gregory Bateson, "A Theory of Play and Phantasy,"[12] in which he directly raised the question of unseriousness and seriousness, allowing us to see what a startling thing experience is, such that a bit of serious activity can be used as a model for putting together unserious versions of the same activity, and that, on occasion, we may not know whether it is play or the real thing that is occurring. (Bateson introduced his own version of the notion of "bracketing," a usable one, and also the argument that individuals can intentionally produce framing confusion in those with whom they are dealing; it is in Bateson's paper that the term "frame" was proposed in roughly the sense in which I want to employ it.)[13] The work of John Austin, who, following Wittgenstein,[14] suggested again that what we mean by "really happening" is complicated, and that although an individual may dream unrealities, it is still proper to say of him on that occasion that he is really dreaming.[15] (I have also drawn on the work of a student of Austin, D. S. Schwayder, and his fine book, *The Stratification of Behavior*.)[16] The efforts of those who study (or at least publish on) fraud, deceit, misidentification, and other "optical" effects, and the work of those who study "strategic interaction," including the way in which concealing and revealing bear upon definitions of the situation. The useful paper by Barney Glaser and Anselm Strauss, "Awareness Contexts and Social Interaction."[17] Finally, the modern effort in linguistically oriented disciplines to employ the notion of a "code" as a device which informs and patterns all events that fall within the boundaries of its application.

I have borrowed extensively from all these sources, claiming really only the bringing of them together. My perspective is situational, meaning here a concern for what one individual can be alive to at a particular moment, this often involving a few other particular individuals and not necessarily restricted to the mutually monitored arena of a face-to-face gathering. I assume that when individuals attend to any current situation, they face the question: "What is it that's going on here?" Whether asked explicitly, as in times of confusion and doubt, or tacitly, during occasions of usual certitude, the question is put and the answer to it is presumed by the way the individuals then proceed to get on with the affairs at hand. Starting, then, with that question, this volume attempts to limn out a framework that could be appealed to for the answer.

Let me say at once that the question "What is it that's going on here?" is considerably suspect. Any event can be described in terms of a focus that includes a wide swath or a narrow one and – as a related but not identical matter – in terms of a focus that is close-up or distant. And no one has a theory as to what particular span and level will come to be the ones employed. To begin with, I must be allowed to proceed by picking my span and level arbitrarily, without special justification.[18]

A similar issue is found in connection with perspective. When participant roles in an activity are differentiated – a common circumstance – the view that one person has of what is going on is likely to be quite different from that of another. There is a sense in which what is play for the golfer is work for the caddy. Different interests will – in Schutz's phrasing – generate different motivational relevancies. (Moreover, variability is complicated here by the fact that those who bring different perspectives to the "same" events are likely to employ different spans and levels of focus.) Of course, in many cases some of those who are committed to differing points of view and focus may still be willing to acknowledge that theirs is not the official or "real" one. Caddies work at golf, as do instructors, but both appreciate that their job is special, since it has to do with servicing persons engaged in play. In any case, again I will initially assume the right to pick my point of view, my motivational relevancies, only limiting this choice of perspective to one that participants would easily recognize to be valid.

Further, it is obvious that in most "situations" many different things are happening simultaneously – things that are likely to have begun at different moments and may terminate dissynchronously.[19] To ask the question "What is it that's going on here?" biases matters in the direction of unitary exposition and simplicity. This bias, too, I must be temporarily allowed.

So, too, to speak of the "current" situation (just as to speak of something going on "here") is to allow reader and writer to continue along easily in their impression that they clearly know and agree on what they are thinking about. The amount of time covered by "current" (just as the amount of space covered by "here") obviously can vary greatly from one occasion to the next and from one participant to another; and the fact that participants seem to have no trouble in quickly coming to the same apparent understanding in this matter does not deny the intellectual importance of our trying to find out what this apparent consensus consists of and how it is established. To speak of something happening before the eyes of observers is to be on firmer ground than usual in the social sciences; but the ground is still shaky, and the crucial question of how a seeming agreement was reached concerning the identity of the "something" and the inclusiveness of "before the eyes" still remains.

Finally, it is plain that retrospective characterization of the "same" event or social occasion may differ very widely, that an individual's role in an undertaking can provide him with a distinctive evaluative assessment of what sort of an instance of the type the particular undertaking was. In that sense it has been argued, for example, that opposing rooters at a football game do not experience the "same" game,[20] and that what makes a party a good one for a participant who is made much of is just what makes it a bad one for a participant who thereby is made little of.

All of which suggests that one should even be uneasy about the easy way in which it is assumed that participants in an activity can be terminologically identified and referred to without issue For surely, a "couple" kissing can also be a "man" greeting his "wife" or "John" being careful with "Mary's" makeup.

I only want to claim that although these questions are very important, they are not the only ones, and that their treatment is not necessarily required before one can proceed. So here, too, I will let sleeping sentences lie.

My aim is to try to isolate some of the basic frameworks of understanding available in our society for making sense out of events and to analyze the special vulnerabilities to which these frames of reference are subject. I start with the fact that from an individual's particular point of view, while one thing may momentarily appear to be what is really going on, in fact what is actually happening is plainly a joke, or a dream, or an accident or a mistake, or a misunderstanding, or a deception, or a theatrical performance, and so forth.

And attention will be directed to what it is about our sense of what is going on that makes it so vulnerable to the need for these various rereadings.

Elementary terms required by the subject matter to be dealt with are provided first. My treatment of these initial terms is abstract, and I am afraid the formulations provided are crude indeed by the standards of modern philosophy. The reader must initially bestow the benefit of mere doubt in order for us both to get to matters that (I feel) are less dubious.

The term "strip" will be used to refer to any arbitrary slice or cut from the stream of ongoing activity, including here sequences of happenings, real or fictive, as seen from the perspective of those subjectively involved in sustaining an interest in them. A strip is not meant to reflect a natural division made by the subjects of inquiry or an analytical division made by students who inquire; it will be used only to refer to any raw batch of occurrences (of whatever status in reality) that one wants to draw attention to as a starting point for analysis.

And of course much use will be made of Bateson's use of the term "frame." I assume that definitions of a situation are built up in accordance with principles of organization which govern events – at least social ones – and our subjective involvement in them; frame is the word I use to refer to such of these basic elements as I am able to identify. That is my definition of frame. My phrase "frame analysis" is a slogan to refer to the examination in these terms of the organization of experience.

In dealing with conventional topics, it is usually practical to develop concepts and themes in some sort of logical sequence: nothing coming earlier depends on something coming later, and, hopefully, terms developed at any one point are actually used in what comes thereafter. Often the complaint of the writer is that linear presentation constrains what is actually a circular affair, ideally requiring simultaneous introduction of terms, and the complaint of the reader is that concepts elaborately defined are not much used beyond the point at which the fuss is made about their meaning. In the analysis of frames, linear presentation is no great embarrassment. Nor is the defining of terms not used thereafter. The problem, in fact, is that once a term is introduced (this occurring at the point at which it is first needed), it begins to have too much bearing, not merely applying to what comes later, but reapplying in each chapter to what it has already applied to. Thus each succeeding section of the study becomes more entangled, until a step can hardly be made because of what must be carried along with it. The process closely follows the horrors of repetition songs, as if – in the case of frame analysis – what Old MacDonald had on his farm were partridge and juniper trees.

Discussions about frame inevitably lead to questions concerning the status of the discussion itself, because here terms applying to what is analyzed ought to apply to the analysis also. I proceed on the commonsense assumption that ordinary language and ordinary writing practices are sufficiently flexible to allow anything that one wants to express to get expressed.[21] Here I follow Carnap's position:

> The sentences, definitions, and rules of the syntax of a language are concerned with the forms of that language. But, now, how are these sentences, definitions, and rules themselves to be correctly expressed? Is a kind of super-language necessary for the purpose? And, again, a third language to explain the syntax of this super-language, and so on to infinity? Or is it possible to formulate the syntax of a language within that language itself? The obvious fear will arise that in the latter case, owing to certain reflexive definitions, contradictions of a nature seemingly similar to those which are familiar both in Cantor's theory of transfinite aggregates and in the pre-Russellian logic might make their appearance. But we shall see later that without any danger of contradictions or antinomies emerging it is possible to express the syntax of a language in that language itself, to an extent which is conditioned by the wealth of means of expression of the language in question.[22]

Thus, even if one took as one's task the examination of the use made in the humanities and the less robust sciences of "examples," "illustrations," and "cases in point," the object being to uncover the folk theories of evidence which underlie resort to these devices, it would still be the case that examples and illustrations would probably have to be used, and they probably could be without entirely vitiating the analysis.

In turning to the issue of reflexivity and in arguing that ordinary language is an adequate resource for discussing it, I do not mean that these particular linguistic matters should block all other concerns. Methodological self-consciousness that is full, immediate, and persistent sets aside all study and analysis except that of the reflexive problem itself, thereby displacing fields of inquiry instead of contributing to them. Thus, I will throughout use quotation marks to suggest a special sense of the word so marked and not concern myself systematically with the fact that this device is routinely used in a variety of quite different ways,[23] that these seem to bear closely on the question of frame, and that I must assume that the context of use will automatically lead my readers and me to have the same understanding, although neither I nor they might be able to explicate the matter further. So, too, with the warning and the lead that ordinary language philosophers have given us. I know that the crucial term "real" may have been permanently Wittgensteined into a blur of slightly different uses, but proceed on the assumption that carefulness can gradually bring us to an understanding of basic themes informing diversity, a diversity which carefulness itself initially establishes, and that what is taken for granted concerning the meaning of this word can safely so be done until it is convenient to attend to what one has been doing.

A further caveat. There are lots of good grounds for doubting the kind of analysis about to be presented. I would do so myself if it weren't my own. It is too bookish, too general, too removed from fieldwork to have a good chance of being anything more than another mentalistic adumbration. And, as will be noted throughout, there are certainly things that cannot be nicely dealt with in the arguments that follow. (I coin a series of terms – some "basic"; but writers have been doing that to not much avail for years.) Nonetheless, some of the things in this world seem to urge the analysis I am here attempting, and the compulsion is strong to try to outline the framework that will perform this job, even if this means some other tasks get handled badly.

Another disclaimer. This book is about the organization of experience – something that an individual actor can take into his mind – and not the organization of society. I make no claim whatsoever to be talking about the core matters of sociology – social organization and social structure. Those matters have been and can continue to be quite nicely studied without reference to frame at all. I am not addressing the structure of social life but the structure of experience individuals have at any moment of their social lives. I personally hold society to be first in every way and any individual's current involvements to be second; this report deals only with matters that are second. This book will have weaknesses enough in the areas it claims to deal with; there is no need to find limitations in regard to what it does not set about to cover. Of course, it can be argued that to focus on the nature of personal experiencing – with the implication this can have for giving equally serious consideration to all matters that might momentarily concern the individual – is itself a standpoint with marked political implications, and that these are conservative ones. The analysis developed does not catch at the differences between the advantaged and disadvantaged classes and can be said to direct attention away from such matters. I think that is true. I can only suggest that he who would combat false consciousness and awaken people to their true interests has much to do, because the sleep is very deep. And I do not intend here to provide a lullaby but merely to sneak in and watch the way the people snore.

Finally, a note about the materials used. First, there is the fact that I deal again in this book with what I have dealt with in others – another go at analyzing fraud, deceit, con games, shows of various kinds, and the like. There are many footnotes to and much repetition of other things I've written.[24] I am trying to order my thoughts on these topics, trying to construct a general statement. That is the excuse.

Second, throughout the book very considerable use is made of anecdotes cited from the press and from popular books in the biographical genre.[25] There could hardly be data with less face value. Obviously, passing events that are typical or representative don't make news just for that reason; only extraordinary ones do, and even these are subject to the editorial violence routinely employed by gentle writers. Our understanding of the world precedes these stories, determining which ones reporters will select and how the ones that are selected will be told. Human interest stories are a caricature of evidence in the very degree of their interest, providing a unity, coherence, pointedness, self-completeness, and drama only crudely sustained, if at all, by everyday living. Each is a cross between an *experimentum crucim* and a sideshow. That is their point. The design of these reported events is fully responsive to our demands

– which are not for facts but for typifications. Their telling demonstrates the power of our conventional understandings to cope with the bizarre potentials of social life, the furthest reaches of experience. What appears, then, to be a threat to our way of making sense of the world turns out to be an ingeniously selected defense of it. We press these stories to the wind; they keep the world from unsettling us. By and large, I do not present these anecdotes, therefore, as evidence or proof, but as clarifying depictions, as frame fantasies which manage, through the hundred liberties taken by their tellers, to celebrate our beliefs about the workings of the world. What was put into these tales is thus what I would like to get out of them.

These data have another weakness. I have culled them over the years on a hit-or-miss basis using principles of selection mysterious to me which, furthermore, changed from year to year and which I could not recover if I wanted to. Here, too, a caricature of systematic sampling is involved.

In addition to clippings as a source of materials, I draw on another, one as questionable as the first. Since this study attempts to deal with the organization of experience as such, whether "actual" or of the other kinds, I will have recourse to the following: cartoons, comics, novels, the cinema, and especially, it turns out, the legitimate stage. I am here involved in no horrors of bias different from the ones already exhibited in the selection of bits of human interest news. But I am led to draw on materials that writers in other traditions use, whether in literary and dramatic criticism of current "high" culture or in the sort of sociological journalism which attempts to read from surface changes in commercially available vicarious experience to the nature of our society at large. In consequence, many of the things I have to say about these materials will have already been said many times and better by fashionable writers. My excuse for brazenly dipping into this preempted domain is that I have a special interest, one that does not recognize a difference in value between a good novel and a bad one, a contemporary play or an ancient one, a comic strip or an opera. All are equally useful in explicating the character of strips of experienced activity. I end up quoting from well-known works recognized as setting standards, and from minor works current at the time of writing, but not because I think these examples of their genre have special cultural worth and warrant endorsement. Critics and reviewers cite the classics of a genre in dealing with current works in order to explicate what if anything is significant and artful in them. I draw clumsily on the same materials – as well as critiques of them – simply because that is what is easy to hand. Indeed, these materials are easy to everyone's hand, providing something of a common fund of familiar experience, something that writers can assume readers know about.

\* \* \* \* \* \*

That is the introduction. Writing one allows a writer to try to set the terms of what he will write about. Accounts, excuses, apologies designed to reframe what follows after them, designed to draw a line between deficiencies in what the author writes and deficiencies in himself, leaving him, he hopes, a little better defended than he might otherwise be.[26] This sort of ritual work can certainly disconnect a hurried pedestrian from a minor inconvenience he might cause a passing stranger. Just as certainly, such efforts are optimistic when their purpose is to recast the way in which a long book is to be taken. (And more optimistic still in the case of a second edition's preface to an already prefaced edition, this being an attempt to recast a recasting.)

\* \* \* \* \* \*

But what about comments on prefaces? Where does such a topic taken up at such a point leave the writer and the reader (or a speaker and an audience)? Does that sort of talk strike at the inclination of the reader to discount or criticize prefacing as an activity? And if it turns out that the preface was written in bad faith, tailored from the beginning to exemplify this use that will have come to be made of it? Will the preface then be retrospectively reframed by the reader into something that really isn't a preface at all but an inappropriately inserted illustration of one? Or if an admission of bad faith is made unconvincingly, leaving open the possibility that the disclosure was an afterthought? What then?

\* \* \* \* \* \*

And does the last comment excuse me in any degree from having been puerile and obvious in commenting on prefaces, as when, in a book analyzing jokes, the writer is excused the badness of the cited jokes but not the badness of the analysis of them? (A novelist who nowadays injects direct address in the body of his work – "Dear Reader, if you've gone this far, you'll know I hate that character . . ." – easily fails to change the footing we allow him; but what if he writes that he would like to succeed in such a device but knows we will not let him?)

\* \* \* \* \* \*

And what about discussions about being puerile and obvious? A word incorrectly spelled can, I think, be successfully used by the misspeller as an illustration of incorrect spelling and analyzed as such. But can a writer posture in his writing and then effectively claim that all along he was only providing an illustration of bad taste and lack of sophistication? Would it be necessary for him to show, and if so, how would he, that his claims were not merely a device hit upon after the fact to make the best out of what he was not able to prevent from being a bad thing?

\* \* \* \* \* \*

And if in the first pages after acknowledging colleagues who had helped, I had said: "Richard C. Jeffrey, on the other hand, did not help." And if I had gone on here (in these later pages) to suggest that the aim had been to make a little joke and incidentally bring awareness to a tacit constraint on acknowledgment writing? Then the explication of this aim could be seen as bad faith – either a post-hoc effort to hedge on having tried to be witty or an admission of having entrapped the reader into accepting a plant, that is, a statement whose reason for inclusion would later be shown to have not been apparent. But if, as is in fact the case, the whole matter is enclosed as a question within a section of the introduction dealing with a consideration of introductions and is therefore not to be seen as having an initial character as a simple, straightforward introduction, what then?

And after all of this, can I get the point across that Richard C. Jeffrey in fact didn't help? Does this last sentence do it? And if so, had a conditional been used, as in: "And after all of this, could I get the point across . . . etc." What then? And would this last comment transform an assertion into an illustration and so once again cast the matter of Richard C. Jeffrey in doubt?

\* \* \* \* \* \*

And if the preface and the comments on the preface and the comments on the comments on the preface are put in question, what about the asterisks which divide up and divide off the various sections in which this is managed? And if the orthography had still been intact, would this last question itself have undermined these framing devices, including the ones which bracket this sentence with the prior one?

\* \* \* \* \* \*

And if above I had said: "What about the \* \* \* \* \* \* which divide up and divide off . . ."; would this be a proper use of print, and can an easy rule be formulated? Given the motivational relevancies of orthographers, a book on orthography can properly use a batch of print to illustrate print, to the neglect of saying something with its meaning. Similarly, a geography book can properly switch from words to maps. But when a mystery writer has his hero find a coded message on a torn bit of paper and then shows the clue to the reader by insetting it in the center of the page as though it were a map in a geography book, so that the reader sees the tear as well as the message, what sort of shift to a nonfictional frame has the writer asked the reader to make, and was he quite within his rights to ask it? Is it overly cute for an anthropologist reporting on the role of metaphor (with special reference to animal sources) to write, "One always feels a bit sheepish, of course, about bringing the metaphor concept into the social sciences and perhaps that is because one always feels there is something soft and wooly about it"?[27] Similarly, if I try to get dodgy with prefaces, is this not different from writing about tricks done with prefaces (which characteristically need not be undertaken at the beginning of a study)? Is this not the difference between doing and writing about the doing? And in considering all of these matters, can I properly draw on my own text ("And if above I had said: 'What about the * * * * * * that divide up and divide off . . .'; would this be . . .") as an illustration? And in this last sentence has not all need to be hesitant about the right to use actual asterisks disappeared, for after all, a doubtful usage cited as an example of doubtful usage ceases to be something that is doubtful to print?

\* \* \* \* \* \*

And if I wanted to comment on the next to last sentence, the one containing a parenthesized quoted sentence and questionably real asterisks, could I quote *that* sentence effectively, that is, employ the apparently required punctuation marks and yet allow the reader an easy comprehension of what was being said about what? Would the limits of doing things in print have been reached?

\* \* \* \* \* \*

That is what frame analysis is about.

### Notes

1. William James, *Principles of Psychology*, vol. 2 (New York: Dover Publications, 1950), chap. 21, pp. 283–324. Here, as throughout, italics in quoted materials are as in the original.
2. *Ibid.*, p. 291.
3. *Ibid.*, p. 293.
4. James' interest in the varieties-of-worlds problem was not fleeting. In his *Varieties of Religious Experience* (New York: Longmans, Green & Co., 1902) he approached the same question but through a different route.
5. "But who does not see that in a disbelieved or doubted or interrogative or conditional proposition, the ideas are combined in the same identical way in which they are in a proposition which is solidly believed" (James, *Principles of Psychology*, 2: 286). Aron Gurwitsch in his *The Field of Consciousness* (Pittsburgh: Duquesne University Press, 1964) makes a similar comment in a discussion of Husserl:

> Among such characters we mentioned those concerning modes of presentation, as when a thing is one time perceived, another time remembered or merely imagined, or when a certain state of affairs (the identical matter of a proposition) is asserted or denied, doubted, questioned, or deemed probable. [p. 327]

6. First appearing in *Philosophy and Phenomenological Research*, V (1945): 533–576; reprinted in his *Collected Papers*, 3 vols. (The Hague: Martinus Nijhoff, 1962), 1: 207–259.) A later version is "The Stratification of the Life-World," in Alfred Schutz and Thomas Luckmann, *The Structures of the Life-World*, trans., Richard M. Zaner and H. Tristram Engelhardt, Jr. (Evanston, Ill.: Northwestern University Press, 1973), pp. 21–98. An influential treatment of Schutz's ideas is Peter L. Berger and Thomas Luckmann, *The Social Construction of Reality* (Garden City, N.Y.: Doubleday & Company, Anchor Books, 1966).

7. Schutz, *Collected Papers*, 1: 231.

8. *Ibid.*, p. 230. See also Alfred Schutz, *Reflections on the Problem of Relevance*, ed. Richard M. Zaner (New Haven, Conn.: Yale University Press, 1970), p. 125. On matters Schutzian I am indebted to Richard Grathoff.

9. From "Symbol, Reality, and Society," Schutz, *Collected Papers*, 1: 294.

10. *Ibid.*, p. 342.

11. Schutz's various pronouncements seem to have hypnotized some students into treating them as definitive rather than suggestive. His version of the "cognitive style" of everyday life he states as follows:

   1. a specific tension of consciousness, namely, wide-awakeness, originating in full attention to life;
   2. a specific *epoché*, namely suspension of doubt;
   3. a prevalent form of spontaneity, namely working (a meaningful spontaneity based upon a project and characterized by the intention of bringing about the projected state of affairs by bodily movements gearing into the outer world);
   4. a specific form of experiencing one's self (the working self as the total self);
   5. a specific form of sociality (the common intersubjective world of communication and social action);
   6. a specific time-perspective (the standard time originating in an interaction between *durée* and cosmic time as the universal temporal structure of the intersubjective world).

   These are at least some of the features of the cognitive style belonging to this particular province of meaning. As long as our experiences of this world – the valid as well as the invalidated ones – partake of this style we may consider this province of meaning as real, we may bestow upon it the accent of reality. [*Ibid.*, pp. 230–231.]

12. *Psychiatric Research Reports 2*, American Psychiatric Association (December 1955), pp. 39–51. Now reprinted in his *Steps to an Ecology of Mind* (New York: Ballantine Books, 1972), pp. 177–193. A useful exegesis is William F. Fry, Jr., *Sweet Madness: A Study of Humor* (Palo Alto, Calif.: Pacific Books, 1968).

13. Edward T. Cone, in the first chapter of his *Musical Form and Musical Performance* (New York: W. W. Norton & Company, 1968), quite explicitly uses the term "frame" in much the same way that Bateson does and suggests some of the same lines of inquiry, but I think quite independently.

14. See, for example, Ludwig Wittgenstein, *Philosophical Investigations*, trans. G. E. M. Anscombe (Oxford: Basil Blackwell, 1958), pt. 2, sec. 7.

15. See, for example, chap. 7 in his *Sense and Sensibilia* (Oxford: Oxford University Press, 1962).

16. London: Routledge & Kegan Paul, 1965.

17. *American Sociological Review*, XXIX (1964): 669–679.

18. See the discussion by Emanuel A. Schegloff, "Notes on a Conversational Practice: Formulating Place," in David Sudnow, ed., *Studies in Social Interaction* (New York: The Free Press, 1972), pp. 75–119. There is a standard criticism of "role" as a concept which presents the same argument.

19. Nicely described by Roger G. Barker and Herbert F. Wright, *Midwest and Its Children* (Evanston, Ill.: Row, Peterson & Company, 1964), chap. 7, "Dividing the Behavior Stream," pp. 225–273.

20. Presented perhaps overstrongly in a well-known early paper by Albert H. Hastorf and Hadley Cantril, "They Saw a Game: A Case Study," *Journal of Abnormal and Social Psychology*, XLIX (1954): 129–234.

21. *Wovan man nicht sprechen kann, ist nicht der satz, "Wovan man nicht sprechen kann, darüber muss man schweigen."*

22. Rudolf Carnap, *The Logical Syntax of Language*, trans. Amethe Smeaton (London: Kegan Paul, Trench, Trubner & Co., 1937), p. 3.

23. I. A. Richards, for example, has a version in his *How to Read a Page* (New York: W. W. Norton & Company, 1942):

> We all recognize – more or less unsystematically – that quotation marks serve varied purposes:
>
> 1. Sometimes they show merely that we are quoting and where our quotation begins and ends.
> 2. Sometimes they imply that the word or words within them are in some way open to question and are only to be taken in some special sense with reference to some special definition.
> 3. Sometimes they suggest further that what is quoted is nonsense or that there is really no such thing as the thing they profess to name.
> 4. Sometimes they suggest that the words are improperly used. The quotation marks are equivalent to *the so-called*.
> 5. Sometimes they only indicate that we are talking of the words as distinguished from their meanings. "Is" and "at" are shorter than "above." "Chien" means what "dog" means, and so forth.
>
> There are many other uses. . . . [p. 66]

24. So much so that I use source abbreviations, a list of which can be found on p. xi.

25. An analysis of incidentally published stories – "fillers" – is provided by Roland Barthes along with an exhibition of literary license in "Structure of *Fait-Divers*," in his *Critical Essays*, trans. Richard Howard (Evanston, Ill.: Northwestern University Press, 1972), pp. 185–195.

26. There is a useful article by Jacob Brackman called "The Put-On" (*The New Yorker*, June 24, 1967, pp. 34–73). In his twelve-page introduction to the paperback edition he writes:

> Updating. If "updating" this essay were to mean exchanging more current jokes and performers for ones since disappeared, and appending how there came to be "put-on" head boutiques, and TV game shows, and a Sears Put-On clothing

shop, and publishers crowing "This is the novel that makes you ask: *Is the author putting me on?*", and thousands of winkful commercials that seemed to say, "I know that you know that I'm trying to sell you. Let's you and me both goof on the product together." – if I were to "update" along these lines, and if I were to add little exegeses of Tiny Tim's wedding, Paul Morrissey's movies, Paul McCartney's death, then the piece would begin to stink of inauthenticity. . . .

I think you must let a piece like this stand – not in its syntax, necessarily, but within the limits of its original awareness – as a fragment of cultural history. It may have been valid to the precise present for a matter of months, or days; who will quibble now that time is so short? Once the vision's devoured, mulched and incorporated, unless it has been frozen somewhere, its moment – when only so much had happened, when only so much had been revealed – is lost forever. All we have left are "updated" reports, grotesquely stretched, debased and freshened up, as what played itself out between haircuts is made to seem the rage of a decade. If I were to do this piece today (which would itself be impossible) hardly anything in it would stay the same. Of things in the real world about which one can try to write, sensibility may be the slipperiest. If I won't write the new piece now, how can I go back and meddle with the old one? [*The Put-On* (New York: Bantam Books, 1972), pp. 10–11.]

Brackman also argues that current items of cultural interest date very rapidly and fully, and, by implication, that writings concerned with these items will date quickly, too. He also suggests that the point of such writings is to bring the not quite consciously appreciated to awareness, and to do this first, and that once again a restatement or republication will sound stale. All of this I think has some truth and correctly describes the contingencies of that kind of subject matter, there being inevitably an unstated element of the reader's interest that derives from the current interest of the item. This element will decline rather quickly, leaving the writer having written something that can no longer be read with interest. In fact, every analyst of jokes has faced this problem, since the current version of a basic joke which he writes about today will sound very dated tomorrow. But given what Brackman is stuck with reprinting, his introduction does the framing work that introductions can do to segregate the producer from his product, in this case arguing that the piece was an expression of his sensibility *then*, not now.

27. James W. Fernandez, "Persuasions and Performances: Of the Beast in Every Body . . . And the Metaphors of Everyman," *Daedalus*, Winter 1972, p. 41.

# 82

# What is Ethnomethodology?

*Harold Garfinkel*

The following studies seek to treat practical activities, practical circumstances, and practical sociological reasoning as topics of empirical study, and by paying to the most commonplace activities of daily life the attention usually accorded extraordinary events, seek to learn about them as phenomena in their own right. Their central recommendation is that the activities whereby members produce and manage settings of organized everyday affairs are identical with members' procedures for making those settings "accountable." The "reflexive," or "incarnate" character of accounting practices and accounts makes up the crux of that recommendation. When I speak of accountable my interests are directed to such matters as the following. I mean observable-and-reportable, *i.e.* available to members as situated practices of looking-and-telling. I mean, too, that such practices consist of an endless, ongoing, contingent accomplishment; that they are carried on under the auspices of, and are made to happen as events in, the same ordinary affairs that in organizing they describe; that the practices are done by parties to those settings whose skill with, knowledge of, and entitlement to the detailed work of that accomplishment – whose competence – they obstinately depend upon, recognize, use, and take for granted; and *that* they take their competence for granted itself furnishes parties with a setting's distinguishing and particular features, and of course it furnishes them as well as resources, troubles, projects, and the rest.

Some structurally equivocal features of the methods and results by persons doing sociology, lay and professional, of making practical activities observable were epitomized by Helmer and Rescher.[1] When members' accounts of everyday activities are used as prescriptions with which to locate, to identify, to analyze, to classify, to make recognizable, or to find one's way around in comparable occasions, the prescriptions, they observe, are law-like, spatiotemporally restricted, and "loose." By "loose" is meant that though they are intendedly conditional in their logical form, "the nature of the conditions is such that they can often not be spelled out completely or fully." The authors cite as an example

---

Source: Harold Garfinkel, *Studies in Ethnomethodology*, (Englewood Cliffs: Prentice-Hall, 1967).

a statement about sailing fleet tactics in the 18th century. They point out the statement carries as a test condition reference to the state of naval ordnance.

> In elaborating conditions (under which such a statement would hold) the historian delineates what is typical of the place and period. The full implications of such reference may be vast and inexhaustible; for instance . . . ordnance soon ramifies *via* metal working technology into metallurgy, mining, etc. Thus, the conditions which are operative in the formulation of an historical law may only be indicated in a general way, and are not necessarily, indeed, in most cases cannot be expected to be exhaustively articulated. This characteristic of such laws is here designed as *looseness*. . . .
>
> A consequence of the looseness of historical laws is that they are not universal, but merely quasi-general in that they admit of exceptions. Since the conditions delimiting the area of application of the law are often not exhaustively articulated, a supposed violation of the law may be explicable by showing that a legitimate, but as yet unformulated, precondition of the law's applicability is not fulfilled in the case under consideration.

Consider that this holds in every *particular* case, and holds not by reason of the meaning of "quasi-law," but because of investigators' actual, particular practices.

Further, Helmer and Rescher point out,

> The laws may be taken to contain a tacit caveat of the "usually" or "other things being equal" type. An historical law is thus not strictly universal in that it must be taken as applicable to all cases falling within the scope of its explicitly formulated or formulable conditions; rather, it may be thought to formulate relationships which obtain generally, or better, which obtain "as a rule."
>
> Such a "law" we will term *quasi-law*. In order for the law to be valid it is not necessary that no apparent exceptions occur. It is only necessary that, if an apparent exception should occur, an adequate explanation be forthcoming, an explanation demonstrating the exceptional characteristic of the case in hand by establishing the violation of an appropriate, if hitherto unformulated, condition of the law's applicability.

These and other features can be cited for the cogency with which they describe members' accounting practices. Thus: (1) Whenever a member is required to demonstrate that an account analyzes an actual situation, he invariably makes use of the practices of "et cetera," "unless," and "let it pass" to demonstrate the rationality of his achievement. (2) The definite and sensible character of the matter that is being reported is settled by an assignment that reporter and auditor make to each other that each will have furnished whatever unstated understandings are required. Much therefore of what is actually reported is not mentioned. (3) Over the time for their delivery accounts are apt to require that "auditors" be willing to wait for what will have been said in order that the present significance of what has been said will have become clear. (4) Like conversations, reputations, and careers, the particulars of accounts are built up step by step over the actual uses of and references to them. (5) An account's materials are apt to depend heavily for sense upon their serial placement, upon their relevance to the auditor's projects, or upon the developing course of the organizational occasions of their use.

In short, *recognizable* sense, or fact, or methodic character, or impersonality, or objectivity of accounts are not independent of the socially organized occasions of their use. Their rational features *consist* of what members do with, what they "make of" the accounts in the socially organized actual occasions of their use. Members' accounts are reflexively and essentially tied for their rational features to the socially organized occasions of their use for they are *features* of the socially organized occasions of their use.

That tie establishes the central topic of our studies: the rational accountability of practical actions as an ongoing, practical accomplishment. I want to specify the topic by reviewing three of its constituent, problematic phenomena. Wherever studies of practical action and practical reasoning are concerned, these consist of the following: (1) the unsatisfied programmatic distinction between and substitutability of objective (context free) for indexical expressions; (2) the "uninteresting" essential reflexivity of accounts of practical actions; and (3) the analyzability of actions-in-context as a practical accomplishment.

### The Unsatisfied Programmatic Distinction Between and Substitutability of Objective for Indexical Expressions

Properties that are exhibited by accounts (by reason of their being features of the socially organized occasions of their use) are available from studies by logicians as the properties of indexical expressions and indexical sentences. Husserl[2] spoke of expressions whose sense cannot be decided by an auditor without his necessarily knowing or assuming something about the biography and the purposes of the user of the expression, the circumstances of the utterance, the previous course of the conversation, or the particular relationship of actual or potential interaction that exists between the expressor and the auditor. Russell[3] observed that descriptions involving them apply on each occasion of use to only one thing, but to different things on different occasions. Such expressions, wrote Goodman,[4] are used to make unequivocal statements that nevertheless seem to change in truth value. Each of their utterances, "tokens," constitutes a word and refers to a certain person, time, or place, but names something not named by some replica of the word. Their denotation is relative to the speaker. Their use depends upon the relation of the user to the object with which the word is concerned. Time for a temporal indexical expression is relevant to what it names. Similarly, just what region a spatial indexical expression names depends upon the location of its utterance. Indexical expressions and statements containing them are not freely repeatable; in a given discourse, not all their replicas therein are also translations of them. The list can be extended indefinitely.

Virtually unanimous agreement exists among students of practical sociological reasoning, laymen and professionals, about the properties of indexical expressions and indexical actions. Impressive agreement exists as well (1) that although indexical expressions "are of enormous utility" they are "awkward for formal discourse"; (2) that a distinction between objective expressions and indexical expressions is not only procedurally proper but unavoidable for whosoever would do science; (3) that without the distinction between objective and indexical expressions, and without the preferred use of objective expressions the victories of generalizing, rigorous, scientific inquiries – logic, mathematics, some of the physical sciences – are unintelligible, the victories would fail, and the inexact sciences would have to abandon their hopes; (4) that the exact sciences are distinguishable from the inexact sciences by the fact that in the case of the exact sciences the distinction between and substitution of objective for indexical expressions for problem formulation, methods, findings, adequate demonstration, adequate evidence and the rest is both an actual task and an actual achievement, whereas in the case of the inexact sciences the availability of the distinction and substitutability to actual tasks, practices, and results remains unrealizably programmatic; (5) that the distinction between objective and indexical expressions, insofar as the distinction consists of inquirers' tasks, ideals, norms, resources, achievements, and the rest describes the difference between sciences and arts – e.g., between biochemistry and documentary filming; (6) that terms and sentences can be distinguished as one or the other in accordance with an assessment procedure that makes decidable their character as indexical or objective expressions; and (7) that in any particular case only practical difficulties prevent the substitution by an objective expression for an indexical expression.

Features of indexical expressions motivate endless methodological studies directed to their remedy. Indeed, attempts to rid the practices of a science of these nuisances lends to each science its distinctive character of preoccupation and productivity with methodological issues. Research practitioners' studies of practical activities of a science, whatever their science, afford them endless occasions to deal rigorously with indexical expressions.

Areas in the social sciences where the promised distinction and promised substitutability occur are countless. The promised distinction and substitutability are supported by and themselves support immense resources directed to developing methods for the strong analysis of practical actions and practical reasoning. Promised applications and benefits are immense.

Nevertheless, *wherever practical actions are topics of study* the promised distinction and substitutability of objective for indexical expressions remains programmatic in every *particular* case and in every *actual* occasion in which the distinction or substitutability must be demonstrated. In every actual case without exception, conditions will be cited that a competent investigator will be required to recognize, such that in *that* particular case the terms of the demonstration can be relaxed and nevertheless the demonstration be counted an adequate one.

We learn from logicians and linguists, who are in virtually unanimous agreement about them, what some of these conditions are. For "long" texts, or "long" courses of action, for events where members' actions are features of the events their actions are accomplishing, or wherever tokens are not used or are not suitable as proxies for indexical expressions, the program's claimed demonstrations are satisfied as matters of practical social management.

Under such conditions indexical expressions, by reason of their prevalence and other properties, present immense, obstinate, and irremediable nuisances to the tasks of dealing rigorously with the phenomena of structure and relevance in theories of consistency proofs and computability, and in attempts to recover actual as compared with supposed common conduct and common talk with full structural particulars. Drawing upon their experience in the uses of sample surveys, and the design and application of measurements of practical actions, statistical analyses, mathematical models, and computer simulations of social processes, professional sociologists are able to document endlessly the ways in which the programmatic distinction and substitutability is satisfied in, and depends upon, professional practices of socially managed demonstration.

In short, wherever studies of practical actions are involved, the distinction and substitutability is always accomplished *only* for all practical purposes. Thereby, the first problematic phenomenon is recommended to consist of the reflexivity of the practices and attainments of sciences in and of the organized activities of everyday life, which is an essential reflexivity.

### The "Uninteresting" Essential Reflexivity of Accounts

For members engaged in practical sociological reasoning – as we shall see in later studies, for staff personnel at the Los Angeles Suicide Prevention Center, for staff users of psychiatric clinic folders at UCLA, for graduate student coders of psychiatric records, for jurors, for an intersexed person managing a sex change, for professional sociological researchers – their concerns are for what is decidable "for practical purposes," "in light of this situation," "given the nature of actual circumstances," and the like. Practical circumstances and practical actions refer for them to many organizationally important and serious matters: to resources, aims, excuses, opportunities, tasks, and of course to grounds for arguing or foretelling the adequacy of procedures and of the findings they yield. One matter, however, is excluded from their interests: practical actions and practical circumstances are not in themselves *a* topic, let alone a sole topic of their inquiries; nor are their inquiries, addressed to the tasks of sociological theorizing, undertaken to formulate what these tasks consist of as practical actions. In no case is the investigation of practical actions undertaken in order that personnel might be able to recognize and describe what they are doing in the first place. Least of all are practical actions investigated in order to explain to practitioners their own talk about what they are doing. For example personnel at the Los Angeles Suicide Prevention Center found it altogether incongruous to consider seriously that they be so engaged in the work of certifying mode of death that a person seeking to commit suicide, and they could concert their efforts to assure the unequivocal recognition of "what really happened."

To say they are "not interested" in the study of practical actions is not to complain, nor to point to an opportunity they miss, nor is it a disclosure of error, nor is it an ironic comment. Neither is it the case that because members are "not interested" that they are "precluded" from sociological theorizing. Nor do their inquiries preclude the use of the rule of doubt, nor are they precluded from making the organized activities of everyday life scientifically problematical, nor does the comment insinuate a difference between "basic" and "applied" interests in research and theorizing.

What does it mean then to say that they are "not interested" in studying practical actions and practical sociological reasoning? And what is the import of such a statement?

There is a feature of members' accounts that for them is of such singular and prevailing relevance that it controls other features in their specific character as recognizable, rational features of practical sociological inquiries. The feature is this. With respect to the problematic character of practical actions and to the practical adequacy of their inquiries, members take for granted that a member must at the outset "know" the settings in which he is to operate if his practices are to serve as measures to bring particular, located features of these settings to recognizable account. They treat as the most passing matter of fact that members' accounts, of every sort, in all their logical modes, with all of their uses, and for every method for their assembly are constituent features of the settings they make observable. Members know, require, count on, and make use of this reflexivity to produce, accomplish, recognize, or demonstrate rational-adequacy-for-all-practical-purposes of their procedures and findings.

Not only do members – the jurors and the others – take that reflexivity for granted, but they recognize, demonstrate, and make observable for each other the rational character of their actual, and that means their occasional, practices while respecting that reflexivity as an unalterable and unavoidable condition of their inquiries.

When I propose that members are "not interested" in studying practical actions, I do not mean that members will have none, a little, or a lot of it. That they are "not interested" has to do with reasonable practices, with plausible argument, and with reasonable findings. It has to do with treating "accountable-for-all-practical-purposes" as a discoverable matter, exclusively, only, and entirely. For members to be "interested" would consist of their undertaking to make the "reflexive" character of practical activities observable; to examine the artful practices of rational inquiry as organizational phenomena without thought for correctives or irony. Members of the Los Angeles Suicide Prevention Center are like members wherever they engage in practical sociological inquiries: though they would, they *can* have none of it.

## The Analyzability of Actions-In-Context as a Practical Accomplishment

In indefinitely many ways members' inquiries are constituent features of the settings they analyze. In the same ways, their inquiries are made recognizable to members as adequate-for-all-practical-purposes. For example, at the Los Angeles Suicide Prevention Center, that deaths are made accountable-for-all-practical-purposes are practical organizational accomplishments. Organizationally, the Suicide Prevention Center consists of practical procedures for accomplishing the rational accountability of suicidal deaths as recognizable features of the settings in which that accountability occurs.

In the actual occasions of interaction that accomplishment is for members omnipresent, unproblematic, and commonplace. For members doing sociology, to make that accomplishment a topic of practical sociological inquiry seems unavoidably to require that they treat the rational properties of practical activities as "anthropologically strange." By this I mean to call attention to "reflexive" practices such as the following: that by his accounting practices the member makes familiar, commonplace activities of everyday life recognizable *as* familiar, commonplace activities; that on each occasion that an account of common activities is used, that they be recognized for "another first time"; that the member treat the processes and attainments of "imagination" as continuous with the *other* observable features of the settings in which they occur; and of proceeding in such a way that at the same time that the member "in the midst" of witnessed actual settings recognizes that witnessed settings have an *accomplished* sense, an accomplished facticity, an accomplished objectivity, an accomplished familiarity, an accomplished accountability, for the member the organizational hows of these accomplishments are unproblematic, are known vaguely, and are known only in the doing which is done skillfully, reliably, uniformly, with enormous standardization and as an unaccountable matter.

That accomplishment consists of members doing, recognizing, and using ethnographies. In unknown ways that accomplishment is for members a commonplace phenomenon. And in the unknown ways that the accomplishment is commonplace it is for our interests, an awesome phenomenon, for in its unknown ways it consists (1) of members' uses of concerted everyday activities as methods with which to recognize and demonstrate the isolatable, typical, uniform, potential repetition, connected appearance, consistency equivalence, substitutability, directionality, anonymously describable, planful – in short, the rational properties of indexical expressions and indexical actions. (2) The phenomenon consists, too, of the analyzability of actions-in-context given that not only does no concept of context-in-general exist, but every use of "context" without exception is itself essentially indexical.

The *recognizedly* rational properties of their common sense inquiries – their recognizedly consistent, or methodic, or uniform, or planful, etc. character – are *somehow* attainments of members' concerted activities. For Suicide Prevention Center staff, for coders, for jurors the rational properties of their practical inquiries *somehow* consist in the concerted work of making evident from fragments, from proverbs, from passing remarks, from rumors, from partial descriptions, from "codified" but essentially vague catalogues of experience and the like how a person died in society, or by what criteria patients were selected for psychiatric treatment, or which among the alternative verdicts was correct. *Somehow* is the problematic crux of the matter.

## What is Ethnomethodology?

The earmark of practical sociological reasoning, wherever it occurs, is that it seeks to remedy the indexical properties of members' talk and conduct. Endless methodological studies are directed to the tasks of providing members a remedy for indexical expressions in members' abiding attempts, with rigorous uses of ideals to demonstrate the observability of organized activities in actual occasions with situated particulars of talk and conduct.

The properties of indexical expressions and indexical actions are ordered properties. These consist of organizationally demonstrable sense, or facticity, or methodic use, or agreement among "cultural colleagues." Their ordered properties consist of organizationally demonstrable rational properties of indexical expressions and indexical actions. Those ordered properties are ongoing achievements of the concerted commonplace activities of investigators. The demonstrable rationality of indexical expressions and indexical actions retains over the course of its managed production by members the character of ordinary, familiar, routinized practical circumstances. As process and attainment the produced rationality of indexical expressions consists of practical tasks subject to every exigency of organizationally situated conduct.

I use the term "ethnomethodology" to refer to the investigation of the rational properties of indexical expressions and other practical actions as contingent ongoing accomplishments of organized artful practices of everyday life. The papers of this volume treat that accomplishment as the phenomenon of interest. They seek to specify its problematic features, to recommend methods for its study, but above all to consider what we might learn definitely about it. My purpose in the remainder of this chapter is to characterize ethnomethodology, which I have done by presenting three studies of the work of that accomplishment together with a concluding recitation of study policies.

*Practical Sociological Reasoning: Doing Accounts in "Common Sense Situations of Choice"*

The Los Angeles Suicide Prevention Center (SPC) and the Los Angeles Medical Examiner-Coroner's Office joined forces in 1957 to furnish Coroner's Death Certificates the warrant of scientific authority "within the limits of practical certainties imposed by the state of the art." Selected cases of "sudden, unnatural death" that were equivocal between "suicide" and other modes of death were referred by the Medical Examiner-Coroner to the SPC with the request that an inquiry, called a "psychological autopsy,"[5] be done.

The practices and concerns by SPC staff to accomplish their inquiries in common sense situations of choice repeated the features of practical inquiries that were encountered in other situations: studies of jury deliberations in negligence cases; clinic staff in selecting patients for out-patient psychiatric treatment; graduate students in sociology coding the contents of clinic folders into a coding sheet by following detailed coding instructions; and countless professional procedures in the conduct of anthropological, linguistic, social psychiatric, and sociological inquiry. The following features in the work at SPC were recognized by staff with frank acknowledgement as prevailing conditions of their work and as matters to consider when assessing the efficacy, efficiency, or intelligibility of their work – and added SPC testimony to that of jurors, survey researchers, and the rest:

(1) An abiding concern on the part of all parties for the temporal concerting of activities; (2) a concern for the practical question *par excellence*: "What to do next?"; (3) a concern on the inquirer's part to give evidence of his grasp of "What Anyone Knows" about how the settings work in which he had to accomplish his inquiries, and his concern to do so in the actual occasions in which the decisions were to be made by his exhibitable conduct in choosing; (4) matters which at the level of talk might be spoken of as "production programs," "laws of conduct," "rules of rational decision-making," "causes," "conditions," "hypothesis testing," "models," "rules of inductive and deductive inference" in the actual situation were taken for granted and were depended upon to consist of recipes, proverbs, slogans, and partially formulated plans of action; (5) inquirers were required to know and be skilled in dealing with situations "of the sort" for which "rules of rational decision-making" and the rest were intended in order to "see" or by what they did to insure the objective, effective, consistent, completely, empirically adequate, *i.e.*, rational character of recipes, prophecies, proverbs, partial descriptions in an actual occasion of the use of rules; (6) for the practical decider the "actual occasion" as a phenomenon in its own right exercised overwhelming priority of relevance to which "decision rules" or theories of decision-making were without exception

subordinated in order to assess their rational features rather than *vice versa*; (7) finally, and perhaps most characteristically, all of the foregoing features, together with an inquirer's "system" of alternatives, his "decision" methods, his information, his choices, and the rationality of his accounts and actions were constituent parts of the same practical circumstances in which inquirers did the work of inquiry – a feature that inquirers if they were to claim and recognize the practicality of their efforts knew of, required, counted on, took for granted, used, and glossed.

The work by SPC members of conducting their inquiries was part and parcel of the day's work. Recognized by staff members as constituent features of the day's work, their inquiries were thereby intimately connected to the terms of employment, to various internal and external chains of reportage, supervision, and review, and to similar organizationally supplied "priorities of relevances" for assessments of what "realistically," "practically," or "reasonably" needed to be done and could be done, how quickly, with what resources, seeing whom, talking about what, for how long, and so on. Such considerations furnished "We did what we could, and for all reasonable interests here is what we came out with" its features of organizationally appropriate sense, fact, impersonality, anonymity of authorship, purpose, reproducibility – i.e., of a *properly* and *visibly* rational account of the inquiry.

Members were required in their occupational capacities to formulate accounts of how a death *really*-for-all-practical-purposes-happened. "Really" made unavoidable reference to daily, ordinary, occupational workings. Members alone were entitled to invoke such workings as appropriate grounds for recommending the reasonable character of the result *without necessity for furnishing specifics.* On occasions of challenge, ordinary occupational workings would be cited explicitly, in "relevant part." Otherwise those features were disengaged from the product. In their place an account of how the inquiry was done made out the how-it-was-actually-done as appropriate to usual demands, usual attainments, usual practices, *and* to usual talk by SPC personnel talking as *bona fide* professional practitioners about usual demands, usual attainments, and usual practices.

One of several titles (relating to mode of death) had to be assigned to each case. The collection consisted of legally possible combinations of four elementary possibilities – natural death, accident, suicide, and homicide.[6] *All* titles were so administered as to not only withstand the varieties of equivocation, ambiguity, and improvisation that arose in every actual occasion of their use, but these titles were so administered as to *invite* that ambiguity, equivocality, and improvisation. It was part of the work not *only* that equivocality is a trouble – is *perhaps* a trouble – but also the practitioners were directed to those circumstances in order to *invite* the ambiguity or the equivocality, to invite the improvisation, or to invite the temporizing, and the rest. It is not that the investigator, having a list of titles performed an inquiry that proceeded stepwise to establish the grounds for electing among them. The formula was not, "Here is what we did, and among the titles as goals of our research *this* title finally interprets in a best fashion what we found out." Instead titles were continually postdicted and foretold. An inquiry was apt to be heavily guided by the inquirer's use of imagined settings in which the title will have been "used" by one or another interested party, including the deceased, and this was done by the inquirers in order to decide, using whatever "datum" might have been searched out, that *that* "datum" could be used to mask if masking needed to be done, or to equivocate, or gloss, or lead, or exemplify if they were needed. The prevailing feature of an inquiry was that nothing about it remained assured aside from the organized occasions of its uses. Thus a routine inquiry was one that the investigator used particular contingencies to accomplish, and depended upon particular contingencies to recognize and to recommend the practical adequacy of his work. When assessed by a member, *i.e.* viewed with respect to actual practices for making it happen, a routine inquiry is not one that is accomplished by rule, or according to rules. It seemed much more to consist of an inquiry that is openly recognized to have fallen short, but in the same ways it falls short its adequacy is acknowledged and for which no one is offering or calling particularly for explanations.

What members are *doing* in their inquiries is always somebody else's business in the sense that particular, organizationally located, locatable persons acquire an interest in light of the SPC member's account of whatever it is that will have been reported to have "really happened." Such considerations contributed heavily to the perceived feature of investigations that they were directed in their course by an account for which the claim will have been advanced that for all practical purposes it is correct. Thus over the path of his inquiry the investigator's task consisted of an account of how a particular person died in society that is adequately told, sufficiently detailed, clear, etc., for all practical purposes.

"What really happened," over the course of arriving at it, as well as after the "what really happened" has been inserted into the file and the title has been decided, may be chronically reviewed as well as chronically foretold in light of what might have been done, or what will have been done with those decisions. It is hardly news that on the way to a decision what a decision will have come to was reviewed and foretold in light of the anticipated consequences of a decision. *After* a recommendation had been made and the coroner had signed the death certificate the result can yet be, as they say, "revised." It can still be made a decision which needs to be reviewed "once more."

Inquirers wanted very much to be able to assure that they could come out at the end with an account of how the person died that would permit the coroner and his staff to withstand claims arguing that that account was incomplete or that the death happened differently than – or in contrast to or in contradiction of – what the members to the arrangement "claimed." The reference is neither only nor entirely to the complaints of the survivors. Those issues are dealt with as a succession of episodes, most being settled fairly quickly. The great contingencies consisted of enduring processes that lay in the fact that the coroner's office is a political office. The coroner's office activities produce continuing records of his office's activities. These records are subject to review as the products of the scientific work of the coroner, his staff, and his consultant. Office activities are methods for accomplishing reports that are scientific-for-all-practical-purposes. This involved "writing" as a warranting procedure in that a report, by reason of being written, is put into a file. That the investigator "does" a report is thereby made a matter for public record for the use of only partially identifiable other persons. Their interests in why or how or what the inquirer did would have in some relevant part to do with his skill and entitlement as a professional. But investigators know too that other interests will inform the "review," for the inquirer's work will be scrutinized to see its scientific-adequacy-for-all-practical-purposes as professionals' socially managed claims. Not only for investigators, but on all sides there is the relevance of "What was really found out for-all-practical-purposes?" which consists unavoidably of how much can you find out, how much can you disclose, how much can you gloss, how much can you conceal, how much can you hold as none of the business of some important persons, *investigators* included. All of them acquired an interest by reason of the fact that investigators, as a matter of occupational duty, were coming up with written reports of how, for-all-practical-purposes persons-really-died-and-are-really-dead-*in*-the-society.

Decisions had an unavoidable consequentiality. By this is meant that investigators needed to say *in so many words*, "What really happened?" The important words were the titles that were assigned to a text to recover that text as the title's "explication." But what an assigned title consists of as an "explicated" title is at any particular time for no one to say with any finality even when it is proposed "in so many words." In fact, *that* it is proposed "in so many words," *that* for example a written text was inserted "into the file of the case," furnishes entitling grounds that can be invoked in order to make something of the "so many words" that will have been used as an account of the death. Viewed with respect to patterns of use, titles and their accompanying texts have an open set of consequences. Upon any occasion of the use of texts it can remain to be seen what can be done with them, or what they will have come to, or what remains done "for the time being" pending the ways in which the environment of that decision may organize itself to "reopen the case," or "issue a complaint," or "find an issue" and so on. Such ways for SPC'ers are, as patterns, certain; but as particular processes for making them happen are in every actual occasion indefinite.

SPC inquiries begin with a death that the coroner finds equivocal as to *mode* of death. That death they use as a precedent with which various ways of living in society that could have terminated with that death are searched out and read "in the remains"; in the scraps of this and that like the body and its trappings, medicine bottles, notes, bits and pieces of clothing, and other memorabilia – stuff that can be photographed, collected, and packaged. Other "remains" are collected too: rumors, passing remarks, and stories – materials in the "repertoires" of whosoever might be consulted via the common work of conversations. These *whatsoever* bits and pieces that a story or a rule or a proverb might make intelligible are used to formulate a recognizably coherent, standard, typical, cogent, uniform, planful, *i.e.*, a professionally defensible, and thereby, for members, a *recognizably* rational account of how the society worked to produce those remains. This point will be easier to make if the reader will consult any standard textbook in forensic pathology. In it he will find the inevitable photograph of a victim with a slashed throat. Were the coroner to use that "sight" to recommend the equivocality of the mode of death he might say something like this: "In the case where a body looks like the one in that picture, you are looking at a suicidal death because the wound shows the 'hesitation cuts' that accompany the great wound. One can imagine these cuts are the remains of a procedure whereby the victim first made several preliminary trials of a hesitating sort and then performed the lethal slash. Other courses of action are imaginable, too, and so cuts that look like hesitation cuts can be produced by other mechanisms. One needs to start with the actual display and imagine how different courses of actions could have been organized such that *that* picture would be compatible with it. One might think of the photographed display as a phase-of-the-action. In any actual display is there a course of action with which that phase is uniquely compatible? *That* is the coroner's question."

The coroner (and SPC'ers) ask this with respect to each *particular* case, and thereby their work of achieving practical decidability seems almost unavoidably to display the following prevailing and important characteristic. SPC'ers must accomplish that decidability with respect to the "this's": they have to start with *this* much; *this* sight; *this* note; *this* collection of whatever is at hand. And *whatever* is there is good enough in the sense that *whatever* is there not only *will* do, but *does*. One makes whatever is there *do*. I do not mean by "making do" that an SPC investigator is too easily content, or that he does not look for more when he should. Instead, I mean: the *whatever* it is that he has to deal with, *that* is what will have been used to have found out, to have made decidable, the way in which the society operated to have produced *that* picture, to have come to *that* scene as its end result. In this way the remains on the slab serve not only as a precedent but as a goal of SPC inquiries. *Whatsoever* SPC members are faced with must serve as the precedent with which to read the remains so as to see how the society could have operated to have produced what it is that the inquirer has "in the end," "in the final analysis," and "in *any* case." What the inquiry can come to is what the death came to.

*Practical Sociological Reasoning: Following Coding Instructions*

Several years ago my co-workers and I undertook to analyze the experience of the UCLA Outpatient Clinic in order to answer the questions "By what criteria are its applicants selected for treatment?" To formulate and to answer this question we used a version of a method of cohort analysis that Kramer and his associates[7] had used to describe load and flow characteristics of patients in mental hospitals. Successive activities of "first contact," "intake interview," "psychological testing," "intake conference," "in-treatment," and "termination" were conceived with the use of the tree diagram of Figure 1. Any path from first contact to termination was called a career.

**Figure 1. Career Paths of Patients of a Psychiatric Clinic**

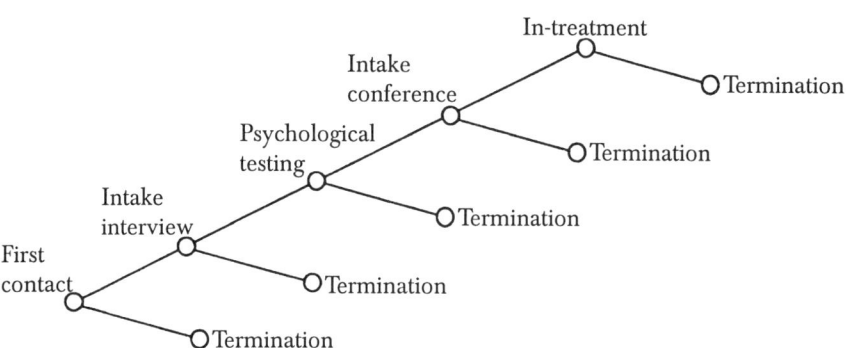

We wished to know what characteristics of patients, of clinical personnel, of their interactions, and of the tree were associated with which careers. Clinic records were our sources of information, the most important of which were intake application forms and case folder contents. In order to obtain a continuing record of patient–clinic case transactions from the time of a patient's initial contact until he terminated a "Clinic Career Form" was designed and inserted into case folders. Because clinic folders contain records that clinic personnel provide of their own activities, almost all of these sources of data were the results of self-reporting procedures.

Two graduate students in Sociology at UCLA examined 1,582 clinic folders for the information to complete the items of a Coding Sheet. A conventional reliability procedure was designed and conducted with the aim of determining the amount of agreement between coders and between successive trials of their coding. According to conventional reasoning, the amount of agreement furnishes one set of grounds for lending credence to coded events as actual clinic events. A critical feature of conventional reliability assessments is that the agreement between coders consists of agreement on the end results.

To no one's surprise, preliminary work showed that in order to accomplish the coding, coders were assuming knowledge of the very organized ways of the clinic that their coding procedures were intended to produce descriptions of. More interestingly, such presupposed knowledge seemed necessary and was most deliberately consulted whenever, for whatever reasons, the coders needed to be satisfied that they had coded "what really happened." *This was so regardless of whether or not they had encountered "ambiguous" folder contents.* Such a procedure undermined any claim that actuarial methods for interrogating the folder contents had been used, no matter how apparently clear the coding instructions were. Agreement in coding results was being produced by a contrasting procedure with unknown characteristics.

To find out more about the procedure that our students used, the reliability procedure was treated as a problematic activity in its own right. The "reliability" of coded results was addressed by asking how the coders had actually brought folder contents under the jurisdiction of the Coding Sheet's item. Via what practices had actual folder contents been assigned the status of answers to the researcher's questions? What actual activities made up those coders' practices called "following coding instruction"?

A procedure was designed that yielded conventional reliability information so that the original interests of the study were preserved. At the same time the procedure permitted the study of how any amount of agreement or disagreement had been produced by the actual ways that the two coders had gone about treating folder contents as answers to the questions formulated by the Coding Sheet. But, instead of assuming that coders, proceeding in whatever ways they did, might have been in error, in greater or lesser amount, the assumption was made that *whatever* they did could be counted correct procedure in *some* coding "game." The question was, what were these "games"? How *ever* coders did it, it was sufficient to produce whatever they got. How did they do it to get what they got?

We soon found the essential relevance to the coders, in their work of interrogating folder contents for answers to their questions, of such considerations as "et cetera," "unless," "let it pass," and "factum valet" (*i.e.*, an action that is otherwise prohibited by a rule is counted correct once it is done). For convenience let me call these "*ad hoc*" considerations, and call their practice "*ad hocing*." Coders used the same *ad hoc* considerations in order to recognize the relevance of the coding instructions to the organized activities of the clinic. Only when this relevance was clear were the coders satisfied that the coding instructions analyzed actually encountered folder contents so as to permit the coders to treat folder contents as reports of "real events." Finally, *ad hoc* considerations were invariant features of the practices of "following coding instructions." Attempts to suppress them while retaining an unequivocal sense to the instructions produced bewilderment on their part.

Various facets of the "new" reliability study were then developed, at first in order to see if these results could be firmly established, and after it was clear, to my satisfaction, that they could, to exploit their consequences for the general sociological character of the coders' methods of interrogation (as well as contrasting methods) as well as for the work that is involved in recognizing or claiming that something had been done by rule – that an action had followed or had been "governed" by instructions.

*Ad hoc* considerations are invariably relevant considerations in deciding the fit between what could be read from the clinic folders and what the coder inserted into the coding sheet. No matter how definitely and elaborately instructions had been written, and despite the fact that strict actuarial coding rules[8] *could* be formulated for every item, and with which folder contents *could* be mapped into the coding sheet, insofar as the claim had to be advanced that Coding Sheet entries reported real events of the clinic's activities, then in every instance, and for every item, "et cetera," "unless," "let it pass" and "factum valet" accompanied the coder's grasp of the coding instructions as ways of analyzing actual folder contents. Their use made it possible, as well, for the coder to read a folder's contents as a report about the events that the Coding Sheet provided and formulated as events of the processing tree.

Ordinarily researchers treat such *ad hoc* procedures as flawed ways of writing, recognizing, or following coding instructions. The prevailing view holds that good work requires researchers, by extending the number and explicitness of their coding rules, to minimize or even eliminate the occasions in which "et cetera" and other such *ad hocing* practices would be used.

To treat instructions as though *ad hoc* features in their use were a nuisance, or to treat their presence as grounds for complaint about the incompleteness of instructions, is very much like complaining that if the walls of a building were only gotten out of the way one could see better what was keeping the roof up. Our studies showed that *ad hoc* considerations are essential features of coding procedures. *Ad hocing* is required if the researcher is to grasp the relevance of the instructions to the particular and actual situation they are intended to analyze. For every particular and actual occasion of search, detection, and assignment of folder contents to a "proper" category – which is to say, over the course of actually coding – such *ad hoc* considerations have irremediable priority over the usually talked about "necessary and sufficient" criteria. It is not the case that the "necessary and sufficient" criteria are procedurally defined by coding instructions. Nor is it the case that *ad hoc* practices such as "et cetera" or "let it pass" are controlled or eliminated in their presence, use, number, or occasions of use by making coding instructions as definite as possible. Instead *ad hoc* considerations are consulted by coders and *ad hocing* practices are *used in order to recognize what the instructions are definitely talking about. Ad hoc* considerations are consulted by coders in order to recognize coding instructions as "operational definitions" of coding categories. They operate as the grounds for and as methods to advance and secure researchers' claims to have coded in accordance with "necessary and sufficient" criteria.

*Ad hocing* occurs (without, I believe, any possibility of remedy), whenever the coder assumes the position of a socially competent member of the arrangement that he seeks to assemble an account of and, when from this "position," he treats actual folder contents as standing in a relationship of trusted signification to the "system" in the clinic activities. Because the coder assumes the "position" of a competent member to the arrangements that he seeks to give an account of, he can "see the system" in the actual content of the folder. This he accomplishes in something like the way that one must know the orderly ways of English usage in order to recognize an utterance as a word-in-English or know the rules of a game to make out a move-in-a-game, given that alternative ways of making out an utterance or a board play are always imaginable. Thereby, the coder recognizes the folder content for "what it actually is," or can "see what a note in the folder 'is really talking about.'"

Given this, if the coder has to be satisfied that he has detected a real clinic occurrence, he must treat actual folder contents as standing proxy for the social-order-in-and-of-clinic-activities. Actual folder contents stand to the socially ordered ways of clinic activities as *representations* of them; they do not describe the order, nor are they evidences of the order. It is the coder's use of folder documents as *sign-functions* to which I mean to be pointing in saying that the coder must know the order of the clinic's activities that he is looking at in order to recognize the actual content as an appearance-of-the-order. Once the coder can "see the system" in the content, it is possible for the coder to extend and to otherwise interpret the coding instructions – to *ad hoc* them – so as to maintain the relevance of the coding instructions to the actual contents, and in this way to formulate the sense of actual content so that its meaning, even though it is transformed by the coding, is preserved in the coder's eyes as a real event of the clinic's actual activities.

There are several important consequences:

(1) Characteristically, coded results would be treated as if they were disinterested descriptions of clinic events, and coding rules are presumed to back up the claim of disinterested description. But if the work of *ad hocing* is required to make such claims intelligible, it can always be argued – and so far I do not see a defensible reply – that the coded results consist of a persuasive version of the socially organized character of the clinic's operations, regardless of what the actual order is, perhaps independently of what the actual order is, and even without the investigator having detected the actual order. Instead of our study of patients' clinic careers (as well as the multitude of studies of various social arrangements that have been carried out in similarly conventional ways) having described the order of the clinic's operations, the account may be argued to consist of a socially invented, persuasive, and proper way of talking about the clinic as an orderly enterprise, since "after all" the account was produced by "scientific procedures." The account would be itself part of the actual order of the clinic's operations, in much the same way that one might treat a person's report on his own activities as a feature of his activities. *The actual order would remain to be described.*

(2) Another consequence arises when we ask what is to be made of the care that nevertheless is so assiduously exercised in the design and use of coding instructions for interrogating actual contents and transforming them into the language of the coding sheet? If the resulting account is itself a feature

of the clinic's activities, then perhaps one ought not read the coding instructions as a way of obtaining a scientific description of the clinic's activities, since this assumes that the coding language, in what it is talking *about*, is independent of the interests of the members that are being served in using it. Coding instructions ought to be read instead as consisting of a grammar of rhetoric; they furnish a "social science" way of talking so as to persuade consensus and action within the practical circumstances of the clinic's organized daily activities, a grasp of which members are expected to have as a matter of course. By referring to an account of the clinic that was obtained by following coding instructions, it is possible for members with different interests to persuade each other and to reconcile their talk about clinic affairs in an impersonal way, while the matters that are really being talked *about* retain their sense, for the "discussants," as a legitimate, or illegitimate, a desirable or undesirable, an advantaged or disadvantaged state of affairs for the "discussants" in their occupational lives. It furnishes an impersonal way of characterizing their affairs without the members relinquishing important organizationally determined interests in what the account, in their eyes, is "after all" all about. What it is all about is the clinic order whose real features, as any member knows that Anyone Knows, are always none of somebody-else-in-that-organization's-business.

*Practical Sociological Reasoning: Common Understanding*

Sociologists distinguish the "product" from the "process" meanings of a common understanding. As "product," a common understanding is thought to consist of a shared agreement on substantive matters; as "process," it consists of various methods whereby something that a person says or does is recognized to accord with a rule. With his concepts of *Begreifen* and *Verstehen*, each with its distinct character as method and knowledge, Weber provided sociologists an authority for this distinction.

An analysis of students' experiences in reporting commonplace conversation suggests that for either case, for "product" or "process," a common understanding consists of an inner-temporal course of interpretive work. Their experiences suggest some strange consequences of the facts that *in either case* a common understanding has necessarily an operational structure.

In Chapter Two research is reported in which students were asked to report common conversations by writing on the left side of a sheet what the parties actually said, and on the right side what they and their partners understood they were talking about. The following colloquy is reported there:

HUSBAND: Dana succeeded in putting a penny in a parking meter today without being picked up.     This afternoon as I was bringing Dana, our four-year-old son, home from the nursery school, he succeeded in reaching high enough to put a penny in a parking meter when we parked in

| | | |
|---|---|---|
| | | a meter zone, whereas before he had always had to be picked up to reach that high. |
| WIFE: | Did you take him to the record store? | Since he put a penny in a meter that means that you stopped while he was with you. I know that you stopped at the record store either on the way to get him or on the way back. Was it on the way back, so that he was with you or did you stop there on the way to get him and somewhere else on the way back? |
| HUSBAND: | No, to the shoe repair shop. | No, I stopped at the record store on the way to get him and stopped at the shoe repair shop on the way home when he was with me. |
| WIFE: | What for? | I know of one reason why you might have stopped at the shoe repair shop. Why did you in fact? |
| HUSBAND: | I got some new shoe laces for my shoes. | As you will remember I broke a shoe lace on one of my brown oxfords the other day so I stopped to get some new laces. |
| WIFE: | Your loafers need new heels badly. | Something else you could have gotten that I was thinking of. You could have taken in your black loafers which need heels badly. You'd better get them taken care of pretty soon. |

Students filled out the left side of the sheet quickly and easily, but found the right side incomparably more difficult. When the assignment was made, many asked how much I wanted them to write. As I progressively imposed accuracy, clarity, and distinctness, the task became increasingly laborious. Finally, when I required that they assume I would know what they had actually talked about only from reading literally what they wrote literally, they gave up with the complaint that the task was impossible.

Although their complaints were concerned with the laboriousness of having to write "more," the frustrating "more" was not made up of the large labor of having to reduce a mountain with buckets. It was not their complaint that what was talked about consisted of bounded contents made so vast by pedantry that they lacked sufficient time, stamina, paper, drive, or good reason to write "all of it." Instead, the complaint and its circumstances seemed to consist of this: *if*, for whatever a student wrote, I was able to persuade him that it was not yet accurate, distinct, or clear enough, and *if* he remained willing to repair the ambiguity, then he returned to the task with the complaint that the writing itself developed the conversation as a branching texture of relevant matters. The very *way* of accomplishing the task multiplied its features.

What task had I set them such that it required that they write "more"; such that the progressive imposition of accuracy, clarity, and literalness made it increasingly difficult and finally impossible; and such that the way of accomplishing the task multiplied its features? If a common understanding consisted of shared agreement on substantive matters, their task would have been identical with one that professional sociologists supposedly address. The task would have been solved as professional sociologists are apt to propose its solution, as follows:

Students would first distinguish *what* was said from *what* was talked about, and set the two contents into a correspondence of sign and referent. *What the parties said* would be treated as a sketchy, partial, incomplete, masked, elliptical, concealed, ambiguous, or misleading version of *what the parties talked about*. The task would consist of filling out the sketchiness of what was said. What was talked about would consist of elaborated and corresponding contents of what the parties said. Thus the format of left and right hand columns would accord with the "fact" that the contents of what was said were recordable by writing what a tape recorder would pick up. The right hand column would require that something "more" be "added." Because the sketchiness of what was said was its defect, it would be necessary for students to look elsewhere than to what was said in order (a) to find the corresponding contents, and (b) to find the grounds to argue – because they would need to argue – for the correctness of the correspondence. Because they were reporting the actual conversation of particular persons, they would look for these further contents in what the conversationalists had "in mind," or what they were "thinking," or what they "believed," or what they "intended." Furthermore, they would need to be assured that they had detected what the conversationalists actually, and not supposedly, hypothetically, imaginarily, or possibly had in mind. That is to say, they would need to cite observed actions – observed ways that the parties conducted themselves – in order to furnish grounds for the claim of "actually." This assurance would be obtained by seeking to establish the presence, in the conversationalists' relationship, of warranting virtues such as their having spoken honestly, openly, candidly, sincerely, and the like. All of which is to say that students would invoke their knowledge of the community of understandings, and their knowledge of shared agreements to recommend the adequacy of their accounts of what the parties had been talking about, *i.e.*, what the parties understood in common. Then, for anything the students wrote, they could assume that I, as a competent co-member of the same community (the conversations were after all commonplace) should be able to see the correspondence and its grounds. If I did not see the correspondence or if I made out the contents differently than they did, then as long as they could continue to assume my competence – *i.e.*, as long as my alternative interpretations did not undermine my right to claim that such alternatives needed to be taken seriously by them and by me – I could be made out by the students as insisting that they furnish me with finer detailing than practical considerations required. In such a case, they should have charged me with blind pedantry and should have complained that because "anyone can see" when, for all practical purposes, enough is enough, none are so blind as those who *will* not see.

This version of their task accounts for their complaints of having to write "more." It also accounts for the task's increasing laboriousness when clarity and the like were progressively imposed. But it does not account very well for the final impossibility, for it explains one facet of the task's "impossibility" as students' unwillingness to go any further, but it does not explain an accompanying sense, namely, that students somehow saw that the task was, in principle, unaccomplishable. Finally, this version of their task does not explain at all their complaint that the way of accomplishing the task multiplied its features.

An alternative conception of the task may do better. Although it may at first appear strange to do so, suppose we drop the assumption that in order to describe a usage as a feature of a community of understandings we must at the outset know what the substantive common understandings consist of. With it, drop the assumption's accompanying theory of signs, according to which a "sign" and "referent" are respectively properties of something said and something talked about, and which in this fashion proposes sign and referent to be related as corresponding contents. By dropping such a theory of signs we drop as well, thereby, the possibility that an invoked shared agreement on substantive matters explains a usage.

If these notions are dropped, then what the parties talked about could not be distinguished from *how* the parties were speaking. An explanation of what the parties were talking about would then consist entirely of describing how the parties had been speaking; of furnishing a method for saying whatever is to be said, like talking synonymously, talking ironically, talking metaphorically, talking cryptically, talking narratively, talking in a questioning or answering way, lying, glossing, double-talking, and the rest.

In the place of and in contrast to a concern for a difference between *what* was said and *what* was talked about, the appropriate difference is between a language-community member's recognition that a person is saying something, *i.e.*, that he was *speaking*, on the one hand, and *how* he was speaking on the other. Then the recognized sense of what a person said consists only and entirely in recognizing the method of his speaking, of *seeing how he spoke*.

I suggest that one not read the right hand column as corresponding contents of the left, and that the students' task of explaining what the conversationalists talked about did not involve them in elaborating the contents of what the conversationalists said. I suggest, instead, that their written explanations consisted of their attempts to instruct me in how to use what the parties said as a method for seeing what the conversationalists said. I suggest that I had asked the students to furnish me with instructions for recognizing what the parties were actually and certainly saying. By persuading them of alternative "interpretations," by insisting that ambiguity still remained, I had persuaded them that they had demonstrated to me only what the parties were supposedly, or probably, or imaginably, or hypothetically saying. *They took this to mean that their instructions were incomplete; that their demonstrations failed by the extent to which their instructions were incomplete; and that the difference between claims of "actually" and "supposedly" depended on the completeness of the instructions.*

We now see what the task was that required them to write "more," that they found increasingly difficult and finally impossible, and that became elaborated in its features by the very procedures for doing it. I had set them the task of formulating these instructions so as to make them "increasingly" accurate, clear, distinct, and finally literal where the meanings of "increasingly" and of clarity, accuracy, distinctness, and literalness were supposedly explained in terms of the properties of the instructions themselves and the instructions alone. I had required them to take on the impossible task of "repairing" the essential incompleteness of *any* set of instructions no matter how carefully or elaborately written they might be. I had required them to formulate the method that the parties had used in speaking as rules of procedure to follow in order to say what the parties said, rules that would withstand every exigency of situation, imagination, and development. I had asked them to describe the parties' methods of speaking as if these methods were isomorphic with actions in strict compliance with a rule of procedure that formulated the method as an instructable matter. To recognize *what* is said *means* to recognize how a person is speaking, *e.g.*, to recognize that the wife in saying "your shoes need heels badly" was speaking narratively, or metaphorically, or euphemistically, or double-talking.

They stumbled over the fact that the question of how a person is speaking, the task of describing a person's method of speaking, is not satisfied by, and is not the same as showing that what he said accords with a rule for demonstrating consistency, compatibility, and coherence of meanings.

For the conduct of their everyday affairs, persons take for granted that what is said will be made out according to methods that the parties use to make out what they are saying for its clear, consistent, coherent, understandable, or planful character, *i.e.*, as subject to some rule's jurisdiction – in a word, as rational. To see the "sense" of what is said is to accord to what was said its character "as a rule." *"Shared agreement" refers to various social methods for accomplishing the member's recognition that something was said-according-to-a-rule and not the demonstrable matching of substantive matters. The appropriate image of a common understanding is therefore an operation rather than a common intersection of overlapping sets.*

A person doing sociology, be it lay or professional sociology, can treat a common understanding as a shared agreement on substantive matters by taking for granted that what is said will be made out in accordance with methods that need not be specified, which is to say that need only be specified on "special" occasions.

Given the discovering character of what the husband and wife were talking about, its recognizable character for both entailed the use by each and the attribution by each to the other of work whereby what was said is or will have been understood to have accorded with their relationship of interaction as an invokable rule of their agreement, as an intersubjectively used grammatical scheme for analyzing each other's talk whose use provided that they *would* understand each other in ways that they *would* be understood. It provides that neither one was entitled to call upon the other to specify how it was being done; neither one was entitled to claim that the other needed to "explain" himself.

In short, a common understanding, entailing as it does an "inner" temporal course of interpretive work, necessarily has an operational structure. For the analyst to disregard its operational structure, is to use common sense knowledge of the society in exactly the ways that members use it when they must decide what persons are really doing or really "talking about," *i.e.*, to use common sense knowledge of social structures as *both* a topic and a resource of inquiry. An alternative would be to assign exclusive priority to the study of the methods of concerted actions and methods of common understanding. Not *a* method of understanding, but immensely various methods of understanding are the professional sociologist's proper and hitherto unstudied and critical phenomena. Their multitude is indicated in the endless list of ways that persons speak. Some indication of their character and their differences occurs in the socially available glosses of a multitude of sign functions as when we take note of marking, labeling, symbolizing, emblemizing, cryptograms, analogies, anagrams, indicating, miniaturizing, imitating, mocking-up, simulating – in short, in recognizing, using, and producing the orderly ways of cultural settings from "within" those settings.[9]

## Policies

That practical actions are problematic in ways not so far seen; how they are problematical; how to make them accessible to study; what we might learn about them – these are proposed tasks. I use the term "ethnomethodology" to refer to the study of practical actions according to policies such as the following, and to the phenomena, issues, findings, and methods that accompany their use.

(1) An indefinitely large domain of appropriate settings can be located if one uses a search policy that *any occasion whatsoever* be examined for the feature that "choice" among alternatives of sense, of facticity, of objectivity, of cause, of explanation, of communality *of practical actions* is a project of members'

actions. Such a policy provides that inquiries of every imaginable kind, from divination to theoretical physics, claim our interest as socially organized artful practices. That the social structures of everyday activities furnish contexts, objects, resources, justifications, problematic topics, etc. to practices and products of inquiries establishes the eligibility for our interest of every way of doing inquiries without exception.

No inquiries can be excluded no matter where or when they occur, no matter how vast or trivial their scope, organization, cost, duration, consequences, whatever their successes, whatever their repute, their practitioners, their claims, their philosophies or philosophers. Procedures and results of water witching, divination, mathematics, sociology – whether done by lay persons or professionals – are addressed according to the policy that every feature of sense, of fact, of method, for every particular case of inquiry without exception, is the managed accomplishment of organized settings of practical actions, and that particular determinations in members' practices of consistency, planfulness, relevance, or reproducibility of their practices and results – from witchcraft to topology – are acquired and assured only through particular, located organizations of artful practices.

(2) Members to an organized arrangement are continually engaged in having to decide, recognize, persuade, or make evident the rational, *i.e.*, the coherent, or consistent, or chosen, or planful, or effective, or methodical, or knowledgeable character of such activities of their inquiries as counting, graphing, interrogation, sampling, recording, reporting, planning, decision-making, and the rest. It is not satisfactory to describe how actual investigative procedures, as constituent features of members' ordinary and organized affairs, are accomplished by members as recognizedly rational actions in *actual occasions* of organizational circumstances by saying that members invoke some rule with which to define the coherent or consistent or planful, *i.e.*, rational, character of their actual activities. Nor is it satisfactory to propose that the rational properties of members' inquiries are produced by members' compliance to rules of inquiry. Instead, "adequate demonstration," "adequate reporting," "sufficient evidence," "plain talk," "making too much of the record," "necessary inference," "frame of restricted alternatives," in short, every topic of "logic" and "methodology," including these two titles as well, are glosses for organizational phenomena. These phenomena are contingent achievements of organizations of common practices, and as contingent achievements they are variously available to members as norms, tasks, troubles. Only in these ways rather than as invariant categories or as general principles do they define "adequate inquiry and discourse."

(3) Thus, a leading policy is to refuse serious consideration to the prevailing proposal that efficiency, efficacy, effectiveness, intelligibility, consistency, planfulness, typicality, uniformity, reproducibility of activities – *i.e.*, that rational properties of practical activities – be assessed, recognized, categorized, described by using a rule or a standard obtained outside actual settings within

which such properties are recognized, used, produced, and talked about by settings' members. All procedures whereby logical and methodological properties of the practices and results of inquiries are assessed in their general characteristics by rule are of interest as *phenomena* for ethnomethodological study but not otherwise. Structurally differing organized practical activities of everyday life are to be sought out and examined for the production, origins, recognition, and representations of rational practices. All "logical" and "methodological" properties of action, every feature of an activity's sense, facticity, objectivity, accountability, communality is to be treated as a contingent accomplishment of socially organized common practices.

(4) The policy is recommended that any social setting be viewed as self-organizing with respect to the intelligible character of its own appearances as either representations of or as evidences-of-a-social-order. Any setting organizes its activities to make its properties as an organized environment of practical activities detectable, countable, recordable, reportable, tell-a-story-aboutable, analyzable – in short, *accountable*.

Organized social arrangements consist of various methods for accomplishing the accountability of a settings' organizational ways as a concerted undertaking. Every claim by practitioners of effectiveness, clarity, consistency, planfulness, or efficiency, and every consideration for adequate evidence, demonstration, description, or relevance obtains its character as a *phenomenon* from the corporate pursuit of this undertaking and from the ways in which various organizational environments, by reason of their characteristics as organizations of activities, "sustain," "facilitate," "resist," etc. these methods for making their affairs accountable-matters-for-all-practical-purposes.

In exactly the ways that a setting is organized, it *consists* of members' methods for making evident that setting's ways as clear, coherent, planful, consistent, chosen, knowable, uniform, reproducible connections, – *i.e.*, rational connections. In exactly the way that persons are members to organized affairs, they are engaged in serious and practical work of detecting, demonstrating, persuading through displays in the ordinary occasions of their interactions the appearances of consistent, coherent, clear, chosen, planful arrangements. In exactly the ways in which a setting is organized, it *consists* of methods whereby its members are provided with accounts of the setting as countable, storyable, proverbial, comparable, picturable, representable – *i.e.*, accountable events.

(5) Every kind of inquiry without exception consists of organized artful practices whereby the rational properties of proverbs, partially formulated advice, partial description, elliptical expressions, passing remarks, fables, cautionary tales, and the like are made evident, are demonstrated.

The demonstrably rational properties of indexical expressions and indexical actions is an ongoing achievement of the organized activities of everyday life. Here is the heart of the matter. The managed production of this phenomenon in every aspect, from every perspective, and in every stage retains the character for members of serious, practical tasks, subject to every exigency of organizationally situated conduct. Each of the papers in this volume, in one way or another, recommends that phenomenon for professional sociological analysis.

## Notes

1. Olaf Helmer and Nicholas Rescher, *On the Epistemology of the Inexact Sciences*, P-1513 (Santa Monica, California: RAND Corporation, October 13, 1958), pp. 8–14.

2. In Marvin Farber, *The Foundation of Phenomenology* (Cambridge, Massachusetts: Harvard University Press, 1943), pp. 237–238.

3. Bertrand Russell, *Inquiry into Meaning and Truth* (New York: W. W. Norton & Company, Inc., 1940), pp. 134–143.

4. Nelson Goodman, *The Structure of Appearance* (Cambridge, Massachusetts: Harvard University Press, 1951), pp. 287–298.

5. The following references contain reports on the "psychological autopsy" procedure developed at the Los Angeles Suicide Prevention Center: Theodore J. Curphey, "The Forensic Pathologist and the Multi-Disciplinary Approach to Death," in *Essays in Self-Destruction*, ed. Edwin S. Shneidman (International Science Press, 1967), in press; Theodore J. Curphey, "The Role of the Social Scientist in the Medico-Legal Certification of Death from Suicide," in *The Cry for Help*, ed. Norman L. Farberow and Edwin S. Shneidman (New York: McGraw-Hill Book Company, 1961); Edwin S. Shneidman and Norman L. Farberow, "Sample Investigations of Equivocal Suicidal Deaths," in *The Cry for Help*; Robert E. Litman, Theodore J. Curphey, Edwin S. Shneidman, Norman L. Farberow, and Norman D. Tabachnick, "Investigations of Equivocal Suicides," *Journal of the American Medical Association*, 184 (1963), 924–929; and Edwin S. Shneidman, "Orientations Toward Death: A Vital Aspect of the Study of Lives," in *The Study of Lives*, ed. Robert W. White (New York: Atherton Press, 1963), reprinted in the *International Journal of Psychiatry*, 2 (1966), 167–200.

6. The possible combinations include the following: natural, accident, suicide, homicide, possible accident, possible suicide, possible natural; (between) accident or suicide, undetermined; (between) natural or suicide, undetermined; (between) natural or accident, undetermined; and (among) natural or accident or suicide, undetermined.

7. M. Kramer, H. Goldstein, R. H. Israel, and N. A. Johnson, "Applications of Life Table Methodology to the Study of Mental Hospital Populations," *Psychiatric Research Reports of the American Psychiatric Association*, June, 1956, pp. 49–76.

8. David Harrah's model of an information-matching game was taken to define the meaning of "strict actuarial method for interrogating." See David Harrah, "A Logic of Questions and Answers," *Philosophy of Science*, 28, No. 1 (January, 1961), 40–46.

9. This note was touched off by Monroe Beardsley's remark in "The Metaphorical Twist," *Philosophy and Phenomenological Research*, March, 1962, to the effect that we do not decide that a word is used metaphorically because we know what a person is thinking; rather we know what he is thinking because we see that a word is used metaphorically. Taking poetry for his case, Beardsley points out that "the clues of this fact must somehow be in the poem itself, or we should seldom be able to read poetry."

# 83

# Doing 'Being Ordinary'

*Harvey Sacks*

Usually I start the course by doing what I do in the course, without any programmatic statements, without any indication of why it should be of any interest to anybody. But – and this may be unfair – the course will turn out to be much more severely technical than most people could possibly be interested in, and some good percentage will drop out, and usually that has the consequence that they get nothing out of the class if they last one time. So I decided to spend the first time telling people something that I take it could hardly *not* be of interest to them. Then, when they drop out, they'd at least have gotten what I figure would be worth the price of the course. And I guess I should say if *this* isn't absorbing, you could hardly imagine how unabsorbing the rest will be.

Now, this is in many ways nothing like the way I'll proceed throughout the rest of the course. In the course I will be taking stories offered in conversation and subjecting them to a type of analysis which is concerned roughly to see whether it's possible to subject the details of actual events to formal investigation, informatively. The loosest message is that the world you live in is much more finely organized than you'd imagine. As well as that loose message, there are some really specific things about how stories work and why they work the way they do. I'll do that from next time on. But in this lecture I won't be studying the organization of telling stories in conversation, and I won't be attempting to prove anything. I'll be saying some things about why the study of storytelling should be of interest to anybody. But people don't have to stay around after that to have caught that message, and to have been armed with some materials that would permit them to wander around noticing things that they might not have noticed, and find them ghastly.

I've been studying the organization of stories, how they work, for some time. And one sort of issue is, what do people make stories out of? In particular, given what they *might* make stories out of, what do they make stories out of? It wasn't of particular interest to me why anybody else should be interested in such an issue, but the question arose and now will constitute the business

---

Source: Gail Jefferson (ed.), *Lectures on Conversation*, vol. II, (Oxford: Blackwell, 1992).

of this lecture: What sort of large-scale interest does what people make stories of or what they don't make stories of, have? A good deal of what I'll say has its obscure intellectual source (I say 'obscure' because if anyone were to read the book it's not likely that they'd find that it says what I say, but with some consideration they might see how it is that I owe what I'm saying to this source) in a novel called *Between Life and Death* by a French novelist, Nathalie Sarraute. The book is absolutely not assigned; I'm just citing a debt.

A kind of remarkable thing is how, in ordinary conversation, in reporting some event, people report what we might see to be not what happened, but the *ordinariness* of what happened. For whole ranges of things that you might figure to be kind of exciting, something like this will be offered (the following sorts of things are not made up but are actual): Somebody talking about a man they met the night before might say "He's very nice. He's very, very nice." Or if they saw a movie they might say "It was really good." If they went away for a weekend, they say something like "We went to Palm Springs. Bud played golf with the guys and I sat around the pool with the girls." The reports do not so much give attributes of the scene, activity, participants but announce the event's ordinariness, its usualness. We might figure that lots of these things *could* be stories, but they're not made into stories. And if you think of literature or poetry you can perfectly well know that out of any such event as is passed off as "It was a nice evening. We sat around and talked," really elaborated characterizations are often presented. So I've been wondering about the *non-production* of stories.

Now I come to the central sorts of assertions I want to make. Whatever we may think about what it is to be an ordinary person in the world, an initial shift is not to think of an 'ordinary person' as some person, but as somebody having as their job, as their constant preoccupation, doing 'being ordinary.' It's not that somebody *is* ordinary, it's perhaps that that's what their business is. And it takes work, as any other business does. And if you just extend the analogy of what you obviously think of as work – as whatever it is that takes analytic, intellectual, emotional energy – then you can come to see that all sorts of nominalized things – personal characteristics and the like – are jobs which are done, which took some kind of effort, training, etc. So I'm not going to be talking about an 'ordinary person' as this or that person, or as some average, i.e., a non-exceptional person on some statistical basis, but as something that is the way somebody constitutes themselves, and, in effect, a job that they do on themselves. They and the people around them may be coordinatively engaged in assuring that each of them are ordinary persons, and that can then be a job that they undertake together, to achieve that each of them, together, are ordinary persons.

The core question is, how do people go about doing 'being an ordinary person'? In the first instance there's an easy answer: Among the ways you go about doing 'being an ordinary person' is spending your time in usual ways, having usual thoughts, having usual interests, etc.; so that all you have to do, to be 'an ordinary person' in the evening, is turn on the TV set. It's not that it *happens* that you're doing what lots of ordinary people are doing, but that you know that the way to do 'having a usual evening' is to do that. It's not just that you're selecting, "Gee I'll watch TV tonight," but you're making a job of, and finding an answer to, how to do 'being ordinary tonight.' Some people, as a matter of kicks, could say "Let's do being ordinary tonight. We'll go watch TV, eat popcorn," etc. – something they know is being done at the same time by millions of others around.

We can see, then, that it's a job. You have to know what anybody/everybody is doing; doing ordinarily. And you have to have that available to do. There are people who don't have that available to do, and who specifically can't be ordinary. If, for example, you're in prison, in a room with no facilities at all – say, it has a bench and a hole in the floor and a spigot – then you find yourself doing things like systematically exploring the cracks in the wall from floor to ceiling over the years, and you come to have information about the wall in that room which ordinary people don't have about their bedroom wall. It's not a usual thing to do, to say "Well this evening I'm going to examine that corner of the ceiling." Of course it may be that prison walls are more interesting than other walls, since among the other things prisoners are occupied with is leaving information on the wall that they've been there, so there's things to read on the walls. But it's perfectly available to anybody to spend an afternoon looking at a wall. You could choose to do that. If you take drugs you're permitted to do that. But unless you take drugs you would not find yourself allowed to do it, though nobody's around. That is to say, in being an 'ordinary person,' that's not a thing you could allow yourself to spend the day doing. And there is an infinite collection of possibilities, of things that you couldn't bring yourself to do; not out of boredom, though that's one way you could formulate it, but in the midst of the most utterly boring afternoon you nonetheless would rather live through the boredom in the usual way – whatever that way is – than see whether it would be less or more boring to examine the wall or to look in some detail at the tree outside the window.

There's a place in Freud where he says, "with regard to matters of chemistry or physics or things like that, laymen would not venture an opinion. With regard to psychology it's quite different; anybody feels free to make psychological remarks." And part of the business he thought he was engaged in was changing that around, i.e., to both develop psychology and educate laymen, co-jointly. So that the laymen would know that they don't know anything about it and that there are people who do, so that they would eventually stop making psychological remarks as they stopped making chemical and physical remarks.

I raise this because while we all can see that's quite so, there's a related and in a way much more interesting thing that I doubt we've noticed. If one were to pick up the notebooks of writers, poets, novelists, you're likely to find elaborated studies of small real objects. Like in the notebooks of the poet Gerard Manley Hopkins there are extended naturalistic observations of a very detailed sort, of, e.g., cloud formations or what a leaf looks like, looking up at it under varying types of light. And for some novelists what you have is extended character observations. Now, my notion is that as it is for chemistry and physics, so it is for making distinctive observations about the world and its persons. That is to say, that's the job of novelists and poets and not an ordinary person. It's just a thing that, in being ordinary, you don't do. For example, considering the situation of the Palm Springs weekend described as "I sat around the pool with the girls," you don't get, from somebody doing 'being ordinary,' a report of what the wind did to the water in the pool, or some character observations other than "She was nice," "She was not so nice," "She's getting older," of the people with whom the afternoon was spent.

And I think it's not only that one doesn't make the story but does perhaps make the observations, it's that the cast of mind of doing 'being ordinary' is essentially this: Your business in life is only to see and report the usual aspects of any possibly usual scene. That is to say, what you look for is to see how any scene you're in can be made an ordinary scene, a usual scene, and that's what it is.

Now plainly that could be a job; it could be work. The scene doesn't in the first instance simply present itself, define itself, as insufferably usual, nothing to be said about it; it's a matter of how you're going to attack it, what you are going to see in it, what you are going to see in it that you can say about it. Plainly, people are monitoring scenes for this storyable possibility. I'll give a gruesome instance of It, from a book called *An Ordinary Camp* by Micheline Maurel. She reports the first day in a concentration camp. The first hours are terribly horrifying, and then there's a lapse.

> Little by little conversation sprang up from bunk to bunk. The rumors were already beginning to circulate. Luckily the news is good. We'll be home soon. We'll have an unusual experience to talk about.

A way in which this event was dealt with while it was taking place – and which, for an experience which might leave one utterly without hope, we can see as wonderfully relevant for being able to survive it – was that in the end it will turn out to have been a good story. And we've all experienced being in scenes the virtue of which was that as we were in them we could see what it was we could later tell people had transpired. And there are presumably lots of things which, at least at some points in people's lives, are done just for that, i.e., it seems fair to suppose that there's a time when kids do 'kissing and telling,' that they're doing the kissing in order to have something to tell, and not that they happen to do kissing and happen to do telling, or that they want to do kissing and happen to do telling, etc., but that a way to get them to like the kissing is via the fact that they like the telling.

It seems plain enough that people monitor the scenes they're in for their storyable characteristics. And yet the awesome, overwhelming fact is that they come away with no storyable characteristics, where presumably any of us with any wit could make of this half hour, or of the next, a rather large array of things to say. But that would take a kind of effort that could make one feel awfully uncomfortable.

So, there's a business of being an 'ordinary person,' and that business includes attending the world, yourself, others, objects, so as to see how it is that it's a usual scene. And when offering what transpired, you present it in its usual 'nothing much' fashion, with whatever variants of banal characterizations you might happen to use, i.e., there's no particular difference between saying "It was nothing much" and "It was outta sight." That is to say, we've all heard the usual characterizations of 'our Protestant society' or 'our Puritan background,' which involve that ordinary people/Americans/Europeans are built in such a way that they are constrained from doing lots of experiences that they might do, were they not repressed. And we think of the kinds of repressions that people have that are sociologically based, i.e., the Puritan ethic involves spending most of your time working, holding off pleasure, etc., which we think of as definitively what it means to be a usual person in Western civilization. Though that's manifestly important, it misses an essential part of the thing, which is: Were you to *have* illegitimate experiences, the characteristic of being an 'ordinary person' is that, having the illegitimate experiences that you shouldn't have, they come off in just the usual way that they come off for anybody doing such an illegitimate experience. When you have an affair, take drugs, commit a crime, etc., you find that it's been the usual experience that others who've done it have had. Reports of the most seemingly outrageous experiences, for which you'd figure you'd be at a loss for words, or would have available extraordinary details of what happened, turn out to present them in a fashion that has them come off as utterly unexceptional. So we could perfectly well remove the Puritan constraints – as people report they're being removed – and our utter usualness, the ordinary cast of mind, would nonetheless be there to preserve the way we go about doing 'being ordinary.'

My guess is that we could now take that point with us, and, watching ourselves live in the world – or watching somebody else if that's more pleasant – we could see them working at finding how to make things ordinary. And presumably it would be from such a sort of perceived awareness of, e.g., the ease with which – after practice – you see only the most usual characteristics of the people passing (that's a married couple and that's a black guy and that's an old lady) or what a sunset looks like or what an afternoon with your girlfriend or boyfriend consists of, that you can begin to appreciate that there's some immensely powerful kind of mechanism operating in handling your perceptions and thoughts, other than the known and immensely powerful things like the chemistry of vision, etc. Those sorts of thing would not explain how it is that, e.g., you can come home day after day and, asked what happened, report without concealing, that nothing happened. And were you concealing something, if it were reported it would turn out to be nothing much. And, as it happens with you, so it happens with those you know. And further, that ventures outside of being ordinary have unknown virtues and unknown costs, i.e., if you come home and report what the grass looked like along the freeway, that there were four noticeable shades of green some of which just appeared yesterday because of the rain, then there may well be some tightening up on the part of your recipient. And if you were to do it routinely, then people might figure that there's something odd about you; that you're pretentious. You might find them jealous of you; you might lose friends. That is to say, you want to ask what are the costs, and if people have checked out the costs of venturing even slightly into making their life an epic.

Now it's also the case that there are people who are entitled to have their lives be an epic. We have assigned a series of storyable people, places, and objects, and they stand as something different from us. It may be that in pretty much every circle there's a somebody who's the source and/or the subject of all neat observations, as there are for the society in general a collection of people about whom detailed reports are made; reports that would never, not merely be ventured about others, they'd never be *thought* of about others. The way in which Elizabeth Taylor turned around is something noticeable, reportable. The way in which your mother turned around is something unseeable, much less nonreportable.

The question is, why in the world should it be that it's almost everybody's business to be occupationally ordinary? Why do they take on the job – it's not that others do it for them – of keeping everything utterly mundane? I'm not going to answer that question, but I guess it has some diagnostic interest, i.e., there are presumably a really large collection of what seem to be serious changes in the world – changes in governments, economies, religions – that would not change the business of being ordinary. Across such changes it is enforced on pretty much everybody that they stay ordinary, finding only how it is that what's going on is usual, with all their effort possible.

And it's really remarkable to see people's efforts to achieve the 'nothing happened' sense of really catastrophic events. I've been collecting fragments out of newspapers, about hijackings and what the airplane passengers think when a hijacking takes place. The latest one I happened to find goes something like this: "I was walking up towards the front of the airplane and by the cabin I saw the stewardess standing, facing the cabin, and a fellow standing with a gun in her back. And my first thought was he's showing her the gun, and then I realized that couldn't be, and then it turned out he was hijacking the plane." And another; a Polish plane is in the midst of being hijacked, and the guy reports, "I thought to myself we just had a Polish hijacking a month ago and they're already making a movie of it." And a classically dramatic instance is that almost universally the initial report of the Kennedy assassination (the first one), was of firecrackers.

Just imagine rewriting the Old Testament in its monumental events, with ordinary people having gone through it. What would they have heard and seen, e.g., when voices called out to them, when it started to rain, etc. There's at least one place in the Old Testament where that happens. Lot was warned of the burning of Sodom and Gomorrah, and given permission to bring his daughters and sons-in-law out. "And Lot went out, and spake unto his sons in law, which married his daughters, and said, Up, get you out of this place; for the Lord will destroy this city. But he seemed as one that mocked unto his sons in law." And they stayed behind.

Here I'm only giving specifically dramatic sorts of things, as compared to seeing the interesting possibilities in an event that can also be seen to be ordinary — which is really a much more fundamental kind of thing. And when we start considering stories, at least one tack we can take is to treat the overwhelming banality of the stories we encounter — in my data, in our own experiences — as not so much something that, e.g., allows for statistical analysis of variation, or that makes them therefore uninteresting to study, but as a specific feature which turns on a kind of attitude; say, an attitude of working at being usual, which is perhaps central to the way our world is organized.

Now there are enormous virtues to seeing the usual in a scene. It permits all kinds of routine ways of dealing with it. Also, if you're dealing with an utter stranger, e.g., somebody in an approaching car when you're about to cross a street, it seems to be awfully useful to know that what he sees, looking at you, is the usual thing anyone would see, with its usual relevancies, and not God only knows what. You do not, then, have to make an each-and-every-time decision whether or not you'll be allowed the right of way. So, then, I'm not saying let's do away with the ways in which we go about being ordinary. Rather, if being ordinary is the sort of thing I'm suggesting it is, then we want to know what importances it has.

# 84

# Treating Method and Form as Phenomena: An Appreciation of Garfinkel's Phenomenology of Social Action

*Lenore Langsdorf*

In the beginning is the deed.... We wish, then, to consider the surrounding lifeworld concretely, in its neglected relativity... the world in which we live intuitively... with its real entities... as they give themselves to us at first in straightforward experience.... Our exclusive task shall be to comprehend precisely... this whole merely subjective and apparently incomprehensible 'Heraclitean flux.' – Edmund Husserl, *The Crisis of European Sciences and Transcendental Philosophy*

In doing sociology, lay and professional, every reference to the 'real world'... is a reference to the organized activities of everyday life. Ethnomethodological studies analyze everyday activities as members' methods for making those same activities visibly-rational-and-reportable-for-all-practical-purposes, i.e. 'accountable'... – Harold Garfinkel, *Studies in Ethnomethodology*

Our everyday world is, from the outset, an intersubjective world of culture... because, from the outset, the lifeworld is a universe of significations... a framework of meaning which we have to interpret, and of interrelations of meaning which we institute only through our action in this life world. – Alfred Schutz, "Phenomenology and the Social Sciences"

The domain of inquiry toward which Harold Garfinkel began to direct us, twenty five years ago, is a domain of our own deeds. Quite a few years later, he characterized that domain as one of "unsuspected" and "radical"

Source: *Human Studies*, 1995, vol. 18, no. 2–3, pp. 177–188.

"phenomena" (1991: 11). After characterizing ethnomethodology's task as one of "searching for, and specifying" those phenomena, and in order that "concreteness not be handed over to generalities" (1991: 15), he went on to list almost 20 investigations that had uncovered such previously undetected phenomena and then to say, quite specifically, just "what is ethnomethodological about these studies" (1991: 16). In these remarks, I want to extend that reflective portrayal by specifying just what is phenomenological about ethnomethodological enquiries – and also, to say something about why that matters.

Ethnomethodology begins with a deliberately-formulated hypothesis that stands Talcott Parsons' assumed hypothesis on its head. The allusion to Marx's claim that he was turning Hegel on his head, and therefore on his feet, is quite deliberate. For Parsons taught us, as Garfinkel (1991: 13) says, "that there was no orderliness in concrete activities." Since the "concreteness of things" does not in itself yield knowledge, Parsons reasoned, we must either abandon scientific study of society, or, we must impose an analytically-arrived-at structure upon concrete, actual social action. The structure will enable us to know the phenomena. Garfinkel accepted Parsons' basic thesis – that social phenomena are knowable by virtue of their structures – but in a radically re-specified way. With Parsons, describing the phenomena in terms of their structural features – their form – makes knowledge of social action possible. But contrary to Parsons' assumption that form or structure is a conceptual story to be added to an edifice of perceptually accessible phenomena – an informing of the phenomena – Garfinkel proposes that structure is a matter of "radical phenomena" that can be uncovered within the phenomena themselves. Social research is to begin with uncovering, not informing.

If we understand radicality as a procedure of going to the roots, then, Garfinkel's proposal can be formulated as this hypothesis: if the structure of social action is to account for the phenomena of social action, it must be uncovered, made apparent, at the roots of the already apparent phenomena. Less metaphorically: very early on in the complex sequence of doings and undergoings that eventually are labelled "social action" is a domain of deeds, ongoingly organized and rarely thought about as such.[1] The structure of social action, then, is a matter of deeds which are hidden at the basic – formative – levels of any social situation (the content or subject matter of sociology). Structure or form is composed of "unsuspected phenomena" that can be thematized – brought into the purview of knowledge. But doing that requires that we cease assuming, with an honored line of sociologists from Durkheim to Parsons, that the "objective reality of social facts is sociology's fundamental principle."[2] Instead, Garfinkel (1991: 11) proposes, that reality is "sociology's fundamental [that is, radical and previously unsuspected] phenomenon." An ethnomethodological attitude thus requires a change in the direction of search: rather than looking for extrinsic *principles*, we look to intrinsic *phenomena*. What does not change is the interest in the social as "objective reality." In Husserl's (1970: 156) terms, this is an interest in the "objective reality" of the "surrounding lifeworld . . . the world in which we live intuitively . . . with its real entities. . . ." In Schutz's (1962: 133) elaboration, this is an interest in the "objective reality" of "an intersubjective world of culture . . . because, from the outset, the lifeworld is a universe of significations. . . ."

Harold Garfinkel taught us to dig for the roots of that "objective reality"; to uncover these new, "unsuspected," "radical" phenomena, instead of devising principles to account for the empirically accessible phenomena focused upon by "formal analytic" sociology. The remarkable body of work he inspired by refocusing research on the very basic level of the deed is an affirmation of how much is to be learned by attending to the doings at the core of social action. In many cases, as Garfinkel has reminded us in regard to the taken-for-granted nature of accomplishments that constitute the lifeworld, assumptions can obscure accomplishments. Here we may well have an instance of an accomplishment obscuring assumptions. In what follows, I want to discuss one such assumption, in order to show the connections I see between ethnomethodology and phenomenology and propose that both those research strategies would benefit from strengthening these connections.

The assumption I'll be focusing on is articulated in the oft-heard characterization that ethnomethodology "just describes"; that it is not concerned to use, develop, or validate a theory; that it has no method and an unscientific, or perhaps only vague, methodology. Alternatively, I've also heard (in both positive and negative tones) that ethnomethodology permits if not advocates a positivistic method of just depicting "the given," without theoretical admixture or influence. Both advocates and opponents are apt to affirm the descriptive (in contrast to explanatory) nature of ethnomethodology – although they do so with a diversity of meanings that's instructive, for those of us who are interested in the plurivocity of communicative action.

On the one hand, complaints about lack of theory are a major theme in disparagement by sociologists who cherish their discipline's scientific status. This status may well be so tenuous as to be threatened by proposals that speak (as Garfinkel in Button, 1991 do), of "respecification" or an "alternative sociology." On the other hand, there are advocates (and I count myself among them) who see ethnomethodology's general disinterest in theory as a virtue, despite the political danger that a non- and even anti-theoretical stance poses to scientific and academic acceptability. For many of us, this positive evaluation has developed against a background of discouragement with a sociology that is theory-laden and method-controlled, perhaps to the point of suffocating "findings" within elegantly fashioned methodological and theoretical quilts. Alternatively, concern with theory can take the form of either quiet or vociferous adoption of theoretical or methodological precedents from the formal or physical sciences. This is unacceptable to many of us who discern differences among formal, physical, and social sciences that should be nurtured rather than suppressed.[3]

When we consider this "just description" remark more closely, we can find an assumption about theory and method obscured within it: if they exist, they must be discussed, explicitly and often at length, as principles and rules that hold generally (even, universally) in abstraction from particular content. Ethnomethodologists don't do that. This seems to me a commendable instance of practice matching preaching: if asked what ethnomethodology is, Garfinkel's response is apt to be in terms of how it goes about what it *does*.[4] That pattern is quite clear in both of the Garfinkel texts that are central to my reflection here. In the 1967 introductory essay, he gives a scant eleven pages to talking about how ethnomethodology generally goes about its practice, before shifting abruptly to lengthy presentations of three examples of uncovering "artful practices" (1967: 11, 34), followed by a brief "recitation of study policies." In the 1991 "Respecification" essay he summarizes the differences between "formal analytic sociology" and ethnomethodology in a few marvelously dense paragraphs and then gives five pages of detail on ethnomethodology's origins in Parsons' "wonderful book" (1991: 11). That account is followed by a listing of "studies . . . that . . . show . . . that, and just how" the actual doings of particular groups of people "produce and exhibit the . . . locally, reflexively accountable orderliness" that structures "their ordinary lives together, in detail" (1991: 17). We have here a clear pattern: rather than general talk about what ethnomethodology is, Garfinkel insists upon telling *how* particular studies go about their inquiries.

In keeping with the phenomenological practice of examining particular cases with the aim of discerning persistent patterns within and across them, I find that the exemplary studies Garfinkel lists and the research policies he recommends display three strategies for ethnomethodological research that carry out Husserl's "wish . . . to consider the surrounding lifeworld concretely, in its neglected relativity." Since these strategies provide evidence for my claim that Garfinkel's program carries out Husserl's program, we need to begin consideration of them by acknowledging the difference between Husserl's and Garfinkel's programs. I'll then go on to describe the aspects of Husserl's program that seem to be both inspiration for, and fulfilled by, Garfinkel's program.

Succinctly stated: Husserl is as thoroughly the theoretician, much occupied with methodology and stingy with actual case studies, as Garfinkel is the practitioner, wary of theory and methodology and quick to redirect us from *talk* about methodology to the actual *work* done in case studies. What we need to do in order to uncover the hidden phenomena that are ethnomethodology's "data," then, is go beyond Husserl's predilection for talking about phenomenology in abstraction from actual cases of phenomenological analysis. Yet we need briefly to recount the revolution in theory and method that Husserl accomplished, so that these contrasts between phenomenology and ethnomethodology may appear as those appropriate to a propaedeutic in contrast to a practice.

Phenomenology's theoretical revolution occurs in refocusing inquiry away from either a concern for "the subject" or "the object," and toward "an experience" in which interaction between those elements occurs. "The subject" here could be understood on the model of a Cartesian ego prevalent in both empiricism and rationalism. Or it could be understood as a social actor, as in traditional sociology. "The object" might be the perceptual or conceptual items prevalent in traditional philosophical inquiry. Or it might be language as in traditional linguistics; or, "the object" might be a particular use of language, such as aborigines documenting sacred sites so as to withstand encroachment from non-indigenous persons, or residents of a halfway house "talking the convict code." In all of these cases, Husserl redirects us toward the encompassing context of doing and undergoing as the proper site for investigation.

The theoretical importance of this redirection emerges when we consider a theory as a body of ideas that presents a comprehensive and systematic view of "what counts" as relevant to investigation of a particular subject matter. Typically, these factors are stated in a series of propositions allowing for validation or falsification. That comprehensive and systematic view could be based on facts about "the object." Or, it might be a view based on imaginative speculation as to what "the object," comprehensively viewed, could be like. Respectively, those two procedures are often called "bottom-up" and "top-down" theorizing. Until quite recently, the dominant mode of theorizing in Western intellectual history has been of the "top-down" variety: a comprehensive view of "the object" is posited, although often on the basis of selection from what has been observed or deduced; it is then imposed upon "the data" as an enlightening and even explanatory matrix.

Husserl's redirection of inquiry toward "experience" begins before "the object" and "the subject" are delineated. In the quotation with which we began, he identifies this beginning as a "whole merely subjective and apparently incomprehensible 'Heraclitean flux'" of deeds; of ongoing doings that pervasively display directedness toward particular events and items that present themselves as instigating, and being influenced by, those doings.[5] He restricts the focus of inquiry to that domain of doings and undergoings in order to discern, in what is present to us, the emerging of "the subject" (an instituting of attention, talk, and action) and "the object" (that which is attended to, talked about, and acted upon). In order to stress the intrinsic transactional status of those experiential aspects as they are constituted within a context, he refuses to speak of them in the traditional, "natural" theoretical terminology of "subject" and "object." For Husserl, inquiry leads to comprehension by beginning from an unnatural (so to speak) reflective focus on doings. Two correlates, "noetic" directedness and "noematic" focus, can be analytically discerned as moments (that is, distinct but not separable aspects) of the phenomena of our experience. These are recognized as constituted in processual experience, but are not granted ontological status as "subject" and "object." Rather, they remain interactive "poles" of relative and interchangeable activity and passivity; of constituting and being constituted.

The revolutionary theoretical status of this redirection appears if we compare it to Kant's "Copernican Revolution," which also focuses attention on phenomena. Kant's accomplishment is often characterized as a "turn to the subject"; as such, there is a clear rejection of predominant theorizing that focuses on "the object." Kant specifies "the object" through a series of steps that expand and contract the process of inquiry. The initial expansion occurs by borrowing the Copernican strategy of taking the location of inquiry's inception into account along with the location of its termination. Then a contraction occurs by positing diverse realms (of noumena and phenomena), the first of which is discarded from scientific consideration. Another expansion occurs as Kant conceptualizes "the object" (now intrinsically joined to "the subject") in terms of "content" to which "form" has been added. This has the curious effect of reminding us that any phenomenon ("the object") is bound to an investigating subjectivity as such ("the subject"), and placing form (more precisely, the forms of intuition and categories of judgment used by that subjectivity) outside the realm of phenomena. We posit the forms and categories as the structure *of* appearance; as the conditions for the possibility of phenomena. But we cannot find them in, and therefore justify them by, the phenomena.

The result of the Kantian revolution is thus a "top-down" theory that Husserl rejects. While praising Kant as well as Descartes for turning toward subjectivity as an intrinsic component of any inquiry, he objected to their failure to ground – to show the roots of – the theoretical structures they used. More generally, he saw the entire history of theory as accepting "the subject" and "the object" as structures given to, rather than discerned in, experience. Phenomenology as a *theory* insists on overturning both everyday and theoretical categories in order to uncover – make apparent – the hidden phenomena from which those "givens" are constituted. Phenomenology as a method justifies all of its claims intrinsically, without recourse to extrinsic, posited structures that inform phenomena – but with very close attention to the sedimenting of structures that intrinsically form phenomena in interactive experience.

To the discomfort of some phenomenologists, this method of tracing the genesis of phenomena from their beginnings in deeds does not lead to univocal, infallible descriptions of things. Instead, a genetic phenomenological method based in Husserl's theory leads to a comprehension of "objective reality" as Schutz's "universe of significations . . . a framework of meaning which we have to interpret, and of interrelations of meaning which we institute only through our action in this lifeworld." To summarize the result of Husserl's theoretical revolution, then: his decisive turn to describing "the things themselves" as they are actively present leads to seeking out the genesis of those phenomena. That search leads to a multiplicity of possible interpretations, rather than to causal or nomological claims. It also leads beyond "significations," to "action."

There is a great danger here: our phenomenological theory and method can leave us at a place that still is unconnected to our ongoing lived experience of "objective reality." In other words, a "bottom-up" theory such as Husserlian phenomenology, elaborated by Schutz as a phenomenology of the lifeworld, provides an alternative theory and method that responds to the interests of sociologists who are preoccupied with how the "organized activities of everyday life" happen. Yet the theory and method of phenomenology also tell us that there are major differences between the interests, practices, and subject-matter of sociologists, and the interests, practices, and subject-matter of social actors themselves.

Phenomenological theory tells us that the orientation of social actors is one of straightforward involvement in the surrounding lifeworld and that our interests are pragmatic. In this "natural attitude" we function without doubting the facts – the "givens" – of our subject-matter. Prominent among our beliefs is the assumption that language is used to communicate about things which exist without need of being talked about. Until we encounter specific and unavoidable doubts, we act with confidence in what appears to be the case, while acknowledging that those appearances may well seem otherwise, to others. Lifeworld practices neglect a lot that is irrelevant to immediate pragmatic needs, and accomplish a lot that is relative to those needs. In short, lifeworld practice takes a good deal for granted.

As sociologists using a phenomenological method, however, we take an analytic distance from the lifeworld that continues to surround us. Our interests are reflective, and our attitude is one of persistent questioning of what we identify as the "objective reality" of social actors. Our attitude toward facts relates more to the etymology of the term – facts are "things done" – than to taking facts as "givens," since the theory directs us to question how and why particular facts are accomplished. Within this orientation, we notice that communication, including linguistic communication, manages the environment so as to carve out things from a manifold of possibilities. We thus may come to suspect that all things come to be on the basis of being spoken – rather than come to be spoken about, because they already exist. As phenomenologists of social action, we avoid both that linguistically-based attitude, and the "natural" attitude (for which things simply are), by beginning with what we might call "conservative phenomena," in two senses of the term. First, they are phenomena that are not "radical" in Garfinkel's sense: they are not hidden and unsuspected, but evident and expected. Also, they are investigated as phenomena that conserve, and even reify, the actions by which they were constituted.

Thus phenomenological sociology begins from the end, so to speak. Rather than being prodded by pragmatic needs to constitute phenomena, the analyst's theoretical needs require a focus on ongoing results of constitutive transactions. Phenomenology then demands that the analyst always look backward, so to speak, in order to discover what is hidden within the evident; what is unsuspected in the midst of the expected. Although "artful practices" peculiar to social inquiry are needed to carry out this "radical" task, the aim is to recover the "things themselves" without admixture of these practices. Rather, the aim is to report on some content as constituted in our social actions, in accord with mundane, "conservative" practices – and without intrusion from the sociologist's method or interests. As mundane actors with diverse interests and needs, we seek change or stability. As phenomenological analysts, we seek to investigate – not to add to, or undo – those actions. In brief, phenomenological practice forbids innovation just as much as lifeworld practice demands it.

Once we discern this considerable gap in the interests, attitudes, and activities of social actors and phenomenological sociologists, the lack of connection between phenomenologically-motivated inquiry and lifeworld practice is unsurprising. Yet without that connection, we have at best an alternative to Parsons' portrayal of the structure of social action. That is, we can propose methods for analyzing phenomena into constituent elements and interactions, forms and methods. But we still don't have ways of thematizing social actors' own methods and forms as phenomena; of discerning our accomplishments as "practicing methodologists." At best, this alternative starts in the middle, rather than at the theory-laden top: it seeks to analyze "the things themselves" in order to discern their intrinsic structure, rather than impose a structure upon them. But it does not truly begin at the beginning, at the level of the deed, in order to discern the genesis of things in ongoing transactional processes.

We can now consider the three strategies for ethnomethodological inquiry that I mentioned earlier in referring to ethnomethodology as the practice which continues Husserl's revolution in theory and method. More to the point in appreciating Garfinkel's work, I want to consider these strategies as ethnomethodology's own "artful practices" (1967: 11, 32, 34) directed by an interest, attitude, and activity inspired by, but quite distinct from, the interests, attitudes, and activities that motivate either social actors or phenomenological sociologists.

The basic strategy for ethnomethodological analysis is adopting an *attitude* that is neither the social actors' "natural attitude" or the phenomenologists' distanciation by means of epoche-and-reduction. Rather, it is a variation of the phenomenological attitude, and it seeks to explicate the natural attitude. Ethnomethodologists institute, instead, what I would call an *archaeological* attitude. It supports their investigative activity, even as the natural attitude supports the social actor's confidence in things being as they seem, and the phenomenologist's "methodical doubt" supports suspending that confidence and analyzing things only as related to, and thus relative to, their experiential contexts. This archaeological attitude requires that ethnomethodologists, in uncovering social actors' methods for organizing the affairs of everyday life, study those new phenomena without re-forming them; which is to say, without replacing mundane "artful practices" with the ethnomethodologist's own "artful practices." This is no more difficult than (but then again no easier than) sifting through the layers of a dig without losing, or leaving behind, or adding, fragments of artifacts. Issues of accessibility, contingency, and plausibility (rather than certainty) of claims are remarkably parallel in traditional physical archaeology and in this radical cultural archaeology.

The strategy for *activity* within ethnomethodology's archaeological attitude is a series of policies for conducting *experiental*, rather than empirical or speculative, research. It is not an empirical strategy in that it does not focus on identifying the events and objects of a domain so as to describe and explain them in order to control and change them, in accord with particular pragmatic interests. Nor is it speculative, in that it does not begin with a story as to what has happened, and then seek support for that story in the "data." Rather than presupposing either a goal of inquiry or a particular pattern, order, or form to be located in the social facts, ethnomethodologists engage the situation: they intervene in the flux of events so as to enable noticing and minutely examining both evident and (initially) hidden phenomena. There are several phenomenological procedures used in this interventionist stance. Perhaps the most important is variation or possibilizing, which the ethnomethodologist uses in gaining access to the variety of choices made by actors as they interpret their situations.

The last strategy for comment here has to do with the *interest* that instigates ethnomethodological inquiry. It is not the pragmatic interest of social actors in the natural attitude. Nor is it the theoretical interest that dominates much of phenomenological investigation. But it is an interest adopted by those phenomenological studies that seek to trace the roots of theoretical entities and practices in the lifeworld processes which generate them. This *processual* interest requires actual or imaginative entry into the very deeds under analysis, rather than reflection upon them or involvement in their products. It is confined to discerning the ongoing organizational practices from which "the things themselves" emerge.

Perhaps this processual interest is most clearly evident in conversation analysis. In order to discern the intrinsic order in that phenomenon, the analyst must actually become another listener. In thus becoming a silent participant in the actual conversation under study, the analyst uses the methods of the originating participants, in order to ongoingly form the phenomena as they do. As analytic participant, the ethnomethodologist is relieved of the originating participants' pragmatic interests, and refrains from taking on theoretical interests. The interest that directs ethnomethodological inquiry thus is confined to reflexively discerning participants' actual methods for forming (constituting) any phenomenon: to treating method and form as phenomena.

My appreciation of Garfinkel's way of studying social action centers on these innovative strategies for discerning new phenomena. They direct us to neglect what we've been told about social action in favor of recognizing and exploring what we always and already know of social action. Garfinkel begins with experiences that we perform (rather than, experiences that we're informed about by a non-performer). He then calls upon the potential for reflexivity that is intrinsic to such action in order to turn our attention from what we do to how we do it. In other words: he reminds us that we could not go about a variety of everyday life activities unless we knew what we are doing. Since we do get through the day, we know what we're doing – and we can develop methods for reflecting on the methods of that doing; on how we organize the experiences that constitute daily life. Through such demonstrations, he redirects our attention to a previously neglected but "fundamental phenomenon." In his words: "the reflexivity of that phenomenon" is the enabling feature which allows us to investigate "the objective reality of social facts as an ongoing accomplishment of the concerted activities of daily life" (1967: vii).

## Notes

1. Inclusion of "undergoings" along with "doings" suggests an affiliation with both American pragmatism's stress on connections and consequences in particular situations and Euro-American hermeneutic scholarship's stress on the human condition as one of "thrownness" (Heidegger) into situations that are always already formed by tradition. "Experience," Dewey (1980: 8–9) finds, "is primarily a process of undergoing . . . [which] is never mere passivity . . . [it] is a matter of *simultaneous* doings and sufferings." He (1980: 26) goes on to say that "experiencing *is* just certain modes of interaction . . . [it] means primarily not knowledge, but ways of doing and suffering."

Schutz (1962: 133), similarly, understands the lifeworld as getting to us (so to speak) before we get to it: we "live in and endure" the lifeworld by means of a "living intentionality" that "supports our thinking, by which we orient ourselves practically . . . and our action, by which we intervene in it."

Garfinkel's analysis of social action, by identifying strategies (ethnomethods) we use in experiencing situations, enables us to resist strong constructionist positions by documenting the extent to which social action responds – often, with considerable ingenuity – to the practices and exigencies of an always already sedimented social reality which we "undergo" or "endure."

2. "For *The Structure of Social Action*, Durkheim's aphorism is intact: 'The objective reality of social facts is sociology's fundamental principle.'" (Garfinkel, 1991: 11).

3. Opting for nurture here is taking a position in favor of multiplicity in the long history of dispute as to whether the *Geisteswissenschaften* are, and/or ought to be, theoretically and/or methodologically differentiated from, or unified with, the *Naturwissenschaften*. Melvin Pollner's (1991) concern (even, lament) in regard to the neglect of "radical referential reflexivity" demonstrates, I'd argue, that this dispute remains significant for how we go about doing, and defending, ethnomethodological research.

Pollner (1991: 370, 372) finds that "appreciation of ethnomethodology as an expression of the very processes it finds suffused in other forms of inquiry has declined," to the point where "contemporary studies view themselves . . . in terms of their capacity to represent empirical structures." Insofar as ethnomethodological studies fail to "challenge the subject/object duality underlying conventional inquiry" (Pollner, 1991: 370) they opt for a unity of science position that makes observation, rather than interaction, the basis of method in both "social" and "natural" science. Insofar as they do continue that challenge, their status as "empirical" sciences is threatened; cf. note 5.

4. Garfinkel's insistence upon definition through instances may be yet another source of traditional sociologists' disapproval and dismissal of ethnomethodological research. In the *Republic* Plato asked "What is justice?" and dismissed efforts to respond

in terms of concrete instantiations rather than verbal generalizations. Philosophy followed that example until Wittgenstein taught us to account for category inclusion on the basis of "family resemblances" rather than conceptual formulations.

5. This way of accessing "experience" suggests that phenomenology both is, and is not, empirical. Traditional empiricism, as developed by Locke and Hume and adopted by "mainstream" social science, holds that all knowledge is based in experience and understands "experience" as a subject's observation of an object (event or thing). Husserl declines to assume these "givens" (subjects observing objects), in favor of an encompassing analysis of occasions in which perceiving (in the broad sense of directed interaction, which includes sensory, affective, and volitional engagement) occurs.

If this alternative understanding of "experience" (in which the sedimented practices of past experience are more prominent than "self" or "sense-data") is acceptable, then phenomenology's claim to be an empirical mode of inquiry should be equally acceptable. But the steadfast focus is on interaction (and thus, participation) rather than observation (and thus, separation of observing subject from observed object; cf. note 3). The result is a methodology that is closer to praxis-based research, such as in Marxist and neo-marxist as well as pragmatic traditions, than to traditional empiricism or, for that matter, rationalism. Husserl frequently refers to "consciousness" and sometimes speaks of the lifeworld as "merely subjective." (The quotation at the start of this essay and the fragment from it that instigates this note are examples of that practice.) This emphasis on one component of interaction (subjectivity), together with his radically revised understanding of "experience" as interactive rather than observational, may well encourage an especially damaging interpretation of phenomenology as an introspective endeavor concerned with mental structures – which is to say, as a species of rationalism and thus, as vulnerable to current criticism of "logocentric" thinking. Perhaps the best way to counter those claims is to do phenomenology, rather than explicate the intellectual situation in which Husserl's particular way of speaking made sense. One could then adopt Garfinkel's strategy of telling how research happens in particular cases, rather than talking about it in the abstract.

## References

Dewey, J. (1980). The need for a recovery of philosophy. In J. A. Boydston (Ed.), *John Dewey: The middle works, 1899–1924*, vol. 10. Carbondale, IL: Southern Illinois University Press.

Garfinkel, H. (1967). *Studies in ethnomethodology.* Englewood Cliffs, NJ: Prentice-Hall.

Garfinkel, H. (1991). Respecification: Evidence for locally produced, naturally accountable phenomena of order, logic, reason, meaning, method, etc. in and as of the essential haecceity of immortal ordinary society, (I) – an announcement of studies. In G. Button (Ed.), *Ethnomethodology and the human sciences.* Cambridge: Cambridge University Press.

Husserl, E. (1970). *The crisis of European sciences and transcendental phenomenology.* Trans. D. Carr. Evanston: Northwestern University Press.

Pollner, M. (1991). Left of ethnomethodology: The rise and decline of radical reflexivity. *American Sociological Review* 56: 370–380.

Schutz, A. (1962). Phenomenology and the social sciences. In M. Natanson (Ed.), *Collected papers*, vol. 1: *The problem of social reality.* The Hague: Martinus Nijhoff.

# Drama as Life: The Significance of Goffman's Changing Use of the Theatrical Metaphor

## Phil Manning

In this paper I discuss three elements of Goffman's work, all of which have been influenced by his view of the role of metaphor in sociology. The first element is his substantive account of face-to-face interaction. At different times he has described everyday behavior in terms of many different metaphors, although the theatrical metaphor is probably the most important of these. One tendency (among others) in his early work is to see face-to-face interaction as a zero-sum game in which individuals manipulate their performances: each person hides behind a "persona" (etymologically a "mask"). According to this account, we are all cynical actors who practice impression management in the pursuit of personal gain. In his writings in the 1960s and thereafter, Goffman placed less and less emphasis on the cynical aspects of impression management and focused more intensely on the importance of trust in everyday encounters. Trust is evident in the rituals that allow routine interaction among strangers in urban settings. Goffman's analysis of the trust displayed in urban anonymity required him to distance himself from the theatrical metaphor.

Caution is needed, however. This brief description of Goffman's early work is an oversimplification. To do full justice to his thought we must consider the impact of Durkheim on his work, as Randall Collins has suggested, and also his debt to Simmel (see Smith 1989). Elements of an account of ritual are present in his doctoral thesis and thereafter. In this paper I want only to show that one tendency in his early work – to view people as cynical manipulators – is influenced by a dramaturgical metaphor which *itself* is used later to challenge this model of human behavior. The transition actually occurs in Goffman's revisions to the second edition of *Presentation of Self* (1956, 1959).

The second aim of this paper is to consider metaphor as a key to Goffman's often puzzling methodology. For understanding of this method, I am greatly indebted to earlier work by Baldamus (1972) and Williams (1988). Combining their work with Goffman's allows us to understand possible connections between social theory and literary theory.

The third aim of this paper is to make some brief observations about the tensions that can be observed in Goffman's later work. His indebtedness to metaphor seems to suggest that sociological analysis has important limits; in particular, it seems to suggest that sociological findings are partial and are informed by the writer's viewpoint. This idea is part of a "neo-Kantian" legacy, observable in the writings of both Simmel and Weber. In his later work, however, Goffman often tried to formalize our knowledge of face-to-face interaction in a way which implies that the limits set by metaphor can be transcended. Nevertheless, on these occasions he frequently parodied these efforts to construct a single explanation of everyday behavior as well. The result is that in some later texts (perhaps most noticeably *Forms of Talk* 1981), it is possible to identify different "voices" arguing about the merits and limitations of metaphorical analysis in sociology. These texts confront the question of rule following in everyday life. The account which emerges from the later Goffman is that rules are both constraints which govern behavior and resources which people use to justify or rationalize their actions. This suggestion brings Goffman close to Wittgensteinian and ethnomethodological schools of thought.

This paper addresses four topics: sociology and metaphor, Goffman and the theatrical metaphor, metaphor as a research method, and metaphor in Goffman's later work.

## Sociology and Metaphor

In this section I suggest, first, that metaphors are understood better as conceptual models than as words and, second, that our ability to understand them is tied to an ability to extend their use to a multiplicity of settings. The implication is that metaphors can be "stretched" across many different examples. Thus, for example, the metaphor "life is a confidence trick" can be shown to apply on all kinds of occasions. I intend here to provide a thumbnail sketch of the issues concerning the role of metaphor in sociology.

In recent years the literature on metaphor has grown to an unmanageable size; my own route through this literature is unavoidably very selective. My intention is simply to draw upon various studies in order to formalize a position that will assist a reading of this aspect of Goffman's work. Borrowing from Richard Brown's *A Poetic for Sociology* (1977), I define metaphor in the following way:

> Metaphor involves the transfer of one term from one system or level of meaning to another; for example, Dante's "Hell is a lake of ice";
> Metaphor is literally absurd;

Metaphors are meant to be understood;
Metaphor is self-consciously "as if" (1977, pp. 80–85).

When metaphors attend to fleeting resemblances between apparently disparate phenomena, they incite us to make a cognitive leap or connection that subsequently appears to be both inspired and self-evident. On such occasions metaphors seem to provide a link to an object's identity: they are ladders leading us to higher forms of understanding. Later still, however, these metaphors can become disappointing, their resemblances unconvincing, their connections wearying, wrong, or patently absurd. Metaphor's nervous energy then is dissipated into loose formulations, and its ladders are transformed back into snakes. More depressing still is the case of metaphors whose energy is not dissipated but simply lost: they "die" and enter speech merely as literal expressions or adjectives. "Skyscrapers" and "feeling lousy" are dead metaphors, now used unthinkingly in everyday talk.

Any metaphor can be given up, allowed to perish, forgotten, or replaced by other metaphors; tropically speaking, change is the norm and permanence a masquerade. This intuitive view suggests that metaphor is valuable only as an appendage to research in the social sciences: it is the crank to start the engine but not the fuel to sustain the car. Advocates of this view hold to what Ricoeur (1986) calls a "substitution" theory of metaphor, which suggests that metaphor is no more than a concise way of expressing ideas.

A sizable body of work recently has taken a rather different view of the role of metaphor and other tropes in both the natural and the social sciences. Different metaphors are not regarded as exemplifying problems and solutions to questions in the natural and social sciences. Instead these problems and solutions themselves are believed to be only examples of the influence of different metaphors – not metaphor in the text of philosophy but philosophy in the text of metaphor, as Derrida suggests at various points in "White Mythology." He acknowledges that this essay owes much to Borges's short story "The Fearful Sphere of Pascal," which describes universal history as the study of the *intonations* of a few metaphors. According to this view, metaphors are indispensable tools – not tropes attending to fleeting resemblances but fully blown perspectives. With this point in mind, Brown (1977) claims that the history of sociology could be rewritten as the investigation of the ramification of a handful of metaphors; furthermore, that this investigation will never exhaust the resources of those metaphors. This view suggests, first, that sociologists must adopt or be adopted by perspectives which then guide and limit their view of the social world; second, it suggests that metaphors constitute rather than exemplify these perspectives. Metaphor is not so much a word or a sentence as a *conceptual system or model*: as Robin Williams puts it, "Metaphor is perspectivism in miniature" (1983, p. 101).

This account of metaphor underpins most of Goffman's first book, *The Presentation of Self in Everyday Life*, in which an analogy between social life and the theater is pursued at length. Goffman's procedure here, as several commentators have pointed out, is remarkably like Kenneth Burke's "perspective by incongruity." Burke developed this idea through his attempt to pursue the implications of Nietzsche's "dartlike" style, which works by its "constant juxtapositioning of incongruous words" (1955, p. 90). By these means Nietzsche invents a variety of ways to order the everyday world. Similarly, Goffman's *Presentation of Self* invents a vocabulary with which to consider anew what are otherwise quite banal daily events. With an array of apt redescriptions, Goffman makes the familiar, everyday world appear strange.

In *Permanence and Change* (1954) Burke argues that the Nietzschean idea of perspective by incongruity transforms the oversimplified classifications of sociological research into creative acts. He also warns, however, that the "great danger" accompanying the use of any trope is that an insightful similarity can be mistaken as evidence of a shared identity (1954, p. 97). This danger is present because the pertinent incongruities underlying metaphor are transported from one word to another, and this state of affairs can lend itself to the mistaken conflation of words and identities. This conflation is given more credence by the distinction between metaphor and simile: whereas the latter states quite explicitly, for example, that love is *like* a red rose, the former states that love *is* a red rose. The risk is that metaphor may be transformed from an insightful resemblance into an all-embracing world view. The suspicion is that metaphor may be both a restriction and a deception. As Derrida puts it, metaphor "orients research and fixes results" (1978a, p. 17); this suggestion originated perhaps in Nietzsche's famous claim that truth is merely "a mobile army of metaphors." Linguists such as George Lakoff and Mark Johnson have pursued this line of inquiry, arguing that particular metaphors generate conceptual systems which are entrenched in interactants' practical consciousness. Hence the metaphor "argument is war" is refracted throughout a host of everyday expressions that in turn help to structure our daily experiences, even though many of us would prefer to view argument in cooperative rather than military terms (Lakoff and Johnson 1980, pp. 3–13). This, then, is a *subversive* view of metaphor.

Particular problems arise, however, when this view is used to interpret the impact of metaphor on sociological research. What credence can metaphorical models be given, because, as Lakoff and Johnson put it, they both "highlight and hide" different aspects of the social world (1980, p. 10)?

Metaphorical models create perspectives that enable people to extend an initial similarity to an indefinite number of other cases. The perspective is invented, and produces a tension between invention and discovery. Although it is true that metaphors invent models of the social world by highlighting and hiding different factors, it is also true that the factors they highlight are often discoveries about the social world. This point is suggested by the fact that when metaphors work well, they appeal to our practical understandings of the everyday world. The analogy between theatrical productions and everyday life indeed makes good sense of some of our experiences; this is the reason both for its relative success and for the relative failure of metaphors that draw analogies between (for example) daily life and bananas.

Nehamas has suggested that another reason for this tension is the individual's need to believe that each new perspective is not merely one useful alternative among many but the best available. A drive to discover underpins the drive to create (1985, p. 59). Weber makes the same observation when he tells us that the height of self-understanding is the tragic knowledge that not only do other people hold beliefs contrary to one's own, but that they do so with neither less conviction nor with less justification (1949, p. 55). Rorty also makes this point when he claims that the citizens of an "ideally liberal state" would see their "highest hopes as contingent products, as literalizations of what were once accidentally-produced metaphors" (1986, p. 14).

## Goffman and the Theatrical Metaphor

As is well known, Goffman produced a significant body of work before the publication of *The Presentation of Self* (1956, 1959). In his early work, we can see two broad accounts of face-to-face interaction: one of these emphasizes manipulation and impression management; the other emphasizes the importance of ritual and tactful accommodation. For the most part, *The Presentation of Self*, especially in its first edition, focused on the first of these accounts and downplayed ritual concerns. Goffman's early analysis of ritual is captured in two essays from *Interaction Rituals: Essays on Face-to-Face Behavior* (1967), "On Face-Work" (1967 [1955]) and "The Nature of Deference and Demeanor" (1967 [1956]). The confrontation between cynicism and trust, however, can be felt throughout these texts. The tension between them is perhaps most acute in his doctoral dissertation.

In this section I want to show how the view of the individual as a cynical manipulator of public performances developed as one strand of Goffman's predramaturgical writings; these writings culminated in the first edition of *The Presentation of Self*, only to be undermined quietly by additions to the second edition of this famous sociological text. These changes mark a transition to his later analysis of the conditions of trust in modern society, and reaffirm strands that can be identified in his work from the early 1950s.

The fluency of the second edition (1959) of *The Presentation of Self* can obscure the fact that it was the outcome of a decade's work. In 1949 Goffman presented his paper "Symbols of Class Status" to the annual meeting of the University of Chicago Society for Social Research. Two years later a modified version (1951) was published in the *British Journal of Sociology*. In this paper Goffman explores a problem that exists in the still waters at the edge of the dramaturgical maelstrom. The crux of the paper is that although symbols of class status *represent* status, they do not *constitute* it. This discrepancy directs attention towards both fraudulent presentations of self and the attempts of legitimate status holders to immunize their symbols against misuse. Goffman explicates the importance of these symbols in Durkheimian terms, arguing that they affirm ritualistically the traditions and moral values of a community (1951, pp. 294–96). He believes that although these symbols are defended by "curator groups" – those who make access to them difficult – nevertheless there is a "circulation of symbols" among modern consumers, during which their uniqueness is obliterated (1951, pp. 300–304). Paradoxically, the effort by a community to adopt new and "untainted" symbols serves only to undermine the traditions it is meant to affirm.

The "Symbols" paper does not draw explicitly on the theater analogy, but it does raise questions about the necessary conditions for authentic presentations of self. A second paper, "On Cooling the Mark Out," published in *Psychiatry* in 1952, comes closer to this topic. Drawing on the idiom of confidence tricksters, Goffman discusses the cynical manipulations of everyday performances in the pursuit of profit. By metaphorical extension he divides the social world into "con artists" and their "marks," in which the former give the latter "instruction in the philosophy of taking a loss" (1952, p. 452). Here he argues that in everyday life we are all self-consciously "marked" men and women, conducting our activities so as to minimize the risk of being "conned" and subsequently of having to be "cooled out"; that is, of having to be reconciled to the "death" of one of our social selves (p. 462). In a memorable image he suggests that modern societies sort but do not segregate the dead, allowing them to continue to walk among the living (p. 463).

These two papers lead Goffman to the theatrical metaphor by providing him with both the occasions and the tools with which to speculate about the management of impressions in everyday life. For our purposes, the main distinction between the papers concerns their different attitudes toward tradition and manipulation: "Symbols" focuses on cooperation and trust, "Cooling the Mark" on the cynical exploitation of circumstances. This is a powerful strand in his early thinking.

*The Presentation of Self in Everyday Life* first was published by the University of Edinburgh in 1956 and later was expanded for a second edition published simultaneously in Great Britain and the United States. The later version contains some cosmetic changes: it is divided into more paragraphs, and the word "one" is substituted for "we." There are also important additions – a new section to the "Performances" chapter and an extension to the conclusion. Later I will suggest that these additions effectively *overturn* the book's main argument and mark a central change of direction for Goffman's work as a whole, but for the moment I want to consider the common core to the two editions.

Goffman describes *The Presentation of Self* as "a sort of handbook," a "report" outlining six dramaturgical "principles." These key terms generate an often bewildering array of definitions and classifications as they reorder the social world according to a theatrical perspective. The six principles are the performance, the team, the region, discrepant roles, communication out of character, and impression management.

Goffman defines a performance as "all the activity of a given participant on a given occasion which serves to influence in any way any of the other participants" (1959, p 26). A few pages later he adds, "I have been using the term 'performance' to refer to all the activity of an individual which occurs during a period marked by his continuous presence before a particular set of observers and which has some influence on the observers" (p. 32). If performances are to be successful, individuals must demonstrate their conviction that what is enacted is "the real reality" (p. 28) while sustaining a viable "front." This "front" comprises stage props (such as desks for lawyers or white coats for doctors) and appropriate facial expressions and role attitudes. By such means, performances are both realized and idealized as our all-too-human selves are transformed into socialized beings capable of expressive control. In the course of a performance, the individual's attributes may be stretched to the needs of the occasion; different audiences will be held at a distance, from which the performer hopes to appear more interesting. In many cases, the only mystery is that there is no mystery, and the dramaturgical problem is to make sure that no one realizes this fact (pp. 75–76).

Successful performances usually are staged not by individuals but by teams, who share both risk and discreditable information in a manner comparable to that of a secret society (1959, p. 108). Teams perform in "front regions" – spaces from which they are observable by their different publics. They rehearse in, relax in, and retreat to "back regions," areas where front-region performances are "knowingly contradicted as a matter of course" (pp. 110–14). Front and back regions are connected by a "guarded passageway." Throughout this discussion Goffman avoids the claim that authenticity can be regionalized; instead he seems to suggest that locations affect our perceptions of behavior in misinformed ways. Sometimes authenticity exists at center stage; sometimes inauthenticity exists in a dimly lit corner. Goffman was acute enough to realize the importance of spatial considerations at a time when these often were thought, quite erroneously, to be inconsequential. Since that time, work by Foucault (1978), Ignatieff (1978), Evans (1982), and many others working within a human geographic tradition have alerted us to the links between space, power, and knowledge.

The regionally variable behavior of team performances provides performers with secrets to keep. When knowledge of back-region activities could be of value, various people with "discrepant roles" attempt to gain access by masquerading as team members. They aim to find out about the different types of secrets held by team members.

Information, however, can be gleaned from performances without would-be intelligence officers misrepresenting themselves: this occurs when performers disclose damaging facts inadvertently. They do so, as Goffman puts it, "out of character." Failures of this sort are often acknowledged by the performers themselves with outbursts such as "Oh God!"; such an intrusion unravels any prior performances. Fearing the disclosure of discreditable information encourages performers to practice the art of impression management and to avoid unpleasant "scenes" in which each individual's *projected* self may become irreconcilable with a *presented* self (1959, p. 206). In such dreadful times an individual depends on the tact and charity of the audience to limit the extent of interactional damage. Audiences then are called upon not only to be tactful, but also to be tactful about their being tactful. Should their collective performance become strained or too self-evident, the "dramaturgical structure of social interaction is suddenly and poignantly laid bare," and outbursts of laughter or remonstration are necessary to cover the rapid realignment of teams and performers (p. 227).

The overall view in *The Presentation of Self* is that of a world in which people, whether individually or in groups, pursue their own ends with a cynical disregard for others. On the rare occasions when audience and performer cooperate, both endeavor to return hastily to the shelter of their various masks and disguises and to avoid disclosing their inner selves. Here Goffman views the individual as a set of performance masks hiding a manipulative and cynical self. I call this view the *two selves thesis*.

In the second edition of the book Goffman chose to include some passages that threaten this characterization of self and metaphor; I now wish to turn to these passages.

Both editions of *The Presentation of Self* outline six theatrical principles that can be used to interpret everyday behavior. An elaborate series of subclassifications and examples represents the person as a cynical manipulator of social encounters. The picture here is of an individual hiding behind a performance. Underpinning this account are the metaphors of the theater and of the confidence trick, both skillfully interwoven in a masterful literary display. Nevertheless, with a series of deft insertions to the second edition, the appropriateness of this imagery is brought into question.

Doubt arises near the beginning of the book: in the introduction to the second edition but not to the first, Goffman distinguishes impressions that individuals *give* from those which they *give off*. The key to this distinction is the intentions of the individual: impressions that are given are used admittedly, whereas those which are given off convey information inadvertently. At issue is the performer's awareness of the performance (1959, p. 14).

Following through the implications of this distinction leads us to the next of Goffman's additions to the second edition of *The Presentation of Self*. This can be seen by looking more closely at the first dramaturgical principle: the "performance," which is subdivided into seven distinct branches. The seventh of these branches is "mystification," a term referring to the ways in which people ("actors") accentuate some aspects of their performance while concealing others (1959, p. 68). Goffman suggests that people do this to keep their audiences at a distance; the assumption is that distance will make them appear enticing and mysterious. He cites the advice given to the King of Norway: avoid familiarity with "the people" in case they are disappointed (p. 68). In this example, mystification is a device used by the King of Norway: it is merely an appendage to him. By regarding the self in this way, dramaturgical analysis reduces the person to a manipulator behind changeable masks and façades. Earlier in the book, Goffman expresses exactly this thought when he comments that the apparent cynicism of professionals is "a means of insulating their *inner selves*" (p. 31, emphasis added). This expression reveals his explicit or implicit willingness to distinguish *two* selves.

When *The Presentation of Self* was reissued in 1959, Goffman reconsidered his earlier account of the self. For the most part he limited his revisions to stylistic changes and the amplification of the general theme. At two key points, however, he appended sections that challenge the *two selves* thesis. In a very curious way these sections are neither introduced nor distinguished from the prior body of text. Instead a second Goffman "voice" intrudes in a quietly disruptive fashion.

The first intervention I want to consider occurs on pages 76–82 of the Penguin edition. This appended section, called "Reality and Contrivance," is entirely new. The first sentence of this section mentions our commonsense acceptance of a model of human behavior based on the confidence trick. The ensuing pages then question this assumption, leading up to an example that profoundly disturbs the account of self on which both editions are built. In almost anecdotal fashion Goffman notes:

> And when we observe a young American middle-class girl playing dumb for the benefit of her boyfriend, we are ready to point to items of guile in her behavior. But like herself and her boyfriend, we accept as an unperformed fact that the performer is a young American middle-class girl. But surely here we neglect the greater part of the performance (1959, p. 81).

It is immensely significant that this example does *not* appear in the earlier edition; it is also likely that Goffman's suggestion that "we" have neglected the greater part of the girl's performance signals his recognition that he had done so himself. Inserting this example discredits the *two selves* thesis by exposing the analytic limitations of a reliance on the existence of a hidden manipulator. The claim that the greater part of the girl's performance is not her guile and contrivance but her enactment of a young American middle-class girl opens up a much more complex analysis of the person, for which a dramaturgical analysis is unsatisfactory.

The ramifications of American dating practices for accounts of self are a cause of concern for Goffman throughout the rewriting of *The Presentation of Self*. At the end of the chapter concerning impression management he appends a new section about the dilemmas facing young American girls in the 1950s. Here he no longer makes any reference to their guile and contrivance; instead he acknowledges that the custom of "playing dumb" leads to "a special kind of alienation from self and a special kind of wariness of others" (p. 229). Goffman cites one American college girl as saying that although occasionally she plays dumb on dates, the experience "leaves a bad taste" (p.229).

The examples of the King of Norway and the young American middle-class girl clarify the reasons for the suspicion that dramaturgical analysis is of limited use: although it is reasonable to classify the king's efforts to keep a distance from "the people" as a performance, it is unreasonable to classify the girl's actions in the same way. This is the case because the king can both *stop* his performance and *separate* himself from it; the girl's "performance" of young American middle-class girl cannot be distinguished so readily from her sense of personhood. Implicit here is the thought that the girl displays a multiplicity of selves which are neither appendages nor masks. This idea invites a picture of the person as a composite of multiple selves, each of which projects a set of claims. Goffman's later work is very much concerned with this. This change of direction reneges on the image of the hidden manipulator.

The 1956 edition of *The Presentation of Self* ends with a suitably cynical conclusion:

> The very obligation and profitability of appearing always in a steady moral light, of being a socialized character, forces one to be the sort of person who is practiced in the ways of the stage (1956, p. 162).

Exactly the same sentence appears towards the end of the second edition (1959, p. 244). In the first edition it is the culmination of the study: the text ends with the thought that moral character is merely a staged achievement. The second edition downplays this cynicism by concluding with the second intervention noted above, a new section titled "Staging and the Self" (pp. 244–47). The first two pages of this section attempt to reformulate the self by distinguishing self-as-performer from self-as-character. The distinction is couched in hesitation; it moves uneasily between the self as a being with "fantasies and dreams" and the self as a "peg on which something of collaborative manufacture will be hung for a time" (p. 245). This appended section, and with it the second edition, end with words of caution about the dramaturgical vocabulary. In the face of his growing dissatisfaction, Goffman informs us that "the language and mask of the stage will be dropped" (1959, p. 246).

One of the key distinctions between the two editions is that the first pursues the theater analogy *optimistically*, whereas the additions to the second edition present the metaphor *pessimistically*, as a line of inquiry that has run its course. I suggest that the atrophy of the trope occurs for two reasons: first, because theatrical interpretations posit a cynical account of the individual as possessor of two selves, one manipulative, the other performative; and second, because Goffman's early use of the theater analogy is better understood *metonymically*, as a figurative exercise that takes a small part of the world as indicative of the whole.

## Metaphor as a Research Method

Like other research strategies, the use of metaphor has advantages and disadvantages. In addition, it raises a series of instructive issues. At various times, Goffman applauded the advantages, bemoaned the disadvantages, and considered the issues raised by metaphor. His comments about metaphor (and even about method) are fragmentary, however, and our understanding of his procedures has been aided more by some commentators than by Goffman himself.

As suggested in the first part of this paper, there are three broad advantages to the extensive use of metaphor in sociological research. The first is that apt metaphors make the social world appear strange, thereby challenging our commonsensical and taken-for-granted ideas. Viewed in this way, *The Presentation of Self* is an extended metaphorical description of everyday behavior which forces us to reconsider mundane social events.

The second advantage is that metaphors suggest more than passing resemblances between apparently different things. Instead they create "semantic maps" to the social world which are best thought of as conceptual systems. Consequently it is possible to extend research to new topics while at the same time developing different aspects of the metaphor. For example, the theatrical metaphor suggests to us that people follow "scripts" in their everyday encounters. It is instructive to consider the extent to which this is done, how it is done, the differences between scripts, and so on.

Third, metaphors can be "played twice": first in terms of what they reveal about the social world and then in terms of their inadequacy as models of social life and behavior. Metaphors produce new insights and questions by this double playing of the social world. Goffman's strategy was to use the theatrical metaphor first as a guide to the social world and then as a falsification of it. This approach exploits the two sides of the metaphor: it is both an insightful (if incongruous) comparison and a literal absurdity. The use of metaphors by sociologists undermines the idea that their work has the objectivity of mathematics and emphasizes the fact that sociology is forged from an uneasy combination of meanings; some of these meanings derive from the people who are being studied, others from sociologists themselves.

The deployment of metaphor also poses problems and has disadvantages. Metaphors, by definition, are literally absurd, and thus require the indulgence of all concerned. However convincing a metaphor appears to be, it nevertheless remains a "category error," an interesting confusion. This fact casts doubt on its validity as a research procedure, even when the metaphor is double played. Related to this criticism is the fact that the resulting analysis cannot really be disproved, and therefore is of little scientific use. How could you show, for example, that dramaturgical analysis is "true" or "false"? Goffman acknowledges this point in his comment at the beginning of *The Presentation of Self* that the justification for his work and for Simmel's is the same.

Clearly, then, metaphors are at best only partial descriptions of social behavior, and these descriptions assume that other descriptions are possible and no less significant. Goffman frequently acknowledged this truth about his own work, as Williams (1988) reminds us. Partiality and a plurality of models, of course, are hallmarks of neo-Kantian thought, and Goffman's use of metaphor should be understood as his contribution to the continuation of this tradition. Metaphors also make us question our aims: are we trying to *discover* things about the social world, or are we trying to *invent* "narratives" about modern life? Goffman seems always to have been hesitant about the status of his findings. To understand this hesitancy, it is instructive to consider Baldamus's discussion of this topic and then to turn to Williams's attempt to use Baldamus's work to clarify Goffman's various methods.

Baldamus's discussion of the tension between invention and discovery in sociological research is based on the idea of "double fitting" (1972). He begins by noting that informal theorizing is indispensable to sociology: it is the day-to-day means of the interminable restructuring, redefining, reinterpreting, and reformulating of conceptual frameworks. Informal theorizing is an example of what one might call "single fitting" (although Baldamus doesn't do so) because it involves the continual alteration of definitions and classifications. Double fitting occurs when empirical examples are chosen or rejected in order either to confirm existing definitions or to support the claims of new definitions. Baldamus explains double fitting by an analogy: carpenters would be like sociologists if they mended a door by altering *both* the shape of the door *and* that of the door frame. By the use of double fitting, it becomes possible over a period of time to make some kind of progress and to accumulate results. In scientific terms, however, Baldamus admits that double fitting is a way of "cooking the books" (1972, p. 295). Later he attempts to justify this remark, saying that by combining the theoretical task of "inventing and articulating conceptual frameworks" with the empirical task of hypothesizing, it becomes possible to produce an insightful merger of theory and research (pp. 296–97).

Robin Williams (1988) uses Baldamus's idea of double fitting to make sense of Goffman's willingness to reformulate and even to discard concepts. In particular, Williams shows the extent to which Goffman alternates between invention and discovery, between conceptual elaboration and hypothesizing, between a refocusing of terms and a refocusing of empirical investigation. In doing so, Goffman alters his vocabulary, his level of abstraction, and his substantive interests in the pursuit of discovery. The result is that the notion of discovery itself must be rethought:

> Sociological discoveries are not then about the anticipated or unanticipated discovery of previously unknown facts; they are much more about the attribution of different significances to what is already known. If sociological discoveries are about re-ordering what is already known, then sociological methods must be those which permit that re-order-

ing to take place as efficiently and reliably as possible (Williams 1988, p. 173).

Williams's elegant argument leads us back directly to Goffman's use of metaphor, as he himself realizes (1988, p. 77), because the theater metaphor is an efficient tool for reordering our views about the social world. In my vocabulary, this metaphor is a *form* of inquiry with which Goffman explored social phenomena. Goffman undermined these investigations by focusing on the inherent limitations of metaphorical descriptions. That is to say, he used the *formless* detail previously hidden by metaphor to promote further "discoveries." The literal absurdity of metaphor ensures that this procedure always will be possible. This image of sociology is suggestive of Weber's methodological writings; Williams ends his paper by arguing that Goffman is very much an heir to the "neo-Kantian" conception of the social sciences as the "continuous process" of ordering and reordering reality through the construction, dissolution, and replacement of concepts in the endless task of sociological inquiry (Weber 1949; Williams 1988, p. 87).

This persuasive and scholarly reading helps to correct the belief of what Williams calls the "critical orthodoxy, " namely that Goffman is an idiosyncratic and unsystematic writer. It also establishes the justification for his widespread use of metaphor. Nevertheless, it is possible to detect an area of uncertainty in Williams's reading. This critical moment occurs as he moves from his elucidation of Baldamus's notion of double fitting to his discussion of Goffman's neo-Kantian acceptance of the demise of ideal-types, sociological perspectives, and extended metaphors. The critical moment – the *fracture* – occurs when Williams hesitates over the question of Goffman's attitude towards progress. Baldamus, who he believes (correctly, in my view) offers valuable insights into Goffman's procedure, holds a paradoxical position with regard to cognitive progress in sociology: on the one hand he believes that double fitting is tantamount to "cooking the books"; on the other, he maintains that progress by modification towards an ever-tighter fit is possible. In fact, this tension becomes even more acute in his later writings.

In his paper, Williams offers a close reading of two passages from Goffman's corpus – the first from the beginning of Goffman's doctorate, finished in 1953, and the second from his final paper, the presidential address to the American Sociological Association. These passages show very neatly that Goffman indeed thought that during the intervening years he had managed to stabilize "a highly integrated hierarchical structure of interlocking definitions" (Williams 1988, p. 76). Yet this view surely is difficult to reconcile with Williams's subsequent claim that Goffman exploited the strengths and the vulnerabilities of different metaphors in a series of well-planned "raids" on the ever-changing flux of social reality. Such raids hardly can be part of a long-term cumulative project. The difficulty is exacerbated by the forcefulness of Williams's earlier reading of Baldamus's ambivalent position regarding the possibility of progress in sociology.

In fact, I think Williams has exposed an important tension within Goffman's work, a tension between a desire for an ever more elaborate description of face-to-face interaction and a refusal to believe that such a formalization is possible. Allen Grimshaw tells us that in his later years, Goffman struggled to find ways to systematize his findings (Grimshaw 1983, p. 147). This "voice" is certainly evident in passages throughout *Frame Analysis* (1974), *Forms of Talk* (1981), and "Felicity's Condition" (1983a) but so, too, is a maverick parodying of such efforts.

### Metaphor in Goffman's Later Work

In this section I argue that beneath Goffman's attempt to establish the conceptual basis to *Frame Analysis* there is a subtextual critique of his earlier dramaturgical model. Goffman held high hopes for *Frame Analysis*, a book with a ten-year gestation period and the trimmings (and quite possibly the content) of a *magnum opus*. In it he attempts to formalize our knowledge about the ways in which context structures our experiences of the world, and thereby to offer a substantive analysis of the true but now weary claim that meaning and understanding are context-dependent. The drive to formalization, however, is accompanied almost invariably by a ruthless parodying of such "foundationalist," indeed structuralist, ambitions. As a result, the book often gives the impression that Goffman is holding an interior monologue with himself about the possibility and the limits of formal knowledge about our everyday practices. The same can be said for *Forms of Talk* and "Felicity's Condition": both contain what Goffman describes as a "call to arms" for the detailed analysis of tacit knowledge, and both mock what he once termed his "clumsy typologies held together with string."

The subtext of *Frame Analysis* is that the theatrical metaphor must be used only cautiously. This warning is signaled on the first page of *Frame Analysis*, where Goffman writes:

> All the world is not a stage – certainly the theater isn't entirely. (Whether you organize a theater or an aircraft factory, you need to find places for cars to park and coats to be checked, and these had better be real places, which, incidentally, had better carry real insurance against theft) (1974, p. 1).

In this passage Goffman attempts to *implode* the theatrical analogy, to show that the theater analogy is not only an inadequate way of analyzing the world of our daily affairs, but also an inadequate way of analyzing the world of the theater.

The key to exploiting the analogy is to limit the definition of a performance. Goffman's initial formulation in *The Presentation of Self* doesn't allow a negative case: according to it, we are acting all the time. Goffman wrote that "*all* the activity of a given participant" is an example of social acting (1959, p. 26; emphasis added). This definition distracts us from the literal absurdity of metaphor. In *Frame Analysis* he offers a different definition, redefining the term "performance" so as to limit its meaning. In doing so he tacitly acknowledges his earlier mistake:

> A performance, *in the restricted sense in which I shall now use the term*, is that arrangement which transforms an individual into a stage performer, the later, in turn, being an object that can be looked at in the round and at length without offense, and looked to for an engaging behavior, by persons in an "audience" role (1974, p. 124; emphasis added).

In this passage Goffman shows that he is quite conscious of his earlier difficulties; this new definition is deliberately more limited and more aware of the ways in which, as he says at the beginning of the book, all the world is not a stage. Tied to this new definition of a performance is a new definition of social acting; both definitions require an account of the ways in which the metaphor is literally absurd. Goffman clarified matters by pointing to the "basic conceptual distinction" between performers and their characters. This clarification allows us to discuss, for example, John Gielgud taking the part of Hamlet. The analogue in everyday life is a remark such as "John Smith is a loyal friend, a bad father, a good plumber," and so forth, because here it seems that John Smith is playing the part or role of friend, father, or plumber. Metonymic readings, of course, imply that it is wrong to say that he *seems* to be playing these roles; in fact he *is* playing them. Yet as Goffman tells us, the analogue is inadequate, albeit inadequate in interesting ways. John Smith playing friend, father, and plumber is a man with a personal identity and a biography, and it is far from clear what it could mean for him to *stop* "playing" these roles. When John Gielgud plays Hamlet, his identity and biography are different from those of Hamlet, whom he stops playing when the curtain falls (1974, pp. 128–29).

The literal absurdity of the theatrical metaphor, now established more clearly, can be used to draw our attention to the differences between face-to-face interaction in social life and on stage. This sort of analytic work points to the importance of a variety of everyday conventions which must be flouted on stage. For example: if an audience is to follow a play, it is usually necessary for actors to finish their lines. In daily life, however, this is manifestly not the case, because interruptions are a necessary and normal part of the "multiple channeling" of interaction (1974, pp. 139–40, 146). Similarly, body alignments differ radically from real life in stage productions because actors must align themselves not for the encounter but for the benefit of the audience (1974, p. 140). Tacit information also must be explicated on stage, whereas in everyday life the silence about such information is part of the manufacture of intimacy; these are the "entrusted secrets" discussed in *The Presentation of Self* (1959, pp. 141–43). On stage the "involvement contour" of participants is much flatter than off stage, where audiences are not present solely for entertainment or enlightenment (1974, pp. 142–44).

Understanding a performance, then, requires a practical or discursive knowledge of the frames that surround it. Frames are vulnerable. They can both *keyed* – that is, transformed from one schema of interpretation into another – and *fabricated* – that is, designed so as to mislead others about actual events. The motivations behind these transformations vary dramatically from the benign fabrications of "leg-pulls" to the exploitative devices of confidence tricks. Benign fabrications maintain the basic interests and rights of their targets; exploitative ones undermine them (1974, p. 102). For sociology the implication of these different frame manipulations is that everyday life can tolerate extraordinarily complex frame structures with the same nonchalances concert pianists display in the midst of frighteningly difficult musical scores. Goffman emphasizes this point by saying that when children "play doctor" for "naughty reasons" they show a childish understanding of medicine but a fully adult competence in framing matters (1974, p. 161, footnote).

The substantive fascination of this metaphor is that it provides an instructive way of reordering familiar information about the organization of everyday experience. Goffman's acute portrayal of the mystification of our performances, of team behavior, of front and back regions, and of the arts of impression management is an intricate and productive way of characterizing social life. Indeed, his analysis almost suggests that the dramaturgical metaphor is more than a metaphorical description of social life, that instead it is almost an accurate portrayal of that life.

In addition, the theatrical metaphor solved a range of methodological issues. Goffman realized that the metaphor, instead of being a convenient shorthand for lengthy descriptions, is a model that can be extended to an indefinite number of cases, generating a wide range of semantic innovations and nurturing new analyses of diverse problems. More provocatively, however, the metaphor negotiated a role merger between the sociologist as inventor and as discoverer. The exhilaration felt when reading *The Presentation of Self* is produced by our realization that in some form we *already knew* everything Goffman suggests in this book. The examples he gives resonate well because readers immediately can think of examples of their own. *The Presentation of Self* is an eloquent statement of ideas that many of us have half grasped, half realized, and half developed. Goffman clarifies and extends an argument that is already compatible with our intuitions.

At this point the works of Williams and of Baldamus become important because they show that discoveries about the social world are *typically* the result of imaginative reconstructions of things that are already known. This process involves a double fitting of redefinitions and the reselection of empirical examples. The issue is not, on this account, whether this activity commendable but how best to achieve more of it (remember: Baldamus acknowledges that he is advocating "cooking the books").

The final chapters of *Frame Analysis* contain a detailed discussion of the organization of everyday talk, and Goffman's work thereafter continued this analysis. These final works, especially *Forms of Talk*, raise many of the issues encountered by ethnomethodologists and conversation analysts. In these writings Goffman encounters a range of substantive problems that *cannot* be accommodated by the theatrical metaphor. Two of these problems are especially important: 1) To what extent can the rules followed in day-to-day life be formalized? 2) To what extent must social life be characterized in terms of the *manipulation* of these rules?

Whenever sociologists analyze social interaction in detail, they discover that people are very capable rule followers. We all show a remarkable ability to follow rules in both verbal and nonverbal communication. In everyday talk, for example, we use standard techniques to begin and end phone calls (Schegloff and Sacks 1974), we follow predictable channels when getting to know strangers (Maynard and Zimmerman 1984), we tell sad stories in predictable ways (Jefferson 1984), and we even allow turns at talk to overlap according to specifiable rules (Emmison 1989). Rule following is also apparent in nonverbal communication, as shown by our wide repertoire of ways of sitting or standing, by our measurement of physical proximity, even by our timed eye contacts (see Kendon 1981). From a wealth of well-documented information, it would be easy to conclude that social conduct is governed by rules, and that we are constrained by them.

The findings of Goffman, Wittgenstein, and the ethnomethodologists, however, make it clear that this is a misleading and only partial characterization of social life. Rules are not only constraints governing behavior; they are also resources used to justify or rationalize behavior. Further, these constraints and resources are only incomplete guides to conduct. In some sense we know that our behavior is interpreted by other people according to sets of rules. This knowledge allows us to manipulate these interpretations. Perhaps the best study of this topic is Wieder's (1974) investigation of the "convict code." Wieder was able to show that juvenile inmates in a correctional institution both follow an informal, unwritten rule book and use this rule book to justify their behavior. The staff knows about these rules and also uses them to make sense of the inmates' actions. For example, in an incident in which a boy's bed was burned, both staff and inmates interpreted this action as meaning that the victim had broken the informal code of conduct. Of course the person who burned the boy's bed knew that the incident would be interpreted in this way; thus he could use the convict code as a screen to cover his actual motivations, which may be unrelated to the victim's failure to abide by the convict code.

Further problems with the idea that everyday behavior is governed by rules are caused by the inability of the convict code to specify appropriate behavior in different situations. As a result, the boys found that their behavior was underdetermined by the code. For example, although the code was clear that inmates should not cooperate with staff, it was unclear about whether they should cooperate with Wieder, who as a sociologist was neither a staff member nor an inmate. The boys frequently found themselves in a quandary as to how to follow the rules of the convict code.

In his later work, Goffman became increasingly aware that the reflexivity of social action meant that it would be impossible to specify a rule book or an algorithm for social life that resembled a rule book for a game such as chess. This problem was acute because Goffman's later works try to say something nonmetaphorical and analytic about the rules governing everyday behavior. Goffman's problem was that he could see *both* that social life is routinized, predictable, and governed by rules *and* that we can all manipulate our common expectations about rule following and the predictability of social encounters.

Whenever Goffman tried to specify some of the rules governing our behavior, he encountered this problem of reflexivity and rule manipulation. Consider, for example, the crux of his paper "Replies and Responses" in *Forms of Talk*. The context of this paper is a range of disagreements between himself and conversation analysts; the paper is as much a reply and a response to them as a study of replies and responses in everyday life. Close to the end of this paper (but, significantly, not at the end) he proposes that for any culture there will be only a limited number of ways in which utterances can be reinterpreted. It is important to recognize how alien this argument would be to his early work, which was indebted so heavily to extended metaphors. Goffman attempts to show that the question "Do you have the time?" can be answered by one of only six classes of response. He claims that this observation offers "a framework of frameworks" with which to analyze social life (1981, p. 68). If he had been successful in this venture, he would have formalized a nonmetaphorical algorithm for social intercourse by showing that an inexhaustible number of actual cases complied with an underlying and finite set of commands.

Schegloff (1988) uses this passage in an important criticism of Goffman's ideas. He points out correctly that throughout Goffman's discussion of a possible framework of reinterpretation schemata, he fails to suggest any *implausible* responses to the question "Do you have the time?" Schegloff uses this observation to criticize Goffman's reliance on data obtained exclusively from thought experiments (1988, pp. 102–103). Schegloff also criticizes Goffman's habit of practicing "sociology by epitome" and "analytic nihilism," of skipping from example to example in order to obtain a good fit between concept and reality. Schegloff's complaint about analytic nihilism is an accurate discussion of the final pages of "Replies and Responses," which turned away from a concern with formalization and towards an analysis of Goffman's second research topic – namely, the ways in which people manipulate rules. By the end of this paper Goffman had convinced himself that these manipulations are so complicated that it is impossible to construct the framework of frameworks he had proposed earlier for reinterpretation schemata. He then likened the project to a Pandora's box, in which the lid can't be closed, and went on to say that there isn't even a box. Schegloff's complaints about "sociology by epitome" and "analytic nihilism" are most appropriate here because the implication of Goffman's argument is that sociological analysis is always an unsatisfactory simplification of actual conduct. As Schegloff points out, by the end of "Replies and Responses" Goffman has reached a position of "considerable ambivalence" (1988, p. 117). This ambivalence should be understood as the result of his hopes for a rule book governing social life (a box) and his realization that rules are not merely constraints but also resources. Consequently, as Schegloff suggests, sociological descriptions of the rules of face-to-face interaction typically underestimate the extent to which meaning is a collective "accomplishment" (1982). The theatrical metaphor cannot remedy this underestimation.

## Conclusion

Much of Goffman's later work questions both the methodological limitations of the theatrical metaphor and the substantive limitations of the dramaturgical assumption that we are all cynical manipulators. This trend affirms a line of inquiry that is present in some of his predramaturgical writings. Goffman's later analysis of everyday talk can be read as an interior monologue in which he debates the feasibility of an accurate portrayal of the complexities of face-to-face interaction. One Goffman voice suggests that these complexities will submit to formal analysis; the other parodies such efforts. Goffman often "resolved" the issue of the complexity of naturally occurring talk by resorting to examples produced by thought experiments. The content of this interior monologue is familiar to many conversation analysts, whose insistence on the use of transcripts forces them to recognize how difficult it is to formalize our practical knowledge of social interaction. As for Goffman, their central problem is to find an appropriate way to describe systematically the ways in which we extend the meaning of the rules of social interaction by breaching and manipulating them. The dramaturgical metaphor was a useful guide to behavior in public settings, but it is not a good way of analyzing how rules in everyday life can be simultaneously constraints, resources, and indeterminate guides to conduct.

## References

Baldamus, W. 1972. "The Role of Discoveries in Social Science." In *The Rules of the Game*, edited by T. Shanin. London: Tavistock.
Baldamus, W. 1976. *The Structure of Sociological Inference*. London: Macmillan.
Black, M. 1962. *Models and Metaphors*. Ithaca: Cornell University Press.
Blumer, H. 1972. "Action vs. Interaction." *Society* 9: 50–53.
Booth, W. 1984 (1979). "Metaphor as Rhetoric: The Problem of Evaluation." In *On Metaphor*, edited by S. Sacks. Chicago: University of Chicago Press.
Brown, R. 1977. *A Poetic for Sociology*. Cambridge: Cambridge University Press.
Burke, K. 1955. *Permanence and Change*. Indianapolis: Bobbs-Merrill.

Cohen, T. 1984 (1979). "Metaphor and the Cultivation of Intimacy." In *On Metaphor*, edited by S. Sacks. Chicago: University of Chicago Press.

Collins, R. 1980. "Erving Goffman and the Development of Modern Social Theory." In *The View from Goffman*, edited by J. Ditton. London: Macmillan.

Collins, R. 1988. "Theoretical Continuities in Goffman's Work." In *Erving Goffman: Exploring the Interaction Order*, edited by P. Drew and A. Wooten. Cambridge: Polity.

Cooper, D. 1985. "Metaphors We Live By." In *Philosophy and Practice*, edited by A. Phillips Griffiths. Cambridge: Cambridge University Press.

Davidson, D. 1984 (1979). "What Metaphors Mean." In *On Metaphor*, edited by S. Sacks. Chicago: University of Chicago Press.

De Man, P. 1984 (1979). "The Epistemology of Metaphor." In *On Metaphor*, edited by S. Sacks. Chicago: University of Chicago Press.

Derrida, J. 1978a. *Writing and Difference*. London: RKP.

Derrida, J. 1978b. "The Retrait of Metaphor." *Enclitic* 2: 5–33.

Derrida, J. 1982. *Margins of Philosophy*. Brighton, UK: Harvester.

Ditton, J. (ed.). 1980. *The View from Goffman*. London: Macmillan.

Drew P. and A. Wootten (eds.). 1988. *Erving Goffman: Exploring the Interaction Order*. Cambridge, UK: Polity.

Emmison, M. 1989. "A Conversation on Trial?" *Journal of Pragmatics* 13: 363–83.

Evans, R. 1982. *The Fabrication of Virtue: English Prison Architecture, 1750–1840*. Cambridge: Cambridge University Press.

Foucault, M. 1978. *Discipline and Punish*. London: Allen Lane.

Garfinkel, H. 1967. *Studies in Ethnomethodology*. Englewood Cliffs, NJ: Prentice-Hall.

Giddens, A. 1984. *The Constitution of Society*. Cambridge, UK: Polity.

Goffman, E. 1949. "Some Characteristics of Response to Depicted Experience." M.A. thesis, University of Chicago.

Goffman, E. 1951. "Symbols of Class Status." *British Journal of Sociology* 11: 294–304.

Goffman, E. 1952. "On Cooling the Mark Out: Some Aspects of Adaptation to Failure." *Psychiatry* 15: 451–63.

Goffman, E. 1953a. *The Service Station Dealer: The Man and His Work*. Chicago: Social Research Incorporated.

Goffman, E. 1953b. "Communication Conduct in an Island Community." Unpublished doctoral dissertation, University of Chicago.

Goffman, E. 1956. *The Presentation of Self in Everyday Life*. Edinburgh: University of Edinburgh Social Sciences Research Centre.

Goffman, E. 1959. *The Presentation of Self in Everyday Life*, Second ed. Harmondsworth, UK: Penguin.

Goffman, E. 1961a. *Encounters: Two Studies in the Sociology of Interaction*. Indianapolis: Bobbs-Merill.

Goffman, E. 1961b. *Asylums*. Harmondsworth, UK: Penguin.

Goffman, E. 1963. *Behavior in Public Places: Notes on the Social Organization of Gatherings*. New York: Free Press.

Goffman, E. 1967. *Interaction Ritual: Essays on Face-to-Face Behavior*. New York: Anchor.

Goffman, E. 1970. *Strategic Interaction*. Oxford: Basil Blackwell.

Goffman, E. 1971. *Relations in Public: Microstudies of the Public Order*. New York: Basic Books.

Goffman, E. 1972. *Encounters*. Harmondsworth, UK: Penguin.

Goffman, E. 1974. *Frame Analysis: An Essay on the Organization of Experience*. New York: Harper and Row.

Goffman, E. 1981. *Forms of Talk*. Oxford: Basil Blackwell.
Goffman, E. 1983a. "Felicity's Condition." *American Journal of Sociology* 89: 1–53.
Goffman, E. 1983b. "The Interaction Order." *American Sociology Review* 48: 1–17.
Grimshaw, A. 1983. "Erving Goffman: A Personal Appreciation." *Language in Society* 12 (1): 147–48.
Heritage, J. 1984. *Garfinkel and Ethnomethodology*. Cambridge, UK: Polity.
Ignatieff, M. 1978. *A Just Measure of Pain*. London: Macmillan.
Jefferson, G. 1984 "On the Organization of Laughter in Talk about Troubles." In *Structures of Social Action*, edited by J. Atkinson and J. Heritage. Cambridge: Cambridge University Press.
Kendon, A. (ed.). 1981. *Nonverbal Communication, Interaction and Gesture*. New York: Mouton.
Lakoff, G. and M. Johnson. 1980. *Metaphors We Live By*. Chicago: University of Chicago Press.
Manning, P. 1988. "More Views of the Lovingly Empirical: Reply to Miller." *Philosophy of the Social Sciences*, 18: 61–4.
Manning, P. 1989. "Resemblances." *History of the Human Sciences* 2: 207–33.
Manning, P. 1989. "Ritual Talk." *Sociology* 19: 365–85.
Maynard, D. and D. Zimmerman 1984. "Topical Talk: Ritual and the Social Organization of Relationships." *Social Psychology Quarterly* 47: 301–16.
Nehamas, A. 1985. *Nietzsche: Literature as Life*. Cambridge: Harvard University Press.
Nietzsche, F. 1968. *The Will to Power*, translated by W. Kaufmann. New York: Vintage.
Richards, I. 1965. *The Philosophy of Rhetoric*. Oxford. Oxford University Press.
Ricouer, P. 1986. *The Rule of Metaphor*. London: RKP.
Rorty, R. 1986. "The Contingency of Community." *London Review of Books*, July 29.
Schegloff, E. 1982. "Discourse as an Interactional Achievement: Some Uses of "Uh Huh" and Other Things That Come between Sentences." Pp. 71–93 in *Georgetown University Roundtable on Languages and Linguistics*, edited by D. Tannen. Washington, DC: Georgetown University Press.
Schegloff, E. 1988. "Goffman and the Analysis of Conversation." In *Erving Goffman: Exploring the Interaction Order*, edited by P. Drew and A. Wooten.
Schegloff, E. and H. Sacks. 1974 "Opening Up Closings." In *Ethnomethodology*, edited by R. Turner. Middlesex, UK: Penguin.
Smith, G. 1989. "A Simmelian Reading of Goffman." Unpublished doctoral dissertation, University of Salford.
Soskice, J. 1985. *Metaphor and Religious Language*. Oxford: Clarendon.
Weber, M. 1949. *The Methodology of the Social Sciences*. New York: Free Press.
Wieder, L. 1974. "Telling the Code." In *Ethnomethodology*, edited by R. Turner. Middlesex: Penguin.
Williams, R. 1980. "Goffman's Sociology of Talk." In *The View from Goffman*, edited by J. Ditton. London: MacMillan.
Williams, R. 1983. "Sociological Tropes: A Tribute to Erving Goffman." *Theory, Culture and Society* 2: 98–101.
Williams, R. 1988. "Understanding Goffman's Methods." In Erving Goffman: Exploring the Interaction Order, edited by P. Drew and A. Wooten. Cambridge, UK: Polity.

# 86

# Rational Choice Theory in Sociology

*Robert J. Holton*

Until very recently, rational choice theory has been far less central to sociology than to economics. Whereas rationality is a fundamental presupposition of mainstream economics, for sociology it has always been problematic. This is partly because irrational or nonrational determinants of social action have been viewed as important, and partly because rationality has been denied a unitary status.[1] In other words, there is not one structure of rationality, but multiple incommensurable rationalities that vary according to the viewpoints, interests, and power of the actors concerned. What is rational to one may be irrational and arbitrary to another.

There is also a normative issue. While economics generally argues that the real-world actor should do what the rational actor would, in order to maximize her interests, sociology lacks such a clear-cut normative presumption. Sociologists often emphasize resistance to rationality, and focus on alternatives to individual self-interest. Utopianism remains a legitimate interest for sociologists, whereas economists tend to shun it.

The late James Coleman's *Foundations of Social Theory* (Cambridge, Mass.: Harvard University Press, 1990), published the year after the launching of the journal *Rationality and Society*, promises to transform this situation. His objective, and that of his collaborators in the journal, such as Michael Hechter and Peter Abell, is not to colonize sociology with an economistic version of rational choice theory. Rather, it is to recast the central concerns of sociology within a framework that brings together the theories of social exchange and rational choice. For Coleman, all types of human action, including norms and much collective behavior that is regarded as irrational or expressive, may plausibly be brought within theories of purposive rationality.

There is immense ambition behind Coleman's project. In the first place, he addresses some of the knottiest issues in social theory. These include what Coleman sees as sociology's microfoundational schism between those who view "modern man" as a robot, and those who see "him" as an irrational participant in collective behavior. Beyond this there is the even greater problem of how to relate micro- and macro- levels of social organization.

The second part of Coleman's ambition is to bridge the gap between social theory, moral philosophy, and social research, so as to enhance the capacity of social science to assist in the resolution of major social problems through institutional design. These include the crisis of the family and the excessive power of corporate actors. As Adrian Favel (1993) has pointed out, Coleman's intention is to be both explanatory and prescriptive, advancing a dialogue between social theory and moral philosophy designed to address questions about rights raised by moral philosophers such as Rawls and Nozick, but in a manner that avoids transcendent metaphysical speculation in favor of a sociology of rational choice.

Fin-de-siècle skepticism towards the claims of rational choice theory to explain and benefit the world may not seem out of place after two world wars, the Gulag, Auschwitz, Pol Pot, and Balkan ethnic cleansing. These tragedies may be read either as proof of the continuing power of irrationalism, or as manifestations of the irrational consequences of the rational pursuit of terror. Coleman, by contrast, limits the normative aspect of his discussion to the functioning of Western liberal democracy in general and the United States in particular. The wider global context is noted but not systematically pursued. It is not immediately apparent how the book's argument might be applied to social actors facing famine, genocide, or civil war.

Indeed, Coleman starts with the optimistic view that we live in the epoch of purposive social organization, constructed through human intention, and therefore capable of being evaluated and reshaped. There is, he claims, a fundamental difference between "natural," primordial ties of family, clan, village, and so forth, on the one hand, and, on the other, a constructed environment embodied in corporate organization, both public and private. The decline of primordialism brings major problems, such as the depletion of the personalized social capital necessary for the socialization of children and for emotional bonding among adults. Yet it also brings opportunities to redesign the allocation of rights and the structure of authority so as to improve corporate organization. Coleman sees his book as "providing the foundation for constructing a viable social structure, as the primordial structure on which persons have depended, vanishes" (652). This objective is of course applicable to any particular society, as well as to the transnational institutions of global society.

Coleman's shift from primordialism to social construction is neither unfamiliar nor unproblematic. It is the shift from Tönnies's (1955) *Gemeinschaft* (community) to *Gesellschaft* (association), and it has close affinities with Durkheim's (1947) discussion of mechanical and organic solidarity. The problems with Coleman's use of this dichotomy are also familiar. Two particular matters are worthy of mention.

First, there are always difficulties in the application of a binary conceptual distinction to complex processes of historical change. Constructed political and legal organizations have coexisted alongside spontaneous institutions, such as language and money, for centuries. Coleman notes certain precursors of modern constructed social organization, such as the legal personality of the corporation in late medieval law. Yet he admits that "the full history of the restructuring of social organization from the thirteenth century to the present has yet to be written" (53).

The lack of a convincing historical sociology in Coleman's theory of organizations is also reflected in his comments on the family. Coleman's foreshortened sense of historical development allows him to present the contemporary transformation of the family as a sudden and dramatic crisis, rather than one phase in a process of longer-term change. The family itself is a rather more complex historical institution than Coleman suggests, with a longer history of instrumental, calculative, individualistic, and at times amoral social action than his rather romantic picture of primordial normativity implies.[2] As with all nostalgic arguments about "the world we have lost," this one also needs to be treated with caution.

A second, related difficulty is the applicability of rational choice theory to premodern societies. It remains unclear whether Coleman intends his rational choice apparatus to apply to what he sees as the long epoch of primordialism. Others have been less reticent. A strong body of opinion suggests that the logic of rational choice applies to a range of actors from medieval farmers to imperial dynasts.[3] But is rational choice compatible with primordialism? Put another way, can people who do not think in terms of the pursuit of instrumental rationality still pursue it? If so, then Coleman's distinction between primordial and constructed social organization is misleading.

Coleman's argument is that how people understand the social environment around them matters, and has changed. Like Anthony Giddens (1990), he wants to draw attention to the reflexivity of contemporary social action. Modern life is constantly subject to monitoring and evaluation through processes of information feedback and analysis, which leads, in turn, to the continual reshaping of individual and institutional activities. It is this active social orientation, rather than the underlying logic of rationality, which distinguishes the modern world from what went before.

For Coleman, modern social reflexivity offers two intellectual opportunities for sociology. First, it may be able to do better than economics where social theorizing is underdeveloped. Second, it can remedy what he sees as the excessively abstract style of reasoning about normative issues found in moral philosophy. Rather than speculate about the optimal character of norms evaluated against transcendent standards of judgment, he prefers a realistic analysis of norms as they have developed in relations between real actors in society.

Like modern society, sociology is reflexive, in that the subject matter of the discipline encompasses itself. A sociological approach to social action and rationality must therefore analyze, *inter alia*, the action of engaging in the construction of social theory. According to Coleman, this radical reflexivity is often missing in classical sociology (and, one might add, mainstream economics). To the extent that this is true, Coleman's version of rational choice theory must not only pass the test of explaining social action, but also of analyzing the action of theorizing, and, in particular, the role of social theoretical knowledge in helping to construct social reality.

## Coleman's Social Theory

In addressing the relationship between individuals and social systems or structures, Coleman attempts to thread his way between what he sees as two major traps in social theory. The first is what might be called radical methodological individualism, which attempts to explain social action as nothing more than the aggregate of individual actions. Coleman rejects this approach because individual actions are interdependent; they generate emergent system level phenomena that are often unintended and unexpected. Yet Coleman also wants to avoid a second trap, that of structuralism, which forecloses on human agency, and, in the process, human freedom. Society is neither the sum of individual choices by actors, nor a supra-organic totality within which individuals are wholly subsumed.

Coleman identifies his own position as a variant of methodological individualism, partly for the pragmatic reason that starting with the individual is the most useful way of connecting human intervention with the purposive construction of social organization. But it is also partly the result of a more substantive intellectual wish to ground the emergence of norms in individual interaction, rather than assuming their presence as an axiom or as an unexplained *deus ex machina*. This strategy brings Coleman very close to rational choice theory, yet he expressly distances himself from the view that norms can be reduced to practices generated by self-serving individuals engaged in repeated exchanges.

Coleman's starting point is certainly the actor, with reason and interests, yet without the resources to realize those interests. This bundle of characteristics requires social exchange with others, which in turn involves both behavioral interdependence and the development of structures of rights. Residual deviations from rationality are possible, as in the case of what Jon Elster (1979) calls precommitment. However, Coleman's initial presumption is that much that has hitherto been regarded as irrational can be recast as rational once the viewpoint of the actors concerned has been discovered.

So far this follows the familiar strategy of rational choice theory. The first bridge between all of this and Coleman's specifically sociological perspective is made through the identification of eleven different structures of social action. While Talcott Parsons (1968) thought in terms of a singular generic structure of action, Coleman offers a far more complex and nuanced discussion. This takes into account the ways in which actions vary according to whether or not they involve transfers of control, or rights of control, over resources; how such transfers, where they exist, differ from one another; and whether such actions produce externalities (third-party effects).

Like economists, Coleman rejects the possibility of any objective interpersonal measure of utility. But he sees individual preferences and standards of utility as generated instead by the kinds of comparisons that grow up within social systems based on unequal distributions of power. Thus utility maximization "cannot be normatively justified, except within the set of values implied by the initial distribution of control among the actors in the system" (42).

Moreover, exchange does not necessarily generate social equilibrium between free-standing actors. Rather, concentrations of power, especially corporate power, are possible. Social exchange takes place not simply in isolated two-person exchanges, or between several individuals within markets, but increasingly within wider social and political systems. The macro-level characteristics of these systems require analysis over and beyond that offered by rational choice theorists.

Put more explicitly, whereas rational choice theory provides a micro-level theory of macro-level institutions, Coleman's sociology offers a theory of micro–macro–micro transitions. Here, micro-level interactions generate unintended macro-level structures, and these structures in turn influence micro-level interactions.

A second bridge between Coleman's theory and conventional sociology is his presumption that the rights that link social actors together are an emergent property of social life, rather than natural presocial endowments. Coleman is impatient with speculative philosophical accounts of the individual as a rights-holder outside society, and with strategies of fictional abstraction such as Rawls's "veil of ignorance." Thus, "individuals have no rights until there is a consensus in the particular social situation involving a rights claim" (596). The task of the theorist is then to locate the rationality of emergent systems of rights, and to use this as a basis for prescribing more optimal allocations of rights in society.

Thus, although Coleman is close to rational choice theory, he subtly tries to distance himself from its typical utilitarian and liberal-individualist formulations. This distancing process, however, is by no means successful.

What Coleman appears to share with the utilitarians is a preference for a unitary conception of social action based on the most parsimonious of premises about self-interest. He assumes that social action cannot be grounded both in the rational pursuit of interests and in norms: one or the other must take precedence. Coleman resists the sociologists' privileging of normativity for two reasons. First, such a starting point precludes the construction of theories about how normative systems develop. Second, this approach would commit him to an oversocialized conception of humankind.

This is unsatisfactory in several respects. First, why should the assumption that action is structured by norms preclude theories about how they are constructed, any more than the presumption of rational interests precludes theories about *their* emergence? Max Weber[4] posited rationality as an ideal type of social action, but this did not preclude either the analysis of deviations from rationality, or the historical analysis of the emergence of rationality. The same methodology is possible with the analysis of norms.

Second, is it necessary, as Coleman believes, that reasoning from normative axioms must lead inexorably to oversocialized conceptions of human agency? One alternative possibility is that normativity can be linked with more purposive conceptions of human agency through emergent universals such as the search for freedom and human dignity. Socialization, in this alternative sense, does not turn individuals into the puppets of strong normative controls. It is rather that agents are socialized to be individuals.

Third, is it really the case that normativity arises only as a result of the rational pursuit of interests? Could it not equally be the other way around, such that rationality is grounded in norms, and that the means-oriented purposive rationality Coleman takes as axiomatic is historically emergent rather than an invariant property of human action?

Underlying these concerns, as Amartya Sen (1977) has pointed out, is an unresolved epistemological issue about the status of the rational pursuit of interest. Is this necessarily axiomatic of all social behavior? If so, it tells us nothing about variations in the substantive reasons behind people's actions, and hence says little about the normative or expressive components of such action. In a given situation, we could say it was equally rational to be controlled, passionate, prudent, emotional, or whatever, where all that is being identified is the imputed reason that seems to best fit the action in question. The rational pursuit of interest thereby becomes the lowest common denominator in the logic of social action, impossible to falsify, and yielding bland and uninteresting results.

On the other hand, there are points where Coleman seems to suggest that rational choice theory is falsifiable: for example, where it claims to eliminate such alternatives as irrational and expressive actions. Insofar as rational choice is testable, then the alternatives must be, too. With few exceptions, however, Coleman is reluctant to allow this, foreclosing on any further analysis once explanations that fit the rational choice model are found. The starting point of the rational pursuit of interest is thus not only theoretically arbitrary, but epistemologically dubious.

It is also sociologically implausible. This is primarily because sociality requires the simultaneous presence of micro and macro levels of social organization. The micro-level pursuit of interests by rational actors must always take place under initial conditions which include human language, patterns of meaning, and norms of socialization that make communication and social interaction possible.

This means that micro and macro are omnipresent from the start, giving the relationship between structure and agency a recursive quality, as Giddens (1979) puts it. Coleman regards the speculative philosophical treatment of questions such as optimal rights as excessively abstract and divorced from social life, but it seems the same criticism might well be made against interest-based rational choice theory itself.

To his credit, Coleman faces up to some of these difficulties midway through the book. Rational choice theory, he argues, has its limits. Although he bypasses the issue of the social constitution of rationality, Coleman is more forthright about the problem of the origin of interests. Asking how individuals come to have the interests they do is not ordinarily seen as possible within utilitarian versions of rational choice theory (292–93). This is because the theory assumes purpose, leaving analysis to concentrate on the issues that arise in its realization.

The problem of the origins of interests remains a serious residual difficulty for rational choice theory. In Coleman's view the theory not only fails to explain how interests arise, but also cannot explain how and why interests change. This residual is a large one. However, Coleman also points to major difficulties with those theories that presume social norms from which individual interests are then derived. In this case the residual problem lies in accounting for human agency and individual choice without recourse to deterministic reasoning. Consequently, "a theory based on rational action has the same deficiency at the level of the individual, as a theory which begins with societal purposes has at the level of the social system" (292–93).

Coleman goes on to argue that the problems associated with the normative starting-point are more intractable and intellectually disabling, but for reasons that appear more to do with pragmatism and normative preferences than anything else. His next intellectual move is not therefore to develop a multi-dimensional social theory grounded in both interests and norms. This option was attempted by earlier writers such as Parsons,[5] and has been further explicated in Jeffrey Alexander's four-volume commentary (1982–84) on classical sociological theory. Coleman, by contrast, looks elsewhere.

Essentially he returns to rational choice theory and seeks to buttress it with additional support. He draws upon two specific resources. The first is Mark Granovetter's (1985) discussion of the embeddedness of rational economic action in networks of personal relations. These personal relations generate the trust and stable expectations necessary for the enforcement of norms. Discussion of these mechanisms is seen as lacking in economic thought and thus as undeveloped in rational choice theory. To dramatize the importance of personal relations Coleman introduces the concept of social capital. This can only accumulate "when the relations among persons change in ways that facilitate action" (304).

## Correcting Rational Choice Theory

It is fair to say that rational choice theory is stronger in dealing with rights than with obligations. Thus, the discussion of social capital may be seen as

Coleman's best attempt to come to grips with the latter. His thesis is that involvement in the development of social capital, within a framework of norms, is necessary for effective socialization. The corollary is that socialization breaks down if the personalized networks of social capital are somehow depleted or eroded, or if norms never emerge in the first place. Coleman cites a number of examples from contemporary family life where he believes such networks are being eroded. Underlying all this is the assumption that social capital does not flow inexorably from rationality and self-interest. The processes through which social capital is generated or depreciated arise elsewhere, in areas such as social closure by groups, stability of the social structure, and ideology (318–21).

The second resource upon which Coleman draws to rectify deficiencies in rational choice theory is a theory of the self. Changes in rational choice theory are called for, not only with respect to its disregard of socialization, but also in relation to its minimalist view of the human actor. Assumptions of utility maximization are too narrow. They cannot explain how social selves come into being. Nor do they address whether the self is a stable, consistent, and unitary structure, or whether it is in some sense subdivided into distinct elements, subject to inconsistency and change.

Coleman argues that we can do better than rational choice theory by developing a sociology of the self. Following earlier sociologists, such as G. H. Mead (1962), he argues that the self is composed of different elements. One way of conceptualizing this is in terms of the distinction between the object self, "me," and the subject or acting self, "I." Whereas the former experiences social life in terms of levels of satisfaction, the latter acts through the mobilization of resources so as to realize interests. This conception of interests links the object and acting self, but there may be discrepancies between the two. This, according to Coleman, is because the object self is ever changing and expanding its scope, raising the possibility of lags between experience and action.

These lags may be further magnified through the increasing complexity of interaction with the social world. Rather than simple interactions between actors in pursuit of tangible divisible goods, Coleman adds greater complexity by including a range of further mechanisms of social action. These include seeking an increase in personal satisfaction through identification with others, sharing with others one's experience of the same events, depending on others, and vesting control over one's actions in others. All of these interactions involve internalizing the interests of others.

However, it is not immediately apparent to Coleman whether there is an overarching sense in which all these mechanisms may be brought together as manifestations of rationality. What is rational about transferring control over one's actions to significant others? In answering this, he is not satisfied by the utilitarian truism that this will occur when the expected benefits exceed the costs. Nor does he believe that individuals have the capacity to discern when such outcomes would eventuate. Instead, Coleman responds to the problem of the complexity of the self by invoking the idea that each person has a different constitution in which are balanced a set of "rights" applying both to oneself and to a range of external actors. Thus "each of the actors from the outside world who participates in a person's internal system of action is endowed with certain rights by that person" (526). Moreover, the external influences that may become internalized are not only particular persons with interests, but also norms, passions, and moral principles.

Where do external influences leave rationality? Does it become merely one influence amongst many upon the self and social action? Or does it occupy a different order of importance than norms, passions, or interests? Coleman adheres to the second of these options, but his elaboration of this point is disappointingly brief. He sees rationality as generated by "a kind of evolutionary feedback process" (526), in which actors learn the consequences of actions taken within the current framework of their internal constitution. Rationality is, in this sense, pre-constitutional, whereas norms and passions are not.

Here Coleman moves onto a very narrow theoretical ledge, with accounts of rationality as presocial on one side, and, on the other, accounts of rationality as a social product on a par with other social products such as norms and moral principles. It is unfortunate that the contours of this ledge are not developed in more depth, for example by a confrontation with Jürgen Habermas's (1984) theory of communicative action.

The challenge to Coleman, implicit in Habermas's work, is that it is possible to conceive of the logic of social action in a nondeterministic way without privileging purposive rationality in the way that Coleman feels obliged to do. For Habermas (1979), purposive rationality is one of two major structures of social action: the other is moral learning, institutionalized in normative frameworks. Thus, the rational choice of means cannot be treated as ontologically prior to the interpersonal formation of values and norms. Both Habermas and Parsons share a sense of society as an action system in which a strong dialectic takes place between structure and agency around the purposive and normative contingencies of social life. In failing to scrutinize this position, Coleman boxes himself into a binary choice between two options, both of which are seen as deficient. In this sense his engagement with the microfoundations of social life is ultimately unsatisfying.

## Coleman on Bureaucracy

If Coleman's study has its limits, it also exhibits some magnificent achievements. The foremost of these is a sophisticated elaboration and extension of the research program of rational choice theory as it applies to corporate actors, both public and private. For Coleman, the corporate actor is not simply an aggregation of individual actors, but rather a system of action embracing one or more principals and one or more agents. Typically, the corporate actor has multiple principals and multiple agents. To act purposefully, however, it must solve two problems. The first is the coordination of the resources and interests of the multiple principals into a coherent set. The second is the deployment of resources and multiple agents so as to realize interests. In addressing these problems, Coleman develops a very interesting critique of Max Weber's classic discussion of rationality in society, with particular reference to bureaucracy.

For Coleman, authority relations constitute major varieties of social action, and may be further subdivided into conjoint and disjoint types of relationships. Each involves individuals giving up certain rights of control over their actions to others. Conjoint authority relationships are those in which rights of control are given up unilaterally with no compensatory benefit, as when people accept the charismatic authority of leaders. Disjoint authority relations are those in which people surrender rights of control in return for a benefit, as in the employment of salaried subordinates within a bureaucracy. It is in the sphere of disjoint authority relations, as manifest in bureaucracy, that Coleman identifies a major problem in Weber's work.

Coleman criticizes Weber for conflating two distinct elements in the bureaucratic complex: the concept of bureaucracy as an impersonal hierarchy of positions, and the notion of bureaucracy as an instrumentally rational authority (that is, the most efficient means to reach a given end). For Coleman, the two are not necessarily connected. Functional efficiency is not necessarily realized through the adoption of an impersonal bureaucratic structure. Weber's conflation effectively forecloses on the question, "What kinds of organizational structure will most effectively realize the purpose for which the organization is designed?" In this manner an opportunity is lost to apply sociology to questions of institutional design. Instead, Weber treats bureaucracy as both efficient and impersonal, and hence necessarily and fatefully dehumanizing. We are left with the fatalistic metaphor of purposive rationality as an Iron Cage (Weber 1978, 181), in which ends have been subordinated to means, and the search for means has become an end in itself.

Coleman follows this criticism of Weber with a powerful *coup de grâce*, arguing that bureaucracy does not necessarily realize functional efficiency due to the mediating influence of its personnel. This influence may be exercised to meet the formal goals of the organization, or it may not. This raises a major question for disjoint authority relations, namely, Why should the subordinate work to maximize the superordinate's interests?

In a general and mostly persuasive review of corporate practice, Coleman notes significant deviations from the Weberian model of impersonal authority in a bureaucracy to address this problem of noncompliance. These include the use of incentive payments to senior managers, and the specific vesting of control over corporate resources in a particular person's hands. Such trends persuade him that corporations now intertwine the interests of the corporation and those of its members so fully that it has become very difficult to separate them. In a provocative argument that challenges both Weber and more recent theorists like Oliver Williamson (1975; 1985), Coleman claims that the modern corporation should not be seen as an impersonal machine, but as a system more like an unconstrained market. Its organizational structure "lies not in defining expectations and obligations, but in structuring reward systems and providing resources" (436). This is interesting because it denies much of Williamson's argument that markets and hierarchies offer contrasting ways of conducting transactions. What Coleman is saying is that corporations have become more like markets in terms of their flexible capacity to link self-interested persons with resources via the distribution of rewards. Of course, Coleman's organizations are not spot markets, but neither are they stable, normatively-bound hierarchies.

The challenge for the internal governance of corporations is therefore how to take into account the interests of agents in the organization of increasingly diffuse and decreasingly hierarchical authority systems. For Coleman, this means that ways must be found to make the pursuit of agents' interests consistent with the realization of corporate interests. This, however, requires more thought about which allocation of rights within a corporation is optimal for corporate interests to be realized. Issues such as this simply do not arise within a Weberian framework.

Coleman's critique of Weber is a powerful one that has implications for both social theory and institutional design. It helps open up organizations to richer empirical analysis of the internal play and rationality of corporate agents, and in the process offers insights into the range of options that exist for organizational norms and governance structures.

Beyond these internal questions for the corporation, Coleman also deals with the problematic and uncertain relationship between corporate actors and the wider society. While he rejects Weber's vision of modern society as an Iron Cage dominated by bureaucracy and instrumental rationality, Coleman emphasizes that corporate actors have massively expanded their power and influence at the expense of direct relations between particular persons. As a result, most of the events in which individuals are interested are no longer under their direct control. The potential danger of this situation is that it creates a dependent population that receives benefits from intangible corporate actions over which they exercise only very distant and indirect means of control. For Coleman, the Iron Cage may not be here yet, but it is not far away either.

How then is the public accountability of corporations to be achieved? Can the model of individual responsibility be applied to corporations?

Coleman explores this possibility by returning to the process of socialization. If individual responsibility is achieved largely through interpersonal socialization, what institutions might socialize the corporation? This question is made more difficult by the depletion of historical family-based and philanthropic sources of socialization. In addition, the detachment of corporate responsibility from individual persons means that forms of socialization applied to natural persons may no longer be an effective means of securing corporate responsibility.

The starting point for any resolution of this issue remains with the interests of those affected by corporate action: customers, employees, neighbours, owners, and investors. In many cases such groups are unorganized. While they may possess the individual power of "exit" from market transactions with a given corporation, they generally lack any power of active "voice" in corporate decision-making.

Coleman goes on to investigate two strategies whereby such interests may socialize the corporation. The first is through the representation of external interests within the governance structures of the corporation, e.g., through external directorships. This strategy has limitations, however, notably a failure to address negative externalities that may be imposed by the corporation. Coleman argues that these are optimally addressed neither by moralizing the corporation, nor necessarily by vesting rights of control over externalities in society as a whole via government agencies. For cases in which persons affected by the externalities are identifiable, he advocates government assistance to eliminate the costs of collective action for such persons, thereby enhancing their capacity to exercise effective voice. Meanwhile, corporations themselves can be induced to act responsibly by such rational means as greater external auditing and appropriate tax incentives, each designed to be responsive to particular interests.

The attractiveness of this proposal, from a liberal democratic viewpoint, is that it retains an emphasis on individual agency and the individual's claim to best know his or her own interests, while adapting these presuppositions to the level of corporate power. This reclaims agency from the fatalistic stasis induced by Weber's Iron Cage scenario, while attempting a fine-grained approach to the reallocation of rights to particular persons in their dealings with corporate bodies.

## The Hazy Promise of Coleman's Sociology

It would be unfair to leave the discussion on a Panglossian note. We live in a world that is very far from the best one possible, and Coleman is aware of this. He diagnoses very serious challenges to the capacity of modern society to reproduce itself. These arise from the decline of the family's role in interpersonal socialization, and the failure of increasingly powerful corporate actors to fill the gap. Persons have replaced households as the units engaging in economic activity, while the welfare activities of the family have been taken over by the state. Taxation-fed redistribution, however, fails to address either the micro-level process of personal socialization, or macro-level free rider problems. Thus "the social structure necessary to suppress the disincentive to contribute is missing" (657). Families were better able to handle free-rider problems through social-psychological mechanisms such as stigma and reputation, but no longer. Where are the new social institutions to replace them?

Perhaps this is just a conservative lament. Does it not sentimentalize the past with views of childhood that are simplistic and historically naive? Does it not gloss over negative features of the long history of the family, such as sexual abuse and patriarchal domination? Coleman's sociology of social action is not in any sense gendered. Women's increasing involvement in the workforce is discussed solely in terms of negative effects on children, and parent-child relations. Similarly the growing autonomy of adolescents from parents is seen as tending to pathology rather than empowerment. In one sense, then, we return full circle to the lack of a convincing historical and theoretical anchorage for Coleman's account of the personalized world we have lost. As a result, Coleman lacks any effective means of explaining the struggle by women and children to obtain rights.

Yet there is far more to it than this. Coleman is on stronger ground in identifying the limits of corporate (i.e. impersonal) institutions as comprehensive models of social organization. In thematizing such issues as responsibility for the socialization of particular persons, Coleman is able to specify problematic features of "the new social structure." The most central of these are taken to hinge on conflict between the family and the corporation (in its widest, impersonal sense, e.g., the state) over responsibility for child rearing. This becomes the core question for the society concerned with its capacity to reproduce itself via the creation of a new generation of socialized individuals.

In terms of public policy, this creates dilemmas. "Should social policy attempt to recreate the conditions which reinforce parents' natural [sic] interest in and responsibility for their own children, or attempt to create conditions which will induce agents of the state to take a long-term personal interest in and responsibility for children who fall into their hands" (608)? The first option would appear to fly in the face of social trends toward individual adult autonomy, while the second, according to Coleman, relies on the dubious capacity of state agents to substitute for parents.

The corner that Coleman boxes himself into here might be less restrictive were he able to conceive of the socialization process itself as a dynamic, historically changing institution. This conceptual shift does not appear possible. Instead, his evaluative standpoint remains steadfastly that of the *Gemeinschaft*.

For all these problems, though, this is an ambitious, highly intelligent, intellectually honest, and morally uplifting book. If it is true that radical conservatives make the best sociologists, then Coleman certainly fits the bill.

### Notes

1. A subtle review of the problems of assuming a unitary or holistic rationality, and of the presence of multiple rationalities or ways of deliberative thinking is contained in Hindess 1988, especially chapter 5.

2. Many contributions to the history of the family and of childhood have challenged the assumptions that (a) the premodern family may be regarded as a high point of interpersonal care and responsibility, and (b) modernity is rapidly destroying this family- and child-centeredness. As far as (a) is concerned, it has been argued, from French evidence, that the idea of childhood and the sentimentalization of family life are modern, i.e., seventeenth-century inventions rather than age old "family values." See, for example, Ariès 1962. Simon Schama (1987) notes high rates of child abandonment in some early modern cities, data that are scarcely comforting to those who would idealize the premodern family. However, like Ariès, he also points out, this time from seventeenth century Dutch evidence, that child-centeredness and concern for the specific needs of children are historical products, sensitive to particular demographic and socio-economic contexts. Given that available data for these judgments is based very largely on the European aristocracy or bourgeoisie, it is hard to tell whether their arguments can be generalized. It is nonetheless difficult to sustain Coleman's idealized premodern family on the basis of such data as exists.

3. For a very judicious review of the historical use of "rational economic man" assumptions see Snooks 1993, especially chapter 6.

4. The major texts are Weber 1978a and 1978b. Additional commentary may be found in Brubaker 1984 and Schluchter 1981.

5. The initial statement of Parsons's attempt at theoretical multi-dimensionality is contained in Parsons, Bales, and Shils 1953. The approach is developed further in Parsons and Smelser 1956. For further commentary see Holton and Turner 1986.

## References

Alexander, Jeffrey C. 1982–1984. *Theoretical Logic in Sociology*. 4 vols. London: Routledge and Kegan Paul.
Ariès, Phillipe. 1962. *Centuries of Childhood: A Social History of Family Life*. New York: Random House.
Brubaker, Rogers. 1984. *The Limits of Rationality*. London: Allen and Unwin.
Coleman, James S. 1990. "Rational Organization." *Rationality and Society* 2:94–105.
Coleman, James. 1990b. *Foundations of Social Theory*. Cambridge, Mass.: Harvard University Press.
Durkheim, Emile. 1947. *The Division of Labor*. New York: Free Press.
Elster, Jon. 1979. *Ulysses and the Sirens*. Cambridge: Cambridge University Press.
Favell, Adrian. 1993. "James Coleman: Social Theorist and Moral Philosopher." *American Journal of Sociology* 99: 590–614.
Giddens, Anthony. 1979. *Central Problems in Social Theory*. London: Macmillan.
Giddens, Anthony. 1990. *The Constitution of Society*. Oxford: Polity.
Granovetter, Mark. 1985. "Economic Action, Social Structure, and Embeddedness." *American Journal of Sociology* 83: 1410–1443.
Habermas, Jürgen. 1979. *Communication and the Evolution of Society*. London: Heinemann.
Habermas, Jürgen. 1984. *Reason and the Rationalization of Society*. Vol. I of *Theory of Communicative Action*. Boston: Beacon Press.
Hindess, Barry. 1988. *Choice, Rationality, and Social Theory*. London: Unwin Hyman.
Holton, Robert, and Brian Turner. 1986. *Talcott Parsons on Economy and Society*. London: Routledge.

Mead, George Herbert. 1962. "Mind, Self, and Society." In *Mind, Self, and Society*, ed. C. W. Morris. Chicago: Chicago University Press.
Parsons, Talcott. 1968. *The Structure of Social Action*. New York: Free Press.
Parsons, Talcott, Robert F. Bales, and Edward A. Shils. 1953. *Working Papers in the Theory of Action*. Glencoe, Ill.: Free Press.
Parsons, Talcott and Neil Smelser. 1956. *Economy and Society*. London: Routledge.
Schama, Simon. 1987. *The Embarrassment of Riches: An Interpretation of Dutch Culture in the Golden Age*. London: Collins.
Schluchter, Wolfgang. 1981. *The Rise of Western Rationality*. Berkeley: University of California Press.
Sen, Amartya. 1977. "Rational Fools: A Critique of the Behavioral Foundations of Economic Theory." *Philosophy and Public Affairs* 6: 317–344.
Snooks, Graeme D. 1993. *Economics without Time: a Science Blind to the Forces of Historical Change*. Basingstoke: Macmillan.
Tönnies, Ferdinand. 1955. *Community and Association*. London: Routledge.
Weber, Max. 1978a. *Economy and Society*. Vol. I. Berkeley: University of California Press.
Weber, Max. 1978b. *The Protestant Ethic and the Spirit of Capitalism*. London: Allen and Unwin.
Williamson, Oliver E. 1975. *Markets and Hierarchies: Analysis and Anti-Trust Implications*. New York: Free Press
Williamson, Oliver E. 1985. *The Economic Institutions of Capitalism: Firms, Markets, Relational Contracting*. London: Macmillan.

# Feminism, Essentialism, and Historical Context

*Rosaria Champagne*

I

As its title suggests, *Conflicts in Feminism* responds to the turmoil within academic feminism. The editors, Marianne Hirsch and Evelyn Fox Keller, write in their conclusion that the "dream of a common language" depends on conflict-free feminism, a political strategy that separates the "us" from the "them." The problem of course, is that the category of "us" – even a feminist "us" – signifies those whose power and privilege remains intact, unquestioned and invisible. Hirsch and Keller write: "Today, we have come to recognize those boundaries we wanted to think of as delineating 'us' from 'them' as conspicuous fault lines among 'us'."[1] This essay worries the category of "us," turning over the terms that have constructed the us/them delineation within feminist critical theory – essentialism and context. I worry (and worry over) these terms because the constructed oppositions among them make certain paradigms, such as "poststructural feminism" and "derridean antiracism" highly suspect.[2]

As Hirsch and Keller point out, debates about poststructuralism's use to feminism are constituted by and inform other critical discourses – Marxism, reader response theory, New Criticism and pluralism – and shape institutional values, as represented most recently by the dismissal of Women's Studies and Black Studies as somehow "overly" ideological by mainstream journals and conservative faculty members and right-wing organizations such as the National Association of Scholars. Both because of and in spite of this disruption of power, feminist theory has flourished. As a feminist teacher, I'm not disturbed by conflicts within feminism (and I would have to quit my job if I were!), but I am distressed that these conflicts are regarded as acts of bad faith. And, a well-dressed, self-fashioned feminist in the 1990s has the goodness and badness of her faith measured against the term "essentialism."

---

Source: *Women's Studies*, 1995, vol. 25, no. 1, pp. 95–108.

Since the 1970s, Women's Studies, the earliest academic manifestation of feminism, has accepted – although not without conflict and turmoil – that Woman is a category and that women, although different and separate (and mediated through categories of class, race, age and sexual orientation) all share a culturally degraded status. Different feminist critical positions have engaged with and debated this issue of essentialism and its place in maintaining the politics of feminism.[3] Having direct bearing on the question of how (and, how we prove that) gender "marks" the text; essentialism has become a weapon and a symbol of intellectual warfare within feminism.

Although Gayatri Spivak wrote in her 1987 essay, "Feminism and Critical Theory," that "essentialism is a trap,"[4] she has since asked that feminist theorists take the "risk" of essence.[5] Spivak's shift exposes a changing critical climate, not a change of heart. Essentialism is neither "good" nor "bad," and its presence in contemporary feminist discourse and practice cannot be simply embraced or dismissed. However, when we focus on how essentialism is used (and by whom) rather than what "it" is, we take a more pro-active approach. Essentialism saps feminist energy when it becomes the tool feminists use to size up other feminists. It further undermines our political strength when we use essentialism as a means to legitimacy, a gesture we no-doubt borrowed from boys in the playground or boardroom who drop their drawers to measure up; this is never a good practice for a political movement that is concerned with social betterment. Furthermore, as Teresa de Lauretis suggests in "Upping the Anti [sic] in Feminist Theory," disputing the size of "essential" gestures has sidetracked feminism: "The currency of the term 'essentialism' may be based on nothing more than its capacity to circumvent this very question – the nature of the specific difference of feminism – and thus polarize feminist thought on what amounts to a red herring."[6] Debating and refuting and engaging with other feminist texts using an anti-essentialist paradigm is not "bad," but when the purpose of feminist reading becomes the act of routing out essentialism, the red herring may turn into a rainbow scare.

My position, echoing that of Diana Fuss in *Essentially Speaking: Feminism, Nature and Difference*, is that essentialism and constructionism, as theoretical positions that determine ways of reading, are not mutually exclusive, but inseparable and interdependent; they are complicated versions of each other. Although the doctrinaire anti-essentialist would necessarily resist this assertion out-of-hand, what we see when filtering the essentialist–constructionist binarism through a psychoanalytic/poststructural frame is that essence (essentialism) is to counter-essence (constructionism) as transference is to counter-transference. In Diana Fuss's words: "To insist that essentialism is always and everywhere reactionary is, for the constructionist, to buy into essentialism in the very act of making the charge: *it is to act as if essentialism has an essence.*"[7] Thus, essentialism is only negatively charged when it operates as a critical return of the repressed.

What interests me in the conflict generated within feminism over the term "essentialism" is the divisions it produces and the way these boundaries protect the category of "context." I would like now, to shift this focus from "essentialism" to the feminist embrace of "context." Unfortunately, the resistance to "conflicts in feminism" has reified "context" as the paternal gatekeeper which has in turn fashioned "context" as feminism's over-determined father. Since contexts are constructed, not discovered, feminism would do well to reconstruct "context" – as an intellectual and political placekeeper, as well as a marker for historical materialism – from a poststructural paradigm.

## II

Jane Marcus in "Daughters of Anger/Material Girls: Con/textualizing Feminist Criticism" states without irony that "perspective makes all the difference."[8] However, it is feminism's unproblematic relationship with "perspective" that I contend has created the climate where an unreconstructed "context" stands as the father of feminist theory. Like the presence of an all-knowing father, the invitation of unreconstructed "context" to a critical debate gives a woman permission to interpret; her utterance suggests that she has a subject position from which to speak, although the half-truth here works in the same fashion as does subtle sexism making it harder to complain because the appearance – the trustworthy signifier – belies the signified.[9] The political ramifications of this unreconstructed "context" have created the climate for Ellen Rooney's assertion that "context is swallowed whole, and women, as subjects, disappear with it, absorbed entirely into their bodies."[10]

According to Mikhail Bakhtin, the definition of "Heteroglossia" explains that contexts assume primacy over texts because "all utterances are heteroglot in that they are functions of a matrix of forces practically impossible to recoup, and therefore impossible to resolve."[11] When used in the spirit of Bakhtin's definition, "context" (via heteroglossia) provides for feminist theories of reading a useful means to explore the social production of women's experiences and writing within specific historical moments. However, context is too often used to prove that women's bodies and texts do not measure up to the standards of white males. Furthermore, context is also used as tool of both intellectual and geographical boundary maintenance.

The boundaries between inside (text) and outside (context) are slippery: although the female body foregrounds and locates experience, we do not stop at our skins. "Erotogenic" zones, places where there are gaps in the body's surface, let precious texts permeate contexts. Because the female body functions as both the container and the contained, we can read sexist arguments that continue to regard women's place in the domestic sphere as an example of how cultural norms privatize the emissions from the erotogenic zones. After all, victim blame is often used to keep women off the streets: what were you doing, walking "our" streets at night? As Patricia J. Williams explores in her wonderful book on feminist legal theory and cultural studies, *The Alchemy of Race and Rights*, the privatization of public space purposely misunderstands the term "public," which really signifies ownership by the privileged:

> Blacks went from being owned by others to having everything around them owned by others . . . this limbo of disownedness keeps blacks beyond the pale of those who are entitled to receive the survival gifts of commerce, the life, liberty and happiness whose fruits our culture locates in the marketplace.[12]

The racism that declares "our" streets the private property of the white privileged reflects our culture's laws regarding the strategic slippage of public and private space. The message is clear: the dispossessed do not own the streets; therefore, unreconstructed context does not empower the dispossessed.

Most collections of feminist literary theory and criticism produced throughout the 1970s and 1980s have understood "context" as woman's license to speak (probably because context often stands for history as a fixed set or linear self-contained unit, which, stands for truth).[13] The ability of "context" to legitimate the speaker or reader sets up "context" as an answer to the always-present question that lurks in the interdictions of textuality – who gave that woman license to speak? This makes victimhood a by-product of unreconstructed context, because the temporary permission unreconstructed context thus offers can be taken away at whim, an exchange we see almost constantly in play in the debate over the inclusion of minority texts to the canon. My view is that if intertextuality means that each text is a rewriting of previous texts, then feminist theory will find context more useful as a system of questions than answers, especially if these questions lend themselves to a feminist reconstruction of context. But, unreconstructed context has, through repeated use, gained such authority that one can hardly challenge it.[14]

Context becomes an intellectual time-out when it closes down the potential for conflict, when it smooths away the wrinkles and determines for the reader the available interpretive possibilities. Because events (most noticeably, the painful crimes of rape and incest) often precede language, and "experience" results from the language available to represent these events (to ourselves and others), feminist work that relies on poststructural redefinitions of the body have much to lose when "context" becomes a privileged placekeeper. Context shuts down important feminist questions about author's lives: how do we begin to frame analyses about incest or lesbianism if a woman writer's context overrides these possibilities? The established and accepted context that constructs a woman writer's biography often determines the available interpretations of her life and work; in my more cynical moods, I feel any interpretative possibility made available by patriarchal logic renders unthinkable important feminist speculations. After all, how do we examine the experiences of a woman writer's body and psyche that stand outside the "definitive" biographical story without being merely speculative or naively essentialist?

This use of context as an intellectual and political time-out relies most visibly on a foundationalist definition of history; encoded in this foundationalism, we also find a cultural prescription to keep in private spheres. Let us begin, then, with Donna Haraway's poststructural definition of history. Rejecting history as a "completed past simply waiting to be applied to deepen a time probe or to give perspective," Haraway regards history as a baggage of "contradictions and multiple material-semiotic processes."[15] Haraway's definition allows us to reclaim history as a narrative which constructs its authority while simultaneously dismantling the seductive appearance of discovered truth.

Is "context" ever a politically safe placekeeper for feminist critics? Yes, if it has been reworked to expose both the seductions of unreconstructed context, and identifies the political possibilities for a feminist reconstitution. Clearly, I do not want to erase "context" (I couldn't even if I wanted to); instead, I desire to expose its affiliation with patriarchal constructions and thus, in Derrida's terms, put it under erasure. The distinction between being erased and being under erasure is significant; the former disregards the term as unimportant (e.g., the reader of this text regards her reading as pure of ideological workings); the latter regards the word as both necessary and simultaneously inaccurate.[16] Context becomes context (crossed out); the term is legible, but its purity is visibly contested.[17] Following Derrida, I would like to offer unreconstructed "context" as a placekeeper which those in power use to falsely legitimize their privilege; social commodification naturalizes constructions so that they appear organic; organic categories become key tools for keeping women in subordinate places.

The argument which I hope to illustrate is this: the desire for context is the desire to be contained or at least to construct our own containers. Furthermore, this desire, which is connected to feminism's concern with coalition politics and strategic essentialism, identifies identity as an activity in exclusion, a set of removals. This agenda compels me to digress and define more terms of my discussion: identity, subject position, subject effect.

## III

The terms "subject-position," "subject-effect," and "identity" and their contemporary use in critical theory rely heavily on Louis Althusser's articulation of the ideological interpellation of individuals as subjects in his now famous "Ideology and Ideological State Apparatuses (Notes Toward an Investigation)." His theory that ideology knows no boundaries is especially useful to exposing the problems of unreconstructed context. He states: "[T]hose who are in ideology believe themselves by definition outside ideology: one of the effects of ideology is the practical denigration of the ideological character of ideology."[18] State Apparatuses "hail" individuals and transform them through this policing into subjects ("the constitutive category of all ideology" [171]). Using feminism, we can understand this material force as a kind of street harassment of women: it can both transform a woman into passivity (if we stop walking the streets at night, an act which becomes both the proof of and the cause to the established context of women's space in the private sphere) and it may recruit her into compliance with the norms and values endorsed by heterosexism (for example, through employing male escorts as protection against other men).[19] Althusser writes: "[Ideology 'acts' or 'functions' in such a way that it 'recruits' subjects among the individuals (it recruits them all)" [174].[20]

If "interpellation" is an act of inclusion, the question remains: is identity a form of self-knowledge or an activity of difference? Here we see where liberal humanism (which invokes the former definition) and deconstruction (which sees difference as the operative term) can both be appropriated on feminist terms. Although one cannot choose one's subject-position (Foucault), one can regulate her subject-effect (Spivak). According to Foucault, a subject position is *assigned*:

> So the subject of the statement should not be regarded as identical with the author of the formulation. . . . He is not in fact the cause, origin, or starting point of the phenomenon. . . . [A subject-position is] a particular, vacant place that may in fact be filled by different individuals.[21]

Identities are (con)textual: neither the woman writer nor the woman character has the privilege of self-diagnoses. Not a confession, a subject-position is also not an admission of our personal biases or commitments. On the other hand, one's "subject-effect" is the text of self-projection in "politics, ideology, economics, history, sexuality, language. . . . [The] configurations of these strands . . . produce the effect of an operating subject."[22]

By juxtaposing interpellation into subjecthood as an act of inclusion (subject-position) with the oppositional assertion of self-identity as a gesture of exclusion (subject-effect), the instability of categories such as "context" or "experience" becomes exposed. I suggest that there is more at stake than the feminist–materialist watchword that all categories ("Woman," "Lesbian," "African-American" and so on) are mediated through class levels.[23] What interests me is the way "identity" becomes interchangeable with "experience." Within this exchange of epistemology for ontology lies a subtle but insidious curtsy to patriarchal constructions of "context," identifiable when "woman's experience" becomes coercive in its invisible exclusions. As Joan W. Scott states in "The Evidence of Experience": "it is not individuals who have experience, but subjects who are constituted through experience."[24]

The feminist desire for context reveals the precarious place women hold within patriarchal discourse. Although identity cannot be named, only constructed, for that construction to become a cultural commodity we repair it to a category, knowing that this act not only provides cultural commodification (as categories have familiar currency) but also neutralizes political potential (category carry the value judgments of the dominant ideology). Categories (like canons) provide authority for the subject and the possibility for representation. As Freud has shown, the desire for representation is a death wish: this becomes a political transmutation when we see that what often gets sacrificed for categorical purity is the germ of radical potential.[25] This relationship between representation and death raises two questions: what are the possible identifications between desire and ideology? and, how can we account for the agency of desire? The overlap between reifying experience as essentialist and representation/death occurs in ways that insinuate the gestures of the former with the latter. It is difficult to tell where the "owning an experience" leaves off and "representation/death" begins.

According to Mikhail Bakhtin, "A context is potentially unfinalized; a code must be finalized. . . . A code is a deliberately killed context."[26] The site for the "killed context" in social and literary texts is often a woman's body. Certainly, this attitude fuels the abortion tactics of the anti-choice movement "Operation Rescue." The implication is that space (womb) is only valuable once filled (appropriated by male presence), at which point the "killed context's" visibility (the desire for reproductive freedom) is only an issue if it fails to function as container (if the fetus is aborted). That "code" signifies a system of restraints is evident in Gothic romances, where the castle, a publicized womb, offers both protections and oppression. Thus, it is not surprising that in *Frankenstein* (1818) two women are sacrificed in an attempt to kill/chase the context (which is in this text the creation of life in a laboratory) back into a woman's body.[27] First, Victor kills his Creature's bride because he fears losing power over him: "I thought with a sensation of madness on my promise of creating another like to him, and, trembling with passion, tore to pieces the thing on which I was engaged." In retaliation the Creature destroys his master's "thing" (his bride). Victor, who has been avoiding all possible contact with women in general and sexual contact with Elizabeth in particular, collapses with relief when the heterosexist context in which he finds himself has been destroyed with/in the body of his wife.

The contextualization/sexualization of marriage as an institution appears also in works of critical theory. Two primary examples are J. L. Austin's *How To Do Things With Words* and Jonathon Culler's critique of this text in *On Deconstruction*.[28] Using Austin's example of marriage as proof that all meaning is context-bound, Culler writes:

> When the minister says "I now pronounce you man and wife," his utterance successfully performs the act of uniting a couple in marriage if the context meets certain conditions. . . . Suppose that the requirements for a marriage ceremony were met but that one of the parties were [sic] under hypnosis, or again that the ceremony were impeccable in all respects but had been called a "rehearsal," or finally, that while the speaker

was a minister licensed to perform weddings and the couple had obtained a license, the three of them were on this occasion acting in a play that, coincidentally, included a wedding ceremony. [122]

But despite Culler's attempt to neutralize the contexts of the institution of marriage, all weddings actually incorporate in their contexts, subtexts and pretexts, examples of all three "confusions." Clearly, some women are interpellated into marriage through its idealization in patriarchal cultures and enticed to attach themselves to men through an economic system that privileges men by thirty-five cents on the dollar – an example of hypnosis in that once the "honeymoon is over," as the popular phrase will have it, the context changes severely. Clearly, weddings are performances where the "real" is always-already in competition with the "rehearsed." Clearly, the activity of following the script of the marriage vows involves playacting. And, although the theoretical point at which Austin arrives through his discussion of marriage – and that which Culler deconstructs – is authorial intention, what interests me is the choice of example. It is hardly news that marriage as an institution encourages woman's material subservience in a patriarchal system; like the castle/womb, it simultaneously enslaves and protects. The ways that politics hides in the interdictions of social institutions (for example, the ontology that naturalizes heterosexism and marriage) call to mind what Mary Jacobus writes in her feminist revision of Stanley Fish's "Is There a Text in this Class?": "One might speculate that the function of the female 'victim' in scenarios of this kind is to provide the mute sacrifice on which theory itself may be founded; the woman is silenced so that the theorist can make the truth come out of her mouth."[29] I agree that a woman in the text is being sacrificed, but rather than regard, in this case, Culler as the oppressor, it is the silencing effect of unreconstructed context which mutes her voice, specifically as this context imbeds itself with ontological and epistemic choices under the guise of ostensibly "natural" orders.

When contexts become overdetermined vis-a-vis institutionalization (as in marriage) the social texts that proliferate are absorbed by these institutions. Derrida in "Signature Event Context" writes: "A context is never absolutely determinable . . . its determination is never certain or saturated."[30] Derrida, later in this essay, asserts that every sign can break with every context in a logocentric/phallocentric culture: "No context can enclose it [a written sign]. Nor can any code, the code being here both the possibility and impossibility of writing, of its essential iterability" [321]. Perhaps, then, the limitations of feminist interventions can be traced to our reliance on an unreconstructed "context" as the witness of our oppressions (proof) and the legitimation of our interpretations (truth).

## IV

One of the reasons "context" has become reified in feminist theory is because feminist theory stops the deconstructive trajectory at inversion. The stakes are high here. If we move feminist theory towards displacement (a gesture of translation in which the original text is changed through the process), what will happen to the material status of women in culture? How can we know that our feminist–poststructural interventions won't become absorbed by patriarchal values which always/already declare, for example, that women lie about hate crimes such as rape and incest? This concern informs the voices in feminist theory that endorse canon constructions: the displacement of context (and of a woman's body as context) threatens to destablize (white, middle-class, heterosexual) women's comfort in both the public sphere and private sphere.

I suggest that we use this discomfort strategically through our intentional production of misreadings – that is, we "do" readings that challenge both the boundaries of accepted contexts as well as question the politics of context as a form of boundary maintenance. This offers feminism a hermeneutical politics enacted to protest the conventional and misogynist traditions of cohesive, unified readings as well as a methodology which will create new ways of representing women in literature. And although we (feminists) borrow this deconstructive turn from post-structural theory, we need not be grateful for the loan because we are turning the deconstructive screw in the way the fathers would not necessarily sanction.

The discomfort to which I refer can be understood as a kind of resisting reading, an activity that regards political readers as criminals of culture and political readings as a projection of strategy, not truth.[31] If the responsibility of the reader is understood in the traditional way – as an ethical accountability for getting the text and the receivable reading "right" – then reading becomes an act of compliance with culture, and culture has a good deal invested in prohibiting our recognition of the social construction of its power. Because texts do not merely reflect social values but, rather, create the representations through which we live, the narrative we seek to deconstruct, receivable readings and misreadings construct and protect "context" as a powerful and important aesthetic.[32]

One means through which the aestheticization of context (and culture) can be undone is through an understanding of the naturalization of constructed social norms and values. Instead of simply defining ideology as that which puts reading and misreading into practice, we can fix on discourse as the agent through which the strategic and political misreadings lodge. Understanding discourse in this way can expose how ideology hides in the sign system through which it gains authority. This understanding overturns the dispute regarding poststructuralism's use-value to feminism, which is traditionally read as a disagreement over the "truth" of poststructural critics. Clearly, there is a more profitable way to understand this debate, namely though the feminist revision of poststructuralism as a strategy. Thus, feminism need not make an overall commitment to poststructuralism to use it towards the realization of feminist goals. Through this dialogue between contemporary feminism and poststructuralism, mediated as all discussions of subject construction are, through psychoanalysis, feminism's fixed relations to the unified subject and transparency of language can loosen without denying authorality and authority to women writers. Furthermore, feminism can expose the poststructural confidence in its own rightness and righteousness (the "vanguardism of theory" in Spivak's words) which undermines its political utility.

"What we need is an ethics of criticism," states Jane Gallop in the conclusion to "Criticizing Feminist Criticism" (a conversation among Gallop, Hirsch and Nancy K. Miller).[33] By appropriating poststructural gestures for feminist gains, we can understand that the ethics of our feminist revolution need not look like a chorus line; that is, we can afford to disagree.[34] A poststructural–feminist intervention has already been mapped out by Donna Haraway in "A Manifesto for Cyborgs: Science, Technology, and Socialist Feminism in the 1980s." Because "taxonomies of feminism produce epistemologies to police deviation from official women's experience," Haraway calls for a non-taxonomic feminism which identifies the "non-innocence of the category 'woman.'"[35] Because ideology relies on its own invisibility, any move which exposes its construction implies that it can be deconstructed. Reading in a way that refuses to accept context as natural (that is, nonideological) or essentialism as always/already "bad" offers one avenue for this "ethics of criticism" because this strategic misreading reveals that political solidarity is not necessary for group cohesion. Specifically if the concern is that the boys are listening, fragmentation within feminism can be strategically useful, especially when our fragmentation of voices means that we are everywhere at once.

### Notes

1. Marianne Hirsch and Evelyn Fox Keller, eds., *Conflicts in Feminism* (New York: Routledge Press, 1990) 379.

2. I would like to thank Laura E. Brown, Janet Gray, and Erin Mackie, whose comments and criticisms have shaped and informed this present draft.

3. See especially Teresa de Lauretis, *Alice Doesn't: Feminism, Semiotics and Cinema* (Bloomington: Indiana UP, 1984); Diana Fuss, *Essentially Speaking: Feminism, Nature, and Difference* (New York: Routledge Press, 1989); Denise Riley, *"Am I that Name?": Feminism and the Category of 'Women' in History* (Minneapolis: University of Minnesota, 1988); Naomi Schor and Elizabeth Weed, eds, special ed. of *Differences* 1.2 (1989).

4. Gayatri Chakravorty Spivak, "Feminism and Critical Theory," *In Other Worlds: Essays in Cultural Politics* (New York: Routledge Press, 1988) 77–95.

5. See *Differences: A Journal of Feminist Cultural Studies* 1.2 (1989). In this special volume entitled "Another Look at Essentialism," Spivak gives an interview, "I A Word" (124–156), in which she discusses "how anti-essentialism . . . more than essentialism, is allowing women to call names and to congratulate themselves" [129].

6. Hirsch and Keller 256.

7. Diana Fuss, *Essentially Speaking: Feminism, Nature, and Difference* (New York: Routledge Press, 1989) 21. Fuss's italics.

8. Jane Marcus, "Daughters of Anger/Material Girls: Con/textualizing Feminist Criticism," *Women's Studies: An Interdisciplinary Journal* 15 (1988) 288.

9. For an analysis of the problematic relationship between narrative discourse and representation, see Jacques Derrida in "Semiology and Grammatology: Interview with Julia Kristeva" (1972) in *Positions*, trans. Alan Bass (Chicago; U of Chicago P, 1981) 15-37. On the confusion of the signifier for the signified, Derrida rejects Saussure's "transcendental signifier" and instead suggests:

> Not only do the signified and signifier seem to unite, but also, in this confusion, the signifier seems to erase itself or to become transparent, in order to allow the concept to present itself as what it is, referring to nothing other than its presence. [22]

10. "In a Word," Interview by Ellen Rooney with Gayatri Spivak. *Differences: A Journal of Feminist Cultural Studies* 1 (1989) 125.

11. M. M. Bakhtin, *The Dialogic Imagination*, trans. Caryl Emerson and Michael Holquist (Austin: University of Texas Press, 1991) 428.

12. Patricia J. Williams, *The Alchemy of Race and Rights* (Cambridge: Harvard University Press, 1991) 71.

13. According to Gerald Graff in *Professing Literature: An Institutional History* (Chicago: University of Chicago Press, 1987), all literary texts rely on cultural contexts. He writes:

> If there is any point of agreement among deconstructionists, structuralists, reader-response critics, pragmatists, phenomenologists, speech-act theorists, and theoretically-minded humanists, it is on the principle that texts are not ... autonomous and self-contained, that the meaning of any text in itself depends for its comprehension on other texts and textualized frames of reference. Current schools of criticism disagree over whether anything like an objective reconstruction of the relevant context of any text is possible. ... But despite these substantive and important disagreements, there is considerable agreement on at least one point: that meaning is not an autonomous essence within the words of a text but something dependent for its comprehension on prior texts and situations [contexts].

14. That "context" acts as the placekeeper for many critical schools is shown in two recent poststructural texts that also employ "context" as license to speak. See Mark Poster, *Critical Theory and Poststructuralism: In Search of a Context* (Ithaca: Cornell University Press, 1989) and Mark Taylor, ed., *Deconstruction in Context: Literature and Philosophy* (Chicago: University of Chicago Press, 1986).

15. Donna Haraway, *Primate Visions* (New York: Routledge, 1989) 172.

16. For a discussion of "sous rature," see Jacques Derrida's *Of Grammatology*. Spivak's "Translator's Preface" is especially helpful. For an accessible introduction to Derridean deconstruction, see Madan Sarup's *An Introductory Guide to Post-structuralism and Postmodernism* (Athens: University of Georgia Press, 1989).

17. Martin Heidegger, *On Time and Being*, trans. Joan Stambaugh (New York: Harper and Row, 1972). In his works, he often crossed out the word "Being" to show that Being has no context; that is, it transcends signification; this was one of the concepts that Derridean deconstruction puts under erasure.

18. Louis Althusser, "Ideology and Ideological State Apparatuses (Notes Toward an Investigation)" (1970), *Lenin and Philosophy and Other Essays*, trans. Ben Brewster (New York: Monthly Review Press, 1971) 175. Further references will appear in the text in square brackets.

19. When feminism removed rape from the category of sexuality and re-categorized it as an act of violence, this contributed to the proliferation of theories which see violence against women as an institutional arm of the patriarchy. In turn, this has created rape education programs on university campuses, where women can and do learn to fight back. To say that our interpellation into ideology does not depend on our conscious submission is not to suggest that we cannot resist.

20. The problem with using Althusser to refashion context is that there is no room for resistance; Althusser cannot accommodate those who break the rules. Nevertheless, feminists can use Althusser's formulation to expose the seductiveness of social inclusion.

21. Michel Foucault, *The Archeology of Knowledge and the Discourse on Language* (1969), trans. A. M. Sgeridan Smith (New York: Pantheon Books, 1972) 95.

22. Gayatri C. Spivak, 'Subaltern Studies: Deconstructing Historiography," *In Other Worlds: Essays in Cultural Politics* (New York and London: Routledge, 1987) 204.

23. Although this concept now has wide currency, one of the best defenses of this gesture can be found in "Toward a Materialist–feminist Criticism," the introduction of Judith Newton and Deborah Rosenfelt, eds., *Feminist Criticism and Social Change: Sex, Class and Race in Literature and Culture* (New York and London: Methuen Press, 1985) xv–xxxix.

24. Joan W. Scott, "The Evidence of Experience," *Critical Inquiry* 17.4 (1991) 779.

25. Nineteenth- and twentieth-century women's literature seems obsessed with this issue. When a woman character has to represent her own desire/action, the woman author often breaks literary boundaries/contexts. In Marilynne Robinson's *Housekeeping* (1981) the narrator represents herself through a refusal to make speech acts and utterances; in Toni Morrison's *Beloved* (1988), Sethe calls the murdered Beloved to life through a discursive cathexis, where the ghostly daughter represents simultaneously the body part of the mother imbued with psychic energy as well as her own autonomous subject; in Mary Shelley's *Frankenstein* (1818), a text ostensibly written for Margaret Saville, the non-categorized Creature who is the living dead says, "I, the miserable, am an abortion." Shelley's use of the present tense – as well as her infiltration of the category in which women are most often perceived as empty vessels waiting to be filled – reacts against both linguistic and social containment. Literature offers a most useful site for theoretical inquiry into both the psyche and society; as critics, our own gesture to "make the text stand still" and our concomitant recognition of this impossibility provides entries into both unconscious and conscious desire

26. Mikhail Bakhtin, "Extracts from Notes (1970–1971)" *Bakhtin: Essays and Dialogues on His Work*, ed. Gary Saul Morson (Chicago: University of Chicago Press, 1986) 179–182.

27. Mary Shelley, *Frankenstein, or the Modern Prometheus*, ed. James Reiger (Indianapolis: Bobbs-Merrill, 1974) 164.

28. J. L. Austin, *How To Do Things with Words* (Cambridge; Harvard University Press, 1975); Jonathan Culler, *On Deconstruction: Theory and Criticism after Structuralism* (Ithaca: Cornell University Press, 1982). All references to these works are included parenthetically within the text.

29. Mary Jacobus, "Is There a Woman in this Text?" (1982) *Reading Woman: Essays in Feminist Criticism* (New York: Columbia University Press, 1986) 83–109.

30. Jacques Derrida, "Signature Event Context" (1977), *Margins of Philosophy*, trans. Allen Bass (Chicago: University of Chicago Press, 1982) 310.

31. My theory of resistance should not be confused with the early articulation of feminist reader response developed by Judith Fetterley in *The Resisting Reader: A Feminist Approach to American Fiction* (Bloomington: Indiana University Press, 1981). While Fetterley privileges the text in a fixed and stable place, and then situates the feminist reader in relation to it, I alter this paradigm through the post-structural notion that both text and reader assume indeterminate positions. Using post-structuralism to redefine reading as resistance, I hope to bypass the problems raised by reading the privileged text of New Criticism and the essentialized reader of reader response criticism. Through this paradigm, I hope to arrive at the place where the text is always the text-in-transference (because as Foucault has shown, desire is always invested in the law) and the reader has the responsibility of reading her own effect/affect the text produces in her, which both informs and is informed by the interpretation she lays on the text.

32. For an excellent explanation of how receivable readings are always apolitical because of their complicity with traditional categories, see Gayatri Spivak, "Displacement and the Discourse of Woman," *Displacement: Derrida and After*, ed. Mark Krupnick (Bloomington: Indiana University Press, 1983) 169–95.

33. Hirsch and Keller 368.

34. This should not be confused with the pluralist gesture which silences voices from the margins in the very act of eliciting them.

35. Donna Haraway, "A Manifesto for Cyborgs: Science, Technology, and Socialist Feminism in the 1980s." *Feminism/Postmodern*, ed. Linda J. Nicholson (New York: Routledge, 1990) 198, 199.

# "I Can't Even Think Straight:" "Queer" Theory and the Missing Sexual Revolution in Sociology*

*Arlene Stein and Ken Plummer*

> *There's nowt so queer as folk*
> —Old Lancashire Saying

Writing in 1985, Judith Stacey and Barrie Thorne provided a useful critique of the "missing feminist revolution" in sociology. Feminists, they charged, had made important contributions to sociology, but had not been successful in "transforming the basic conceptual frameworks of the field" (Stacey and Thorne 1985: 301). In fact, feminist sociologists had been less successful than their counterparts in anthropology, history, and literature in effecting a "paradigm shift."

We believe that much the same could be said for the state of lesbian and gay sociology today. Even though a few sociologists have been studying lesbian/gay life for at least 25 years (at least since the publication of Mary McIntosh's [1968] seminal article), these concerns continue to inhabit the margins of the discipline.[1]

Studies of lesbian/gay life occur almost exclusively within the areas of deviance, gender, or sexuality, and have barely made their mark on the discipline as a whole. Many sociologists tend to labor under the assumption that lesbian and gay concerns are particularistic, and have little relevance to them, even though the lesbian/gay movement is among the most vibrant and well-organized social movements in the United States and Europe today. Clearly, there is a story here that we are missing; not only does its absence further marginalize "sexual minorities," but it also weakens sociological explanations as a whole.

There may be a glimmer of hope in an intellectual movement which is currently taking place in the humanities, called "queer theory." It is less and less possible today to take a course in anthropology, literature, film studies, or

---

Source: *Sociological Theory*, 1994, vol. 12, no. 2, pp. 178–187.

cultural history in the United States (and, to a much lesser extent, in Britain) without encountering the writings of so-called queer theorists. These scholars are succeeding in placing sexual difference at the center of intellectual inquiry in many fields – a "sexual revolution" which has been, for the most part, absent in sociology. Their success is particularly striking and even ironic in view of the fact that they are using social constructionism as if it were a new discovery, when it was sociologists who first generated this perspective.

How can sociologists redress this imbalance, and build upon the work that has already been done, to rethink sexual (and gender) nonconformity in ways that do not reproduce marginality? Toward this goal, we will briefly review the legacy of the sociology of homosexuality, consider what queer theory is, examine why it has been relatively successful in deghettoizing lesbian/gay studies, and ask what, if anything, we might learn from those efforts.

## The Legacy of the Sociology of Homosexuality

Although conducted on the margins, the sociology of homosexuality falls into two broad camps. The first is primarily empirical; the second tends to be more theoretically oriented. The first tends to accept sexual categories; the second often problematizes these categories.[2]

The first strand of homosexual studies, the empirical, has quite a long history. Emerging out of the nineteenth century, it seeks to describe and classify etiologies of homosexuality. Much of the earliest work was focused on "the homosexual" as an object of sociological survey, but increasingly, from the 1960s onwards, it has turned to the investigation of every nook and cranny of lesbian and gay life: bars, communities, identities, tearooms, and the like. It still continues, for example, in sociological accounts of identity stages (Troiden 1988).

Useful as they can be, empirical studies have tended to be unreflective about the nature of sexuality as a social category.[3] Such studies tend to replicate social divisions, implicitly reasserting the exotica of difference. At times, one is left with the sense that lesbian and gay individuals inhabit communities that are completely set off from the rest of society, that they are members of an altogether different culture and even a different species, if one follows the long-standing obsession with isolating the "cause" of homosexuality.[4]

The second strand of sociological studies problematizes the category "homosexual." It was present in some early writings, including those of Freud and Kinsey, but it was brought to the fore in the heyday of deviancy theory, the 1960s. The first generation of constructionist studies of sociology was conducted by American labeling theorists and U.K. "new deviancy theorists," young radical scholars who rejected the orthodoxies of criminology and traditional deviance study. Instead they challenged the very categories of deviance, locating "deviance" – not deviants – within frameworks of power.[5]

At this time a few key papers helped refocus the questions. McIntosh's (1968) highly influential contribution asked questions about the functions of the homosexual role, and shifted attention away from the homosexual "condition." Gagnon and Simon's (1967) reformulation brought matters of meaning, gender, and social organization to the fore. Kitsuse (1962) highlighted the powerful role of societal reaction and labeling. By the 1970s, a more theoretically informed study had commenced, and some research explicitly linked theorization with empirical work (Warren 1974).

Through labeling theory, the whole categorization process of homosexuality became problematized in what was later to be called "constructionism" and "deconstructionism." (The term *social constructionism* was rarely used in this literature, even though Berger and Luckman [1967] first popularized the phrase. It was widely used in other fields, and antedates Michel Foucault [1978] by more than a decade.) Through symbolic interactionism, the notions of meaning, process, "invented identities," and the cultural construction of communities became central – long before their current popularity in cultural studies. A lesser strand focused on "the stranger," "marginality," and "outsiders," describing homosexuality as a form of liberating consciousness.[6] Borrowing some ideas from U.S. sociology, it was seen as radically critical and challenging of the status quo, although with hindsight the ideas may not now seem so challenging.[7]

The sociology of homosexuality has also been influenced by feminism, which has conceptualized sexuality as a terrain of power. Lesbian feminists provided a powerful critique of compulsory homosexuality and what Rubin (1975) called the "sex/gender system." Adrienne Rich's ([1980] 1983) conception of a "lesbian continuum" was highly influential in reexamining the relationship between gender and sexuality. This literature broadened the definition of lesbianism, emphasizing the relational aspects of lesbian sexuality and universalizing the possibility of lesbianism. Challenging medicalized conceptions that focused upon gender inversion and masculinized sexual desire, these theories blurred the boundaries between gay and straight women, and hardened the boundaries separating lesbians and gay men.

Although enormously valuable, feminist sociology has an unfortunate tendency to conflate gender and sexuality, erasing the specificity of lesbian and gay existence. As Rubin remarked:

> Gender affects the operation of the sexual system, and the sexual system has had gender-specific manifestations. But although sex and gender are related, they are not the same thing, and they form the basis of two distinct arenas of social practice. . . . Lesbian feminist ideology has mostly analyzed the oppression of lesbians in terms of the oppression of women. However, lesbians are also oppressed as queers and perverts by the operation of sexual, not gender, stratifications (1984: 33).

This conflation of gender and sexuality continues to occur in feminist work. For example, a recent book on "never married women" barely mentions that many women in that category are lesbians (Simon 1987). A book on cross-gender occupations – women in the military and male nurses – mentions homosexuality only in passing, understating the prevalence of lesbians and gay men in nonnormative occupations (Williams 1989).

Collectively, the sociology of homosexuality, particularly the more theoretically oriented variety, may be seen as a kind of "standpoint theorizing" (McIntosh 1993). It assumes that studying and theorizing from the perspective of those who have been systematically denied access to power will inform our knowledge of the center. Yet in terms of the concerns of sociologists, the center has hardly budged. When studies of lesbian/gay life appear today, they are almost exclusively within the areas of deviance, gender, or sexuality, and have barely made their mark on the discipline as a whole. Though a few male theorists – but only a few – have made some nodding gestures towards feminist theory, there are virtually none who take lesbian and gay concerns seriously. Sometimes this is due to overt antagonisms and homophobia. Often it is due to theoretical blind spots.

Yet the "radical" theories of this period anticipated a number of ideas which would emerge again in the new queer theory, albeit somewhat more boldly, and even more resolutely committed to problematizing sexual categories.

## From Constructionism to Queer Theory

Queer theory, an academic movement – indeed, an elite academic movement centered least initially in the most prestigious U.S. institutions – is indirectly related to the emergence of an increasingly visible queer politics, a confrontational form of grass-roots activism embodied in ACT UP, Queer Nation, and other direct-action groups during the last decade. Queer theory emerged in the late 1980s, publicized through a series of academic conferences held at Yale and other Ivy League universities, in which scholars, primarily from history and the humanities, presented their work on lesbian/gay subjects (Fuss 1991).

Queer theory became a rallying cry for new ways of thinking and theorizing. For many, the term *lesbian and gay studies* did not seem inclusive enough; it did not encapsulate the ambivalence toward sexual categorization which many lesbian/gay scholars felt, and the difficulties they faced in fitting sexuality into the "ethnicity model" which provided the template for such fields as African-American and women's studies, and indeed for identity politics in general. Gay men and (to a lesser extent) lesbians had organized themselves along the lines of an ethnic group at least since the early 1970s, following the example of the black civil rights movement. Sexuality, however, defines a political interest constituency unlike those of gender and race. Membership in the group is fluctuating and largely invisible; identity as a lesbian or a gay man is, as Warner describes it,

> ambiguously given and chosen, in some ways ascribed and in other ways the product of the performative act of coming out. . . . In many

respects, queer people are a kind of social group fundamentally unlike others, a status group only insofar as they are not a class (1991: 15).

Against attempts to define the lesbian and gay population and to organize a politics around it, queer theory, at least ideally, embraces the indeterminacy of the gay category and suggests "the difficulty in defining the population whose interests are at stake in queer politics" (Warner 1991: 16).

Clues as to what queer theory looks like can be glimpsed through some of its (emerging) canonical works, which come mainly from philosophy, literature, and cultural studies. Judith Butler (1990) describes the "unwritten and written codes of heterosexualized gender systems". (Drawing upon the queer practices of drag, cross-dressing, and butch-femme, she develops a conception of gender as performance, and of gender parodies as subversive acts.) Through readings of modern literature, Eve Sedgwick (1990) describes new ways of knowing and not knowing based on secrecy and outings, arguing that such knowledges constitute a medium of domination that is not reducible to other forms of domination, and that finds its paradigmatic case in the homosexual and the closet. Andrew Parker (1991) rereads Marx's *Eighteenth Blumaire*, calling our attention to the homosocial dynamics of the collaboration between Marx and Engels and arguing that we need a "sex-inflected analysis of class formations," an understanding of how sexuality is constitutive of class categories.

In texts like these we start to see the following hallmarks of queer theory: 1) a conceptualization of sexuality which sees sexual power embodied in different levels of social life, expressed discursively and enforced through boundaries and binary divides; 2) the problematization of sexual and gender categories, and of identities in general. Identities are always on uncertain ground, entailing displacements of identification and knowing; 3) a rejection of civil rights strategies in favor of a politics of carnival, transgression, and parody which leads to deconstruction, decentering, revisionist readings, and an anti-assimilationist politics; 4) a willingness to interrogate areas which normally would not be seen as the terrain of sexuality, and to conduct queer "readings" of ostensibly heterosexual or nonsexualized texts.

At its widest, tallest, and Wilde(st), queer theory is a plea for massive transgression of all conventional categorizations and analyses – a Sadean/Nietzschean breaking of boundaries around gender/the erotic/the interpersonal, and a plea for dissidence. More narrowly, it is a political play on the word *queer*, long identified with "homosexuality," and the newest in a series of "reverse affirmations" in which the categories constructed through medicalization are turned against themselves. Often there is overlap between the more narrow (i.e., lesbian and gay) focus and the wider focus on transgression: they are far from separate.

Queer theorists claim that existing gay strategies, and minority group strategies in general, have tended to rely on conceptual dualisms (male/female gender models, natural/artificial ontological systems, or essentialist/constructionist intellectual frameworks) that reinforce the notion of minority as "other" and create binary oppositions which leave the "center" intact. As Teresa de Lauretis has written:

> Homosexuality is no longer to be seen simply as marginal with regard to a dominant, stable form of sexuality (heterosexuality) against which it would be defined . . . it is no longer to be seen as transgressive or deviant vis-a-vis a proper, natural sexuality (i.e. institutionalized reproductive sexuality) according to the older, pathological model, or as just another, optional "lifestyle," according to the model of contemporary North American pluralism (1991:iii).

Not content to study the "lesbian community" or the "gay community" as the exclusive site of sexual difference, queer theorists interrogate aspects of social life – the family, intimate relationships – but also look at places not typically thought of as sexualized – the economy, for example.

The homo/hetero divide so artfully assembled in the nineteenth century comes to be a strategy for deconstructing and rereading texts previously assembled through heterosexuality. "The sexual order overlaps with a wide range of institutions and social ideologies," writes Michael Warner (1991: 5), so that "to challenge the sexual order is sooner or later to encounter those institutions as problems." Much as feminists began treating gender as a primary lens for understanding problems that did not initially look gender-specific, for queer theorists the personal life is sexualized – and heterosexualized – and so are politics and economics, and just about everything else under the sun.

Queer theorists turn their deconstructive zeal against heterosexuality with a particular vengeance. When lesbian/gay theorists analyzed normative heterosexuality in the past, they envisioned it as a sex/gender system which was largely monolithic. Gayle Rubin (1975), in her classic article "The Traffic in Women," located heterosexuality as central to the reproduction of gender and sexual inequality. Queer theorists, on the other hand, locate within the institution of heterosexuality the seeds of its own demise. As Butler has suggested.

> That heterosexuality is always in the act of elaborating itself that it is perpetually at risk, that is, that it "knows" its own possibility of being undone (1991: 23).

Heterosexuality, in this vision, is a highly unstable system, subject to various slippages, reliant upon carefully constructed individual performances of identity, and dependent upon the exclusion of homosexuality for its very identity. One could say that queer theory normalizes homosexuality by making heterosexuality deviant. Homosexuality ceases to be the exclusive site of sexual difference.

The figure whose influence looms large in this literature is Michel Foucault. His sweeping *History of Sexuality* (1978) details the construction of sexuality through institutional discourses, which come to constitute "regimes of truth." As the result of the Victorian era's "discursive explosion," Foucault argues, sexuality became a mainstay of identity, heterosexual monogamy came to function as a norm, and sexual deviants began to see themselves as distinct persons, possessing particular "natures." Foucault problematizes the belief in a continuous history of homosexuality, arguing that the differences between the homosexuality we know today and previous arrangements of same-sex relations may be so profound as to call into question a defining "essence" of homosexuality. Much the same could be said of sexuality in general. Modern sexuality is a product of modern discourses of sexuality. Knowledge about sexuality can scarcely be a transparent window onto a separate realm of sexuality; rather, it constitutes that sexuality itself.

It has been argued that Foucault's intellectual influence, and certainly the fact that he himself was gay, may be largely responsible for the recent movement of queer theory out of the ghetto (Duggan 1992). It might be argued that lesbians and gay men have long been cultural innovators, but with the influence of Foucault and the rise of postmodernism they emerge, more visibly than ever before, as intellectual innovators and social theorists.[8]

Certainly an affinity between queer culture and postmodernism, which today is perhaps the dominant theoretical approach in the humanities, is clear. Some observers have suggested that the typical postmodernist artifact is playful, self-ironizing, and even schizoid. In much the same way, lesbian/gay culture has often made use of camp, drag, and other cultural strategies to celebrate alienation, distance, and incongruity (Ross 1989). If the goal of the modernist project was to rationally organize social life, postmodernists see rationality as a lie – something which many lesbians and gay men have been saying all along.

## Toward a More Queer Sociology

What does the seemingly antirational project of queer theory have to do with sociology, and how could it possibly inform the sociology of homosexuality? As we saw, the idea that sexuality is socially constructed was promoted by interpretive sociologists and feminist theorists at least two decades before queer theory emerged on the intellectual scene. Even if they lacked the elaborate theories of postmodernism, one could say that symbolic interactionist approaches, along with some strains of lesbian feminism, were protodeconstructionist. Problematizing taken-for-granted linguistic codes and categories, they had an "elective affinity" with some versions of postmodernism (Denzin 1989).

In the 1980s and 1990s, the terrain of identities has been further problematized. The feminist sex debates, the critique of the false universalism of feminism lodged primarily by women of color, and scholarly work on masculinity (Brittan 1989; Connell 1987) have questioned the tendency among many feminists to subsume sexuality (and race) under gender. At the same time, partly through the experience of the AIDS crisis, many activists and scholars have come to believe that lesbians and gay men, in Sedgwick's words, "may share important though contested aspects of one another's histories, cultures, identities, politics, and destinies" (1990: 255).

Before these intellectual and political challenges emerged, the solution to cultural exclusion seemed to be the construction of social groups whose taken-for-granted identities simply needed to be made visible. Today, things appear to be a great deal more complicated. The existence of groups as essential entities is no longer taken for granted (Bourdieu 1985; Stein 1992). Rather than simply devising a politics which privileges one identity over others, it has become more apparent that different oppressions are differently structured and intersecting. It is impossible to separate one's sexuality from one's class, one's gender, and so forth. There has been a growing acknowledgment of the multiple, shifting character of sexual identities.

Sociology suffers from endless domain assumptions of the time and place in which it is written. Its own "sociology of knowledge" claims should make it sensitive to this, but it often fails to be sensitive in this way. Reading the sociology of the past often reveals how it is lodged in its own time warp, capturing specific times and places in the hidden assumptions it harbors.[9] Sociology can benefit from a more focused analysis of its assumptions. It can also benefit from the challenges of queer theory. In turn, it can contribute to forming a conception of lesbian/gay life, and of all its interconnections with social life more generally, that is deeper and more grounded than the approach of "queer theory."

First, we can take the question of "culture" much more seriously than we do now, but without ceding experience to the play of "texts." Symbolic interactionists rightly claimed that sexuality was constructed situationally, though they may have understated the extent to which individual agency is constrained by the power of institutionalized discourses such as medicine, and by the proliferation of the mass media.

Queer theorists, on the other hand, appreciate the extent to which the texts of literature and mass culture shape sexuality, but their weakness is that they rarely, if ever, move beyond the text. There is a dangerous tendency for the new queer theorists to ignore "real" queer life as it is materially experienced across the world, while they play with the free-floating signifiers of texts. What can the rereading of a nineteenth-century novel really tell us about the pains of gay Chicanos or West Indian lesbians now, for example? Indeed, such postmodern readings may well tell us more about the lives of middle-class radical intellectuals than about anything else! Sociology's key concerns – inequality, modernity, institutional analysis – can bring a clearer focus to queer theory.[10]

Although sexuality is constructed through various discourses, individuals are not simply passive recipients of these cultural constructions. They use them creatively, accepting parts of them, rejecting others, to actively construct their lives. Queer theorists have attuned us to the importance of looking at texts, but as sociologists we need to look at how identities are constituted in the cultural practices of everyday life, though mediated by texts. We are, as McRobbie reminds us, "more than just audiences for texts" (1992: 730). We would agree with her that what is required is a new paradigm for conceptualizing "identity-in-culture," developing an understanding of how sexuality, along with gender, race, ethnicity, class, and generation, is articulated and experienced within a terrain of social practices.[11]

The second thing we can learn from queer theory is how important it is to study the center and not just the margins. The "theoretical universalism" of the sociological approach smacks of a lingering functionalism in which all deviations from the norm must be explained. Homosexuality becomes the marked category; heterosexuality recedes into the background, normalized and naturalized. Queer theory's universalization of "queerness," and its willingness to look at the social construction of heterosexuality as well as homosexuality, reconceptualize sexuality in ways which could be taken up fruitfully by sociologists, though it may be a bit premature to reject the conception of deviance altogether.

As sociologists we should incorporate the best insights of the queer theory project – its attention to the terrain of culture, and its willingness to venture into areas typically not considered "homosexual" or even sexual – into our own work, and into sociological theorizing more generally. At the same time, we could deepen its insights by providing a more grounded, more accessible approach. We offer some initial suggestions for doing this.

*Reconsidering the Issues*

How can sociology seriously purport to understand the social stratification system, for example, while ignoring quite profound social processes connected to heterosexism, homophobia, erotic hierarchies, and so forth (Rubin 1984)? Sexuality does not operate simply in the family, or through gender dynamics. Moreover, lesbians and gay men are not simply persons with sexual identities; they also are raced, classed, and situated in a wide array of different life contexts.

Many questions arise from this. What, for example, happens to stratification theory if gay and lesbian concerns are recognized? What are the mobility patterns of lesbians? How do these patterns intersect with race, age, region, and other factors? What happens to market structure analysis if gays are placed into it? To consumption studies? To education? To social gerontology? We need to reconsider whole fields of inquiry with differences of sexuality in mind. The narrowness of so much sociology has to leave us aghast!

*Rereading the Classics*

What happens to Giddens's structuration theory if hetero/homo issues are brought into the foreground? How might *Street Corner Society* or *Learning to*

*Labor* look if homo/hetero issues were placed at center stage? How would the work of a Smelser, a Habermas, or an Alexander look if they lost their heterosexual and heterosexist assumptions and placed "queer" concerns in their frame of analysis?

An initial way of approaching this could be by rereading sociological classics. As we bring "bring the lesbians and gays back in," however, we should also be problematizing the heterosexual center. The goal, as Michael Warner puts it, is "to make theory queer, and not just to have a theory about queers" (1991: 18). We need to challenge the assumption that sexuality is necessarily organized around a binary division between homosexuality and heterosexuality.

### Rethinking Pedagogy

Enter the queer student, and his or her not-so-queer classmates. In addition to revising the notion of who is the subject of a sociology of homosexuality, reflecting upon and rethinking pedagogical practice is in order. Mary Bryson (1992) designed a course at the University of British Columbia which incorporates what she calls "queer pedagogy," a way of teaching against the grain. She starts from the assumption that classrooms are always heterosexualized, but rather than simply organizing the course on lesbian and gay topics narrowly defined, she purposely never defines "lesbian" or "sexual orientation" so as to avoid ghettoizing lesbian and gay concerns and reifying the categories. Other approaches may be relevant as well, depending on the teaching context (Giroux 1992; Lather 1992). The point here is that we need to reflect upon how classrooms, like all other social spaces, are "heterosexualized."

These are only a few ideas, but they suggest a rethinking of some of sociology's core assumptions in a fashion which goes beyond the current tendency to treat sexuality (at worst) as peripheral and unimportant, and (at best) as something which can be conveniently tacked onto course syllabi or research designs without considering how it reshapes the questions that are being asked.

The process of paradigm shifting entails two dimensions: 1) the transformation of existing conceptual frameworks and 2) the acceptance of those transformations by others in the fields (Stacey and Thorne 1985). In terms of the "missing sexual revolution," sociologists have made some very preliminary progress toward the first goal, but the second – the acceptance of those transformations by others in the field – continues to impede progress. These innovations, however, will not only allow us to better represent those who are marginalized by current frameworks of theorizing; they will also make for better sociology.

## Notes

* Presented at The 1993 ASA Meetings, held in Miami Beach. Thanks to R.W. Connell, Steve Epstein, Becky Thompson, and Steven Seidman for their comments on an earlier draft. Arlene Stein also wishes to thank the Fuller Fund at the University of Essex.

1. There are a few earlier studies: in the United Kingdom, Schofield (1966); in the United States, Leznoff and Westley (1956). There are a few hints as well in the early Chicago School (Murray 1984: 65), but it is McIntosh (1968) that is widely cited as the first major statement.

2. Though the authors of this article come from different generational cohorts (Plummer, from the first generation of constructionists; Stein, from the second), we share a general sympathy for the latter tradition. Plummer was active in the early London-based Gay Liberation Front. He first published an article on the sociology of homosexuality in 1973, which used a symbolic interactionist perspective (Plummer 1973). His subsequent work, *Sexual Stigma* (Plummer 1975), was an attempt to apply the core ideas of social constructionism to sex diversity. Stein's lineage is more recent. She came of age between the lesbian feminist and the "queer" movements and received her training at Berkeley, publishing her first article on the subject 16 years after Plummer – a survey of approaches to the sociology of sexuality (Stein 1989). She has continued these interests in her work on lesbian identity (Stein 1992). For a useful discussion of generational differences in lesbian/gay theory, see Escoffier (1992).

3. For an early statement of this criticism, see Gagnon and Simon (1967). Some recent work on the social aspects of AIDS, however, manages to be empirically as well as theoretically sophisticated. Because HIV transmission itself does not tend to respect sexual categories, many researchers in this area have come to recognize the problematic nature of sexual categories. See, for example, Connell and Kippax (1990).

4. See, for example, LeVay (1993), the latest in a century-long obsession with linking homosexuality with particular genes and chromosomes.

5. See, for instance, Stan Cohen, "Footsteps in the Sand," in McIntosh and Rock (1974).

6. The theme of the "outsider" is important but will not be taken up here. There is a long tradition of concern with marginality and outsiders in sociology – via Simmel, Stonequist, Park, Becker, Goffman, Garfinkle, and others – and it anticipates yet another theme of queer theory: the transgressive.

7. The tension between these two schools of lesbian/gay sociology may mirror the political tension which has long existed within the movement, between nationalism and assimilation, between fixing homosexuals as a stable minority group and seeking to liberate the "homosexual" in everyone (Epstein 1992: Stein 1992).

8. There were two previous "moments" when "out" lesbians and gay men – particularly gay men – were visible intellectual innovators. The first was in the 1890s and early 1900s, when Magnus Hirschfeld and Edward Carpenter were in the vanguard of an intellectual and cultural movement to remake gender and sexuality (see Rowbotham and Weeks 1977). The second "moment" was half a century later, when gay liberation began to raise questions about power and sexuality (see Fernbach 1981; Hocquenghem 1978). Thanks to R.W. Connell for reminding us of this.

9. Feminism has shown this only too clearly. More recently, the analysis of race has revealed a hidden structure which is potentially racist. See, for example, Collins (1990) and Gilroy (1993).

10. Similarly, though queer theory deghettoizes queer concerns within the academy, it tends to restrict access to those outside. Resolutely and unapologetically laden with theoretical jargon, it limits its audience to only the most theory-literate. In contrast, sociology has been more accessible to nonintellectuals, and should continue to strive for greater accessibility.

11. For a related understanding of culture which looks at symbols, stories, and other cultural products as tools in persistent "strategies of action," and points to a way of understanding identities in culture, see Swidler (1986).

## References

Berger, Peter and Thomas Luckmann. 1967. *The Social Construction of Reality.* New York: Penguin.
Bourdieu, Pierre. 1985. "Social Space and the Genesis of Groups." *Theory and Society* 14 (6): 723–44.
Britain, Arthur. 1989. *Masculinities and Power.* Oxford: Blackwell.
Bryson, Mary. 1992. "Queer Pedagogy: Praxis Makes Imperfect." Presented at Meetings of The American Educational Research Association, San Francisco.
Butler, Judith. 1990. *Gender Trouble: Feminism and the Subversion of Identity.* New York: Routledge.
Butler, Judith. 1991. "Imitation and Gender Insubordination." Pp. 13–31 in *Inside/Out: Lesbian Theories, Gay Theories,* edited by Diana Fuss. New York: Routledge.
Collins, Patricia Hill. 1990. *Black Feminist Thought.* New York: Routledge.
Connell, R.W. 1987. *Gender and Power.* Oxford: Polity.
Connell, R.W. 1992. "A Very Straight Gay: Masculinity, Homosexual Experience and the Dynamics of Gender." *American Sociological Review* 57 (6): 735–51.
Connell, R.W. and S. Kippax. 1990. "Sexuality in the AIDS Crisis: Patterns of Sexual Practice and Pleasure in a Sample of Australian Gay and Bisexual Men." *Journal of Sex Research* 27 (2): 167–98.
de Lauretis, Teresa. 1991. "Queer Theory: Lesbian and Gay Sexualities." *Differences* 3: iii–xviii.
Denzin, Norman, ed. 1989. *Studies in Symbolic Interactionism* Vol. 10. Greenwich, Conn.: JAI Press.
Dollimore, Jonathan. 1991. *Sexual Dissidence.* Oxford: Clarendon.
Duggan, Lisa. 1992. "Making It Perfectly Queer." *Socialist Review* 22 (1) 11–31.
Epstein, Steven. 1992. "Gay Politics, Ethnic Identity: The Limits of Social Constructionism." Pp. 239–93 in *Forms of Desire,* edited by E. Stein. New York: Routledge.
Escoffier, Jeffrey. 1992. "Generations and Paradigms: Mainstreams in Lesbian and Gay Studies." *Journal of Homosexuality* 24(1–2): 7–27.
Ferguson, Russell, Martha Gever, Trinh T. Minh-Ha, and Cornel West. 1990. *Out There: Marginalization and Contemporary Cultures.* New York: New Museum.
Fernbach, David. 1981. *The Spiral Path.* London: Gay Men's Press.
Foucault, Michel. 1978. *The History of Sexuality.* New York: Vintage.
Fuss, Diana. 1989. *Essentially Speaking: Feminism, Nature and Difference,* New York: Routledge.
Fuss, Diana. 1991. *Inside/Out: Lesbian Theories, Gay Theories.* New York: Routledge.

Gagnon, John and William Simon. 1967. "Homosexuals: The Formation of a Sociological Perspective." *Journal of Health and Social Behavior* 8: 177–85.
Gilroy, Paul. 1993. *The Black Atlantic.* London: Verso.
Giroux, Henry. 1992. *Border Crossings: Cultural Workers and the Politics of Education.* New York: Routledge.
Hocquenghem, Guy. 1978. *Homosexual Desire.* London: Allison and Busby.
Katz, Jonathan. 1990. "The Invention of Heterosexuality." *Socialist Review* 20 (1): 7–34.
Kitsuse, J. 1962. "Societal Reaction to Deviant Behavior." *Social Problems* 9: 247–56.
Lather, Patti. 1992. *Getting Smart.* London: Routledge.
LeVay, Simon. 1993. *The Sexual Brain.* Boston: MIT Press.
Leznoff, M. and W.A. Westley. 1956. "The Homosexual Community." *Social Problems* 3: 257–63.
McIntosh, Mary. 1968. The Homosexual Role." *Social Problems* 17: 182–92.
McIntosh, Mary. 1992. "Feminism and Cultural Studies." *New Statesman and Society* vol. 5. Presentation at Feminist Theory conference, University of Essex.
McIntosh, Mary and P. Rock. 1974. *Deviance and Control.* London: Tavistock.
Murray, Stephen. 1984. *Social Theory, Homosexual Realities.* New York: Gai Saber.
Parker, Andrew. 1991. "Unthinking Sex: Marx, Engels and the Scene of Writing." *Social Text* 9 (11): 28–45.
Plummer, Ken. 1973. "Awareness of Homosexuality." In *Contemporary Social Problems in Britain*, edited by R. Bailey and J. Young. Lexington, UK: Saxon House.
Plummer, Ken. 1975. *Sexual Stigma: An Interactionist Account.* London: Routledge.
Plummer, Ken. ed. 1992. *Modern Homosexualities: Fragments of Lesbian and Gay Experience.* London: Routledge.
Plummer, Ken. Forthcoming. *Telling Sexual Stories.* London: Routledge.
Rich, Adrienne. (1980) 1983. "Compulsory Heterosexuality and Lesbian Existence." Pp. 177–205 in *Powers of Desire: The Politics of Sexuality*, edited by A. Snitow, C. Stansell, and S. Thompson. New York: Monthly Review Press.
Ross, Andrew. 1989. *No Respect: Intellectuals and Popular Culture.* New York: Routledge.
Rowbotham, Sheila and Jeffrey Weeks. 1977. *Socialism and the New Life.* London: Pluto.
Rubin, Gayle. 1975. "The Traffic in Women." Pp. 157–210 in *Toward an Anthropology of Women*, edited by R. Reiter. New York: Monthly Review Press.
Rubin, Gayle. (1984) 1993. "Thinking Sex." Pp. 267–319 in *The Lesbian and Gay Studies Reader*, edited by: H. Abelove, M. Barale, and D. Halperin. New York: Routledge.
Schofield, Michael. 1966. *Sociological Aspects of Homosexuality.* London: Longman.
Sedgwick, Eve. 1990. *Epistemology of the Closet.* Berkeley: University of California Press.
Simon, Barbara Levy. 1987. *Never Married Women.* Philadelphia: Temple University Press.
Stacey, Judith and Barrie Thorne. 1985. "The Missing Feminist Revolution in Sociology." *Social Problems* 32 (4): 301–16.
Stein, Arlene. 1989. "Three Models of Sexuality: Drives, Identities and Practices." *Sociological Theory* 7 (1): 1–13.
Stein, Arlene. 1992. "Sisters and Queers: The Decentering of Lesbian Feminism." *Socialist Review* 22 (1): 33–55.
Swidler, Ann. 1986. "Culture in Action: Symbols and Strategies." *American Sociological Review* 52: 401–1:
Thorne, Barrie, 1993. *Gender Play: Girls and Boys in School.* New Brunswick: Rutgers University Press.

Troiden, Richard R. 1988. *Gay and Lesbian Identity: A Sociological Analysis.* New York: General Hall.
Warner, Michael. 1991. "Fear of a Queer Planet." *Social Text* 9 (14): 3–17.
Warren, Carol A.B. 1974. *Identity and Community in the Gay World.* New York: Wiley.
Williams, Christine. 1989. *Gender Differences at Work: Women and Men in Nontraditional Occupations.* Berkeley: University of California Press.

# Social Postmodernism: Beyond Identity Politics

*Linda Nicholson and Steven Seidman*

It is perhaps ironic that the very intellectuals thought to have originated postmodern theory – we mean of course Baudrillard, Foucault, and Derrida (Lyotard being the exception) – have refused this characterization of their work. It is again not entirely without paradox that postmodern theory has found its most welcoming reception and home not in France but in the United States – the nation of pragmatism, empiricism, and a much vaunted liberal consensus. And notwithstanding Rorty's liberal pragmatic version of postmodernism, it is among the American left, among neo- and post-Marxists, feminists, queers, and Third World and postcolonial intellectuals, that postmodernism has been most enthusiastically embraced. Why have Americans, mostly left academic intellectuals but also some outside America (for example, in Britain and Australia) come to advocate a politics and social theory in a postmodern mode?

We think that this is an important question but it cannot be productively engaged by approaching postmodernism in an ahistorical way. Postmodernism is best spoken about in the plural and its meaning best clarified by understanding those who use it in a particular social and discursive setting. So, we submit two stories, our stories, of "why postmodernism." Of course, we know that these are not the whole story or the only ones – indeed they are not even the only stories we could tell but they are, we hope, stories that are suggestive beyond the tales of two left American academic intellectuals.

### Why Postmodernism: Steve's Story

Before I was a postmodernist, I was a Marxist. Why the change? My "conversion" pivoted on my disillusionment with Marxism which broadened into a disenchantment with key aspects of the Western Enlightenment tradition.

---

Source: Linda Nicholson and Steven Seidman, *Social Postmodernism: Beyond Identity Politics*, (Cambridge: Cambridge University Press, 1995).

Marxism was a natural for me. White, middle class, culturally alienated – a 1960s radical. For me, Marxism was entangled in an oedipal and generational rebellion – against a successful but distant father and against an "affluent" society that promised little more than family, consumerism, and career. Marxism allowed me to stake out a rebellious identity in opposition to the liberalism of my parents and an American national identity. It furnished a standpoint from which to criticize my elders – to expose their hypocrisy by exposing America's social inequalities and its illusions of freedom by appealing to the reign of capital and class. Marxism allowed me a ferocious critique of America and liberal intellectuals that could not be so easily refused as my previously held hippie critique. Moreover, Marx's vision of a fully realized self, especially as elaborated by such neo-Marxist gurus as Erich Fromm and Herbert Marcuse, resonated perfectly with the folk beliefs I absorbed from mainstream and countercultural America. So, I became a Marxist of the Frankfurt School persuasion.

As the 1960s passed into the 1970s, and establishing an academic career moved to the center of my life, my enthusiasm for Marxism waned. Undoubtedly, the failed institutionalization of Marxism in the United States worked against sustaining Marxism in a post-crisis social setting. Moreover, as the heroic days of rebellion passed, and as my education included a serious engagement with classical sociology, my assessment of Marxism proved decidedly mixed. I continued to value Marx's historicist and political critique of ideology and his view of science as in the service of social change. However, I was critical of Marx's collapse of the social into class conflict, which hardly spoke to my radical political impulses which pivoted on issues of the subjective and the cultural, e.g., the body, the psyche, sexuality, and the "spiritual."

By the middle of the 1970s, the spirit of revolution had, for me, given way to a more sobering consideration of political prospects. I thought that progressive social change in the United States pivoted on a liberal-left alliance which went beyond the division between Marxism and liberalism. I imagined that in some of the writings of Durkheim and Weber there was to be found a social liberal ideal that had some kinship with a social democratic reading of Marx. I believed that a reconstruction of European social theory could provide intellectual resources for a social democratic political culture. Although I was questioning Marxism and liberalism, I remained firm in my faith in the Enlightenment – for example, in the link between science, truth, and social progress, in millennial notions of human liberation, in the West as the site of human progress, and in the self as the ultimate ground of knowledge and action.

My belief in the Enlightenment was seriously shaken in the early 1980s. Why? Of course, the succession of Republican administrations dampened my hopes of a liberal-left progressive front. The renewal of Cold War politics under Reagan and the vigor of the new right and neoconservatism further marginalized the left. I, once again, felt like a stranger in America. These developments shaped a context favorable to putting my belief in the Enlightenment into crisis. Personal considerations proved fateful.

As the world left my dreams of change tattered and almost mocked my high-minded European criticalness, my own personal life, despite an academic appointment and higher levels of consumerism, landed me in psychoanalysis. And my analysis brought me face to face with the web of delusions, inner otherness, and just plain psychic craziness that unconsciously drove my life. I initially undertook analysis with the Enlightenment faith that it would replace delusion with reality, opaqueness with scientific insight, unconscious compulsion with deliberate willfulness, and distress with happiness. Wasn't this its promise and indeed the promise of scientific Enlightenment? To be sure, analysis (thankfully) released me from certain inner constraints and did give me an understanding of particular feelings and psychic patterns. Yet, even as my daily life has been less brooding and anguished, my analytical experience contributed to putting my Enlightenment faith into doubt. Analysis revealed a self or "subject" which was de-centered, a psyche populated by multiple, often conflicted identities, selves who were hitherto strange to my conscious life, and a self driven by unconscious desires. Moreover, despite many years of analysis my psyche remained dense and opaque, ruthlessly refusing truth in favor of narratives whose value came to be judged by me – and my analyst – less by their validity than by whether they "worked" or were enabling or hopeful or permitted a provisional psychic coherence. In short, psychoanalysis disposed me to think of subjectivity less in a "modern" language of centered, unified, rational subjects than in a "postmodern" vocabulary of de-centered, multiple selves impelled by unconscious structures. Psychoanalytic understandings looked decidedly less like "science" or "reason" than pragmatic narratives or literary-poetic texts.

My analysis transpired side by side with coming out as gay. I don't of course assume any necessary tie between this event and a postmodern standpoint. Nevertheless, coming out had for me far-reaching epistemological consequences. While I was already well read in critiques of scientism, my coming out put me in a daily political relation to science and, indeed, pressured me to rethink the politics of knowledge beyond Enlightenment frameworks.

In its servicing of a heterosexist society, science denied me a range of legal and civil rights; it shaped a context which made me a target of ridicule and violence. It did this by constructing homosexuality as a disease and as marking a pathological, deviant, morally damaged personage. I did not conclude that science was an evil social force. I knew that it could be invoked to justify "normalization." I did conclude, though, that science is a powerful social force. This power, moreover, lay not only in its capacity to rationalize the denial of basic civil and social rights and to enforce social marginalization. More importantly, by virtue of its ties to institutional practices (e.g., education, medicine, law, government, mass media, therapeutic regimes), science had the power to inscribe in our bodies and minds a sexual and social regime. This regime made sexual object choice into a master category of sexual and social identity and that purified a heterosexual life while polluting a homosexual one. Science helped to create a regime of sexual and social order which organizes and regulates our bodies, desires, identities, and social behavior. Foucault of course provided the full conceptual articulation of this perspective, but my personal experience allowed me to hear his arguments about power/knowledge and the productive and disciplining aspects of power. It followed that if the regime of sexuality is a disciplinary order, if the assertion – even affirmatively – of gay identity reinforces this regime, the Enlightenment project of announcing and liberating the homosexual is in doubt.

My suspicion toward a Western culture of Enlightenment was further nourished by internal developments within the gay community during the 1980s. This was a time of enormous turmoil and division within the gay movement. The ethnic model of identity that grounded community and politics was under serious scrutiny. An antigay backlash exposed the political costs of an insulated community pursuing a single-interest gay politic. Moreover, voices of difference within the gay movement threatened to unravel the fragile bonds of solidarity that rested upon the assertion of a common gay identity. Hitherto excluded segments of the lesbian and gay community – people of color, sexual rebels, Third World gays, working-class gays, butches, and fems – protested their silencing and marginalization by the gay mainstream. They exposed the repressive politics entailed in asserting a unified gay subject. Rebelling against the disciplining effects of a politics of identity, a new celebration of multiple, composite identities became the rallying cry of a queer politics of difference. While some saw this as threatening the gains of lesbians and gays, I imagined the new queer politics as potentially recovering the radical impulse of gay liberationism, namely, the ideal of a truly coalitional politic and a politic that goes beyond legitimating homosexual identities to remaking bodies and everyday life. In this regard, I saw the language of postmodernism as resonant with a new queer politics challenging normalization and a routinized politics of respectability.

## Why Postmodernism: Linda's Story

As with Steve, Marxism was for me a means of making sense of many of the political and psychological sentiments which came out of my early years. I was a "red diaper baby" in the sense that my parents gave to me and my brother a strong sense of identification with the underdog and a certain disdain for what they regarded as the shallow and overly consumer-oriented elements of much of American life. My parents' contempt for mainstream American life was also mixed with a not untypical second-generation immigrant desire for their children to succeed, particularly in that arena they viewed with unqualified regard, education. So I became a Marxist academic, using my academic studies both to create a career and refine my understanding of

Marxism. In the course of my work in philosophy as an undergraduate and then in the History of Ideas program at Brandeis University, this refinement led to a particular perspective on what was worthwhile in Marx's writings: his critique of capitalism; his vision of a democratic socialist society; and his strong sense of the historicity of all ideas. Against many reigning liberal ideas about "reason" and "objectivity," and in accord with ideas which were beginning to emerge in nascent form in academic and new left culture of the time, Marxism also sensitized me to the power dynamics involved in the production and distribution of knowledges. That sensitivity, and the developing critique of positivism and scientism I was deriving from my studies in the early 1970s, led me to think of the Marxism that saw itself as "a science of society" as not only wrong-headed but as allied with the authoritarianism I identified with the Marxism-Leninism of the Soviet Union and of the Eastern bloc countries. I became, in short, a child of that segment of the new left who thought the words "class" and "Marxism" had political relevance but who also rejected the kind of Marxism associated with the parties of the old left. Not surprisingly, I became attracted to many of the writings of those associated with the Frankfurt School. In 1973, I found in Jürgen Habermas's *Knowledge and Human Interests* the elegant expression of many of my developing ideas about politics and knowledge. One idea in that book I found particularly compelling was Habermas's way of thinking about the two different Marxes. Habermas drew a distinction between the Marx who provided a powerful historical narrative about the development of capitalism and the Marx who saw himself as providing a philosophical theory about the nature and meaning of human history. I started to think about how this latter Marx, this Marx who thought he could provide a perch upon which to view all of human history, was a Marx who had not taken seriously enough his own ideas about the historicity and power dynamics of the production of ideas.

But in 1973 Marxism was not the only issue on my political and intellectual agenda. Feminism was emerging as a force which both excited me and demanded that I carve some place for it in my intellectual, political, and emotional life. While my Marxist commitments had initially led me to characterize this new movement as a manifestation of "bourgeois" interests, by 1973 such a characterization could no longer fit with the excitement and energy I found from this movement. But, of course, as an academic philosopher I could not just call myself a "feminist." I needed to decide just what kind of feminist I was. I came to describe myself as a "socialist-feminist." In large part this self-description emerged out of my earlier commitment to Marxism. It enabled me to declare myself a feminist while also remaining publicly committed to many of those ideas of Marx's I still found viable: his critique of capitalism, his vision of a future socialist society, and his sense of the historicity of all ideas. But other psychic factors were also at work. As someone who had a deep emotional connection to a father who died when I was just entering adolescence and as one who has always been strongly connected to an older brother, the alternative beckoning theory of radical feminism was never completely attractive. While in the late 1970s I certainly could not use public declarations of allegiances to men to defend any theoretical commitment, I could use the strong sense of historicity I derived from Marx to undermine what I was also seeing as the ahistoricity and lack of attention to differences among women in many radical feminist accounts. Of course at the time I was also being powerfully affected by many of the ideas that were coming out of radical feminism, ideas which were both deepening my commitment to feminism and accentuating my turn away from Marxism. At a certain point, and at least in part because of feminism, I stopped calling myself a Marxist.

It was somewhere in the 1980s, probably through work on my book *Gender and History*, that I began to put together theoretically my criticisms of Marxism and of radical feminism. I began to think that what was wrong with both could be expressed in the same terms. Moreover, this common language could also be used to account for each not being able to include what was important in the other. It was Marxism's tendency to see itself as providing a grand theory of history and social organization constituted around such categories as "production" and "labor" which precluded it from adequately theorizing the situation of women. Simultaneously, it was radical feminism's tendency to develop grand theories about "patriarchy" and women which precluded it from seeing differences among women which were, amongst other things, differences of class.

It was around this time that the word "postmodernism" was beginning to enter my intellectual world. It attracted me because it seemed to provide a label by which to name this common problem I saw in Marxism, feminism, and liberal understandings of reason and knowledge: the tendency in elements of all to forget that what they were calling "reason" or "history" or "women" came out of a particular context and were implicated in relations of power. It made sense that liberalism, Marxism, and feminism might suffer from such a common problem. All had emerged within a certain period in Europe and North America where this part of the world had exercised a great amount of power over other parts of the world. As this power was coming into question, so might also the ways of theorizing knowledge which had attended it. The term "postmodern" seemed to provide a name for this break.

## Why Social Postmodernism

We do not think that these two stories exclude other accounts of postmodernism. In particular, we value macrosocial perspectives which, for example, feature the importance of changes in systems of production, technology, and information systems, or perspectives which underscore the importance of deterritorialization or globalization. Yet we are convinced that shifts in left public cultures, in particular, the rise and development of the new social movements and their encounter with Marxist and liberal Enlightenment traditions are one crucial matrix for understanding the formation of postmodern theories in America and perhaps elsewhere. Moreover, we believe that at least certain strains of postmodern thinking are a key resource for rethinking a democratic social theory and politics. While it is understandable that some might be suspicious of perspectives that announce the de-centering of the subject, the end of metanarratives (including Marxism), the interlocking of knowledge and power, and the substitution of a politics of difference for a millennial liberationist politic, we believe that the postmodern turn offers a potentially useful vantage point from which to rethink theory and politics in at least some Western nations.

And yet, we have come to see that while the term "postmodernism" had its benefits, it also had its problems. Some of the problems seemed to us to emerge from those places where postmodernism overlapped with poststructuralism. Such overlaps occurred particularly in relation to thinking about language. For example, as Jean François Lyotard talked about the power dynamics in the play of discourse, so also did Jacques Derrida talk about linguistic and social meaning in relation to the regime of power of "logocentrism." But the concern with undoing reigning beliefs about logocentrism or troubling textual authority on the part of many poststructuralists meant that poststructuralism in particular, but postmodernism also, became significantly associated with a critical mode of analyzing texts. At times, the social was collapsed into the textual, and critique often meant "deconstructing" texts or exposing the instability of those foundational categories and binaries which structured texts and which were said to be carriers of ideological meanings. As important as deconstruction was to politicizing language and knowledge, this "textualizing" turn of the postmodern meant that many of the issues that have been pivotal to social theorists were neglected. In short, the whole field of institutions, social classes, political organizations, political economic processes, and social movements appeared to remain in the hands of Marxists or other theorists whose perspectives were often untouched by postmodern concerns. For Steve Seidman, with his background in social theory, and for Linda Nicholson, with her background in political philosophy, this separation of the "postmodern" and the "social" seemed to mark a wrong turn.

This slippage between postmodern critical analysis and "social" theory seemed to us further accentuated by the nature of postmodernism's critical engagement with the new social movements. For us, and for many others who were also sympathetic to postmodern ideas, the ways that these movements maintained the legacy of modernism was to naturalize or essentialize categories of identity. Thus, Nicholson, as well as other feminists, critiqued those tendencies in feminism which naturalized or essentialized the concept of "woman." Seidman, as well as other gay and lesbian theorists, challenged ahistorical constructions of "the homosexual." Our project was to demonstrate the constructed, historically variable, and varied meanings of such categories, that is, to "genealogize" or "deconstruct" these categories. But many such attempts also seemed to us to turn away from "the social." By focusing on what was wrong in the understanding of specific categories of identity, our attention remained fixed on the individual categories themselves. We were paying little attention to the ways in which the genealogies we and others were constructing intertwined with each other. Many of us had abandoned broader, systematic, and integrating perspectives on social processes and dynamics. Postmodern critique narrowed into a critique of representations or knowledges, leaving relatively unattended their social and historical contexts.

But one of the serious causes of the turn from the social appeared to us as the pronounced negative or critical aspect of much postmodern theorizing. It is difficult to focus on the interrelation of social patterns when one is fixed on avoiding totalizing or essentializing analyses. This negative bent of much postmodern intellectual work was quickly perceived by its critics and soon became described as a sign not only of its theoretical weakness but also of its political weakness. Postmodernism, it was claimed, could show only what was wrong: it could provide no positive directions either intellectually or politically. After all, was it not impossible to generate strong political movements while also deconstructing the categories such movements were based upon?

In this volume, we wish to show that it is possible for postmodern thinkers to focus on institutions as well as texts, to think about the interrelations of social patterns without being essentializing or totalizing, and to create constructive as well as deconstructive analyses of the social. The positive possibilities of postmodern theorizing can be matched, we believe, by constructive ideas about political action. Such ideas may seriously challenge and expand our ideas about how political change can take place. But, to transform present understandings of "the political" is not equivalent to abandoning politics altogether. Rather, through the following essays we hope to begin the process of imagining what "postmodern" social analysis can be and of how "postmodern" political action can be understood.

## Critiques of Identity

This volume begins this task by looking at the critique postmodernism has made of identity politics. As the three essays in the first section show, the critique is a complex one. Those who reject the postmodern turn often equate the postmodern or poststructural term "deconstruction" with the ordinary-language term "destruction." But the postmodern move to "deconstruct" does not translate into a move to destroy or abandon. Rather, as Linda Nicholson demonstrates in her opening essay "Interpreting Gender," a feminist deconstructive analysis of the concept of "gender" does not mean eliminating it. Rather, it entails a critical examination of its history to see what baggage the term carries from that history and the political effects of that baggage. It means "redeploying" the meaning of the term so that feminists can accomplish their political ends without encountering some of the difficulties past uses of the term have generated.

Nicholson argues that even after the development of the concept of "gender," many feminists continued to hold onto the idea that the male/female distinction is rooted in some fundamental features of biology. "Gender" was introduced to undermine widely held beliefs in the biological basis of many of the traits associated with women and men, beliefs expressed through the concept of "sex." However, insofar as "gender" was understood to supplement rather than supplant "sex," the idea of some biological basis of the male/female distinction remained. The conjunction of "gender" and "sex" was made possible by what Nicholson describes as an implicit "coat-rack" understanding of human identity: where biological givens distinguishing women and men constitute the basic "rack" upon which different societies "throw" different interpretations, the latter constituting "gender." Nicholson argues that this understanding of human identity articulates a particular worldview developed in the early modern period in Western Europe and North America where biology rather than the Bible came to be seen as the "cause" or "basis" of socially given distinctions. While this transformation had many manifestations, including the development of the biologically based concept of "race," in relation to the male/female distinction, it generated an understanding of differences between women and men both as more rigidly binary than had previously been the case and as the direct manifestation of the "facts" of biology. While the feminist introduction of the concept of "gender" represented a move to get beyond this worldview, keeping "sex" as a supplementary term has prevented feminists from wholly doing so. Nicholson depicts this limited transcendence in feminist theory by pointing to what she describes as "biological foundationalism." While the latter is not equivalent to "biological determinism," it shares with the latter the ideas that certain givens of biology exist cross-culturally and are always potential contributors to the social understanding of the male/female distinction.

Nicholson claims that it is this idea that there are certain cross-cultural givens of biology, albeit always subject to possibly diverse social interpretations, which provided the theoretical grounds for the elaboration of "difference feminism," that is, that feminism which stressed the similarities among women and their differences from men. "Difference feminism," however, has been most at fault in ignoring differences among women. Nicholson argues that adequately to get beyond this erasure of differences requires that we get beyond biological foundationalism as well. Doing so means abandoning the idea of differences as that which supplements certain basic similarities. It means coming to see differences as that which "go all the way down" affecting the very criteria of what it means to be a man or a woman in diverse societies. This does not mean abandoning attention to the body; instead, it means seeing the meaning given to the body and how this meaning is related to the male/female distinction as historically variable. This way of thinking about the "body" supports an understanding of the term "woman" not as reflective of some one determinate meaning, but rather as reflective of a diverse set of meanings related through a complex set of "family resemblances."

While Nicholson's essay focuses on the grounding of "woman" in biology as a contributor to essentialist tendencies within feminism, Chandra Talpade Mohanty's "Feminist Encounters: Locating the Politics of Experience" focuses on essentialism itself and its relation to politics. Even in the absence of "biological foundationalism," "essential" or "unitary" characteristics can be attributed to the category of "woman." For example, it could be argued that while the meaning of "woman" is completely socially constructed, this construction has been similar in central ways throughout a long span of human history. Mohanty's essay elaborates many of the problems inherent in such an essential or unitary understanding of "woman."

Most basically, such an assumption erases social, historical differences among women, differences which are those of power. Using Robin Morgan's essay, "Planetary Feminism: The Politics of the 21st Century" as an example, Mohanty illustrates how this kind of assumption affects such an erasure. It does so by placing women outside history and, as related, by employing a problematic, individualized conception of experience.

Mohanty argues that Morgan, by eliding the difference between history as a written record and history as a course of events, depicts "history" as a male construction. Consequently, women are portrayed as having no part in history and as ahistorically endowed with certain traits, for example, as being "truth tellers." Such a depiction ignores the ways in which women have been differently situated in history and in the ways such differences have affected both the lives they have lived and the truth and power of the stories they have told.

Allied to this depiction of women as outside history is a conception of women's experience as given and individual. There is in Morgan's essay, according to Mohanty, no sense of experience as socially constructed in accord with different historical contexts.

> The *experience* of struggle is thus defined as both personal and ahistorical. In other words, the political is *limited to* the personal and all conflicts among and within women are flattened. If sisterhood itself is defined on the basis of personal intentions, attitudes, or desires, conflict is also automatically constructed on only the psychological level. Experience is thus written in as simultaneously individual (that is, located in the individual body/psyche of woman) and general (located in women as a preconstituted collective).

Mohanty draws on Bernice Johnson Reagon's "Coalition Politics: Turning the Century" to generate ideas about identity and politics which are different from those of Morgan. Particularly, Mohanty points to Reagon's idea of political struggle as being based on a recognition of difference rather than on imputed commonalities in experience. This idea of political struggle opposes metaphors of "coalition" to metaphors of "home." Whereas the latter suggested criteria of unity separating those on the inside from those on the outside, the former suggest constructed and contingent comings together which can coexist with differences. In short, it represents a notion of political struggle where alliances are made around explicit goals rather than presumed on the basis of imputed commonalities. It represents "sisterhood" as that which needs to be achieved rather than that which can be assumed.

While the first two essays in this volume focus on problems in feminism as a site of identity politics, similar kinds of problems have been found in many post-1960s social struggles, in those of the gay and lesbian movement, and in struggles by African-Americans in the United States and in nationalist and postcolonial struggles around the world. The essay by Gyan Prakash provides a framework for understanding the genesis of such problems. In "Postcolonial Criticism and Indian Historiography," as Prakash makes explicit, oppositional discourses emerge within a complex relationship to the discourses of domination they seek to overthrow.

Focusing on Marxism as an example of this point, Prakash shows how this discourse can be seen as a continuation of the very territorial imperialism it sought to overthrow. By employing a unified concept of "capitalism" and by making this concept foundational to the analysis of all those societies which have been affected by it, Marxism effectively homogenized the histories of these societies.

> In fact, like many other nineteenth-century European ideas, the staging of the Eurocentric mode-of-production narrative as History should be seen as an analogue of nineteenth-century territorial imperialism. From this point of view, Marx's ideas on changeless India – theorized, for example in his concept of the "Asiatic mode of production" – appear not so much mistaken as the discursive form produced by the universalization of Europe, by its appropriation of the absolute other into a domesticated other.

The point here is not to abandon an analysis of capitalism nor to stop using the concept of "class" but to understand how the dynamics of capitalism and class intersect with other determinations. By doing so, it becomes possible to recognize "the irreducible heterogeneity of metropolitan capital with the colonial subaltern" and consequently to extricate Marxism from the imperialistic elements of its nineteenth-century Western European heritage.

However, a word of caution is in order. As Prakash emphasizes, the idea here is not to idealize heterogeneity per se. It is not to emphasize difference for the sake of difference nor to include a list of determinations, such as those of gender, race, ethnicity, etc., for the sake of some current ideal of what is politically appropriate. Rather, it is to recognize that all categories of analysis – even those used in the service of political opposition – are the affects of specific relations of power. In the case of postcolonial discourse this means recognizing that an emphasis on difference emerges from the ambivalence produced in the very enunciation of colonial discourses. As colonial discourses asserted unchanging identities both to the colonizer and colonized, they also acknowledged differences and potential disruptions to these forms of identity. They thus created the very stress points which their critics can employ against them. Consequently, the lesson here is not some absolute celebration of difference but a sensitivity to the relations of power which make a focus on difference both possible and an effective tool of subversion.

If the above essays begin to show some of the complexities involved in the critique of identity politics, the essays in the second section illustrate the limits of some versions of this critique.

## Critiques of the Deconstruction of Identity

As the above comments make clear, we see the force of at least some critiques of identity politics as both theoretical and political. Nicholson's, Mohanty's, and Prakash's essays underscore the theoretical and political gains of a critique of identity, for example as creating a space for imagining the possibility of a coalitional politics of difference and a reflexive critique of power/knowledge regimes. Although such critiques of identity have been productive, especially as they have leaned on postmodern or poststructural conceptual strategies, others have revealed certain stress points. This section reviews some of these tensions.

Kwame Anthony Appiah's essay "African Identities" illustrates the need to preserve the deconstructive critique of identity and yet retain some kind of politic of identity. Appiah comments on the personal and political impulses behind his theoretical reckoning with questions of identity and politics. As the son of an African father and a European mother, and as someone who grew up in both Ghana and Britain and who now lives in the United States, Appiah was personally troubled by the way individual and national identity has been framed by the African/European binary. This binary leaves no "home" or coherent cultural space for Appiah's own experience. Deconstructing such unitary, totalizing identities as "African" and "European" was integral to his own personal struggle for psychological and cultural coherence. The African/European binary was disturbing for political reasons as well. It interferes with the effectiveness of a Pan-African antiracist movement. On the one hand, the construction of an "African identity" is inevitably normative and exclusionary; it has the effect of impeding African solidarity and mobilization. On the other hand, this binary obstructs the formation of alliances with Americans and Europeans committed to antiracist struggle. Appiah believes that only the deconstruction of essentialized group identities and totalizing binaries makes possible the kinds of coalition building and political mobilization strategies that can create an effective Pan-African movement.

Deconstructing the notion of a unitary, essentially fixed African identity is pivotal then to his political project. Appiah considers three key strategies that have given cultural and intellectual currency to an essentialized, totalizing concept of group identity. A racial strategy appeals to a common biological foundation; an historical strategy invokes a shared history; a metaphysical strategy imagines a unique common culture or African spirit. Appiah exposes the inconsistencies and conceptual flaws of each strategy as well as underscoring the undesirable moral and political consequences of an essentialist concept of African identity.

Does criticizing a unitary essentializing approach to African identity mean abandoning identity categories and politics? No. Recall that Appiah wishes to defend the conceptual and political possibilities of a Pan-African antiracist movement. Toward this goal, Appiah proposes to substitute for an essentialized group identity a concept of identity that insists upon its irreducibly heterogeneous, plural, changeable, and ultimately chosen and "fictitious" character. Although African peoples and cultures are quite different, even contradictory, within the continent and across the diaspora, the idea of an African identity and movement continues to be invented and given personal and social force through myths and political organizations. Such a social fact cannot be denied or devalued simply because it is not true or real in some fundamental philosophical sense. African identities are very real in their personal and social effect and in their political consequences. Appiah believes that we can and should defend such socially constructed realities but always with an eye to their strategic social and political gains. We should never, however, surrender our criticalness toward constructions which essentialize and totalize group identities.

Appiah engages then in a deconstructive critique of group identity and politics in the style of poststructural critics. Nevertheless, he gestures toward the limits of such a deconstructive strategy in two ways. First, he argues that it is not enough to point to the general instability, heterogeneity, and exclusionary character of identity categories. We need to analyze simultaneously the precise historical context and the economic, political, and cultural forces which are intertwined with identity categories and politics. "Identities are complex and multiple and grow out of a history of changing responses to economic, political, and cultural forces, almost always in opposition to other identities." For example, Appiah notes that the three central ethnic identities of modern Nigerian political life – Hausa-Fulani, Yoruba, Igbo – materialized in the transition from colonial to postcolonial status.

> David Laitin has pointed out that "the idea that there was a single Hausa-Fulani tribe . . . was largely a political claim of the NPC [Northern Peoples' Congress] in their battle against the South," while "many elders intimately involved in rural Yoruba society today recall that, as late as the 1930s, 'Yoruba' was not a common form of political identification."
> . . . [And as] Johannes Fabian has observed, the powerful Lingala- and Swahili-speaking identities of modern Zaire exist "because spheres of

political and economic interest were established before the Belgians took full control, and continued to inform relations between regions under colonial rule." Modern Ghana witnesses the development of an Akan identity, as speakers of the three major regional dialects of Twi – Asante, Fante, Akuapem – organize themselves into a corporation against an (equally novel) Ewe unity.

Departing from the deconstructive critiques of many poststructuralists, Appiah advises intellectuals to analyze identity formations and movements in their precise sociohistorical context and in relation to institutional and political forces.

In a second departure, Appiah argues that whereas many postmodern analysts approach identities only as disciplinary, constraining structures, he underscores the affirmative political possibilities of identity-based movements. For example, "[b]ecause the value of identities is thus relative, we must argue for and against them case by case. And given the current situation in Africa, I think it remains clear that another Pan-Africanism – . . . *not* the project of a racialized Negro nationalism – however false or muddled its theoretical roots, can be a progressive force." This would entail building alliances among, say, African-Americans, African-Caribbeans, African-Latins, and continental Africans to struggle against racism and to intervene into various regional conflicts. Such a Pan African movement, finally, is not a mere idea but articulates concrete developments, for example, common problems due to a similar positioning in a world economy, common discourses, or symbolic resources, and the existence of already regional Pan-African organizations such as the African Development Bank or the African caucuses serving in the UN or the World Bank.

A similar impulse, both appreciative of the deconstruction of identity and yet aiming to expose its theoretical and political limits, is central to Steve Seidman's and Rosemary Hennessy's essays – both of which address the theoretical and political significance of queer theory and politics. If decolonialization and the subsequent resurgence of racially based nationalist movements were a key juncture in shaping the rise of a deconstructive-styled race theory, the feeble efforts at coalition building in the 1970s exposed in the antigay backlash and the explicit assimilationism of gay politics in the context of AIDS and the renewal of HIV radicalism, shaped the context of the "postmodern" turn in queer theory.

In Seidman's essay, "Deconstructing Queer Theory or the Under-Theorization of the Social and the Ethical," mainstream lesbian and gay theory and politics is distinguished from queer theory. The former is characterized by the ethnic modeling of homosexuality. Homosexuals are seen as forming an ethnic minority with their own distinctive identities, cultures, and political interests. Gay theory analyzes the formation of homosexual identities and their functioning as the foundations for community development and politics. Such minoritizing concepts of homosexuality are viewed as part of the consolidation of affirmative lesbian and gay identities in the 1970s. Seidman argues that minoritizing approaches have been valuable in legitimating homosexuality in American culture and serving as symbolic resources for the successful community-building efforts of the 1970s and 1980s.

And, yet, the limits of the ethnic nationalist model became apparent in the failure of the lesbian and gay movement effectively to form coalitions to respond to the antigay backlash and the AIDS crisis. Similarly, internal solidarity was unraveling with as much intensity as the antigay backlash. The growing discontent within the lesbian and gay mainstream for its excluding and marginalizing of segments of the community who were different, for example, not white or not middle class or involved in nonconventional sexual or gender practices – a discontent exhibited in the sex and race debates – exposed the limits of a minority model of gay identity and politics.

The deconstructive turn that characterizes much so-called queer theory is, at once, a response to the crisis of a minority model, and an effort to imagine an alternative model of homosexual theory and politics. In the former role, Seidman insists on the considerable social and political importance of queer theory. It exposes the assertion of a unitary gay or lesbian identity anchored in a common experience or set of values as normative and having disciplinary effects. In this regard, queer theory does not so much press to abandon identity categories but rethinks them as open to conflicting and multiple meanings and as always interlocking with categories of gender, race, class, and so on. This theoretical move makes possible newly imagined composite or hybrid and fluid identities which, in turn, facilitate both coalition building and a politics of difference.

Queer theory does more than rethink categories and strategies of identity and politics. It shifts the very center of theorizing homosexuality.

> Queer theorists argue that homosexuality should not be treated as an issue of the lives and fate of a social minority . . . [They] urge an epistemological shift. They propose to focus on a cultural level . . . Specifically, their object of analysis is the hetero/homosexual opposition. This is understood as a category of knowledge, a way of defining and organizing selves, desires, behaviors, and social relations. Through the articulation of this hetero/homosexual figure in texts and social practices . . . it contributes to producing mutually exclusive heterosexualized and homosexualized subjects and social worlds.

Queer theory shifts the center of analysis from viewing homosexuality as a minority identity to a cultural figure. The hetero/homo binary is imagined, parallel to the masculine/feminine trope, as a symbolic code structured into the texts of daily life, from popular culture (e.g., television sitcoms or popular songs) to disciplinary knowledges, law, therapeutic practices, criminal justice, and state policies. It frames the way we know and organize personal and social experience, with the effect of reproducing heteronormativity. Queer theory aims to expose the operation of the hetero/homo code in the center of society and to contribute to destabilizing its operation. Queer theory aspires to imagine a sexual and social regime beyond the hetero/homo code and beyond heteronormativity – a regime organized around the tolerance, indeed the celebration, of social differences.

Seidman interprets queer theory as marking a valuable shift in lesbian and gay thinking. It opens up the possibility of gay theory as a general social theory and critique, not just a theory of a social minority. Similarly, it opens up the possibility of a politics beyond minority rights and representation to a politics contesting normative heterosexuality and, indeed, contesting a sexual and social regime organized around hetero/homosexuality as master categories of desire, identity, and social life. While appreciating its theoretical and political gains, Seidman criticizes queer theory for its failure to go beyond its "critique of knowledge" to a critique of the social conditions which make such hetero/homo knowledges possible. In a series of critical readings of queer theorists, Seidman tries to show that while each theorist deconstructs identities and dominant sexual knowledges, each fails to provide an account of the social conditions making such a critique and oppositional politics possible. Similarly, while these queer theorists tie their critical theory to a politics of difference against the normalizing politics of mainstream straight and gay America, none of them articulates the ethical standpoint that guides their ideas and that might give coherence to their view of social difference.

Queer theory was made possible by particular social conditions, even if queer theorists have not analyzed them. For example, Seidman emphasizes changes in the feminist and gay movements in response to both internal and external developments. In particular, Seidman points to the fact that queer theory formed in the university which, in the past few decades, has become arguably the major site in the production and legitimation of knowledges. This explains, in part, the shape of queer theory and its importance – as a participant in the struggle over power/knowledge regimes as they are centered or originate in the academe.

Queer theory has only recently exploded onto the public scene. Inevitably, it is becoming the site of important critical disputes over the meaning of queer and, more generally, over the project of a gay theory and politic. Rosemary Hennessy's "Queer Visibility in Commodity Culture" suggests a somewhat different social account and interpretation, though her essay parallels Seidman's general point that queer theory has failed to articulate its cultural critique into a social critique.

Hennessy appreciates the renewal of radical social criticism intended by queer theory, in particular, its aim to trace the operation of heterosexuality in daily life and its insistence on the socially constructed, politically produced character of desire and sexual identities. Yet it is less queer theory's failure to realize its radical project that she criticizes than a kind of "false consciousness" that attends to queer theory. Despite its radical intentions, the structure of queer theory never really escapes a certain middle-class or "bourgeois individualism." Class is the absent reflexive moment in queer theory. Unfortunately, says Hennessy, it is indicative of the general abandonment of materialism and, therewith, queer theory surrenders its warrant as a serious critical social theory.

For Hennessy, queer theory arises and never gets beyond a preoccupation with analyzing and problematizing subjectivity and cultural representations. Whether it is queer theory's deconstruction of the gay or lesbian subject or Queer Nation's "visibility" actions, it is the surface of society – the realm of subjectivity, cultural image, or social appearance – that is the object of analysis or political intervention. Like Seidman, Hennessy criticizes queer theory and politics for neglecting the relation between identity and symbolic politics and the sociohistorical conditions making queer subjects and visibility possible. However, for Hennessy, it is a specific articulation of the social that drives her critique. Queer theory has failed to incorporate in any serious way a materialist theory of society – that is, a framework which links identity to class, capitalism, and patriarchy.

In a series of critical readings of Judith Butler, Diana Fuss, and Teresa de Lauretis, Hennessy proposes that these theorists never go beyond a critical discursive analysis of questions of subjectivity, identity, and representation. Where, Hennessy asks, are the efforts to articulate discursive orders with the sexual division of labor or multinational corporate economies or patriarchy? Without such efforts to link questions of identity to institutional contexts and interlocking systems of domination, queer theory resembles those Western avant-garde movements, from Dadaism to the Situationists, whose "radical" cultural project of aestheticizing daily life or performatively parodying "the natural," fit all too well within consumer capitalism.

> Many of the aesthetic features of the avant-garde reverberate in this more worldly [queer] "social postmodernism": a tendency toward formalist modes of reading, a focus on performance and aesthetic experimentation, an idealist retreat to mythic/psychic spirituality, and the disparity between a professed agenda for broad social change and a practice focused exclusively on cultural politics. One way to begin to understand this gravitation toward cultural politics . . . is to consider it in relation to the more general aestheticization of everyday life in consumer capitalism.

The aestheticization of daily life is part of the saturation of the everyday with the commodity as a carrier of images, signs, and meanings. Many of these meanings focus on fashioning or stylizing the self and everyday reality, suggesting a highly voluntaristic and protean concept of subjectivity not unlike that of queer theory. This fetishizing of appearance and an active subjectivity conceals and legitimates the underlying social relations of class and gender domination that remain at the core of capitalist patriarchy. By remaining at the level of "the sphere of circulation" or the play of images, discourses, and subjectivity, queer theory and politics engage in a form of "opposition" that ironically perpetuates the illusion of freedom in commodity culture while concealing the material reality of domination and oppression. Thus the new queer visibility in the mass media is less a serious challenge to heteronormativity or a sign of a new acceptance of queers than a recognition of new market strategies and sites to be colonized by capital. Queer visibility has not contested heteronormativity or patriarchy or capitalism but perhaps is indicative of a new type of capitalist integration and political neutralization of queer people. Only by exposing the middle-class status of much queer theory and politics, says Hennessy, can we hope to revive a truly critical historical materialist queer theory and politics.

The essays in parts I and II cohere around a dual impulse: first, to take seriously but not uncritically the assertion of identity as a basis of political mobilization. We cannot ignore that identity-based movements in the United States and elsewhere have become pivotal agents of change and political contestation. And yet, we cannot ignore that identity can be a fulcrum for both coalitionally based movements and narrow single-interest group movements. The "postmodern" turn is intended to articulate identity politics in a way that pressures it to move in the former direction. Second, these essays have maintained that the framing of identities must be attentive to the historical context in which they are a part and articulated in relation to the social forces – classes, institutions, status groups, social processes such as globalization or commodification – which give coherence to questions of identity. In the next section, we introduce a series of essays which explore possible social articulations of postmodern analysis and critique.

## Postmodern Approaches to the Social

The question thus becomes: how do we generate ways of understanding identity as central to personal and group formation while avoiding essentialism? And, how do we articulate identity so that it can be understood in relation to sociohistorical dynamics? The contributors to part III address these questions by formulating postmodern approaches to the social.

Iris Marion Young begins with the dilemma that the use of identity categories raises: how can we use group labels without attributing to them any essential characteristics? On the one hand, we need group labels. Social analyses which are not merely accounts of individual intentions and actions must speak in the language of groups. On the other hand, group labels suggest common characteristics, a suggestion negated by the often amorphous criteria defining group membership. In reference to the category of "woman," this dilemma has given rise to the suggestion that we think of this category only as designating political affiliation. But, according to Young, this suggestion will not work. The identification of "woman" with a self-conscious political movement seems to designate arbitrarily what, from the vantage point of common sense, seems merely a specific group of women. Moreover, it also appears to restrict in a disciplinary way who gets to be counted as a "woman."

Borrowing Sartre's concept of seriality, Young proposes an alternative way out of the dilemma. Whereas the idea of a "group" suggests shared characteristics, a series has no such determining characteristics; its vaguer and more amorphous unity is derived only from its shared passive relationship to a specific material milieu. This milieu both constrains and enables individual actions but neither defines nor determines them. Thus the series lacks defining attributes or characteristics:

> Membership in serial collectives defines an individual's being, in a sense – one "is" a farmer, or a commuter, or a radio listener, and so on, together in series with others similarly positioned. But the definition is anonymous, and the unity of the series is amorphous, without determinate limits, attributes, or intentions. Sartre calls it a unity "in flight," a collective gathering that slips away at the edges, whose qualities and characteristics are impossible to pin down because they are an inert result of the confluence of actions. There is no concept of the series, no specific set of attributes that form the sufficient conditions for membership in it.

In relation to gender, bodies constitute one of the types of "practico-inert" objects that position individuals as women or men. But bodies themselves gain their meaning through specific structural arrangements. And Young claims that it is the set of meanings, rules, and practices that comprise institutionalized heterosexuality which form the material milieu enabling the differentiation of female from male bodies. But bodies are only one of the types of "practico-inert" objects that position women as gendered beings. Also involved are such other "materialized historical products" as pronouns, verbal and visual representations, clothes, tools, spaces, etc., which Young claims are themselves structured in relation to gender through the sexual division of labor. While some sexual division of labor and the system of institutionalized heterosexuality set the parameters for the series "woman," because the specific content of both varies historically and because in any given context neither determines what it means to be a woman, the series "woman" exists without defining characteristics.

In short, Young responds to the dilemma of identity by proposing a conceptual strategy which avoids both nominalism and essentialism. In the concept of the "series," Young suggests a way of conceptualizing group identity which allows for a conception of "the social" where patterns can be described but which are fluid in nature.

Whereas Young argues for a new analytical approach to social groups, other contributors to this section rearticulate "the social" more by emphasizing the historicity of the categories by which social life is constituted. They argue that particular categories of identity must be understood within the context of a given historical setting. This move is intended to avoid certain poststructuralist analyses which theorize identity in relation to ahistorical theories of language or of psychoanalysis. Instead the coherence of identity categories becomes a "social" issue requiring attention to the specific sociohistorical context such categories emerge out of and help shape.

This type of focus is pivotal in the essay by Cindy Patton where the political context of identity categories, as used by theorists and political agents, is examined in some detail. In "Refiguring Social Space," Patton argues that it was a particular set of social and historical circumstances which made the postulation of social identity a useful mechanism for making political claims. However, those circumstances have changed, requiring the reassessment of identity politics.

Patton's essay provides a novel analysis of the historical rise of identity politics and of the present circumstances which challenge its utility. She points to the emergence of identity politics out of the space provided by the civil rights movement. As the civil rights movement transformed the African-American population from a group to a claimant for political rights, so the later women's and gay and lesbian movements used the concept of civil rights to make a similar move. "Civil rights was no longer a compensatory, temporary conduit designed to incorporate a class of bodies viewed as historically always present but excluded as subjects, but an open door that permitted more bodies to make different claims to subject status." By employing the concept of civil rights as a means to make claims on the body politic, feminists and gays and lesbians could, to use the language of Bourdieu, transform social into political capital. This move, while reaping important results, also generated its own reactions. One of the consequences of situating civil rights as an open door was the suggestion of an endless proliferation of identities, all of which could make social claims for rights and representation. The new right has seized on this political logic. In response, it has reconfigured "civil rights" as that which belongs properly to "true Americans," identifying the claims of the excluded as requests for "special privileges." Social space became redefined from an expanding sphere open to new configurations to a bounded sphere identified with the family and those operating by the values the new right has associated with it. This bounded sphere became depicted as the space of a beleaguered minority threatened by the increasing claims of "special interests." The new right has thus worked to reconstitute the social whole in a binary mode which differentiates an "us" who truly belong from a "them" who threaten to engulf and destroy.

One of the benefits of Patton's analysis is that it enables us to understand the advantages and disadvantages of identity politics in historically specific ways. As she emphasizes, identity politics has reaped important political rewards. However, that success rested on a very particular and not necessarily enduring sociohistorical context. "The difficulty with 'identity politics' is not so much that we mistakenly 'believed' in our self-namings but that we believed in the promise of inalienable rights, rights which would accrue once our status as political subjects was secured." The task facing us today, accordingly, may involve less the question of defending or rejecting identity politics than it is in figuring out how to generate its positive possibilities in an environment where civil rights has a different meaning than in an earlier time.

Patton's essay underlines the point that categories of analysis are social constructs whose meanings and consequences shift in different contexts. The essay by Ali Rattansi, "Just Framing: Ethnicities and Racisms in a 'Postmodern' Framework," elaborates this point in relation to the concepts of racism and ethnicity. Rattansi rejects definitions of racism or ethnicity that ignore the myriad of differences among racial and ethnic categorizations. Concepts of race and ethnicity vary not only in relation to the degree of centrality of biology but also in relation to their intersection with concepts of nationality, sexual difference, and class. Nor, Rattansi claims, does the language of cultural difference even have any "necessary political belonging," being employed as means for political resistance as well as for projects of domination.

The point to be deduced from such an argument, however, is not merely to urge complexity, to add more differentiations to the theorist's understanding of race or of other categorizations of social life. Rather, what emerges from Rattansi's essay, as well as from Patton's, is a new understanding of the social world and consequently of the categories which the social theorist can best employ to depict it. This is an understanding of social reality as itself being continually reshaped by the changing categories social actors use to understand themselves, others, and the spaces they share.

> A "postmodern" framing conceptualizes *ethnicity* as part of a *cultural politics of representation*, involving processes of "self-identification" as well as formation by disciplinary agencies such as the state and including the involvement of the social sciences, given their incorporation in the categorization and redistributive activities of the state and campaigning organizations.

Social life becomes no longer, as it tended to be in much modern social theory, a relatively static field, understandable through the use of abstract categories. Rather, it becomes a field continually in shift where the very categories actors are using to depict it are productive of the shifts themselves. Following this understanding, the social theorist becomes, with the social worker, the state agent, the journalist, and the protester, one more social actor in the process of social production.

Therefore, as the above essays reveal, a postmodern social analysis involves the rethinking of the very nature of the basic categories through which the social whole is viewed and constituted. Such a postmodern approach rejects an understanding of such categories as the family, the state, the individual, and the homosexual as "natural." This move de-essentializes such categories by placing them within specific historical and political contexts. It thus avoids the essentialist disposition of some modern modes of understanding; it also avoids those poststructuralist arguments which often ignore the institutional context of discursive practices.

A "social postmodern" turn is evident in Nancy Fraser's "Politics, Culture, and the Public Sphere: Toward a Postmodern Conception." Fraser aims to retrieve the concept of the public sphere from modern discourses. She claims that this concept is a useful one, enabling us to situate discourse in institutionalized settings. It thus provides an alternative to those kinds of theoretical approaches which "dissociate cultural studies from critical social theory." The problem, however, is the way in which modern theory has tended to employ this concept. Such theory has often been organized around three prevailing assumptions: that democratic public spaces can exist without social equality; that a multiplicity of competing publics are necessarily a threat to democracy; and that public discourse need be about the common good.

Fraser questions all of these assumptions and their usefulness for a concept of the public sphere. Instead she develops a postliberal, postmodern conception of the public which recognizes the necessity of social equality for political democracy; which accepts the idea that a multiplicity of counterpublics may at times expand democratic, discursive space; and which includes rather than excludes interests that have been understood as "private."

In elaborating the point of the admissibility of "private" issues into public debate, Fraser takes on the broad question of how we understand the concept of "public" and the counterconcept of "private." She argues that these concepts do not designate naturally given or preexisting social spheres. "[R]ather, they are cultural classifications and rhetorical labels. In political discourse, they are frequently deployed to delegitimate some interests, views, and topics and to valorize others."

Fraser develops this argument by focusing on the confirmation process of Associate Supreme Court Justice Clarence Thomas. Here she emphasizes that a central element in the struggle was contesting battles over where the line between public and private was to be drawn. These battles were staged differently and had different consequences for Clarence Thomas and Anita Hill. While Thomas' prior sexual habits were successfully defended as "off-limits to public debate," this claim was not achieved on behalf of Anita Hill. These different consequences point to the need for understanding publicity not only as a cultural categorization emerging out of particular political struggles, but also as a multivalent one, having, as a consequence of such struggles, different meanings for different groups.

> Such a conception takes as its starting point the multivalent, contested character of the categories of privacy and publicity with their gendered and racialized subtexts. It acknowledges that in highly stratified late

capitalist societies, not everyone stands in the same relation to privacy and publicity; some have more power than others to draw and defend the line.

In short, "publicity" like "identity" must be viewed as a cultural construction whose deployment must be assessed in relation to a particular context. At issue in the use of both the categories of "identity" and "publicity," as well as other categories of social life, is the question of "for whom" and "in relation to what specific consequences."

Postmodernism, therefore, does not represent an abandonment of "the social." Rather, it represents new ways of conceptualizing it. A postmodern conceptualization deviates from a modern one in understanding the categories by which social life is organized as historically emergent rather than naturally given, as multivalent rather than unified in meaning, and as the frequent result and possible present instrument in struggles of power. Whereas in the context of modernist understandings, a negative or "deconstructionist" emphasis may have been and still is necessary, such an emphasis need not be either all that a postmodern approach includes nor understood as that which is removed from institutional social analysis. As the essays in this section illustrate, postmodern approaches can be seen not as those which avoid the social but rather as those which reinterpret its meaning.

## Postmodern Approaches to the Political

If postmodern thinkers are now feeling pressed to articulate a concept of the social that goes beyond textual meanings or sign systems, perhaps this is so, in part, because of their perception of a narrow identity-based politics and an exclusively discursively based theory. In addition, we would like to think that, at least for many parts of the world, we are leaving a period of social and political conservatism. We hope that many of the events in the last decade or so, such as the end of the Soviet empire and of apartheid in South Africa or the revival of radical social activism in the United States (e.g., ACT-UP or Queer Nation) open new possibilities for democratic social change. If we are right, there will be a heightened demand for theories which focus on social institutions and processes such as changes in the public sphere, nationalism, social movements. information systems, and the globalization of capital. Once again, social theory and politics might go hand in hand. But what would a postmodern politics look like?

Some critics of the postmodern turn have called into question the very idea of a postmodern politics. They argue that a theoretical perspective which announces the "death of the subject" or refuses a concept of the self as unified or coherent surrenders any basis for political mobilization. In "Feminism, Citizenship, and Radical Democratic Politics," Chantal Mouffe addresses this critique directly.

> Many feminists believe that, without seeing women as a coherent identity, we cannot ground the possibility of a feminist political movement in which women could unite as women in order to formulate and pursue specific feminist aims. Contrary to that view, I will argue that, for those feminists who are committed to a radical democratic politics, the deconstruction of essential identities should be seen as the necessary condition for an adequate understanding of the variety of social relations where the principles of liberty and equality should apply.

Mouffe disputes the feminist view which assumes that only a concept of woman as a coherent identity makes feminist politics possible. To be sure, essentialist constructions of womanhood make possible certain kinds of feminist struggles, for example, a liberal feminism which asserts demands for women's equal rights or a radical feminism which might promote a distinctively feminine concept of citizenship or politics. However, Mouffe argues that the de-centering of the unity of the category of "woman" encourages a "radical democratic politics."

If feminists conceive of women as a distinct unitary group grounded in some presumed common experiences or values, politics is imagined as articulating these shared ways of being or thinking. Thus, if women's experiences are seen as similar to men's, feminist politics may well center on demands for equal opportunities, representations, and rights for women. If, on the other hand, women's experience is imagined as different in some fundamental way from men's, feminist politics may focus on asserting and legitimating women's uniquely feminine values. The limits of a feminist epistemology grounded in a concept of essential female identity are that it cannot give expression to all of women's experiences, i.e., it is normative and exclusionary. The limits of a feminist politics grounded in a notion of unitary gender identity are that it weakens coalition-building efforts and surrenders to a single-interest group politic of either assimilationism or separatism. In both cases, coalitional politics is either abandoned or rendered feeble. Moreover, such a feminist politic does not challenge the dominant masculine liberal model of citizenship and politics.

By contrast, Mouffe argues, if feminists approach identities as always multiple or, to use Mouffe's poststructural language, as always framed in discourses and practices in multiple, sometimes contradictory ways e.g., simultaneously gender-subordinate but racially dominant – we can imagine a feminist politics that is part of a broader radical democratic project. How so? If we cannot separate gender identity easily, if at all, from racial, sexual, national, or class positioning, then "women" as a category cannot be thought apart from these other social identities. There would be no separate, independent "women's" experience that could be marked off and presumed as the ground of feminist politics. Rather, "women's" interests would be viewed as always inflected by particular race, class, sexual, or national concerns. There is no "woman" in general, only women who simultaneously occupy particular race, class, sexual, or national social positions. This deconstruction of identity politics suggests a new approach to politics: less a politics organized exclusively around separate identities than a politics organized around specific issues, struggles, goals, and broad democratic principles which bring together interested parties.

What does such a concept of radical democratic politics mean for feminism? It does not mean abandoning a concept of "women" or gender-based politics. We can reject a notion of gender identity as a common essence while retaining a nonessentialist framing of women. "The absence of a female essential identity and of a pregiven unity . . . does not preclude the construction of multiple forms of unity and common action. As the result of the construction of nodal points, partial fixations can take place and precarious forms of identification can be established around the category 'women' that provide the basis for a feminist identity and a feminist struggle." Such struggles, however, would not be focused exclusively on gender since gender is viewed as interlocking with class, sexuality, race, nationality, and so on. Mouffe's idea of democratic politics aspires to recover an expansive transformative political vision in the tradition of Western Marxism while recognizing that individuals will continue to organize under the identities of women, gay, black, or working class. Her model of politics suggests that alliances between selves differently positioned will be promoted by viewing identities as multiple and interlocking and by a more issues-centered, coalitional politics. Moreover, in a suggestive proposal, Mouffe offers as a common bond uniting such a democratic project the notion of a collective political identity based on the principle of "liberty and equality for all."

Indicative perhaps of a new sense of democratic prospects in the United States and elsewhere, theorists and activists are exploring the contours of a positive progressive politics. This is what we find exciting and hopeful about Mouffe's proposal for a radical democratic politics. She begins to imagine such a politics without appealing to essentialized identities or the evolutionary theory of Marxism. This same project informs Shane Phelan's "A Space for Justice: Lesbians and Democratic Politics."

Phelan considers the prospects of a lesbian democratic politics that no longer trades on the essentialism of lesbian-feminism and is impatient with the refusal of poststructuralist queer theory to go beyond deconstructive critique. She sketches some of the conceptual underpinnings of a postmodern lesbian politics.

Drawing on the poststructural critique of essential identities and the parallel critique by people of color, Phelan describes a conceptual strategy to make coherent a postmodern coalitional politics. Given the diversity of lesbians' lives and values, the appeal to a common experience and interest cannot ground lesbian politics. If the assumption of a common lesbian experience is made problematic, so too is the idea of a common lesbian interest and therefore the very foundation of "modern" lesbian politics. In other words, Phelan aims to trouble what she perceives as the operative logic in contemporary lesbian politics: an assumed homology between experience, interest, identity, and politics. Although such a lesbian politics has been historically important, serious limitations have been attached to it. In particular, coalition building is seriously weakened as alliances appear as the stringing together of separate identity-based groups – women, lesbians, gay men, blacks, Latinos and Latinas – around a particular struggle. Such coalitions are temporary and unified only by a utilitarian calculus which assumes that groups support each other with the expectation of a future payback.

However, if we assume that identities are multiple, unstable, and interlocking, the logic of identity politics is made problematic. Although such arguments evoke fears of the unraveling of sexual politics, Phelan sees productive possibilities. Central to her proposal is the suggestion to approach the concept of "lesbian interest" not as grounded in common experiences or shared values but as an expression of a demand for public recognition and inclusion advanced by lesbians making claims as citizens.

> The formal claim of an interest – say as a lesbian – does not yet commit a lesbian to a particular desire or need. It establishes lesbianism as a relevant political identity from which to proceed. This provides the space to articulate a "lesbian good" without predetermining what that good will be. It also opens the category of "lesbian" to negotiation – claiming lesbianism as a relevant identity cannot simply avoid "common sense" notions of what such an identity is, but it need not rest with those notions either. The identity itself becomes open to politics.

Phelan wishes to view the assertion of lesbian identity, in part, as a civic act. In this formulation, the concept of lesbian interest loses any essentializing connotations and instead suggests a public political identity. The advantage of this formulation of lesbian interest is that it does not render it exclusive or captive to narrow concerns but allows an assertion of lesbian interest to attach to a wide range of social and political issues and struggles. For example, from this perspective Phelan imagines lesbians articulating an "interest" in decent, affordable housing. This would not be seen as an issue for all lesbians or as one grounded in anything defining of a lesbian. Moreover, it would not be an exclusively lesbian issue but would be an issue potentially for all individuals for whom the lack of decent, affordable housing is a concern. Lesbians would need to work on housing issues along with many nonlesbians and would do so by articulating their unique housing concerns, just as those positioned in unique class or racial terms would clarify their specific concerns.

Recognizing the multiplicity of lesbian experiences, interests, and therefore political identities does not mean surrendering all claims to commonality. Phelan sees the reframing of lesbian identity as a political demand for recognition and participation as equal citizens as providing a kind of unifying political force. The focus on social issues, specific goals, and coalitional struggles based on affinities of interest means that public officials will be pressured to take as seriously the lives and issues of lesbians as they would other citizens. The concept of citizenship and political identity provides a unifying reference for lesbians without repressing their differences. Like Mouffe, Phelan imagines a lesbian politic as part of a broader politics. "In the end, our goal should be to articulate a lesbian agenda as part of a radical democratic creed shared across sexualities and other differences."

Phelan sees in Queer Nation a movement with a decidedly postmodern temper. In its politics against normalization and its assertion of a hybrid, composite identity based on loose affinities of interests and aims, Queer Nation suggests a postmodern movement. However, whereas Queer Nation is somewhat compromised by a nationalist strain, Stanley Aronowitz argues that no such nationalism characterizes ACT-UP, perhaps a better exemplar of a postmodern social movement today.

In "Against the Liberal State: ACT-UP and the Emergence of Postmodern Politics," Aronowitz suggests that the political logic and success of ACT-UP mark a shift to a postmodern political culture. Modern liberal politics has been organized around the logic of electoral, majoritarian rule. Citizens elect representatives and expect them to enact social policy which reflects majority electoral sentiment. The mobilization of electoral majorities which elect public officials legitimates public representatives and their legislation. This liberal political logic is now in doubt.

> In contrast to the leading premise of modern politics, namely, that the legitimacy of the liberal state is guaranteed by electoral majorities, ACT-UP tacitly challenges the *ethical* legitimacy of the majority – just as business interests have buried the majority interest in areas such as tax policy, national health care, and environmental protection. Although ACT-UP eschews doctrinal pronouncements, it insists on and seeks to impose a *substantive* rather than procedural criterion upon claims to representation. If the majority accepts or otherwise acquiesces to the institutionalized homophobia of the state ... citizens are under no obligation to obey the law and rules of conduct prescribed in its name.

On the one hand, liberal majoritarian politics is threatened by business interests which increasingly dictate public policy – demanding tax breaks or deferment of public investment – by its threat to relocate or significantly reduce their present investments. This capturing of public policy by corporate interest is evident in urban policies across the country. On the other hand, movements such as ACT-UP are similarly placing liberal politics in doubt by their ability to shape public policy through successful social and media, not electoral, mobilization. Both of these developments suggest, says Aronowitz, that the legitimacy of public policies is increasingly grounded not in majority rule, whose legitimacy is established by electoral procedures, but in the ability of groups to impose a substantive standard upon claims to representation or to win public support for their particular substantive interests. The indeterminate relation between elections and public policy spells a potential crisis of modern liberal politics and a shift to a postmodern politics where power is responsive to substantive concerns and where the media becomes a key site for political mobilization. Aronowitz suggests that these developments have ambivalent moral implications. If business-driven policies underscore illiberal possibilities, ACT-UP suggests the democratic potential of a postmodern political culture.

The future of American politics significantly depends upon the outcome of the struggles of contemporary social movements. In this regard, Aronowitz perceives in ACT-UP radical democratic social possibilities. Whereas the history of many progressive social movements in postwar America has been either to become part of the Democratic Party as a pressure group (e.g., labor), thereby losing much of their radical democratic force, or to become part of the state in the form of a service agency (Gay Men's Health Crisis), thereby becoming part of the politics of management, ACT-UP has not – yet – surrendered its politics of protest and radical confrontation. This movement continues to engage in direct-action practices, refuses to bow to economically driven public policy, and has not reduced politics to electoral practices. ACT-UP demands shared power, input into decision-making processes, and asserts that substantive criteria should guide public policy. Indeed, in its organizational structure, for example, its rejection of a bureaucratic centralized mode of decision making, its engagement with the politics of science, its de-centralized, voluntary, action-oriented style of practice, and its demand to be involved in institutional decision making, even in "expert" realms (e.g., medicine and science), ACT-UP exemplifies a radical democratic styling of a postmodern politic.

Whether the argument for a postmodern politics takes the form of Mouffe's call for a deconstruction of essentialized identities or Phelan's rethinking of identity and interest, or Aronowitz's advocacy of social movements as carriers of substantive reason, there is unanimity on one overriding point that we feel should be underlined: a postmodern politics is conceived as radically democratic. A postmodern politics suggests less an abandonment of modern values (e.g., liberty, equality, citizenship, autonomy, public participation) than an effort to preserve these values by rethinking the premises of modern culture and politics. Nor in these versions of postmodern politics is there a refusal to articulate common grounds or unifying points in politics. Rather, these proposals criticize efforts to deduce such commonality from some general principle or to ground them in a quasi-transcendental foundational philosophy or a philosophical anthropology. This articulation of the premises and goals of a postmodern political project is reaffirmed in R. W. Connell's "Democracies of Pleasure: Thoughts on the Goals of Radical Sexual Politics."

Connell suggests that "postmodernity" means the end of the politics of sexual liberation. This is so because postmodern perspectives deconstruct the very idea of a sexuality to be liberated. "There is no thing there to liberate." This does not mean sexual politics must surrender a political direction or positive project. In this regard, Connell is critical of efforts to substitute a politics of discursive and body play for a liberatory sexual politics. Connell advocates a return to strong social approaches to analyzing sexuality and a sexual politics tied to social structural change.

Criticizing liberationist sexual politics by deconstructing sexuality has led some poststructuralists into an exclusively discursive sex theory and playful sexual politic. With regard to the former, Connell wishes to preserve the deconstructive turn which denaturalizes the body and desire but he aims to avoid an exclusively discourse-centered approach to "sexuality." He urges instead that the body and desire be approached not only in relation to discourse but also in relation to institutions and organizations such as the state, families, the church, or the corporation. In place of discourse as the site of sexual analysis, he proposes the guiding idea of "sexual social relations." From this sociological standpoint, "sexuality" can be analyzed in terms of the creation of and struggles around hierarchies of power and legitimation, inequalities in desires, behaviors, and relations, and issues of constraint and scarcity. Sexual practices should be studied, he concludes, like any other social practice, in terms of questions of power, inequality, legitimacy, domination, scarcity, and so on.

Deploying the concept of sexual social relations, Connell frames sexual politics in terms similar to other spheres of politics. "To understand sexuality neither as nature nor discourse, but as a sphere of social practices that constitute social relations, helps clarify the goal of sexual politics." If the goal is not the liberation of sexuality, it is, he says, the liberation of people, and sexual politics means freeing people from unnecessary constraints and inequities in the realm of the body and desire. "It is meaningful to speak of 'sexual liberation' where oppression is accomplished in the sexual social relations between groups of people. What 'liberation' then means is that the oppressed gain power over their own lives, power that was formerly exercised by other groups." In other words, sexual politics is not all that different from gender, race, or class politics: it is about equality, empowerment, and democratization through altering sexual social relations, i.e., changes in social institutions. The goal of sexual liberation is not the end of repression or the end of the social structuring of desire, but the democratization of sexual social relations. "This means a search for equality and empowerment across the whole social terrain of the body-reflexive practices relating to erotic pleasure and reproduction." Democracies of pleasure involve sexual resource sharing, shared decision making, equitable distribution of knowledge, and social respect; like any process of democratization, sexual democracy entails social structural changes, e.g., changes in schools, AIDS policies, and mass media.

## Social Postmodernism:
## A Language of Radical Democratic Theory and Politics

As a way of thinking about knowledge, self, society, and politics, postmodernism has roots in the struggles over social life that have been at the center of many Western societies in the past few decades. We should not forget that deconstruction made its appearance as part of the revolts against the disciplinary, normalized order of French society in the late 1960s. Similarly, the articulation of self-conscious postmodern social theories in the United States emerged in relation to developments in the new social movements, especially in the 1980s and 1990s. With regard to the latter, the postmodern turn is closely connected to the failure of the new social movements to forge coalitions in the face of a well-organized backlash against progressive democratic change. Simultaneously, the surfacing of voices of difference within the movements was pivotal in facilitating the deconstruction of essentialized identities and advocating a radical cultural politics of difference.

Many of us who have adopted a postmodern perspective have drawn positively on such critical traditions as Marxism, feminism, or gay liberationism. However, we have also believed that such radical "modernist" theories frequently have absorbed the assumptions of the society they criticized, limiting their contemporary oppositional force. We believe that to preserve a democratic critical tradition requires a radical rethinking of the premises and language of social knowledge and politics. We have sought to refashion the political culture of the left so that intellectuals could speak to the multiplicity of oppositional movements, be attentive to their specific struggles, be coalitional, and affirm strategies and social goals that valued difference. For us, and many contributors to this volume, the best available language was, and perhaps remains, that of postmodernism.

But, as the essays in this volume argue, this involves a postmodern perspective of a certain type, one which attends to histories, institutions, and social processes. In this regard, we have sought to overcome the limits of those "poststructuralist" or "deconstructionist" approaches which have failed to articulate the interconnections between oppositional movements, refused to state a positive, transformative social and political project, and neglected the institutional, social structural contexts of discursive, textual meanings. This does not mean, however, that a poststructural strain of critical social analysis which has relied heavily on deconstructing texts has not been very important in pressuring a critical reflexivity regarding knowledge, society, and politics. The problematizing of essentialized identities, the de-centering of the subject and society, the re-centering of the social around analyzing power/knowledge regimes, are major resources for critical analysis and a democratic politics. In contrast to many of its detractors, we believe that deconstruction makes possible a politics of coalition building, a cultural politics of social tolerance and difference, a critical politics of knowledge, and an affirmation of particular, local struggles without disavowing the possibilities of broader forms of social solidarity and political mobilization. The critique of deconstruction, therefore, should not lead to its abandonment but to its absorption in a "social postmodernism," as at least one strategy for imagining a democratic social theory and politics as we approach the end of the second millennium.

*Social postmodernism* makes the case for a type of social thinking which integrates deconstruction while simultaneously incorporating some of the analytically synthesizing and expansive political hopes of the modernist tradition of social theorizing. We think this move might be productive for generating conceptual and political strategies that can continue to expose inequalities, oppressions, forms of social injustice, and sites of conflict and change in societies that mix modern and postmodern features.

This volume is at best suggestive of one direction for theory and politics. Indeed, there is hardly unity among those who mark out the terrain of "social postmodernism" beyond the need to move beyond the current impasse in theory and politics. Nevertheless, we hope that this volume suggests at least one possible move beyond the antinomy of "radical modernism" (Marxism, feminism, Afrocentrism, gay liberationism) and postmodern deconstruction: a theoretical perspective which refashions both into a new language of radical democratic theory and politics.

# The Promise of a Cultural Sociology: Technological Discourse and the Sacred and Profane Information Machine

*Jeffrey C. Alexander*

The gradual permeation of the computer into the pores of modern life deepens what Max Weber called the "rationalization of the world." The computer converts every message – regardless of its substantive meaning, metaphysical remoteness, or emotional allure – into a series of numerical bits and bytes. These series are connected to others through electrical impulses. Eventually these impulses are converted back into the media of human life.

Can there be any better example of the subjection of worldly activity to impersonal rational control? Can there be any more forceful illustration of the disenchantment of the world that Weber warned would be the result? Much depends on the answer to this portentous question, for discourse about the meaning of advanced technology demarcates one of the central ideological penumbra of the age. If the answer is yes, we are not only trapped inside of Weber's cage of iron but also bound by the laws of exchange that Marx asserted would eventually force everything human into a commodity form.

This query about the rationalization of the world poses theoretical questions, not just existential ones. Can there really exist a world of purely technical rationality? Although this question may be ideologically compelling for critics of the modern world, I will argue that the theory underlying such a proposition is not correct. Because both action and its environments (Alexander 1982-1983, 1988a) are indelibly interpenetrated by the nonrational, a pure technically rational world cannot exist. Certainly the growing centrality of the digital computer is an empirical fact. This fact, however, remains to be interpreted and explained.

It is theory that provides the framework for interpretation and explanation. In the following section I outline a theoretical model that provides a more accurate understanding and that points to a more culturally sensitive sociology.

---

Source: Jeffrey C. Alexander (ed.), *Theory of Culture*, (Berkeley, CA.: University of California Press, 1992).

On the basis of this model, I will argue against the validity of Weber's conception of rationalization. First, I critically examine sociological accounts of technology in general, arguing that by eliminating technology's symbolic status, these accounts reduce it to a cog in the social system. From there I turn to an empirical examination of the social understandings of the computer that have emerged over the last half century. Far from leading to (or from) the rationalization of society, this prototype of modern technology has been caught within a deep and traditional cultural web. I conclude that the rationalization thesis is a reflection of this web of symbolism rather than an explanation of it. It crystallizes the sentiments and symbolic meanings that underlie what is perceived to be peculiarly modern about our world.

## Taking Meaning Seriously

Contemporary sociology is almost entirely the study of social elements from the perspective of their place in the social system. The promise of a cultural sociology is that a more multidimensional perspective can be attained. From this multidimensional perspective, social elements would no longer be seen naturalistically, as things that can exist, in and of themselves, without the mediation of cultural codes. Although this naturalistic view seems pragmatically justified in terms of how we experience the world (Rochberg-Halton 1986), in fact, it reifies persons and institutions.[1]

Such reification is most obvious in the theoretical traditions that have emerged from the dichotomies of the post-Parsonian world (Alexander 1987: chaps. 8–20). Microtheorists tend to see actors as omni-powerful meaning-creators, as hard-headed rationalizers, as participants in networks that have immediate situational relevance. Macrotheorists are inclined to see the world in terms of *Realpolitik*.[2] In more subtle ways, this pragmatic reification has vitiated the contributions of theorists who have given the cultural realm more serious attention. From Simmel to Parsons, theorists have justified an exclusively social system reference for sociology – its self-limitation to institutions, interactions, and institutionalized values – by apportioning disciplinary specialties. Anthropology or literary studies explain symbolic patterns; sociologists focus on real interactions.[3]

While Simmel and Parsons described this specialization as an analytic one, the argument is closely connected to the approach that makes culture into a concrete variable. In the worst case this variable is high culture. From this perspective, "cultural sociologists" are limited to research on art museums and musical taste, and mass society theorists speak about the decline of culture in the modern world.[4] More common, but just as misleading, culture is equated with ideological attitudes and contrasted to – measured against the effect of – economic interests; it is equated with values and contrasted with norms; it is equated with religion and weighted against the effects of political position. Common to all these approaches is the "everything else" argument. Other than this particular variable, their adherents suggest, everything else is noncultural. Everything else exists in its social system form.

The alternative to such "type analysis" is an analytic approach, but one that will not relegate symbolic status to disciplines outside sociology. This approach, rather than understanding symbolic and material forces in a pluralistic and "generous" way, assumes that both are always present as analytical dimensions of the same empirical unit. From the analytic perspective, every social object can be analyzed as a cultural object, every social structure as a "culture structure" (for this concept, see Rambo and Chan 1990; for a general defense of the analytic approach to culture, see Kane 1991). Events, actors, roles, groups, and institutions, as elements in a concrete society, are part of a social system; they are simultaneously, however, part of a cultural system that overlaps, but is not contiguous with, the society. I define culture as an organized set of meaningfully understood symbolic patterns. It is because of their location in such an organized set that every social interaction can also be understood as a text (Ricoeur 1971).

Only if these analytical transformations are made, can the thickness of human life (Geertz 1973), its dimensionality and nuance, enter into the language of social science. Dilthey (1976) prepared us to respect this density by insisting that all social action rests upon the reservoir of our inner experience of life. Because we experience the world rather than simply behave in it, the world is meaningful. As social scientists, we must describe the world's inner life or we will fail to describe "it" at all. We cannot, moreover, handle the problem of meaning cavalierly, taking its character for granted as something obvious and shifting our attention to this meaning's cause or effects, as does the culture-as-variable approach.[5] Rather, we must willingly inhabit the world of meaning itself.

To try to inhabit this world does not mean orienting ourselves to the idiosyncratic attitudes of individuals. This is the "getting into the actor's head" approach advocated by microtheorists such as symbolic interactionists.[6] Because culture is an environment of every action, to inhabit the world of meaning is, rather, to enter into the organized sets of symbolic patterns that these actors meaningfully understand. This is not to say that social science aims to describe cultural patterns in and of themselves. In the first place, mere description is impossible; cultural analysis consists of interpretation and reconstruction. In the second place, to attempt a complex understanding of meaningful sets is not to eschew a fuller explanatory goal. Indeed, my contention here is quite the opposite. Only with a more muscular understanding of culture can we gain a real, multidimensional understanding of the relation between symbolic systems and more traditional sociological referents.[7]

We cannot enter this world of meaning armed only with methodologies, our sensibilities and hermeneutical circles well in hand. We can do so only with strong theories about how the cultural system actually works. For this, hermeneutics, whether Dilthey's or Gadamer's, is hopelessly unprepared.

Sociological theories of modern culture are not much better. Beyond the death of meaning, Weber (1958) suggests its fragmentation into autonomous spheres of cognitive, moral, and aesthetic knowledge. This perspective leads us to understand the antagonism, or paradoxes, between different beliefs and competing social actions (Schluchter 1979). It does not lead us to pattern-interpretation, the effort to understand these patterns in and of themselves.[8] For his part, Durkheim (1951) often endorses a complementary view of the dissolution of meaning. In the best-known examples to the contrary, he (1933, 1973) theorizes the generalization and growing abstraction of the collective conscience. This approach lends itself to the blurring and vulgarization of the symbolic patterns in organized sets, leading the analyst to look at culture from the outside, in terms of its social effects.

Parsons draws on both Weber's and Durkheim's theories, transmuting them (for example, Parsons 1966) into accounts of cultural differentiation and value generalization. The precision of his theorizing makes the implications of this approach much clearer than in classical work. Parsons (for example, Parsons and Shils 1951) declares that he is not concerned with the internal geography of the culture structure, which he calls *symbol systems*. Rather, he says, sociology should study only the institutionalized segment of culture, in Parsons's terms not the *cultural system*, but the *latency*, or *pattern maintenance*, *subsystem* of the social system. These specialized elements are called *values* in Parsons's theory.[9] Parsons examined socialization and specification to study the manner in which differentiated and generalized values affect the organization of the social system: the support for politics, the motivation for work, the nature of professions, and the operation of universities. He studied, in other words, not the internal structure of symbolic systems, but the processes by which a given culture structure becomes institutionalized in society.[10]

Contemporary critical theory is similar in surprising respects, though it hardly gives institutionalization its due. For Habermas, neither meaning nor culture structure is the real object of analysis. On the basis of Weber's and Parsons's evolutionary theory, the existence of a small number of abstract, differentiated, and specific normative patterns is assumed (Habermas 1984). The concern is not with interpreting normative patterns but with tracing how actors refer to patterns and, particularly, with the effect this reference has on the relations between actors and institutions. Recreating the inner world of modern objects, however, involves much more rigorous and internally complex theoretical resources. To acquire these resources, we must turn to extrasociological traditions and to sociological theories of premodern life.

If we begin with the notion that culture is a form of language, we can make use of the conceptual architecture provided by Saussure's semiotics, his "science of signs." Though they perhaps are not as tightly organized as real languages (but see Barthes 1983), cultural sets have definite codelike properties. They are composed of strongly structured symbolic relationships that are largely independent of any particular actor's volition or speech. Cultural codes, like linguistic languages, are built upon signs, which contain both signifier and signified. Technology, for example, is not only a thing, a signified object to which others refer, it is also a signifier, a signal, an internal expectation. The relation between signifier and signified, Saussure insists, is "arbitrary." When he writes (1964) that the former "has no natural connection with the signified," he is suggesting that the meaning or nature of the sign – its name or internal dimension – cannot be understood as being dictated by the nature of the signified, that is, by the sign's external, material dimension.

If the meaning of the sign cannot be observed or induced from examining the signified, or objective, referents, then how is it established? By its relation to other signifiers, Saussure insists. Systems of signs are composed of endless such relationships. At their most primitive, these relationships are binary. In any actual system of cultural sets, they become long strings, or webs, of interwoven analogies and antitheses, what Eco (1979) calls the "similitude of signifiers" that compose the "global semantic field."[11] Structural anthropology has illustrated the usefulness of this architecture, most famously in the work of Lévi-Strauss (1967) and most usefully in the work of Sahlins (1976, 1981).

Yet, even at its most socially embedded, semiotics can never be enough. By definition it abstracts from the social world, taking organized symbolic sets as psychologically unmotivated and as socially uncaused. By contrast, for the purposes of cultural sociology, semiotic codes must be tied into both social and psychological environments and into action itself. I will term the result of this specification *discourses*, in appreciation of, though not identification with, the phenomena conceptualized by Foucault. Discourses are symbolic sets that embody clear references to social system relationships, whether defined in terms of power, solidarity, or other organizational forms (cf. Sewell 1980; Hunt 1984).[12] As social languages, they relate binary symbolic associations with social forms. In doing so, they provide a vocabulary for members to speak graphically about a society's highest values, its relevant groups, its boundaries vis-à-vis conflict, creativity, and internal dissent. Discourse socializes semiotic codes and emerges as a series of narratives (Ricoeur 1984) – myths that specify and stereotype a society's founding and founders (Eliade 1959, Bellah 1970a), its critical events (Alexander 1988b), and utopian aspirations (Smith 1950).

In their theories of premodern cultures, classical sociologists constructed powerful models of how this social construction of semiotic codes can proceed. They did so in terms of their theories of religion. Thus, drawing from primitive totemism, Durkheim (1964) argued that every religion organizes social things into both binary relations and deeply felt antitheses between sacred and profane. Because sacred objects have to be protected, the "society" maintains a distance between them and other objects, either routine or profane. Actors not only try to protect themselves from coming into contact with polluted (Douglas 1966) or profane (Caillois 1959) objects, but also seek a real, if mediated, contact with the sacred. This is one primary function of ritual behavior (Turner 1969; cf. Alexander 1988c).

While Weber's better-known theory of religion overlaps with Durkheim's, it is historically and comparatively specific. Given the emergence of a more formal and rationalized religion, the goal of believers becomes salvation from worldly suffering (Weber 1946a). Salvation creates the problem of theodicy, "from what" and "for what" one will be saved. Theodicy involves the image of God. If the gods or God is immanent, worshipers seek salvation through an internal experience of mystical contact. If God is transcendent, salvation is achieved more ascetically, by correctly divining God's will and following his commands. Each of these mandates can be pursued, moreover, in either a this-worldly or an otherworldly direction.

While Durkheim and Weber generally limited the application of these cultural theories to premodern religious life, it is possible to extend them to secular phenomena. This possibility is clarified when we define religions as types of semiotic systems, as discourses that reveal how the psychological and social structuring of culture proceeds.[13]

In this section I have briefly sketched a model for examining the cultural dimension of social life. I hope merely that this discussion provides an introduction to what follows. Before examining the construction of the computer as a cultural object in the postwar world, however, I look at a range of earlier sociological treatments of technology to sense the difficulties that a more culturally sensitive approach must overcome.

## Sociological Accounts of Technology: The Dead Hand of the Social System

Considered in its social system reference, technology is a thing that can be touched, observed, interacted with, and calculated in an objectively rational way. Analytically, however, technology is also part of the cultural system. It is a sign, both a signifier and a signified, in relation to which actors cannot entirely separate their subjective states of mind. Social scientists have not usually considered technology in this more subjective way. Indeed, they have not typically considered it as a cultural object at all. It has appeared as the material variable par excellence, not as a point of sacrality, but as the most routine of the routine, not a sign, but an antisign, the essence of a modernity that has undermined the very possibility for cultural understanding itself.

In the postmodern era, Marx has become infamous for his effusive praise in *The Communist Manifesto* of technology as the embodiment of scientific rationality. Marx believed that modern industrial technique, as the harbinger of progress, was breaking down the barriers of primitive and magical thought. Stripped of its capitalist integument, Marx predicted, advanced technology would be the mainspring of industrial communism, which he defined as the administration of *things* rather than *people*.[14] Despite the central role he gives to technology, for Marx it is not a form of knowledge, even of the most rational sort. It is a material variable, a "force of production" (Marx 1962). As an element of the base, technology is something actors relate to mechanistically. It is produced because the laws of the capitalist economy force factory owners to lower their costs. The effects of this incorporation are equally objective. As technology replaces human labor, the organic composition of capital changes and the rate of profit falls; barring mitigating factors, this falling rate causes the collapse of the capitalist system.

While neo-Marxism has revised the determining relationship Marx posits between economy and technology, it continues to accept Marx's view of technology as a purely material fact. In Rueschemeyer's recent work on the relation between power and the division of labor, for example, neither general symbolic patterns nor the internal trajectory of rational knowledge are conceived of as affecting technological growth. "It is the inexorability of interest and power constellations," Rueschemeyer (1986: 117–118) argues, "which shape even fundamental research and which determine translations of knowledge into new products and new ways of production." We would expect modern functionalism to view technology very differently, but this is true in an only limited sense. Of course, Parsons (1967) criticized Marx for putting technology into the base; functionalists have always been aware that technology belongs in a more intermediate position in the social system. They have, however, never looked at it as anything other than the product of rational knowledge, and they have often conceived of its efficient causes and specific effects in material terms.

In *Science, Technology, and Society in Seventeenth-Century England*, Merton emphasizes the role that puritanism played in inspiring scientific inventions. Within the context of this inventive climate, however, the immediate cause of technology was economic benefit. The "relation between a problem raised by economic development and technologic endeavor is clear-cut and definite," Merton argues (1970: 144), suggesting that "importance in the realm of technology is often concretely allied with economic estimations." It was the "vigorous economic development" of the time that led to effective inventions, because it "posed the most imperative problems for solution" (146). In Smelser's (1959) later account of the industrial revolution, the perspective is exactly the same. Methodist values form a background input to technological innovation, but they are not involved in the creation or the effects of technology itself: Innovation is problem driven, not culture driven, and the immediate cause is economic demand. The effect of technology is also concrete and material. By resolving strain at the social system level, innovation allows collective behavior to leave the level of generalized behavior – wish fulfillment, fantasy, utopian aspirations – and return to the more mundane and rational attitudes of the everyday (Smelser 1959: 21–50).

Parsons himself is more sensitive to the subjective environment of technology. While acknowledging that it is "a product of productive processes," he insists (1960: 135) that it depends ultimately on cultural resources. In a characteristic move, he turns his discussion of technology from economic issues to a focus on the origins of "usable knowledge." He describes the latter as "produced by two processes which, though economic factors play a part, are clearly predominantly noneconomic, namely research and education" (135). In other words, while Parsons recognizes that technology is, in the most important sense, a product of subjective knowledge rather than material force, this recognition leads him, not to the analysis of symbolic processes, but to the study of institutional processes, namely research and education. When Parsons and Platt explore these processes in *The American University* (1973), they take the input from culture – the "rationality value" – as a given, focusing instead on how this value becomes institutionalized in the social system.

Critical theory, drawing from Weber's rationalization theme, differs from orthodox Marxism in its attention to the relation between technology and consciousness. But whereas Weber (for example, 1946b) viewed the machine as the objectification of discipline, calculation, and rational organization, critical theorists reverse the causal relation, asserting that it is technology that creates rationalized culture by virtue of its brute physical and economic power. "If we follow the path taken by labour in its development from handicraft [to] manufacture to machine industry," Lukács writes (1971: 88), "we can see a continuous trend toward greater rationalization [as] the process of labour is progressively broken down into abstract, rational, specialized operations." This technologically driven rationalization eventually spreads to all social spheres, leading to the objectification of society and the "reified mind" (93). Lukacs insists that he is concerned "with the *principle* at work here" (88, original italics), but the principle is the result of technology conceived as a material force.

This shift toward the pivotal ideological role of technology, without giving up its materialist conceptualization or its economic cause, culminates in Marcuse's later work. To explain the reasons for "one-dimensional society," Marcuse actually focuses more on technological production per se than on its capitalist form. Again, that technology is a purely instrumental, rational phenomenon Marcuse takes completely for granted. Its "sweeping rationality," Marcuse writes (1963: xiii), "propels efficiency and growth." The problem, once again, is that this "technical progress [is] extended to a whole system of domination and coordination" (xii). When it is, it institutionalizes throughout the society a purely formal and abstract norm of rationality. This technological "culture" suppresses any ability to imagine social alternatives. As Marcuse states (xvi), "technological rationality has become political rationality."

New class and postindustrial theories make this critical theory more nuanced and sophisticated, but they do not overcome its fatal anticultural flaw. Gouldner accepts the notion that scientists, engineers, and government planners have a rational worldview because of the technical nature of their work. Technocratic competence depends on higher education, and the expansion of higher education depends in the last analysis on production driven by technology. Indeed, Gouldner finds no fault with technocratic competence in and of itself; he takes it as a paradigm of universalism, criticism, and rationality. When he attacks the technocrats' false consciousness, he does so because they extend this rationality beyond their sphere of technical competence: "The new ideology holds [that] the *society*'s problems are solvable on a technological basis, with the use of educationally acquired technical competence" (1979: 24, italics added). By pretending to understand society at large, the new class can provide a patina of rationality for the entire society. Gouldner also emphasizes, of course, that this very expansion of technical rationality can create a new kind of class conflict and a "rational" source of social change. This notion, of course, is simply the old contradiction between (technological) forces and relations of production, dressed in postindustrial garb. When Szelenyi and Martin (1987) criticize Gouldner's theory as economistic, they have touched its theoretical core.

Using similar theoretical distinctions, conservative theorists have reached different ideological conclusions. In his postindustrial theory, Bell (1976) also emphasizes the growing cultural rationality of modern societies, a cultural pattern he, too, ties directly to technological and productive demands. In order to produce and maintain the advanced technologies that are at the basis of postindustrial economic and political institutions, scientific values and scientific education have become central to modern life. In the political and economic spheres of modern societies, therefore, sober, rational, and instrumental culture is the rule. It is only in reaction against this technological sphere that there develop, according to Bell (1976), irrational, postmodern values, which create the cultural contradictions of capitalist society. Here the contradiction between (technological) forces and relations is dressed in other garb. Because Ellul, the other, more conservative, theorist of "technological society," wrote before the 1960s, he views the social effects of technology as more thoroughly instrumental and rational than does Bell. Propelled by "the search for greater efficiency" (Ellul 1964: 19), technique "clarifies, arranges, and rationalizes" (5). It exists in "the domain of the abstract" (5) and has no relation to cultural values or to the real needs of human life.

It is fitting to close this section with Habermas, for the distinction between the world of technique (variously defined as work, organization, or system) and the world of humanity (communication, norms, or lifeworld) has marked a fateful contrast throughout his work. Habermas (1968a: 57) defines technology in what is by now a familiar way. He believes it to be the "scientifically rationalized control of objectified processes" and contrasts it with phenomena that are related to "the practical question of how men can and want to live." With the increasing centrality of technology, the meaningful organization of the world is displaced by purposive-rational organization. "To the extent that technology and science permeate social institutions and thus transform them," Habermas (1968b: 81) insists, "old legitimations are destroyed."

These old legitimations were based on tradition, "the older mythic, religious, and metaphysical worldviews" that addressed "the central questions of men's collective existence [for example] justice and freedom, violence and oppression, happiness and gratification . . . love and hate, salvation and damnation

(96)." After technology has done its work, however, these questions can no longer be asked: "The culturally defined self-understanding of a social lifeworld is replaced by the self-reification of men under categories of purposive-rational action and adaptive behavior" (105–6). There has ensued a "horizontal extension of subsystems of purposive-rational action," such that "traditional structures are increasingly subordinated to conditions of instrumental or strategic rationality" (98). In this particular sense, Habermas (111) argues, the ideology of technology has displaced all previous ideologies. Because it is so stubbornly rationalistic, this new ideology does not exhibit "the opaque force of a delusion" or a "wish-fulfilling fantasy," nor is it "based in the same way [as earlier ideologies] on the causality of dissociated symbols and unconscious motives." This ideology, Habermas believes, has abandoned any attempt to "express a projection of the 'good life.'"

In the discussion that follows, I will demonstrate that these suppositions about technological consciousness are false. Only because Habermas has accepted the possibility of a radical historicization of consciousness can he believe them to be true. My own discussion begins from quite the opposite understanding. It is impossible for a society to be dominated by technical rationality because the mental structures of humankind cannot be radically historicized; in crucial respects, they are unchanging. Human beings continue to experience the need to invest the world with metaphysical meaning and to experience solidarity with objects outside the self. Certainly, the ability to calculate objectively and impersonally is perhaps the clearest demarcation of modernity. But this remains one institutionalized complex (Parsons 1951) of motives, actions, and meanings among many others. Individuals can exercise scientifically rational orientations in certain situations, but even in these instances their actions are not scientifically rational as such. Objectivity is a cultural norm, a system of social sanctions and rewards, a motivational impulse of the personality. It remains nested, however, within deeply irrational systems of psychological defense and cultural systems of an enduringly primordial kind.

This is not to deny that technological production has become more central with the advent of postindustrial society. There has been a quickening in the substitution of information for physical energy, which Marx described as a shift in the organic composition of capital, with dramatic consequences. The shift from manual to mental labor has transformed the class structure and the typical strains of capitalist and socialist societies. The increased capacity for storing information has strengthened the control of bureaucracy over the information that it constantly needs. But the sociological approaches to technology, which we have examined in this section, extend much further than such empirical observations. The stronger version of Marxist and critical theory describes a technologically obsessed society whose consciousness is so narrowed that the meaningful concerns of traditional life are no longer possible. The weaker versions of functionalist and postindustrial theory describe technology as a variable that has a merely material status and orientations to technology as cognitively rational and routine. From my point of view, however, neither of these positions is correct. The ideas that inform even modern society are not cognitive repositories of verified facts; they are symbols that continue to be shaped by deep emotional impulses and molded by meaningful constraints.

## Technological Discourse and Salvation

We must learn to see technology as a discourse, as a sign system that is subject to semiotic constraints and responsive to social and psychological demands. The first step to this alternative conception of modern technology is to reconceptualize its introduction so that it is open to metaphysical terms. Ironically, perhaps, Weber himself provided the best indication of how this can be done.

Weber argued that those who created modern industrial society did so in order to pursue salvation. The Puritan capitalists practiced what Weber (1958) called *this-worldly asceticism*. Through hard work and self-denial they produced wealth as proof that God had predestined them to be saved. Weber (1963) demonstrated, indeed, that salvation has been a central concern of humankind for millennia. Whether it be heaven or nirvana, the great religions have promised human beings an escape from toil and suffering and a release from earthly constraints – only if humans conceived of the world in certain terms and strove to act in certain ways. In order to historicize this conception of salvation and to allow comparative explanation of it, Weber developed the typology of this-worldly versus otherworldly paths to salvation, which he interwove with the distinction between ascetic and mystical. The disciplined, self-denying, and impersonal action upon which modernization depended, Weber argued, could be achieved only by acting in a this-worldly, ascetic way. Compared to Buddhist or Hindu holy men, the Puritan saints focused their attention much more completely on this world. Rather than allowing themselves the direct experience of God and striving to become vessels of his spirit, they believed that they would be saved by becoming practical instruments for carrying out his will. This-worldly salvation was the cultural precursor for the impersonal rationality and objectivism that, in Weber's view (1958: 181–183), eventually dominated the world.

While Weber's religious theory is of fundamental importance, it has two substantial weaknesses. First, Weber conceived the modern style of salvation in a caricatured way. It has never been as one-sidedly ascetic as he suggests. This-worldly activity is permeated by desires to escape from the world, just as the ascetic self-denial of grace is punctuated by episodes of mystical intimacy. In an anomalous strain in his writing about modernity (Alexander 1986), Weber acknowledged that industrial society is shot through with "flights from the world," in which category he included things such as the surrender by moderns to religious belief or ideological fanaticism and the escape provided by eroticism or aestheticism. Although Weber condemned these flights as irresponsible, however, he was never able to incorporate them into his sociology of modern life. They represented a force with which his historicist and overly ideal-typical theory could not contend.

In truth, modern attempts to pursue salvation in purely ascetic ways have always short-circuited, not only in overtly escapist forms but also in the everyday world itself. We would never know from Weber's account, for example, that the Puritans conceived of their relationship to God in terms of the intimacies of holy matrimony (Morgan 1958); nor would we be aware that outbursts of mystical "antinomianism" were a constant, recurring danger in Puritan life. The post-Puritan tradition of evangelical Protestantism, which developed in Germany, England, and the United States in the late eighteenth and early nineteenth centuries, was distinguished by its significant opening to mystical experience. One of its cultural offshoots, the modern ideology of romantic love (Lewis 1983), reflected the continuing demand for immediate, transformative salvation in the very heart of the industrial age.

This last example points to the second major problem in Weber's religious theory, its historicism. Weber believed that a concern with salvation could permeate and organize worldly experience only so long as scientific understanding had not undermined the possibility of accepting an extramundane, divine telos for progress on earth. As I suggested previously, this mistaken effort to rationalize contemporary discourse can be corrected by incorporating the more structural understandings of Durkheim's religious sociology. Durkheim believed that human beings continue to divide the world into sacred and profane and that even modern men and women need to experience mystical centers directly through ritual encounters with the sacred. In the modern context, then, Weber's salvation theory can be elaborated and sustained only by turning to Durkheim. The fit can be made even tighter if we make the alteration in Durkheim's theory suggested by Caillois (1959), who argued that alongside sacred and profane there was a third term, *routine*. Whereas routine life does not partake of ritual experience, sacred and profane experiences are both highly charged. Whereas the sacred provides an image of the good with which social actors seek community and strive to protect, the profane defines an image of evil from which human beings must be saved. This conception allows us to be more true to Weber's understanding of theodicy, even when we shift it onto the modern state. Secular salvation "religions" provide escape not only from earthly suffering in general but also more specifically from evil. Every salvation religion has conceived not only God and death, in other words, but also the devil.

It is in terms of these reconstructed arenas for symbolic discourse that our examination of the introduction of technology will proceed.

## The Sacred and Profane Information Machine

Expectations for salvation were inseparable from the technological innovations of industrial capitalism. Major inventions like the steam engine, railroad, telegraph, and telephone (Pool 1983) were hailed by elites and masses as vehicles for secular transcendence. Their speed and power, it was widely proclaimed, would undermine the earthly constraints of time, space, and scarcity. In their early halcyon days, they became vessels for experiencing ecstatic release, instruments for bringing the glories of heaven down to earth. The technicians and engineers who understood this new technology were elevated to the status of worldly priests. In this technological discourse, however, the machine has been not only God but also the devil. In the early nineteenth century, Luddites lashed out at spinning machines as if they were the idols that the Hebrew fathers had condemned. William Blake decried "dark Satanic mills." Mary Shelley wrote *Frankenstein, or, the Modern Prometheus*, about the terrifying results of Victor Frankenstein's effort to build the world's most "gigantic" machine. The Gothic genre presented a revolt against the Age of Reason and insisted that dark forces were still brewing, forces that were often embodied by the engine of technology itself. It was, ironically, from such forces that the modern age had to be saved. There is a direct line from that gothic revival to Steven Spielberg's wildly popular movie, *Star Wars* (Pynchon 1984). Today's science fiction mixes technology with medieval Gothic themes, pits evil against good, and promises salvation from space, from time, and even from mortality itself.

The computer is the newest and certainly one of the most potent technological innovations of the modern age, but its symbolization has been much the same. The culture structure of technological discourse has been firmly set. In theoretical terms, the introduction of the computer into Western society resembles the much more tumultuous entrance of Captain Cook into the Sandwich Islands: it was an event "given significance and effect by the system in place" (Sahlins 1981: 21).[15]

While there were certainly "routine" assessments of the computer from 1944 to 1975 – assessments that talked about it in rational, scientific, and "realistic" tones – they paled in comparison to the transcendental and mythical discourse that was filled with wish-fulfilling rhetoric of salvation and damnation. In a *Time* magazine report on the first encounter between computer and public in 1944, the machine was treated as a sacred and mysterious object. What was "unveiled" was a "bewildering 50-foot panel of knobs, wires, counters, gears and switches." The connection to higher, even cosmic, forces immediately suggested itself. *Time* described it as having been unveiled "in the presence of high officers in the Navy" and promised its readers that the new machine would solve problems "on earth as well as those posed by the celestial universe" (T8/44). This sacred status was elaborated in the years that followed. To be sacred, an object must be sharply separated from contact with the routine world. Popular literature continually recounted the distance that separated the computer from the lay public and the mystery attendant on this. In another report on the 1944 unveiling, for example, *Popular Science*, a leading lay technology magazine, described the first computer as an electrical brain whirring "behind its polished panels" secluded in "an air-conditioned basement" (PS10/44). Twenty years later the image had not changed. In 1965, a new and far more powerful computer was conceptualized in the same way, as an "isolated marvel" working in "the air-conditioned seclusion of the company's data-programming room." In unmistakable terms, *Time* elaborated this discourse of the sacred technology.

> Arranged row upon row in air-conditioned rooms, waited upon by crisp young white-shirted men who move softly among them like priests serving in a shrine, the computers go about their work quietly and, for the most part, unseen from the public (T4/65).

Objects are isolated because they are thought to possess mysterious power. The connection between computer and established centers of charismatic power is repeated constantly in the popular literature. Occasionally, an analogy is made between the computer and sacred things on earth. Reporting on the unveiling of a new and more sophisticated computer in 1949, *Newsweek* called it "the real hero" of the occasion and described it, like royalty, as "holding court in the computer lab upstairs" (11/49). Often, however, more direct references to the computer's cosmic powers and even to its extrahuman status were made. In an article about the first computer, *Popular Science* reported that "everybody's notion of the universe and everything in it will be upset by the columns of figures this monster will type out" (PS10/44). Fifteen years later, a famous technical expert asserted in a widely circulated feature magazine that "forces will be set in motion whose ultimate effects for good and evil are incalculable" (RD3/60).

As the machine became more sophisticated, and more awesome, references to godly powers were openly made. The new computers "render unto Caesar by sending out the monthly bills and . . . unto God by counting the ballots of the world's Catholic bishops" (T4/65). A joke circulated to the effect that a scientist tried to stump his computer with the question: Is there a God? "The computer was silent for a moment. Then it answered: 'Now there is'" (N1/66). After describing the computer in superhuman terms – "infallible in memory, incredibly swift in math [and] utterly impartial in judgment" – a mass weekly made the obvious deduction: "This transistorized prophet can help the church adapt to modern spiritual needs" (T3/68). A leader of one national church described the Bible as a "distillation of human experience" and asserted that computers are capable of correlating an even greater range "of experience about how people ought to behave." The conclusion that was drawn underscored the deeply established connection between the computer and cosmic power: "When we want to consult the deity, we go to the computer because it's the closest thing to God to come along" (T3/68).

If an object is sacred and sealed off from the profane world, gaining access to its powers becomes a problem in itself. Priests emerge as intermediaries between divinity and laity. As one leading expert suggested, while there were many who appreciated the computer, "only specialists yet realize how these elements will all be combined and [the] far-reaching social, economic, and political implications" (RD5/60). Typically, erroneous predictions about the computer were usually attributed to "nonspecialists" (BW3/65). To possess knowledge of computing, it was emphasized time and again, requires incredible training and seclusion. Difficult new procedures must be developed. To learn how to operate a new computer introduced in 1949, specialists "spent months literally studying day and night" (N8/49). The number of people capable of undergoing such rigorous training was highly restricted. The forging of "links between human society and the robot brain" (N9/49) called for "a new race of scientists." The "new breed of specialists [which] has grown up to tend the machines," *Time* wrote sixteen years later, "have formed themselves into a solemn priesthood of the computer, purposely separated from ordinary laymen [and] speak[ing] an esoteric language that some suspect is just their way of mystifying outsiders" (T4/65). The article predicted. "There will be a small, almost separate society of people in rapport with the advanced computer. They will have established a relationship with their machines that cannot be shared with the average man. Those with talent for the work will have to develop it from childhood and will be trained as intensively as the classical ballerina." Is it surprising that, reporting on computer news ten years later, *Time* (1/74) decided its readers would be interested in learning that among this esoteric group of programmers there had emerged a new and wildly popular computer game called "the game of life"? The identification of the computer with God and of computer operators with sacred intermediaries signifies culture structures that had not changed in forty years.

The contact with the cosmic computer that these technological priests provided would, then, certainly transform earthly life. Like the revolutionary technologies that preceded it, however, the computer embodied within itself both superhuman evil and superhuman good. As Lévi-Strauss (1963) emphasized, it is through naming that the cultural codes defining an object are first constructed. In the years immediately following the introduction of the computer, efforts to name this new thinking machine were intense, and they followed the binary pattern that Durkheim and Lévi-Strauss described. The result was a "similitude of signifiers," an amplified series of sacred and profane associations that created for technological discourse a thick semantic field. One series revealed dreadful proportions and dire implications. The computer was called a "colossal gadget" (T8/44, N8/49), a "figure factory" (PS10/44), a "mountain of machinery" (PS10/44), a "monster" (PS10/44, SEP2/50), a "mathematical dreadnought" (PS10/44), a "portentous contrivance" (PS10/44), a "giant" (N8/49), a "math robot" (N8/49), a "wonder-working robot" (SEP2/50), the "Maniac" (SEP2/50), and the "Frankenstein-monster" (SEP2/50). In announcing a new and bigger computer in 1949, *Time* (9/49) hailed the "great machines that eat their way through oceans of figures like whale grazing on plankton" and described them as roaring like "a hive of mechanical insects."

In direct opposition to this profane realm, journalists and technicians also named the computer and its parts through analogies to the presumptively innocent and assuredly sacred human being. It was called a "super-brain" (PS10/44) and a "giant brain" (N8/49). Attached to an audio instrument, it was described as "a brain child with a temporary voice" and as "the only mechanical brain with a soft heart" (N10/49). Its "physiology" (SEP2/50) became a topic of debate. Computers were given an "inner memory" (T9/49), "eyes," a "nervous system" (SEP2/50), a "spinning heart" (T2/51), and a "female temperament" (SEP2/50) in addition to the brain with which they were already endowed. It was announced that they were to have "descendants" (N4/50), and in later years "families" and "generations" (T4/65) emerged. Finally, there were the developmental phrases. "Just out of its teens," *Time* announced (T4/65), the computer was about to enter a "formidable adulthood." It might do so, however, in a neurotic way, for its designers had "made a pampered and all but adored child" out of him (or her).[16]

The period of compulsive naming quickly abated, but the awesome forces for good and evil that the names symbolized have been locked in deadly combat to this day. Salvation rhetoric overcomes this dualism in one direction, apocalyptic rhetoric in another. Both moves can be seen in structural terms as overcoming binary opposition by providing a third term. But more profound emotional and metaphysical issues are also at stake. Computer discourse was eschatological because the computer was seen as involving matters of life and death.

At first, salvation was defined in narrowly mathematical terms. The new computer would "solve in a flash" (T9/49) problems that had "baffled men for years" (PS10/44). By 1950, salvation had already become much more broadly defined. "Come the Revolution!" read the headline to a story about these new predictions (T11/50). A broad and visionary ideal of progress was laid out: "Thinking machines will bring a healthier, happier civilization than any known heretofore" (SEP2/50). People would now be able to "solve their problems the painless electronic way" (N7/54). Airplanes, for example, would be able to reach their destinations "without one bit of help from the pilot" (PS1/55).

By 1960, public discourse about the computer had become truly millennial. "A new age in human relations has opened," a reigning expert announced (RD3/60). Like all eschatological rhetoric, the timing of this promised salvation is imprecise. It has not yet occurred, but it has already begun. It is coming in five years or ten, its effects will be felt soon, the transformation is imminent. Whatever the timing, the end result is certain. "There will be a social effect of unbelievable proportions" (RD3/60). "By surmounting the last great barrier of distance," the computer's effect on the natural world will be just as great (RD3/60). Most human labor will be eliminated, and people will finally be set "free to undertake completely new tasks, most of them directed toward perfecting ourselves, creating beauty, and understanding one another" (Mc5/65).[17]

The convictions were confirmed in still more sweeping tones in the late 1960s and early 1970s. The new computers had such "awesome power" (RD5/71) that, as God was recorded in the book of Genesis, they would bring "order out of chaos" (BW7/71). That "the computer age is dawning" is certain. One sign of this millennium will be that "the common way of thinking in terms of cause and effect [will be] replaced by a new awareness" (RD5/71). That this was the stuff of which "dreams are made" (USN6/67) cannot be denied. Computers would transform all natural forces. They would cure diseases and guarantee long life. They would allow everyone to know everything at all times. They would allow all students to learn easily and the best to learn perfectly. They would produce a world community and end war. They would overturn stratification and allow equality to reign. They would make government responsible and efficient, business productive and profitable, work creative, and leisure endlessly satisfying.

As for apocalypse, there was also much to say. The machine has always embodied not only the transcendental hopes but also the fear and loathing generated by industrial society. *Time* once articulated this deep ambiguity in a truly Gothic way. Viewed from the front, computers exhibit a "clean, serene dignity." This is deceptive, however, for "behind there hides a nightmare of pulsing, twitching, flashing complexity" (9/49).

Whereas contact with the sacred side of the computer is the vehicle for salvation, the profane side threatens destruction. It is something from which human beings must be saved. First, the computer creates the fear of degradation. "People are scared" (N8/68) because the computer has the power to "blot or diminish man" (RD3/60). People feel "rage and helpless frustration" (N9/69). The computer degrades because it objectifies; this is the second great fear. It will "lead to mechanical men who replace humans" (T11/50). Students will be "treated as impersonal machines" (RD1/71). Computers are inseparable from "the image of slavery" (USN11/67). It is because they are seen as objectifying human beings that computers present a concrete danger. In 1975, one popular author described his personal computer as a "humming thing poised to rip me apart" (RD11/75). More typically the danger is not mutilation but manipulation. With computers "markets can be scientifically rigged. . . with an efficiency that would make dictators blush" (SEP2/50). Their intelligence can turn them into "instruments for massive subversion" (RD3/60). They could "lead us to that ultimate horror – chains of plastic tape" (N8/66).

Finally there is the cataclysm, the final judgment on earthly technological folly that has been predicted from 1944 until the present day. Computers are "Frankenstein (monsters) which can . . . wreck the very foundations of our society" (T11/50). They can lead to "disorders [that may] pass beyond control" (RD4/60). There is a "storm brewing" (BW1/68). There are "nightmarish stories" about the "light that failed" (BW7/71). "Incapable of making allowances for error," the "Christian notion of redemption is incomprehensible to the computer" (N8/66). The computer has become the Antichrist.

I have taken the computer story to 1975. This was the eve of the "personal computer," the very name of which demonstrates how the battle between human and antihuman continued to fuel the discourse that surrounded the computer's birth. In the decade of discussion that followed, utopian and antiutopian themes remained prominent (for example, Turkle 1984: 165–196). Disappointment and "realism," however, also became more frequently expressed. In the present day, computer news has passed from the cover of *Time* to advertisements in the sports pages of daily newspapers. This is routinization. We may, indeed, be watching this latest episode in the history of technological discourse pass into history.

## Conclusion

Social scientists have looked at the computer through the framework of their rationalizing discourse on modernity. For Ellul (1964: 89), it represented a phase of "technical progress" that "seems limitless" because it "consists primarily in the efficient systematization of society and the conquest of the human being." In the analysis of Lyotard, who proposes a postmodern theory, the same kind of extravagant modernizing claims are made. "It is common knowledge," according to Lyotard (1984: 4), "that the miniaturization and commercialization of machines is already changing the way in which learning is acquired, classified, made available, and exploited." With the advent of computerization, learning that cannot be "translated into quantities of information" will be abandoned. In contrast to the opacity of traditional culture, computerization produces "the ideology of communicational 'transparency'" (5), which signals the decline of the "grand narrative" and will lead to a crisis of legitimation (66–67).

I have tried to refute such rationalistic theorizing, first by developing a framework for cultural sociology and second by applying it to the technological domain. In theoretical terms, I have shown that technology is never in the social system alone. It is also a sign and possesses an internal subjective referent. Technology, in other words, is an element in the culture and the personality systems as well; it is both meaningful and motivated. In my examination of the popular literature about the computer, I have shown that this ideology is rarely factual, rational, or abstract. It is concrete, imagistic, utopian, and satanic – a discourse that is filled, indeed, with the grand narratives of life.

Let us return, in conclusion, to the sociological understandings of technology I have recounted above. Far from being empirical accounts based on objective observations and interpretations, they represent simply another version of technocratic discourse itself. The apocalyptic strain of that discourse fears degradation, objectification, slavery, and manipulation. Has not critical theory merely translated this evaluation into the empirical language of social science? The same goes for those sociological analyses that take a more benign form: they provide social scientific translations of the discourse about salvation.[18]

At stake is more than the accuracy or the distortion of social scientific statements. That the rationalization hypothesis is wrong does not make technology a benign force. The great danger that technology poses to modern life is neither the flattening out of human consciousness nor its enslavement to economic or political reality. To the contrary, it is because technology is lodged in the unreal fantasies of salvation and apocalypse that the dangers are real.

For Freud, psychoanalysis was a rational theory of the irrational, even while it did not promise an ultimate escape from unconscious life. Psychoanalysis aimed to provide a distance from irrationality, if not the high ground of conscious rationality itself. Cultural sociology can provide a similar distance and some of the same cure. Only by understanding the omnipresent shaping of technological consciousness by discourse can we hope to gain control over technology in its material form. To do so, we must gain some distance from the visions of salvation and apocalypse in which technology is so deeply embedded.[19]

## Notes

1. In this respect, I could not disagree more with Rochberg-Halton's assertion that it is the semiotic and Parsonian position that leads to reification and that the pragmatic one is their antidote. It is Rochberg-Halton's commitment to Piercean semiotics that underlines his naturalism. Saussurian semiotics, by contrast, make it possible to see naturalism's fatal weaknesses. Where Saussure and Parsons emphasize the constructed meaning of objects, Peirce (1985) is obsessed with the relative "realness" of signs, in the sense of both their scientific truthfulness and their tactile representatives. On the one hand, this emphasis on the motivated, rather than the arbitrary, relation of signifier and signified (see the discussion of Saussure below) is an advantage, as demonstrated by Peirce's extremely interesting theorizing about icons and indexes. At the same rime, Peirce's emphasis on the growing truthfulness of signs – *symbols* in his vocabulary – and their relationship to experience can cause serious problems, allowing Peircean analysts to emphasize the pragmatics of culture in place of the semiotics.

2. Mann's (1985) work attempts to blend micro and macro sides of the post-Parsonian response, even while it begins to move beyond them. While I believe the historical aspects of his account of the Western world are not only highly original but also largely correct, the work suffers from an anticultural theoretical bias despite the significant empirical openings it makes to religion. Mann insists that one can and should study the infrastructures of ideas, the concrete networks and communications systems through which ideas are expressed rather than the ideas themselves. His premise is that ideas are not in themselves legitimate social causes. Yet one of the major sociological explanations for these infrastructures must always be the influence of the ideas themselves.

3. I have criticized Parsons's repeated effort to apportion different variables to different disciplines in Alexander 1983: 272–276. In that discussion, however, I related this

tendency to Parsons's idealism, for he apportioned to sociology the specialization in normative rather than material forces (in his later work, it was the study of the integrative subsystem of general action, which specializes in affect). Here I criticize this disciplinary apportionment because it allowed Parsons to escape from a true confrontation with symbolic codes. Although Parsons provided the baseline for any contemporary effort to create a multidimensional cultural sociology, he blocked its development by insisting that sociology focus only on the institutionalized segment of culture, in his terms not the *cultural system*, but the *latency*, or *pattern maintenance*, *subsystem* of the social system. Only these specialized elements are called *values* in Parsons's theory, as Bellah (1970b) makes particularly clear in some of his work. Yet, as I have argued elsewhere (1988a, 1990), values are only one of several areas of focus for a true cultural sociology.

4. This concrete approach to culture as high culture has been subject to criticism by Greenfield (1987) in a recent round of discussion about approaches to cultural sociology in the newsletter of the Culture Section of the American Sociological Association.

5. Such a treatment is manifest, for example, in much of Wuthnow's (1987) recent work. Although Wuthnow sets out to reinsert culture into sociology, and provides some important illustrations of how to do so, he throws a roadblock in his own path by insisting that cultural analysis should take an "objective" approach that avoids the problem of meaning. This avoidance is epistemologically impossible, for any effort to understand a social element, even from the outside, is based upon assumptions about its subjective orientation or inner patterns, that is, its meaning (see Alexander 1987: 281–301). An analyst can no more avoid the meaning problem than an actor can. Indeed, in the methodologically ideal case, the same organized set provides a reference point for both.

The principle of avoiding meaning allows Wuthnow a rationale for not entering into the "thicket of symbolism." With some important exceptions (1987: 66–96), this has the effect of undermining the authenticity of his references to cultural patterns, which he often reduces to such vague and general themes as *individualism, socialism,* and *rationality* (for example, 1987: 187–214), that is, he glosses over meaningful sets rather than attempts to understand them. Not surprisingly, as his book progresses, Wuthnow's theorizing of culture as variable gives increasing, and eventually almost exclusive, attention to the institutional and ecological forces in culture's environment. For an insightful discussion of the limitations of what they call Wuthnow's "positive structuralism," see Rambo and Chan 1990.

6. By orthodox interactionists, I am referring to those, such as Blumer who manifest the individualist current (see Alexander 1987: 215–237). An attractive counterexample within the interactionist tradition is found in Fine's (1987) interpretation of the culture of little league baseball players in the United States. Motivated by interactionist theory, Fine develops the concept of *idioculture* to describe the specific and unique belief set developed within each team; yet this individualizing variant is placed deftly within a more general cultural framework that Fine interprets and finds to be widely shared.

7. Swidler takes quite the opposite position, criticizing recent movements toward thicker cultural analysis as mere efforts "to *describe* the features of cultural products and experiences" (italics added) in contrast to efforts at "*cultural explanation*," which she prefers (Swidler 1986: 273, original italics). By searching for "effects" and "causes" and by offering "an image of culture as a 'tool kit' of symbols," Swidler moves from culture

to the levels of social system and action. Her essay actually reinforces the very tendencies that have prevented social science from taking culture seriously. Kane's (1991) theoretical essay is the most systematic and successful effort to argue that the analytic autonomy of culture is essential for any realistic assessment of its relation to more structural variables to be attained.

8. Indeed, rather than investigate the texture of new meaning configurations, most contemporary Weberians take over the ideal-typical patterns of modernity that Weber identified at the beginning of this century, for example, value rationality, ethic of responsibility, and so on.

9. Bellah emphasized this distinction between symbols and values in his early work on Japan (Bellah 1970b). As he moved toward symbolic realism and his civil religion concept, this distinction became blurred for he became less interested in institutionalized systems and more interested in symbolic references in and of themselves. In Bellah's most recent work, the internal analysis of meaning systems has received less attention.

10. Eisenstadt is one of the few contemporary sociologists of culture who continues this early Parsonian focus on institutionalization. By incorporating elements of Shils's more cultural program and by expanding the Weberian elements that are incorporated into institutionalization theory, however, Eisenstadt has significantly extended the Parsonian cultural program (see Alexander and Colomy 1985). For a critique by Eisenstadt of contemporary macro-sociological analyses on the grounds they take an *ontological* approach to culture rather than an analytical one – a critique parallel to my discussion of the problems with the culture-as-variable approach – see Eisenstadt 1987.

11. For an extremely interesting study of contemporary society that makes use of Eco's conception of an interwoven web of symbols, see Edles's (1990) study of Spanish political culture in the transition to democracy after Franco's death.

12. Rather than a relation between symbolic and social systems, Foucault would call this the manner in which discourse is shaped by discursive relations.

> Discursive relations are, in a sense, at the limit of discourse: they offer it objects of which it can speak, or rather . . . they determine the group of relations that discourse must establish in order to speak of this or that object, in order to deal with them, name them, analyze them, classify them, explain them, etc. These relations characterize . . . rules that are immanent in a practice, and define it in its specificity (1972: 47).

This last sentence shows the difficulty in Foucault's approach. After defining discursive relations as something that offers objects to discourse, he collapses the distinction between these relations and discursive patterns by calling relations *rules*, on the one hand, and arguing that they (these rules, or symbolic codes) are at the same time immanent in practices, on the other. Reductionistic idealism and materialism are both at work in Foucault's analysis, for reasons of both theoretical confusion and ideological interest. Rather than following Foucault's lead to establish the "power-culture link," as Lamont (1988) advises, we must learn how to separate the two spheres analytically in order to understand just what it is that power links to.

13. Among contemporary social theorists, Shils (for example, 1975) is virtually alone in his effort to elaborate the secular extension of Durkheim's and Weber's religious theories. Shils argues that modern societies still retain "centers" of sacred and transcendent significance and that social status is determined by the distribution of charisma from

these sacred centers. The power of this vocabulary to clarify cultural sociology is partly neutralized by the awkward concreteness of Shils's vocabulary, its concentration on charisma, its inexplicable rejection of Durkheimian theory, and its failure to consider more general issues of semiotic thought.

14. As Habermas (1968a: 58) wonderingly puts it, "Marx equates the practical insight of a political public with successful technical control."

15. The data in the following are samples from the thousands of articles written about the computer from its introduction in 1944 up until 1984. I selected for analysis ninety-seven articles drawn from ten popular American mass magazines: *Time* (T), *Newsweek* (N), *Business Week* (BW), *Fortune* (F), *The Saturday Evening Post* (SEP), *Popular Science* (PS), *Reader's Digest* (RD), *U.S. News and World Report* (USN), *McCall's* (Mc), and *Esquire* (E). In quoting or referring to these sources, I cite first the magazine, then the month and year; for example, T8/63 indicates an article in *Time* magazine that appeared in August 1963. These sampled articles were not randomly selected but chosen by their value relevance to the interpretive themes of this work. I would like to thank David Wooline for his assistance.

16. Many of these anthropomorphic references, which originated in the "charismatic" phase of the computer, have since become routine in the technical literature, for example, in terms such as *memory* and *generations*.

17. Technological discourse has always portrayed a transformation that would eliminate human labor and allow human perfection, love, and mutual understanding, as the rhetoric of Marx's descriptions of communism amply demonstrates.

18. While we examined several neutral accounts of technology, we did not spend much time on truly benign accounts. Marx was the only writer we examined who qualifies for this category, and his account is double-edged. An outstanding recent example of the social scientific translation of salvation discourse is Turkle's (1984) widely read pop-sociology discussion. Her account presented as objective data gleaned from her informants, is breathless in its sense of imminent possibility.

> Technology catalyzes changes not only in what we do but in how we think. It changes people's awareness of themselves, of one another, of their relationship with the world. The new machine that stands beyond the flashing digital signal, unlike the clock, the telescope, or the train, is a machine that "thinks." It challenges our notions not only of time and distance, but of mind (1984: 13).

Among a wide range of adults, getting involved with computers opens up long-closed questions. It can stimulate them to reconsider ideas about themselves and can provide a bias for thinking about large and puzzling philosophical issues (165).

The effect is subversive. It calls into question our ways of thinking about ourselves (308).

19. World War II was brought to an end on 10 August 1945 by the surrender of Japan, which followed quickly after the atomic bomb attacks on Hiroshima and Nagasaki. The very next day there appeared in *The Times* of London an article by Niels Bohr, which presented a prescient perspective on how efforts to control the bomb should proceed. Even while he notes the apocalyptic strain in the public's comprehension of this terrible technological achievement, Bohr warns that, above all, a distance from this fantasy is necessary if rational control efforts are to be made.

The grim realities which are being revealed to the world in these days will no doubt, in the minds of many, revive terrifying prospects forecast in fiction. With all admiration for such imagination, it is, however, most essential to appreciate the contrast between these fantasies and the actual situation confronting us (1985 [1945]: 264).

Bohr was just as concerned to counter the utopian discourse so prevalent among Los Alamos scientists during the war, which portrayed the much hoped for bomb as the only means for ensuring future peace (Rhoades 1987: 528–538).

## References

Alexander, Jeffrey C. 1982–1983. *Theoretical Logic in Sociology.* 4 Vols. Berkeley and Los Angeles: University of California Press.
Alexander, Jeffrey C. 1983. *The Modern Reconstruction of Classical Thought: Talcott Parsons.* Berkeley and Los Angeles: University of California Press.
Alexander, Jeffrey C. 1986. "The Dialectic of Individuation and Domination: Max Weber's Rationalization Theory and Beyond." In *Max Weber and Rationality*, edited by Sam Whipster and Scott Lash. London: Allen and Unwin.
Alexander, Jeffrey C. 1987. *Twenty Lectures: Sociological Theory Since World War II.* New York: Columbia University Press.
Alexander, Jeffrey C. 1988a. "Action and Its Environments." In *Action and Its Environments: Toward a New Synthesis*, edited by J. Alexander, 301–333. New York: Columbia University Press.
Alexander, Jeffrey C. 1988b. "Culture and Political Crisis: 'Watergate' and Durkheimian Sociology." In *Durkheimian Sociology: Cultural Studies.* edited by J. Alexander, 187–224. New York: Cambridge University Press.
Alexander, Jeffrey C., ed. 1988c. *Durkheimian Sociology: Cultural Studies.* New York: Cambridge University Press.
Alexander, Jeffrey C. 1990. "Analytic Debates: Understanding the Autonomy of Culture." In *Culture and Society: Contemporary Debates*, edited by J. Alexander and Steven Seidman. New York: Cambridge University Press.
Alexander, Jeffrey C., and Paul Colomy. 1985. "Towards Neofunctionalism: Eisenstadt's Change Theory and Symbolic Interaction." *Sociological Theory* 3 (2) 11–23.
Barthes, Roland. 1983. *The Fashion System.* New York: Hill and Wang.
Bell, Daniel. 1973. *The Coming of Post-Industrial Society.* New York: Basic Books.
Bell, Daniel. 1976. *The Cultural Contradictions of Capitalism.* New York: Basic Books.
Bellah, Robert. 1970a. "Civil Religion in America." In Bellah, *Beyond Belief,* 168–189. New York: Harper and Row.
Bellah, Robert. 1970b. "Values and Social Change in Modern Japan." In Bellah, *Beyond Belief,* 114–145. New York: Harper and Row.
Bohr, Niels. 1985 [1945]. "Energy from the Atom: An Opportunity and a Challenge." In *Niels Bohr: A Centenary Volume*, edited by A. P. French and P. J. Kennedy, 261–265. Cambridge: Harvard University Press.
Caillois, Roger. 1959 [1939]. Man and the Sacred. New York: Free Press.
Dilthey, Wilhelm. 1976. "The Construction of the Historical World in the Human Studies." In *Selected Writings*, 168–245. New York and Cambridge: Cambridge University Press.

Douglas, Mary. 1966. *Purity and Danger*. London: Penguin.
Durkheim, Emile. 1933. *The Division of Labor in Society*. New York: Free Press.
Durkheim, Emile. 1951. *Suicide*. New York: Free Press.
Durkheim, Emile. 1963. *The Elementary Forms of Religious Life*. New York: Free Press.
Durkheim, Emile. 1973. "Individualism and the Intellectuals." In *Emile Durkheim on Morality and Society*, edited by Robert N. Bellah, 48–56. Chicago: University of Chicago Press.
Eco, Umberto. 1979. "The Semantics of Metaphor." In *The Role of the Reader*, edited by U. Eco. Bloomington: Indiana University Press.
Edles, Laura. 1990. "Political Culture and the Transition to Democracy in Spain." Unpublished Ph.D. Dissertation, Department of Sociology, UCLA.
Eisenstadt, S. N. 1987. "Macrosociology and Sociological Theory: Some New Directions." *Contemporary Sociology* 16: 602–610.
Eisenstadt, S. N. 1987. *International Sociology*.
Eliade, Mircea. 1959. *The Sacred and the Profane*. New York: Harcourt, Brace, and World.
Ellul, Jacques. 1964. *The Technological Society*. New York: Vintage.
Fine, Gary Alan. 1987. *With the Boys: Little League and Preadolescent Culture*. Chicago: University of Chicago Press.
Foucault, Michel. 1972. *The Archaeology of Knowledge*. New York: Pantheon Books.
Geertz, Clifford. 1973. "Thick Description: Toward an Interpretive Theory of Culture." In Geertz, *The Interpretation of Cultures*, 3–32. New York: Basic Books.
Gouldner, Alvin. 1979. *The Future of Intellectuals and the Rise of the New Class*. New York: Seabury.
Greenfeld, Liah. 1987. "Sociology of Culture: Perspective Not Speciality." *Newsletter of the Culture Section of the American Sociological Association* 2 (1): 2.
Habermas, Jürgen. 1968a. "Technical Progress and the Social Life-World." In Habermas, *Toward a Rational Society*, 50–61. Boston: Beacon.
Habermas, Jürgen. 1968b. "Technology and Science as 'Ideology'." In Habermas, *Toward a Rational Society*, 31–122. Boston: Beacon.
Habermas, Jürgen. 1981. *The Theory of Communicative Action*. Vol. 1, *Reason and the Rationalization of Society*. Boston: Beacon.
Hunt, Lynn. 1984. *Politics, Culture, and Class in the French Revolution*. Berkeley and Los Angeles: University of California Press.
Kane, Anne. 1991. "Cultural Analysis in Historical Sociology: The Analytic and Concrete Forms of the Autonomy of Culture." *Sociological Theory* 9:1 (spring): 53–69.
Lamont, Michele. 1988. "The Power-Culture Link in a Comparative Perspective." Paper prepared for the Third German-American Theory Conference in Bremen, West Germany.
Lévi-Strauss, Claude. 1963. *Structural Anthropology*. New York: Basic Books.
Lévi-Strauss, Claude. 1967. *The Savage Mind*. Chicago: University of Chicago Press.
Lewis, Jan. 1983. *The Pursuit of Happiness: Family and Values in Jefferson's Virginia*. New York: Cambridge University Press.
Lukács, Georg. 1971. "Reification and the Consciousness of the Proletariat." In Lukács, *History and Class Consciousness*, Cambridge, Mass.: MIT Press.
Lyotard, Jean-François. 1984. *The Postmodern Condition: A Report on Knowledge*. Minneapolis: University of Minnesota Press.
Mann, Michael. 1985. *The Origins of Social Power*. Vol. 1. New York: Cambridge University Press.

Marcuse, Herbert. 1963. *One-Dimensional Man.* Boston: Beacon.
Marx, Karl. 1962. "Preface to a Contribution to the Critique of Political Economy." In *Selected Works*, Vol. 1, K. Marx and F. Engels, 361–365. Moscow: International Publishing House.
Merton, Robert K. 1970. *Science, Technology and Society in Seventeenth-Century England.* New York: Harper and Row.
Morgan, Edmund. 1958. *The Puritan Dilemma.* Boston: Little, Brown.
Parsons, Talcott. 1937. *The Structure of Social Action.* New York: Free Press.
Parsons, Talcott. 1951. *The Social System.* New York: Free Press.
Parsons, Talcott. 1960. "Some Principal Characteristics of Industrial Societies." In *Structure and Process in Modern Societies*, edited by T. Parsons, 132–168. New York: Free Press.
Parsons, Talcott. 1966. *Societies: Evolutionary and Comparative Perspectives.* Englewood Cliffs, N.J.: Prentice-Hall.
Parsons, Talcott. 1967. "Some Comments on the Sociology of Karl Marx." In *Sociological Theory and Modern Society*, edited by T. Parsons. New York: Free Press.
Parsons, Talcott, and Gerald Platt. 1973. *The American University.* Cambridge: Harvard University Press.
Parsons, Talcott, and Edward Shils. 1951. "Values, Motives, and Systems of Action." In *Towards a General Theory of Action*, edited by T. Parsons and E. Shils. New York: Harper and Row.
Peirce, Charles. 1985. "Logic as Semiotic: The Theory of Signs." In *Semiotics*, edited by Robert E. Innis, 1–23. Bloomington: Indiana University Press.
Pool, Ithiel de Sola. 1983. *Forecasting the Telephone.* Norwood, N.J.: Ablex.
Pynchon, Thomas. 1984. "Is It O.K. to Be a Luddite?" *New York Times Book Review*, 23 October, 1.
Rambo, Eric, and Elaine Chan. 1990. "Text, Structure, and Action in Cultural Sociology: A Commentary on 'Positive Objectivity' in Wuthnow and Archer." *Theory and Society* 19 (1990): 635–648.
Rhoades, Richard. 1987. *The Making of the Atomic Bomb.* New York: Simon and Schuster.
Ricoeur, Paul. 1984. *Time and Narrative*, Vol. 1. Chicago: University of Chicago Press.
Ricoeur, Paul. 1971. "The Model of a Text: Meaningful Action Considered as a Text." *Social Research* 38: 529–562.
Rochberg-Halton, E. 1986. *Meaning and Modernity.* Chicago: University of Chicago Press.
Rueschemeyer, Dietrich. 1986. *Power and the Division of Labor.* Stanford: Stanford University Press.
Sahlins, Marshall. 1976. *Culture and Practical Reason.* Chicago: University of Chicago Press.
Sahlins, Marshall. 1981. *Historical Metaphors and Mythical Realities: Structure in the Early History of the Sandwich Islands Kingdom.* Ann Arbor: University of Michigan Press.
Saussure, Ferdinand de. 1964. *A Course in General Linguistics.* London: Owen.
Schluchter, Wolfgang. 1979. "The Paradoxes of Rationalization." In *Max Weber's Vision of History*, edited by Guenther Roth and W. Schluchter, 1164. Berkeley and Los Angeles: University of California Press.
Sewell, William, Jr. 1980. *Work and Revolution in France.* New York: Cambridge University Press.
Shils, Edward. 1975. *Center and Periphery: Essays in Macrosociology.* Chicago: University of Chicago Press.

Smelser, Neil. 1959. *Social Change in the Industrial Revolution.* Chicago: University of Chicago Press.

Smith, Henry Nash. 1950. *Virgin Land.* Cambridge: Harvard University Press.

Swidler, Ann. 1986. "Culture in Action: Symbols and Strategies." *American Sociological Review* 51: 273–286.

Szelenyi, Ivan, and Bill Martin. 1987. "Theories of Cultural Capital and Beyond." In *Intellectuals, Universities, and the State in Western Modern Societies,* edited by Ron Eyerman, L. G. Svensson, and T. Soderquist, 16–49. Berkeley and Los Angeles: University of California Press.

Turkle, Sherry. 1984. *The Second Self: Computers and the Human Spirit.* New York: Simon and Schuster.

Turner, Victor. 1969. *The Ritual Process.* Chicago: Aldine.

Weber, Max. 1946a. "Religious Rejections of the World and Their Directions." In *From Max Weber,* edited by Hans Berth and C. Wright Mills, 323–359. New York: Oxford University Press.

Weber, Max. 1946b. "The Meaning of Discipline." In *From Max Weber,* edited by H. Gerth and C. W. Mills, 253–264. New York: Oxford University Press.

Weber, Max. 1958. *The Protestant Ethic and the Spirit of Capitalism.* New York: Scribners.

Weber, Max. 1963. *The Sociology of Religion.* Boston: Beacon Press.

Wuthnow, Robert. 1987. *Meaning and Moral Order.* Berkeley and Los Angeles: University of California Press.